D1191224

# DON'T BUY ANOTHER VOTE, I WON'T PAY FOR A LANDSLIDE

*The Sordid and Continuing History of Political Corruption in West Virginia*

# DON'T BUY ANOTHER VOTE, I WON'T PAY FOR A LANDSLIDE

*The Sordid and Continuing History*
*of Political Corruption in West Virginia*

By

Dr. ALLEN H. LOUGHRY II

International Standard Book Number 0-87012-748-9
Library of Congress Control Number 2006925448
Printed in the United States of America
Copyright © 2003 by Allen H. Loughry II
Copyright © 2006 by Allen H. Loughry II
Charleston, WV
All Rights Reserved
2006

McClain Printing Company
Parsons, WV 26287
www.mcclainprinting.com
2006

To the People of West Virginia

# CONTENTS

## PART THREE
### THE ROAD TO REFORM

# FOREWORD
## By
# United States Senator John McCain

Allen Loughry has issued a reminder that there are watchdogs and whistle-blowers willing to defy intimidation and do the difficult and necessary work of defending our American ideals. He approaches his work with an idealism thought impossible for someone involved in politics so many years.

Few Americans believe their government to be a place of moral sanctity. Many accept corruption as the rule. Actual wrongdoing is not as flagrant as Hollywood movies would portray, but that subtlety also makes it more difficult to identify the real-life political villains. They do not lurk in the dark, dressed in black. They can be our neighbors, friends and coworkers. They are not necessarily bad people, but rather people who have been held to low standards a long time. They are merely playing the game that has evolved over years of transgressions going unchecked.

Dr. Loughry is not simply making a "naughty" list. He reaches beyond his examples and poses questions that seem like black and white moral issues on the surface, but upon closer inspection we are forced to examine the other side of the coin. He points to West Virginia, the Robin Hood of states, where gold was stolen to finance separation from Virginia and the Confederate ideology of slavery and separatism. We inevitably start to question, if the only way for good to prevail is to play the corruption game, does the end justify the means, and can the virtuous path ever be the successful path?

Ultimately, we find ourselves mired in Dr. Loughry's Catch-22: to find political success it seems one has to play the game and ignore ethical quagmires, but by engaging in such behavior, one must accept the consequences of making voters apathetic and weakening our democracy.

Dr. Loughry provides us with disturbing evidence of widespread dishonesty, but also supplies a remedy. I believe virtue and success can coexist, and that belief has been proven to me time and time again by many of my colleagues. We cannot deny the existence of corruption, but we shouldn't assume that every government official is in his or her position because of backroom deals and tainted elections. In every election season there are candidates looking to highlight their records rather than their opponents' shortcomings, and on occasion there are babies kissed without a camera in sight.

Americans should vote for candidates we believe to be honorable and decent. In concert, lawmaking bodies should commit to making changes in election law that will diminish the opportunities for fraud. We may never have a perfect government, but Dr. Loughry reminds us we should never stop striving for one.

*John McCain*

# FOREWORD
## By
# United States Senator Robert C. Byrd

In politics, money, it seems, drives everything. Fundraisers are at the top of people's schedules as they run for public office. That constant cycle of asking for money has helped to erode the people's faith in the ability of their elected representatives.

In 1946, when I started out in politics, if we had the current system of funding campaigns, I would not be in the United States Senate. I came out at the very bottom of the ladder. I came out of a coal camp with my fiddle and my brain. I held firmly to my belief in our system of government, a system where a person who didn't have anything, who was poor, who came from humble beginnings, could run for office. My father was a coal miner. He was honest, but he did not have great political connections. I just had a high school education. And yet the system that we had in that day allowed me–a coal miner's son–to run for office. Could I have done that today? I'd go to the political leaders and tell them, "I'd like to run for the House of Delegates" or "I'd like to run for the House of Representatives." Those leaders would look at me and say, "Who are you? Do you have any money?" I would have been out if it had depended on money. I would never have gotten to first base.

That's the problem with today's political system. The money cycle in politics too often corrupts political discourse. It makes us slaves to the dollar rather than the servants of the people we all aspire to be. If one doesn't have the money, forget going to the House of Representatives or the U.S. Senate. And, unfortunately, the United States Supreme Court has given this system First Amendment protection. In *Buckley v. Valeo*, the Court made it extraordinarily difficult for the public to have what it wants: reasonable regulations of campaign expenditures which do not–either directly or indirectly–limit the ideas that may be expressed in the public realm. In fact, I would submit that such regulations would actually broaden the public debate on a number of issues by freeing it from the narrow confines dictated by special interest money.

Consider for a moment the sheer costs involved. According to the Congressional Research Service, aggregate costs of House and Senate campaigns increased eightfold between 1976 and 2004, from $115.5 million to $1.16 billion, while the cost of living rose threefold. Campaign costs for average winning candidates, a useful measure of the real cost of seeking office, show an increase in the House from $87,000 in 1976 to $1.0 million in 2004; a winning Senate race went from $609,000 in 1976 to $7.0 million in 2004. The figures are astounding, and lend themselves to the mistrust that people have for the political process.

The American people are more than aware that both political parties abuse the current system and that both political parties fear to change that system. Each party wants to preserve its advantages under the system. But the insidious system of campaign fundraising will eventually undermine the very foundations of this Republic. For our own sakes, and for the sake of the people, we must find a way to stop this political minuet. We must come to grips with the fact that the campaign finance system, in its current form, is simply unworthy of preservation.

I have spoken in the Senate many times about the exponential increase in campaign expenditures since I first ran for the U.S. Senate in 1958. It was not too long ago that Warren Buffet, one of the richest men in America, said that political access is "undervalued" in the campaign finance market. Campaign contributions will continue to increase until a "market valuation" is achieved, thus causing the cost of a reasonably effective campaign to continue to skyrocket. It already costs tens of millions of dollars to run an effective campaign for the Senate in many States. What do we tell a poor kid from the hollows who has the capacity and drive to be a good Senator? A campaign for the Senate will be beyond his or her personal means, and beyond the means of friends and associates. We must act to put the United States Senate, the House of Representatives, and the Presidency within the reach of anyone with the brains, with the spirit, with the spine, and with the desire to go for it.

In 2002, the Congress tried again to rein in the out-of-control campaign costs and enacted the Bipartisan Campaign Reform Act (BCRA) of 2002, more commonly known as the McCain-Feingold Campaign Finance Reform Act. Making the most significant changes in the Federal Election Campaign Act since its creation in 1971, McCain-Feingold featured higher contribution limits, a ban on the raising of soft money by political parties and federal candidates, and a restriction on broadcast ads by outside groups in the closing days of an election. Most of the McCain-Feingold provisions survived a Supreme Court challenge (*McConnell v. FEC*, December 10, 2003).

However, there are loopholes in McCain-Feingold–and those loopholes are making for significant problems and still-escalating campaign costs. In the end, I expect that it will take a Constitutional amendment to finally put an end to the money chase in campaigns.

One of the great ironies of the campaign financing system is that it puts more distance between candidates and the very people they hope to represent. Campaigns of today are technologically sophisticated. They rely, increasingly, on mass media. The whole point of current campaigns has become raising enough money to pay to more people, more times, over the airwaves.

There is no argument that there is an efficiency consideration here. People's lives today are complicated. They have to run from work, to school activities, to the grocery store or the dry cleaner, cook dinner, put the kids to bed, and so on, over and over again. Families do not have the time, or the inclination, to attend community functions like they used to attend years ago. I have had recent campaign events in some of West Virginia's communities where people still come out to hear candidates and to celebrate our electoral system. But, in our nation today, such events are the exception, not the rule.

So, to influence voters, candidates pay high-priced consultants to produce high-priced ads and to buy high-priced television and radio time to air them. The other side does the same. It is a vicious cycle that requires candidates to spend more and more time raising money and less and less time listening to the people they wish to represent.

The result is that, today, there are fewer rallies. There is less knocking on doors, less face-to-face time with the voters, less handshaking. No wonder the people think that politicians are out of touch; through the creative use of film and audio tape, politicians have made themselves intangible.

Some argue that money will find a way to control the process, regardless of what we do. I respond that a simple and straightforward limit on campaign expenditures is much more difficult to circumvent than the maze of regulations to which we have had to resort. I wonder, too, whether these opponents of campaign finance reform are willing to permit money to buy anything on the grounds that it is difficult to control.

Even without a constitutional amendment, we can, of course, tinker around the edges. But we cannot enact comprehensive legislation that will get to the heart of the problem. I wish we could. But the fact is we cannot get the kind of legislation we really need unless we first adopt an amendment to the Constitution.

Fear is a very terrible thing. Fear paralyzes, it clouds judgment. Fear of losing advantage is what has driven both parties to be reluctant to enact meaningful expenditure reforms. But the fixation with maintaining advantage is blinding us to the dangers to our credibility. Credibility is a precious commodity, more important to a politician than, yes, money! When we lose our credibility, no amount of money will enable us to buy it back. Already many of our citizens do not vote. They don't feel that their vote counts. I hope that more public officials fear the further erosion of our democracy, not the loss of fleeting financial advantages.

Our democratic system of government is based on public trust. Nothing alienates that trust faster and more completely than the taint–or the suggestion of taint–connected with big money. Where, once, an individual election campaign for the Senate cost a few thousand dollars, such campaigns currently cost millions.

In 1958, I ran for the first time for a full term as a U.S. Senator from West Virginia, together with Senator Jennings Randolph, who was running for the Senate to fill the unexpired term of the late Senator M.M. Neely. The combined costs of that campaign for two U.S. Senate seats amounted to, roughly, $50,000.

The kind of campaign system that we have today sends the clear message to the American people that it is money, not ideas and not principles, that reigns supreme in our political system. We must bring into check the obscene spending that occurs in pursuit of public office, and put the U.S. Senate back within the reach of anyone with the desire to make a difference, the spirit of public service, the dedication, and the intelligence to serve.

*Robert C. Byrd*

# INTRODUCTION

*Few will have the greatness to bend history itself, but each of us can work to change a small portion of events and in the total of all those acts will be written the history of this generation.*

Robert F. Kennedy

From the rushing waters of Blackwater Falls to the healing waters of Berkeley Springs, West Virginia is a burst of fresh air that breathes life into the very soul of all who experience her. It only takes one visit to see why the State is known as "Wild, Wonderful West Virginia." People all over the world have heard of the State through John Denver's song *Country Roads,* which begins, "Almost Heaven, West Virginia." Yet unfortunately, in spite of its wealth in beauty, the citizens of West Virginia have been subjected to never-ending political corruption and money dominance over a government that has pervaded the culture of its national, state, and locally elected officials.

People of the State are traditionally known as Mountaineers. A Mountaineer, by definition, is not only a native of a mountainous region, but also one who climbs mountains, and indeed, West Virginians are a strong, hardworking, proud people who have emerged from the dark and dirty coal mines and have risen to the top of the Blue Ridge Mountains. West Virginians almost universally have a cynical view of politics and after reviewing the history of political corruption in the State, at all levels of government, it is easy to understand those feelings, for if political corruption were an Olympic event, West Virginia would have won the Gold Medal many times over.

Notwithstanding such a dismal past, recognizing and accepting the State's history of plutocracy and corruption will provide the incentive as well as the framework for reforming the State's politics. The result will be that West Virginia will provide the supreme model for national reform. With the countless examples of corrupt politicians throughout West Virginia's history, the State has also had its share of nationally recognized and exceptional politicians who have worked diligently to improve the lives of many of its citizens. One example is former United States Senator Jennings Randolph who authored the Twenty-Sixth Amendment to the United States Constitution which gave eighteen-year-olds the right to vote.

At the outset, I certainly recognize that every state in the Union has low level political hacks who are petty thieves. Unfortunately though, West Virginia has had much more than its fair share of corrupt political felons as countless state, county, and city elected officials have spent time in federal and state penitentiaries. West Virginians have also witnessed generations of well-intentioned elected officials getting their voices squelched by corrupt politicians who have abused their positions for personal gain. I often try to imagine the opportunities that have been lost by citizens of West Virginia in so many areas of concern such as education, healthcare, and infrastructure as a result of a long line of corrupt elected officials. The people of the State who proudly call themselves Mountaineers have never been truly free from the depredations of political and financial corruption.

Amazingly, while my research demonstrates that West Virginia elections have been among the most corrupt in America, peculiarly, the vast majority of its citizens are not corrupt; they are honest people seeking to make better lives for their families. Nonetheless, these same straightforward and sincere people seem to have become so desensitized to corruption that many of them laugh at the thought of the countless elected officials who later became felons. Many simply ignore the State's unfortunate long line of felons which only serves to condone, promote, and perpetuate such behavior. I have heard so many times during my career from numerous politicians that "everything in West Virginia is political except politics and that's personal."

I grew up near Parsons, West Virginia, a town of approximately 1,200 people. My upbringing was in a middle class family where politics was an integral part of our daily lives. My father was a partner in a construction company, later a small business owner, and then served as the Tucker County Assessor. My mother worked several years at the local shoe factory, first assembling shoes and later working as a secretary in the administrative office. She currently works as a secretary at a federal laboratory and research center just outside of Parsons. From an early stage, my father taught me that politics in one way or another affects everything in our lives and that we have no other choice but to get involved.

Recently, while visiting my parents, I also revisited my past by going through drawers and boxes that still hold childhood memories and mementos of school accomplishments. I couldn't help but feel the veil of pride being lifted as I sifted through piles of certificates presented to me by numerous West Virginia elected officials for my participation in activities such as school fairs, sports, and graduation. Now, as a State taxpayer, I realize that I have joined the ranks of the generations before me who paid for such campaigning tools cleverly disguised as tokens of recognition. As a voter, I wonder which officials I have helped keep in office who used my hard earned money to pay for, not only certificates, but also countless pill boxes, combs, pencils, magnets, and key chains that prominently displayed their names.

Moreover, throughout the many years I have been involved with West Virginia politics, I have heard the pleas from teachers who requested salary increases, more money for adequate computers, and other progressive educational supplies for their classrooms. I have learned of the issues surrounding a failing healthcare system, a workers' compensation system that has plummeted to a debt of billions, a State retirement system in distress, and a lack of adequate infrastructure in the many rural sections of the State. As I drive the picturesque country roads outlined with redbud and aging hardwoods, my attention is drawn to the potholes and general signs of neglect from town to town. When I hear of schools that struggle to provide adequate heating and air conditioning or meet even the most basic safety requirements for their students, I question why we continue to have no money for these necessities, but we can spend staggering amounts of valuable tax dollars on certificates and trinkets for these same children.

It is time to reexamine the basic assumptions of our laws and consider election and political reform in general. We often talk of empowerment of the people and nothing empowers people more than having an effective voice in government. But how do you tackle such an immense problem in a state that has been plagued with corruption since its beginnings? Before confronting the issue or even the question itself, one must better understand the events surrounding the State's inception, the circumstances of its people, and the effect of geography on its political growth.

Although oftentimes troubling, West Virginia has had a unique and fascinating past. For a State that broke free from Confederate Virginia and took a stand against slavery, it is ironic that it began enslaving its own. The owners of the early coal companies became like the plantation owners of the South, keeping workers uneducated, underpaid and isolated, while at the same time, controlling elections and even the very culture of its people.

West Virginia is also unique in that it is the only state to be completely within the boundaries of the Appalachian Mountains or "Appalachia." The State's geography, coupled with a lack of infrastructure, is what made the State such a beautiful and untouched haven for those who traveled there to start a new life. At the same time, however, the land made the isolation of its people all too easy for the lingering control by coal companies. And, since the coal barons controlled everything in that era, even the elections, promoting roadways and development in order to decrease alienation, were not important issues on their agenda.

The very history of the State is the reason why it should take the lead in the reform process. To rise from the worst to one of the best in the nation with regard to clean politics would be the greatest way to prove that true change can occur in every state. In recent years, while money is still changing hands to buy individual votes in southern West Virginia, the influx of multi-millions of legal dollars gushing into political campaigns provides the greatest threat to reforming elections. When candidates, special interest groups, or even the leaders of large corporations (purportedly in their private capacity since corporate contributions are illegal) are able to spend countless sums of money on scathing television commercials with the intent to completely destroy the reputations of candidates for office with virtually no regulation to check the veracity of such advertise-ments, then intervention is necessary.

The fight to reform the corruption in West Virginia's politics as well as the role of money in campaigns will not revitalize the democratic process overnight. Not until the system is purged of big money and corrupt politicians are not only removed from office, but jailed and banned for life from participat-ing in West Virginia politics, will there be hope for a decent democratic future. And, given the difficulties of securing any significant reforms at a national level, states must take the lead with reform. They must develop creative legislation with the teeth necessary to insure that politicians comply with the election laws and the criminal laws of the State while at the same time there must be enforce-ment mechanisms with effective preventative incentives and sanctions.

A recurring theme from the many individuals with whom I have spoken while writing this book was that they had often given money to candidates because they felt they had to contribute to campaigns or else they "would pay the political price." Of course, for the very same reasons–fear of political revenge and retribution–those individuals wished to remain anonymous. Likewise, many West Virginia citizens fear that if they don't contribute to various campaigns, or if they support the losing candidate, or if businesses refuse to contribute to inau-gural activities of a newly elected governor, it will be detrimental to their busi-nesses, jobs, and friendships.

The real people of power in campaigns today are the fundraisers and campaign donors. Money buys name recognition, for unless you already have name recognition, have recently won a state lottery, or are a multi-millionaire, then you have to raise big money early if you plan to be taken seriously as a legitimate candidate. When you do not fall into one of the categories enumerated above, then you have to ask people wealthy enough to risk their money at the early stages of your speculative venture which often allows those contributors to assert control of your candidacy. Or, as is the case with some West Virginia public officials, they compete with wealthy candidates by spending or giving away millions of State tax dollars to secure re-election.

Part of the problem in politics today is that massive amounts of money must be collected in order to buy television, radio, and newspaper advertisements in addition to the cash funneled to every precinct captain in southern West Virginia to buy votes. Recognizing their constant need for campaign funds, special interest groups contribute generously to campaigns and use their wealth to build relationships with lawmakers that give them unparalleled access to influence legislation. The average citizen without bags of cash to hand out is often left outside the realm of elite political access. Moreover, with the strings of scandal attached to campaign money, reforms are necessary to prevent money from continually buying legislative favors such as loopholes and advantages for certain influential groups. Furthermore, it is nearly impossible to attract the best people to serve in public office when special interest groups constantly undermine the integrity of the legislative process. It is fine to buy a business, but it should not be permissible to buy a political office.

When someone donates thousands of dollars to a political campaign it is naive to believe that the recipient of such cash will not immediately take the contributor's telephone calls. Money clearly buys access that the average person is unable to attain. What it really amounts to is a few hundred lobbyists and wealthy individuals having a much louder voice than 1.8 million West Virginians who are largely absent from the lists of donors to political campaigns. On the other hand, campaign donor lists read like a who's who among corporate executives and wealthy individuals. For an entrenched politician, it's likely they will receive money from companies such as tobacco, oil and gas, telephone, various utilities, real estate, securities and investments, computer/Internet, an abundance of law firms, and numerous airlines. For a beginner to politics, that trough of money usually isn't as readily available.

West Virginians believe government is a process that is out of their control and something that they cannot effectively impact in a positive manner. Moreover, after countless indiscretions by West Virginia politicians, the appearance is that everything is for sale. West Virginia and other states must consider all possible changes to reform their systems of elections and state government. While some have suggested that during General Elections, Congress should pass a federal holiday for election day to ensure higher voter turnout, others suggest allowing voting by mail, changing election day to Saturday, or utilizing the Internet for voting as possible steps to improving the election process and voter turnout. None of these suggestions, or any other ideas of reform, regardless of their possible utility, would make the slightest difference in an election unless the causes of corruption in West Virginia and other states are fully recognized, taken seriously, and addressed. Making it easier to vote and other "feel good" changes will do nothing to alter the fact that many of those votes will still be tainted by corruption.

This book is by no means an all-inclusive list of every act of malfeasance by every elected official in West Virginia. A book of that size outlining the countless small-scale political bandits who have scammed citizens throughout their time in public office would have to be held at the Library of Congress. Instead, this is a compilation of some of the more glaring examples of political corruption and indiscretions, many of which, such as the nose-biting judge, are unique to West Virginia. Moreover, many of these individuals I have known personally for years and not all of them are so-called hardened criminals. As citizens hear continuous negative stories about their elected officials, those instances of corrupt activities, perceptively-corrupt activities, and even inauspicious or questionable behaviors in elected officials' personal lives all become completely intertwined whether actually corrupt or not. It becomes just another string in a big ball of yarn and once trust in government is lost it can be enormously difficult to recover, but often the more difficult the hurdle or challenge to overcome, the greater the reward.

I have been so fortunate during my young life to have had such unique political experiences. I grew up watching politics while others my age were watching their favorite singers or movie stars. I followed politics on a state and national level and began to slowly form my opinions as more information filtered in my direction. My grandfather was my county's Democratic Party Chairman, which back in those days meant a lot more in State politics than it does today. For instance, when any prominent politician came to the county they always met with the leaders of their party. That's how I first met United States Senator Robert C. Byrd. Years later, as a young man just out of college, I became a Direct Aide to West Virginia Governor Gaston Caperton. To follow was a wonderful experience as a Special Assistant and Deputy Press Secretary to United States Congressman Harley O. Staggers, Jr. I developed a personal relationship with Staggers, known to many as "Bucky," and learned a great deal during my time in his office. I went on to work as a Senior Assistant Attorney General gaining many experiences during my several years there that I will have for a lifetime. Today, I am an attorney with the West Virginia Supreme Court, working for Justice Elliott "Spike" Maynard, a position that is equally interesting and challenging. I have also had the opportunity to work on political campaigns on national, statewide, county, and city levels, including being a Regional Coordinator in the Clinton/Gore 1992 presidential campaign. Some of my other less political jobs included road construction, building construction, managing my father's business, and writing for newspapers. All of these provided the real world and sometimes backbreaking experiences which–for better or worse–helped shape me into the person I am today. My construction jobs gave me an appreciation for how individuals work hard day after day in physically demanding positions to support themselves and their families, while my journalism experiences opened my mind to many new situations and pushed me to ask more questions about everything, especially my government and my state.

Each of my experiences in one way or another has affected the path I have taken in life. I remember one day, in particular, when I was working for Congressman Staggers when he and I were meeting with constituents in Morgantown, in the north-central part of the State. I was touched and saddened as several senior citizens, who were crying and grabbing onto both of us, told their stories and pleaded desperately for help. They were scared because of an issue surrounding a plant closing and a union dispute wherein the workers lost their jobs and were without money or food. I remember one elderly woman clinging to me as the tears streamed down her cheeks saying, "Help me! Help me! I don't know what to do!" I really felt for all of them, but I knew they needed more help than I could give them. It was a time when the importance of public service was driven home to me more clearly than at any moment in my life. It was also at that moment when I decided to stop prolonging law school, believing that the education would give me more tools to better help individuals like the ones I had met that day.

Now, years later, I have completed four separate law degrees and was fortunate enough to have studied law during one summer at Oxford University. It was while I was working toward one of those law degrees at American University that the beginnings of this book became a reality. I was working on a paper for Law Professor and author Jamin Raskin on campaign finance reform and the amount of money in politics. It has always been a topic of personal concern, but it was Raskin who helped me look outside the box and gear my research more toward identifying, rather than just complaining about, the problems with West Virginia's politics and to create sound solutions toward correcting those problems.

I have been told by several friends, family members, and those in the world of academia that publishing this book, due to the number of powerful individuals named herein, is the equivalent of committing political suicide, particularly if I have any personal political aspirations or simply plan to work or do business with State government. I have also been told that I might in some way be considered disloyal to the people for whom I have worked in their political offices. In fact, a very close family member pleaded with me, "Please don't do this. No one will hire you and you and Kelly (my wife) will have to leave the State." Another person suggested: "If I were you, I'd have someone else start my car and taste my food after the book gets published."

People have very strong and very real fears when it comes to voicing their opinions or just speaking out about problems within West Virginia's government and it's not a fear that has developed overnight. It was developed by reading the newspaper stories, many of which are briefed in this book, and seeing people who spoke out about an injustice get destroyed by the establishment. It was also developed after experiencing it personally by people like my grandfather and several other workers who, in the 1950s, were fired by Governor Cecil H. Underwood from their jobs with the State Road (Division of Highways) simply because they were registered Democrats. I don't dismiss these concerns as I have witnessed the firing of individuals on numerous occasions simply because it was in some way politically advantageous to a particular officeholder. Many politicians will do absolutely anything to stay in office and if they see you as a threat they will take you down by destroying you personally as well as professionally. I fully expect some retribution for this book and, in fact, have already been threatened by one powerful individual who said their name "had better not appear anywhere in print." In fact, this person told me if their name appeared in this book, they would "deny the information, sue me, and destroy my reputation." I was unable to oblige with that person's "request." Politics in West Virginia is not a profession for the weak-hearted.

Given the nature of the political scene, as well as the personal friendships I have garnered with myriad elected officials throughout the years, I do feel the need to specifically address some of the concerns surrounding this publication. I would've preferred to write about strangers; that certainly would've been easier. Many of these people I have known for a lifetime and have been to their homes, had lunch or dinner with, or sat beside them at countless political events. It wasn't easy naming names, but it would be impossible to write this book in any other way and still retain my credibility. I am not a traitor or an enemy of either political party, nor are the majority of honest West Virginians who are tired of a destructive and corrupt system of State politics. There is also a lot of information I have learned throughout the years that I am simply unable to include in this book because the sources of that information would surely lose their jobs.

I have included information on West Virginia elected officials regardless of their political party affiliations and a fair reading of this book in its entirety will lead the reader to no other conclusion. If someone is a filthy corrupt scoundrel stealing State money from the good people of this State, then it means absolutely nothing to me whether he or she is a Democrat or Republican as corruption should not be protected by the veil of either party. This book lists many allegations as well as convictions of State officers as seen through the eyes of the citizens by way of public records. In point of fact, all of the information provided with regard to an elected official's corrupt behavior came directly from state and federal recorded court cases, legislative journals, newspapers, historical books, government records, magazines, and other public sources. Therefore, not a single sentence detailing the corrupt activities of named individuals resulted from any of my previous or current work experiences or conversations with any of my previous or current employers. Those private conversations with those individuals are, indeed, private and I hold a deep professional responsibility not to betray that trust.

As far as this book being so-called political suicide, I say if that is the consequence I must pay for highlighting generations of corruption and stressing the immediate need for comprehensive reform, then I am more than willing to shoulder that burden. Corruption in politics as well as the enormous amounts of money pouring into political campaigns are the most important issues surrounding the future success of West Virginia and our entire country. It was once said, "You can't plow a field without plowing the ground." Thus, if I make a few politicians mad and they seek retribution, I have paid the price for my politics in the past and I am sure it won't be the last time.

Sometimes you even have to pay a political price when you didn't do anything to deserve it. I remember one occasion in 1996 while I was working toward one of my law degrees in Columbus, Ohio, when I filled out an application and submitted it for a legal externship in then-Governor George Voinovich's office. It was a position highly sought after by my fellow classmates, but one that I really didn't expect to get because I was just a West Virginia country boy who had no political connections in Ohio. Much to my surprise, I was chosen by the school's faculty and my name and application were sent to Voinovich's office. Soon afterward, I received a call from the Governor's Office. I was told the Governor had reviewed my information, noticed I had worked as a Direct Aide to West Virginia Governor Gaston Caperton, was impressed with my other work experiences, and looked forward to having me work with him during the next semester. I was then told to send the Governor's Office my latest resume just because they thought it would be "a good idea to have it on file." I sent it that day. Within days, the Governor's Office called the law school and said Governor Voinovich was "furious." A Governor's Office employee told a member of the faculty that my resume indicated I had been a Regional Coordinator for President Clinton in 1992 and had the Governor known that, he never would have chosen me. The man said they wanted to cancel the externship relationship with the law school because it was believed I was a "subversive" sent by President Clinton to spy on the Governor, who was planning his run for the United States Senate.

Although not a joke, I still laugh about it today whenever I see now-Senator Voinovich on television. I can't imagine what would lead him to think that a sitting President would be trying to place a student in his office for one semester of law school to spy on him. The law school and the Governor's Office discussed the issue back and forth for days, finally agreeing to "allow me" to work there; however, the Governor explained I would be "closely watched." I then explained in very clear terms what I thought about his offer, and instead accepted a position in the Master Commissioner's Office, which is the legal counsel to the Ohio Supreme Court. The Master Commissioner, John Dilenschneider, was a former federal bankruptcy judge, a lawyer at two of Ohio's largest law firms, and had been a former aide to United States Senator John Glenn. He took me under his wing, and I certainly learned a lot from him. In any case, even though that particular situation worked out positively for me, it sent the clear message that there is always a lack of job security associated with any political position at any given moment from the highest to lowest levels of employment.

This book is applicable to everyone. Candidates and those already elected to a public office should read carefully the information contained throughout this book and keep in mind that many well-meaning individuals began their political careers with the best of intentions. Many started out determined to remain honest and fight a long history of political corruption only to find themselves years later receiving the same negative headlines that originally caused them to enter into public service. Candidates should also understand that, thanks to their corrupt predecessors, even questionable conduct in their personal lives becomes a serious issue. The information included herein also provides to elected officials the framework for complete reformation of West Virginia politics. No longer will candidates or entrenched politicians have any acceptable excuses for not enacting or supporting reform measures. No longer can they play ignorant with regard to reform ideas because they are spelled out in simple and easy to read language in the chapters to follow.

This book also reinforces the fact that newspaper reporters and editors in West Virginia have a unique responsibility to report the fact that corruptive practices have occurred year after year from the State's very inception. The press

is the one constant check on the system. It is the one avenue to get the most information to the people about the misgivings of politicians or even the uselessness
of a government entity such as the State's Ethics Commission. At times though,
editorials and reporters have not always been as proactive as they need to be in
reporting West Virginia's corruption. At other times it seems they too have
become desensitized to the excessive amount and perpetual nature of State corruption. For instance, a 1998 *Charleston Gazette* editorial headline began, "Keep
your fingers crossed, but corruption seems to be fading in West Virginia."[1] I
found the editorial baffling and almost inconceivable considering the events that
preceded it. I have even found that some State newspapers have reported that the
history of corruption in West Virginia was systemic, while just days later the same
newspapers wrote stories declaring that corruption was not a major problem in
the State. Regardless of some of their failures, West Virginia newspapers have
been instrumental in helping to keep at least some governmental actors in check.

        In talking with various reporters from around the State, many have told
me that while they report some widely known corrupt practices, they ignore many
negative facts because they don't want to lose access to the elected officials or
that their newspapers' editors have expressed, without giving the reporter any further explanation, that they don't want certain stories reported. One reporter said,
"Are you crazy? I am careful what I write about because I want to keep my job
and I want to be able to call the Governor and actually get my calls returned. If
I don't have access, I don't have a story. And, if I don't have a story, I don't have
a job." Another former reporter told me about being followed and even stopped
on the street by strangers who called her by name and made veiled threats toward
her that if she continued to report on a certain West Virginia public official, "You
never know when drugs could be found in your desk at work." She was so
alarmed that soon afterward she left journalism forever, telling me it wasn't worth
destroying her life and her family.

        Political leaders from both of West Virginia's major political parties also
should read this book with particular interest. Corruption and clean politics should
unquestionably be a non-partisan issue. Political parties should openly support the
plenitude of people who are not corrupt that would stand strongly on their respective
issues if given the opportunity and stand firmly against candidates who are known to
have taken liberties with their ethical behavior. I simply don't understand why members of either political party justify the corrupt actions of some public officials within their political parties by strongly supporting them in an election, while they readily criticize those from opposing parties who share similar unscrupulous conduct.

        A book like this has never been written in the State's history chronicling
so many of the sordid details of various elected officials. My hope is that it will

serve as a glaring reminder to elected officials that their indiscretions will forever be memorialized in print when they are involved in wrongdoing. Furthermore, even if some elected officials are not primarily concerned with their own reputations, they should realize such negative headlines will follow their family members throughout their lives. Thus, the son or daughter of a convicted ex-politician, who is interested in running for elected office, will more often than not be perceived by many to be corrupt since most voters believe the fruit doesn't fall far from the tree.

Inaction only contributes to allowing many of the corrupt politicians to remain in power, so citizens throughout this nation, particularly those who are registered, but still don't vote, should also consider these pages carefully. Some will say this book doesn't apply to people who don't vote. The truth is, many West Virginians hunger for change and have simply lost faith in the system, while others feel their votes will simply be tainted by the ones bought and sold during each election. Many of these non-voters are actually well informed and truly do care about the issues, but unfortunately feel helpless with the choices during an election and have no faith in the validity of many of the ballots cast. Until people stand up and make their voices heard the system will not change. A grass roots effort promoting my Contract With The Voter[2] will provide the motivation and framework necessary for everyone to get involved, particularly if my suggestion of adding "None of the Above" as a choice on every General Election ballot is enacted.

The purpose of my chapters outlining many of the indiscretions in the executive, legislative, and judicial branches of government, as well as county by county corruption, is not to conclude that all West Virginia politicians are corrupt individuals or to malign the character of any particular politician. It must also be recognized that sometimes the claims made against elected officials are filtered to citizens through the news media who on occasion may report a story without any known evidentiary foundations for such claims. Nonetheless, such assertions, whether true or not, necessarily hone the already tainted image of elected officials. Moreover, some people might even try to argue there is no good reason to keep bringing up the State's negative past. Scholars may even attempt to simply explain away the various indiscretions and criminal behaviors of State politicians as problems that people have the opportunity to correct on election day. In the first place, as it has been said in many different contexts, ignoring or forgetting the past will only lead to repeating those same mistakes. More than that though, we have never at any point in the State's history left behind the corrupt practices of the past. They continue year after year filling countless column inches in newspapers throughout the State. And, without significant reform, simply having elections every two years will do nothing to cleanup West Virginia's politics and restore voter confidence.

I will never forget the words of one of my political science professors while I was attending undergraduate school at West Virginia University. He theorized that voters have *only* three choices when voting for candidates. He said voters must either choose an honest politician who accomplishes nothing for his constituents, a corrupt politician who accomplishes nothing for his constituents, or a corrupt politician who accomplishes something for his constituents after first taking care of himself and his family. I remember thinking how much I disagreed with his statement and that it seemed so jaded and completely without merit. I also found it troubling that this was a person in a position to shape the opinions of many of his undergraduate students for years to come. Many years later though–after the numerous governmental positions I've held–the views espoused by my former professor are, at the very least, more easily understandable. It is difficult not to become discouraged after observing the high number of West Virginia Governors, Attorneys General, Treasurers, Auditors, Delegates, Senators, Judges, and county and city elected officials committing egregious violations of federal and state law.

Part of the driving force behind my decision to write this book is the fact that I am so outraged with my State's political corruption. The countless disgusting examples of politicians violating the people's trust are not just embarrassing and disheartening, but have completely shattered my confidence in my State's government. I considered the situation and decided that I had a choice, walk away from any thought of public service, which if performed by honest people is the most noble of all professions, or try in some way to do something about these problems. My choice was to put together the framework for reform for all West Virginians so that together we would be able to regain confidence in the system. I have spent years researching West Virginia's past and present indiscretions and developed suggested reforms to help rid the State of its corrupt politics. I no longer just want to complain about our problems, I want to come up with solutions. As I consider the possibility of successfully reforming West Virginia politics, I believe that if one of the most corrupt states in the nation can become one of the cleanest states, then that would set the stage for more individuals in other states to recognize that reform is possible. Those individuals will then have a framework to begin to develop strategies to cleanup their own state governments.

One of my favorite movies is *Mr. Smith Goes to Washington*, a 1939 movie staring James "Jimmy" Stewart. Stewart's character represents the powerful forces of democracy, morality, and freedom, versus the forces of oppression and evil. Stewart's role is an emotional depiction of an optimistic, naive, patriotic young politician who, after being sent to Washington, D.C. as a junior United States Senator from an un-named state, fights political corruption within his state's political machine, and guards American values as a moral hero. I have asked myself countless times if such a person could stand up against the millions of dollars provided by special interests to defeat such a candidacy and actually get elected to serve the people with no strings attached.

Throughout the years, I have had many conversations with numerous elected officials about the future of West Virginia politics and how to effectuate change and if such change was even possible. One of those individuals was former State Speaker of the House of Delegates Lewis McManus, who I have always considered a political giant with unfettered integrity worthy of any citizen's admiration. I first developed what later became a cherished friendship with Lew while I was working in the Governor's Office in 1992 and continued that friendship until his unfortunate death in 2002. He was an incredible man who touched countless lives with his work in the Legislature, with education as the President of the University of Charleston, and with his immeasurable hours as a volunteer to the Ohio-West Virginia YMCA Hi-Y youth program which promotes participation and ethical civic leadership. Lew and I often discussed the problems with politics and the possibilities of change. At some point during the latter part of the 1990s I spoke with him about writing this book. I expressed my concerns about the possible consequences of political retribution toward me and even my family members. Lew, who was a very kind and gentle man, began answering me in a stronger tone than he had ever spoken to me. He pointed his finger in my direction and sternly said, "You don't for a second have a choice in the matter. You have a responsibility to write this book regardless of any potential consequences and I will hear no discussion to the contrary."

On another occasion just before he died, I spoke with Lew in his hospital room. I had loaned him a book on tape about Abraham Lincoln and even though he was near his death–and knew it–he still wanted to learn about people and politics and relished sharing his knowledge and experiences. He wanted to talk at length that day about my book. I just wanted to let him relax, but he would hear none of that. We talked for hours about politics and how important it was to get involved and stay involved regardless of how discouraging it can be at times. Lew, who believed strongly in the people of West Virginia, told me to stand with my convictions and trust the people. He said political corruption and money dominance in politics has historically played a dangerous role in electing candidates to office, but he could foresee a day when people would at last stand up and make the choice to take back their government. He also told me that with regard to the inclusion of hundreds of pages of information detailing the indiscretions of numerous elected officials, to leave every word I had written and asked, "Why do you seem to be apologizing for standing up against those who have tainted this great State's reputation? They are the ones who should be apologizing to each and every West Virginian." Lew then said the final words I ever heard from him and which still resonate with me to this day, "Allen, don't you for a second believe that political courage is political suicide. Those words are not synonymous. Now, write your book and make me proud." I hope he would have been.

# PART ONE

# THE EARLY YEARS

# CHAPTER ONE

# John F. Kennedy's 1960 Primary Election and a Culture of Corruption in Southern West Virginia

*He [Joe Kennedy] bought West Virginia. I don't know how much it cost him; he's a tightfisted old son of a bitch; so he didn't [spend] any more than he had to, but he bought West Virginia, and that's how his boy won the Primary over Humphrey.*

President Harry S. Truman

The 1960 Presidential Primary brought the national spotlight to West Virginia. To seize the nomination, John F. Kennedy, the forty-three-year-old Catholic United States Senator from Massachusetts, needed to defeat Minnesota's United States Senator Hubert Humphrey in the West Virginia Primary to prove to the national convention delegates that a Catholic could collect votes in this deeply religious and ninety-five percent Protestant state.[3]  It was widely held that "a defeat in West Virginia would all but end John F. Kennedy's chance of nomination."[4]  In his book, *John F. Kennedy: The Presidential Portfolio: History as told through the collection of the John F. Kennedy Library and Museum*, author Charles Kenney explains:

> The archives of the John F. Kennedy Library offer eloquent and extensive testimony to the anti-Catholic bias that confronted Senator Kennedy in the presidential campaign of 1960.  One bulging file after another preserves the collection of articles, pamphlets, letters, and resolutions attacking Kennedy because

of his religion. In February 1960 one of Senator Kennedy's aides sought the counsel of a leading West Virginia politician concerning Kennedy's prospects in the state's pivotal presidential primary. The library preserves the memo in which the politician flatly predicted Kennedy would be "whipped" in West Virginia. Why? "Because the senator is a Roman Catholic."[5]

With regard to Kennedy's 1960 victory, Charles Kenney added: "West Virginia proved decisive in the race for the Democratic nomination. Humphrey withdrew from the contest and Kennedy went on to Los Angeles, where he was cheered as the party's nominee."[6] West Virginia was clearly a critical state given the fact that prior to the Primary many in the national press had discounted Kennedy's chances in West Virginia and had already conceded the State to Humphrey. In fact, the *Washington Post* surrendered West Virginia to Humphrey based on "the issue of religion" as it stated, "With one or two exceptions, every West Virginia political newspaper writer that this reporter has interviewed has predicted a victory for Senator Humphrey." The *Charleston Gazette* reported: "U.S. Sen. John F. Kennedy made his first campaign swing through West Virginia Monday amid growing indications that his opponents were gathering en masse to stop him here."[7] Even one of Kennedy's closest aides in the White House, Kenneth P. O'Donnell, explained that the issue of religion was so real that he, Robert F. Kennedy, and the other campaign members,

> went into the [West Virginia] campaign in a gloomy mood, fig-
> uring that odds were stacked against us and praying that Jack
> might at least be able to keep Humphrey from winning more
> than 60 percent of the votes, so that we could claim the moral
> victory that Hubert had claimed in Wisconsin.[8]

O'Donnell said that originally the people of West Virginia had supported Kennedy until they realized he was Catholic when "overnight our whole situation in West Virginia had changed [as the entire campaign then became] on the brink of going down the drain." He recalled attending a meeting of a group of people who had been "working enthusiastically for Kennedy" for several months and had just learned that Kennedy was Catholic. O'Donnell said Robert F. Kennedy addressed the group and asked, "What are our problems?" to which a man stood up and shouted, "There's only one problem. He's a Catholic. That's our God-damned problem!" O'Donnell described another moment when John

Kennedy walked to the Kanawha County Courthouse when only two people from a large crowd that had gathered to get a look at the Presidential candidate approached him and shook his hand. Kennedy quipped to O'Donnell, "Those two guys must have been a couple of visiting Catholics from Pennsylvania."[9]

The widespread predictions of a loss were wrong and the negative sentiment did not reflect the final vote totals as Kennedy was victorious in fifty of the State's fifty-five counties, garnering a sixty-one to thirty-nine percent statewide margin. Kennedy's large margin of victory in the May 10, 1960, West Virginia Democratic Presidential Primary left him with 236,510 votes and Humphrey with 152,510.[10] The 84,000 vote victory, however, came with much controversy. Kennedy was particularly successful in the southern coal counties such as Mingo, Logan, McDowell, Lincoln, and Boone, all of which were dominated by political factions.

One reason cited by the *New York Times* for the victory was far-reaching associations with local political leaders who agreed to slate[11] Kennedy along with favored local candidates.[12] It has often been reported that Kennedy's West Virginia victory "was paid for through bribes and organized crime," and vote-buying.[13] Such campaign practices were not new to John F. Kennedy whose maternal grandfather John F. Fitzgerald's "contentious two terms as mayor of Boston [were] marked by sworn testimony of payoffs and cronyism."[14] Kennedy, nevertheless, attributed his West Virginia victory to voters who cast their vote "on the basis of the issues and not on any religious prejudice."[15] Others have said that Kennedy's success resulted from the "excitement in the hills" that was spread by the likes of "Jack, Jackie, Bobby, Teddy, Franklin D. Roosevelt, Jr., and perhaps Jimmy Hoffa running around the Mountain State."[16] Even Rose Kennedy, John Kennedy's mother, came to Logan County and stayed at the Aracoma Hotel and ate her meals at the Smoke House Restaurant, both located in the City of Logan.[17] Kennedy spent so much time in West Virginia during the campaign that "West Virginia was the third word that his daughter Caroline learned to pronounce."[18] Keith Davis, author of *West Virginia Tough Boys: Vote Buying, Fist Fighting, And A President Named JFK*, who is also the general manager of the *Logan Banner*, a southern West Virginia newspaper since 1888, said, "It was a common thing to see the Kennedys walking the streets of Logan. They used their charm, and they knew how to work people."[19]

Following the Primary, the many allegations of voting corruption in Logan County were investigated by the FBI to determine if federal voting laws were violated. The Attorney General and numerous State newspapers also investigated as newspapers across the nation and throughout the State depicted headlines such as "County Machines Helped to Swell Vote for Kennedy in Primary,"[20]

"Plenty of Votes Bought in W. Virginia Primary,"[21] and "Votes Bought and Sold Openly on Streets."[22]

A story in the *New York World-Telegram and Sun* quoted a Logan County resident, who had been defeated in his bid for Justice of the Peace, as declaring that many voters "wouldn't go inside the house [polling place] unless they were paid. They would just sit in their cars until they got their money." Furthermore, a Chapmanville policeman asserted, "I saw men standing outside the polling place with large stacks of $1 bills. I saw money change hands."[23] Author Peter Mass, when writing for the *Saturday Evening Post*, interviewed a political operative "in one dirt-poor town in West Virginia" who initially told him that his county would be supporting Humphrey. "A few weeks later, I interviewed him again and he said the county was for Jack. I asked what had changed, and he said with a smile, 'My workers each got $20, and I got $150. We're for Kennedy.'"[24] In his book *Kennedy vs. Humphrey, West Virginia, 1960*, well-respected historian Dan Fleming told of "three young reformers" from the southern part of Logan County who "were also in revolt against the voting system." Fleming writes:

> Dr. Luke Combs, a physician, 30; Sam Hatfield, 31, of the famous 'feudin' clan, a teacher at Man High School; and Ned Grubb, 25, an attorney, organized a petition signed by a thousand residents requesting federal officials to oversee the fall 1960 general elections.[25]

The *Pittsburgh Post Gazette* reported that the petition alleged:

> mass selling and buying of votes with money, whiskey, and moonshine; the entering of polling places by candidates and other persons; the forcible denial of voters to vote in privacy by some election officials, and the flagrant operation of the voting machines by some election officials without the consent of the voter and often against his overt protests.[26]

After the petition was presented, the FBI sent agents to Logan County to investigate. "Unfortunately there were few federal laws governing Primary Elections, particularly vote-buying," Fleming asserts. The three individuals thought their efforts with the petition were "non-partisan in nature [and would] insure a comparatively honest election in the fall." Grubb, the twenty-five year-old Logan County lawyer, was described by Fleming as "just someone who wanted to reform the entire corrupt system."[27]

Ironically, even though Grubb led what appeared to be an admirable fight for clean elections in Logan County following the Kennedy 1960 Primary victory, he later earned the unfortunate distinction of being West Virginia's first circuit judge to be convicted of a felony.[28] Grubb was convicted in 1992 of aiding and abetting the payment of a bribe, two counts of aiding and abetting mail fraud, conspiracy to commit fraud, tampering with a witness, obstruction of justice, and operating his judicial office as a racketeering enterprise.[29] Essentially, Grubb was convicted for the same unethical and corrupt political activities that he so gallantly seemed to stand against years earlier.

Wally Barron, then-Attorney General and later Governor, also weighed in on the 1960 election by assigning an Assistant Attorney General to investigate. The extent of Barron's investigation is unknown given the fact that he was reported to have been heavily involved with slating during his own election for Attorney General.[30] Barron's credibility was further tainted in 1968 when he was charged and acquitted on bribery and conspiracy accusations involving kickbacks he and his aides had taken while Barron was Governor. A few years later, Barron was sentenced to a five-year prison term for tampering with the jury that had earlier acquitted him of the corruption charges.[31]

Logan County was described as being like "hungry hogs going to the trough" with regard to the amount of money being spent buying votes. The day after the Primary, the *Logan Banner* maintained that the election was a spree of "flagrant vote-buying, whiskey flowing like water, and coercion of voters . . . . You name it and we just about had it."[32] Soon after the Primary, John F. Kennedy joked that he had received a telegram from his father pleading, "Don't buy another vote, I won't pay for a landslide."[33] Likewise, on other occasions, in an effort to further defuse the criticism about his father's money being used in the campaign, Kennedy expanded his earlier remark by saying, "I have just received the following telegram from my generous father: 'Dear Jack: Don't buy a single vote more than is necessary. I'll help you win this election, but I'll be damned if I'm going to pay for a landslide!"[34]

Just prior to the Primary, *Life* magazine published an article entitled, "The Half-Pint Vote, Slating and the Lever Brothers." It described how votes were bought with money and whiskey, how election officials actually participated by "helping" voters cast a ballot, and how slating was used to win an election.[35] Soon after the article appeared, the *Logan Banner* said it was "rather rough on Logan County;" however, it did not refute many of the troublesome charges.[36]

In his book, *The Making of the President, 1960*, Pulitzer Prize winner, Theodore White, described the people of West Virginia during the Kennedy election as, handsome people and, beyond doubt, the best-mannered and most courteous in the nation. These are people who teach their children to say "Sir" and "Thank you" to their elders; . . . speak in soft and gentle tones; their relations with . . . Negroes are the best of any state with any significant Negro population, north or south. The Negroes, being treated with respect and good manners, reciprocate with a bearing of good manners and respect. Whether on a West Virginia bus or in a crowded West Virginia store, men and women are well-behaved and friendly. Moreover, these are brave people–no state of the union contributed more heavily to the armed forces of the United States in proportion to population than did this state of mountain men; nor did any state suffer more casualties in proportion to its population. That they should live as they do is a scar and shame on American life, an indictment of the national political system as well as of their own.[37]

Nonetheless, White maintains that West Virginia politics at the time was extraordinarily corrupt. He says,

If one were to choose those states whose politics . . . are the most squalid, corrupt and despicable, then one would add West Virginia to the Jukes family of American politics. . . . West Virginia politics rise from hunger, and they are sordid politics. . . . Politics in West Virginia involves money–hot money, under-the-table money, open money. . . . Politics in West Virginia can be violent. . . . The local bosses, the union chiefs, the statewide candidates, the education-board candidates, even the veterans organizations, all make cross-alliances to settle on, then print a 'slate' of approved candidates . . . and money is spent lavishly–and legally–in providing such 'slates' [to the voters].[38]

Charlie Peters, a former West Virginia legislator and editor of the political journal *The Washington Monthly*, maintains, "Votes are bought in every West Virginia election" and contends that "in the culture of Appalachia, it's a severe problem–like the old moonshining tradition."[39] Peters, who served as one of four members of the committee who approved my dissertation at American University, witnessed much of West Virginia's colorful political past when he worked on Kennedy's campaign in 1960, while he successfully and simultane-ously campaigned for himself to be elected to the West Virginia House of Delegates. Peters is also credited as the man who urged his Peace Corps friend, current United States Senator Jay Rockefeller, to go to West Virginia to learn about poverty and other problems that existed in the State.

Current City of Logan Mayor, former Deputy County Assessor, Magistrate candidate, and political faction leader Claude "Big Daddy" Ellis, described the vote-buying in Logan County as "simply a way of life." Ellis said, "I've known people who turn around and go back home if you didn't have something for them [to buy their vote]." He added that election time "is Christmas for a lot of people still."[40]   Ellis, who handled Kennedy's campaign in Logan County and worked closely with Teddy and Robert Kennedy, has been described as "a rough and tough individual in 1960, [who] exercised his own particular brand of politics, which often involved his clenched fist or the influence he commanded by carrying a crowbar."[41]   Raymond Chafin, another longtime Democratic faction leader and "political boss" in Logan County agreed with Ellis saying, "there were folks around Logan who would be nearly offended if you didn't offer them at least something for their vote. Something was expected. They were used to being paid. It's the way it was done. I didn't plan to disappoint them."[42]

According to the autobiography of Raymond Chafin, the Kennedy vic-tory in southern West Virginia was aided by a long-established system of voter bribery in the boss-dominated coalfields.[43]  Chafin's autobiography adds a unique perspective on a practice that is often discussed, but with few details. Chafin, nephew of the infamous Devil Anse Hatfield, also claims to have "spread money and influence around southern West Virginia" in order to help many other politi-cians such as United States Senator Robert C. Byrd, and at least three Governors.[44]  Chafin said that he spent money on Byrd because he liked him per-sonally and that Byrd was one of only a "few fellers who abstained from that sort of thing." Chafin has said, "You'd be surprised how many local and state elec-tions have been decided on the back deck of my home. In times gone by, we have argued and nearly fist-fought in my yard over the strategy and outcome of Primary Elections." As for the Kennedy election, Chafin says,

> John F. Kennedy took the State of West Virginia by storm. It's
> now history. However, what people should remember is that it
> was a presidential race that was bought and paid for—cold cash
> for nearly every voter. The Kennedys were well aware of our
> brand of politics. I guess it was their brand, too.[45]

Chafin describes from his perspective the election practices in Logan County during the 1930s and continuing to the present-day. Political factions such as the one in Logan County illustrate just how readily large numbers of votes could be controlled by a small number of individuals. Chafin, whose own father-in-law was killed in an Election Day shooting, recalls times when some politicians needed armed guards and remembers when the various political deals were contrived at night along the rural roads of southern West Virginia.[46]

Chafin had originally supported Minnesota Senator and presidential candidate Hubert Humphrey for the 1960 Democratic Presidential nomination after receiving $2,500 from him to buy votes on his behalf; however, after being handed $35,000 stuffed in sealed briefcases by Kennedy operatives just days before the Primary, Chafin switched his support to Kennedy.[47] With regard to double-crossing Humphrey, Chafin said,

> Seriously, twenty-five hundred dollars ain't nothin! Jeez, what could we have really done with that? Humphrey knew he lost his position because he didn't have the kind of finances to pull things off. He gave me a measly $2,500; you can't barely buy a used car for that kind of money nowadays.

Chafin added that the,

> Kennedy campaign was a tough one–and a dangerous one, at that. When you go to foolin' around with that kind of folk who were in that campaign, it gets mighty risky. Both sides, Humphrey and Kennedy campaigners, had people involved who would tear you up in a heartbeat if need be. I'm talkin' both local and national politicians, now. Plus, when youse got big money–cash–'round ya, you get mighty squirrelly.[48]

Chafin was called a few days prior to the Primary Election by the Kennedy campaign and told to bring bodyguards with him to retrieve "something to work with" that the campaign was sending to him on a plane later that day.[49] Upon arriving at the landing strip at Taplin Airport in Logan County, Chafin recalled:

> It was rainin', and the tiny plane circled the runway before it landed. We were soaked and I could hardly see through my glasses 'cause of the constant drizzle. The pilot landed the

small aircraft and two fellas jumped out of the plane, holding
two sealed bags. When they got up to us, they handed the sop-
ping-wet bags over to Bus [Perry] and me.[50]

Chafin explained that when he told the Kennedy campaign that he needed "about
thirty-five," that he actually meant $3,500 and not the $35,000 he received in
packages of five, ten, and twenty-dollar bills. Chafin said, "There were fives, tens,
and twenties–all wrapped up. The money was in crisp, new bills. The bags were
soaking wet, and when we counted it all, there was even some green ink left on the
sheets of the bed." Upon learning exactly how much money the Kennedys gave
to Chafin to buy votes, Bus Perry, who drove Chafin to the airport that day, said,
"I've already been in the penitentiary once! I'm not going back! I haven't seen
anything–nothing! I don't want anything to do with this!"[51] Chafin calmed Perry
down and called the Kennedy campaign and told them that they may have made a
mistake. To this the campaign responded, "Hell no! There's no mistake! We know
you're doing your job!"[52] Chafin explained that Kennedy campaign big-wheel
Jim McCahey chuckled and said, "I don't know where the money came from, but
you have a job to do there. We know you'll be able to take care of things with
those two bags of . . . uh . . . literature, right?"[53] Kennedy's brother-in-law Robert
Sargent Shriver is quoted as saying he "vividly" remembered a 1960 meeting with
a "top Logan County official a few days before the May 10 voting and being able
to persuade the leader to switch from Humphrey to Kennedy."[54] Chafin said,

Nobody will ever know where that money came from. Never!

But I'll tell you what we did with it. We bought votes with it!
Regardless of what you want to believe, that's the way real politics works. We used up all that money from the bags and won
the whole dang election. It takes large amounts of money to
sweep an election. We had it, all right!

I'd say there were about two thousand dollars worth of two-
dollar bills, besides the other money. I wish now I would have
kept the two-dollar bills. They'd be worth a fortune now.[55]

Chafin recalls traveling to McDowell, Wyoming, Mingo, and Boone
counties to deliver the "Kennedy campaign money" to pay for election day operations in those counties as well. Chafin said,

People are still trying to determine how John F. Kennedy did so
well in southern West Virginia, the heart of the 'anti-Catholic'
Bible Belt. McDowell County gave him eighty-four percent of
the vote, the highest in the state. The second highest was
Wyoming County, with seventy-eight percent of the vote.
Logan and Mingo each delivered more than fifty-five percent
for Kennedy, and as a result he carried the entire state by more
than 84,000 votes.[56]

Chafin said people sold their votes for cash or personal items such as
payment for a driver's license for someone who could not afford it, or payment
for someone's electric bill as "free-flowing liquor and crisp bills were commonly involved on Election Day." Chafin added that with regard to the influx of
Kennedy money, "where we originally had two hundred dollars designated for a
precinct, we might put four hundred or even five hundred, maybe a thousand.
Where we had five hundred dollars planned, we switched it to eight hundred, a
thousand, maybe two thousand dollars."[57]

Chafin said he used a hotel room at the Aracoma Hotel as his headquarters which was where the money was divided and the cash was placed inside
manila envelopes and shopping bags and eventually given to precinct captains
who then helped to deliver votes for the slate. Chafin explained that at his
request, Logan County Sheriff Ed McDonald placed two deputies to guard the
hotel room during the day as two more replaced them to guard Chafin and his
campaign money during the night. Chafin said his headquarters in Room 220 of
the Aracoma Hotel was "overflowing with swollen envelopes of cash, slate cards,
campaign posters, and literature." He said John Kennedy and his brothers "had
a firm understanding of how to pull a grumbling faction together and how to win
in a state like West Virginia. The key: cash, and lots of it. It always works."[58]

Chafin writes of distributing money freely in buying votes and how he
used his political leverage to get Logan County what it needed, such as roads,
bridges, schools and even a new courthouse.[59] Chafin said many people routinely sold their votes to the highest bidder for cash, moonshine, jobs, or "about anything they could get out of it."[60] Chafin's father, however, believed, "You don't
work in politics for no money! You sell your soul when you do that–and you
don't do that!"[61] Chafin explained that in order to get people to vote for his political faction, he would promise and later deliver new bridges, roads, and even new
schools.[62] Moreover, Chafin said the importance of winning was driven by jobs:
"Back then, if Democrats won, they got the jobs. If the Republicans won, they
got the jobs."[63]

The *Logan Banner's* Keith Davis said: "In Logan County, it was common to pay voters to pull the lever in the voting booth the way the local political bosses wanted it pulled." In Davis' book, he said the Kennedy family used West Virginia's political machinery and used former political bosses to describe money drops, vote-buying, and other political shenanigans. Davis said the political bosses, "were just following through on politics as they had always known it. But I was shocked that it was such a blatant thing. There is a certain amount of pride these fellows have in explaining how they pulled it off."[64] Davis also said that the political bosses were not above using violence to get their way and that: "Natives of the area grew up with voting corruption as a part of their mountain culture, and many believed that a campaign, regardless of how organized and professional it may have seemed, wasn't really a campaign at all unless it included cash or liquor at the precincts."[65]

Seventy-nine-year-old Logan County political boss Claude Ellis, known as one of the most notorious machine politicians in his younger days, takes credit for helping John Kennedy win Logan County on a platform of "saw bucks and half-pints" during the 1960 Primary. He says that buying votes during that time period was an easy task and that: "Back in those days, it was wide open. You could do anything you wanted." He added, "It was widely known that the Kennedy campaign blanketed the Logan County area with $10 bills and half-pints for the 1960 campaign."[66] Ellis claims the Kennedy campaign gave him between $50,000 and $60,000 in cash to purchase votes in Logan County precincts and most of that money was given to him by Kennedy campaign staffer Kenneth P. O'Donnell.[67] Ellis explained that voters would stand outside the polling place making deals for whom to vote and what they would receive in return. Then, if a voter agreed to sell his or her vote, a precinct worker inside would get the sign and watch for the seller's ballot.[68] He said, "They'd give a sign–thumbs up or tug their ear, whatever they had worked out–that the person had voted right. Then they got their money or their whiskey." Ellis said the corrupt system of politics in rural Appalachia was "all we ever knew." Ellis also said,

> *Scripps Howard News Service* had reporters in here in 1960. I was working up at Stratton Hollow precinct. When it was all over, a news writer said that we went in and out of the polls more times than the election officers did. It was the way it was done then, and the way we handled it was TOUGH! It was all politics, paid in a bundle, and whoever could buy the most votes wound up with the precinct when the polls closed.[69]

After reflecting on his many years as a political kingpin in Logan County, Ellis said, "I knew there was a job to be done; and I did whatever it took to get the job done–and then I let the chips fall where they may. Period." Ellis said, "It took thousands of dollars, thousands of handshakes, and plenty of corn whiskey to do it, but we got people out to the precincts." Ellis also said, "Folks need to be passionate enough to fight over their candidate or do whatever it takes to make 'em win–even if it involves buying the election. Believe me, I knows what I'm talkin' 'bout. I wouldn't steer ya wrong–that's for dang sure." He added,

> I'd do it all the same way again–so my politicians would be successful. Being victorious is important. It's the final outcome that counts. Yes, we may have bought votes and handed out whiskey in pint bottles; but I also know that we were partly responsible for John Kennedy's victory. The outcome was worth the methods we used.[70]

Likewise, Chafin explains that the key to winning an election is controlling the precincts and that there were more than a hundred precincts in Logan County during those days. Chafin said precinct captains were chosen who, in turn, were responsible for hiring all of the campaign workers and for determining "the amount of money they needed to pay people in order [to] 'win' their boss's candidates." Chafin describes the captains as people with political jobs and political knowledge who either had the largest families or who had developed solid relationships with everyone in their neighborhoods. Captains coordinated cars to get people to the polls, managed the money necessary to win the precinct and "in some cases, the captains were the ones who paid for votes."[71] This explains why Chafin believed that precinct captains were so vital on election day and why he was able to wield so much power. Chafin writes:

> Now most southern West Virginia voters took pride in voting for its own sake, while others took pride in what they were going to get for it–money, a job, a pint of whiskey, or some favor from a politician. Everyone had a good reason to get to the polls on election day, though, and most of the competition for votes was right there at the precincts–among those party captains. They did anything and everything they could to get the votes in for their people. At times, things could get pretty rough around the polling places.[72]

Chafin said the mechanics of vote-buying requires the cooperation of both Republicans and Democrats at the polling places. Voters willing to sell their ballot simply asked an election commissioner (who by law are from both political parties) for "assistance." The election commissioners then "assisted" the voter by casting the ballot in favor of a particular political slate of which the voter was going to be paid to vote; then, the commissioner signaled outside the "house" (voting precinct) that the vote had been cast, allowing campaign workers in the yard to make the promised payment. Chafin said that occasionally a Republican in the highly outnumbered Democratic areas would receive a token job as a reward for participation in the corrupt system. Chafin added:

> If someone was selling his vote, one of the commissioners would take him over to a table and he'd watch that voter fill out his ballot. Or the voter might just let the commissioner do it for him. (Some of those fellows could vote a ticket faster than a chicken pickin' up corn!) When that voter came out of the building, a commissioner in the doorway gave a sign, which changed every hour or so. That commissioner might tug on his nose or scratch his ear or something to show his faction's people outside that the voter had done what they wanted. Then the precinct captain signed off to somebody else, who met that voter and paid him off.[73]

The production of slates was a big part of an election during that period. Many politicians during those days declared that you were either on the slates or you lost the election. In some counties there were competing political factions with separate slates. Each faction would raise money by levying a hefty fee, or "contribution," for each candidate who wished to be included on the slate. That money was typically used to print the slates as well as to pay voters. Money played an intricate role in slating of candidates as a candidate with limited funds might not be able to raise the money and thus, typically would be left off the slates, often losing the election as a result. Those candidates with money would often buy placement onto more than one slate.

Chafin's nonchalant attitude toward southern West Virginia politics demonstrates this was simply a way of life for politicians throughout various communities. It also demonstrates how easy it was for Chafin to control the votes for Kennedy in the 1960 Election. He remembers one election in which an argument began with regard to whether or not a group was voting in the correct precinct. Chafin says the event turned so violent that one man was shot in the head and killed. While two men were tried for the murder, one was declared innocent and the other was later pardoned, possibly not even serving a day in prison.[74]

Raymond Chafin has yet to retire from politics. Former *Charleston Gazette* political columnist Fanny Seiler said that Chafin, the long-time Logan County political boss who supported former Governor Cecil Underwood, was instrumental in getting his administration to pave a private road just prior to the General Election in November 2000 when Underwood was running for re-election. The Logan County road supervisor, Curley Belcher, said Chafin aided his friend in getting the road paved by directing him to pave the private road under an "emergency order."[75]

In describing politics of the 1960s and before, Chafin said, "If you wanted to win an election, it was fist-and-skull back then. If you didn't go out there and risk getting shot or killed, you didn't work an election at all. It was dangerous in those days." Chafin believes that elections are much different today, particularly in light of the limitations on the amount a candidate can pay election workers as well as the fact they can no longer campaign at the polls.[76] In addition, many local residents described Logan County politics as a "great game," a "sport," and a "way of life."[77]

Chafin believes that while those limitations are in place in today's elections, there are no limits placed on the amounts that someone can pay for television advertising. He says one difference in candidates today is that they are more concerned with how they will look on television than actually going from county to county, door to door, or by campaigning at different meetings around the State. He further believes that only a rich man has a chance to win a campaign today as they can purchase substantial television buys that make it difficult for the average person to compete. Chafin said,

> The way it is now, nobody but the rich man's got a chance to win. You pay hundreds of thousands of dollars to the advertisers, and they'll say anything you want them to about the other side. A poor person running for office doesn't have any way to fight a campaign like that. There's no way they can compete.[78]

In addition, Chafin expressed that the television campaign commercials don't tell the potential voter anything about the candidate and that many are not even fit for public consumption. He said, "If you had [said] such things about one of our candidates in the old days, he'd have knocked your head off." Chafin further asserted that the coal companies' only concern was with which candidate would allow them to "get away with more." He said,

These coal companies and big businesses are all the same. Their money people ask, 'Which man is going to let me dump the most in the creek?,' 'Who's going to let me strip coal and scrape the trees over the hillside the way I want?,' or 'Who'll let me get by this law or that one?'[79]

Joe Savage, a former United States Attorney for the Southern District of West Virginia, said there were no successful vote-buying prosecutions in West Virginia until the late 1980s in part because of a sense that juries would be unlikely to condemn such behavior by their neighbors and friends. Savage referred to a time when, "[o]ne drug-dealing fire chief and local political boss [was] met by the fire truck and paraded through town for a hero's welcome during a brief release from custody as he awaited the start of a ten year sentence."[80] It seems that as a society, we consistently continue to tolerate misconduct by local officials.

Chafin's description of life in Logan County during that time period confirms Savage's belief. Chafin depicts a time of lawlessness depending on whose side of the political fence a person belonged. He recalled a time when his friend John was fighting a man who had just arrived in town to promote the union. The sheriff arrested both of them and said, "Now, John, I've told you about starting trouble down here. . . . You already killed four or five people and here you are beating up on this fellow. I believe we're gonna have to put you in jail this time." The Sheriff, however, let John go when he promised not to fight anymore.[81]

Chafin explained the political nature and risk of holding a State job when he recalled a time when he and an associate were fired personally from their Division of Highways jobs by Governor Matthew Mansfield Neely for not joining a different political faction in Logan County. Chafin quoted the Governor as declaring, "[n]ow, both of you work for the state roads, and you'll do exactly as I say, or you won't have a job in my administration!"[82] The use of the Division of Highways as a political tool of the Governor's Office was common during those days. Even my grandfather, Scott Hovatter, who was a strong Democratic leader in Tucker County politics, fell victim to the political axe based upon his political party affiliation. He has told me on several occasions how then-Governor Cecil H. Underwood fired him from his position with the State Road (Division of Highways) in Tucker County because he had supported the Democratic candidate who lost to Underwood during the 1956 election. He said, "It was just the way it was done back then. We all knew our jobs depended on who won the Governor's Office and that's why we fought so hard for our candidates. It didn't make it any easier losing my job, but it wasn't unexpected."

Strong political machines weren't only in southern West Virginia during the Kennedy Election.  The Northern Panhandle of West Virginia had a
strong and well-financed political organization just as the north-central part of
West Virginia also had strong political factions.[83]  For instance, in Harrison
County, "Humphrey never had a chance since he was opposed by the powerful
county machine, lacked support from labor, and was swamped by the well-
organized Kennedy operation."  Author Dan Fleming quoted Harry Pauley, the
Speaker of the House of Delegates in West Virginia in 1960, as saying that
Kennedy leaders offered so much money that it "would pay for the next couple
of elections in Harrison County."[84]

Fleming asserts that West Virginia's largest county, Kanawha County,
had several independent voters and was not a "machine-controlled county like
Logan or McDowell."  He did admit, however, there were still several precincts
that were so called "machine-controlled."  Fleming also included comments from
Kanawha County resident Edward W. Hiserman to describe his view of a typical
Kanawha County election.

> There is an inside man and an outside man at every bought
> precinct.  There's also a 'rider' who goes around from precinct
> to precinct with money.  The side man has some token–often
> it's baseball tickets.  When a purchasable voter comes into the
> polls, the inside man goes into the booth with him and makes
> certain how he votes–or votes for him.  Then the inside man
> gives the voter a baseball ticket.  The voter takes this token to
> the outside man and gets paid for voting–$2 or $3 usually.
> When the outside man runs out of money, he gets more by giv-
> ing the rider the tickets he has collected as proof that he used
> the money in the agreed way.[85]

Much speculation exists even today about exactly how much money
poured into the hills of West Virginia during the 1960 Presidential Election.
Pulitzer Prize-winning and investigative journalist Seymour Hersh asserts in his
book *The Dark Side of Camelot* that $2 million was dumped into West Virginia
by the Kennedy campaign.[86]  Hersh explained that "political payoffs in West
Virginia had begun in October 1959, when young Teddy Kennedy traveled across
the State distributing cash to the Democratic committeeman in each county."[87]
Hersh said:

Bonn Brown of Elkins was the personal attorney to W.W. 'Wally' Barron, who was elected Democratic Governor of West Virginia in 1960. He estimated the Kennedy outlay at between $3 million and $5 million, with some sheriffs being paid as much as $50,000. Asked how he knew, Brown told me curtly, 'I know. If you don't get those guys'–the sheriffs–'they will really fight you.' In his role as adviser to the Democratic gubernatorial candidate, Brown met with Robert Kennedy and other campaign officials 'and told them who to see and what to do, but stayed clear of it myself. Bobby was as smart and mean as a snake. I think he had more to do with West Virginia'–the victory there, and the payoffs–'than any other person. Bobby ran it; he was the one who set it up.' Governor Barron was later convicted on bribery charges, and Brown was later convicted of the attempted bribery of a juror in the case.[88]

Hersh added, "In West Virginia, the Kennedys spent at least $2 million (nearly $11 million in today's dollars), and possibly twice that amount–much of it in direct payoffs to state and local officials." Hersh said:

Many West Virginia county and state officials revealed that the Kennedy family spent upward of $2 million in bribes and other payoffs before the May 10, 1960 primary, with some sheriffs in key counties collecting more than $50,000 apiece in cash in return for placing Kennedy's name at the top of their election slate. Much of the money was distributed personally by Bobby and Teddy Kennedy. The Kennedy campaign would publicly claim after the convention that only $100,000 had been spent in West Virginia (out of $912,500 in expenses claimed for the entire campaign).

Hersh also wrote:

Buying votes was nothing new in West Virginia, where political control was tightly held by sheriffs or political committeemen in each of the state's fifty-five counties. . . . The sheriffs and party leaders were also responsible for hiring precinct workers and poll watchers for election day. Political tradition in the state called for the statewide candidates to pay some or all of the county's election expenses in return for being placed at the top of a political leader's slate. Paying a few dollars per vote on election day was widespread in some areas, as was the payment for 'Lever Brothers' (named after the popular detergent maker)—election officers in various precincts who were instructed to actually walk into the ballot booth with voters and cast their ballots for them.[89]

In Dan Fleming's book on the Kennedy election, he quotes Kennedy's brother-in-law, Sargent Shriver, explaining how he compelled southern West Virginia officials to support Kennedy: "We played the West Virginia game by the West Virginia rules."[90] When I spoke with Sargent Shriver in 2000, as he and United States Senator Ted Kennedy were campaigning in Logan County for the Democratic Party ticket, he repeated those remarks to me. He told me with a mischievous smile on his face that he remembered many of the people from southern West Virginia "vividly" and he simply helped them to facilitate a Kennedy victory "in the only way they knew how to do it." In Keith Davis' book, he provides the words of a former newspaper reporter who covered the 1960 election. The former reporter, who only spoke to Davis with the condition of anonymity, said at least $2.5 million in cash was delivered on one occasion to a Charleston motel. He added:

> I arrived at a Charleston motel a few minutes after the money had arrived. Several powerful people were there, and they all were talking and laughing about the cash. I was young and bold at the time. I asked if I could lift one of the containers, an aluminum suitcase. After I received a lackluster nod, I grabbed up one of the bags, and I honestly couldn't believe how heavy the suitcase was. Later the cases were opened and my jaw dropped.[91]

Former President Harry S. Truman even weighed in on the election, calling Joe Kennedy "as big a crook as we've got anywhere in this country" and stated, "He [Joe Kennedy] bought West Virginia. I don't know how much it cost him; he's a tightfisted old son of a bitch; so he didn't [spend] any more than he had to, but he bought West Virginia, and that's how his boy won the Primary over Humphrey."[92] Likewise, former Speaker of the United States House of Representatives Tip O'Neill said Joe Kennedy made all of the arrangements and that in West Virginia, "they passed money around like it was never seen." O'Neill said Eddie Ford, a successful Boston real estate man, went out there [with] a pocket full of money [and would] see the sheriff, and he'd say, 'Sheriff, I'm from Chicago. I'm on my way south. I love this young Kennedy boy. He can help this nation, by God. He's got the feeling for it, you know. He'll do things for West Virginians. I'll tell you what. Here's $3,000 [or] here's $5,000. You carry your village for him or your county for him, and I'll give you a little reward when I'm on my way back.[93]

When asked if Kennedy bought the 1960 West Virginia Primary Election, Claude Ellis, who directed Kennedy's winning campaign in Logan County, said with a wink and a smile, "I'd have to check if the statute of limitations ran out yet." Ellis added, "He didn't want to buy West Virginia, he just rented it for a day." Kennedy opponent Hubert Humphrey said, "I can't afford to run around this State with a little black bag and a checkbook. I don't have a daddy to pay the bills. I don't have an open checkbook." The Kennedy campaign, however, only declared to have spent $55,000 for advertising; $10,000 for traveling; and $5,000 for printing and mailings in West Virginia for the entire campaign.[94]

Ken Hechler, former United States Congressman, West Virginia Secretary of State, and speechwriter for President Harry S. Truman, said claims of the Kennedys spending millions of dollars in West Virginia were "outrageous" and typically used to sell books. Hechler said Kennedy didn't need to buy votes in West Virginia because his campaign was more cohesive and better organized than Humphrey's.[95] Hechler believed much of his success was due to the many Kennedy family members who toured the State–as did the popular Franklin D. Roosevelt, Jr.–on behalf of Kennedy, while Humphrey traveled primarily with his wife.[96] During his comments in the United States House of Representatives, then-Congressman Hechler stated:

Mr. Speaker, it was a glorious spring in 1960 in West Virginia. The laurel-decked hillsides sparkled. When the early morning fog had lifted from the mountaintop airports, plane-loads of news commentators, political experts, and curious visitors debarked and headed for the hills and hollows. This was political primary time in West Virginia, the primary which started John F. Kennedy on the road to the White House.

West Virginia, the 35th State in the Union, made John F. Kennedy the 35th President of the United States. It was on this battleground on the 10th day of May 1960 that the future President scored a smashing victory which buried the so-called religious issue.[97]

With regard to buying votes in the West Virginia Primary, Raymond Chafin's autobiography states:

> Ever since the last vote was tallied that spring, analysts have speculated about the effects of vote-buying and 'out-of-state' wealth on JFK's victory. Investigations were carried out by the U.S. Justice Department, the FBI, anti-Kennedy Democrats, the *Wall Street Journal*, local newspapers, and Washington espouser Jack Anderson. Invariably the conclusion was, as one former state governor declared (intending no apparent irony), that Kennedy had 'sold himself' to the voters, not bought them.[98]

Speculation continues to this day, however, with regard to the details surrounding the West Virginia Primary that propelled John F. Kennedy, despite his religion, into the national spotlight as a feasible candidate. In 1995, Pierre Salinger, who worked on Kennedy's campaign and later became his press secretary, confirmed that money went to local officials (including a number of sheriffs) in order to get Kennedy's name on printed campaign material.[99]

In *The Kennedys: Dynasty and Disaster*, John H. Davis maintains:

> In December, 1961, FBI listening devices picked up evidence of large Mafia donations to the West Virginia campaign that had apparently been disbursed through Frank Sinatra. It was this under-the-table money, used to make payoffs to key election officials, that was to be the deciding factor in the contest.[100]

On October 8, 2000, Tina Sinatra told *60 Minutes* that her father, Frank Sinatra, had been approached by Kennedy's multimillionaire father, Joseph P. Kennedy, to contact Chicago mob kingpin Sam Giancana, to help secure the union vote in the 1960 West Virginia Presidential Primary.[101] Sinatra always publicly denied such allegations of his complicity in a scandal involving mafia association in the 1960 West Virginia Primary Election.[102] Sinatra's assertion that the Mafia's help to Kennedy was crucial in bringing a Kennedy victory over Humphrey in the 1960 Primary Election only reinforced the image of corruption in West Virginia's political system. News of Sinatra's allegations with regard to the West Virginia Primary has been documented *ad nauseam* in papers around the world.[103] It must be noted that while Frank Sinatra's daughter's book may not be given the same credibility as a finding of fact provided by a court, it nonetheless is a further example of the continued perception of incessant corruption surrounding West Virginia elections.

Moreover, according to author Nellie Bly, "Judy Campbell [who claimed she was a mistress of President Kennedy] arranged a meeting for [John Kennedy] with Sam Giancana at the Fontainebleau [a hotel in Miami Beach, Florida]. Giancana agreed to use his influence with West Virginia officials to ensure victory there. In all, Judy Campbell arranged ten meetings between the President and the mob boss. She acted as their courier, carrying plain sealed manila envelopes among JFK [and] Giancana. . . ." Then, "Giancana sent his lieutenant, Paul 'Skinny' D'Amato, into West Virginia to get out the vote. D'Amato met with the sheriffs who controlled the State's political machine. He forgave debts many of them had run up at his 500 Club in Atlantic City and handed cash payments to others." In addition, "FBI wiretaps reveal that Frank Sinatra also disbursed large mob donations to pay off election officials."[104]

The situation of the Kennedy election in West Virginia has not faded from headlines throughout the country. In 1993, for example, federal and state prosecutors launched investigations into the election of then-New Jersey Republican Governor Christine Todd Whitman. The allegations were that as much as $500,000 in "walking-around money" under her control was paid to curtail the traditionally Democratic black vote in the gubernatorial election. The *Baltimore Sun* reported:

> The handing out of "walking-around money" has fallen off, some consultants say, as appeals by direct mail, radio and television have increased. In the past, it has not been restricted to local or state elections. It has been used, or rumored to have been used, in presidential campaigns as well, notably in the West Virginia presidential primary of 1960 by supporters of John F. Kennedy against Hubert H. Humphrey. In Chicago, Democrats tell the story that Franklin D. Roosevelt used to say that when he died he wanted to be buried in the Windy city so that he could keep on voting–and be paid for it.[105]

Kennedy did take an interest in West Virginia after he was elected President. The first food stamps were distributed in McDowell County soon after the election and Kennedy also doubled the surplus food allotment and extended welfare benefits for the poor in West Virginia. Perhaps the most significant benefit to the State came from Kennedy's support for Interstate 79 which runs from the north to the south of West Virginia.[106]

In any case, many people in West Virginia to this day, particularly in the southern counties, think of the Kennedys as royalty. They feel responsible for putting John Kennedy into the White House and are proud of West Virginia's involvement during the 1960 campaign. In fact, Massachusetts United States Senator Ted Kennedy is often referred to as West Virginia's third United States Senator. The people of southern West Virginia feel an excitement and warmth surrounding the Kennedys and any discussion of vote-buying doesn't seem to taint that image in the least.

Recognizing their enormous popularity in a state far away from their own, the Kennedys often campaign in the hills of West Virginia on behalf of national candidates. On one such occasion during the 2000 Presidential campaign, Senator Ted Kennedy campaigned in southern West Virginia on behalf of Presidential candidate Al Gore. At the time I was a Senior Assistant Attorney General in West Virginia and attended various political events throughout the State on behalf of the Attorney General. At one such campaign rally, held at a high school gymnasium in Chapmanville, West Virginia [Logan County], I was alone in a room with Senator Kennedy prior to the beginning of the political event. Senator Kennedy and I talked about his campaigning in West Virginia during the 1960 election and he said to me at least ten times, "The Kennedys love West Virginia." He said it so many times that it was a little bit awkward as I found myself running out of ways to respond. In fact, he even wrote "The Kennedys love West Virginia" on a picture he later signed and sent to my grandfather for his eighty-sixth birthday. My grandfather had worked for the Kennedy campaign in Tucker County, which is located in north-central West Virginia. At one point, Senator Kennedy suddenly seemed to change to a more serious demeanor and said that with the exception of Massachusetts, there simply was no place like West Virginia and "without West Virginia, Jack would not have been President. It's that simple!"

While we waited for the other dignitaries to arrive so the event could begin, Senator Kennedy and I spoke about the first time we had met, which was shortly after a huge flood occurred on November 4, 1985. The flood devastated my family's business as well as most of the other businesses and homes located in my small hometown of Parsons, West Virginia. Senator Kennedy at the time was skiing just twenty-four miles away with his family at a resort in Canaan Valley. He and his two sons, Edward Moore Kennedy, Jr. and Patrick Kennedy, drove to the area to look at the extensive damage and decided to address the community, which was both confused and scared because of the devastation left behind. It was a natural disaster that gained international attention. The Senator spoke at my church and I remember the day vividly even though I was just fifteen years old. We only had one microphone and I was the person who carried it back and forth between Senator Kennedy and the community members. Before his address, Senator Kennedy, his two sons, a friend of mine named Arlie Davis, and I, all sat in a small room on boxes of Army rations that had been provided by the government to feed the people who had lost everything. In 2000, as we once again sat in a small room prior to Kennedy addressing a large crowd of people, the Senator remembered the 1985 day and described the church, some of the people, and much of the devastation. He spoke to me with vivid recollection and concern about what had happened and what that small town and others like it had been through.

When it was finally time to begin the political rally, Senator Kennedy and several other political dignitaries proceeded to the stage in the gym. As I was standing behind Senator Kennedy and Senator John D. Rockefeller, IV, who were seated on the stage, I couldn't believe what I was seeing. There must have been two or three thousand people in the audience completely energized. While that may not sound like a lot of people for a political rally, the fact was that the Kennedy visit to Logan County happened with virtually no notice to anyone. I didn't even find out about his visit until nearly two hours before he arrived and I had been communicating daily with the State Democratic Party and Al Gore Presidential Campaign State leader Patrick Baskette. I was the Democratic Party's contact with regard to coordinating the Attorney General's schedule, whom they wanted to appear at various political functions as he was considered the highest ranking State Democrat due to the fact that Governor Cecil Underwood was a Republican. In any case, with virtually no notice of Kennedy's arrival, people dropped everything the second they heard the news and swarmed to the local high school gym to see him. As I looked at the jam-packed crowd, I saw John F. Kennedy campaign signs from the 1960 election as well as political signs from Robert F. Kennedy's 1968 election. I could only imagine that the signs had been prominently displayed in the homes of many of these people ever since the days of those elections many years ago. People even brought gifts for the Senator. One such gift was a framed painting of John F. Kennedy and Robert F. Kennedy that was presented to Senator Kennedy after he spoke to the crowd and was preparing to leave. He was very gracious to the individual and he turned to me as I was talking with his brother-in-law Sargent Shriver, and ask me to mail the portrait to him because he didn't want it to get broken during his return trip to Washington, D.C. Of course I agreed and mailed it to Senator Kennedy the next day at my expense, which, back then, was a surprising cost of more than $50. As I paid for the packing and postage, I couldn't help but wonder exactly how many votes that would have bought for his brother John in southern West Virginia in 1960.

Senator Kennedy has made plenty of other appearances in West Virginia throughout the years. In fact, during the 2004 Presidential Election he again traveled the hills and hollows of the State trying to garner votes for Senator John F. Kerry. He went from city to city drawing large crowds everywhere he went. It has been my experience that when people show up to see any of the Kennedys in West Virginia they immediately become energized as they cling to the image of Camelot following the tragedies suffered by the family.

I remember another time during the 2000 election when Joe Kennedy, former United States Congressman from Massachusetts and son of Robert F. Kennedy, arrived in Bluefield, West Virginia for a campaign rally. Joe, who has the Kennedy family smile, was flanked by his wife Beth, a very attractive, tall, and extremely friendly woman. The courtroom was packed with people who wanted to meet a Kennedy. Most of the people I talked with that day didn't even know who Joe Kennedy was as I must have heard at least thirty-five different people say: "Which Kennedy is he?" They didn't care. They just wanted to shake the hands of a Kennedy–any Kennedy–and tell them what their family meant to West Virginia. Joe Kennedy and I had met in years past while I was working for former Congressman Harley O. Staggers, Jr. Joe, his wife, and I talked about Harley that day and shared a few stories about how much we both liked him as a person and hated that he was forced out of politics due to West Virginia's loss of one Congressman following the 1990 redistricting.

I asked Beth what she thought about the attention her husband was receiving from people in a state far away from Massachusetts who had never met him and weren't even exactly sure who he was. She smiled brightly and said, "I don't really know what to say, but it is amazing. It is clear to me that his father and brothers certainly left a huge impression on these people." Joe then delivered a speech on the importance of voting and I will readily admit that I was impressed with it, and with him on that day. I really don't say that lightly because I have written my share of political speeches and have followed politics long enough that most speeches seem to run together in my mind as they tend to be filled with the same old political jargon. This speech, however, was refreshing and powerful.

A few days later, people showed up in Charleston, West Virginia in large numbers to meet Congressman Patrick Kennedy (D-RI) to shake his hand. At that function I found the same phenomena; people didn't know who he was, but he was a Kennedy and that was all that mattered. As I was talking with Congressman Kennedy, just like his father, he remembered in great detail the day we spent together in 1985 sitting on boxes with his father and brother following the flood.

The Kennedy connection to West Virginia is strong. I have struggled with my thoughts on the family for quite some time. I have asked myself how I could feel so strongly against corruption while at the same time have a picture of myself with Senator Ted Kennedy hanging on my wall in my office given the facts surrounding the open vote-buying of the 1960 election. Initially, I do believe–whether or not you agree with them philosophically–that John Kennedy, Robert Kennedy, and Teddy Kennedy's involvement in politics stemmed from a conviction to help people. Their family has more money than I could possibly fathom, yet they have dedicated their lives to fighting for the average person. Even so, I also believe that the vote-buying activities surrounding the 1960 election in West Virginia–while certainly fascinating–are absolutely and unequivocally a blemish and embarrassment to the State. However, being perfectly honest about it, this was by no means anything new to West Virginia politics. It was politics as usual, only more cash traded hands in buying votes than in previous years. The Kennedys didn't come into southern West Virginia and develop a system of vote-buying. The system of elections was already so corrupt at the time that if you didn't buy onto the slates, you didn't get elected. That certainly doesn't make it right, but it does explain the actions of the campaign. Every successful major candidate either paid to play or they lost the election. It's that simple. So, the blame cannot be confined to one family and one election. Much of the culpability rests with State lawmakers and statewide elected officials who were–and are today–in the position to change these longstanding rules, but have chosen not to, probably for fear of not being able to get on a slate in a subsequent election. It was already a flourishing system that was well-entrenched and had controlled elections since the State's very inception. The Kennedys–as Sargent Shriver once said to me–were simply playing the game by the West Virginia rules.

# CHAPTER TWO

# The Birth of West Virginia and the Controversy that Surrounded it

*I see in the near future a crisis approaching that unnerves me and causes me to tremble for the safety of my country. As a result of the war, corporations have been enthroned and an era of corruption in high places will follow, and the money power of the country will endeavor to prolong its reign by working upon the prejudices of the people until all wealth is aggregated in a few hands and the Republic is destroyed.*

President Abraham Lincoln
*(Nov. 21, 1864, in letter to Colonel William Elkins)*

As thirty-five brightly costumed schoolgirls, who represented each state in the Union, sang the national anthem, Arthur Boreman delivered West Virginia's first inaugural address in Wheeling on June 20, 1863, as the new State's first Governor.[107] The picture of Boreman, a solemn-faced attorney with a full beard, still hangs in the State Capitol today and is more often than not believed by onlookers to be a picture of Abraham Lincoln.

The new Governor declared in his first inaugural message to the Legislature: "In the midst of the great rebellion we all deplore so much, we rejoice in the fact accomplished of separate statehood. For thirty years and more, the people west of the mountains in Virginia have justly complained of bitter wrongs done them by the governmental majority, in the East." In light of the turmoil during that time period, Governor Boreman, recognizing both present and future troubles, proposed that, "citizens organize themselves into squads of twelve or fifteen armed men 'on duty in every neighborhood in the

State all the time [to] keep down guerilla warfare or major raids by the rebels."[108]

West Virginia was a state born during the Civil War as the Union side was carved from the western counties of Confederate Virginia. However, its unique history began well before the War. Even as long ago as 1747, much of West Virginia's present-day territory was surveyed for the first time by none other than George Washington.[109] Nearly sixty years later, from 1805 to 1806, Blennerhassett Mansion, near present-day Parkersburg, West Virginia, was the site of meetings between Aaron Burr and Harman Blennerhassett who developed plans to break away from the United States and build their own empire which would have included western sections of the United States and some of the Mexican territory. Their plans were quickly ended when Ohio militiamen invaded the island on December 11, 1806, after President Thomas Jefferson announced that Aaron Burr and his supporters were plotting treason against the United States. Burr was arrested and charged with treason in a trial presided over by Chief Justice of the United States, John Marshall, the namesake of West Virginia's Marshall University.[110]

Years later, on October 16, 1859, just four years before West Virginia was recognized as a state, John Brown led his infamous raid on Harpers Ferry. Brown, whose neighbors knew him as Isaac Smith (known throughout the country as "Old Brown of Osawatomie"), seized the federal arsenal and the rifle works and blocked all the bridges leading to the town. A few years later, this historic town would be included in the Eastern Panhandle of the newly formed State of West Virginia. Brown claimed to be God's agent in freeing the slaves and said he began his crusade to start a national insurrection against the inhumane activity of slavery. On December 2, 1859, Brown, who some considered "one of the most dangerous men in America," was executed in Charles Town, Virginia (present-day West Virginia and named for George Washington's brother Charles) for murder, insurrection, and treason against the Commonwealth of Virginia.[111] The John Brown saga was just one example of the intense emotions and situations of the Virginia region at the time.

Just a few short years later, on May 13, 1861, only two months and nine days after President Abraham Lincoln was inaugurated, the First Wheeling Convention met in Wheeling, the largest city in the western part of Virginia at the time. The attendees voted to hold a General Election on June 4, 1861, to formally elect delegates for a Second Wheeling Convention if Virginia approved the Ordinance of Secession from the Union.[112] Many of the members of the First Wheeling Convention vehemently opposed separating from Virginia. Nonetheless, after the Virginia delegates met in Richmond for the

Commonwealth of Virginia's Convention for an Ordinance of Secession, and approved secession from the Union by a vote of eighty-six to fifty-five, and a May 23, 1861, Virginia statewide referendum confirmed the notion, the creation of a new "western" state suddenly became a real possibility. Members of the Richmond Convention from the present-day West Virginia region voted thirty-two to eleven (with four not voting) against secession.[113]

Days later, on June 3, 1861, Philippi, present-day West Virginia, which is approximately twenty miles from my hometown of Parsons, was the site of the first land battle of the Civil War between the North and South.[114] It is difficult to imagine any area that faced as much of a dilemma as the citizens of the Commonwealth of Virginia and the citizens of the soon-to-be newly formed territory of the Restored Government of Virginia. Neighbors and family members were simultaneously faced with dissension over loyalty to Virginia and loyalty to the United States. To further illustrate this point, during the Civil War, West Virginia provided to the Union Army 31,872 regular army troops, 133 sailors and marines, and 196 United States "Colored" Troops, while it is estimated that somewhere between 16,000 and 20,000 men from West Virginia served in the Confederate Army in this war of brother versus brother.[115]

The next week, the Second Wheeling Convention met on June 11, 1861, with thirty-nine counties being represented. By a unanimous vote on June 20, 1861, they authorized the establishment of the Restored Government of Virginia, also known as the Pierpont Government, named after Francis Harrison Pierpont, the first and only governor of the Reorganized Government of Virginia. On August 20, 1861, the Wheeling Convention passed an ordinance providing for the formation of the "State of Kanawha," and on October 24, 1861, the voters ratified the ordinance. Another Convention assembled in Wheeling on November 26, 1861, and framed a Constitution with a view of becoming a separate and independent state. On April 4, 1862, voters in the "State of Kanawha" approved, by a vote of 18,062 to 514, a new Constitution as well as a name change to "West Virginia."[116]

On May 13, 1862, the soon-to-be State petitioned the United States Congress for admission to the Union. On December 10, 1862, the United States House of Representatives approved a United States Senate bill to create the State of West Virginia, which was to take effect sixty days after the President's proclamation and subsequent approval. On April 20, 1863, President Lincoln, whose mother Nancy Hanks was actually born within the boundaries of what soon would become the new State, issued a proclamation making West Virginia the thirty-fifth state in the Union, effective sixty days thereafter. Thus, on June 20, 1863, exactly two years after the First Wheeling Convention gathered to discuss the prospects of breaking away from the eastern segment of Virginia, the State of West Virginia was born.[117]

West Virginia's ninth Governor, William Alexander MacCorkle, once described the newly formed State as:

> a vision of mountains, dark wilderness, the beetling crag, some smiling valleys, wild deer, and the mountain people, the latter living in their one room, punch and daub log cabin, cultivating on the hillside a patch of yellow corn for food, raising the razor-back hog or shooting the squirrels or of the fox pulling down the wild grape and muscadine; or the possum making his muddy footprints in the soft bands of the streams as he hunts for crawfish or stains his fur with the juice of the pokeberry.[118]

Governor MacCorkle also said:

> It is true that we are of the mountain and valley, but our mountains are filled with coal and clothed with timber, rich enough for a king's heritage, and our wildernesses are active with the whirr of wheels, with the thunder of the locomotive, and the stroke of the pick and ax, while our active, happy and intelligent people attest our determination to more than equal the old time glory of the Mother State in all the acts of peace.[119]

West Virginia played an important role in helping the Union prevail in the Civil War. Even Rutherford B. Hayes and William McKinley, two men who would later become Presidents of the United States, fought as Union soldiers in Civil War activities which centered around Charleston, the present-day Capital of West Virginia.[120] As President Lincoln said, "The admission of the new state turns that much slave soil to free; and thus, is a certain, and irrevocable encroachment upon the cause of the rebellion."[121]

From its controversial beginning as a State to its regrettable reputation of political corruption that survives to this day, West Virginia has indeed had a rich history, literally and figuratively. A group of Lewis County historians reenacting the "Great Gold Robbery of 1861" assert that if $27,000 in gold coins had not been stolen from a bank in Weston (present-day West Virginia) in June of 1861, just two months after Virginia seceded from the Union and joined the Confederacy, West Virginia may not have become a state. The money was obtained following a telegraph from Union General George B. McClellan, then chief of the Western Virginia command and later the leader of the Army of the Potomac, sent to Colonel Erastus Tyler, commander of the 7th Ohio Infantry, dictating: "Get your troops to Weston, Lewis County, at once. Confiscate all the gold in the Weston Bank, by force if necessary. Ship it to Governor Pierpont at Wheeling. Hurrah for New Virginia!" The day after the twenty-seven draw-string-fastened leather pouches containing $1,000 each were obtained from the bank, they were transferred under military guard to Clarksburg where the gold coins were then placed on a train to Wheeling. This money, with a present-day value of at least $600,000, was used to finance the activities of the Restored Government of Virginia with necessary expenses such as payment of salaries, the renting of a building, and buying office supplies. The money was essential to the formation of the new State given the fact that tax collections were disrupted by the outbreak of the Civil War.[122]

While many believe the Civil War was the sole reason for the split of Virginia, in reality it was just the final straw as differences between eastern and western Virginia were present long before the war. Geographical differences played a significant role. For instance, in eastern Virginia, the flat landscape with its deep rivers connected with the Atlantic Ocean making for easy and cheap transportation, while the farming land was more suitable for growing tobacco and accommodating large plantations worked by slave labor. Conversely, the western part of Virginia was vastly mountainous with small farms not suited for slavery. The rivers were also useful for transportation although many costly improvements were necessary. Moreover, while most of the eastern Virginians were of English backgrounds, those of western Virginia were of German, Scotch-Irish, Dutch, and Welsh, as well as English heritage, and most had never been to the eastern region of Virginia. Many of those geographical and ethnical differences also led to abundant political differences between the two regions that existed long before and after 1861.[123]

The young State's formation was surrounded by controversy. For instance, even though President Lincoln's 1863 signature officially legitimized the State of West Virginia, the actual boundary lines would not be settled for several years. One boundary line battle between Virginia and West Virginia ended with an 1870 decision by the United States Supreme Court.[124] Moreover, in 1906, Virginia sued West Virginia for payment of its share of debts owed by Virginia at the start of the Civil War in 1861 and it was not until July 1, 1939, that the debt of $14,562,867.16 was finally paid by West Virginia to Virginia.[125] Governor William A. MacCorkle, who served from 1893 to 1897, maintained that the debt could have been settled for less than $1 million when he was Governor, but that public sentiment was strongly against giving any money to Virginia. MacCorkle explained that he was in favor of a settlement of the debt, but that "opposition made me afraid to advocate openly the Virginia debt, and in fact, like many men in public life, I was afraid to face a question which was loaded with political disaster."[126]

During the early years, West Virginians also experienced indecision with regard to the fixed location of where their governors and legislators would meet to do the work of the people. From 1863 to 1870, West Virginia's first State Capitol was located in Wheeling.[127] On February 26, 1869, the legislature passed a law making Charleston the permanent seat of government effective April 1, 1870, and the State's important records were then transferred from Wheeling to Charleston by a steamboat named "The Mountain Boy," which journeyed down the Ohio River and up the Great Kanawha River to the new capital city.[128] Just five years later, on May 21, 1875, the Capitol would once again be relocated to Wheeling as the legislature for the second time reversed itself. It should be noted that the distance between Charleston and Wheeling is not insignificant. Even by today's standards using the interstate highway system it is still a four hour drive between the two cities. It was not until May 1, 1885 (twenty-two years after becoming a state), that a statewide referendum with choices between Charleston, Clarksburg, and Martinsburg, settled the question once and for all as Charleston became the permanent and present-day Capital of West Virginia.[129]

From the State's origination in 1863 to 1873, the Governor's Office was controlled by the Republicans while the Democrats were in power for twenty-four continuous years thereafter, from 1873 to 1897. Republicans then controlled the office from 1897 to 1933, with the exception of only one Democrat. Democrats, however, controlled the Legislature in West Virginia from 1863 to 1896, followed by Republican control until the election of Franklin D. Roosevelt in 1932. Since 1932, Democrats have held strong domination, leaving few Republicans elected to any statewide offices.[130]

Even after becoming a state, not all of West Virginia's citizens had a right to vote. Following the close of the Civil War in 1865, the young State Legislature passed laws requiring voters and officeholders to swear that they had never aided or fought for the Confederacy. While citizens could register to vote, they could not cast their ballot unless they took the prescribed oaths. The law was next to impossible to enforce, resulting in the West Virginia Constitution being amended to strengthen the law by preventing ex-Confederates not only from voting, but also from holding any elected office.[131]

The turbulence and uncertainty of the young State continued for many years. In 1871, the inauguration of John J. Jacobs, the first Democratic Governor and the first to take the oath of office in Charleston, was reported by newspapers as "general disorder" on the Capitol steps "with some spectators pulling out revolvers and knives when a fight broke out while the new Governor spoke. Several people received cuts and the crowd could not be held back from the Senate chamber, where champagne was being served." Perhaps a more pressing example of the turmoil was the telegram sent to President Rutherford B. Hayes in 1877 by Governor Henry Mason Mathews requesting the President to send at least 200 to 300 soldiers from "the U.S. military to protect the law-abiding people of this State against domestic violence and to maintain supremacy of the law."[132]   Governor Mathews said troops were necessary: "Owing to unlawful combinations and domestic violence now existing at Martinsburg and at other points along the line of the B&O railroad, it is impossible with any force at my command to execute the laws of the State."[133]

The very fact that West Virginia was a state conceived from another state during the Civil War was not an event without controversy. Some scholars even today continue to argue that it was created illegally, calling its formation "a mere illegal breakaway province of the Commonwealth of Virginia."[134]   It has also been said that the people of present-day West Virginia capitalized on a national crisis to acquire statehood. The legality of the State's creation and admission to the Union was obviously in doubt even by President Lincoln, who signed the Proclamation creating West Virginia. President Lincoln declared:

> We can scarcely dispense with the aid of West Virginia in this struggle, much less can we afford to have her against us, in Congress and in the field. Her brave and good men regard her admission into the Union as a matter of life and death. They have been true to the Union under many severe trials. The division of a state is dreaded as a precedent but a measure expedient by a war is no precedent for times of peace.

> It is said that the admission of West Virginia is secession, and tolerated only because it is our secession. Well, if we call it by that name, there is still difference enough between secession against the Constitution and secession in favor of the Constitution. I believe the admission of West Virginia into the Union is expedient.[135]

Following West Virginia's admission to the Union, United States Senator Garrett Davis of Kentucky objected to seating any of West Virginia's chosen United States Senators. He argued:

I hold that there is, legally and constitutionally no such state in existence as the State of West Virginia and consequently no Senators from such a state. My object is simply to raise a question to be put upon the record, and to have my name as a Senator recorded against the recognition of West Virginia as a state of the United States. I do not believe that the Old Dominion, like a polypus, can be separated into different segments, and each segment become a living constitutional organism in this node. The present State of West Virginia as it has been organized, and as it is seeking representation on the floor of the Senate, is a flagrant violation of the Constitution.[136]

Moreover, Jefferson Davis in his memoirs wrote, with considerable bitterness, on the creation of West Virginia:

When the state convention at Richmond passed an ordinance of secession, which was subsequently ratified by a 60,000 majority, it was as valid an act for the people of Virginia as was ever passed by a representative body. The legally expressed decision of the majority was the true voice of the state. When, therefore, disorderly persons in the northwest counties assembled and declared the ordinance of secession "to be null and void," they rose up against the authority of the state. . . . The subsequent organization of the state of West Virginia and its separation from the state of Virginia were acts of secession. Thus we have, in their movements, insurrection, revolution and secession. . . . To admit a state under such a government is entirely unauthorized, revolutionary, subversive of the constitution and destructive of the Union of States.[137]

The controversy surrounds a provision of the United States Constitution which provides that a new state cannot be formed within the boundaries of another state without the full approval of Congress and by the Legislature of the original state of which it is being formed.[138] It is this point that scholars argue as West Virginia's formation occurred unique to the formation of any other state in the history of the United States.   It was the Restored Government of Virginia located in Wheeling which was recognized by the United States Congress as the legal government of Virginia instead of the Virginia Legislature in Richmond which voted to secede from the Union.   Thus, it was the Restored Government of

Virginia in Wheeling that granted itself permission in 1862 for the formation of the new State.

It is difficult to imagine the birth of a state during such tumultuous times of fierce struggle, only to be magnified by the bitterly divided sympathies of its populace as a result of the Civil War. I try to picture my great-great grandfather Nathan A.W. Loughry and his brother William Loughry as they were soldiers fighting for the Union Army and for West Virginia's freedom. Both survived the bloody encounter and went back to farming their land and rearing their children on the same hillside where my father was born. I now own Uncle William's Civil War medal and as I look at it I can only guess what went through the minds of the individuals who–even though they were still very much a part of the Commonwealth of Virginia–left their homes, farms, and families and traveled by horseback to Wheeling, in the northwestern part of Virginia, to discuss forming a new government even before Virginia officially voted to secede. Many of these men struggled with the idea of breaking away from the only state they had ever known and had pledged their loyalty. Many of those same men remained loyal to Virginia while others fought for the creation of a new state. The confusion is unimaginable to me as people went from farming their land as loyal Virginians to hearing the man elected as their new State's Governor telling them to organize into squads of armed men to keep down guerilla warfare by the rebels. The rebels, of course, were often friends and family members from their former State of Virginia. Day by day I am sure they struggled with whom they could or could not trust. Even after the new State was formed and the Civil War had ended, West Virginians watched as the Capital moved back and forth like a teeter-totter as well as waiting several years for courts to determine controversies surrounding the State's boundary and unpaid debts to Virginia. Then, even though West Virginia statehood became a reality, many of its citizens were forbidden to participate in the government due to the loyalty oaths. Those controversies compounded with West Virginia's vast wilderness areas and geographical barriers set the stage for a history unmatched by any other state.

# CHAPTER THREE

# The Hatfields and McCoys

*. . . when his family were finally driven out by the flames, one son, in an attempt to escape, was shot and killed, and his daughter, while begging for mercy and perfectly defenseless, was shot down. His wife was most cruelly beaten, and the escape of the father from death seems almost miraculous . . . to find a more cruel and inhuman murder we must leave our own civilization and resort to the annals of savage life.*

Kentucky Supreme Court 1889

West Virginia's early years were besieged by individuals and stories that became an enduring part of our national folklore. Perhaps America's most mythic and bloody events surrounded the feud between the Hatfields and the McCoys. It was not long after the Civil War and West Virginia statehood that Mingo County (then Logan County) became the murderous site of the world famous feud of the two clans. The numerous books and reports discussing the feud vary widely with regard to the names of the people, actual spelling of names, dates and specific details of the major events, and even the actual cause or causes of the feud.[139] After extensive research, I believe the feud was not caused by a single event which is often suggested by many scholars. Instead, it seems clear that it resulted from an escalation of several events throughout many years.

It would be a mistake to believe the Hatfields and McCoys were simply gun-toting mountain men who killed anyone who wasn't related to them, taught their children how to shoot a gun before they even mastered walking, and completely ignored the courts and any form of law. Likewise, while many people make light of the feud as a skirmish between a bunch of tobacco chewing and overall-wearing hillbillies, it can never be forgotten that these were real people who suffered misfortune and tragedy that changed the lives of both families forever.

The Hatfields of West Virginia had engaged in the long and well-known feud with the McCoys from nearby Kentucky due to many factors among which were the death of a McCoy following Civil War hostilities believed to be at the hands of the Hatfields; the alleged theft of a McCoy razor-back pig by Floyd Hatfield; the love affair between Johnse Hatfield and Roseanna McCoy, the son and daughter of the patriarchs of both families; and the election day murder of Ellison Hatfield, which was followed by severe retribution resulting in the killing of three young McCoys.[140]

The Hatfields were led by William Anderson "Devil Anse" Hatfield (1839-1921), while the McCoys were led by Randolph "Ran'l" McCoy (1825-1914). Devil Anse, described as "six feet of devil and one hundred eighty pounds of hell," was a tall, imposing man with broad shoulders and a shaggy-haired reddish brown beard that extended at least five inches below his chin. In addtion to being a skilled horse rider, he was a self-reliant and rugged man with little if any formal education, which was not uncommon during those days. Randolph McCoy appeared to be shorter than Devil Anse, but had the same broad shoulders. He was said to have been a serious man without a sense of humor, while Devil Anse was just the opposite with a sharp witticism and an active sense of humor as he was known for challenging people to wresting matches. Randolph had grey eyes and a scruffy full grey beard that extended just below his chin. Devil Anse and his wife Louvicey "Vicie" Chafin had thirteen children consisting of nine sons and four daughters. Their first son Johnson "Johnse" Hatfield, was named for William Johnson McCoy, one of Louvicey's brothers-in-law. Randolph McCoy and his wife Sarah, who was also his first cousin, had sixteen children, one daughter dying at birth, with nine sons and six daughters who survived. While their appearances and lifestyles provided little evidence of their wealth, each family was involved in the manufacture and sale of illegal whiskey and owned thousands of acres of prime timberland. Devil Anse was more successful with his timber operations than Randolph, which may have added to the quarrels between the families.

Both clans were among the first wave of pioneers to settle in this wilderness territory later known as the Tug Valley. This region was a rural and isolated terrain with limited access prior to the building of the railroad in 1889. The Hatfields lived along the valley of the Tug Fork River, off the Big Sandy River, on the West Virginia side of the Kentucky-West Virginia border near present-day Matewan, West Virginia. The McCoys lived on the Kentucky side of the river. It was also the same territory explored and hunted by frontiersman Daniel Boone during the days when Indians were prevalent throughout the region.[141]

The people who settled these areas during the Hatfield days lived their lives in crudely built log cabins as they farmed, gathered ginseng, hunted, fished, and logged timber, in the remoteness of the heavily forested valleys. They became skilled with guns, were usually intelligent, but illiterate, had huge families and enjoyed their freedom. It was so isolated that inhabitants often communicated with each other with so-called backwoods wireless telegraph which included numerous animal sounds and birdcalls signifying everything from the arrival of a stranger to a family gathering.

They lived in backwoods areas not easily accessible to the outside world, which meant that courts were few and police protection was almost non-existent. As such, they learned to protect themselves and handle their guns as well as their farm tools. They were so far removed from communication with the outside world and so isolated physically, that they were unable to witness the quickly changing developments of the region around them. Devil Anse's grandson, Coleman A. Hatfield (Cap Hatfield's son), said,

> As you might expect, one who was born and reared in the mountains more than a century ago, when the forest furnished food for every form of life that lived among the virgin trees and mighty rocks, a boy was well equipped by his nature to meet every condition of the wild life which surrounded him. This was true of Anse Hatfield, a man of the timberland, one who loved the deep recesses of the forest, the clear waters and the food supply, not only game, but also every form of edible fruit and nut that he encountered.[142]

Prior to the Civil War, it seems that the feud was non-existent as these families frequently crossed the Tug River in search of romance due to the few families who lived in the vicinity. It was a time when cousins often married cousins and Hatfields often married McCoys. Both the Hatfields and the majority of the McCoys were active sympathizers with the Confederates during the Civil War. Even Devil Anse and Randolph worked together to kill Captain Bill France, a Union officer that both men considered "one of the worst menaces to the borderland" during the War.[143] Nonetheless, two years after the start of the War, Randolph's brother Asa Harmon McCoy, even though he was a slave owner, enlisted in the Union army where he served for twelve months under the control of Captain Bill France. According to some reports he was shot, while others indicate that he had a broken shoulder, resulting in his discharge on Christmas Eve, 1864. It is believed that he was killed by Devil Anse's uncle, Jim Vance, a member of a Confederate guerilla unit, known as the Logan Wildcats and led by Devil Anse Hatfield. Devil Anse formed the Wildcats following West Virginia's admittance to the Union in 1863 fearing that as a Southern sympathizer, his family and property were in danger. Even today the Logan County High School mascot is the Logan Wildcat.

Asa Harmon McCoy had received word that the Logan Wildcats would be paying him a visit so he hid in a nearby cave and instructed his slave Pete to bring food and water to him. Soon afterward, Pete's tracks were followed to the cave and on January 8, 1865, Asa was shot and killed. No one was brought to trial, possibly because Asa Harmon McCoy's military service with the Union was considered an act of disloyalty, even to his family. Many years later, in 1888, Asa's son, Asa Harmon McCoy, Jr., shot and killed Jim Vance. Asa Harmon McCoy is the great-great grandfather of my current boss, West Virginia Supreme Court Justice Elliott "Spike" Maynard.

During the fall of 1878, several years after the killing of Asa McCoy, Randolph McCoy believed that his wife's brother-in-law, Floyd Hatfield, had stolen his pig. Pigs generally roamed freely during those days and were marked on their ears to indicate who owned them. The case went to trial and was presided over by Reverend Anderson Hatfield, a "hardshell" Baptist minister and justice of the peace. The jury consisted of six McCoys and six Hatfields and hinged on the testimony of Randolph's nephew, Bill Staton, who told the jurors the pig belonged to Floyd Hatfield. Floyd was a cousin to Devil Anse and the son of John Hatfield, a brother to Devil Anse's father "Big Eph" Hatfield. The situation was particularly confusing because in one way or another it seemed that everybody was related to each other. Floyd was married to Esther Staton, the sister of Bill Staton, who was the key witness in the case. Esther, or Easter as some historians have referred to her, was also a great-granddaughter of "Old" William McCoy, the grandfather of Randolph McCoy. The jury voted seven to five in favor of the Hatfields as Selkirk McCoy, a relative to the McCoys, was the swing vote against Randolph McCoy.

Soon after the pig trial, on June 18, 1880, Bill Staton was shot to death by Paris and "Big" Sam "Squirrel Huntin'" McCoy, who were later acquitted of murder charges based upon a plea of self-defense. Staton saw the McCoys in the woods and believed they were there seeking revenge due to his testimony during the trial. On the day he was killed, Paris and Sam claimed they were hunting squirrels along the Tug River when Bill Staton fired upon them and they were simply firing back to save their own lives. Charges were initially brought against Paris and Sam by Ellison Hatfield, the husband of Bill Staton's sister. Ellison was a former First Lieutenant with the Confederate Army who fought in the Battle of

Gettysburg and Appomattox. It was believed that Devil Anse helped arrange for the acquittal in the trial, presided over by his brother Valentine "River Wall" Hatfield, in an attempt to keep peace between the families. Nonetheless, the McCoys were incensed that they were even forced to face charges for the killing.

Soon afterward, during the 1880 elections for Pike County, Kentucky, Devil Anse's two oldest sons, Johnson "Johnse" and William Anderson "Cap" Hatfield, appeared for the festivities. Election day during that time period was described as "the most important social event of the year [as] everyone in the community was fully aware, not only of everyone else's political beliefs, but of their status as landowners or tenants and their families' connections. Men came to the elections prepared to state and defend their politics as well as their reputations, if necessary."[144] It was also a time of food, family, and friends gathering together. The eighteen-year-old Johnse, known as a stylish dresser who was popular with the women, was captivated by Randolph McCoy's tall and black haired buxom daughter Roseanna, who was believed to be nineteen-years-old at the time. The two talked as if there was no animosity between their families and Roseanna returned with Johnse that night to live with him in his cabin. Randolph was furious with regard to the couple's relationship and became even more upset by their break-up months later which left Roseanna a "ruined" woman. Roseanna returned to live with Randolph, but found life so unbearable she moved in with her aunt, Betty McCoy. While living with Betty, Johnse and Roseanna once again rekindled their love affair. On one night as the couple was sleeping together, Roseanna's brothers took Johnse prisoner. They told Roseanna they were taking him to jail for bootlegging violations, however, she knew they would kill him. Roseanna borrowed a neighbor's horse and rode bareback, hatless, and coatless to Devil Anse and pleaded for his help. Devil Anse organized his family and neighbors and rescued Johnse. Although the couple were never together again, Roseanna learned she was pregnant with Johnse's child. It has been written that Roseanna miscarried the child after she contracted measles, while others believe her infant child, Sarah Elizabeth, was born, but died sometime later. Making the situation worse for Roseanna, Johnse later married her sixteen-year-old cousin, Nancy McCoy. It is said Roseanna died eight years later from a broken heart.

The eruption of hostilities continued during the next election which occurred in August 1882, at the Blackberry Creek voting precinct in Pike County, Kentucky, as the Hatfields and McCoys had one of their first major encounters that escalated the feud to new levels of danger. On this election day, "Big" Ellison Hatfield and his brother Elias had a confrontation with Roseanna's brothers, twenty-one-year-old Tolbert, nineteen-year-old Phanner, and fifteen-year-old Randolph (Randall) McCoy, Jr.[145] Coleman A. Hatfield writes,

The fifth day of August 1882, which was Saturday, was Election Day in Kentucky and the time when Randall McCoy had sworn vengeance against Ellison Hatfield because Ellison had testified against McCoy's two nephews, Sam and Paris, who were tried on charges of killing Bill Staton on the West Virginia side. Ellison Hatfield's testimony had made him a marked man, as far as the McCoys were concerned.[146]

During the argument, two of the McCoys stabbed Ellison, while the third McCoy shot him. Following the stabbing, the three McCoy men were immediately arrested by special constable Floyd Hatfield and placed in the custody of Tolbert Hatfield and Joseph Hatfield, two justices of the peace from Pike County, Kentucky. All three men, Floyd, Tolbert, and Joseph, were related to Ellison Hatfield. While the three Hatfield officers of the law attempted to transport the three McCoy prisoners to the county seat to be tried for their crimes, they were overtaken by numerous other Hatfields who lived across the border in West Virginia.[147]

One such West Virginia Hatfield was Valentine Hatfield, a West Virginia justice of the peace, who in conjunction with a posse of armed men, confiscated the three McCoys and delivered them to West Virginia. Valentine had also presided over the trial of Sam and Paris McCoy years earlier. The McCoys were tied together by a rope and taken to Reverend Anderson Hatfield's home, where everyone sat down for dinner. Then, the McCoys were confined in a schoolhouse in West Virginia while the Hatfields waited to find out if Ellison would survive from the stabbing and gunshot wounds.[148] In the meantime they permitted the McCoys' mother Sarah to visit them whereby the Kentucky Supreme Court explained, "seeing that human law was powerless to save her boys, on bended knees [she] implored the interposition of Divine Providence for the protection of her offspring from the brutal resolves of these merciless men." Valentine, following Sarah's fervent plea to save her sons' lives, told her "to make less noise and leave."[149]

Only two days had passed since his stabbing when Ellison, the father of eleven children, died from the twenty-six stab wounds and a bullet in the back. After learning of Ellison's death, the three McCoys were taken from the schoolhouse to the Kentucky side of the river, tied to pawpaw bushes, and surrounded for the purpose, as they proclaimed, of having "a shooting match." According to the Kentucky Supreme Court, the men then cocked their guns, "blew the top of the smaller boy's head off, shot Tolbert some 15 times, and Phanner 11 times, and then made the night hideous by hooting as the owl, in contempt, doubtless, on the law and those who administer it." The Supreme Court further proclaimed that "to find a more cruel and inhuman murder we must leave our own civilization and resort to the annals of savage life."[150] On August 10, 1882, funerals were held on both sides of the Tug River as Ellison Hatfield and the three young McCoys were buried by their respective families. The controversy continued even into 2003 when Hatfield relative John Vance denied the McCoy descendants access to the McCoy cemetery where the three boys are buried, claiming that the access road to the cemetery was his private driveway.[151] Ellison Hatfield, incidentally, is the great-grandfather of current State Senate Majority Leader Truman Chafin.

Soon after the 1882 brutal encounters, some of the Hatfields broke into the home of Mary McCoy Daniels and whipped Mary and her daughter with a cow's tail. The Hatfields believed that even though Mary was related to both the Hatfields and McCoys, she was leaking information to the McCoys about the Hatfields. When Mary's brother, Jeff McCoy, sought revenge for his sister's whippings, he was shot and killed by Cap Hatfield, Devil Anse's son.

Everything seemed to calm down for a few years until the Kentucky Governor decided to reopen the case with regard to the deaths of Tolbert, Phanner, and Randall McCoy. The case was reopened approximately five years after the killings at the urging of Randolph McCoy and his brother-in-law Perry Cline, a Pikeville, Kentucky attorney who disliked Devil Anse because he had lost a court battle and 5,000 acres of prime timberland to him in 1877.[152] Devil Anse's land and timber holdings made him one of the richest Logan County residents. Cline was the brother of Martha McCoy, the widow of Asa Harmon McCoy (Randolph McCoy's brother), who was killed years earlier for his support of the Union during the Civil War. Following the renewed interest in the case, warrants were sworn out for numerous West Virginia Hatfields and their relatives. Coleman A. Hatfield described Cline as a "long-haired, bewhiskered, gaunt man whose ill-fitting clothes made him appear more ancient than his years."[153] Hatfield believed that Cline used his political influence as prosecuting attorney in Pike County with the Governor of Kentucky to reissue the murder indictments against the Hatfields.

On September 10, 1887, Kentucky Governor Simon Bolivar Buckner, a heavy man with a thick mustache and beard with a white comb-over haircut, filed a requisition under the seal of the Commonwealth of Kentucky demanding West Virginia Governor Emanuel Willis Wilson arrest the individuals who killed the three McCoys. The West Virginia Governor refused to serve warrants on the Hatfields "because they were not guilty, in his opinion."[154] The Kentucky Governor then appointed an agent, Pike County Deputy Sheriff, "Bad" Frank Phillips, to receive the fugitives from justice from West Virginia. Phillips then formed a posse of twenty-five to thirty men and crossed the Tug River into West Virginia and "with force and arms, violently seized" some of the Hatfields.[155] The first capture was Selkirk McCoy, who had sided with the Hatfields during the pig trial and then moved to West Virginia fearing for his safety. Subsequently, Governor Wilson demanded their release from a Kentucky prison and safe return to West Virginia; however, Governor Buckner refused.[156] Governor Wilson was furious and called up the National Guard, which was followed by Governor Buckner taking the same action.

On February 6, 1888, Governor Buckner was presented a one-sided story surrounding the events of the feud by his Adjutant General Sam E. Hill, who described the Hatfields as follows: "The assertion that Anderson Hatfield and his sons, Johnson [Johnse] and Cap, are reputable, law-abiding people, is not sustained, for the stories of their lawlessness and brutality, vouched for by credible persons, would fill a volume." With regard to the McCoys, Hill said, "while, on the other hand, old man McCoy and his boys are represented as law-abiding, honest people by reputable men."[157]

Because of the involvement of the Governors of both Kentucky and West Virginia, the United States Supreme Court was forced to weigh in on part of the Hatfield and McCoy feud. West Virginia carried the case to the United States Supreme Court arguing that the Hatfields had been kidnapped without due process, but Kentucky prevailed. The Court said that West Virginia had no Constitutional remedy to have its citizens returned as they were being held in Kentucky on legitimate indictments charging them with murder. The Court did, however, call Phillips' actions "lawless and indefensible acts, for which Phillips and his aides may justly be punished under the laws of West Virginia."[158]

Following the news that the arrested Hatfields would not be returned to West Virginia and would have to stand trial in the Kentucky courts, the Hatfields believed that they needed to kill anyone who might testify against them. Thereafter, on January 1, 1888, the West Virginia Hatfields traveled to Kentucky with the intention of killing Randolph McCoy, the head of the large McCoy family, and his son George. After Randolph and his family had gone to bed for the start of a new year, his small log house was surrounded by the West Virginia natives, including Johnse Hatfield, Ellison "Cotton Top" Mounts (illegitimate son of the murdered Ellison Hatfield), Valentine "River Wall" Hatfield, Cap Hatfield, Robert Hatfield, Selkirk McCoy, as well as several other Hatfield sympathizers who demanded that Randolph come outside of his cabin and surrender.[159] When Randolph did not leave the cabin, his house was repeatedly fired into from both sides, and finally set on fire. Then, according to the Kentucky Supreme Court, "when his family [was] finally driven out by the flames, one son [Calvin], in an attempt to escape, was shot and killed, and his daughter [Alifair], while begging for mercy and perfectly defenseless, was shot down. His wife [Sarah] was most cruelly beaten, and the escape of the father from death seems almost miraculous." Randolph testified that "by the light of the moon and the flames of his burning dwelling he distinctly recognized [Johnse Hatfield] as one of the party which surrounded his house, and that as he came out he was shot in the shoulder with a shotgun, and that this diversion enabled him to escape." Sarah was found the next morning with broken ribs and her head frozen to the ground by her own blood.[160] On February 18, 1890, after being convicted in the McCoy killings, Ellison Mounts died by a hanging that was witnessed by thousands of Pike County, Kentucky spectators. The individual charged with hanging Mounts was Sheriff William Harmon Maynard. Valentine Hatfield was also convicted for killing the three McCoys. Valentine later died in prison. His two sons-in-law, Doc Mayhorn and Plyant Mayhorn, were also convicted of those murders. Their convictions were affirmed by the Kentucky Supreme Court on November 9, 1889.

After the burning of the house and killing Randolph's children, Johnse Hatfield fled from his home to the far-off State of Washington where he lived for several years. He later moved to British Columbia, Canada and sent word back to Kentucky that he had died, in hopes that he would no longer be pursued by the authorities on murder charges. Prior to fleeing from West Virginia, Johnse and Nancy McCoy divorced. Nancy later married the Kentucky Governor's agent, Frank Phillips, who by illegally crossing into West Virginia to seize various Hatfields years earlier, may have escalated the feud to the murderous heights it finally reached. Due to Johnse Hatfield's ten-year withdrawal to Washington and British Columbia, it was not until the September Term of Court in 1898, that he was arraigned for trial and later convicted for the murder of Alifair McCoy.[161] Soon afterward, Johnse was paroled for saving the life of the prison warden by slitting the throat of an inmate who attacked the warden. Johnse was later elected and served as a constable in Mingo County. He then was employed as a detective by the United States Coal and Coke Company, a subsidiary of United States Steel Corporation.

Following Johnse's conviction, but prior to his parole, his brother Elias H. Hatfield, a man with black hair and Scottish blue eyes, sought retribution against H.E. "Doc" Ellis, who at the time had been a business rival of Johnse as both men had been involved in the development and marketing of timber. When Johnse was kidnapped by six men as he walked along the river in July 1898 and brought back to Kentucky to stand trial, it was believed that Doc Ellis had organized the ambush.[162] According to Devil Anse's grandson, Coleman A. Hatfield,

"[Doc] Ellis returned to his business in the timber area and often boasted triumphantly to his friends that he had been responsible for getting rid of Johnse Hatfield. He stated that he felt no fear and that his money would see him through."[163] On July 4, 1889, during a day of festivities in Williamson, West Virginia, Elias Hatfield, confronted Doc Ellis as he was getting off the train, asking, "Hello, Doc. Do you think you can take me to Kentucky as easy as you did my brother, Johnse?" The two exchanged more words on the busy train platform before shots were fired. Doc Ellis fired the first shot which just missed Hatfield's head. Elias Hatfield then shot at Doc Ellis and reportedly "hit a gold cufflink on Ellis' wrist, but the bullet ricocheted upward and broke Ellis' neck. Ellis fell dying to the train platform."[164] Elias Hatfield was arrested and indicted for murder on June 1, 1899.[165]

On August 30, 1899, the *Charleston Gazette* reported, "A few minutes before midnight last night Governor Atkinson received a telegram from Bob Hatfield, brother of Elias Hatfield, who is now on trial at Williamson for the murder of Doc Ellis, stating that a mob had gathered at Logan yesterday morning and was on its way to lynch the prisoner, and asking the Governor to instruct the officers what to do."[166] Fearing for his brother's life, Cap Hatfield arranged for Elias to escape from jail as both men then fled West Virginia and went to Oklahoma. Cap Hatfield had been accused of a different murder for the killings of John and Elliott Rutherford on November 3, 1896.[167] Elias later returned to West Virginia and was convicted of murder, but only spent a short period of time in jail before being paroled by Governor George W. Atkinson, who earlier, as a lawyer, persuaded Elias to surrender to the authorities. Nearly ten years later, Elias and his brother Detroit "Troy" Hatfield faced more trouble following their move to the City of Boomer in Fayette County to open a saloon. On October 17, 1911, Elias and Troy were involved in an argument with a man named Octavia Gerone resulting in all three men dying of gunshot wounds.[168]

Cap Hatfield later became an attorney and was admitted to the West Virginia bar. His granddaughter Elizabeth graduated from law school and in 1932 became the first woman admitted to the Logan County Bar Association. Cap also was a Deputy United States Marshal before becoming a deputy sheriff for his brothers Tennyson "Tennis" Hatfield and Joe Hatfield who served separate terms as Sheriff of Logan County. Tennis was first elected sheriff in 1924; however, he didn't begin his term until 1926 because the election results were challenged and the results were ultimately decided by the West Virginia Supreme Court.[169] Tennis was also the subject of a messy divorce that became final on January 11, 1932, resulting in the Circuit Court of Logan County sustaining his adulterous charge against his wife, Sadie Hatfield. Tennis was granted the divorce and the custody of his three infant children. The case ultimately went before the West Virginia Supreme Court where Sadie Hatfield said that Tennis was "a person of vicious habits and character and addicted to the use of intoxicants [and] the acme of cruelty." She told the Court of one occasion when Tennis began striking her with a whip so hard that it "cut the blood out clear around." Tennis denied such conduct. The Supreme Court upheld the circuit court's ruling, but detailed testimony of sexual and adulterous conduct by both individuals.[170] Greenway Hatfield, brother to Governor Henry D. Hatfield, and son to Devil Anse's brother Elias, was also a sheriff and was elected twice as a Republican and once as a Democrat in Mingo County. Devil Anse's other son Robert E. Lee Hatfield became a merchant and acquired a great deal of property, while Robert's brother Elliott studied medicine and graduated in 1898 from City College of Louisville, Kentucky.

Randolph McCoy, having lost many of his sons and family members at an early age, lived to the age of eighty-eight, dying from burns from a fire in the home of his nephew on March 28, 1914. Devil Anse, who became a baptized, born-again Christian in 1911, died of pneumonia on January 6, 1921, at the age of eighty. During his lifetime he was only arrested once and that arrest didn't have anything to do with the famous feud. Instead, Devil Anse was brought into federal court on charges of selling liquor illegally following an indictment brought by Dan Cunningham, a notorious detective of the period. Cunningham and other detectives invested many hours trying to track and capture Hatfield family members. Even Bill Baldwin, who later formed the infamous Baldwin-Felts Detective Agency, reportedly said, "I have never seen Cap and Johnse, two of the Hatfield brothers, and I would give five years of my life to get a shot at either of them at sixty yards, off-hand, and furthermore, I could collect more than a thousand dollars for either." Federal District Judge John Jay Jackson, Jr. dismissed the charges against Devil Anse believing it was a "ruse to get Anse out of Logan County where he could be kidnapped."[171] Devil Anse died with several warrants for his arrest still in force. His funeral was attended by more than 5,000 people making it the largest funeral in Logan County history. Even his grave site, which includes a life-size monument, has been dedicated as a national monument.

The Hatfield-McCoy feud made sensational headlines in newspapers throughout the country only furthering the already widespread negative image of Appalachia during the late 1800s. Newspapers such as the *New York Times* used headlines such as "Dark and Bloody Ground" describing "family feuds" where victims were hanged from trees and sprawled across courthouse steps. According to the *Times*, "Murder [in 1878] was so commonplace that Kentuckians didn't view it with 'the horror with which it is regarded in civilized communities.'"[172]

When Devil Anse's nephew, Dr. Henry Drury Hatfield, ran for Governor in 1912, opponents were exceptionally critical. Henry, the double-cousin to the infamous Johnse and Cap Hatfield, was the son of Elias Hatfield, who was involved in the 1882 election day fight that resulted in the stabbing and shooting of Elias' brother Ellison Hatfield. Elias was the brother to Devil Anse. Their wives, Louvicey and Elizabeth Chafin, were sisters. Just as Dr. Hatfield announced his intention to run for governor, Willis Hatfield was arrested for killing Dr. E.O. Thornhill when the doctor refused to give Willis a prescription for whiskey so that he could buy it at the drugstore. When Dr. Thornhill refused, seeing that he didn't need it for medical purposes, Willis "drew his six-shooter and emptied its contents into the body of the physician."[173] Willis was later convicted of voluntary manslaughter and sentenced to serve four years in the penitentiary. Willis was the brother to Elias and Troy Hatfield who had been killed in a shootout months earlier. Due to those incidents as well as his family's well-known history, one campaign advertisement printed against Dr. Hatfield in the *Charleston Daily Mail* proclaimed:

> Many thousand loyal Republicans in Kanawha County are thoroughly convinced that the best interests of the Republican party demand the overwhelming defeat of Dr. Hatfield on next Thursday. Their reasons are numerous. Their minds are made up, . . . To elect Dr. Hatfield unmistakably means not only the return to Hatfieldism . . . the greatest political menace to WV . . . but it surely and definitely gives to Hallanan the political domination and control of the Rep. organization of WV.[174]

Much to their disfavor, Dr. Henry D. Hatfield was successful in becoming the fourteenth Governor of West Virginia. Dr. Hatfield, however, dispelled any notions that his term in office would resemble the rowdy days of his famous family members as his inauguration day was a strait-laced event. Hatfield, who was the first West Virginia Governor to ride in an automobile in an inaugural parade, declared that the only dance that would be permitted at his inaugural ball would be the two-step waltz. Hatfield's aides announced, "Such dances as the turkey trot, grizzly bear, wine jelly roll, angle worm wiggle and kindred animal dances, along with dances which have been tabooed everywhere except in shanty boats and cabarets, are prohibited."[175] Prior to serving as Governor, Hatfield was a member of the McDowell County Court and the State Senate.[176] Following his term as Governor, he served West Virginia in the United States Senate until 1934. He graduated from medical school in

Kentucky in 1893 even though the Hatfields were not the most popular people in that State.

The times of the region were constantly changing with the completion of the railroad in the 1890s and the expansion of coal mining at an astronomical rate. By the early 1900s southern West Virginia was rapidly becoming a place far different from how it was when Governor Hatfield was a child as a massive influx of people from many states and around the world moved there to find work. Suddenly, instead of a region of vast wilderness with families few and far between, coal towns began appearing in hollow after hollow. Moreover, coal production increased daily resulting in even more people moving to the area in what was becoming a region of ethnically diverse people with an ever growing population of people of Austrian, Bohemian, Canadian, Croatian, English, Finnish, Greek, Hungarian, Italian, Irish, Lithuanian, Polish, Romanian, Russian, Scottish, Serbian, Slovenian, Ukrainian, and Welsh ancestries. While the fighting continued, it was a different kind of fighting. No longer was it simply family versus family, it was now the working people versus the coal companies in a new economic and political climate.

# CHAPTER FOUR

# Mother Jones and the Bloodshed in the Southern West Virginia Coalfields

*But I warn this little Governor that unless he rids Paint Creek and Cabin Creek of these goddamned Baldwin-Felts mine-guard thugs, there is going to be one hell of a lot of bloodletting in these hills. Arm yourselves, return home and kill every goddamned mine guard on the creeks, blow up the mines, and drive the damned scabs out of the valleys.*

Mother Jones

During the early 1900s, West Virginia gained national attention and became the subject of concern following seemingly endless periods of martial law that included bloodshed, disorderliness, and death resulting from the mining wars in southern West Virginia. The most notable individuals and episodes featured Mother Jones and the fierce battles throughout the mining communities including the bloody Matewan Massacre involving the Baldwin-Felts Detective Agency and Chief of Police Sid Hatfield.

During one instance of unrest on September 2, 1912, in light of the dangers of the day because of mining confrontations and strikes, Governor William E. Glasscock placed the entire strike district under martial law,[177] bringing 1,200 state militia into those areas of southern West Virginia. Governor Glasscock ordered a proclamation disallowing the "congregating" of miners and thereafter, ordered a military court to be set up and a freight house converted into a temporary jail often referred to as a bullpen. These coal mining "military prisoners" were held in this stockade until their cases were disposed of by the military court.[178] Judges of the military courts acted without knowledge of law and pre-

scribed penalties for various offenses while completely ignoring the state and federal Constitutions.  For instance, long sentences of incarceration were imposed
for misdemeanors that were only punishable by small fines under State law.[179]
When two victims of the military courts sought their release from the penitentiary
in habeas corpus,[180] the West Virginia Supreme Court of Appeals upheld their
convictions on the theory that the Governor "in the event of invasion, insurrection, rebellion, or riot [may] declare a state or war."[181]

Military courts ruled southern West Virginia even though the State civil
and criminal courts remained unclogged and available to address the very same
charges being made against the miners.  They also operated notwithstanding
Sections 4 and 12 of Article III of the West Virginia Constitution which provide:

> Section 4: The privilege of the writ of habeas corpus shall not
> be suspended.  No person shall be held to answer to treason,
> felony, or other crime not cognizable by a justice, unless on a
> presentment or indictment of a grand jury.

> Section 12: The military shall be subordinate to the civil power,
> and no citizen, unless in the military service of the State, shall
> be tried or punished by any military court, for any offense that
> is cognizable by the civil courts of the State.[182]

Years later, during another interval of martial law, one union organizer,
a Mr. Lavender, was successful with his petition for habeas corpus and was
released from jail.  The West Virginia Supreme Court of Appeals said, "Martial
law cannot exist . . . where the State fails to employ its military arm to enforce
it."  The Court's ruling sparked the Governor to ask the President for immediate
military aid which resulted in 1,000 "battle-equipped army troops into the strike
district."[183]

On February 10, 1913, Governor Glasscock issued a third proclamation
placing parts of certain counties in southern West Virginia under martial law,
leaving military forces to once again occupy the territory.[184]  Not surprisingly, it
was reported that "much rioting and lawlessness existed" in southern West
Virginia at the time.  The West Virginia Supreme Court of Appeals found "that
many lives and much property had been destroyed, and that riot and bloodshed
was then rampant and pending, and that the State had spent about one-half million dollars in trying to restore peace and order and due execution of the laws."[185]

Much of the disorder was due to attempts to unionize miners by Mary
Harris Jones, better known as "Mother Jones," who ignited many of the miners

and other laborers in strikes and uprisings against their employers.[186]  She was born near Cork, Ireland in 1830[187] and became known as a fighter for the working class everywhere.  She often said she was "born in revolution."  As a child in Ireland, she witnessed deadly clashes between British soldiers and peasant farmers, which included her own family such as her grandfather who was hanged for revolting against British colonialism.  She also witnessed those same British soldiers in Ireland carrying the heads of decapitated rebel Irishmen on the tips of their bayonets.  While still a young girl, her family moved to Toronto, Canada.  It was a welcomed move.[188]

Jones began her long history of fighting for the working class following the death of her husband, George E. Jones, an iron molder, who was a staunch member of the Iron Molders' Union.  Her life changed drastically during a one week period in 1867 when, at thirty-seven-years-old, she lost her husband and four children to a yellow fever epidemic.  Tragedy hit again in 1871 when the Great Chicago Fire destroyed all of her belongings.  It is said she never had a permanent address again as she traveled for the next fifty years from state to state in support of workers.  While testifying before the United States Congress in 1910, she said she lived "in the United States, but I do not know exactly where.  My address is wherever there is a fight against oppression."  She added, "My address is like my shoes.  It travels with me.  I abide where there is a fight against wrong."[189]  She would tie whatever possessions she had in her black shawl and travel wherever she was needed as she fought in every imaginable labor battle, attempting to create a public outcry with regard to the inhumane treatment of workers.  She would live with workers in tent colonies or in shanty towns near the numerous mines, mills, or factories she was attempting to help unionize.

Jones fought against West Virginia's current United States Senator Jay Rockefeller's grandfather, John Davidson Rockefeller, Jr., who had a large stake in the Colorado mines and refused to negotiate or even acknowledge the union.  She was arrested and imprisoned twice for participating in strikes at Rockefeller's mines.  Following one arrest Mother Jones was taken before the Governor of Colorado, Ellias M. Ammons, who said, "I am going to turn you free, but you must not go back to the strike zone! [and] I think you ought to take my advice."  Mother Jones responded, "Governor, if Washington took instructions from such as you, we would be under King George's descendants yet!  If Lincoln took instructions from you, Grant would never have gone to Gettysburg.  I think I had better not take your orders."  Soon afterward, she was put in the cellar under the courthouse in what she referred to as one of Rockefeller's prisons.  "It was a cold, terrible place, without heat, damp and dark.  I slept in my clothes by day, and at night I fought great sewer rats with a beer bottle," she said.  According to her autobiography, as she sat in the prison she thought: "If I were out of this dungeon, I would be fighting the human sewer rats anyway!" She explained:

> For twenty-six days I was held a military prisoner in that black hole. I would not give in. I would not leave the State. At any time, if I would do so, I could have my freedom. General Chase and his bandits thought that by keeping me in that cold cellar, I would catch the flue [sic] or pneumonia, and that would settle for them what to do with "old Mother Jones."[190]

In January of 1914, she returned to Colorado and was arrested as soon as she got off the train. She was taken by the militia to a hotel where they had their headquarters. As she was getting her morning meal she asked, "Who is paying for my breakfast?" The officers responded, "The State." Mother Jones said, "Then as the guest of the State of Colorado I'll order a good breakfast. And I did–all the way from bacon to pie."[191]

"It is all an outrage. 'Tis an outrage indeed that Rockefeller should own the coal that God put in the earth for all the people. 'Tis an outrage that gunmen and soldiers are here protecting mines against workmen who ask a bit more than a crust, a bit more than bondage! 'Tis an ocean of outrage," Mother Jones said. She added that many of the outrages that occurred at Rockefeller's mines were never reported until the Ludlow Massacre where "little children roasted alive" and miners were "dying by inches of starvation and exposure." Machine guns were used on miners, their tents were burned, and barbed wire was stuffed into the well, the miners' only water supply. Mother Jones said Rockefeller hired public relations people to cover up the situation.

> Rockefeller got busy. Writers were hired to write pamphlets which were sent [sic] broadcast to every editor in the country, bulletins. In these leaflets, it was shown how perfectly happy was the life of the miner until the agitators came; how joyous he was with the company's saloon, the company's pigstys for homes, the company's teachers and preachers and coroners. How the miners hated the state law of an eight-hour working day, begging to be allowed to work ten, twelve. How they hated the state law that they should have their own check weigh-man to see that they were not cheated at the tipple.[192]

Thus, as the propaganda was being circulated about the positive environment of Rockefeller's mines, the mothers of the children who died at Ludlow were mourning and burying their dead. Jones said, "John Rockefeller, Jr. is a nice young man but . . . he could not possibly understand the aspirations of the working class. He was as alien as is one species from another; as alien as is stone from wheat." She said she sent a letter to Rockefeller, who she referred to as "Oily John," alerting him of conditions in the mines because she had "heard he was a good young man and read the Bible, and I thought I'd take a chance." The letter came back with "Refused" written across the envelope.[193]

In rallying miners' wives, Jones often said, "No matter what the fight, don't be ladylike! God almighty made women and the Rockefeller gang of thieves made the ladies." She told women, who at the time didn't even have the right to vote, that: "I have never had a vote, and I have raised hell all over this country! You don't need a vote to raise hell! You need convictions and a voice!" She also said, "I asked a man in prison once how he happened to be there and he said he had stolen a pair of shoes. I told him if he had stolen a railroad he would be a United States Senator." She believed that, "[t]he miners [often] lost because they had only the constitution [while] the other side had bayonets [and] in the end, bayonets always win."[194]

In 1890, she joined the newly-formed United Mine Workers of America as a paid organizer even though she had already been an organizer in the labor movement for nearly thirty years. Mother Jones had the quiet, gentle appearance of a sweet grandmother with her snow-white hair gathered in a knot at her neckline. But that quickly changed when she began addressing crowds with her strong rhetoric against the people she believed were the oppressors of the miners who she treated like her own children. Mother Jones described one occasion when she met for the first time with a group of miners in the Fairmont district of West Virginia who asked her to come and speak with them about unionizing. Unaware of where the meeting was being held, she was taken to a church where she saw a priest holding money. When the president of the local union told her the miners had rented the church for the meeting, she reached over and took the money from the priest, turned to the miners and said, "Boys, this is a praying institution. You should not commercialize it. Get up every one of you and go out in the open fields." The group then went outside to an open field and held the meeting. She then said,

> Your ancestors fought for you to have a share in that institution
> over there. It's yours. See the school board, and every Friday
> night hold your meetings there. Have your wives clean it up

Saturday morning for the children to enter Monday. Your organization is not a praying institution. It's a fighting institution. It's an educational institution along industrial lines. Pray for the dead and fight like hell for the living![195]

On June 7, 1902, Mother Jones was holding a meeting of the bituminous coal miners of Clarksburg, West Virginia. She was talking about striking as she and nine organizers sat under a tree. As she was speaking, a United States Marshal notified one of the men to tell Jones she was under arrest. One of the men approached her saying, "Mother, you're under arrest. They've got an injunction against your speaking." She then looked at the Marshal and said, "I will be right with you. Wait 'til I run down." She continued until she finished her speech and said, "Goodbye, boys; I'm under arrest. I may have to go to jail. I may not see you for a long time. Keep up this fight! Don't surrender! Pay no attention to the injunction machine at Parkersburg. The federal judge is a scab anyhow. While you starve he plays golf. While you serve humanity, he serves injunctions for the money powers."[196]

Jones and the miners were taken to the Federal District Court for trial in front of Federal Judge John Jay "Iron Judge" Jackson, Jr., who had been appointed to the federal bench by Abraham Lincoln on July 26, 1861. Jackson was a stern looking man with a full, but scraggly beard, a mustache that extended well below his chin, and a comb-over haircut that left much of his shiny forehead exposed. His family was very prominent in West Virginia politics. He and his father were members of the First Wheeling Convention, which was organized to decide whether to secede from the Union following Virginia's vote to secede; both were vigorously opposed to secession. His brother James M. Jackson served as a circuit judge and a member of the United States House of Representatives, his brother Jacob Beeson Jackson served as West Virginia's sixth Governor, and his cousin was the prominent General Thomas Jonathan "Stonewall" Jackson.

During her trial, a woman was put on the stand against Mother Jones who testified that Jones "had told the miners to go into the mines and throw out the scabs." Mother Jones described the witness as "a poor skinny woman with scared eyes and she wore her best dress, as if she were in church." She said: "I looked at the miserable slave of the coal company and I felt sorry for her; sorry that there was a creature so low who would perjure herself for a handful of coppers."

When Mother Jones was put on the stand, Judge Jackson asked her if she gave such advice to the miners telling them to use violence. She replied, "You know, sir, that it would be suicidal for me to make such a statement in public. I am more careful than that. You've been on the bench forty years, have you not, judge?" When Judge Jackson said "Yes," Mother Jones proceeded to ask him, "And in forty years you learn to discern between a lie and the truth, judge?" Following the exchange, the United States Attorney jumped to his feet shaking his finger at her and said, "Your honor–there is the most dangerous woman in the country today. She called your honor a scab. But I will recommend mercy of the court–if she will consent to leave the state and never return." Mother Jones replied that she didn't come into the court asking for mercy, but that she came there looking for justice, adding, "And I will not leave this state so long as there is a single little child that asks me to stay and fight his battle for bread." Judge Jackson inquired, "Did you call me a scab?" She responded, "I certainly did, judge" to which Jackson further asked, "How [come] you call[ed] me a scab?" Mother Jones replied,

> When you had me arrested I was only talking about the consti-
> tution, speaking to a lot of men about life and liberty and a
> chance for happiness; to men who had been robbed for years by
> their masters, who had been made industrial slaves. I was
> thinking of the immortal Lincoln. And it occurred to me that I
> had read in the papers that when Lincoln made the appointment
> of Federal judge to this bench, he did not designate senior or
> junior. You and your father bore the same initials. Your father
> was away when the appointment came. You took the appoint-
> ment. Wasn't that scabbing on your father, judge?

Judge Jackson denied the allegation saying, "I never heard that before." The bailiff then approached Mother Jones and whispered, "Madam, don't say 'judge' or 'sir' to the court. Say 'Your Honor.'" Mother Jones answered, "Are you refer-ring to the old chap behind the justice counter? Well, I can't call him 'your honor' until I know how honorable he is. You know I took an oath to tell the truth when I took the witness stand."

When the court session ended, the bailiff told Jones that the judge want-ed to see her in his chambers. As soon as she entered his judicial chambers, Judge Jackson reached out his hand and took hold of hers and said, "I wish to give you proof that I am not a scab; that I didn't scab on my father." Jackson handed her documents which proved the reports were wrong and had been circulated by his enemies. "Judge," Mother Jones said, "I apologize. And I am glad to be tried by so human a judge who resents being called a scab. And who would not want to be one. You probably understand how we working people feel about it." Judge

Jackson did not sentence her, but he did give the men who were arrested with her sixty and ninety days in jail.[197] The so-called "scabs" were people who came from faraway places and were hired without any knowledge of the strikes. Once they arrived they were forced to work at the mine in spite of the dangerous conditions and threats from the striking miners who were attempting to unionize. The company thugs had no problem killing coal miners and their supporters.

On another occasion, the sixty-seven-year-old, five-foot tall Jones, in her black dress with lace that extended to her throat and wrists and her black hat trimmed with ribbons, was arrested for military despotism, inciting riot, and conspiring to commit murder. She was sentenced to twenty years in prison by a military tribunal.[198] Prior to her arrest she told striking miners to "Buy guns, and buy good ones; have them where you can lay your hands on them at any minute, and I will tell you when and where to use them."[199] Jones' arrest and conviction followed her speeches in the strike zone of Cabin Creek, West Virginia, referred to as "Russia." She said, "The miners had been peons for years, kept in slavery by the guns of the coal company, and by the system of paying in scrip so that a miner never had any money should he wish to leave the district." She added that miners were

> cheated of wages when his coal was weighed, cheated in the company store where he was forced to purchase his food, charged an exorbitant rent for his kennel in which he lived and bred, docked for school tax and burial tax and physician and for 'protection,' which meant the gunmen who shot him back into the mines if he rebelled or so much as murmured against his outrageous exploitation.

During those days, no one was allowed in the Cabin Creek district without a good explanation for being there. When the Cabin Creek miners went on strike and the Paint Creek miners followed, gunmen patrolled the roads, all of which belonged to the coal company. In addition to all civil and constitutional rights being suspended, the miners were removed from their company owned homes at gunpoint and left without any place to live. The miners established a tent colony, but they were not safe from the assaults of the "gunmen criminals." Mother Jones said, "To protect their women and children, who were being shot with poisoned bullets, whose houses were entered and rough-housed, the miners armed themselves as did the early settlers against the attacks of wild Indians."[200]

When she arrived at Paint Creek, the train brakeman told her, "Mother, it will be sure death for you to go into the Creeks. Not an organizer dares go in there now. They have machine guns on the highway, and those gunmen don't care whom they kill." As she exited the train she noticed a lot of gunmen, "armed to the teeth." She said, "Everything was still and no one would know of the bloody war that was raging in those silent hills, except for the sight of those guns and the strange, terrified look on everyone's face."

Almost immediately, a young boy ran screaming and crying as he rubbed his eyes with his dirty little fist and said, "Oh Mother Jones! Mother Jones! Did you come to stay with us?" When she said "Yes," the young boy threw his arms around her knees and held her tight. He said, "Oh Mother, Mother, they drove my papa away and we don't know where he is, and they threw my mama and all the kids out of the house and they beat my mama and they beat me." As he continued to cry, he added, "See, Mother, I'm all sore where the gunmen hit me," as he pulled down his cotton shirt revealing his shoulders which were black and blue. She asked, "The gunmen did that?" The boy responded, "Yes, and my mama's worse'n that! The gunmen! The gunmen! Mother, when I'm a man I'm going to kill twenty gunmen for hurting my mama! I'm going to kill them dead–all dead!"[201] Mother Jones certainly shared the young boy's sentiment as on one occasion she held up the bloody coat of a mine guard and said, "This is the first time I ever saw a goddamned mine guard's coat decorated to suit me." The coat was cut into pieces that the miners later wore as souvenirs.

Soon after meeting the boy, Jones arrived at the miners' camp in Holly Grove where "all through the winter, through snow and ice and blizzard, men and women and little children had shuddered in canvas tents that America might be a better country to live in." They lived in an almost feudal society as their thin tents stood atop mud floors. As Mother Jones listened to their stories, she recalled talking to Mrs. Sevilla "whose unborn child had been kicked dead by gunmen while her husband was out looking for work." She talked with widows, "whose husbands had been shot by the gunmen; with children whose frightened faces talked more effectively than their baby tongues [and] learned how the scabs had been recruited in the cities, locked in boxcars, and delivered to the mines like so much pork." An old miner whose son had been killed told her, "I think the strike is lost, Mother," to which she replied, "Lost! Not until your souls are lost!"[202]

Mother Jones was then approached and asked to go to nearby Cabin Creek to speak to those miners. She said, "I knew all about Cabin Creek–old Russia. Labor organizer after organizer had been beaten into insensibility, thrown into the creek, tossed into some desolate ravine. The creek ran with the blood of brave men, of workers who had tried to escape their bondage." As Jones left the train, she noticed a detective behind her. She walked up to him and said, "Isn't your name Corcoran? Aren't you the Corcoran who followed me up New River in the strike of 1902? You were working for the Chesapeake and Ohio Railroad and the coal company then." The man said, "Why, yes, but you know people change!" She told him, "Not sewer rats, A sewer rat never changes!"[203]

That night she met with the miners and they discussed a possible strike. She told the men to go to work and try to get their fellow miners to join them. When the miners went to work the next day, each man who attended the meeting was fired. According to Mother Jones, "That caused the strike, a long, bitter, cruel strike. Bullpens came. Flags came. The militia came. More hungry, more cold, more starving, more ragged than Washington's army that fought against tyranny were the miners of the Kanawha Mountains. And just as grim. Just as heroic. Men died in those hills so that others might be free." The militia prohibited all meetings, suspended every civil right, and arrested scores of miners and tried them in military courts without juries and arbitrarily sentenced them to ten or fifteen years in the Moundsville prison.[204]

Days later while in Charleston, "a big elephant" named Dan Cunningham, grabbed Mother Jones by the arm and arrested her.[205] Cunningham was the same person who had taken Devil Anse Hatfield into custody years earlier and brought him before Judge Jackson's court. Mother Jones was taken by train to Pratt, West Virginia, and handed over to the military. She waited for several weeks before she was taken before the judge advocate. Jones, who refused the attorneys appointed for her military trial said, "I don't recognize the jurisdiction of a military court. I am not a soldier. Don't you feel like idiots sentencing me to prison for 20 years?"[206] This arrest and conviction occurred during the term of Governor Glasscock, whom Mother Jones referred to as "Crystal Peter."

When Governor Henry Drury Hatfield, the nephew to Devil Anse Hatfield, took office on March 14, 1913, Mother Jones was still imprisoned and West Virginia was plagued with constant disorderliness no longer limited to the tragic family feuds involving Hatfield's family members. The day after his inauguration, Governor Hatfield, who was also a doctor, packed his doctor's bag and went to the strike zone to see the situation for himself. The coal operators were upset with Hatfield and accused him of being overly conciliatory to the miners. Unfortunately for the coal operators, they mistakenly believed that they could control Hatfield just as they controlled his predecessor Governor Glasscock.

Upon his arrival, Hatfield witnessed the illnesses caused by the unsanitary conditions in the coal camps. Hatfield personally examined Mother Jones, who was still under house arrest and was suffering from pneumonia. Initially he refused to release the elderly Jones; however, he changed his mind and released her following negative press coverage on a national level as well as the initiation of a Congressional investigation of the strike. It was the first time that a United

States Senate subcommittee was appointed to investigate a labor controversy. She said her guards "were nice young men, respectful and courteous with the exception of a fellow called Lafferty, and another sewer rat whose name I have not taxed my mind with."[207]

Mother Jones recalled a later time when she was in Washington, D.C. and a man approached her and said that General Elliott had sent him to meet her. General Elliott was the military man who was in charge of the prisoners who were sentenced to the penitentiary following their court martial during the strike. Mother Jones recalled, "Never would I forget that scene on the station platform of Pratt when the men were being taken to Moundsville; the wives screaming frantically; the little children not allowed to kiss or caress their fathers. Neither the screams nor the sobs touched the stone heart of General Elliott." The man explained that General Elliott sent him to her to ask for a letter endorsing him for Congress. She explained that since he was Elliott's friend, to "tell the general that nothing would give me more pleasure than to give you a letter, but it would be a letter to go to hell and not to Congress!"[208]

Jones spoke to the miners in a language they could understand, using fiery rhetoric that aroused the workers to strike and fight for better working conditions. During the Cabin Creek and Paint Creek strikes, in a 1912 speech on the steps of the State Capitol, Mother Jones called West Virginia's Governor Glasscock "a goddamned dirty coward" and proclaimed:

> But I warn this little Governor [Governor William E. Glasscock] that unless he rids Paint Creek and Cabin Creek of these goddamned Baldwin-Felts mine-guard thugs, there is going to be one hell of a lot of bloodletting in these hills.

> Arm yourselves, return home and kill every goddamned mine guard on the creeks, blow up the mines, and drive the damned scabs out of the valleys.[209]

Prior to the speech she met with Governor Glasscock and asked him to come out and address the crowd. Governor Glasscock said, "I can't come with you but I am not as bad as you may think." She pulled him by his coattail and again asked him to join her. She said, "He looked like a scared child and I felt sorry for him; a man without the courage of his emotions; a good, weak man who could not measure up to a position that took great strength of mind, a character of granite." She left the Governor's Office and delivered a lengthy speech on the Capitol steps requesting the Governor to put a stop to the Baldwin-Felts guards and murderous gunmen.

"We asked him to reestablish America and American traditions in West Virginia," she said. In finishing her speech she told the crowd, "Go home now. Keep away from the saloons. Save your money. You're going to need it." Someone from the crowd shouted, "What will we need it for, Mother?" She explained, "For guns. Go home and read the immortal Washington's words to the colonists. He told those who were struggling for liberty against those who would not heed or hear 'to buy guns.'" She said the men left the meeting peacefully and bought every gun in the hardware stores of Charleston. "They took down the old hammerlocks from their cabin walls. Like the Minute Men of New England, they marched up the creeks to their homes with the grimness of the soldiers of the revolution," she said.[210]

Day after day, constant turmoil continued as the mine operators refused to negotiate with the union, while at the same time relying on violence and intimidation in their attempts to control the miners and their families. The mine operators often used machine guns to defend the company offices as mine guards were ordered to shoot to kill those considered to be a threat to their mining operations. Due to the isolation of the mines, violence escalated without the risk of heavy public outcry. As a result of the constant periods of conflict, the West Virginia State Police was established in 1919, under the reign of Governor John J. Cornwell, "to help enforce State laws in violent coal mining disputes. . . ."[211]

The coal companies strongly opposed unions. Companies forced union miners to move from their homes while many of them had no choice but to live with their families in tents along public highways. Mother Jones said, "There is never peace in West Virginia because there is never justice. Injunctions and guns, like morphia, produce a temporary quiet. Then the pain, agonizing and more severe, comes again. So it is with West Virginia." She added, "Medieval West Virginia! With its tent colonies on the bleak hills? With its grim men and women? When I get to the other side, I shall tell God Almighty about West Virginia!"[212]

It was a time of economic depression with skyrocketing levels of unemployment and homelessness in spite of considerable financial gains of corporations mining coal in West Virginia. Successful corporations controlled their workers' lives and controlled or were able to override local laws making it next to impossible to unionize workers. Mother Jones described the living conditions in West Virginia mine towns as terrible where there was no care for the sick as the people lived in a condition of desolate poverty. She described the homes as slave huts. According to Mother Jones,

> Men who joined the union were blacklisted throughout the entire section. Their families were thrown out on the highways. Men were shot. They were beaten. Numbers disappeared and no trace of them found. Store keepers were ordered not to sell

to union men or their families. Meetings had to be held in the woods at night, in abandoned mines, in barns.[213]

She said, "There are no limits to which powers of privilege will not go to keep the workers in slavery." The conditions were in direct conflict of the vision of President Abraham Lincoln who said in 1860 that the admission of West Virginia as a new state to the Union, "turns that much slave soil to free."[214]

In spite of the horrid conditions, Mother Jones continued the fight. She was arrested countless times and faced numerous death threats as the number one enemy of wealthy business owners. She said in her autobiography she had been in West Virginia "more or less for the past twenty-three years, taking part in the interminable conflicts that arose between the industrial slaves and their masters." The conflicts were always bitter and mining was cruel work. Further describing the conditions she witnessed in the mines, she said, "Men are down in utter darkness hours on end. They have no life in the sun. They come up from the silence of the earth utterly wearied. Sleep and work, work and sleep. No time or strength for education, no money for books. No leisure for thought." She added, "With the primitive tools of pick and shovel they gut out the insides of the old earth. Their shoulders are stooped from bending. Their eyes are narrowed to the tiny crevices through which they crawl. Evolution, development, is turned backward. Miners become less erect, less wide-eyed." She further explained,

> Like all things that live under ground, away from the sun, they become waxen. Their light is the tiny lamp in their caps. It lights up only work. It lights but a few steps ahead. Their children will follow them down into these strange chambers after they have gone down into the earth forever. Cruel is the life of the miners with the weight of the world upon their backs. And cruel are their strikes. Miners are accustomed to cruelty. They know no other law. They are like primitive men struggling in his ferocious jungle–for himself, for his children, for the race of men.[215]

The blue-eyed "Miners' Angel," who nearly always had a kindly expression on her face, said of herself on countless occasions, "I'm not a humanitarian. I'm a hellraiser." She controlled her audience and could easily bring her listeners to laughter or tears as she discussed the blatant economic and social inequities that existed at the time. Prior to addressing one crowd the police informed her that if anyone was killed that she would be held responsible and hanged. She told the crowd, "If they want to hang me, let them. And on the scaffold I will shout

'Freedom for the working class!' And when I meet God Almighty I will tell him to damn my accusers and the accusers of the working class, the people who tend and develop and beautify His world."[216] When Mother Jones died in 1930 at the age of one hundred, she was buried in the United Mine Workers Union Cemetery in Mount Olive, Illinois. More than 20,000 people attended her funeral. Even today, more than seventy-five years later, her name is still a part of our daily culture as the title of a magazine, *Mother Jones*, an independent non-profit magazine dedicated to social justice. The magazine has a paid circulation of more than 226,000.

Former West Virginia Attorney General Howard B. Lee described the southern West Virginia coalfields where Mother Jones spent much of her life as a place of deplorable living conditions and upheaval. Attorney General Lee wrote:

> At the peak of production the industry employed in excess of 125,000 miners. These workers and their families made up a population of 750,000 people who huddled in the grimy mining camps, and lived in company owned houses, which were little better than cow stables in many camps. These deplorable living conditions, starvation wages, illegal, oppressive, and often dis-honest practices of many of the early coal operators frequently brought on bloody uprisings that bordered on civil war; and on four occasions required the presence of United States regular army troops to restore order in the troubled mountains.[217]

Ironically, many of the workers were enticed from Europe to the West Virginia coalfields by pamphlets portraying the glowing conditions and economic advantages of becoming a coal miner. To further entice people to relocate to south-ern West Virginia, expert writers and translators were employed by coal companies to prepare the brochures in the language of the numerous countries. With little to no restrictions on immigration, thousands of new workers migrated to New York and then traveled by labor trains to the West Virginia coalfields.[218] A company recruiter in New York, working to bring men, many of them "just off the boat," to work in the "dark holes" of West Virginia during the early part of the last century said,

> We understand labor is nothing but a commodity, and it is gov-erned not by [unions] but by supply and demand. . . . In the wintertime, I can get a half a million men for any kind of work–[breaking] strikes or any [other] kind–because outside work is closed and people are starving in the big towns.[219]

Topper Sherwood, co-author of the book *Just Good Politics: the Life of Raymond Chafin, Appalachian Boss*, explained:

> To attract these poor workers, coal companies built community houses, stores, schools, and churches. They hired teachers, preachers, and storekeepers. Later, when workers demanded certain rights–including payment in real American dollars, as opposed to credit at the company store–the coal company could use its power to ride all dissidents and their families out of town. Evictions were carried out by the sheriff's deputies, often working in league with private company police. Anyone linked to union organizing–or even suspected of it–was liable to be jailed, beaten, or killed.[220]

Virtually overnight, due to the completion of the railroad, towns were being created throughout the region wherever coal could be mined. The economy quickly shifted from agricultural to industrial as the massive influx of people and new towns were controlled by the coal companies. Before the coalfields were unionized, the coal companies used a variety of devices to oppress the miners. They paid the miners in scrip instead of legal tender currency. As such, miners were forced to accept scrip as payment to buy food, clothing, and tools. And, even before they received their scrip, the company would deduct from their pay numerous company expenses such as a doctor fee, rent, and even the price of a load of coal used to heat their homes. Furthermore, the only stores that accepted the scrip were owned by the coal companies, who capitalized on the miners with inflated prices that were said to be as much as four or five times what the items actually cost the company store. Moreover, even when miners received an increase in pay, the prices coincidentally increased at the company store. The companies owned all of the housing and would evict "trouble makers." They employed thugs to beat and kill workers they didn't like and they ignored the laws restricting child labor and providing for mine safety.

Coal companies also cheated miners out of pay by using a process known as cribbing. Miners were paid based upon the tons of coal they mined and each coal car that a miner filled was supposed to equal a certain number of pounds. Nonetheless, coal cars were altered to hold more coal than the specific amount the cars were supposed to hold. For instance, a coal car could have been reported to hold 2,500 pounds of coal and the miner would be paid for mining 2,500 pounds, when in actuality it held more than 3,000 pounds of coal. The coal companies also docked pay from the miners for any slate and rock they found with the mined coal. And, as a condition of employment, miners would be forced to sign contracts for employment stating they weren't members of the United Mine Workers of America and would not become members.[221]

Mining in West Virginia was dangerous. The State had more mining deaths than any other state between 1890 and 1912. On one occasion, December 6, 1907, an explosion at the Fairmont Coal Company in Monongah, West Virginia, killed 361 people, making it the nation's worst coal disaster. Coal companies controlled everything and didn't want unions to have any say on mining conditions. In exchange for keeping the union out, county sheriffs were financially rewarded by coal executives, allowing them to maintain strong political organizations on their behalf. The county sheriff in Logan County, who was conveniently employed by the coal companies, was none other than the infamous Don Chafin, a cousin to Devil Anse Hatfield's wife Louvicey Chafin Hatfield. In 1922, "one United States prosecutor reported 'enormous sums of money' going to Sheriff Don Chafin to maintain 'complete political control of [Logan] County,' keeping voters from expressing any real preference at the polls."[222]

"[Sheriff Don] Chafin with his deputies absolutely dominates practically all of the polling places," the United States Attorney wrote. "Only such voters are allowed to vote as suit the organization. Election results are figured up and given out in advance. . . ." When coal miners remained under close watch, professionals in Logan County praised Don Chafin's work to protect them from the "evil" of unions. Chafin's security forces patrolled the roads and railway stations, making sure outsiders carried not so much as a leaflet into Logan County. Local people were also encouraged to report any suspected betrayers of Chafin's one-party State.[223]

Chafin controlled Logan County with the full knowledge and support from many politicians. Among those was Governor John J. Cornwell who served from 1917 to 1921. On one occasion when miners attempted to march on Logan County, Cromwell threatened the intervention of federal troops as well as charging the miners with treason on the United States. He later bragged that he had broken up "a deliberate plan to discard the work of Washington and Jefferson, of Madison, and Monroe, of Lincoln, of Cleveland, of Roosevelt and . . . substitute the ideas of Karl Marx, of Nicola [sic] Lenin and Leon Trotsky."[224] Governor Cornwell's loyalty to the coal companies was rewarded after leaving office as he served as a director and general counsel for the Baltimore and Ohio Railroad Company.

It was in 1920 that the tensions of the mine wars seemed to reach an all-time high. That was the year the famous Mingo County Matewan Massacre occurred involving the showdown between the Baldwin-Felts detectives hired by the coal companies and the tall and slender Matewan Chief of Police Sid Hatfield.

The battle occurred on May 19, 1920, in an area that was once home to the Hatfields of the Hatfield and McCoy feud. It began as Albert Felts, the head of the Baldwin-Felts Detective Agency, came to Matewan with eleven armed agents planning to evict miners who had joined the strike. When he arrived he instructed Chief of Police "Smiling" Sid Hatfield to evict the miners from their homes, which were owned by the Stone Mountain Coal Company. Hatfield, who had large bulging ears, along with Mayor Cabell C. Testerman, a shorter and heavier man, refused and intervened on behalf of the evicted families and deputized twelve men, including a McCoy, to defend the town.

Given the pervasiveness of corruption in West Virginia, it was unusual for a local police chief and a mayor to side with the union miners as the coal company operators dominated West Virginia politics, controlling both the Republican and Democratic parties. Moreover, it was common for elected officials to also be executives of the coal companies being paid directly by the companies in addition to the salary they received from the State. During the standoff, one reminiscent of a Hollywood western movie played out on the big screen, the Mayor of Matewan, two miners and seven armed coal company strong-arm men, including Albert and Lee Felts, were all killed in a shootout on the main street of Matewan.[225] Shortly after the battle, Hatfield married Jessie, the widow of Mayor Testerman, fueling speculation propagated by coal operators that Hatfield actually shot the mayor to be with his wife. To most miners though, Hatfield became an inspiration and folk hero for standing up for them when most others in a position of authority caved to the pressure of the coal operators.

The speculation and accounts vary as to who fired the first shot and exactly what happened that day probably because shots were being fired from all directions. Most accounts do agree though that seconds after the first shots were fired, Mayor Testerman was dead from a bullet through his stomach while Alberts Felts died following a bullet to his head. Ninety-six-year-old Marie Cooley Robinette, the daughter and wife of railroad workers, is the last surviving witness of the events of that day. When the ten-year-old girl left her home on that cloudy and dreary day on the way to the town grocery, she had no idea she would find herself as a witness to one of the most famous gun battles in history. She remembered going into the grocery store, which was owned and operated by Mayor Testerman, who she described as a kind and friendly man. As she left the store, she walked beside the old Matewan railroad depot. She said,

> When I got just a few feet past the railroad depot, the shooting
> began. It seemed as though bullets were flying everywhere. I could
> hear the bullets whizzing by me. One of the bullets hit the railroad

ties just a foot or so in front of me. The shooting lasted quite a while. Many shots were fired initially, with the shooting becoming more sporadic after a few minutes. I still recall how scared I was, and I remember running on home as fast as I could.[226]

Following the shootout, Sid Hatfield and the other miners were charged with murder. After a two-month trial, however, they were acquitted of the charges. Tom Felts became the head of the Baldwin-Felts Detective Agency due to the deaths of his brothers Albert and Lee and vowed to seek revenge against Hatfield. Soon after his acquittal, Hatfield was charged for another shooting at the Mohawk Coal Camp in McDowell County. Then, on August 1, 1921, as Hatfield and fellow defendant Ed Chambers walked up the steps of the McDowell County Courthouse in Welch, West Virginia, both were murdered by Baldwin-Felts detectives. Hatfield was "shot down like a dog on the Court House steps at Welch . . . in front of [his wife]" by company operatives because of his role in the Matewan Massacre.[227] The *Wheeling Intelligencer* called the murder "the most glaring and outrageous expression of contempt for law that has ever stained the history of West Virginia."[228]

Hatfield's murder triggered even more violence. Because he became known as a hero to miners, on August 7, 1921, a crowd of thousands gathered at the State Capitol to protest the murder. Coal operators didn't seem fazed by the event even though it garnered much national attention. It was looked at as just one more battle in the Great Coal Field War to which they simply upped the stakes by sending thousands of armed guards and strike-breakers to West Virginia.

The coal miners, for their part in the mine wars, blew up mines and other coal company property. In 1921, no fewer than 10,000 miners fought a pitched battle with company forces at Logan, West Virginia, gaining the upper hand for the moment.[229] It was then that President Warren G. Harding declared martial law in West Virginia and sent in federal troops to break the strike.[230] This era of strife in Mingo County, causing federal troops to attempt to restore calm to Bloody Mingo and surrounding counties, only continued to spark confrontations and violence between operators and miners.

On March 4, 1921, E.F. Morgan was inaugurated as Governor and once again part of West Virginia was declared under martial law as troops were sent to enforce his proclamation. Mother Jones referred to Morgan as nothing more than "a tool of the goddamned coal operators." Attorney General Lee explains:

'A state of war, insurrection, and riot is, and has been for some time, in existence in Mingo County,' said the proclamation, 'and

many lives and much property have been destroyed as a result
thereof, and riot and bloodshed are rampant and pending.' Even
freedom of the press was suspended. 'No publication,' continued the decree, 'either newspaper, pamphlet, handbill, or otherwise, reflecting in any way upon the United States, or the State
of West Virginia, or their officers, may be published, displayed,
or circulated within the zone of martial law.'[231]

Governor Morgan, who sent the telegram to President Harding calling
for the federal troops, said "Nothing short of 100 percent martial law" could
restore order. Calling Mingo County a "smouldering volcano," Governor
Morgan said no fewer than 500 troops would be necessary "to prevent wanton
slaughter of innocent citizens." Secretary of War John W. Weeks was sent a
telegraph by a Huntington, West Virginia man proclaiming, "In the name of
GOD, please hurry Federal aid to Matewan. Our citizens are being shot down
like rats."[232] President Harding, recognizing insurrection in West Virginia,
issued a proclamation giving miners less than forty-eight hours to disband:

> Now, therefore, I, Warren G. Harding, President of the United
> States, do hereby make Proclamation and I do hereby com-
> mand all persons engaged in said insurrection to disperse and
> retire peaceably to their respective abodes on or before 12
> o'clock, noon, of the first day of September, 1921, and here-
> after abandon said combinations and submit themselves to the
> laws and constituted authorities of said State. . . .[233]

President Harding later signed a second proclamation establishing martial law in the disturbed areas of West Virginia, but it was to be used only if necessary. The Battle of Blair Mountain in Logan County that followed was referred
to as a Civil War and depicted as:

> Fully ten thousand men—and some estimates go to twice that
> number—were involved as the two armies began exchanging
> shots along a ten-mile front. George Washington had fewer
> soldiers at the Battle of Trenton, the engagement which
> changed the course of the American Revolution.[234]

As the thousands of miners marched toward Logan County, they wore red ban-
danas, which resulted in the nickname, "red necks." On September 4, 1921, with

more than 6,000 federal soldiers assisted by twenty airplanes under the command of Brigadier General Billy Mitchell, the miners eventually surrendered when faced with the alternative of fighting against United States troops. Hundreds of men were indicted by a Logan County Grand Jury on charges of treason and murder.

In all, in September and October of 1921, Logan County Grand Juries returned 1,217 indictments against various individuals for complicity in the insurrection, which included 325 murder charges and 24 indictments for treason against the State of West Virginia. Perhaps the most watched trial was that of United Mine Workers Organizer Billy Blizzard, who was tried for treason. It was in April and May of 1922, following a change of venue, when Blizzard was tried in Charles Town, located in West Virginia's Eastern Panhandle, in the same courthouse where John Brown was convicted of treason and hanged in 1859. Blizzard, after a thirty-day trial, was found not guilty.[235]

Mother Jones' time in West Virginia illustrates that since the latter part of the 1800s, coal, railroad, power, and chemical companies with out-of-state headquarters have dominated West Virginia economically and politically. Their presence is immeasurable. For instance, between 1897 and 1928, more than 10,000 men died in West Virginia's coal mines, a rate of more than 330 per year, with 475 in 1928 alone.[236] Because of such control by big business, the state of the State throughout much of West Virginia's history was that of lawlessness as they often controlled those who were supposed to be enforcing the law. One such example was in January 1931, when Logan County Circuit Judge Naaman Jackson privately appealed to Governor Conley to intervene in his county to help restore the rule of law. Jackson feared that the murderer of the Logan City Police Chief "would be acquitted by a Logan County jury because of the intimidating tactics of the sheriff's department and the willingness of the army of 'special constables' to testify to anything."[237]

I believe that once a corrupt system is in place and a majority of people operate within that system, individuals have no incentive to try to change it or to refrain from taking part in it, even if everyone would benefit from the elimination of the illicit behavior. When corruption has become ingrained, as it has in West Virginia, it is difficult to eradicate it. Corruption is allowed by West Virginians accepting lower standards. The problem with corrupt government officials is that there are few ways to fight back other than making more informed choices on election day as corruption has no political face, age, has no color, religion, or creed.

When I think back to my grade school and high school history classes, I wonder why I was never taught about the West Virginia mine wars. Quite frankly it amazes me that the injustices that occurred in southern West Virginia aren't being taught in history classes in every high school in America today. We all learned in history class that World War I lasted from 1914 through 1918 and until World War II, it was the war to end all wars. What we weren't taught was that the wartime conditions placed a great demand on the coal industry as more and more coal was needed and more and more miners were needed to mine the coal. Coal demand increased dramatically during that period to feed the furnaces of industrial plants while immigrants, who were perceived as easier to manipulate, were recruited heavily to mine coal in southern West Virginia. In many cases, immigrants, who often were unable to speak English, were approached the second they arrived on American soil and offered a job with promises of great pay and benefits and provided transportation to a West Virginia mine. Of course when they arrived they quickly learned that it was a different situation. They even had their transportation costs to West Virginia deducted from their first pay.

Miners were told through patriotic rhetoric that the success of the war depended on how much coal they mined which would require greater efficiency and greater output from every industry that was essential to winning the war. Coal operators, who profited heavily by the increase in demand for coal, also did their part to ensure that miners produced more coal. For instance, if a coal operator decided that a miner hadn't produced enough coal, he was fired which resulted in the miner losing his draft exemption. It was a dangerous time when miners feared getting their heads cracked or even killed if they didn't renounce the union. Even the company ministers were hired to preach anti-union sermons resulting in control of the miners' religious and political beliefs. Miners also secured the politicians they wanted in power by rigging the votes. They often had mine guards assigned as pollsters who either inspected miners' ballots or handed the miners ballots that had already been marked. If a miner voted contrary to his company's choice, he was fired and removed from his company home immediately.

Again, I wonder why we weren't taught in school that as we fought for the freedom of others in Europe, West Virginia coal miners were living in poverty and pre-Civil War slave-like conditions. The miners worked fourteen hour days and lived in fear of the mine guards who patrolled the towns and surrounding roads preventing miners from even congregating. They lived in an area where the local law enforcement was paid for by the coal companies leaving them with nowhere to turn to address their grievances. They were left living in a state of suspended rights as the numerous proclamations of martial law resulted in a denial of virtually any constitutional rights. Southern West Virginia was under the control of the coal companies, who in turn, controlled many of the politicians.

It was also a time when communication in general was often difficult as people lived without television, radio, or a telephone in every home as is the case today. Moreover, the very nature of the rural towns that surrounded the coal mines prevented contact with the media and civilization.

Every teacher in America should tell their students that thousands of miners were threatened with treason by the President of the United States who sent federal troops into West Virginia. This era in West Virginia's history was a dramatic shift from just a few years earlier when mountaineers roamed freely in sparsely populated areas and hunted, fished, raised crops, and cut and sold timber to feed their families. As I look at the history of the mine wars, which I believe is a dark chapter of United States history due to the lack of adequate intervention in assisting an enslaved group of workers, I have often wondered whether soldiers in World War I had a better chance of surviving in Europe than a coal miner's chances of surviving in southern West Virginia's mines.

# CHAPTER FIVE

# Nineteenth Century History of Political Corruption in West Virginia

*Goff took [the] oath of office, claiming election by 110 votes, Fleming laid claim to the governorship, Carr insisted that the Senate president should be in charge, and the outgoing governor, Wilson, refused to step out of office until his successor was legally determined.*

Shirley Donnelly
*Beckley Post-Herald*

From the First Wheeling Convention in May 1861 and the Second Wheeling Convention in June 1861, to the referendum on separation from Virginia, uncertainty in West Virginia's election process undeniably existed. A Boone County resident, a Mr. Hagar, who was an elected Delegate to the First Constitutional Convention, observed problems with even the way in which he and his fellow Delegates were selected. Hagar states:

> If . . . Cabell County, which borders on the Ohio River, had to have a military force to hold an election there; if Boone [County] had to have a military force to hold an election at two points [out of the usual eight]; if a detachment went up and got into a corner of Raleigh [County] and held an election there, with what difficulty are the counties represented![238]

It was also clear that Civil War disturbances interfered with the vote in Calhoun, Clay, Fayette, Logan, McDowell, Mercer, Nicholas, and Wyoming counties, while Webster and Monroe counties did not even send Delegates to the First Constitutional Convention in Wheeling. Further evidence of disarray was when "Dr. D.W. Gibson of Pocahontas County was elected [to the Convention] by refugees at Buckhannon in Upshur County."[239] In Wyoming and Fayette counties, citizens did not even hold an election to select their Delegates. Instead, those areas were represented by Delegates who came to the Convention bearing petitions signed by county residents.[240]

With such early questionable election practices it is not surprising that some believe the vote surrounding the first Constitution of West Virginia was tainted as it "was adopted by the suspiciously large majority of 20,442 to 440." Moreover, Greenbrier, Logan, McDowell, Mercer, Monroe, Raleigh, and Wyoming counties did not even report returns *for* or *against* the first Constitution. In fact, from the first election as a recognized state, many West Virginia citizens were prohibited from even participating in the new State's government. As previously discussed, so-called "test oaths" or "loyalty oaths" became mandatory for many elected positions which rewarded those loyal to the Union and prevented any ex-Confederates from holding a political office or even voting in an election.[241]

James H. Fergueson of Cabell County, the author of the bill that required the oath, made clear his intentions by stating: "'I do not want the rebels to have any share in government. If they do I shall be defeated by five hundred votes.'"[242] Merely three years after becoming a state, the West Virginia Supreme Court upheld the constitutionality of the "test oath" in the case of William Stratton, a former Confederate who was elected Circuit Clerk of Logan County. In spite of his valid election, the circuit judge would not qualify Stratton for office when he refused to take the loyalty oath.[243]

The oath was also responsible for removing from office John McCraw, who was chosen by the voters of the Sixth Delegate District in the election of 1868. The Legislature of 1869 unseated him concluding, "John McCraw, the sitting member from the sixth delegate district, is not entitled to his seat in this House. . . ." On February 2, 1869, the House of Delegates voted thirty-five to sixteen to remove McCraw, a forebear of current West Virginia Attorney General Darrell Vivian McGraw, Jr. and former State Supreme Court Chief Justice Warren McGraw. The spelling McCraw was changed by family members to McGraw years later.[244]

The situation which prevented ex-confederates from becoming full participants in the political process prevailed until August of 1871 when West

Virginians voted 30,220 to 27,658 in favor of a new constitutional convention. According to a 1999 Opinion of the West Virginia Supreme Court, ironically authored by Justice Warren McGraw, "[p]reventing the abuses and self-dealing of the 'carpetbaggers' of the Reconstruction period must have been foremost in [the] minds" of the men who drafted the 1872 Constitution. Further delineating this point, Justice McGraw said that for "an example of the evil they sought to prevent, one may examine the story of Judge Nathaniel Harrison of what was the 7th Judicial Circuit, which encompassed Greenbrier, Nicholas, Monroe, and Pocahontas counties–an area that was substantially pro-Confederate during the war." He explained that,

> Among various abuses, Judge Harrison ejected all former Confederates from office, even though they had been popularly elected in the elections of 1865; enforced the 'test oath' and 'forfeiture' acts relentlessly; demanded that all legal ads be placed in a paper that he owned; suggested parties use a particular lawyer, from whom Harrison received a percentage of the fees; sat in cases in which he, himself was an interested party; and charged cash for approving pardon applications for ex-Confederates.[245]

Justice McGraw further said,

> When a former confederate officer sought Harrison's impeachment in the House of Delegates in February of 1866, members or staff of the House beat him, ejected him from the chamber, and called his formal request for Harrison's impeachment 'a paper which was deemed by this House a malicious attempt to publicly slander one of the Circuit Judges of this State.' Others attempted to remove Harrison from office, but he managed to hold on to his position until the Legislature of 1870 adopted articles of impeachment against him.[246]

Even after the 1872 Constitutional Convention, while only a state for nine years, questions about the West Virginia electoral process continued. One such example arose north of the coalfields as George Loomis contested the August 1872 election of his opponent James Monroe Jackson to the position of circuit judge for the Fifth Judicial Circuit. James Jackson (1825-1901), who argued that he had properly been elected to serve as circuit judge, was a former member of the West Virginia House of Delegates from 1870-1871 and served as a Delegate to the West Virginia Constitutional Convention of 1872. The new Constitution authorized nine circuit judge positions and divided the State into nine judicial districts. Thus, the circuit court contest would be decided under the new Constitution, of which Jackson had helped write as a Delegate.

The battle between Loomis and Jackson involved one of West Virginia's most influential and politically entrenched families whose connections with other notable and powerful individuals also added to their influence. James Jackson's father, General John Jay Jackson, Sr. (1800-1877), was a Delegate to the Richmond Convention, where he voted against West Virginia's secession from the Union. Both General Jackson and James' brother John Jay Jackson, Jr. served in the First Wheeling Convention in the creation of West Virginia. Also serving on the First Wheeling Convention was George Loomis, James' 1872 opponent. James' grandfather, John George Jackson (1777-1825), replaced his father, Colonel George Jackson, in the United States Congress and was a close friend and ally to President James Madison. In fact, Judge John G. Jackson's first marriage was to a Miss Payne, a sister to the wife of President James Madison, while his second wife was the only daughter of R.J. Meigs, Governor of Ohio, United States Senator, and postmaster general of the United States. Colonel Jackson and his father John Jackson, who arrived in Maryland in 1748 from Ireland, both served during the American Revolution. Colonel Jackson was also a member of that state Convention in which Virginia accepted the United States Constitution and was the first representative from his district to the first Congress of the United States. In addition, John Jackson was the great-grandfather of Lieutenant-General Thomas Jonathan "Stonewall" Jackson, making Stonewall Jackson, James' cousin. James Jackson's brother, Judge John Jay "Iron Judge" Jackson Jr. (1824-1907), served as a Federal Judge appointed by President Abraham Lincoln. Among those most notable to appear in front of the "Iron Judge" were Devil Anse Hatfield and Mother Jones. James Jackson's other brother, Jacob Beeson Jackson (1829-1893), served as West Virginia's Governor from 1881-1885.

The battle between Jackson and Loomis was the first documented case in the history of the State to challenge before the State Supreme Court the election of a judge of the circuit court. Loomis contended that he had received more votes, that there was "malconduct at the respective voting places" on the part of the officers conducting the election, and there was an unlawful destruction of many ballots that directly affected the result of the election. Loomis also contended that certificates in various counties were incorrectly certified with regard to the number of actual votes received, and that ballot boxes were opened several times and ballots were handled, examined, and tampered with by persons having "no authority to do so." Among Loomis' other accusations were claims that minors and nonresidents voted and that polls were closed in some areas at 4:00 p.m. "and not kept open until sundown of that day as required by the law."[247]

In response to the charges, Jackson declared he received more votes and was fairly elected.  He then lodged allegations of his own asserting that Loomis or his agents "had access to said ballots, have handled and examined and counted the same contrary to law . . . leading to well grounded suspicions of unfairness and fraud," and that voting places were held in locations not specified by law.  He further alleged that the officers conducting the election committed numerous violations such as opening ballot boxes inappropriately while the election was ongoing, counting ballots without the presence of the election supervisor, failing to close the polls at sundown as required by law, and the failing of election officers to be legally and properly sworn to perform their duties.  Jackson called the allegations "negligence and misconduct amounting to fraud" and further charged that minors, non-residents of the voting district, non-residents of West Virginia, and non-citizens of the United States cast votes for his opponent.[248]

Judge Jackson eventually won the lengthy election dispute and served as the circuit judge until 1888 when he was chosen as the United States Representative from the Fourth District of West Virginia.  He only served one term in that position and was succeeded on February 3, 1890, by Charles B. Smith, who successfully contested the congressional election.  Smith had initially lost the election to Jackson by only three votes–19,834 to 19,837.  Smith's election contest resulted in the victor ultimately being decided by the United States House of Representatives.

On January 29, 1890, a resolution was brought to the House floor that concerned who should be seated: James M. Jackson, the Democrat, or Charles B. Smith, the Republican.  Fortunately for Smith, the Republicans held a slight majority in the House of Representatives and submitted a resolution in favor of Smith.  The Speaker of the House, Thomas B. Reed, asked, "Will the House now consider the resolution?" The Democrats objected, arguing the election challenge was being unjustly decided and described the Speaker's action with such words as "tyranny," "scandal," and "revolution."[249]  When a vote was called, the yeas and nays were recorded as 162 yeas, 3 nays, and 163 not voting.

Up until that point, a quorum in the House of Representatives could only be established by counting actual voting members and a quorum was necessary to take any action.  The Democrats declared that the absence of a quorum (a quorum being 179 voting members) prevented the House from making a decision on the election.  Nonetheless, the Speaker of the House directed the Clerk to record as "present but not voting" a sufficient number of members to constitute an official quorum for the transaction of legislative business. The Speaker's action resulted in an angry debate that lasted for several days. The Speaker remained firm and even ordered the doors of the House Chamber locked when Democrats tried to exit. Following five days of arguments, on February 3, 1890, the contested election case was voted on and Republican Smith was declared the winner by a vote of 166 yeas, 0 nays, and 162 not voting.[250] During that same election cycle, another Republican United States House of Delegates candidate, George W. Atkinson, successfully challenged his Democratic opponent, John O. Pendleton, in the First Congressional District. While it appeared that Pendleton had been chosen by the voters, Atkinson, who later served as West Virginia's tenth Governor, was chosen as the State's newest member of Congress on February 26, 1890.

In 1875, three years after James Jackson's first election challenge, mistrust surrounded two of West Virginia's statewide elected officials as impeachment proceedings were held against State Auditor Edward A. Bennett and State Treasurer John S. Burdett. Both were charged with improperly using interest on State money loaned to various banks. After finding sufficient charges against both the Treasurer and Auditor, the House of Delegates impeached them and sent their cases to the State Senate for trial. On January 30, 1876, Burdett, a former member of the Second Wheeling Convention who spoke against secession, was ousted by the Senate, while Bennett was retained by only one vote.[251] Bennett remained in office until the expiration of his term.

The scam arose as Treasurer Burdett began depositing thousands of State dollars in specific banks throughout West Virginia in exchange for direct, secret, and illegal cash payments from the banks to him. State Auditor Bennett was implicated for failing to file semi-annual records that would have exposed the Treasurer's dealings. During the Senate trial of both men, their lawyers argued "the prosecution was political and arose out of differences and animosities" and that the Treasurer and Auditor were upstanding citizens and respected politicians.[252] Both Bennett and Burdett served from 1871 until 1876.

The image of politics throughout West Virginia was further tarnished with year after year of uncertain election returns and unscrupulous politicians making election day anything but boring for spectators and participants. For instance, in 1882, Bassel Branen was charged with distributing pure liquor to various voters on election day during the Gilmer County General Election. He was also accused of being intoxicated as he "rode his horse recklessly about and made a great deal of noise." Following Branen's conviction, Edward Miller was found guilty of perjury for his testimony against Branen and was sentenced to a one year imprisonment and a five dollar fine.[253]

During the next election cycle, in 1884, the Fayette County elections were questioned as the candidates for prosecuting attorney, circuit clerk, and county commission challenged the election returns. They argued that unqualified voters throughout the county cast countless fraudulent ballots in the election.[254] The 1884 election returns were also questioned in Nicholas County as an election commissioner at a voting precinct failed to take the required oath which resulted in the courthouse commissioners rejecting and refusing to count any of the votes cast at the entire precinct. The drastic remedy of refusing to count any of those votes shifted the victory from one circuit clerk candidate to the other candidate.[255]

Even when the legitimacy of the election itself was not in question, the propriety of those elected was often suspect. In 1887 the West Virginia Supreme Court found that the Clarksburg town council possessed the power to try their Mayor and remove him from office if they deemed such action appropriate. The charges stemmed from a report provided to the Mayor detailing that several individuals, including Martin Feemy, planned to attend the local circus on June 23, 1887, and intended to assault W.M. Maphis. According to the West Virginia Supreme Court, the Mayor instructed the police force and others to either kill or inflict great bodily injury upon the named individuals "who might assault or attempt to assault said Maphis, instead of directing such policemen and others to preserve the peace of said town by proper and legitimate means." The Mayor ordered the officers,

> to make no arrests of any person or persons who might attempt to make such assault while they had life in them; meaning and intending thereby that said members of the police force and others should either kill or inflict great bodily injury upon such persons, including Feemy, who might assault or attempt to assault said Maphis, but to club such persons as might attempt to assault or injure said Maphis, but to club such persons as might attempt to make such assault while they had life in them (kill them).[256]

That same year, in another early West Virginia election challenge, the issue stretched beyond the border of the State once again as the election of United States Senator Charles J. Faulkner, Jr. was contested in the United States Senate. Until the ratification of the Seventeenth Amendment to the United States Constitution on April 8, 1913, United States Senators were not directly elected by voters during a statewide election; instead, they were chosen by their respective state's Legislatures.[257]

The contest involved Charles J. Faulkner, Jr. and Daniel Bedinger Lucas, both of whom were strong Confederates who descended from prominent Virginia families. Faulkner Jr. and Lucas also fought tenaciously against the Union, and therefore against West Virginia's statehood during the Civil War. In 1862, Faulkner, Jr., while only fifteen, entered the Virginia Military Institute at Lexington. Faulkner's father, Charles James Faulkner, Sr., was a congressman, a minister of the United States to France (appointed by President James Buchannon), and an assistant adjutant-general to "Stonewall" Jackson. Faulkner, Sr. was also a former Virginia State Delegate and was elected as a State Senator. He served as a member of Virginia's 1850 Constitutional Convention and later served as a member of the West Virginia Constitutional Convention of 1872. He also served in the United States House of Representatives from Virginia from 1851 until 1859 and served in the United States House of Representatives from West Virginia from 1875 to 1877. He was unsuccessful in attempts to become a United States Senator as well as West Virginia Governor. Likewise, Judge Lucas was a descendant of the prominent Virginian families of Bedinger and Lucas, both of whom were connected with the history of the colony and State of Virginia during the Indian wars, the Revolutionary period, and the Confederate fight to secede from the Union.

The complication began on March 5, 1887, when West Virginia Governor Emanuel Willis Wilson appointed Daniel B. Lucas to fill the seat in the Senate left vacant two days earlier by the unsuccessful attempt to re-elect Senator Johnson N. Camden. The Governor had the authority to temporarily appoint someone "until the next meeting of the legislature" who then would have the authority to fill the vacancy of Senator Camden's term.[258] Since West Virginia had a biennial Legislature during those days, Wilson expected his appointment to last for at least the next two years. Soon after Lucas' March 5, 1887, appointment, Governor Wilson called the Legislature to meet for a special session to consider eight specific objects, none of which was the election of a United States Senator. The Governor was attempting to usurp the State Legislature's constitutional power to select the open seat of United States Senator as the Legislature was only authorized during a special session to act upon the specific issues set forth by the Governor. In spite of the Governor's actions, the State Senate chose to elect Charles A. Faulkner, Jr. to be United States Senator instead of Governor Wilson's choice of Lucas. Faulkner resigned his position as a judge to accept the Senate position.

Lucas, who had resigned his seat in the State House of Delegates to accept the appointment, challenged the Legislature's selection of Faulkner, arguing that the Constitution of West Virginia provided that "[t]he Governor may, on extraordinary occasions convene, at his own instance, the Legislature; but when so convened, it shall enter upon no business except that stated in the proclamation by which it was called together." In spite of Lucas' argument that the State Senate had no authority to appoint Faulkner, the United States Senate held the Faulkner appointment to be valid. The United States Senate report said the West Virginia Constitution could not have intended to "prohibit the performance of duties imposed upon it by the supreme authority of the Constitution of the United States."[259] Faulkner served as Senator for West Virginia in the United States Congress from 1887-1899. Lucas, on the other hand, was appointed until the next election cycle to fill a seat on the State Supreme Court in 1889 following the death of Justice Thomas C. Green, who was Faulkner's former law partner. In 1890 Lucas ran for his seat on the Court and was elected by an overwhelming majority of the popular vote.

The year after the Faulkner-Lucas United Senate seat battle, Governor Wilson again found himself in the middle of a quagmire as the election of the West Virginia Governor was so tumultuous it became a story that even today is simply too perplexing to imagine. The result of the November 6, 1888, gubernatorial election, sometimes referred to as "A Tale of Four Governors," remained in limbo until February 6, 1890.[260] The gubernatorial contest began as a contest between candidates Aretus Brooks Fleming and Nathan Goff. Before it was over, no fewer than four men claimed the Governor's Office, including two men who weren't even on the ballot running for Governor that year. This infamous election included West Virginia Legislature intervention, State Supreme Court decisions, and the calling of the National Guard as E. Willis Wilson, A.B. Fleming, Nathan Goff, and Robert S. Carr claimed the Governor's Office.[261] As "Goff took [the] oath of office, claiming election by 110 votes, Fleming [also] laid claim to the governorship, [while] Carr insisted that the Senate president should be in charge, and the outgoing Governor, Wilson, refused to step out of office until his successor was legally determined."[262]

The new Governor was scheduled to take office on March 4, 1889. The certificate of returns showed Goff, a Republican, with 78,714 votes, while Fleming, a Democrat, received 78,604 votes.[263] Fleming, a clean-shaven serious looking man with wire-rimmed glasses, was a circuit judge from the Marion district prior to running for Governor. He contested the election by charging fraud and various irregularities which resulted in a recount in three counties.[264] On December 27, 1888, Fleming said he felt the people of West Virginia demanded the election contest. He said, "From the bottom of my heart I did not seek the gubernatorial nomination; but being a candidate I believe it . . . my duty to my State and to my party to see that the result of the election is honestly obtained. I have entered upon this contest from these motives alone. . . ."[265]

On March 4, 1889, with the contest incomplete, Goff, the former Union General as well as Secretary of the Navy under President Rutherford B. Hayes, took the oath of office from future West Virginia Supreme Court Justice Henry C. McWhorter. He then went to the Governor's Office where E.W. Wilson, who had been elected Governor in 1884, refused to yield the Governor's Office to Goff arguing that the contest was incomplete.[266] When it was rumored that Goff, with a great number of his supporters were armed and planned to take over the Governor's Office, armed men were placed throughout the Capitol to keep the office in the hands of Governor Wilson.[267]

According to William MacCorkle, who four years later became West Virginia's ninth Governor, sixteen men were placed in the vaults in the Governor's Office with loaded rifles protecting Governor Wilson, while "[t]hree or four hundred of Goff's friends were there armed, and it looked like a clash, where many men would be killed, but better counsel prevailed."[268] The *Beckley Post-Herald*, reported that: "Wilson called out the West Virginia National Guard and stationed the men in the Capitol with rifles and live ammunition. They had orders to resist attempts of any man or group of men to take forcible possession of the governor's office."[269]

The contest followed Fleming's dispute of the lead held by Goff as he "contended the election had been stolen or bought, and ex-Confederate soldiers and sympathizers who had just regained their right to vote with the adoption of the 1872 Constitution were especially bitter."[270] On March 7, 1889, Goff, who was described as a magnetic and strong leader, petitioned the West Virginia Supreme Court of Appeals to declare him Governor of West Virginia and force Wilson to leave the office because the Legislature would not take action since the contest of the results was not completed. The Court held that such power was exclusively retained by the West Virginia Legislature and "beyond the control or interference of the courts in any manner."[271]

Meanwhile, President of the State Senate Robert S. Carr, a hefty man who frequently smoked cigars and wore a cowboy hat and tight suits with pants that stuck to his bulging stomach, filed a petition with the West Virginia Supreme Court of Appeals stating that as of March 4, 1889, the office of Governor remained vacant and that he, not Governor Wilson, Goff, nor Flemming, should be declared Governor until the contest was finalized. Carr, just as Goff had attempted, asked the Supreme Court to compel Wilson to surrender the office to him and to further declare Goff's act of taking the oath of office as void, therefore having absolutely no effect on his claim to the Governor's Office.[272] Governor Wilson filed a response stating that there simply was no vacancy in the office and that he was bound by a constitutional duty to "continue in the discharge of the powers of the office until his successor should be declared elected and qualified." Conversely, Carr argued that neither Fleming nor Goff had been declared elected and thus were ineligible to take the office. As a result, Carr asserted he should be declared Governor since the State Constitution provides that, "in case of the death, conviction on impeachment, failure to qualify, resignation, or other disability of the Governor, the President of the Senate shall act as Governor." The Supreme Court disagreed with Carr holding that the provision of the Constitution didn't apply to this situation.[273] Carr also declared that Wilson was ineligible to remain for the term succeeding his elected term of office as the State Constitution provided that a Governor could not succeed himself.[274] The Court held that Wilson was not starting a new term in office, but was simply a holdover under his old term.[275]

More State Supreme Court action occurred on January 10, 1889, when Fleming filed a petition asking the Court to prevent Secretary of State Henry S. Walker from delivering to the Legislature the certificate of the County Commission of Kanawha County, purporting to ascertain the results of the election. Fleming had obtained an injunction from Cabell County Circuit Judge A.N. Campbell against Secretary Walker preventing him from delivering the Kanawha County results; however, Goff had obtained a separate ruling from Kanawha County Circuit Judge Francis A. Guthrie, commanding Secretary Walker "to forthwith deliver said certificate to the speaker of the house of delegates of the legislature." On January 12, 1889, the Supreme Court denied Fleming's petition finding that neither ruling by the circuit judges were proper and that court intervention was not necessary for the Secretary of State to perform his constitutional duties.[276] On January 22, 1889, prior to legislative action of the election contest, Governor Wilson delivered his biennial message to the Legislature entitled "Fraud and Corruption in Elections." Wilson said the misuse of the ballot was "more dangerous than open revolt [to the] foundation [of the] superstructure of our political fabric." He said it defiled the ballot box when candidates raised money for campaign expenses and spent money "to corrupt the voter and defeat the public will."[277]

As the uncertainty continued, the Legislature formed a Joint Contest Committee to consider the evidence presented by Fleming and Goff and to decide who would be declared Governor.[278] Even the formation of such a committee was difficult because the State Senate was composed of thirteen Republicans, twelve Democrats, and one Independent. The Senators spent twelve days attempting to elect a President, casting 125 different ballots during the time, and finally elected Carr on the 126th ballot.[279] Shortly thereafter, on February 19, 1889, the Senate chose Republicans Presley W. Morris of Ritchie County and

Edwin Maxwell of Harrison County, who was Goff's former law partner, a former Supreme Court Justice and a State Attorney General, as its two members allotted under the Constitution.[280] The following day the House of Delegates chose Democrats William L. Kee of Randolph County, William E. Lively of Lewis County, and Joseph Sprigg of Hardy County, as its members of the Joint Contest Committee.[281] Charges of whiskey and money buying votes, people voting more than once, non-residents illegally casting votes, and minors not eligible to vote, tainted the election. According to the *Clarksburg Exponent*: "Probably thousands of individual cases were cited, each of which had to be investigated by the committee."[282]

With the Legislature so closely aligned to favor the Democrats by a single representative, one vote could select the next Governor. The political pressure in the Capitol was without precedent. Future Governor MacCorkle explains in his autobiographical book, *The Recollections of Fifty Years*, that Azel Ford, a Democrat and member of the House of Delegates was poised to vote for Goff until MacCorkle went to Philadelphia by train and convinced L.C. Bullett, who was in charge of the Norfolk & Western Railroad, to come to West Virginia and persuade Ford to vote for Fleming.[283] MacCorkle said that due to Bullett's conversation with Ford, "[m]y recollection was that the vote finally stood forty-three for Fleming and forty for Goff, and Ford's vote was vital to the result." MacCorkle, who was Kanawha County Prosecuting Attorney at the time of the gubernatorial quandary, said his "candidacy for the office of Governor [in 1894] grew out of this contest" due to his help in securing Ford's vote.[284] As such, on February 6, 1890, more than eleven months after the term of the next Governor was scheduled to commence, the Democratic candidate, Fleming, became West Virginia's eighth Governor even though Republican candidate Goff initially was declared the victor after the votes were tallied on election day. As a result, Governor Wilson actually served nearly five years in office in spite of being elected to a term of only four years.[285]

That same year, another investigation resulted after misdeeds were alleged in two southern West Virginia counties involving Nathan Goff's consideration for another political office other than Governor. A.B. Shelton, a Delegate from Lincoln County, charged that A.C. Ray, a Republican from Lincoln County, had attempted to bribe him to be absent from the assembly, and that Henry Poteet, a Republican controlled Democrat from the City of Barboursville in Cabell County, had similarly approached him after that body was organized to choose a United States Senator. Both attempts, he claimed, were aimed to facilitate Nathan Goff's selection as United States Senator, which would have been chosen by the Legislature. Even though Goff was engaged in a bitter fight for Governor, he also sought to be chosen by the Legislature for the United States Senate. On February 21, 1889, the Legislature chose to re-elect John E. Kenna to the Senate by casting forty-six votes for Kenna and forty-five votes for Goff. When all of the contests were completed, Goff ended up losing both the Governor's Office and his bid for the United States Senate during the same year. A few years after suffering those defeats, he was named a United States Circuit Judge for the Fourth Judicial Circuit and served in that capacity from 1892-1913. Finally, in 1913, his dream of becoming a United States Senator came true. He served as Senator until March 3, 1919.[286]

The 1888 elections, however, were replete with problems beyond the gubernatorial contest which the West Virginia Legislature was forced to examine. Another controversial issue which roused acrimony involved contested seats in the House of Delegates in Mercer and Putnam counties and in the Third Delegate District, comprising McDowell and Wyoming counties.[287] There were also contested seats in the State Senate along with a legislative committee investigation launched when the certificate of election from Webster County for State Attorney General and the certificate of election from Wood County for State Auditor were incomplete.[288] West Virginia's Congressional seats as well as just about all elected offices were in question that year.[289] One Congressional uncertainty centered around the Third Congressional District as candidates John D. Alderson and James H. McGinnis were left in limbo with regard to the results until well after election night. As recounts were sought in Kanawha County, West Virginia's largest populated county, the votes of several precincts became deeply involved in controversy. According to the State Supreme Court, the county commissioners, who would decide the ultimate vote totals, acted "in a very unusual and very arbitrary manner" as they accepted some of the recount totals from select precincts while not accepting the recount totals from other precincts.[290] The result of the commissioners' conduct was intended to declare McGinnis the winner in spite of the actual recount vote totals indicating Alderson had been elected. John D. Alderson was ultimately selected as the winner following a battle in the circuit court. The actions of the Kanawha County Commissioners resulted in four separate State Supreme Court opinions, with the final opinion written by Justice Daniel B. Lucas, who had lost his bitter battle for the United States Senate seat the previous year against Charles J. Faulkner, Jr.[291]

For many years, questions surrounding other elections were prevalent from its most southern border to the Northern Panhandle of the young State. A letter to the editor printed in the *Wheeling Intelligencer* in December 1888 illuminated such problems as attorney D.W. McClaugherty said that 260 individuals were indicted for illegal voting and that all of them voted at the two strongest

Republican precincts in the county. The letter charged that although "the number of votes cast at the other precincts in the county were largely in excess of the number of names upon the assessor's books, nowhere else [referring to Democratic Precincts] was the vote questioned in the same way."[292]  Then, in Gilmer County, in 1889, H.B. Griggs and N.B. Floyd were found guilty for betting on an election.  The statute preventing betting is said to have two effects—"one to prevent betting; the other to promote purity in elections, and prevention of betting which may affect the result, not only by corruption of voters while the polling is going on, but by promoting, or tending to promote, a false ascertainment of the result."[293]

A few years later in Lincoln County, in 1892, J.M. Dial and J.M. Hollandsworth were candidates for sheriff and on election night Hollandsworth was declared the victor.  The Board of Canvassers affirmed that Hollandsworth had been elected and Dial contested the election.  The county commission then found Dial to have been elected by the totals of the vote cast at Precinct No. 1, in Hart's Creek district, where Hollandsworth received 148 votes and Dial received 57 votes.  The concerns surrounding the votes of Precinct No. 1 were that additional poll clerks were chosen at about 1:00 p.m. on election day to work the precinct in violation of West Virginia Code.  Also, it was charged that one of the unauthorized poll clerks, a Mr. Brumfield, "acted all the afternoon in aiding voters to prepare tickets, and [was] constantly occupied, as, from illiteracy or because of the newly-introduced method of voting, more than three-fourths received [his] aid."  Receiving "aid" while voting often meant that a voter had sold his or her vote and would request so-called assistance from a poll worker who would verify to the political faction leaders waiting just outside of the polling place that the voter had in fact voted according to the slate of which he agreed to vote.  Thus, Brumfield "extensively, constantly participated by going alone, without any other poll clerk, into the booths, and prepar[ed] tickets for dozens of illiterate voters."  Nonetheless, the circuit court reversed the county commission and determined that Hollandsworth had been elected.  The State Supreme Court affirmed the decision of the circuit court.[294]

Election questions surfaced again in 1893 with regard to the location of a county seat.  A special election was called on April 28, 1893, in Tucker County, for the purpose of deciding whether to move the county seat from St. George, six miles away to the City of Parsons.  I grew up in Tucker County and more than 110 years later many people continue to fiercely argue that the county seat was illegally moved from St. George to Parsons.  I have been told countless times that the "records were stolen at gunpoint and transported to Parsons during the early hours of the morning.  It was a shock to everyone.  The people from Parsons were brutal." Once I performed some research of my own I learned that the records were in fact taken from St. George and moved to Parsons, but only after a valid county election was held and Parsons was overwhelmingly chosen as the new county seat. Nonetheless, there was plenty of contention surrounding the election including gunfights and two decisions of the West Virginia Supreme Court upholding the election as valid and enforceable.[295]

On May 4, 1893, the county commission canvassed the returns of the election, and declared that more than three-fifths of the votes cast were in favor of relocation to Parsons. Subsequently, on July 10, 1893, the county commission entered an order providing that the contract with Poling Brothers, the company chosen for the removal of the county records, papers, and property to be moved from St. George to Parsons, was to occur promptly on August 7, 1893. Tensions were high surrounding the move, and people in St. George vowed to stop it by whatever means necessary.

During the evening of August 1, 1893, and morning of August 2, 1893, Poling Brothers, along with nearly 300 men, left Parsons to forcibly remove the county records from St. George a few days early, hoping for the element of surprise; however, it was a poorly kept secret. "While traveling along the lonely road to St. George several shots were fired at the crowd by the St. George picket guards along the path."[296] As they approached the St. George Courthouse several blasts of dynamite were discharged as squads of St. George citizens armed with rifles congregated along the street corners. The Sheriff ordered the groups to disband. However, his orders were ignored as windows were broken and the courthouse was raided. The contents were then taken to Parsons where a large crowd of people anxiously awaited their arrival, including more than seventy people from Davis (a Tucker County city sixteen miles from Parsons) who bought train tickets to Parsons to watch the episode.[297]

On August 7, 1893, at 9:00 p.m., word was received in Parsons that the St. George citizens were gathering to attempt to forcibly remove the records and return them to their town. As word was received, the new courthouse bell rang for twenty minutes. Within the first five minutes, more than fifty armed men appeared and began to fortify the area surrounding the temporary Parsons courthouse. The men were "armed with rifles, repeaters, old army muskets, hatchets, and acid," but the St. George citizens decided not to show up that night.[298]

That same day, even though the records were supposed to be located in Parsons pursuant to the commission's earlier order, the county commission said that the earlier raid was illegal and ordered all of the county records returned to St. George. The case then was brought to the State Supreme Court. Several additional arguments were made including charges that the election was illegally held in violation of West Virginia law and that numerous other violations nullified the election. It was further argued that the validity of various votes cast were in doubt, the illegitimacy of various election officials caused an unfair election, and that a lack of notice for the special election was properly provided to county residents.[299] The State Supreme Court upheld the election results and declared the county commission's order to return the records to St. George to be without merit.

In addition to election violations and resulting disagreements, citizens were also faced with situations of moral conduct to digest with regard to their elected officials. For example, in 1898, J.H. Strickling, the Prosecuting Attorney of Tyler County was found guilty of gross immorality by the circuit court for dissolute conduct and removed from office. The charge against Strickling provided:

> That he did on divers occasions visit a certain house of ill fame in the town of Sistersville, county of Tyler in the State of West Virginia, then and there kept by one Nellie White; that on several occasions during the year 1897 he remained in the said house of ill fame all night, drinking excessively, and conducting himself in a grossly immoral manner with a number of lewd men and women living and associating together in the said house.[300]

The West Virginia Supreme Court found:

> It is shown that during the year 1897, while prosecuting attorney, he visited the house of ill fame kept by Nellie White, in the town of Sistersville, not on business, but for the purpose of prostitution, that he drank, caroused, and slept with the inmates, and promised the mistress immunity from prosecution, or that he would let her know when the house was to be raided. He denies this, but admits that he visited and drank there, and slept with one of the "girls," before he was elected prosecuting attorney.

The Court further wrote:

> If frequenting a house of ill fame, for the purpose of drinking and sleeping with the unfortunate inmates, more sinned against than sinning, by a prosecuting attorney of the county, whose duty it is to prosecute the keeper of such house and the inmates

and patrons thereof, is not gross immorality, then such a thing is not known to the law. On the question of immorality, although the punishment is not so severe, almost any other crime is preferable. It is the most debasing and harmful to society, as it tends to destroy all respect for decency and virtue, and drags womanhood down to the lowest depths of degradation, and its demoralizing influence for evil upon the young is beyond computation, and the aged offender finds it the pit of destruction. While it is a harsh measure to remove an incumbent from office, yet he accepted the office on condition of upright behavior, as required in the constitution and laws, and he has no one to blame but himself.[301]

The problems surrounding West Virginia's elections and elected officials during the nineteenth century were constant and affected all levels of government from city, county, state, and federal elections. While it does not serve as justification for the election issues, there certainly were contributing factors perpetuating the State's political struggles such as the ever-present underdeveloped system of transportation and struggling economy. The terrain made communication very difficult in most places and next to impossible in some parts of the young State. For instance, in 1860, of the forty-three newspapers that existed in the counties comprising present-day West Virginia, only three of those were daily publications, while thirty-six were weekly, two were tri-weekly, and two were monthly publications.[302]

One additional problem with communication during the early years of statehood was that even though newspapers, books, and pamphlets were available, "thousands of people could not read and write and had little use for a newspaper."[303] Likewise, many potential readers lived long distances from towns where the papers were printed and mail service during those years was uncertain. You also had the leftover battles that ensued in this daughter of the Civil War State well after the actual end of the war evidenced by the test oaths which attempted to choke the voices of former Confederates. The problem with the test oaths was that some estimate that half of the State's population either fought for or was sympathetic to the Confederate position. These early elections were chaotic as many areas of the State needed a military presence to even hold an election. Then, even after elected, many of the victorious candidates were thrown out of office by the courts and the Legislature for not taking an oath proclaiming they were not involved with the Confederate Army. In 1872, however, a shift in power occurred in West Virginia as the new Constitution ended the loyalty oaths.

As a result, many of the people who fought for secession from the Union and against West Virginia's statehood were now being elected to the State's highest offices.

Nonetheless, election after election was in question as it seemed that the candidate who received more votes on election day often ended up losing the election. The results of the people were overturned by county commissions, circuit courts, the State Supreme Court, the Legislature, and even the United States Congress. This left the impression that the victorious candidates were being chosen by other elected officials who were already in office and whose initial election by the people may have even been in question. Moreover, as the election results were constantly being contested, results of those elections were not determined in many cases for more than a year after the election leading to more uncertainty.

On some level, it is amazing that people even bothered to vote during those days. The buying and selling of votes was relentless, mayors were ordering citizens killed at public events just like in a bad western movie, people were betting on elections, and citizens arming themselves with "rifles, repeaters, old army muskets, hatchets, and acid" were willing to die with regard to the location of their county courthouse. The unrest throughout the early years of statehood resulted in many West Virginians viewing politics as entertainment while others simply saw it as a way of life. These years set the stage for the beginning of a culture of corruption and apathy in the election process that still exists in many of West Virginia's counties today.

# CHAPTER SIX

# Early Twentieth Century Corruption and the Beginning of the Rule of Coal

*Everywhere one goes down in this country he hears the name Don Chafin, high sheriff of Logan County. One can see that he struck terror in the hearts of the people of the union fields. Although a state officer, they do not trust him. Every kind of crime is charged to him and his deputies. He is king of the 'Kingdom of Logan.' He reigns supreme by virtue of a state machine backed by the power of the operators. It is Don Chafin upon whom the miners and the people of this section place the blame for this latest blot in the State's history.*

*Washington Star*

The new century brought with it many of the same problems of corruption and uncertainty in the political process as election results throughout the young State continued to be viewed with skepticism. In 1902, in the State's Eastern Panhandle, the Berkeley County General Election results fell under scrutiny as the validity of the ballots again brought court intervention. The results of the election left I.L. Bender the victor in the circuit clerk race by a mere four votes over challenger Frank W. Doll. A recount gave Bender a victory by eleven votes, while the circuit court later found Bender the winner by five votes. The final results were not known until two years and three months later when the West Virginia Supreme Court of Appeals gave Bender a three vote victory.[304] In 1903, in the southern part of the State, the Fayette County elections were once again decided by the State Supreme Court as the legitimacy of "scores of ballots" were challenged.[305]

Subsequently, in 1904, the election of the judge to the Twelfth Judicial Circuit was contested as sundry charges were made including fraud, corruption for buying votes, bribing poll clerks and election commissioners, and providing alcohol as payment for votes. It was not until 1905 that the West Virginia Supreme Court upheld the November, 1904 election of J.C. McWhorter as circuit court judge for the Twelfth Circuit. The challenger, J.B. Morrison, brought twenty-one separate charges of bribery and corruption of the general electorate used by McWhorter in order to win the election. It was said that money was paid directly to individuals for votes and to other influential people to secure numerous votes. Morrison also said poll clerks in Upshur County were paid to "secure the votes and influence" and that $5,000 was used by McWhorter to buy votes.[306]

That same year, the 1904 Mingo County Sheriff's election swung back and forth like a pendulum. H.H. Williamson was declared the winner after the tabulated ballots were canvassed, followed by E.E. Musick being declared the winner after a recount. A trial of the election contest then declared Musick the victor, while an appeal to the Mingo County Circuit Court found in favor of Williamson. Yet again, the West Virginia Supreme Court was called upon to sort through the election confusion. At the heart of the contest was the Matewan Precinct where the Court considered charges of "fraud, trickery, corruption, and irregularity" including guns present in the election room, whiskey provided and consumed by election commissioners and candidates, a wager by an election commissioner on the outcome of the election, a hole in the top of the ballot box providing easy access to ballots, and the refusal to allow certain individuals to vote. The West Virginia Supreme Court reversed the circuit court's decision and declared Musick the winner.[307]

The following year, with just three hours remaining in the 1905 regular session of the West Virginia Legislature and with only nine days remaining in his term as West Virginia Governor, Albert B. White sent a message to the House of Delegates requesting that it investigate the charges made against him by a member of the State Senate a few days earlier. The charges in question were that Governor White had appointed a Secretary of State only after agreeing to a payment for the appointment from the would-be-appointed Secretary of State. White was also accused of inappropriate involvement with a proposal to reduce taxes on non-resident domestic corporations.[308]

At the Governor's request, the House of Delegates appointed a committee to investigate the charges and began compelling the attendance of witnesses and documents and employing the necessary people to conduct the investigation. When one individual was summoned as a witness and failed to appear, he was arrested and jailed in Wood County. Consequently, a subsequent petition for a writ of habeas corpus was heard in federal court, whereby the individual arrested sought his release from prison. The federal court held that the Legislature was without power to put the man in jail and that he had to be released immediately since Governor White was out of office and thus, beyond the powers of impeachment or removal possessed by the Legislature. The Court wrote that since the Governor's term ended, "the only tribunals under the Constitution where these things can be legally investigated are the courts of the State."[309]

A few years later, W.S. Laidley wrote in his 1911 book, *History of Charleston and Kanawha County*, that both Republicans and Democrats were accountable for the fact that Kanawha County had become a "by-word for political infamy" and that the odors of Kanawha County political practices "would drive a polecat into bankruptcy." Kanawha County election returns are always particularly important during any election year because the county is the largest in the State with one-ninth of the entire State's population within its border. Laidley, however, wrote that the evils practiced by one party in obtaining power–irrespective of the methods–were quickly adopted by the other party.[310]

That same year, a political battle ensued following the February 4, 1911, death of Republican United States Senator Stephen Elkins, in which a vacancy in the United States Senate proved difficult to fill. As previously discussed, in those days, United States Senators were elected by each state's legislatures and not by a direct vote of the people as they are today.[311] The death of Senator Elkins meant the State Legislature had a chance to elect two replacements as Elkins' Republican colleague in the Senate, Nathan Scott, did not run for re-election.[312]

The controversy resulted from the fact that the West Virginia House of Delegates was controlled by Democrats, while an equal number of Democrats and Republicans served in the State Senate. Fearing Democrats would win both United States Senate seats, all fifteen Republican State Senators locked themselves in Republican Governor William Glasscock's office, preventing the State Senate from convening and choosing the Senators.[313] The Republicans decided this was the only way to stop the appointments as the Senate would not be able to form a quorum and the appointments would have then been left to the Governor, who would certainly choose two Republicans. "For 48 hours the Governor's Office was a virtual boarding house and jail. The situation became tense and nationwide attention was attracted," as the fifteen Republicans seized refuge in Governor Glasscock's office, with the assurance that the National Guard would step in if necessary.

When the Democrats were poised to use a State law to compel the absent Republicans' appearance in the Legislature, Glasscock's security officer secretly transported the State Senators by horse-drawn cabs to Cincinnati, Ohio as high-level Democrats followed them after learning of the Republicans' plan. When twenty armed Kentucky woodsmen appeared at their plush hotel, the Republican

State Senators feared West Virginia Democrats had conspired to kidnap them and agreed to negotiate.[314] The two sides finally reached a compromise, which included future Governor Henry D. Hatfield, a Republican, getting selected as State Senate President, while the Democrats were able to choose the two United States Senators.[315] The two United States Senators appointed were the editor and publisher of the *Charleston Gazette*, W. E. Chilton,[316] who succeeded Senator Scott, and coal baron Clarence Watson of Fairmont, who replaced Senator Elkins.[317]

Election problems continued during subsequent years including a county commissioner from Tyler County who sued the ex-county clerk and ex-commissioner in 1915 to recover monies unlawfully paid by the commissioner to the clerk.[318] In 1916, the soundness of the election of the Cabell County Sheriff was placed in question as citizens argued it was procured by corrupt practices.[319]

That same year, the June 6, 1916, West Virginia Primary Election was considered by the United States Supreme Court who reviewed the circumstances surrounding the nomination of candidates for the United States Senate. It was the first year that the voters directly chose their United States Senators, but it was not without controversy. Among the allegations was the charge that voter fraud during the election amounted to conspiring to "injure, oppress, threaten, or intimidate any citizen in the free exercise or enjoyment of any right or privilege secured to him by the Constitution or laws of the United States. . . ."[320] It was contended that as many as 1,000 unqualified voters voted in the election while 400 of those illegal voters were able to vote twice.

United States Senate Republican candidate Howard Sutherland was victorious in the Primary; however, he was among the candidates said to have been injured by the twenty individuals charged with conspiracy. The United States Supreme Court upheld the Federal District Court in saying the term "election" in federal law was in reference to a General Election and not a state's nominating Primary. As such, the Supreme Court found no violation of federal law by West Virginia's corrupt practices during the Primary Election.[321]

Later that year, during the General Election, more allegations were asserted with regard to "election money or other things of value in excess of the amount allowed . . . sufficient to influence materially the result of the election."[322] On November 7, 1916, Howard Sutherland received 144,243 votes compared to William E. Chilton's 138,585 votes. Chilton filed a petition with Circuit Judge James H. Miller, seeking a judicial inquiry by the judge into the correctness of the charges made against Sutherland and asking the judge to issue an appropriate remedy, by declaring Chilton the actual winner. Instead of answering the charges against him, Sutherland filed a writ of prohibition asking the State Supreme Court to prohibit a judicial inquiry into the results of the election.

The Supreme Court recognized that the Legislature provided in the State Statutes a remedy of judicial inquiry in a section of the West Virginia Code known as the *Corrupt Practice Act*. Nonetheless, the Supreme Court held that the West Virginia legislative restriction was "wholly beyond its legitimate jurisdiction" and declared it unconstitutional and prohibited Judge Miller from investigating charges of corruption surrounding the election.[323]  Thus, Sutherland was declared the winner and served until 1923.

Soon after the Senate dispute, on February 17, 1919, the State House of Delegates Judiciary Committee recommended the impeachment of Monongalia County Circuit Judge George C. Sturgiss, saying he was "biased, prejudiced, dishonest and wholly unfit to sit as judge of the circuit court and that he was guilty of misconduct in the administration of the duties of his office." The Committee said,

> We are further of the opinion that Judge Sturgiss's efforts to qualify himself to sit in the case of Lemley against the Morgantown and Wheeling Railway Company was a plain case of corruption. If not bribery in itself. Another instance of corruption was his efforts to increase his court reporter's salary.[324]

The Committee said, "numerous incidents have been shown of the delinquency of the judge: His failure to enter orders, his unlawful arrests, his oppressive and arbitrary judgments, his taking the law into his own hands, [and] his total disregard of the law. . . ." It added that his conduct, "all of which show conclusively that Judge Sturgiss has been guilty of arbitrary, [o]ppressive and unlawful conduct while sitting as a judge, and stamp him as wholly unfit to hold the office of judge." Judge Sturgiss denied the charges against him; however, the perception of State politicians controlled by powerful industrial interests was becoming more and more prevalent.[325]

Many of the questions of political graft among West Virginia's politicians surrounded southern West Virginia and the increasing control wielded by the coal operators as the need for coal and the number of coal mines and coal miners increased dramatically.  In 1919, Governor John Jacob Cornwell appointed a commission to investigate conditions in Logan County coalfields and determined that the "treasurer of the Logan County Coal Operators Association paid the Logan Sheriff the sum of $32,000, and in 1920, the sum of $46,630, for salaries of deputy sheriffs." Chafin, who received money directly from coal companies in addition to his county paid $3,500 Sheriff's salary, reported a net worth of $350,000 in 1921. A separate investigation began in the United States Senate to explore the situation in the West Virginia coalfields. In discussing the deputy sheriff system in Logan County, United States Senator William S. Kenyon's Committee on Education and Labor said, "The system of paying deputy sheriffs out of funds contributed by the operators, as the testimony shows has been done in Logan County . . . is a vicious and un-American policy. Public officers should be paid out of the public treasury." The Committee added, "It is freely admitted that the purpose of the plan is to prevent men from coming into the county to organize the United Mine Workers. Men have been driven out of the county who attempted to do so. . . ." Finally, the Senate Committee said, "It would be just as logical to have members of Congress paid by certain interests, or to have judges paid by other interests."[326]

The control of the law in southern West Virginia necessarily led to the control of the elections. Much of the controversy surrounded Logan County Sheriff Don Chafin, who was known nationally as the "Indomitable Sheriff of Logan County." Even though Chafin received positive news coverage in West Virginia's largest newspaper by virtue of becoming a candidate for a Delegate-at-large to the Democratic National Convention, newspapers outside of the State presented Chafin in a much different light.[327] A reporter for the *Washington Star* who was covering the 1921 bloody coalfield battle in southern West Virginia sent a dispatch to his paper maintaining:

> Everywhere one goes down in this country he hears the name Don Chafin, high sheriff of Logan County. One can see that he struck terror in the hearts of the people of the union fields. Although a state officer, they do not trust him. Every kind of crime is charged to him and his deputies. He is king of the 'Kingdom of Logan.' He reigns supreme by virtue of a state machine backed by the power of the operators. It is Don Chafin upon whom the miners and the people of this section place the blame for this latest blot in the State's history.[328]

Former West Virginia Attorney General Howard Lee, who served from 1925 to 1933, explains how the early voting procedures and elections in the West Virginia coalfields were controlled entirely by people like Chafin and the coal operators. Lee said, "Under non-union conditions, the operators could say, and many did say, to their workers: 'You vote for the candidates we have selected, or get off the job.'" Lee wrote:

> In many camps, free primary elections were most favorably disposed toward their interests and required their miners to vote for

thcm. Under the caption 'I WANT TO VOTE FOR THE FOL-LOWING CANDIDATES,' they printed the names of all approved candidates on slips of paper called 'THE SLATE' and, on election mornings, company-paid deputy sheriffs handed a copy of THE SLATE to each voter as he approached the polls. The voter in turn passed the list to the election officials, also company employees, who marked his ballot accordingly.[329]

A good example of the methods used was exemplified in 1924, when a Mr. Thompson, a Logan County voter, challenged the process by which elections had been held during the previous twelve years and presumptively in future elections in his county. Thompson said Logan County officials had "failed and refused to provide election booths furnished with proper counters or shelves and supplies, together with guard rails, for the proper conduct of the numerous elections." Thompson also maintained that the required secrecy of the ballots had been prevented, multiple other election frauds had been committed, and that partisan workers remained in election rooms observing how the voters cast their ballots.[330]

Thompson sought a writ of mandamus[331] to force Logan County officials to comply with State law by the November 1924 General Election and to have proper voting booths in which voters could cast their votes without the intimidation that usually existed. The Court granted Thompson's writ, saying that a "persistent public demand for the performance of a duty designed to preserve free and unbiased expression of the voters will be met, so far as this court can do so. The purity of our elections should be preserved. They are designed to insure our liberties and promote the general welfare." The Court added that all persons, particularly public officers, "should heartily join in any step designed to preserve the purity of the ballot. One who by acts, or omissions of duty, seeks to corrupt the electorate, defeat the will of the voters, and destroy public confidence in our system of government makes a dagger thrust at the heart of liberty."[332]

Just two years after the State Supreme Court issued the writ requiring Logan County to comply with State election regulations, the Court was forced to write a subsequent Opinion outlining how Chafin and other Logan County officials completely disregarded its order. The Court found "a clear case of intimidation of the voters by Chafin and his armed deputies, so far reaching as to render doubtful what the result of the vote at this precinct would have been had there been no intimidation." The Court was referring to Chafin's conduct during the 1924 General Election in Logan County–the very election the Court's earlier Opinion specifically ordered to be free from the usual transgressions.[333]

While the results for every elective office were in question, a particular interest surrounded who would be elected as the new Sheriff. The Sheriff's Office in those days was, without question, the most powerful and lucrative political office in a county. One candidate for Sheriff was Republican Tennis Hatfield, son of Devil Anse Hatfield.[334] Don Chafin, a cousin to Tennis' mother Louvicey Chafin Hatfield, supported the Democratic ticket against Hatfield, who initially was declared to have lost the election. After four separate written Opinions from the State Supreme Court, Hatfield was finally declared the winner and began serving his term in 1926, two years after being elected.

Chafin's lack of support of Tennis surrounded Chafin's conviction in federal district court on October 24, 1924, for conspiring with Tennis to violate the National Prohibition Act. Early in the 1920s, Tennis, who had previously been Chafin's Deputy Sheriff, resigned his position with Chafin and established the Blue Goose, an open barroom at Barnabus, approximately twelve miles south of the City of Logan. Tennis began amassing significant amounts of money and even had more than $100,000 in cash deposited in banks within a short period of time after opening the bar. According to George Swain, an author and close friend of Chafin, Tennis was initially sent to prison, but was released on probation "after spilling his guts on Chafin." Tennis told investigators that Chafin was a silent partner in the Blue Goose and was paid between $200 and $300 per month to help keep the illegal business operating.[335]

Chafin was a feared man who was politically active and well-connected from an early age. His father Francis Marion Chafin had served as Logan County Sheriff from 1884-1888, while his brother John served as Circuit Clerk for eighteen years and his other brother James was the Mingo County Clerk from 1896 until 1900. In 1908, at just twenty-one, Chafin was elected Logan County Assessor. In 1912, he was elected to the powerful position of Sheriff, but could only serve until 1916 because the State had a prohibition of serving successive terms as Sheriff. In 1916, he was appointed Logan County Clerk, while in 1920, he once again was elected Sheriff. George Swain said Chafin was courageous and undaunted by any situation. He recalled a time when a man pulled a gun on Chafin and said, "Say your final words." Swain said Chafin calmly pulled out his revolver and told the man, "Now, damn you, pull the trigger and we'll both hop into hell together." Chafin was so fearless that World Heavyweight champion boxer Jack Dempsey chose Chafin as his personal bodyguard when he fought Tommy Gibbons in Shelby, Montana in 1923.[336]

Chafin was running the Mud Fork Precinct polling place that election day and was assisted by seven or eight of his armed deputy sheriffs. Deputy

United States Marshal Hugh Deskins, a Republican, was at the polls in an attempt to prevent some of the violations of the law that commonly occurred in Logan County on election day. Sometime between the hours of 9:00 a.m. and 10:00 a.m., Sheriff Chafin arrived at the precinct and announced that he was in charge. When Marshal Deskins announced his presence, Chafin struck him in the face in the presence of potential voters as Chafin's deputies were standing in full view with their weapons drawn. Deskins did not resist Chafin's attack; however, he later deputized four citizens and gave each a pistol. Chafin promptly arrested the four appointed deputies and put them in jail in spite of their federal authority to be there.[337]

Following the arrival of Chafin, the vote totals for Democratic candidates increased significantly. Not surprisingly, the Supreme Court found that Chafin's actions inside the election room destroyed the opportunity for secret balloting. The Court also ruled that Logan County officials violated the State Constitution in requiring voters to cast open ballots in another precinct, the Shamrock Precinct. Voters were brought in pairs and forced to sit at school desks located one in front of the other while the ballots were marked openly at the desks. W.F. Butcher, one of the Democratic Commissioners, testified that "practically all the ballots were marked by the clerks [and] that when the voters came in they would either call for a ticket or would be handed one, and then the clerks would complete the ballots [instead of the voters]." The Court rejected the precinct's entire vote, finding that it was "conducted in such a way as to prevent the free expression of the will of the voters."[338]

Chafin, also known as "The Czar" in Logan County, exercised his control during elections to prevent unionizing. By controlling the elections, Chafin could control the people who would help him enforce–or not enforce–the law. Chafin even converted one room of the courthouse "into an arsenal in which he kept scores of pistols and high-power rifles, and a half-dozen machine guns, all ready for instant use."[339]

Another tactic Chafin used was to arrest Republican election officers the night before an election on false charges, replacing them on election morning with so-called "Chafin Democrats" who would do exactly what Chafin asked of them. In other instances, he would not permit predominately Republican precincts to even open on the day of the election, while in cases where he allowed the precincts to open, he would seize and burn the ballots after they had been cast.[340]

Even after Chafin's October 24, 1924, conviction in federal district court and sentence of a fine of $10,000 and two years in the penitentiary for his violation of the liquor laws (bootlegging), he used his powerful influence and received a Presidential parole cutting short his sentence by several months as he was released in July 1925. Moreover, after being released from prison, Chafin returned to a homecoming celebration in Logan County in his honor that included "a parade, band music, and welcoming speeches by leading Democratic politicians of the city and county."[341] Chafin was never convicted for any of his election violations.

As Attorney General Lee explained, the circumstances surrounding Chafin were just one illustration of the political influence of the early coal "oligarchy." Lee believed the coal operators' influence certainly wasn't limited to southern West Virginia. To this end, he said after the 1928 General Election, the coal operators held dominion over, not only the Governor's Office, but both branches of the West Virginia Legislature as well. In order to maintain control, coal operators directed much of their focus toward electing the county sheriffs and assessors. The sheriffs had the authority to appoint deputy sheriffs who could suppress union activities, while the assessors were responsible for fixing the value of the coal properties at a minimum for taxation purposes saving the coal companies enormous amounts of money.[342]

Further evidence that these problems weren't limited to Logan County is proven by the fact that there were plenty of questionable election results throughout the 1920s outside of Chafin's control. For instance, in 1924, the ballots in four Boone County precincts were said to have been "handled in such a way as to lose their integrity." According to the West Virginia Supreme Court, an examination of the ballots, aided by a magnifying glass, showed clear proof of ballot tampering as the marks used to cast votes in three different precincts were made by the same hand and pencil as were the markings on several of the ballots.[343] The very next year, in the neighboring county of Mingo, the citizens of Kermit, during the election day of May 19, 1925, were met with more than 200 gun shots as they attempted to vote. Minutes before the shooting, election official Floyd E. Morris had returned to his home for some election supplies, avoiding the shots that left two men dead, two men critically wounded, and others with flesh wounds. A few years later, in 1934, Mingo County Circuit Judge B.F. Howard appealed from the bench for an orderly election in the City of Williamson, referring to it as the "hell hole of creation."[344]

In addition to the chaotic election day events and the coal companies' control of southern West Virginia elections, in 1926, people from one end of the State to the other witnessed yet another statewide elected official who left office in disgrace. That year, Governor Howard Gore concluded that public funds had been illegally withdrawn from the West Virginia State Treasury which resulted in his decision to immediately suspend and remove State Auditor John C. Bond for malfeasance. Governor Gore charged Bond with: "neglect of official duty, illegal and unwarranted withdrawal of public funds from the state treasury." Governor Gore said, "I further request the attorney general to institute proper proceedings for the recovery of all funds believed to have been illegally withdrawn from the treasury of the State of West Virginia by Auditor John C. Bond."

It was State Treasurer W.S. Johnson who in 1926 alerted Governor Gore that Auditor Bond had been "removing money from state coffers and distributing it to friends, relatives and fictitious names."[345] During a later inquiry of the then-ousted Auditor Bond, several of the clerks in the Auditor's Office declared that several persons had been receiving substantial paychecks from the Auditor's Office who didn't even work there. It was then discovered that many other checks were going directly to Bond's friends and family members, who didn't work for the State nor perform any work for the Auditor's Office. Bond was also charged with issuing checks to fictitious people and forcing his employees to cash the checks and return the money to him.[346]

The House of Delegates was unanimous in its vote to impeach Bond. He resigned one day prior to the Senate vote to convict him and was later declared "insane" by a Kanawha County Circuit Court and sent to a State hospital where–if he had remained–he would not have been forced to face the charges of embezzlement, forgery, and larceny while in office.[347] Unfortunately for Bond, after only a brief stay at Huntington State Hospital, he was released and later convicted of embezzlement and larceny of State funds and sentenced to six years in the State Penitentiary. It was a sad ending to what initially appeared to be the beginning of a long and productive political career as Bond "was considered one of West Virginia's most promising young politicians [who] was a veteran of the Spanish-American War [and] who rose to the rank of major during World War I."[348]

This period of West Virginia's history demonstrates much of the same uncertainty in election results brought about by the constant charges of fraud and buying and selling of votes existent in every election since the State's very inception. Throughout the beginning of the new century, both state and federal courts–including the United States Supreme Court–were called upon to try and sort out who actually won and lost many of the elections as the integrity of some judges, statewide officials, and countless individuals were continually placed in question. It was politics as usual for citizens seeing convictions of politicians they suspected were corrupt, but it amounted to just another disappointment when a politician believed to be honest was later convicted. The early years were again filled with skepticism that flowed freely from the previous century.

The early 1900s, however, added the new element of direct control of many of the ballots cast by miners and citizens of coal mining areas. While there was certainly control of a substantial number of votes during previous years, it was much more prevalent during this period because of the explosion in population throughout the coalfields. In order to control the miners and control any potential regulation of coal or their properties and other interests, the coal companies knew it was in their best interests to control the politicians. The politicians, in turn, even though they received a public salary, worked directly for the coal companies who paid them an additional salary significantly larger than their governmental salary. At the direction of the coal companies, with enforcement by local sheriffs and deputies, individuals cast their ballots openly for predetermined candidates. To vote otherwise, an individual would risk losing his job or maybe even his life. Voters were sent the clear message that they had better not cross the local sheriff who was in complete control regardless of whatever outside authorities may be present.

This lack of accountability for illegal behavior was evidenced by Sheriff Chafin striking the United States Marshal with a gun and then jailing the Marshal's deputies. Anyone who watched that event, or heard about it later, understood clearly that if Chafin couldn't be stopped by federal law enforcement, then his complete domination and persistent corruption couldn't be stopped by anyone. Those beliefs were only further substantiated by Chafin's complete disregard for the State Supreme Court's written Opinion directing the common corrupt practices to end in Logan County elections.

As there was no accountability for lawless behavior by those supposed to uphold the law, a person from southern West Virginia probably asked himself, "What is the problem with taking five dollars at the polls to vote against someone I really believe in when the election outcome is predetermined anyway?" It is clear to me that ethical behavior becomes at risk out of a need for survival when someone is concerned with how they are going to feed their family. Consider these inherent problems in conducting elections under conditions as tumultuous as those which ushered in West Virginia's statehood. The Mountain State has endured an ungainly history marred with many episodes of corruption and disappointment along with the outrages which occurred during the bloody mine wars in southern West Virginia between labor activists and union-busting mine owners during the 1920s which received national attention.

While it is apparent that election problems existed throughout the State during the beginning of the century, it is equally important to note that the problems which burdened early West Virginia elections and the various influences of coal have not subsided. Coal companies have long ruled the day in West Virginia as many of the controversies from earlier years have continued throughout the last century to present-day. For instance, thirty-four-year-old Governor William

Casey Marland, who served from 1953 to 1957, faced immediate battles as he attempted to implement a tax on coal. The *Charleston Daily Mail* reported: "[Marland's] first effort in office was to try to pass a severance tax on coal, an unsuccessful move that shocked legislators and rocked his administration. The wrath of the coal industry was swift."[349]

It was argued that coal companies handicapped and impeded Governor Marland's full term in office because of the potential loss of jobs to southern West Virginia if Marland's five percent proposed tax on coal was successful. The tax increase was put forward to provide money for a college education to West Virginia high school graduates; however, coal companies feared that as younger people received their education they would leave southern West Virginia creating a void in the workforce.[350] Following his term as Governor, Marland never won another election. After leaving the Governor's Office, he was later discovered driving a cab in Chicago, Illinois. He described driving a taxi as "a vehicle to help me compose my character, which had fallen apart."[351] The ruination of Marland's career proved too much for him to endure as he ultimately fell prey to alcohol, a problem which plagued him to the end.[352]

Winding the clock forward to the beginning of this century, Governor Bob Wise received a great deal of negative press for approving a $50 million settlement paid by mining contractors for unpaid workers' compensation premiums. The agreement forgave approximately $295 million in interest and penalties the coal companies owed the State. Steve White, Affiliated Construction Trades Foundation Executive Director, said, "We are disappointed the state is settling for so little, for less than 15 cents on a dollar. And we are concerned that the settlements send the wrong message to businesses that faithfully paid their premiums."[353] The perception was that once again, *King Coal* wins. It is a cyclical pattern that has existed since the very beginning of West Virginia's statehood, throughout the last century, and is still present today. It seems that one administration after another is faced with the challenges of coal companies who donate large sums of money to candidates. In 1989, when my former boss Governor Gaston Caperton was elected, "he made a horrifying discovery: Coal companies were getting hundreds of millions of dollars in Super Tax Credits for 'creating jobs'–but the firms reaping the giveaways actually were cutting payrolls. Some earned credits by investing in machines that eliminated jobs."[354]

I mention a few of the recent examples in this chapter to illustrate this is a problem that started years ago, but has survived year after year and election after election to present-day. Money, money, money–seems to be the driving force in the illicit behavior of West Virginia's corrupt political history. It also appears to be the basis for control of the people. A prime example of control is the poverty-stricken man during the early years of statehood who couldn't afford to leave his coal mining job because his only pay was in scrip, who couldn't escape to a place nearby to live for it would also be coal company owned, who couldn't speak out against the problems to the local sheriff because the sheriff's salary was paid by the very company committing the injustices. Even today, West Virginia elections are controlled by a small number of individuals and corporations. The only difference may be that campaign contributors are at least somewhat more accountable with increased reporting regulations.

The bigger problem surrounding year after year of corruption is how the countless transgressions have become woven into our culture and are an expected occurrence in each and every election. It has happened for so long that people just accept it. They either hold their noses and vote and ignore it, don't vote because they know the system is tainted, or just become a part of the corrupt process and profit from it. As long ago as 1904, the West Virginia Supreme Court wrote that a laissez faire attitude toward political corruption would only lead to a breakdown in State government. Justice Marmaduke Dent said the sentiment "held and being fostered by politicians, through a corruptible vote, that crime against the election laws is no crime, should be firmly met and vigorously repelled before it becomes a floodtide, destructive of popular government. Courts of justice, at least, should give no countenance to such a false and dangerous sentiment."[355] It is now just more than 100 years after those words were written and Justice Dent's warnings were not heeded and have become a solid reality in our system of politics. The unfortunate result is that the corrupt conduct of West Virginia politicians has become a cultural norm during State elections while the sense of outrage with regard to such conduct diminishes year after year.

# PART TWO

## RECENT HISTORY

# CHAPTER SEVEN

# Election Fraud and Southern West Virginia

*Election fraud in the counties south of U.S. 60 is part and parcel of West Virginia history. There is no way of knowing to what extent vote-buying has shaped the state's—indeed, the nation's—political leadership.*

*Charleston Daily Mail*

West Virginia has certainly had its share of corrupt elected officials; southern West Virginia, however, has had more than its share. In fact, between 1984 and 1991, more than seventy-five public officials in southern West Virginia were convicted of a variety of crimes such as extortion, fraud, arson, drugs, tax evasion, and seemingly countless other illegal and corrupt activities. During that period,

> six sheriffs, eleven deputy sheriffs, three county commissioners, eight police officers, three mayors, two members of county school boards, two county prosecuting attorneys, four members of the West Virginia Legislature (including two senate presidents), four lobbyists, three housing officials, a former governor of the state, and a multitude of other public officials and related persons [were] convicted for abusing the trust of their office.[356]

One of the most common West Virginia election problems is vote-buying. The *Charleston Daily Mail* says that vote-buying is "a seasonal business, if you will–an economic opportunity that comes around every four years and puts a little zip in the local economy."[357]  In addition, a separate *Daily Mail* editorial asserts, "Election fraud in the counties south of U.S. 60 is part and parcel of West Virginia history.  There is no way of knowing to what extent vote-buying has shaped the state's–indeed, the nation's–political leadership."[358]

Kasey Warner, former United States Attorney for the Southern District of West Virginia, said that during the 2004 elections, voting fraud was "running rampant across the State" as votes were commonly being sold for between $15 and $20.  According to Warner, "It's extensive.  I have no doubt that there's election fraud in virtually every county in this State," adding that his office had received calls from throughout the State reporting election violations.  Calls also came from individuals who had previously sold their votes or tried to buy votes and decided to stop committing fraud.  "They say, 'we've seen what fraudulent elections have gotten us.'  They just get tired of it," Warner said.  He also stated that in many of the precincts known to have been areas where votes are often bought and sold, there is a very low voter turnout as people consistently respond, "We don't care, the election's already been decided."[359]

That same year, Kasey Warner's brothers Kris, the State Republican Chairman, and Monty, a Republican candidate for Governor, said they were tar-gets of death threats they believed came from people who disliked the Republican Party's pledge to root out voter fraud in the southern part of the State.[360] Additional election-related threats surfaced that September when Lincoln County residents, thirty-five-year-old Paul Rodney Lowe and thirty-two-year-old Matthew Riffe, were arrested after allegedly forcing Steve and Regina Hensley off the road and accusing the couple of being federal informants in the ongoing vote-buying investigation by United States Attorney Warner.[361]  In a sworn state-ment, State Police Senior Trooper Anthony Perdue said, "Riffe struck Steve Hensley in the mouth claiming the Hensleys were 'ratting' on everyone in Harts Creek."  Lowe then approached Regina Hensley, cursed her, and "placed his hand on a nickel-plated pistol which he was carrying in his front pocket and threatened to kill [her] and throw her in the creek."  Trooper Perdue said Lowe then pushed Regina against the car and said "people who rat for the Feds need killed."[362] According to Assistant United States Attorney Karen George, Rodney Lowe and Matthew Riffe avoided the federal charges by pleading guilty to State crimes in the Circuit Court of Lincoln County on December 6, 2004.  Lowe pled guilty to assaulting Regina Hensley, while Riffe pled guilty to battering Steve Hensley.[363]

One of the common election problems in southern West Virginia is votes being cast in the name of people who have been dead for many years.  For instance, during the 2004 elections, Lincoln County had 18,580 registered voters.

The problem, however, is that Lincoln County only had 16,899 eligible voters.[364] That means there were nearly a couple thousand people who were registered to vote, but who were either dead or no longer lived in Lincoln County. Either way, it is a problem that only assists dirty politicians in recording votes posthumously.

On July 27, 2004, the United States Attorney's Office had the voting records from Lincoln County boxed up and sent to its Charleston office.[365] Then, on May 5, 2005, forty-eight-year-old Lincoln County Circuit Clerk Greg Stowers was arrested for directing a conspiracy to buy votes and participating in the vote-buying process during the elections held in 1990, 1992, 1994, 1996, 1998, 2000, 2002, and 2004. The federal grand jury also indicted Clifford "Groundhog" Vance, Toney "Zeke" Dingess, Wandell "Rocky" Adkins, and Jackie Adkins, for working with Stowers to buy votes. On one occasion in 1994, Stowers allegedly drove to Kentucky to purchase a pickup truck full of liquor that was used to buy votes. Two years later, Stowers was charged with giving a local person $25,000 to buy votes for his political faction. In October of 2005, in a separate matter, Vance was convicted of being a felon in possession of a firearm.[366]

Greg Stowers and his brother Lyle are the sons of Lincoln County political power broker Wiley Stowers, who served for many years as Lincoln County's Democratic Party Chairman. Greg is a member of the State Democratic Party Executive Committee, while his brother Lyle is second vice president of the State Democratic Party. Lyle was also a volunteer for current Governor Joe Manchin's campaign for Governor in 2004.

The indictment stated that Greg Stowers, Vance, Dingess, and others would meet in a barn on Greg Stowers' farm each election cycle to organize their vote-buying efforts. During the meeting, Stowers provided cash and slates with the candidates' names of which his family's political faction was supporting. The money and slates were to be provided to precinct captains to buy votes. Stowers was charged with buying votes to maintain his elected office and to keep political power for hiring and firing decisions, for paving roads, for fixing traffic tickets, for controlling property taxes, and for controlling the use of millions of dollars in public money in Lincoln County. In addition to controlling the flow of public money, Stowers even set up private businesses which collected public money.[367] For instance, following the June 8, 2001, flooding disasters in Wyoming and McDowell counties, a company called "Lincoln Leasing" collected more than $4.1 million in "no bid" or "emergency" flood cleanup contracts. Lincoln Leasing is owned by Greg and Lyle Stowers. The company was awarded the contracts by then-Governor Bob Wise who ran on Stowers' slate in the 2000 election.[368] The Stowers' support was critical to Wise, who faced incumbent Governor Cecil Underwood in a close election battle.

Current Governor Joe Manchin, III was also on Stowers' 2004 slate, but denies having any knowledge of vote-buying on his behalf.[369] In 2005, Lyle Stowers held vehicle license plate number 5, a highly coveted digit. The Governor controls the first 2,000 license plate numbers in West Virginia and personally awards them to his friends and supporters. I remember the fights that occurred for low license plate numbers when I worked as a Direct Aide to Governor Gaston Caperton. While it might not seem like a big deal, people sincerely believe getting a low license plate number is a serious issue and fight hard for one. It is believed that the lower the number on the license plate is equivalent to the amount of political clout a person has in State government, particularly with the Governor. The number 1 license plate always goes to the Governor, number 2 to the President of the Senate, and number 3 to the Speaker of the House of Delegates. Stowers' number 5 plate that was given to him by Governor Wise, was reissued by Governor Manchin, and is lower than former Governor Caperton's number 10, former Governor Hulett Smith's 11, United States Senator Robert C. Byrd's 48, or Supreme Court Justice Larry V. Starcher's number 125.[370] In 2005, Governor Manchin awarded plate number 37 to Greg Stowers even though he was under arrest for buying elections. Manchin also awarded number 13 to John Hey, the former Kanawha County Circuit Judge who was forced to retire because of inappropriate behavior while performing his judicial duties.

One of the other individuals charged along with Stowers was a thirty-year-old Lincoln County woman named Jojena Adkins who pled guilty in October 2004 to making false declarations before a federal grand jury during its continuing investigation of corrupt politics in Logan, Lincoln, and surrounding counties. She was sentenced to a year in jail. Adkins initially testified that she never saw money change hands to buy votes, then admitted to lying when she answered "no" to the question of whether she had seen anyone pay her father to vote or whether anyone had offered to buy her vote. Adkins explained that when she and her father were together on their way to the polling place, her father stopped along the road when a person, identified as "the known person," approached "our car and he leaned in the window and put a piece of paper in my dad's pocket." Adkins said that the paper was a slate wrapped around cash.[371]

Thirty-five-year-old Jackie David Adkins of Harts was also charged with conspiracy to buy votes in southern West Virginia. Adkins, a State Department of Highways employee, was indicted on charges of bribing voters, while forty-nine-year-old Wandell "Rocky" Adkins, of Ferrellsburg, no relation, was charged with conspiracy to buy votes and eight separate counts of vote-buying.[372] Assistant United States Attorney Karen George asserts that Jackie and Wandell Adkins "have tried to intimidate potential witnesses against them. The pair even followed investigators into a Harts pizza parlor."[373]  On August 2, 2005, the case against Jackie Adkins was dropped by prosecutors who reserved the right to re-file charges against him in the future.  Although charges have yet to be re-filed against Adkins, the December 29, 2005, guilty pleas of Toney Dingess and Wandell Adkins, implicated him for numerous vote-buying activities.

An informant working with the United States Attorneys alleged that Lincoln County Assessor Jerry Weaver gave him $5,000 in cash and a pile of slates to buy votes in the 2002 Primary Election.  Instead of buying votes, the informant said he spent most of the cash Weaver gave him on drugs.  He also said that a cocaine-buying trip to Huntington, West Virginia, forced him to miss a large political dinner prior to the 2002 General Election.  He alleged that he went to Greg Stowers' barn where Stowers gave him $5,000 in cash to buy votes.

In May 2005, federal investigators subpoenaed all of the property and tax records from Assessor Weaver's office dating back to 1990.  Among the records, it was shown that in 1982, Stowers & Sons Land Co., owned by Wylie Stowers and his sons Greg and Lyle, bought a vacant lot in Hamlin that had property taxes assessed at $82.02 per year.  Soon after purchasing the land, the Stowers' built a building on the lot and rented it to a utility firm.  The building was later remodeled into a gasoline station.  In 2004, twenty-two years later, the Lincoln County property records showed the land was still valued at $2,700 with no structure on it while property taxes remained at $82.02.[374]  On August 3, 2005, Weaver and another county resident, Ralph Dale Adkins, were indicted, and thus added to the host of others alleged to be involved in an election fraud conspiracy, "including allegations one of the group gave protection to a marijuana grower."  The indictment alleged that Weaver, Adkins, Greg Stowers, and four others "conspired to buy votes, control who was hired for public jobs, decide whose roads were repaired, fix traffic tickets and arrange for lower taxes for those involved in the conspiracy in order to control public offices."[375]

On December 27, 2005, Weaver pled guilty to a charge of conspiracy for his part in the ring of county politicos who bribed voters in order to maintain power in the region.  Weaver told United States District Judge John Copenhaver Jr. that he had "received money from Greg Stowers in order to buy votes, I would say in every election from 1990 to 2004."  Weaver said he would pass along Stowers' money to precinct captains instructed to pay voters.  He also stated that he received $5,000 in 1990 from then-House Speaker Pro Tempore William E. Anderson to bribe voters.  According to Assistant United States Attorney Karen George, Weaver also received $4,000 from current Delegate Joe C. Ferrell in 1990 to buy votes.  Weaver said he could not recall Ferrell giving him money, "but there's a strong indication that he did."  With regard to the allegations of fixing tickets for supporters, Weaver said, "Mr. Stowers would bring me a ticket and lay it on my desk, and I would take it upstairs and get it dismissed, or try to get it dismissed. I would ask the trooper if I knew him, [or] I would ask the prosecutor to dismiss the ticket."[376]

On December 28, 2005, Clifford Vance pled guilty in federal court by admitting that he bribed voters with pints of Kessler Whiskey, $10 to $15 in cash or both during the 1988 or 1990 Democratic Primary. Vance said he could not recall which year he purchased the votes, but told Judge Copenhaver that he would hand slates to voters with the names of the candidates for which to vote. Vance also alleged that Lincoln County Commission President Charles McCann, the county's former longtime schools superintendent, provided the $400 to $500 he received to buy votes. McCann responded, "I don't know where he gets his information, but it's the furthest thing from the truth. There's no truth to it." At the time of publication of this book, McCann had not been charged with any crime.[377]

The next day, on December 29th, Greg Stowers pled guilty to a felony vote-buying charge by admitting that he led a criminal enterprise and abused a position of public trust. Stowers resigned his office and then admitted that he funneled $7,000 into the 2004 Democratic Party Primary to bribe county voters. Stowers admitted giving the cash to Wandell Adkins, who then passed it along to others. Following his guilty plea, Stowers joined Acting United States Attorney Chuck Miller at a press conference to denounce his past crimes. In a statement read by his lawyer, Richard Glaser, Stowers said, "I'm here today to say that what I did has to stop. We can't continue to go down the path I willingly followed over these years."

Also pleading guilty that day were Toney Dingess and Ralph Dale Adkins, who admitted to helping buy votes with Stowers' money. Dingess said, "I know I've done wrong, and I just want to bring the truth out." Dingess said he helped Rocky Adkins bribe voters outside the Ferrellsburg polling place. Dingess explained that to signal an exiting voter who was to be paid for his vote, Rocky Adkins would nod his head or give a hand signal: one finger meant $20, two fingers meant $40. Dingess estimated that between paying voters and resupplying two other precinct captains with more cash, he and Adkins passed out as much as $5,000 during the election.[378]

On December 30, 2005, Wandell Adkins admitted that he distributed $6,000 in cash to two precinct captains to buy votes during the 2004 Democratic Primary. He said that bribed voters were given a slate of candidates for which to vote. In exchange for his plea agreement, the federal prosecutors agreed to dismiss the six counts in the indictment which had been pending against him.

Wandell said he received the money from Greg Stowers. Just one day prior to Wandell's guilty plea, Stowers admitted: "I've collected and given out cash to buy votes [and have even] given gravel for votes."[379]

The problems with southern West Virginia elections are certainly not limited to Lincoln County. Just following the 2004 Primary Election, Mingo County Circuit Judge Michael Thornsbury sent police to precincts around the county to seize ballots cast before the Primary Election, due to election officials complaining of voting irregularities.[380] Judge Thornsbury said there "exists the possibility of criminal investigations and possible presentation to the grand jury" of the allegedly corrupt ballots.[381] The day before the Primary, Thornsbury issued a temporary injunction against Doffie Hall, a Democratic ballot commissioner, barring him from entering the polling places during the election except to cast his vote.[382] Hall was accused of distributing fraudulent ballots at a Williamson senior citizens' home the weekend prior to the election. The phony ballots omitted the names of two school board candidates, and swapped the ballot numbers of two magistrate candidates.[383]

Not even a month prior to the 2004 General Election, the *Charleston Daily Mail*, referring to the United States Attorney's Office investigations, said, "So far, the most recent probe of trashy electoral habits in southern West Virginia–the last bout was in the early 1990s–is shaping up nicely. Here's to more of it."[384] The editorial said that while Logan County clearly had its problems with poverty and a dwindling population, "the county suffers additional harm from this moral bankruptcy."[385] According to the *Daily Mail*, "The corruption scandal now unfolding in Logan shows just how termite-infested the pillars of a community had become. Federal prosecutors are investigating a vote-buying scheme that is disheartening to anyone who thought–hoped–that West Virginia had outgrown dirty politics." Soon afterward, newspaper stories filled countless column inches detailing numerous southern West Virginia individuals who had been arrested for various election violations.[386]

For instance, then-Logan County Sheriff Johnny "Big John" Mendez resigned on July 19, 2004, after pleading guilty to two federal charges that he conspired with at least four other individuals to buy votes in the 2000 and 2004 Democratic Primaries.[387] Mendez was sentenced to home confinement and probation. On March 24, 2004, Mendez received $2,000 in cash from two different people to buy votes for himself and for Lidella Hrutkay, a first-time candidate for the House of Delegates.[388] Testimony during his United States District Court hearing conveyed that Mendez and unnamed co-conspirators paid between $10 to individual voters and $100 to heads of families who could deliver several votes.[389]

The United States Attorney's Office said Mendez met with his co-conspirators several times between late 1999 and May 2000 to discuss buying votes in that year's Primary. Mendez accepted $10,000 from Mark Hrutkay, then-husband to Delegate Lidella Hrutkay, to bribe voters in March 2000. He then passed along money to a second individual on the day of the Primary Election to be used for paying others to vote.[390] This was not Mendez's first conviction for political corruption in southern West Virginia politics. In 1993, Mendez was convicted of illegally paying poll workers $5,000 during his successful 1988 Primary campaign for magistrate. He resigned as magistrate that year, but recaptured the seat in 1994 by running for his own unexpired term and held it until running for sheriff in 2000. Mendez had been a magistrate for twenty-two years when he pled guilty to the 1993 election-fraud charges. He had also been censured at least twice by the West Virginia Supreme Court for his conduct as a magistrate, once for his 1993 criminal conviction and another time for improperly suspending a defendant's 1985 jail sentence.[391]

Following Mendez's 2004 conviction, it was announced that there was an unnamed House of Delegates candidate implicated in the federal vote-buying charges against him. Delegate Joe C. Ferrell (D-Logan), who gave $1,000 to Mendez's campaign, quickly announced he was not the unnamed Delegate. Years earlier, in October of 1992, Ferrell pled guilty in the Circuit Court of Kanawha County to distributing $58,000 in cash during four elections and paid a $174,000 fine and agreed not to run for office again. With regard to the rumors that he was the unnamed candidate, Ferrell said, "Oh no, definitely not. No, sir. The word is no, I'm not trying to avoid anything, but I don't have any knowledge of what went on."[392] On October 19, 2005, it was learned that Ferrell was, in fact, listed as a co-conspirator in the pending cases surrounding the charges against the numerous Lincoln County officials for scheming to buy votes during more than a dozen elections.[393] With regard to Ferrell's 1992 promise to the United States Attorneys never to run for political office again, he ran in 1998, was re-elected, and currently serves in the House of Delegates. It was just three months after Ferrell's 1992 conviction that Mendez pled guilty in Kanawha County Circuit Court to similar charges, admitting he paid $5,000 to election workers in Logan County's 1988 Democratic Primary. He was subsequently fined $15,000. Even though Mendez was convicted while serving as magistrate, he was later elected Logan County Sheriff in 2000, where he continued his illegal ways.[394]

On January 7, 2005, multi-millionaire workers' compensation attorney Mark Hrutkay, of Logan County, pled guilty to two counts of mail fraud in connection with the ongoing federal investigation of election fraud in southern West Virginia.[395] While acting as treasurer for the 2000 House of Delegates campaign of his now-ex-wife, Lidella Wilson-Hrutkay, Mark Hrutkay mailed false campaign finance statements to the West Virginia Secretary of State's Office, hiding illegal cash expenditures he made in connection with the campaign.[396] Those expenditures included the $10,000 in cash he paid to ex-Logan County Sheriff Johnny Mendez to buy votes for Lidella and for Mendez in the 2000 Primary.[397] Mendez and Lidella Hrutkay both won their respective races.[398] Delegate Hrutkay (D-Logan), said she did not know Mark had bought votes for her in 2000 and that it was "a huge mistake."[399] The Delegate further said, "The acts my ex-husband states he committed are extremely serious. According to his statement . . . he has accepted sole responsibility for the actions set forth in the [United States Attorney's charge]. This statement verifies I had no personal knowledge of his actions."[400] Delegate Hrutkay added that one of the reasons she divorced Mark Hrutkay in 2003 was because he never included her in his life and therefore "it's no surprise that she was unaware at the time of what he was doing."[401] In spite of the fraud surrounding her first election, Delegate Hrutkay was easily re-elected in 2004.

Mark Hrutkay had plenty of money to buy votes for Lidella as his and Lidella's law firm won $78 million for its clients from the State Workers' Compensation Commission from 2001 to 2004.[402] The millions of dollars his firm collected was enough to buy two helicopters and a second home in Charleston, West Virginia. Nonetheless, Hrutkay's $10,000 vote purchases cost him his law license, forced him to sell his law firm, to plead guilty to a federal mail fraud charge, and subjected himself to a prison sentence.

Mark Hrutkay initially gained control of Delegate Hrutkay's father Amos C. Wilson's law firm in 1991 after Wilson "got caught ripping off the State." Wilson's crimes began by altering portions of a client's medical report in order to make more from the State on a worker's compensation case. Following his conviction in the Circuit Court of Kanawha County for obtaining money by false pretenses, Wilson returned to the law office; however, because he no longer had a law license, he was forbidden from having direct contact with his clients or practicing law. Mark and Lidella paid Wilson to be a $120,000-a-year paralegal even though he was legally only allowed to assist his daughter Lidella and son-in-law Mark behind the scenes. Soon afterward, in spite of the prohibition against practicing law, a 1993 State Bar investigation found that Wilson picked doctors for clients, wrote letters and even decided whether or not to appeal decisions. To hide his involvement, he stamped letters and briefs with Mark Hrutkay's signature. Delegate Hrutkay, accepting no responsibility for her father's actions, merely said, "We were constantly telling him, 'No, you can't do that.'" The Hrutkays never offered to repay the potentially millions of dollars they received from Wilson's illegal practice of law nor were they forced to do so.[403]

Prior to his conviction, Hrutkay's willingness to give substantial political contributions as well as providing his helicopters for campaigns, made him a valued supporter for politicians such as then-Governor Bob Wise, whose administration gave Hrutkay license plate number 23. In fact, current Governor Joe Manchin even used the helicopters during his 2004 campaign for Governor while Hrutkay was under investigation.[404] Hrutkay was sentenced to a year in prison for buying votes for his ex-wife's election to the House of Delegates and ordered to pay $45,000 in restitution to the Legislature, pay a $20,000 fine and serve three years' supervised release following completion of his prison term. He told the federal court, "I'm sorry for what I've done, I can't put in enough words how remorseful I am." He further said, "In Logan County . . . the system is very corrupt," and that it is controlled by two political factions, and that candidates who aren't a member of either have a "very slim" chance of getting elected. United States District Judge David Faber told Hrutkay, "You allowed yourself to become part of significant corruption [and] in light of this, I find it difficult to feel sorry for you." United States Attorney Kasey Warner said, "I hope the sentence today will help cause people to see what they are doing to themselves and to their society when they sell their vote or fail to report to high-level law enforcement their knowledge of corrupt election practices."[405]

Another Mendez associate was Logan City Police Chief Alvin R. "Chipper" Porter Jr., who was charged by the United States Attorney's Office with buying votes for a slate of candidates in the 2002 Democratic Primary.[406] On December 7, 2004, Porter pled guilty to a federal vote-buying charge in United States Magistrate Court in Charleston, West Virginia. According to a letter outlining his plea deal, forty-one-year-old Porter said an unidentified person gave him $500 to buy votes for a slate of candidates in the 2002 Democratic Primary.[407] He was sentenced to one year probation and a $1,000 fine. He was also ordered to spend the next three years giving monthly speeches to eighth grade civics classes, parent-teacher organizations, and other groups, talking about his experience with political corruption. Porter said he was pressured into buying votes by politically powerful figures in Logan County who controlled courthouse jobs. He added that when he refused to buy votes during the 1988 election, he lost his job as a process server for three months and was told this was to "get him in line."[408]

Likewise, Ernest J. Stapleton, a Logan County resident, was involved in the ongoing scheme to buy and sell southern West Virginia elections. He was charged by the United States Attorney's Office for skimming money from a

Logan County Veterans of Foreign Wars Post (VFW) in order to illegally raise cash to buy votes for political candidates.[409] Stapleton embezzled at least $35,000 from tip raffles held at the VFW Post 4523 and distributed the cash to numerous political campaigns in Logan County. Stapleton was Commander and President of the VFW Post at the time the crimes occurred between January 1999 and January 2001.[410]

On July 21, 2005, longtime Logan County Clerk Glen "Hound Dog" Adkins was added to the list of public officials charged with vote-buying. He was charged with conspiring to buy votes for certain candidates from 1992 until 2002. It was even alleged that in addition to simply providing cash, one individual even paid $4,173 for the college tuition at Marshall University and the University of Charleston, between 1998 and 2001, for one of Adkins' relatives in order to be placed on Adkins' political slate. Adkins was charged with conspiring to buy votes during a ten year period for certain candidates including those for the offices of magistrate, sheriff, and the House of Delegates.

On December 13, 2005, Adkins pled guilty in federal court to selling his vote for $500 in the 1996 Democratic Party Primary. In light of "Hound Dog" Adkins' guilty plea and Lincoln County politico "Groundhog" Vance, who pled guilty soon after Adkins, the *Charleston Gazette*, quipped, "By the time the federal probe is over, there may not be a political critter left in Southern West Virginia."[411] The *Gazette* also said, "Colorful nicknames put a cornpone face on a deeply corrupt political culture that involved vote-buying, ticket fixing, controlling access to jobs, suppressing the taxes of some, graveling the roads of others. It's a pathetic spectacle."[412]

Also that same day, Logan County resident Perry French Harvey Jr., pled guilty to conspiring to buy votes during the 2004 Democratic Primary. The fifty-six-year-old Harvey, Jr. accepted $1,000 from a House of Delegates candidate to buy votes. Unbeknownst to Harvey, the House of Delegates candidate, former City of Logan Mayor Tom Esposito, was secretly working for federal investigators. On February 28, 2006, Harvey was sentenced to three years probation and fined $1,000 for his role in the vote-buying scandal.[413]

During the Logan County 2004 Primary Election, Joe Spradling was victorious on election night for the office of Logan County Prosecuting Attorney. He defeated incumbent Prosecutor Brian Abraham by nearly 200 votes. Then, two days after the election, the new results were revealed and Spradling was said to have lost by almost 200 votes. Election officials blamed a ballot error and certified the results with incumbent Brian Abraham as the winner. Spradling said, "It would be easier to take that if there wasn't so much corruption. Everybody knows elections down here are notoriously crooked. Most people in Logan

County don't believe the results when they see them." Spradling added, "If I was prosecutor, I'd clean it up. But if you aren't allowed to win if you're not part of the system, [then you can't win, and without the United States Attorneys] it will never get cleaned up on this end. Somebody from the outside is going to have to do it."[414]

In spite of Spradling's claims and while intervention by the United States Attorney's Office is an important aspect to curbing corruption in West Virginia elections, a complete overhaul of State laws is also necessary for true change to occur. For example, statewide candidates are legally allowed to pay nearly 2,000 so-called campaign workers $50 a piece to work for them during an election.[415] Such a law amounts to lawfully paying a limited number of people to vote for a particular candidate. Citizens should settle for nothing less than candidates who are willing to bring integrity to the election process and work to end the State's long-standing abuses.

The numerous 2004 convictions created much speculation with regard to who might be the next public official to be arrested. *Charleston Gazette* reporter Phil Kabler said that: "The buzz from the south is that there still will be about 30 indictments coming out of the federal vote-buying investigation in Logan and Lincoln counties, mostly involving county-level offices, although word is at least one state delegate is involved."[416] *MetroNews Talkline* host Hoppy Kercheval said, "Federal prosecutors aren't talking, but Logan County is buzzing with talk about who has been called to testify and who might be the target of the investigations. Clearly, some politicians in Logan County are nervous."[417] Likewise, the *Charleston Daily Mail* observed:

> Folks in Lincoln, Logan, Boone and Mingo counties are watching what and who comes out of the federal courthouse closely.
>
> Always fractious and distrustful, the world of downstate politics is turning downright paranoid. The old-timers have seen this show before, and know that the third act can always have a twist or two that leaves the audience shocked.
>
> At the next party unity day celebration down that way, politicians will be patting each other down for wires instead of shaking hands.[418]

West Virginia has consistently fulfilled its reputation of corrupt politics throughout the years. Moreover, such stories of political misdeeds are passed from generation to generation and only add to the frustrations experienced by many citizens as a result of today's political indiscretions. Earlier chapters have revealed that election violations were commonplace and occurred consistently from the State's birth continuing into the early twentieth century. Unfortunately, the corruption didn't end there. It has consistently continued to haunt West Virginia elections from that point right up until present day. Moreover, such political graft has become expected and is often ignored as just a regular course of business in conducting West Virginia elections. For instance, in the 1940s, elder statesmen of both the Republican and Democratic parties conceded expansively that votes had been bought in West Virginia for as long as they could remember. They offered the following so-called redeeming argument: "Since both parties compete to buy an equal number of votes in the contested precincts, the non-bought votes really decide the election outcome." A few years later, in his 1946 visit to the State, *The Nation* magazine editor Carey McWilliams said that what visitors to West Virginia find "mystifying about the politics of the State is how the citizenry really know who won an election [before election day.] It would be accurate to say, that there are rotten boroughs in West Virginia, but it would be closer to the truth to say that the State itself is a rotten borough." McWilliams confessed he was "impressed with the nonchalant manner in which voting frauds are taken for granted."[419]

In 1952, the *Charleston Gazette* reported that during the Primary Election it investigated and "found evidence of the dead and the insane voting, and widespread vote-buying."[420] That same election produced Governor William Casey Marland, who served from 1953 to 1957. Marland won the gubernatorial election in a very tight race despite Republican charges of statehouse corruption.[421] Though Marland received praise for taking on the big industries by proposing a severance tax and foraging the country for industries inclined to relocate in West Virginia, his term as Governor was not without controversy and a continued sense of a violation of public trust. Paul Lutz writes in his book illustrating the life of Governor Marland:

> Some examples of his actions that irked the public were: his father was given the St. George wine account, worth an estimated $17,000 to $25,000 a year under the state's monopoly system for control of sales; his brother Robert, a retired Army officer, was made the assistant State Purchasing Director; he had the State Road Commission build a limestone road to his Dutch Ridge apple orchard in a sparsely settled section of Kanawha County some fourteen miles up Elk River from

Charleston. These old-style 'political doings' combined with the Governor's abrupt manner and his penchant for alcohol gave rise to serious political and personal difficulties.[422]

During the 1952 election, Marland's Republican challenger Rush Holt charged, "The present State Administration [which Marland as the Governor's appointed Attorney General was certainly a part of] is one of corruption, waste, and misgovernment!"[423] Holt unveiled a "fifteen-point" platform in which eleven of the fifteen positions underscored corruption and the need to clean "a dirty bundle of linen." Holt alleged "political favoritism in the Department of Public Assistance, the 'squandering' of money in the Road Commission, favoritism in the insurance and liquor sales racket, the 'rotten' State Purchasing Commission and the practice of forced 'kick-ins' to political campaigns by state employees." Marland responded to some of Holt's allegations by saying that Holt was "a person who stands in a rowboat in the middle of the river, rocking the boat and trying to make the people think there's a storm."[424]

A few years later, following the 1960 Primary Election, one Logan County citizen proclaimed: "With $5,000 you can elect a man to any office except sheriff in this county. This costs $40,000. Why, heck, all you need to do is have the right boys pulling the levers and you can't miss."[425] *Life* magazine wrote:

> Anything from $2 to $5 buys a vote on election day, and sometimes they are delivered in wholesale lots. Moonshine is still used as payment for a vote, but it is now risky business. Last election day Democratic worker Harry ("Geets") Johnson was caught by a revenue officer in Coal Branch Creek with a load of moonshine. Geets was arrested and sent to jail, although not before he had bitten off most of the revenuer's nose. A variation is the 'half-pint vote' in the area–a straight swap arrangement, bottles for votes–but it too causes a problem for politicians because state law prohibits the sale of half pints of whiskey over the counter. Most of the half pints used in elections are brought in by truck illegally from nearby Kentucky.[426]

In 1964, a Wayne County constable and candidate for re-election in the November 6, 1962, General Election brought back a despicable tactic mastered by Sheriff Don Chafin of Logan County. The constable used a fictitious warrant issued by his wife, a Justice of the Peace, to arrest and jail Homer Fraley on election day. Fraley was an election official in the largest precinct in the Grant

District and "had become active in an effort to challenge registrations in the precinct and had consulted the county prosecutor and circuit clerk, requesting of the latter blanks to use in challenging voters." Fraley was arrested on the fictitious charge of rape at 3:30 a.m. election morning and kept in jail until noon and thus, did not serve as an election official.[427]

In 1966, the *Charleston Daily Mail* proclaimed: "If you don't vote your own ballot someone else will."[428] The article referred to several citizens whose votes were recorded even though they had not been to the voting precinct. One such individual, Lenora B. Withrow, responded: "You're not serious! No, I didn't go to the polls at all—you mean I'm recorded as voting?" After reviewing a copy of her signed poll slip, Withrow noted: "That's not my signature—that's not even near it."[429]

In 1968, citizens continued to witness many of the same disconcerting election violations from years past. For instance,

> In Lincoln County, north of Mingo . . . voters had been threatened with guns at two polling places. An armed state employee, who was not even a law enforcement official, ordered an elderly couple to 'vote the way I told you to, or you will get hurt.' At another precinct, a man drew his pistol and held it close to the chest of a poll watcher who was carrying a camera. 'If you take any picture,' he warned, 'you will get shot.'[430]

With regard to that same election, Republican Sheriff William Abraham also charged that, "'a good majority' of some 1,200 absentee votes were cast illegally." He further contended: "The Democratic organization . . . tried to vote absentee 'every known drunk, wino, or otherwise human derelict in our county. . . . If the Justice Department doesn't send its investigators, our case down here is hopeless.'" The next year, a 1969 *Charleston Sunday Gazette-Mail* article outlined the continuing problem with special interest groups that amounted to a legal form of vote-buying. It says:

> Special interests groups have long played inordinately powerful roles in these colonies. From the beginning, coal operators have bought politicians, who in turn bought elections. Doctors and lawyers have had their influential associations. Labor unions—the UMW of A in particular—have been in the game for years. Teachers are now learning a few tricks. Almost everybody has had his pressure group except, of course, the forgotten people in the hollows.[431]

Even as the endless cycle of the routine corruption, scandals, and polling place disruptions continue to flourish, the technology of innovative voting procedures designed to prevent corrupt practices of the past has resulted in perpetuating new types of fraud. For example, the results of the 1970 Logan County Primary Elections were again the subject of distrust. In this particular case, a vote fraud scheme involved the use of voting machines to cast an entire slate of votes, including votes for the races for the United States Senate, the United States House of Representatives, and the entire ballot of the various state and county public offices.[432]

In 1971, seven Democratic officials were charged with vote-buying during the 1968 General Election. Four of them, including Delegate T.I. Varney, former State Senator Noah Floyd, Sheriff Harry Artis, and Mingo Assessor Arnold Star, were charged with spending approximately $50,000 on vote-buying for "conspiring to control the outcome of the 1968 General Election."[433] All four of the accused were acquitted after a seven-day federal trial in which forty witnesses testified.

The 1968 election was also responsible for the election of Logan County native William Bernard Smith, who holds the unfortunate distinction of being the only West Virginia lawmaker to ever be expelled from the State Legislature. In 1961, Governor Wally W. Barron appointed Smith as the West Virginia Welfare Commissioner, a cabinet level position. Smith was among various former Governor Barron department heads who were indicted on bribery charges.[434]

Smith served in the capacity of State Senator from his 1968 election until his removal in 1972. The *Charleston Gazette* reported: "Smith attained statewide prominence in the scandal-wracked administration of Gov. W.W. Barron."[435] He was indicted on the bribery charges in 1970 in the Circuit Court of Kanawha County. During a 1970 trial, witnesses described the delivering of bags of cash to Smith and others at the Capitol. Smith was tried twice on the bribery charges, but both trials ended in a hung jury.

Later that year, with regard to a situation completely unrelated to the earlier bribery charges, Smith and four other Logan County politicians, known as "the Logan Five," were charged with violating § 241 of Title 18 of the United States Code which made it unlawful to conspire to injure any citizen in the free exercise or enjoyment of any right or privilege secured by the Constitution or the laws of the United States. The indictment charged that Smith and his co-defendants "caused fraudulent and fictitious votes to be cast . . . all with the purpose and intent that the illegal, fraudulent, and fictitious ballots would be counted, returned and certified as a part of the total vote cast." The Court explained: "In other words, [Smith] was charged with 'stuffing' the ballot box with fraudulent and fictitious ballots."[436]

On December 13, 1971, Smith was acquitted on federal perjury charges, but was convicted of the other charges against him relating to rigging elections by conspiring to cast fictitious votes for federal, state, and local candidates during the 1970 Primary Election. He and the other members of "the Logan Five" were sentenced to brief federal prison terms after being convicted of election-rigging.[437] The five men were convicted for "bribing and threatening precinct officials to cast illegal votes in the 1970 Democratic Primary to ensure the nomination of Okey Hager for Logan County [Commission]."[438] The Logan County convicted politicians included William Anderson, a former County Clerk; John Browning, a former Circuit Clerk; Earl Tomblin, a former Sheriff; Ernest Hager, a former Deputy Sheriff; and of course, Bernard Smith, the former Logan County State Senator.[439] Smith continued to practice law in Logan County while he appealed his conviction to the United States Court of Appeals for the Fourth Circuit and then to the United States Supreme Court.[440] The United States Supreme Court affirmed the convictions of each of the defendants.

Smith remained in office as a State Senator even after his conviction and refused to resign from the State Legislature. On January 25, 1972, an Attorney's General Opinion, written by then-Attorney General Chauncey Browning, concluded that a federal conviction did not require a State Senator to resign from office; however, Attorney General Browning said that the State Senate could cause such removal with a concurrence of two-thirds of the members elected to that body.[441] Attorney General Browning himself was under investigation for corrupt activities at the time and had taken the Fifth Amendment against self-incrimination and refused to testify before a 1972 grand jury investigating bribery and State purchasing abuses.[442]

In spite of Browning's Opinion, the Senate voted for Smith's expulsion in 1972.[443] Former Supreme Court Chief Justice Richard Neely was a young legislator in 1972 and believed Smith was innocent. Smith himself fought to remain a Senator and according to State Senator William Sharpe, Smith was upset at his expulsion which only passed the State Senate by a single vote. Senator Sharpe said he voted against expulsion because the appeals process had not been complete at the time. He added that the only reason Smith was removed from the Senate was due to then-Senate President Hansford McCourt who promised to vote against the expulsion, but changed his mind at the last minute.

In 1973, Smith was publicly reprimanded for "procrastination and delay in handling" a legal matter and in 1974, the State Bar revoked his license to practice law.[444] Then, in 1980, Smith's law license was returned to him. The West Virginia Supreme Court held that "the nature of the original offense for which [Smith] was disbarred was reprehensible, but it was completely unrelated to

[Smith's] law practice or activities as an officer of the Court." The Supreme Court also found that "Smith had been rehabilitated" and therefore, restored his law license. The Court further said, "Although his conviction was widely publicized and generally known, he had a substantial practice at the time of his disbarment [and that] the criteria of character, maturity, and experience are basically designed to permit forgiveness of a young man who has been stupid in his youth and can demonstrate that over the course of years he has become wiser and stronger."[445]

Smith's law licence was restored in spite of the United States Supreme Court's finding that there was ample evidence that Smith, Earl Tomblin, and others engaged in the conspiracy to cast false votes for candidates for all offices including United States Senator Robert C. Byrd and United States Congressman Ken Hechler. The Court outlined how the vote fraud was carried out, such as joining voters in the voting booths and voting for specific candidates regardless of the actual voter's wishes. Others such as Cecil Elswick, an unindicted co-conspirator, who served as the Republican election officer at the Mount Gay precinct, "simply went into the voting machine on his own and cast many fictitious ballots. Through a comparison between the reported returns and the number of persons who actually voted, false votes were shown to have been cast for every office–federal, state, and local."[446]

In 1982, just two years after his law license had been returned, Smith won a landmark case which ruled that property must be taxed at real market value. Later, in 1990, Smith again received a one-year suspension of his law license for his handling of an estate and for threatening to deny benefits to those beneficiaries who filed legal ethics complaints against him.[447]

A few years later, in 1992, Earl Tomblin, the former Logan County Sheriff and member of the "Logan Five," once again faced federal charges for his election-related activities. In federal court, Tomblin pled guilty to bribery charges related to the election of former Logan County Sheriff Oval Adams. Also involved with Tomblin in the corrupt plot to control Logan County elections was then-sitting Circuit Court Judge Ned Grubb who was sentenced to more than five years in prison for bribery, obstruction of justice, mail fraud, tampering with a witness, and racketeering.[448]

With regard to the never-ending situation of vote-buying in southern West Virginia, in 1976, another Logan County Grand Jury returned a multiple count joint indictment against Vernon Dingess, Anthony P. Cristiani, Roy Stollings, Amos Godby, Betty Lunsford, Jack Hobbs, and Harold K. Whitman for various violations of the election laws including deceiving, defrauding, and intimidating voters.[449]

While there were numerous court-imposed judgments against these individuals, both Hobbs and Whitman were convicted of making false returns of the results of the votes cast for candidates during the Primary Election on May 11, 1976, in order to benefit the candidates of their choice. Hobbs and Whitman were appointed election commissioners of Logan County and approached several voters and asked if they needed assistance in voting. Several voters testified that Hobbs entered the voting booth with them and pulled the voting levers for them. Other witnesses testified that Hobbs "pulled the [voting] levers so fast" that they did not know for whom they actually voted, while another said she was unaware that Hobbs was actually voting for her.[450] Hobbs entered the voting booths with the individuals as he disregarded the sample voting machine set up outside of the booths to assist voters.

Many of the same charges were raised against Whitman, including allegations that he had voted for candidates of whom the voters had asked him not to vote. The "assistance" in voting that Hobbs and Whitman gave to voters was given without an election commissioner from the other political party as required by law. In effect, both Hobbs and Whitman "intimidated, tricked or deceived" many Logan County voters into voting for unintended candidates. They then counted and recorded these votes even though they knew them to be false.[451]

In describing a history of voting corruption in southern West Virginia, the *Charleston Daily Mail*, the State's second largest newspaper, wrote: "Dead people voting, cash and liquor-bought ballots, a process controlled by the slick political party machine." The article described "decades-old scandals that have sullied the region's reputation" and "years of purchased votes and coercion by county officials who would actually escort people into the [voting] booths and push buttons for them." It detailed the lasting effect of the illegal election practices that plagued the region in years past and said that people old enough "who still remember what it was like in those days [still] remain wary of their government." A good example of this is eighty-two-year-old Herb Smith of Williamson, West Virginia who explained, "People would come in and vote and you'd have to vote them under somebody else's name because they'd already voted."[452]

Throughout the years, election fraud in certain counties has been scandalously common and the 1980 West Virginia General Election was no exception to the rule. Just after the election, NBC television stations aired nationally a tape which showed alleged vote-buying in Logan and Mingo counties.[453] Then-Secretary of State A. James Manchin, who was later impeached as State Treasurer, said NBC "either contrived the vote-buying story or staged it."[454] Charges of voting irregularities that same year were abundantly visible in Kanawha, Clay, Jackson, Putnam, Boone, Cabell, McDowell, Wayne, Wirt,

Wyoming, Roane, Logan, Marion, as well as in many other West Virginia counties.[455]   In Boone County, for example, officials went to the United States
Attorney's Office arguing that the election results as reported by the computer
provided impossibly inaccurate results.   Cited as an example was that some
Democratic candidates received no votes in two precincts where 250 straight-
ticket Democratic votes were cast.[456]  Another example was the fact that one vote
print-out gave 7,787 votes to Assessor Robert Totten while another vote tally
credited Totten with 6,380 votes.   Boone County Commissioners certified the
results even though "gross discrepancies [had] appeared."[457]

It was argued that Miller manipulated computer toggle switches during
the election totals in an attempt to alter vote counts.[460]   Computer Election
Systems salesman Carl Clough was also seen placing a phone receiver into his
briefcase, an activity consistent with the use of a portable modem,[461] perhaps in
an effort to change vote totals.  It was further contended that "numerous irregularities occurred after the election, including improper handling of the ballots and
release of exact returns prior to the canvass, and destruction of ballots" in violation of the West Virginia Code.  Steven L. Miller was also accused of removing
computer cards from his coat pocket, giving them to his wife, Margaret Miller,
who in turn fed the cards into the computer.[462]   In January 2006, Steven,
Margaret's now-ex-husband, who in the 1980s was a Kanawha County
Republican Chairman who was in the running for United States Attorney for the
Southern District of West Virginia, pled guilty to tax evasion by using some of his
employees' withholdings to pay for his current wife's Mercedes-Benz.  Miller
admitted that he "evaded and defeated approximately $38,000 of the federal per-

Also that year, voting machines were an issue as questions surrounded
the soundness of the 1980 Boone County and Kanawha County elections as allegations of conspiracies by elected officials and others to fix the election were disclosed.  The charge was that the results were predetermined due to a conspiracy
perpetrated through the use of new electronic voting equipment.[458]  The Kanawha
County Commission denied one candidate's request for a recount of all comput-
er ballots and the West Virginia Supreme Court further refused the recount.[459]
Among those charged for election violations were Kanawha County Clerk
Margaret "Peggy" Miller and her employees Carolyn Critchfield, Ann Carroll,
Darlene Dotson, Clayton Spangler; James Roark, the Kanawha County
Prosecuting Attorney; Boone County Clerk employee Bernard Meadows; David
Staton, the successful Congressional candidate in the 1980 election; John
Cavacini, who was associated with the campaign of Governor John D.
Rockefeller, IV; and Computer Election Systems, Inc., which provided the com-
puter vote-tabulating systems in Kanawha County.

sonal income taxes, trust fund taxes and Trust Fund Recovery Penalties due and owing by him" to the federal government.[463]

The Kanawha County Commission initially agreed to pay Margaret's $216,126 legal bills surrounding the 1980 election dispute; however, they later refused to make the payments even though a Kanawha County jury cleared her of all charges.[464] Nonetheless, the consequences of manipulating ballots in one or two counties cannot be overstated. For example, Kanawha County has a population of more than 200,000, which is significant considering the entire population of West Virginia is only 1.8 million.

A few years later, in 1988, Mingo County seized the headlines as fifteen public officials were charged by the United States Attorney's Office for the Southern District of West Virginia on political corruption charges. Democratic Chairman Johnnie Owens was known as the linchpin of the massive corruption case. In sentencing Owens, the United States District Judge remarked, "I despise your acts of public corruption." Once again, West Virginia gained negative national exposure as the *Chicago Tribune* reported: "Nearly 50 public officials or employees in southern West Virginia have been charged or convicted in corruption or drug cases over the past three years."[465]

Owens and numerous other county officials were charged with conspiring to control the Mingo County corruption-plagued elections of 1984. The Sheriff in Mingo County pled guilty to the charges against him, while Owens, the man who sold the Sheriff's post, was sentenced to fourteen years in federal prison for conspiracy and tax evasion. Owens successfully defeated the State's attempt to try him in Mingo County with a group of jurors summoned from Cabell County. He admitted to quitting the Sheriff's position in 1982 after accepting $50,000 from Charles "Eddie" Hilbert to aid Hilbert in obtaining the Sheriff's post. Hilbert pled guilty to buying his job for $100,000 and faced up to thirteen years in jail and $351,000 in fines after striking a plea bargain with federal prosecutors. Subsequently, he pled guilty to conspiracy, mail fraud, failure to report income and he agreed to resign as Sheriff as well as forfeit his pension. Included in the fifteen indictments was a State Senator, the Prosecuting Attorney, the Mayor of Williamson, two County Commissioners, two county school board members, three former Delegates to the State Legislature, one Magistrate, one former Magistrate, a former Circuit Clerk, a former County Clerk, and a former school board member who was also director of the county anti-poverty agency.[466]

Former Federal Prosecutor Joseph F. Savage, Jr. was involved in the corruption probes throughout southern West Virginia, including the investigations and subsequent convictions of former Governor Arch Moore, two Senate presidents and a Senate Majority Leader. Savage, currently an attorney in Boston,

Massachusetts, called the corruption in southern West Virginia a systemic problem. He recalled a situation that quickly introduced him to the ways of Mingo County when Wig Preece, along with his wife and several of their thirteen children, parked a trailer across from the police chief's office to sell drugs. Savage said business was so good that Preece would often run out of drugs and would then place a sign on the front of the trailer declaring, "Out of pot, back in 30 minutes."[467]

Continuing the trend of corruption, on March 20, 2002, Mingo County Prosecuting Attorney Ron Rumora asked the West Virginia Prosecuting Attorney's Institute to appoint a special prosecutor to examine corruption allegations against Mingo County Government officials. Among the allegations were "improper use of county property, improper disposition of county property, and the improper use of county funds."[468] An *Associated Press* article described Mingo County as follows:

> The Hatfield-McCoy feud started it more than a century ago. Later, there was armed insurrection over organizing coal mines. Later, the sheriff and more than 50 officials went to federal prison for corruption.
>
> No wonder they called Mingo County 'Bloody Mingo.'
>
> Now a homecoming queen is shot dead at a sewage treatment plant. A state senator again faces federal charges for wiretapping his ex-wife's home. And a high school science teacher is accused of being in a drug ring.
>
> High-profile, mostly-federal cases can make it seem that life is particularly hard in this tough Appalachian coal county of about 33,000 against the Tug Fork River and Kentucky, about two hours south of Charleston.[469]

In 1989, the *Washington Post* reported that Dan Tonkovich, the West Virginia State Senate President, pled guilty to charges of taking a $5,000 payoff from a casino company in an attempt to pass a legalized gambling bill. The story stated: "Since July, the State's treasurer, attorney general, a former Senate majority leader, and Tonkovich's successor as Senate President, also have resigned, pleaded guilty or agreed to plead guilty in various investigations."[470] Such corrupt election practices and constant convictions have been fused with the State's political system as hallowed custom and technique. Irrespective of who wins or loses the election it is a destructive and devastating game. Democracy is at risk as two out of three eligible West Virginians don't bother to vote. In 1992, West Virginia was among the worst in the nation in voter turnout as it ranked forty-second for that year's election.[471] That same year, the *Charleston Daily Mail* maintained: "West Virginia's image is changing. Barefoot hillbillies are surrendering the limelight to disgraced politicians—an almost unending procession of officeholders whose careers have crumbled because of drug abuse, greed, illicit sex or extortion."[472]

Even as recently as the 2004 election cycle the use of ballot slating was still prevalent. Numerous State Senate and House of Delegate candidates illegally paid money to be included on a list of candidates (a slate) where those controlling the slate asserted they controlled a certain number of votes. Candidates are fearful if they are not included on the slate, their opponent will be included and thus, the election could be swayed in their favor. According to my sources, at least one United States congressional candidate for West Virginia's second congressional district spent several thousand dollars on slating during the 2002 election.[473] Years earlier, in 1984, it cost as much as $7,000 to be included on the Kanawha County Primary Election slates which recommended candidates as "outstanding candidates" or "good Democrats worthy of your vote."[474]

Shortly after becoming the United States Attorney for the Southern District of West Virginia in 2002, Kasey Warner, in recognition of widespread presence of vote fraud, said, "It's embarrassing. The truth is that some West Virginians are so wimpy they will sell their birthright to vote—and others refuse to stand up for truth, justice and the American way." Warner also noted: "These are people who might not be participating and might not approve of what's going on, but they may be beneficiaries of a corrupt system. They're in jobs with good pay, good benefits and security. They know that they could be putting all that in jeopardy if they speak out."[475] Ironically, Warner was later fired by President Bush for, among other things, his questionable election conduct in 2004.[476]

It is clearly recognized that some people are afraid to expose corrupt activities because they are fearful of reprisals against themselves or to their families. Such fears will last as long as some West Virginians sell, and others buy, political power. Many of the economic and social ills of which West Virginians complain can be traced to the willingness of some who sell out to those who seek the power, and the willingness of others to ignore criminal violations for the sake of short-term gain.[477]

People are sometimes more concerned about how they are personally affected by their relationship with an elected official instead of a particular criminal action against the State committed by that same elected official. For instance, many West Virginians may hold a greater concern with regard to whether or not their elected officials are able to help them with personal issues, such as a workers' compensation claim, or a problem with a bridge in need of repair, than whether a politician may be taking money from an illegal source. When considering the political criminal conduct and the indifference by many of the State's citizens to such actions, it has been said, "You can't eat democracy." Furthermore, as Theodore White, who wrote about West Virginians during the 1960 Presidential Primary, explained:

> When men are unemployed, any job looks good, and govern-
> ment in many West Virginia counties is the chief source of jobs.
> The county sheriffs' offices, by antique tradition, still operate
> on the fee system, and the jobs of several county sheriffs are
> estimated to be worth about $30,000 a year in 'take'; some
> county assessor offices are worth more–up to $70,000 a year in
> take.  Posts on the local school boards are bitterly contested,
> from one end of the state to the other. 'Hell,' one local politi-
> cian answered me, 'curriculum? They don't give a damn about
> curriculum, half of them don't know what the word 'curricu-
> lum' means.  School board means jobs–it means teachers' jobs,
> janitors' jobs, bus-driver jobs.  They'll pass the curriculum in
> five minutes and spend two hours arguing about who's gonna
> be bus driver on Peapot Route Number One.  Bus driver means
> a hundred and sixty dollars a month for a part-time job.'[478]

West Virginians have generally considered poverty as a personal moral failing rather than a social injustice.  From the earliest days when our forefathers chose our future leaders, it was believed that wealth, judgment and power natu-rally flowed together.  Thus, from the very beginning our leaders were the so-called elite as sturdy fortunes became indications of social status. Although West Virginia ranks among the lowest for education, healthcare, employment and salaries, citizens often choose their leaders from the ranks of wealth and privi-lege.[479]  Moreover, they often settle for dishonest elected officials. Many believe that the so-called *voting the dead* is an ancient and honorable election day prac-tice in West Virginia.  Nonetheless, it is a practice lawmakers and West Virginia citizenry should no longer tolerate.

Corruption has an impact well beyond the amount of money that may have been stolen or the decisions influenced by bribery.  The real costs come in the form of a breakdown in societal morality caused by prominent examples of corrupt behavior. The headline from a front page *Charleston Daily Mail* news story in 2002 said: "Deceased's vote counted in Mingo." The article discussed out-of-date county voting lists and cited as an example Brooke Franklin, who was supposedly "a good citizen, voting long into the golden years of her life." The problem was that Franklin, who died in 1993, somehow managed to vote during the 1994 Primary Election. In addition, during the last statewide election, Mingo County, just like neighboring Lincoln County, had more people registered to vote than actual citizens living in the county who were eligible to vote.[480]

The *Charleston Daily Mail* declared, "Perhaps if the State worked harder to make sure that voting is not just convenient, but also clean and fair, turnout would take care of itself." It further asserted, "West Virginians have sold their votes for as little as a pint of liquor, and we continue to joke about dead people voting."[481] The *Daily Mail* attributes the State's "decades-old scandals that have sullied the region's reputation," as a reason many residents remain wary of their government.[482] I recall one day when I was driving through southern West Virginia to collect information for this book. As I drove past the large "Lincoln County" sign upon entering the county, I noticed a smaller sign attached to it which said, "Keep It Clean." I know that it was referring to littering, but it could also be interpreted as a cruel joke on the residents of the county who want clean elections, but feel helpless as those around them accept cash and whiskey for their votes.

No West Virginian should be discouraged from voting because they worry that their vote will not be counted. Moreover, they should not be forced to vote on old voting machines that further such skepticism coupled with year after year of widespread reports of irregularities and questionable practices by election officials. People need to know that their vote counted–and thus their voice counted–and that they stood in line to vote for a reason. No longer can West Virginians stand quietly and watch as their well-founded election concerns are swept under the rug. They must demand more from the Secretary of State, Attorney General, Governor, and Legislature.

In particular, the Legislature must play a proactive role in reforming West Virginia elections. Simply making it easier to vote as the Legislature did with so-called early voting isn't enough to fix a broken system. Moreover, the early voting system which allows people to take advantage of a fifteen-day early voting period, while enormously convenient, leaves me great concern for votes that are cast by southern West Virginians which are then left sitting in a box for more than two weeks prior to election day. Several scenarios of election fraud and ballot tampering enter my mind and when you consider that 126,504 West

Virginians cast their ballots during the early voting period in 2004 (16 percent of the total ballots cast),[483] it creates a great deal of unrest that not only local elections could be affected, but that we could also be deciding statewide or even national elections based upon fraudulent ballots. For example, just more than 5,000 votes was the margin of victory in the 2004 race for Attorney General. I would imagine that 5,000 votes wouldn't be that hard to come up with in counties with a history of voting the dead. I also find the complicity with vote-buying to be a huge problem in West Virginia, a problem that needs to be remedied.

A friend of mine who is a political science professor at West Virginia University said to me that vote-buying "isn't that big of a deal anymore in West Virginia and even if it does happen in a few counties today it isn't a statewide problem." I have tremendous respect for this individual, but I couldn't disagree more with his impressions of the destructiveness of election corruption, particularly vote-buying. My example from the previous paragraph with the approximate 5,000 vote difference in the Attorney General's race in 2004 is the perfect illustration of how buying and stealing votes in a few counties can affect an entire state's election results.

I often wonder how many political races have been settled by illegal votes in West Virginia. During the last election in Lincoln County, federal prosecutors charge that votes were bought for the Democratic candidate for county commission who only beat the Republican challenger by 216 votes. Had that election been a clean election the challenger may have won. Moreover, during the 2004 Primary and General Elections, the Lincoln County Circuit Clerk, who was later convicted for buying votes, was also in charge of safely keeping 2,532 early and absentee votes cast by that county's voters prior to the election.[484] Since the circuit clerk was found guilty of buying votes during each of the past elections since 1990, it doesn't seem like much of a stretch to believe that the votes within his actual possession could also have been tainted.

How many West Virginia governors, attorneys general, state senators, or any elected officials have been elected because of bought votes? It absolutely makes me sick to know that every election I have voted in during my entire lifetime has been tainted by vote-buying. These political hacks have denied me, as well as most good and honest West Virginians, a basic right to fair elections. What didn't happen in West Virginia as a result of this disgusting habit? Who did or didn't become President because of illegal vote-buying in West Virginia? It clearly is a problem of which the consequences of southern West Virginia's vote-buying extends far beyond the State's border. Who didn't become governor and what destructive policies were pursued by these illegal inhibitors who gained the State's highest office by buying votes? How would my life in West Virginia be different if people didn't sell their votes and people didn't buy them? The so-called cemetery voting precinct should no longer be a joke. Likewise, this long and sorry history of dirty elections should no longer be a well-accepted tradition ignored by honest people who watch the loathsome compact between powerful politicians and prideless voters.

Many West Virginians, however, feel completely helpless when they watch blatant corruption occur each election cycle followed by little or no enforcement. Then, when an elected official actually is arrested and convicted, it usually only amounts to a slap on the wrist with little or no jail time. Unfortunately though, a strict conclusion that all citizens view the light sentences as a complete lack of accountability for corrupt behavior is presumptuous as such an assumption infers that all West Virginia citizens have an initial respect for the law. People are often more concerned with their personal problems, and to some, in resolving issues important to them, the end justifies the means–even if illegal. Furthermore, such acceptance of illicit behavior creates a feeling of inevitability based upon a long history of political corruption.

It simply amazes me that in 2006 people still sell their votes for a paltry pint of liquor. In addition, county officials have failed to cleanup their voters' registration rolls allowing dead people to continue to vote in elections. Despite the State's motto "Almost Heaven," it shouldn't mean dead people should continue to vote. It seems like a simple solution, i.e., when someone dies or moves away from the county, their name should immediately be removed from the eligible voting lists. There may or may not be life after death, but in southern West Virginia, the use of dead people's names should no longer be allowed to dilute the votes of living people.

Every time I read another story about vote-buying it reminds me of a day years ago when my father and I went to our private property to cut firewood. As we unlocked the gate to enter our property, we heard several gunshots one after another. This was confusing because our land was clearly posted as private property and it wasn't even hunting season. As we continued up the hill, we parked the truck and got out to find five bearded and burly individuals we didn't know who were shooting squirrels. My dad said, "What are you doing?" One of the men raised his shotgun toward me and yelled, "What are you fellows doing? You are trespassing and you need to get out of here NOW!" My dad reached under his coat and into the back of his pants, which is where someone carrying a pistol would often keep it. He kept his hand concealed, but the problem was that he was bluffing. We were both unarmed. Dad said, "No, in fact, it's my property and you have five minutes to find the main road and never come back." The man stood in place for about a minute not saying anything. He eventually lowered his gun and he and the other four men left the area without saying another word. I was twelve or thirteen years old at the time and I will never forget it. It was a tense situation and I felt violated. I remember having a sick feeling in my stomach after being held at gunpoint on my own property by people I didn't even know.

I tell that story because I get that same feeling every time I vote in a West Virginia election. I have love for my country and love for my State, but as I said earlier, it disgusts me as I have come to realize that every election I have ever participated in–and I do mean every election–has been tainted by the buying and selling of votes as well as other corrupt election practices. Just like the five trespassers with their guns who stripped the safe and comfortable feelings I felt on my own property, people I don't even know continue to sell their votes and buy votes in every election taking away my feelings of clean government of the people, for the people, and by the people.

In addition to vote-buying, these same repulsive individuals commit many other blatant fraudulent acts that have altered the election results from the city, county, state, and national levels of government. Those same violated feelings that I had years ago return every election as I consider that politicians are chosen to run my State while I never know if they are actually chosen by a legitimate vote from the majority of West Virginia's good and honest people or if they are ultimately chosen by a select group of slimy individuals who have tainted the entire process. Where is the outrage? As a nation we often talk about helping to bring fair elections to myriad parts of the world, but why don't we consider doing that same thing right here in West Virginia?

# CHAPTER EIGHT

# Governor Arch A. Moore, Jr.
## "Corruption–with a Capitol 'C'"

*Arch laid down in the back seat of my car holding $12,000 up in his hand like a common criminal and he begged me to take it [to buy votes in Mingo County].*

Mingo County Democratic Chairman Johnnie Owens

Bob Brunner, a Charleston-Huntington television news celebrity for most of his thirty years in West Virginia, said of Republican Governor Arch Alfred Moore, Jr.:

> I covered four governors. Arch Moore is one of the most brilliant and yet most flawed people I've ever met. In his heart, he doesn't believe he's a crook. He believed he needed to accumulate money to maintain his political life and he did it by any means possible. He had a phenomenal memory for faces and an incredible ability to know every detail of state government. I don't think we will ever have again a governor who has his pulse on so much of state government as Arch Moore.[485]

Governor Moore, who served longer than any West Virginia Governor, was convicted in 1990 of numerous criminal charges and convicted in federal court in 1996 of additional civil charges. Still today, in spite of those convictions combined with the other corrupt allegations that surround his tenure in State politics, many West Virginians keep an old State road map in their automobile featuring a prominent picture of Moore with an underlying quote where he declares, "West Virginia represents the best of America's timeless traditions–home, family, community."[486] Unfortunately though, the picture and message from Moore only reinforce West Virginia's more unsavory timeless traditions of bribery investigations, indictments, and convictions in State politics.

Moore, who served from 1957 until 1968 as a six-term United States Congressman, said his decision to run for Governor in 1968 "was an attempt to cleanup corruption in State government following a decade of political scandal." Soon after filing for Governor, during a speech to the South Charleston Rotary Club, he declared: "I've had supporters plead with me, 'Don't get involved in State government. It's dirty. It's corrupt.'" He explained, "I'm in the race to try to restore public confidence."[487]

Governor Moore was a sharp dressed man with expensive looking suits and slanted striped ties. In all of the times I was around Governor Moore, I never remember a single one of his slick-backed whitish-greyish hairs out of place. When he spoke, you could see the concern in his eyes which he kept focused on you at all times during the conversation. He had a commanding appearance and stood out in a crowd in spite of his short stature. He had a shiny forehead, blue eyes, and slightly sagging jaws that during his later years made him appear to look a bit like Richard Nixon.

Moore defeated Democratic challenger James Marshall Sprouse in the 1968 General Election by only 12,785 votes in one of the closest gubernatorial elections in the State's history. Following the election, Sprouse, a former CIA agent, filed a lawsuit against the *Charleston Daily Mail,* the State's second largest in general circulation and first among Republican affiliated newspapers. He sought damages from the newspaper for publishing a series of damaging articles just prior to the election that implied he had engaged in corrupt real estate transactions.[488]

A Fayette County jury agreed with Sprouse and awarded him $250,000 in actual damages. In a 1975 Decision upholding the award, the West Virginia Supreme Court said, "the evidence in this case demonstrates that the statements of Arch A. Moore, Jr. were closely coordinated with the stories generated by the [*Daily Mail*] as part of an overall plan or scheme, the purpose of which was to discredit [Sprouse]."[489] The Court wrote that the *Daily Mail* capitalized on the public's particular sensitivity to "allegations of political graft" in impugning Sprouse's integrity, in light of the numerous prison terms served by corrupt West Virginia politicians including Governor Wally Barron and numerous other high-ranking officials.[490] The Court further said the evidence supported a jury verdict that the *Daily Mail* "knowingly used the pretext of a legitimate business transaction to lead the electorate to what it again knew to be a false conclusion" and employed "grossly exaggerated and patently untrue assertions embodied primarily in headlines, to destroy the character of Sprouse." Some of the headlines from the *Daily Mail* series included: "Seneca Rocks Tourist Project Property Enriching Candidate Sprouse;" "Pendleton Realty Bonanza By Jim Sprouse Disclosed;" "Cleanup of Nearly $500,000 in View;" "Moore Asks Federal Probe Into Sprouse's Pendleton Land Grab;" "'Dummy Firm' Seen Proving Corruption;" "Where Governor Candidate 'Cleans Up;'" "Fortune To Jim Sprouse But Pittance For Seneca;" and "Sprouse Owns Choice Land Beside $30 Million U.S. Resort."[491]

Governor Moore's first inaugural address expressed a consistent theme of his intent to be honest and dedicated to the public trust of which West Virginia citizens elected him. While all politicians proclaim to be honest, Moore seemed to obsessively talk about his good name and his quest to reform a corrupt West Virginia system of government. Moore arrived at the podium by "striding confidently down a long red carpet unfurled for the occasion."[492] He announced that his election represented "a new beginning for all West Virginians." He said the people bestowed upon him "a supreme trust" and "confidence" and he planned to provide the type of leadership and action the people had a right to expect. Moore said, "Society is built upon trust, and without trust, there can be little more than discouragement. Without trust, hope is small and we must understand distrust and progress are incompatible." He added, "We must make integrity in State government a tradition in West Virginia, and the time to begin to build such respect is now. Like an individual, a state can have no asset more valuable than a reputation for honesty. West Virginians deserve honorable government, and I will demand it."[493]

Early in Moore's first term, the *Charleston Daily Mail*, an obviously strong supporter of Moore, came to the defense of the new Governor following a story published nationally by the *Chicago Daily News Service* and *Knight Newspapers*.[494] The *Daily Mail* chastised the news services for putting Governor Moore's "name under a cloud in a cruel way that once again damaged the reputation of the State of West Virginia." The editorial further defended Moore as follows: "Through no fault of the governor's, his reputation the last two or three years has been sullied by charges against public officials and convictions of public officials, all of which were reported nationally."[495]

Soon afterward, State newspapers showed additional support for Governor Moore due to his alleged fight to defend the State's reputation by urging the State Legislature to support more stringent laws by passing "a conspiracy law that will stand up in court and make it a crime for a state employee to accept a bribe or for anyone to offer such a bribe." Moore said, "We have slept far too long in regard to abuses and excesses relating to honest handling of the business

of our state." Moore added that, "official chicanery in the past has accounted for
more than $100 million that has been stolen from the State in just a few years."
He said, "If politics is to be the order of the day, you lose, I lose as Governor, but,
tragically, the people of West Virginia lose."[496]

In spite of his tough rhetoric with regard to the honesty of other elected
officials, Governor Moore himself became the target of considerable speculation
concerning his own honesty. In 1973, he was investigated for tax evasion, but
was not convicted. Later, in 1975, Moore and his 1972 campaign manager were
indicted on federal charges of extorting $25,000 from a company that wished to
obtain a bank charter in West Virginia. Both Moore and his campaign manager
were acquitted in 1976 by a federal court; however, the trial did reveal that Moore
kept between $180,000 and $200,000 in cash "crammed" in his desk drawer in
the Governor's Office.[497]

When Moore was first elected, the West Virginia Constitution prohibited a Governor from serving consecutive terms in office, which would have prevented him from running for re-election for Governor in 1972. Almost immediately, however, he pushed to change the State's Constitution to allow Governors
to run for election to consecutive terms. In 1970, at the urging of Moore, the voters of West Virginia approved a Constitutional Amendment allowing a Governor
to serve a second consecutive term in office. He immediately benefitted from the
Constitutional Amendment with his 1972 gubernatorial campaign and subsequent
victory, making him the first West Virginia Governor to serve two consecutive
terms of office.[498]

In 1976, however, Governor Moore decided he wanted more than two
consecutive terms in office even though he was clearly aware of the State
Constitution's prohibition of a third consecutive term. Consequently, he filed for
Governor anyway seeking a third consecutive term and argued before the State
Supreme Court that he had a right to run because not allowing him to run for
another consecutive term was a deprivation of votes for members of the public
and violated "the Fourteenth Amendment to the Constitution of the United States
by denying equal protection of the laws to those persons who would wish to elect
Arch A. Moore, Jr. as Governor for a third successive term."

The West Virginia Supreme Court held the term limitation constitutional
and denied Moore a spot on the ballot in 1976. It said, "it has long been felt that a
limitation upon succession of incumbents removes the temptation to prostitute the
government to the perpetuation of a particular administration. . . . While elections
are won by 51 percent of the vote, all of the people of a state must be served." The
Court added, "Meretricious policies which sacrifice the well-being of economic,
social, racial, or geographical minorities are most likely where a political figure,

political party, or political interest group can rely upon electorate inertia fostered by the hopelessness of encountering a seemingly invincible political machine."[499]

What happened after the Court's decision was surprising for a man who had served longer than any previous West Virginia Governor. First, Moore refused to meet with Governor-elect John D. "Jay" Rockefeller, IV, prior to leaving office. Then, when Moore did leave office, the newly elected Governor Rockefeller found that the Governor's Office was trashed. Rockefeller was faced with missing furniture, files, unscrewed light bulbs, jammed electrical outlets, plugged toilets, a phone system that didn't work, the emergency panic button disconnected from his desk and not working, not a pad or pencil to be found, the typewriter ribbons removed from the typewriters, and unpaid and hidden bills totaling millions of dollars. Nonetheless, Moore ran for the Governor's Office again in 1980 against Rockefeller and narrowly lost as Rockefeller was forced to spend an unheard of $12 million to defeat his popular predecessor. Undeterred, Moore ran again in 1984 and was successful in becoming West Virginia's first and only Governor to serve three terms in office. Moore won the election in spite of relentless rumors that circulated with regard to impending criminal charges.

Governor Moore's luck in evading the law eventually ran out in 1990 as news of his corrupt actions traveled well beyond the border of West Virginia. A 1990 front page story in the *Los Angeles Times* proclaimed "Corruption in West Virginia: Scandals as Thick as Coal Dust." It said:

> West Virginia is suffering from an extraordinary run of corruption. But perhaps more unusual is that politicians are finally getting caught.

> Charleston, West Virginia – As governor, Arch Alfred Moore, Jr. may have been dirty through and through, but he knew how to keep his fingernails clean. "Arch" was always a well-barbered sort, with nary a lick of silver hair out of place and the proper neckties to match the $1000 suits that hung just so.

> His manner was so unruffled and respectable that even West Virginians suspicious of his failings are shocked at the sleaziness suggested by a recent indictment – among the allegations: that he bought votes with fistfuls of cash and hid out back of a municipal incinerator concocting stories to give the slip to a Federal grand jury.[500]

Governor Moore, unfortunately, was not the only West Virginia elected official involved in corrupt activities at that time as people from throughout the State and country learned the sordid details of a crooked government from top to bottom. The year surrounding Moore's guilty plea included the conviction of a State Attorney General, a State Treasurer, two State Senate Presidents, a Senate Majority Leader, a top aide to a Senate President, a House of Delegates member and two lobbyists.[501]

Initially, Moore pled guilty on May 8, 1990, in the United States District Court for the Southern District of West Virginia to criminal charges against him including mail fraud, extortion, filing false tax returns and obstruction of justice.[502] Specifically, he admitted he obtained the Office of Governor of the State of West Virginia in 1984 by defrauding the State of its salary and benefits by accepting illegal cash contributions of at least $100,000 and illegally distributing that money to influence the election; extorting $573,000 from a coal operator, H. Paul Kizer, in 1985 in exchange for Moore's illegal promise to help secure a refund from the West Virginia Black Lung Fund; filing false income tax returns in 1984 and 1985 by failing to report as income, money which he received through his illegal actions; and obstructing justice by lying and arranging for others to lie to cover up his unlawful acts. As his term as Governor was ending on January 16, 1989, Moore even attempted to block the federal grand jury that was investigating him.[503]

Moore's campaign violations were yet another instance of a West Virginia politician demonstrating a manifest lack of respect for both the law and the citizens. Johnnie Owens, the former political boss in Mingo County who was convicted for selling his job as Sheriff for $100,000, said, "Arch laid down in the back seat of my car holding $12,000 up in his hand like a common criminal and he begged me to take it" to buy votes in Mingo County.[504] Moreover, H. Paul Kizer, a millionaire coal executive, outlined another despicable act when he explained that while his company was expecting a $2.3 million refund from the State Black Lung Fund with the possibility of payment nowhere in sight, Governor Moore promised to "slice through a lot of red tape, for a twenty-five percent cut of the dough."[505]

Moore could have been sentenced to thirty-six years in prison and could have been forced to pay fines totaling $1.2 million. Nonetheless, he was sentenced by a federal district judge to just five years and ten months in prison and fined $170,000. He served only thirty-three months of his sentence at a minimum security federal prison camp and then served four months of his sentence in home confinement in Glen Dale, West Virginia; Moore was paroled one year later.[506]

During Moore's years in office, he often gave coal companies a great deal of deference. A national political magazine, *The Nation*, charges that Moore could have prevented some of the devastating mine disasters had the Governor forced coal companies to abide by the law. *The Nation* says the "disaster at Buffalo Creek (Logan County) in February 1972 should be called murder, or at least manslaughter. . . . The disaster which leaves 103 dead and 79 missing a month later is being called 'an act of God' by the vice president of the Pittston Company." The Pittston Coal Company owned the mine and the dam that broke and killed the miners. *The Nation* says, "The dam was actually a dump that contained 5 million cubic feet of water held back by a mine refuse pile of slate, slag, sludge, coal dust, low-grade coal, silt & other debris. State law forbids the erection of any structure more than fifteen feet high across any waterway without approval of the State Public Service Commission." According to *The Nation*, "[t]he Pittston Coal dam was seventy feet high. Federal coal regulations required that hazardous impoundments be inspected at least once a week. In 1966, William Davis of the Geological Survey, found at least seventy-five poorly constructed waste piles at coal sites in five different states including the dam at Buffalo Creek." Finally, the article asserts that: "As a member of Congress, now Governor Arch A. Moore, Jr., received a copy of the report but failed to heed its warnings. Sentiment is that the government has failed to consider that Appalachians are people who are human."[507]

The Buffalo Creek tragedy resulted in the deaths of 125 people and destroyed a fifteen-mile valley. Bob Brunner covered the story for WSAZ television news and recalled being a twenty-seven-year-old reporter surrounded by bodies as a makeshift morgue was created to house the bodies. Brunner said he was "on the verge of tears for most of the newscast."[508] After the tragedy, Governor Moore's Office requested that the Army Corps of Engineers perform recovery work at the State's expense. The Army Corps of Engineers performed the work and incessantly submitted bills to the State in the amount of $3.7 million; however, the Governor not only failed to pay the invoices, he also kept them hidden. Then, in 1977, five years after the tragedy and just three days before the end of Moore's term as Governor, he signed a secret settlement agreement with Pittston Coal Company for $1 million which absolved the coal company of any further liability. Just one week prior to the signed settlement, the Army Corps of Engineers had sent the State a bill in a registered letter for the $3.7 million that it owed on behalf of Pittston as well as notification that it planned to sue the State to recover the money.[509]

Moore testified during a deposition that he had in fact received the letter regarding the debt; however, he then testified during the trial that he did not receive the letter. Then-Senate President William T. Brotherton said that Moore was aware of the Corps' efforts to recover the money because he and former West Virginia Speaker of the House Lewis McManus "had discussed it with him on many, many occasions." Brotherton added, "There is no excuse for Governor Moore to say that he did not know about the U.S. Army Corps of Engineers' claim." The total debt was not revealed to the public until after Governor John D. Rockefeller, IV had taken office and discovered the unpaid bills. By 1987, after losses in the United States District Court, the United States Fourth Circuit Court of Appeals, and the United States Supreme Court, West Virginia was ordered to pay the $3.7 million plus an estimated $10 million in interest. In 1989, as reparation, West Virginia paid a reduced amount of $9.5 million to the Corps of Engineers after then-Attorney General Charlie Brown's successful negotiations.[510]

In 1995, the West Virginia Attorney General's Office filed a civil suit against Moore in an attempt to recover the $2 million it claimed he had pocketed through illegal acts of defrauding the State of West Virginia. As part of the $2 million, the State was specifically seeking the return of $100,000 that Moore illegally used in his 1984 campaign for Governor as well as a $30,000 illegal contribution he received in 1988. The contributions were not reported in Moore's campaign disclosure forms and were used toward an underground campaign "to buy votes and influence voters."[511] In a nine page affidavit, Moore admitted he violated State election laws, but contended the illegal cash did not influence the election and thus he could not have defrauded the State. He said the money was distributed in four southern counties where politicians did not want it known that they were using money from Republicans and he had "failed to carry those four affected counties anyway, so I won the election wholly irrespectively of these actions."[512]

On July 31, 1995, the State settled the lawsuit resulting in Moore paying $750,000 in damages. Deputy Attorney General Silas Taylor, who has worked in the Attorney General's Office for more than twenty years, was instrumental in settlement negotiations. Taylor, whom I personally worked with on many occasions during my years as a Senior Assistant Attorney General, stated, "Although the amount of the settlement was not the most important aspect of this case, it was a fair settlement in light of the myriad circumstances. Most importantly, the State received compensation from Governor Moore for his breech of duty to the State of West Virginia."[513] Moore fought to have all of the documents involved in the case against him kept secret.[514]

On October 31, 1991, the West Virginia Supreme Court annulled Moore's law license. Justice William T. Brotherton, Jr. authored the Opinion of the Court and wrote that, "[Moore] was entrusted with the right to practice law and the privilege to govern this state [and he] violated both oaths of office. Can there be any more serious breach of trust than the violation of these two oaths?"[515] Additional details of the sordid Moore circumstance surfaced the following year during the State Supreme Court's attorney disciplinary proceedings against his former executive assistant Thomas L. Craig, Jr. Craig reported that while working in the 1984 campaign, Moore counted out $100,000 in $100 bills and, in violation of the election laws, instructed Craig to give the money to J. Richard "Dickie" Barber, Moore's liquor commissioner from 1970 through 1976, to distribute to campaign workers. After winning the election, Moore gave Craig $5,000 in cash which was not reported as income. As reparation, the West Virginia Supreme Court suspended Craig's license to practice law for three years. Justice Brotherton dissented in the Opinion believing that Craig should have received more severe consequences and that the three year suspension "reduces the ethical standards of our profession to a level that is embarrassingly low and encourages the image of the law, not as a profession, but as a business with limited accountability to the public we are meant to serve."[516]

Barber, who distributed the illegal cash on behalf of Moore, was convicted on twenty federal charges of racketeering, mail fraud, and extortion in 1979 for "shaking down liquor companies for cash and liquor during Arch Moore's first two terms as Governor." He was sentenced to three years in prison; however, he only served nine months in an Allentown, Pennsylvania federal correctional facility, then performed eighteen months of public service for the Kanawha County Board of Education.

Barber currently owns a beer wholesale business named Central Distributing Company, and in May 2005, he, along with current Governor Joe Manchin; Chris Jarrett, former president of West Virginia-American Water Co; and Manchin's former neighbor, Roger Ramsey, all purchased a fifty-four foot yacht called "The Black Tie" for $566,000. The yacht was located in Mobile, Alabama and the four men originally booked a commercial flight to Alabama to retrieve it. When the commercial flight was delayed, Barber, Governor Manchin, Jarrett, Ramsey, and a State Police officer serving as Manchin's security detail, used the State's private airplane and flew to Alabama. Following questions from the *Charleston Gazette* with regard to the use of the State airplane for a personal trip, Manchin wrote a $5,400 personal check to reimburse the State for the flight.[517]

On March 5, 2006, the *Charleston Gazette* reported that Governor Manchin had originally bought the fifty-four-foot Sea Ray Sundancer 540 yacht in February 2003 with Massachusetts residents Charles "Chuck" Luensmann III (who died in 2004) and his wife, Diane Dileo Luensmann, for $620,000. At the same time, the Luensmanns and Manchins formed a company called Harbor Side Marine and incorporated in Delaware. Manchin was West Virginia's Secretary of State at the time.

In May 2005, Manchin, Barber, Jarrett, and Ramsey bought the yacht after Diane Luensmann sold her half interest in it. Luensmann and her husband had filed for bankruptcy in November 2003 in federal court in Massachusetts. Initially, they did not disclose the $620,000 yacht or a $15,000 wine cellar as assets. In 2004, a bankruptcy trustee alleged that the Luensmanns, "apparently lived an extravagant lifestyle," made "material misstatements" on their bankruptcy filing, and committed "substantial abuse" of federal bankruptcy provisions. On the actual bankruptcy forms, the Luensmanns checked "none" on a question about whether they owned a boat even though they owned The Black Tie at the time with Manchin.

Bankruptcy records also showed they had racked up $248,800 in debt, including credit card bills totaling $27,000 and leases on two Mercedes Benzes. During the proceedings, a federal trustee found documents showing the Luensmanns owned $185,000 worth of jewelry, $100,000 worth of furniture, a $15,000 wine cellar, and the yacht. None of these items had been disclosed on the Luensmanns' bankruptcy schedule. After the bankruptcy trustee concluded the Luensmanns had more than enough assets to cover their debts, he asked the judge to dismiss the case. Richard King, an assistant U.S. bankruptcy court trustee, said, "The record as a whole indicates [the Luensmanns'] financial condition does not warrant the discharge of their debts because they apparently live an extravagant lifestyle, may have made material misstatements, and are not needy." The case was dismissed after the Luensmanns withdrew their bankruptcy petition and agreed to make repayment arrangements with creditors.

After selling her interest in the boat to Manchin, Barber, and the others, Luensmann moved to West Virginia and stayed with Manchin and his wife Gayle for an undisclosed period of time in the Governor's Mansion. She now works in Charleston as Manchin's liaison to the Democratic Governors Association. She was hired in December 2005 when Manchin recommended her for the job, according to Penny Lee, the Association's executive director. Lee said Luensmann brought a strong business background to the job and had experience as a campaign volunteer in Massachusetts. When questioned by reporters in March 2006, Manchin said he was unaware that Luensmann had filed for bankruptcy and said he recommended her for the liaison job because she's a "nice lady, well educated and hard-working," and added, "The poor girl had nothing." In her job working for Manchin, she is paid $90,000 per year.[518]

Governors, past and present, have certainly had more than their share of news-worthy stories surrounding the impropriety or even just the perception of questionable legal behavior of themselves or of their staff members, but Governor Moore has to rank at the top of the list. In 1998, Moore, dubbed "as crooked as a pretzel" by one West Virginia legislator, filed a petition in the West Virginia Supreme Court and began a letter writing campaign in his quest for the return of his law license.[519] The opening pages of the petition contained more than sixty "heavy hitting" lawyers and non-lawyers supporting his cause including such prestigious West Virginians as Secretary of State Ken Hechler; retired State Supreme Court Chief Justice Richard Neely; former State Bar President Thomas Flaherty; West Virginia University Law Professor and former State Supreme Court Justice Franklin Cleckley; West Virginia University Law Professor Forest "Jack" Bowman, who teaches, among other subjects, "Professional Responsibility;" Reverend Thomas S. Acker, President of Wheeling Jesuit University; and numerous other prominent attorneys and politicians.[520] Former Justice Cleckley wrote: "In my few conversations with him, I have noted a grave sense of remorsefulness and a greater sense of one who was truly seeking atonement for his sins." The *Daily Mail* responded to Cleckley's comments:

> Sorry, but the best atonement for his transgressions would be to continue to suffer the consequences of his criminal behavior. Lowering the standards for lawyers to allow him to practice again at the Bar is wrong.

> No matter how sorry or remorseful he may wish to appear, Arch Moore will never be trusted again even to vote. Why should he be allowed to practice the law he violated when he was governor?[521]

Moore filed a motion stating he did not want his petition for reinstatement to become a public document. Sherri Goodman, then-State Bar Chief Disciplinary Counsel, called Moore's reasoning for secrecy "completely spurious." Goodman explained that "reinstatement proceedings are public proceedings as set forth in the rules promulgated by the Supreme Court."[522] In 1998, the *Charleston Daily Mail*, which staunchly supported Governor Moore in years past, spoke strongly against the re-admission of Moore to the State's Bar proclaiming: "Committing felonies is inconsistent with the privilege of practicing law." A *Daily Mail* editorial said, "ours is a forgiving nation" before declaring: "Be that as it may, there are some crimes that can't be overlooked. The violation of the public trust by an elected official is atop the list."[523]

During his quest for the return of his law license, in 2003, the Office of Disciplinary Counsel of the West Virginia State Bar outlined various questionable transactions by Moore including a "fondness for dealing in large amounts of cash." "Thousands of dollars in cash routinely were available to Moore and were used for political campaigns" including the $100,000 in cash that was used by Governor Moore "to support an underground effort of maintaining integrity in the (1984) election process in as many as eleven counties in southern West Virginia, and that was a cash campaign." The Disciplinary Panel's report also said that Moore used cash transactions to pay for purchases of personal items such as expensive clothing and for family trips to Europe including: "a 1986 trip to London for himself and his wife, Shelley Riley Moore, as well as his two daughters, [Congresswoman] Shelley Moore Capito and Lucy Moore Durbin, and their husbands;" a flight from Frankfurt, Germany, to Istanbul; the purchase of a $3,500 carpet in Turkey in 1985; and a trip to Taiwan, South Korea and Japan in 1987. To explain the large amounts of cash Moore kept in his dresser drawer, Moore claimed to have received cash gifts from unnamed individuals.[524]

The report from the Disciplinary Panel also concluded, "[b]ased on the evidence, [Governor Moore] continues to profit personally by using his political influence in his work as a consultant." The Panel further found, "This raises questions as to whether Moore currently understands the line between lawful and unlawful political influence, a line he crossed as a public official [by] trad[ing] unreported cash for political influence." [525] In its conclusion in the fifty-five-page report, the Panel pronounced that Moore, "has failed to establish that he presently possesses the integrity and moral character to resume the practice of law." The Panel recommended that the Supreme Court deny Governor Moore's reinstatement.[526]

On the day of his November 2003 oral argument before the State Supreme Court, a *Charleston Gazette* editorial said that after former Governor Wally Barron went to prison for corruption, instead of seeking the return of his license, he "quietly moved out of state and lived in seclusion until his death." The *Gazette* then explained, however, "former Gov. Arch Moore–equally corrupt, equally disgraced–has a different personality. Imperiously, Moore acts almost self-righteous as he contradicts himself and seeks restoration to the bar." The editorial further elaborated:

> In effect, Moore says he deserves to regain his law license because he was lying in 1990 when he pleaded guilty to extortion, mail fraud, tax evasion and obstruction of justice–crimes that put him in prison three years.

In truth, he pleaded guilty to avoid indictment on 16 felony charges that federal agents were prepared to bring. The U.S. Attorney's Office had written a 120-page summation of his crimes, but his plea kept the report secret. Today, Republican U.S. Attorney Kasey Warner–who owes his job partly to Moore's daughter in Congress–won't reveal the 120 page report, although it has great importance to West Virginians.[527]

The editorial further pleaded with Moore to make full disclosure about the many scandals that hounded his political career, including: "whether he was paid privately for closing the State's lawsuit in the Buffalo Creek tragedy, letting a coal company off the hook and leaving taxpayers stuck for $9.5 million;" to disclose the donors who gave him "$200,000 cash–illicit money that came to light in his 1976 bribery trial;" to "reveal whether he actually got the alleged $25,000 bribe for a bank charter that was the central issue" in the 1976 trial; and that he should "reveal whether he still holds the 900 shares of Exxon stock he took from a dead recluse's estate–securities that were central to an IRS investigation of Moore."[528]

In spite of Moore's widespread support from prominent individuals, on December 12, 2003, the West Virginia Supreme Court denied his request for the return of his license.[529] Many commentators feared that Moore's request wouldn't fall on deaf ears as the West Virginia Supreme Court has on numerous occasions throughout the years been very forgiving of those who have disregarded the public's trust and disgraced the image of West Virginia. For example, Bernard Smith, a former scandal figure who was involved in two bribery trials, a perjury trial, and a vote fraud trial in the early 1970s, and was expelled from the State Senate, was given his law license back by the Court.[530] The *Charleston Gazette* reported at the time that the Court's ruling returning Smith's license may have set the stage for "the return of the licenses of eight other criminal lawyers who were disbarred in bribery and fraud scandals that followed the term of ex-Governor W.W. Barron."[531] In addition, Moore's license request was denied even though just two months earlier the State Supreme Court returned the law license to disgraced former Circuit Court Judge John Hey who was prosecuted on sexual assault charges that led to his 1995 guilty plea to misdemeanor battery. Among the many charges against Judge Hey were that he had sexually harassed women during his career and was often drunk while on the bench.[532]

In her Concurring Opinion, Justice Robin Davis said that with Moore continuing to make "preposterous" claims of innocence, the Court had no choice but to keep him out of the practice of law. Justice Davis added, "If this Court reinstated Mr. Moore's license we would, in effect, be exonerating him from all guilt for the crimes to which he pled guilty." Justice Davis also said, "I find it rather disheartening to know that among the supporters for Mr. Moore's reinstatement was a member of the Bar who proclaims to be an expert in ethics." Davis explained that the so-called expert proclaimed: "Governor Moore has accepted responsibility for the actions which resulted in the loss of his law license [and that],"

> [m]y experience as a teacher of legal ethics, a frequent lecturer on the subject for CLE organizations throughout the country, and as an expert witness in legal ethics cases in West Virginia and a dozen other states leads me to the firm conclusion that, in this case, reinstatement to the practice of law is not only appropriate but highly desirable.[533]

Justice Davis pointed out that "[t]he Majority Opinion in this case has aptly demonstrated that Mr. Moore has not accepted responsibility for his unlawful actions that led to his disbarment. Thus, in order to support Moore's reinstatement, this ethics 'expert' had to ignore not only the true and well-documented facts of this case, but also the established law of this jurisdiction." Davis maintained:

> The integrity of our legal system simply cannot tolerate 'hired gun' advocacy in lawyer disciplinary proceedings. The position taken by Mr. Moore, in his quest for reinstatement, tramples upon fundamental principles of ethics. In spite of the clear ethical flaw in Mr. Moore's position, he successfully found a purported ethics expert to support his position. This is troubling to me. This Court has an uncompromising duty to make certain that honest and morally upright persons are representing the legal affairs of the public. To that end, 'hired gun' proponents have no place in lawyer disciplinary proceedings.[534]

Within Davis' Opinion, she explained the ramifications of the Court's decision in light of the Court's decision to return former Circuit Judge John Hey's law license a month prior to the Moore decision. She said that by denying Moore's petition for reinstatement, while nevertheless granting reinstatement to Judge Hey, "This Court has sent the message that crimes perpetrated for financial gain are more egregious than crimes against women. I find this blatant disregard for the treatment of women in this State to be barbaric and reprehensible."[535]

Following the State Supreme Court's denial of his law license, the former Governor and convicted felon, sought to have the State's insurance company reimburse him for $1 million in legal costs he claims he paid when the State sued him in a civil action in 1990. The State's civil lawsuit against Moore was based solely upon his guilty plea earlier that year in federal court to the criminal charges of extortion, obstruction of justice, mail fraud, and tax evasion.[536] Moore filed his lawsuit one day prior to the ten-year statute of limitations that applies to contract claims. The insurance company responded to his complaint arguing that the State's insurance policy only provided a legal defense for acts he performed as a State official and that "the felonies that Moore pleaded guilty to, which the State sued him over, were not a part of his official duties." The Court also found that finding for Moore and requiring the State's insurer to be liable for his legal costs, "would have created a nearly unlimited duty to defend in future cases and would require insurers to defend an insured regardless of the circumstances . . . and would expose them unfairly to boundless claims of bad faith."[537]

I remember the first time I spoke with Governor Moore for a significant length of time. It was in March of 1988 and I had just returned from a week in Washington, D.C., where I had attended a national conference called the Presidential Classroom, which was a political forum for high school students from every state as well as numerous countries. I was sitting in class at Tucker County High School and was informed that the county superintendent of schools was on the telephone and wanted to speak with me. She said, "You're our Presidential Classroom student and we're proud of you. Governor Moore is in Parsons today so you'll be leaving school early to come to Parsons and introduce the Governor to the crowd." I left school early that day, stopping first at my home to change into my only suit, a grey J.C. Penney's two-button suit with a matching grey tie. Unfortunately I had to put on my tennis shoes with the suit (hoping no one would notice) because I had broken the sole completely off on my only pair of dress shoes the previous week in Washington, D.C. Even though I now wear suits and ties on a daily basis, I had little use for them at the time as a boy in Tucker County who was more preoccupied with girls and sports.

I arrived at the senior center where Governor Moore was presenting them with a new van. I had the opportunity to speak with him privately for a few minutes prior to the actual ceremony and found him enormously personable. We spoke for a while as he asked a lot of questions and focused his eyes on me the entire time. He made you feel like you were the only person in the room when he spoke with you. The only other politician I have ever personally met who had better communication skills was President Bill Clinton.

I remember so many other occasions when I talked with him whether it was at a local fair or festival where he was handing out pepperoni rolls or at a parade where he was intensely shaking every hand he passed. Each time I saw Governor Moore, who had an amazing memory, he would call me by name and even recall the last time we had spoken. On one occasion, at a West Virginia University (WVU) football game, I saw the Governor as he had just handed out his last pepperoni roll. I was joking with him and said, "Fine, I guess I will remember this at election time." I was a freshman in college at WVU at the time and approximately two weeks later I received a package in the mail at my dormitory containing six large pepperoni rolls. I thought to myself that this was certainly a man of great detail. First, he remembered my last name, which isn't the easiest name to remember, then managed to find my address on a college campus, then, spent the time and money to mail the pepperoni rolls to me. Sadly though, I now wonder if the money came from the hundreds of thousands of illicit cash that he kept in his Governor's Office desk drawer.

At that time though, I was young and unaware of the controversy surrounding Moore, who soon afterward would serve a federal prison sentence. Likewise, I had no idea that *Newsweek* would soon be referring to West Virginia as "Corruption–with a Capitol 'C'" based upon Arch Moore and the many other politicians who began serving jail sentences during the latter part of the 1980s and early 1990s.[538] I readily admit that Moore certainly had a presence in a room that is somewhat difficult to explain. When he entered a room you knew it and it wasn't an overbearing entrance. People were drawn to him and couldn't wait to greet him and shake his hand. He is still regarded very highly among so many people throughout the State and sadly, if he ran again for public office, he would either win or he would receive a significant number of votes.

It seems that West Virginians are a very forgiving people. As recently as April 23, 2003, the *Parsons Advocate*, a Parsons, West Virginia weekly newspaper where I worked for several years writing articles, included a large headline and a sizable picture of former Governor Moore on its front page announcing that Moore would be the guest speaker at their annual Republican political dinner.[539] With regard to other speaking engagements, the *Charleston Daily Mail* maintains:

> Former Gov. Arch Moore, a convicted criminal, was an honored guest last month at a Republican Legislature Committee fundraiser.

> Some years earlier, former governor Wally Barron, a convicted criminal of the Democratic persuasion, re-visited the state Capitol. He was warmly greeted by officeholders.

> To honor our ex-convicts, how about a Felons Day?[540]

While I agree that it is important to forgive those who have committed wrongs who recognize the consequences of their actions, it seems that some citizens don't even become upset when the wrongs are committed in the first place. In 1980, the *Charleston Gazette* in an editorial entitled "An honest governor" asked:

Why not re-elect an honest governor?

If West Virginians were to elect a series of governors who gave them honest government, it's very likely most citizens would savor the benefits, treasure them and conclude that honest government is, the best government. At that point, when honest government is taken for granted and no need exists, as is the case today, to nurture it lovingly and tenderly, the body politic will be able to afford the luxury of choosing between gubernatorial candidates whose ideologies clash. Today, alas, the prudent voter must ask: 'Which candidate is honest?'[541]

As far as Arch Moore's place in West Virginia politics, I initially want to point out that I certainly honor his service to our country during World War II. As an Army combat sergeant in World War II, Moore earned a Bronze Star and Purple Heart. I don't for one second view his service to our country lightly. In fact, in 1994, I was in Europe with one of my friends, Jed Drenning. We were staying in Dusseldorf, Germany, where Jed was playing "American Football" for the Dusseldorf Bulldozers. Neither Jed nor I had very much money, yet there was one thing we wanted to do more than anything else while in Europe. We were determined to travel to the beaches where the Allied forces landed in the Normandy region of France. I also wanted to go to Brittany Cemetery, a World War II American Cemetery, where my cousin, who grew up living in my father's home before entering the military, is buried. In spite of the language barrier, Jed and I worked for people in the small Dusseldorf neighborhood to raise the gas and toll money we needed for the trip. We packed peanut butter and jelly sandwiches and drove the back roads to avoid as many of the tolls on the major roadways as possible. Of the six weeks I spent in Europe that summer, my most memorable experience was spending those two days and two nights (sleeping in the car) at Omaha Beach, one of the deadliest landing spots for the United States invasion. We spent the days climbing the cliffs and walking the shores of the English Channel trying to imagine what it was like on that day. It was one of the most moving experiences of my life and I don't take the sacrifices of any of our veterans for granted. I respect any person who has ever served our country during a time of war or peace.

Nonetheless, Governor Moore's service to our country and his service to West Virginia as Governor are clearly two distinguishable circumstances and I simply don't understand how anyone could condone his brazen and corrupt behavior year after year. He was elected on a platform of anti-corruption and during his inaugural address he vowed to rid the State of corruption. Soon afterward, he pushed for tougher laws to deal with corruption because he was one of the only honest elected officials setting the standard for integrity. Unfortunately though, Moore set that standard at an exceptionally low level.

When Moore was defeated by Jay Rockefeller in 1976, he refused to even meet with the incoming Governor, which was unprecedented at the time. Then, when Governor Rockefeller showed up for his first day at the Governor's Office, he encountered a mess that could only be expected from a drunken fraternity house whose members had lost their charter. To me, such behavior demonstrated a total lack of respect for all West Virginians and cannot simply be dismissed as sour grapes directed toward the incoming Governor. The Governor's Office is the people's office and I believe the actions of whoever committed such childish and destructive acts should have been prosecuted for destruction of State property and should have served time in jail. I am tired of public officials getting a free ride. Public office holders and their staff members should be held at the highest level of scrutiny.

In spite of this, Moore ran again for Governor in 1984 and was elected. It seemed that all was forgiven. In 1988, however, he was defeated by political newcomer Gaston Caperton, who spent millions of dollars of his own money to defeat Moore. After Caperton was elected, "he discovered millions of dollars in unpaid bills, many of them stuffed in boxes under desks in the Governor's Office."[542] He called the condition of the State "a total mess," explaining that the gas company was poised to shut off the gas at the Governor's Mansion because of unpaid bills. Governor Caperton also found that the teacher's retirement fund was insolvent and millions more in State income tax refunds had gone unpaid for lack of cash. As a result, he was forced to raise taxes in what was reported as "the largest tax increase in the State's history."[543] "The West Virginia Poll," taken by three news organizations in the midst of a teachers' strike and after the tax increase, found that only 1 percent of those surveyed rated the Governor's performance as excellent. Only 13 percent considered his job performance as good and 29 percent felt it to be fair, while 53 percent considered his job rating as poor. It was the lowest overall score any governor had received since the poll began rating the State's chief executive in 1981.[544] Caperton, however, left office eight years later with the State fiscally sound and as a very popular governor.

I was fortunate enough to work for Governor Caperton. It truly was a dream job. I initiated "A Governor's View" column that was published in thirty-five weekly West Virginia newspapers, prepared briefing materials for him, represented and accompanied him at numerous meetings throughout the State, advanced and organized special events, and coordinated bill signing and photo opportunities between the Governor, Legislators, broadcast and print media, as well as among the citizens of West Virginia.

I remember having a continuous argument with one of the Governor's Executive Assistants who had a picture of ex-Governor Moore on his wall. It all started when I placed on my wall a picture of Mary Lou Retton, a 1980 Olympic Gold Medal winner and West Virginia native. It was given to me by the State Library Commissioner and I actually had planned to leave it on my wall for that day only because the Commissioner was coming to my office to meet with me about an upcoming event and I wanted to show him that I appreciated his gift. Following that meeting, I was then going to take the poster down, take it home, give it away . . . I don't exactly remember. It wasn't that I didn't like the poster. In fact, I was very fond of Mary Lou and if the truth be known, had a crush on her like most other young men at the time, but I hadn't planned to keep it hanging on my office wall. In any case, when my colleague approached me and told me to take it down because it was unprofessional to have such a poster on my Governor's Office wall, I guess my twenty-one-year-old stubbornness surfaced. I refused to remove the poster, raised my voice, and said, "Why do you have a picture of convicted felon Arch Moore on your wall? He violated the trust of every West Virginian in ways never before seen by a Governor of this State." He quickly and sternly responded that Governor Moore was a personal friend of his and he made no apologies for the picture.

Our picture-poster argument continued until I left the Governor's Office with my colleague asking me on a daily basis when I was taking the "unprofessional picture" off the wall followed by my consistent response of, "the day you remove the felon's picture from your wall." On my final day in the Governor's Office I taped the poster of Mary Lou to his wall. A few weeks later it arrived in the mail at my new office in Washington, D.C. where I had taken a position as a Special Assistant to Congressman Harley O. Staggers, Jr. It had been signed by my colleague as well as the Governor and all of the office staff and I still have it today.

I think of that story and laugh, but mainly, with fourteen more years under my belt, I better understand my former colleague's actions with regard to Governor Moore's photo. I still don't condone it, but I have since learned that personal relationships with the State's elected officials are extremely important to many people.  I have found that many people ignore so many of the corrupt actions of these individuals after they have gotten to know them on a personal level and have sat with them for a meal or simply have met with them at several political functions.  That personal contact often becomes so important to people that it overshadows a lot of bad acts.  Moreover, with headline after headline of political graft and conviction after conviction of so many of West Virginia's elected officials, such conduct has become expected and even accepted behavior.  It is equally true that many people feel the most successful politicians have to be corrupt and willing to get down into the mud to maneuver in a dirty political environment.  Likewise, many people see a squeaky clean politician as potentially ineffectual.

    With regard to Governor Moore, who sat in the back seat of a car "like a common criminal" buying votes in southern West Virginia, he committed such egregious acts that the usual blanket forgiveness should not be an issue.  His story is one of disappointment after disappointment and people should no longer tolerate such a disrespect for public office.  Even after admitting his guilt to a federal judge he changed his mind and tried to withdraw his plea.  Then, he had the nerve to wait one day shy of the ten-year statute of limitations for suing on a contract claim and sued the State's insurance carrier for not defending him in the State's civil suit against him.  Moore sought damages of more than $1 million.  He had already pled guilty to the underlying crimes in federal court and the State had absolutely no obligation to defend him in any subsequent proceeding.  His audacity is amazing to me.  To this day he still denies the well-documented bribes, ignores the questions surrounding the closing of the State's lawsuit against the Pittston Coal Company for the Buffalo Creek tragedy (that later left West Virginia taxpayers stuck for a $9.5 million debt that should have been paid by Pittston), and denies the bags of unmarked cash and illegal campaign contributions it has been proven he solicited and received.  In fact, even ex-coal operator H. Paul Kizer, who played a central role in the indictment of Moore, supported his efforts to regain his law license because "[Moore] has suffered enough."[545]

    Perhaps even more amazing to me is the fact that Moore is still a featured speaker at many Republican political party events.  The Republican Party should take a stand and disfavor Governor Moore until he accepts full and unconditional responsibility for his actions.  This same message goes for the Democratic Party when its candidates and elected officials are determined to be corrupt.  Corruption is not a partisan issue and should not be treated that way with blame assessed only to those in opposition to your political beliefs.  His popularity though goes beyond the Republican Party.  In August of 2005, I attended an event where Moore and another former State Governor were in attendance.  Even though the other Governor had served more recently, Moore overwhelmingly received a louder and longer ovation.

It seems that money is always surrounding the corrupt events of West Virginia's elected officials in one way or another. In Moore's case, it seems likely that he felt he was simply doing what he had to do for what he saw as political survival. He knew that someone like Rockefeller could spend millions of dollars against him and he had to be prepared for that. Thus, he used whatever resources he had in order to get as much cash as possible to play West Virginia's political game the way it had been played for so many years. Moore knew that votes were for sale in southern West Virginia and if he bought enough of them he could retain his seat of power. Or, it is equally possible that he feared if he didn't buy those votes that his opponent might buy them and defeat him in the election. Unfortunately for Moore, his corrupt behavior was so widespread that it was easy for the United States Attorney's Office to convict him.

I was warned by several of my friends not to write about Governor Moore due to his continued popularity with many groups around the State. However, his actions have been unbelievably corrupt and absolutely inexcusable and people should no longer be afraid to openly say, "It's wrong!" When will people stand proudly against the corrupt politicians who have stolen from them year after year and tainted the State's image with their disgusting and relentless examples of corrupt behavior?

I wonder if Governor Moore will ever realize the consequences of his actions. It is obvious to me that he is a man who cares about his image. Just prior to leaving office in 1977, he reimbursed the Governor's Contingency Fund $4,000 for a portrait of himself which he didn't like and canceled the State's contract with A. Henry Nordhausen of Columbus, Georgia, who painted the official portrait. He then commissioned David Philip Wilson to paint a $7,000 portrait of Moore which now hangs in the hallway of the State Capitol.[546] Then, during myriad court battles questioning his integrity, he fought hard to have the sordid details hidden from public view. Governor Moore would only improve his standing in history if he would firmly and finally admit his wrongdoings and apologize directly to the people of West Virginia.

# CHAPTER NINE

# Senators Byrd and Rockefeller
# "The Aristocracy of the Money Bag"

*If 55 years ago, when I started out in politics, we had had the current system of funding campaigns, somebody else would be standing at this desk.*

United States Senator Robert C. Byrd

I can't imagine any two United States Senators from the same State with such stark contrasts in upbringing and life experiences as West Virginia's Senator John Davison "Jay" Rockefeller, IV and Senator Robert Carlyle Byrd. Senator Rockefeller's great grandfather, John D. Rockefeller, Sr., was founder and President of Standard Oil, which by 1878 held about 90 percent of the refining capacity in the United States. By 1901, John Rockefeller, Sr.'s estimated wealth was more than $900 million, making him possibly the richest man in the world at the time. Byrd, on the other hand, lived his early life in crushing poverty in a coal mining community in southern West Virginia without even having the luxury of running water or electricity. Both men have attained one of the highest political offices in the country while at the same time becoming national figures, but not surprisingly have achieved this feat differently.

Each time I speak with Senator Rockefeller, I recall a conversation I had with my friend Bob Brunner who worked for nearly thirty years as a news reporter and anchor for WSAZ, West Virginia's largest television news station. Bob and I worked together in 1992 in Governor Gaston Caperton's Office. Bob had left WSAZ and was serving as an Executive Assistant as well as the Communications Director to Governor Caperton. Bob and I ate lunch together on a daily basis and often discussed his many years of reporting on West Virginia's long history of unique and colorful politicians. He always took into account the fact that I had just finished college and was living paycheck to paycheck so he would cut coupons from the newspaper for fast food restaurants. If we didn't have any coupons, or if Shoney's wasn't having their $2.99 buffet special, we wouldn't eat lunch that day.

Bob told me on several occasions about a discussion he had with Rockefeller in 1980 when Rockefeller was running for re-election as Governor. He began the story by providing the background that during Rockefeller's first failed campaign for Governor in 1972 against incumbent Arch A. Moore, Jr., his campaign spending became a statewide issue. In the loss to Governor Moore in 1972, Rockefeller spent $1.5 million, which was–at the time–the largest expenditure ever in a gubernatorial campaign in West Virginia. Then, in 1976, he spent $2.8 million to successfully win the Office of Governor. This was nothing compared to his campaign spending in 1980 when he faced Governor Moore for the second time in eight years as a challenger for the Office of Governor. It was during that same year when President Jimmy Carter qualified for federal matching funds and was spending $29 million nationwide in his re-election campaign, that Rockefeller's spending reports showed he was spending $12 million for his gubernatorial re-election bid in a tiny state with not even 1 percent of the population of America.[547]

Bob, in addition to his work as a television news anchor, was writing a statewide political column for nine newspapers at the time and had railed incessantly against Rockefeller's unprecedented campaign spending. He recalled that during the late summer, Rockefeller invited a few reporters to join him and his political inner circle for beer and a swim at his house on Barberry Lane in South Hills, an affluent section of Charleston, West Virginia. Bob said, "I remember Tom Knight of the *Gazette* was there, and Herb Little of the *Associated Press*. I think Dick Grimes of the *Daily Mail* was around as well as two or three others." During the course of the evening, Bob made a reference to Jay about his spending. He said, "I challenged Jay about his profligate spending and wondered aloud just how it was possible to spend this much in a tiny state where political machines and political ads are so cheap." Then, after demurring for a few moments and being polite, "Jay finally retorted, asking me if I had any idea how much $12 million was to him." Bob remembered that: "Ever the smart ass, I made some grandiose reply about how it would buy food for all the hungry babies or something like that and [Rockefeller] persisted. 'I'll tell you what it means,' he told me. 'It means that for six months, I don't get any richer. That's all.'" Bob said, "I was dumbfounded. That shut me up. I quickly did some rough math about the size of his reputed personal fortune then and realized he was being very accurate." Following the conversation, Bob concluded that to Rockefeller, "money was an abstract, a tool. The fact that his fortune did not continue its growth for a few months meant nothing to him but an academic exercise. It wasn't until that moment I think it began to dawn on me the impact of big money on politics."[548]

Senator Jay Rockefeller, born June 18, 1937, in New York City, has been surrounded by wealthy and influential people his entire life. Senator Rockefeller's uncle, Nelson Rockefeller, was Vice President of the United States under President Gerald Ford, while another uncle, Winthrop Rockefeller, served as Governor of Arkansas, and his Uncle David Rockefeller was head of the Chase Manhattan Bank. Even Jay's in-laws are cut from the upper crust of society following his 1967 marriage to Sharon Percy, the daughter of former United States Senator Charles Percy. Jay and Sharon have four children: John, Valerie,[549] Charles, and Justin. Jay's father-in-law, Senator Percy, even had ambitions of being President of the United States. On one such occasion, in 1968, Senator Percy dropped out of the race to support Jay's Uncle Nelson Rockefeller's bid for the nomination. Percy served Illinois as United States Senator until 1984, the same year Jay Rockefeller was elected to the Senate.

Robert C. Byrd, on the other hand, traveled quite a different path in life. He was born on November 20, 1917, in North Wilkesboro, North Carolina. At only one year old, he was left a virtual orphan following the death of his mother Ada Kirby Sale, who died of the influenza pandemic of 1918. Byrd was one of five children to Cornelius Calvin Sale and his wife, Ada Mae Kirby, and was named Cornelius Calvin Sale, Jr. at birth. At the request of his mother on her deathbed, Sale, Jr. was sent to live with his natural father's sister Vlurma Byrd and brother-in-law Titus Dalton Byrd. He was later re-named Robert Carlyle Byrd and reared as their own. Soon afterward, Titus, Vlurma, and Robert moved to West Virginia, where Robert Byrd grew up as the only child in the home. Vlurma and Titus' first child, Robert Madison Byrd, died of scarlet fever while the couple was still living in North Carolina and prior to Robert C. Byrd's birth. Titus was a coal miner who worked in numerous mines throughout southern West Virginia and according to Senator Byrd, was a humble man who paid his debts, never spoke ill of a neighbor, and never used God's name in vain. Byrd, who has worked with numerous Presidents and has interacted with Kings, Queens, and countless other dignitaries during his career in public service, says that Vlurma was one of the few great people he has known in his life. He said she was a strong woman who impressed upon him a strong work ethic. He said that both Vlurma and Titus had great hearts, honest minds, and stressed to him a respect for the Bible and for religion. Byrd, who was the first person in all of his family who had even graduated from elementary school, did not learn that Vlurma and Titus were not his biological parents until the year of his graduation as valedictorian of his high school.

Byrd says that growing up during the Great Depression on Wolf Creek Hollow in Mercer County, West Virginia was tough as his home didn't have electricity or running water. He recalled being a young man and taking bags of corn on the back of his pony to the mill to grind the corn into meal so that his mother could make a cake of cornbread. His family owned one cow and he recalled that on occasion his mother would squeeze milk directly from the cow into his cup for him to drink.[550] I can easily picture Senator Byrd drinking his milk from the cow without a second thought as he then tended to his daily chores. To the contrary, when I try to envision the six-foot-six multi-millionaire Jay Rockefeller, as a young boy, drinking milk directly from a cow, I actually laugh out loud. I would venture a guess that such an event never occurred and would have been an unimaginable happening for the young aristocrat.

Byrd also learned to play the fiddle during his early years and while in the United States Senate, even recorded an album of his fiddling. When I met with him in his Washington, D.C. office in 1988, as one of two West Virginia high school students attending the Presidential Classroom, a national conference of high school students from the United States and around the world, Senator Byrd gave me an eight-track tape of his fiddling he had recorded in the 1970s titled: *"Senator Robert Byrd: Mountain Fiddler."* I still have the tape, but as I was a senior in high school at the time, I had no idea of the true history surrounding this man. Moreover, I had no idea where I would find an eight-track player to listen to it as even at that time I grew up with cassettes. In fact, the only eight-track tapes I had ever seen were from recordings my grandfather had made many years earlier with his gospel singing group. So I guess I have always thought of Senator Byrd in the same light as I have my grandfather Scott Hovatter, who coincidentally was Byrd's friend. Both of them are roughly the same age and shared many of the same life experiences. My grandfather was Byrd's campaign chairman for my home county during his first campaign for the United States Senate and for several of his subsequent campaigns. When Senator Byrd would come to Tucker County for any reason, he would always meet with my grandfather and I would "conveniently" be there. That is actually how I met the Senator for the first time during the 1970s, when I was just a young boy. In subsequent years, whenever I would see Senator Byrd at some event around the State during the 1980s or early 1990s, we would inevitably speak of my grandfather. Without fail, later that evening he would call my grandfather to tell him he had spoken with his grandson and would proceed to tell him about whatever "young lady" I may have been with when he had seen me. Even to this day, when I see Senator Byrd, we discuss my grandfather and he always corrects me on the pronunciation of my grandfather's name. When I tell him "my grandfather Scott Hovatter says hello and wishes you well," the Senator usually says, "Don't you mean Hovatter?" as he stresses the "o" and the first "t" therefore pronouncing it differently than my family actually does. I, of course, never argue and just smile, saying "Hovatter" the same way he does.

As for the other Presidential Classroom student from West Virginia who sat patiently with me in Senator Byrd's office waiting for him to arrive on that day in March of 1988, I ended up marrying her several years later. It was the first time I had met my future bride Kelly as the two of us sat and talked about our great Senator and looked at some of the many interesting pictures that hung from his wall of him with notable individuals. This actually took place on a day that the Senator had been called away to an unscheduled meeting in the United States Senate and was unavailable for quite some time. It didn't matter to me as Kelly and I sat for a couple of hours in his reception room and became friends. It may have been the only time I actually enjoyed waiting in anyone's reception room. I have never officially thanked him for being late that day.

Senator Byrd's roots in West Virginia grew strong. He lived a difficult life just as many West Virginians did during those years. He worked hard at whatever job he had at the time and made enough money to make ends meet and provide for his family. When Byrd and his high school sweetheart, a coal miner's daughter, Erma Ora James, were married in 1937, he worked as a produce boy in a coal company store. He said he remembered the day he brought an empty orange crate home and nailed it to the wall outside the kitchen window, which served as the couple's first refrigerator.[551] Byrd, who was unable to afford college tuition worked in many different professions including pumping gas at a filling station and working as a meat cutter. Conversely, Senator Rockefeller was not a product of public schools and did not face the issue of money being a factor in his education. Instead, he graduated from the Phillips Exeter Academy in 1954, a prestigious southern New Hampshire institution founded in 1781. Rockefeller then graduated from Harvard University in 1961 with a Bachelor of Arts degree in Far Eastern Languages and History, after having spent three years studying Japanese at the International Christian University in Tokyo.

Byrd, on the other hand, began working after the start of World War II as a welder on "Liberty" and "Victory" ships in construction yards in Baltimore, Maryland, and Tampa, Florida. Following the war's end, Byrd returned to West Virginia and in 1946, he ran for his first political office and was elected to the West Virginia House of Delegates. It was around this time period when it was learned that Byrd had a brief membership in the KKK in 1942. Byrd said,

"Becoming involved with the KKK was the most egregious mistake I have ever made." On countless occasions throughout his career Byrd has publicly admitted his huge mistake calling it the "albatross around my neck" and saying "I know now I was wrong. Intolerance had no place in America. I apologized a thousand times . . . and I don't mind apologizing over and over again. I can't erase what happened." Byrd added, "It has emerged throughout my life to haunt and embarrass me and has taught me in a very graphic way what one major mistake can do to one's life, career, and reputation."[552]

Following two terms in the West Virginia House of Delegates, he was elected to the West Virginia State Senate, then to the United States House of Representatives for three terms, and finally, in 1958, he was elected to the United States Senate where he continues to serve. During Byrd's early campaigns, he often told voters that West Virginia's best friends were "God, Carter's Little Liver Pills, and Robert C. Byrd." Only one other member of the United States Congress has served longer than Senator Byrd. Moreover, even though he suffers from Parkinson's disease, he continues to speak for hours on the Senate Floor often reciting poems and quotes from historical figures such as Cicero and Edmund Burke in often unforgettable oratory, the likes of which might seem reminiscent of a masterful performance at Shakespeare's Theater at Stratford Upon Avon in England.

By most standards I would say Senator Byrd is a self-taught genius, but that never stopped him from excelling in a formal education setting. In fact, even though he was already working countless hours serving West Virginia in Congress, and spending his days developing and pushing important national legislation, he filled out an application and was accepted to American University, The Washington College of Law. He later became the first sitting member of either House of Congress who began and completed his law degree while serving in Congress. Perhaps even more impressive, he graduated *cum laude* from American University in 1963 and was presented his diploma by President John F. Kennedy.

I obtained two of my law degrees from American University and I always felt a sense of pride and motivation as I worked on several of my class projects in the Robert C. Byrd computer room. I often thought of the story that the Senator had told me of how he would work throughout the day in the United States Congress and would attend law school at night surviving on the peanut butter and jelly sandwiches that Erma would pack him for his dinner. Continuing his drive toward learning, Senator Byrd was also awarded a Bachelor of Arts degree in political science, *summa cum laude*, from Marshall University in 1994. If the Senator's story isn't an inspiration to any young person who has grown up during challenging times, then I am not sure what that story would be. Senator Byrd and Erma even managed the time to parent two daughters, Mona and Marjorie, and now have six grandchildren and six great-grandchildren.

Senator Byrd's tenure in the United States Senate is without parallel. As the "Father of the Senate" (the Senator with the longest continuous service), he has held more leadership positions in the Senate than anyone in the United States Senate history, including six years as Senate Majority Leader and six years as Senate Minority Leader. He was also elected President Pro Tempore of the Senate five times between January 3, 1989 and January 3, 2003, a post that placed him third in line of succession to the Presidency.[553] Imagine being a poor boy from southern West Virginia growing up in the coal fields during oppressive times just hoping to make ends meet, and years later finding yourself sitting in the position of being third in line of succession to one of the most powerful jobs in the world.

Senator Byrd is sometimes referred to on a national level as "The King of Pork" because of the huge amounts of the money he has allocated for West Virginia. The majority of the people of West Virginia, however, don't mind that title as Byrd has been instrumental in helping the State, which is the only state wholly within the rugged terrain of Appalachia, develop an infrastructure that connects it to the outside world in spite of the many geographical barriers of the mountainous region. In bringing such change to West Virginia, he has cast more votes than any other Senator in the history of the Republic–more than 17,000 votes in his Senatorial career.

Byrd's accomplishments have not gone unnoticed by his fellow West Virginians. In May 2001, Governor Bob Wise and both Houses of the West Virginia Legislature named him "West Virginian of the 20th Century." In fact, he is so popular among West Virginians that in his 1970 re-election for Senate, he became the first West Virginian to win all fifty-five counties in an election, a feat he has repeated twice since.[554] Senator Edward M. Kennedy (D-MA), often referred to as "West Virginia's third United States Senator" due to the impact of his role in the 1960 Presidential campaign of John F. Kennedy in West Virginia, has said of Byrd: "Bob Byrd personifies what our Founding Fathers were thinking about when they were thinking about a United States Senate. He brings the kind of qualities that the Founding Fathers believed were so important for service to the Nation."[555]

Byrd has authored several books including his most recent bestseller *Losing America: Confronting a Reckless and Arrogant Presidency*. Moreover, in 2005, he released his autobiography titled: *Robert C. Byrd: Child of the Appalachian Coalfields*. He is often referred to by commentators and political pundits as the man who has written the book on the United States Senate due to his longstanding tenure. Unbeknownst to many of those commentators, Senator Byrd literally did write the preeminent book on the United States Senate as he authored *The Senate: 1789-1989*, a four-volume history that covers notable speeches, topics such as impeachment and judicial nominations, and even the Senate's role in American film and literature. His impact on his home State should also be apparent to anyone who has ever driven through West Virginia where his name is affixed (often called Byrd droppings) to countless buildings and roads, with even a high school named in his honor.[556]

Senator Byrd's impact has also extended well beyond the border of West Virginia as he has become known as one of the United States Congress' most staunch and outspoken defenders of the United States Constitution. President Richard Nixon even strongly considered selecting Senator Byrd to fill a vacancy on the United States Supreme Court created by the retirement of Justice Hugo Black in 1971. Also on the national scene, in 1976, at the time he was serving as Senate Majority Whip, Byrd announced that he would run for President of the United States as a "favorite son" candidate, only campaigning in his home State of West Virginia. Byrd was never really a serious national candidate for President, but thought that perhaps if the Democratic Convention were dead-locked, he could use his delegates to hold some influence in the selection of a nominee. He won by a near 9-1 margin in West Virginia.

Approximately fifteen years later, Jay Rockefeller, West Virginia's Junior United States Senator, also considered a run for the nation's highest office. It was 1991, as news reports began to circulate on a national level that Rockefeller was strongly considering running for President during the 1992 election.[557] In fact, I remember receiving a telephone call from a friend of mine who worked for him at the time, telling me, "You can't tell anyone and I mean no one about this, but Jay is running. They've been in meetings all morning and they're announcing it soon." I had a huge secret and I couldn't tell anyone. I even began wondering if I would be able to use some of my contacts close to the Senator to get a job in the White House. Prior to learning of Rockefeller's soon-to-be announcement, the thought of being able to work in the White House was an impossible dream for someone from a rural area of West Virginia with the clos-est city having a population of just more than 1,000. My imagination started playing out all of the different scenarios in my head, from special assistant to the President, to caretaker of the White House lawn. Being twenty-one years old at the time it just didn't matter to me what job I would have to do as I simply want-ed to serve and work in the same building as those who worked so hard to build this country. Soon afterward, my friend's off-the-record comments to me seemed to be becoming a reality as it was announced that Lane Bailey, Rockefeller's long-time aide, began splitting his time on Senate matters with the other half of his time spent preparing for a national campaign.[558] He then became the guest on various national forums and often repeated the joke,

> the good news is I have 100 percent name identification in Iowa. The bad news is one-third of the people think I'm the banker who foreclosed on their farm, one-third think I run the oil company that raised the price of gasoline and one-third think I'm the guy who sold Manhattan to the Japanese.[559]

I waited day after day to hear the official announcement, and it wasn't long after opinion polls surfaced showing President George Bush with an approval rating above 80 percent, that Jay's announcement came. Unfortunately, it was not the announcement I had been expecting as Senator Rockefeller said that he would not be running for President that year. I was told later by my friend that Rockefeller decided that Bush's approval rating was simply too high and that no Democrat would beat him that year so it was time to concentrate on 1996. Rockefeller, however, miscalculated the 1992 election as then-Governor Bill Clinton defeated President Bush.

So, as fate would have it in 1992, instead of working on Senator Rockefeller's Presidential campaign, I found myself working as a regional coordinator for the Clinton/Gore Presidential campaign and was headquartered in Durham, North Carolina. I temporarily moved to North Carolina to work on the campaign after discussing it thoroughly with my then-employer and friend, Congressman Harley O. Staggers, Jr. of West Virginia, where I was serving as his Special Assistant at the time in Washington, D.C. While in North Carolina, I was responsible for a ten county region with a population of more than two million people which is larger than the entire population of the State of West Virginia. I was living near the beautiful Duke University campus. I vividly remember one campaign event I put on at the North Carolina Central University attended by Bill, Hillary, and Chelsea Clinton as well as Al and Tipper Gore. Then-candidate Clinton was more than three hours late for the political rally, but the more than 15,000 people who attended were still excited and eager to hear him speak. I have never seen anything like it. It was just about a week before the General Election and people were energized in a way that I had never before witnessed.

As I was making sure everything surrounding the event was going according to a strict plan, I noticed that for some reason, standing on the stage at my North Carolina event, was Senator Jay Rockefeller. I was puzzled why he was so far away from home campaigning for a candidate when he actually wished he would have been the candidate himself. After the rally, we had a small birthday party for Hillary Clinton and I counted 47 people in the room including myself. At that time, I was able to have a private conversation with Governor Clinton about politics and about the corruption within it. I have never met another politician in my lifetime who made me feel as if I was the only person in the room as was the case with President Clinton. He would often reach out and grab you by the shoulder or the upper arm displaying his wide smile as he looked directly into your eyes without scouring the room for the next hand to shake. At some point, Senator Rockefeller walked by and entered the conversation and we began talking about West Virginia. I started telling both of them about how I thought everything had changed so drastically from when I had first met Governor Clinton on May 6, 1992, while I was working as a Direct Aide to Governor Caperton. I said it was amazing how in just six months I had witnessed a transformation from seeing a lot of people showing up to see Clinton at campaign events who were somewhat excited, to seeing them months later at my North Carolina event fighting as hard as they could just for the opportunity to shake his hand. There was no doubt in my mind on that day that he was going to be President. In fact, the type of energy I saw during the waning days of the 1992 election I haven't seen since in a Presidential campaign.

As Governor Clinton became engrossed in a conversation with another person, I began talking with Senator Rockefeller about politics. I asked him if he would run for President in the future. Of course, he gave me the typical non-committal political answer when someone is asked such a question. He talked about how his only concerns were electing the Democratic nominee and then concentrating on his re-election to the Senate. I began asking him about the enormous amounts of money spent in elections and if he thought anything would be done about it on a national scale. Even though the Senator and I were the only two people in the discussion, he acted as if he didn't hear the question and changed the discussion topic to something else related to West Virginia. I brought up the topic again, but he began talking about the importance of healthcare and the importance of that issue on the nation's seniors. I didn't attempt to discuss money in politics again that day.

As Hillary's birthday party ended, everyone was heading toward the buses to get ready to leave for the next campaign stop in Winston-Salem, North Carolina. In a moment that could only be played out on the big screen, President Clinton turned to me with his beaming smile and told me to get on the campaign bus. I climbed on the bus not even knowing at the time where exactly it was going. I had been so tied up with my event that I didn't know where the next event was even being held. Nonetheless, given the excitement of the moment, I jumped on the bus anyway and arrived at the next campaign stop. Afterward, I was able to catch a ride with a State Police trooper who was going back toward the Durham area. I have replayed that evening in my mind countless times. Particularly, I have thought about my conversation with Senator Rockefeller and how the topic of money in politics wasn't something that seemed to be of interest to him. I have often thought that because of the fact that money has played such an integral role in his elections, he just may not want to talk about it.

Senator Rockefeller's climb to the United States Senate began in West Virginia during the mid 1960s. It started when Rockefeller finished college and began working for the Peace Corps in Washington, D.C., where he served as the operations director for their largest overseas program in the Philippines. He continued his public service in 1964-1965 as a VISTA volunteer (Volunteers In Service To America), during which he moved to Emmons, in southern West Virginia. He quickly began his escalation in State politics as he used his personal wealth and was elected to his first public office in 1966, the West Virginia House of Delegates. In 1968, Rockefeller became West Virginia's Secretary of State and then ran an unsuccessful 1972 election for Governor. His 1972 election was his only political defeat at the hands of the West Virginia voters and it was against challenger and incumbent Governor Arch A. Moore, Jr., whose campaign spots featured interviews of average people who said things such as: "that makes as much sense to me as having the next Governor of West Virginia be a New Yorker." Rockefeller spent approximately $1.5 million (a State record) while incumbent opponent Arch Moore spent about $700,000. Instead of leaving the State after his defeat, as many people believed he would, Rockefeller accepted the position of President of West Virginia Wesleyan College from 1973 to 1976. He then ran for Governor again in 1976 and spent as much as $2.8 million to capture the Governor's seat by defeating former Governor Cecil Underwood.[560]

Accordingly, from 1977 to 1985, the West Virginia Governor's Mansion became the transplanted home to an heir to one of the world's greatest fortunes. Rockefeller's first inaugural address, in which he spoke of new jobs, new roads, and new politics, lasted only seventeen minutes in sub-zero temperatures. My grandfather attended the inauguration and said that even though reports said it was approximately seven below zero, it seemed to him as if it was forty below. He said it was so cold that when he cut his hand on something that he grabbed onto, his hand didn't even bleed. Rockefeller told those in attendance, "[t]he free rides are over" as he pledged an honest government and directed citizens to "[r]each out, reach out West Virginia, for your fair share of the American Dream."[561]

Unfortunately for Rockefeller, his transition to Governor was not a seamless one as his unsuccessful opponent Governor Arch Moore fled the State's highest office in disgraceful fashion. Moore refused to meet with Rockefeller prior to the inauguration which limited Rockefeller's ability to prepare for his new position as Governor as he was not provided access to any information about the affairs of the State.[562] Then, as explained by Richard Grimes, former *Charleston Daily Mail* reporter and Capitol bureau chief as well as author of the book *Jay Rockefeller, Old Money, New Politics*, "[t]here sat Jay Rockefeller, probably the State's most prestigious governor, with hardly any lights, no phones, no paper, no pencils, no files, no toilets, no coffee and a room-full of furniture he was too big to use."[563] Grimes, who began covering politics at the State Capitol in 1968, said:

> [Governor] Moore took most of the furniture and left Rockefeller with odd pieces from surplus that didn't match. The desk was far too small for Rockefeller. The pictures were stripped from the walls. Moore didn't even leave a scratch pad for his predecessor. All the file drawers were empty. There weren't any pencils. Even the light bulbs in the outer offices were unscrewed. It was like someone had taken a ladder and loosened them.

Grimes continues:

> The governor's office had a 10-line phone system. But even it was disconnected. Every time Jay wanted to talk to his secretary, he had to get up and walk out of the room. Jay said that he had never felt so isolated in his life. There is an elaborate emergency alert system that sounds off if an unauthorized person enters the corridor leading to the governor's office. Even that had been disconnected. When some of the Rockefeller staffers tried to plug in a coffee pot, they found that someone had stuffed the outlets, so that an electrician had to be called to clean them out. Female employees complained that the toilets had been stuffed with newspapers, so they overflowed when flushed.[564]

The newly appointed Rockefeller staff members even discovered that the ribbons had been removed from the typewriters, and that most desks were completely empty.  Sandra Lopinsky, the Governor's new administrative assistant, said, "There's not even a scratch pad left in a desk."  With regard to his first day on the job, Rockefeller said, "I've enjoyed it, but it's frustrating because I can't call anyone.  I haven't had a call all day, but I'm sure I've had 500."[565]  This was of course before the days of cell phones.

Leading up to this disgrace, "[g]overnment in the 1960s had not been good to West Virginians.  One Governor had gone to prison [Governor Wally Barron] and several other State officials also had served time.  Politics and scandal were synonymous."  Rockefeller, in an effort to promote his honesty to citizens and to divert criticism from his massive campaign spending proclaimed he was "too rich to steal."[566]  On the one hand, his arguments are compelling as a self-financed candidate is less likely to be controlled by special interests.  This view is supported in an article published in major newspapers across the country including the *Los Angeles Times*, *Pittsburgh Post-Gazette*, and *Arizona Republic*, where reporter Bruce Shulman states that:

> great wealth inoculates candidates against charges of corruption.  In West Virginia, a state with a long history of petty corruption that has sent more than its share of office holders to jail, Sen. John D. 'Jay' Rockefeller IV campaigned as a politician immune to the blandishments of lobbyists and special interests.  Everyone may have theirs, but who could afford a Rockefeller?  In an age of White House coffees and shakedowns at Buddhist temples, [Al] Checchi's candidacy taps this same faith in the incorruptibility of the super-rich.  With a cool $550 million in the bank, he does not need to sell access.[567]

Nonetheless, even with the arguably positive benefits of limiting special interest access, the negatives clearly outweigh any potential positives.  Adding millions of dollars to the mix serves to make it nearly impossible for the average citizen to even consider getting involved in politics on a statewide or national level when they know they could face a well-financed multi-millionaire candidate.  Equally important, the influx of massive amounts of money pouring into West Virginia elections only further cultivates apathy in State politics and results in lower voter turn-out.  In May of 2004, "[o]nly 39.4 percent of registered voters [in West Virginia] went to the polls in the Primary.  That's down from 41.32 percent in 2000, 52.53 percent in 1996, and 54.02 percent in 1992."[568]  According to a United States Census Bureau report, West Virginia finished dead last in the percentage of voters who went to the polls during the 2002 Primary Election.[569]  Moreover, during the final days before the West Virginia 2004

Primary Election, an *Associated Press* survey indicated "about one-fifth of the more than 140 residents polled across the State could not name a single candidate for Governor, Secretary of State or the Supreme Court." Furthermore, not a single participant in the poll could name all of the candidates running for those offices. In fact, the driver of Republican gubernatorial candidate Dan Moore's campaign bus said that "at almost every stop, people ask if he drives for Arch Moore, the former three-term Republican governor." When asked to name a Supreme Court candidate, a race in which sitting Justice Warren McGraw was running for re-election, Willis Valtine, of Wheeling, said, "Ain't Tim McGraw one of them?" Many of those polled said they had blocked out all of the political advertising since they were so negative, while others polled were suspicious of the amount of money spent in the campaigns as State resident James Phillips said, "I figure, if a man spends a million dollars to get them a job that pays nothing, something has got to be crooked or he's got to be stupid."[570]

Unfortunately, many West Virginians question why they should even vote in a system in which it seems they cannot participate due to the millions of dollars spent by candidates during their campaigns. The *Charleston Sunday Gazette-Mail* purports:

> Nowhere is the need to control campaign spending more apparent than in West Virginia. Although poor and small–the state ranks 49th in per-capita income and 41st in land size–it is fourth in the nation for spending on gubernatorial campaigns. Candidates for governor in 1988 spent a combined total of $9 million–$13.12 for each vote cast.[571]

Even if you believe you have an important message and want to become a candidate for a statewide office, you still face the challenge of getting your message to the people. With campaigns of today, if you don't have money, you don't have a voice. Governor Rockefeller has never faced such a dilemma as Richard Grimes explains:

> He bought every conceivable kind of ad. His face was everywhere. Major West Virginia television stations were running his ads as often as 18 times a day. He cranked out so much mail that the Post Office started complaining it was having to work its people overtime. He published newspapers and magazines about himself. He set up telephone banks around the state. Just about everybody got a call, a letter and a personal invitation to one of Jay's picnics. It well may have been the only campaign where every household in the state was reached.[572]

Rockefeller's run for re-election in 1980 cost approximately $12 million in a state with fewer than two million people, while opponent former Governor Arch Moore spent nearly $1.1 million. Rockefeller spent at least $28.92 per vote in a statewide election, most of which was his own money.[573] Bumper stickers surfaced during the campaign that said, "Make him spend it all Arch!" In 1984, he spent $12.1 million on his election to the United States Senate and still holds the distinction of running two of West Virginia's most expensive campaigns in State history. Rockefeller's entrance into West Virginia politics began the astronomical increases in gubernatorial spending and even helped drive up the price of other State campaigns. For example, in 1976, when Rockefeller was first elected Governor, candidates spent a total of $154,953 on all races for the State Senate, while in 1986 the total had soared to $1.5 million.[574] The enormous amounts of money spent sent a clear message to future candidates that if they spent enough money they could buy whichever political office they wanted.

Grimes proclaims that Rockefeller's "campaign spending reports, when stacked together, resembled the federal budget." When confronted with the large amounts of money he spent for re-election, Rockefeller frequently proclaimed that "West Virginians don't sell their votes. West Virginians can't be bought" and called such charges "an insult to the State."[575] Then, soon after spending $12 million on his re-election, he traveled around the country announcing that, "Democrats had to do something to offset the outrageous campaign spending by the Republicans."[576]

Rockefeller's position on corruption and vote-buying in West Virginia politics seemed to change drastically from twelve years earlier when he traveled the State lecturing on clean elections as Secretary of State. It was after that 1968 election that Rockefeller decided to take a public stance on the issue of corruption in West Virginia politics. Shortly after the election he attempted to promote his clean elections campaign by holding a seminar in Mingo County on "How to steal an election and get away with it." Rockefeller won the Democratic nomination in 1968 in every West Virginia county except Mingo County.

During the seminar, citizens described events of the previous election, such as one housewife who said "only 54 of 294 voters in her precinct had voted on their own and the rest asked for assistance in the voting booths."[577] It was widely known that when a voter was asking for assistance from a poll clerk, they were more often than not selling their votes to a political faction. Many of the poll clerks were involved with the vote-buying scheme and would provide confirmation to the election faction leaders who would be waiting just outside of the polling place. After a faction leader received verification that a person voted their slate, the voter would then receive payment.

Rockefeller learned from polling official Okey Spence that nobody in the county knew where the precinct boundaries were and that Mingo County law enforcement officials confiscated cameras from people who took them to the polling places. An elderly man also advised Rockefeller that a justice of the peace had been defeated at the polls, but that he later bought the job back from the winner. Even a former circuit clerk told Rockefeller that 90 percent of the people who had voted absentee ballots during the past election had sought assistance as only 15 of the 397 voters went into secret voting quarters without assistance. The clerk explained that others voted openly, oftentimes with someone looking over their shoulders. In one precinct, 511 people cast votes in spite of the fact that only about 200 people lived in that precinct.

The voting irregularities were not confined to Mingo County as the number of registered voters in 1968 outnumbered eligible voters in thirty-three of the State's fifty-five counties. In fact, in 1960 there were 19,879 eligible voters in Mingo County, while actual registered voters in Mingo County totaled 30,331. Illustrating how the so-called "posthumous ballotings" contributes to the corrupt political situation, Mingo County resident Oakey Hatfield reported that although his brother had been killed in a car accident in 1964, he was recorded as voting in a Mingo County election months later. After hearing their stories, Jay called it a "national disgrace and a local tragedy," and promised he would correct it.[578]

Nonetheless, many county officials denounced Rockefeller's assertions and "accused him of doing what they were doing: buying off elections." During a May 1970 speech to students at Matewan High School, Congressional candidate Hawey Wells declared: "Mr. Rockefeller is screaming clean elections in Mingo County and yet, by his own admission, is financially supporting a notorious group of ballot burners and a rigged machine in McDowell County."[579] While Rockefeller's administration did not face the same scandalous accusations as previous administrations, his campaigns of 1972, 1976, 1980, and his United States Senate campaign in 1984 did introduce West Virginia to a new level of political spending.

Moreover, according to Grimes, even though Rockefeller spoke about cleaning up West Virginia's elections, his staff had "set up a trailer in southern West Virginia and was handing out dollar bills to aid local politicians." Another high ranking Rockefeller aide was quoted as saying, "It became general knowledge among members of the Rockefeller staff that money was being passed out" and "[h]eck, our man [Rockefeller] told me he was passing out money." Yet another associate explained: "The buying and selling of an election was just another business for him. He simply didn't want to be bothered with the details." Others had claimed that he had contributed to select groups and that he would not disclose some of those contributions because it would be too embarrassing for him to report that he had given to these organizations. It has also been insisted that promises to some precinct captains were fashioned that "if their areas produced enough voters on election day, they could keep the cars given to them to haul voters to the polls."[580] Another source expressed:

> Jay pays out a lot of what is called up front money. It's not the money that directly goes into an election, or the money that is reported. But it has an effect on the outcome. It goes to organize the outlying areas. We used to sit around and calculate that Rockefeller probably reported about 70 cents on the dollar. He couldn't really report the other 30 percent. It was ground money. There was always a buffer.[581]

I have personally spoken with individuals on the condition of anonymity who were involved with stuffing cash in little yellow envelopes that were later delivered to various political faction leaders and precinct captains, primarily in southern West Virginia, on behalf of Rockefeller. One of those individuals said he sat in a large room with nothing but people, cash, and tables, and he stuffed a predetermined amount of cash in specially marked small yellow envelopes. He told me, "you couldn't find a $1, $2, $5, or $10 bill at any bank in Charleston that day because we had all of them."

Stuffing envelopes with cash was not something new to West Virginia politics brought about by Rockefeller. In southern West Virginia it is a time-honored tradition that has been around as long as anyone can remember but reached new heights in 1960 during the John F. Kennedy election. Nonetheless, Logan County political boss Raymond Chafin, who openly discusses providing money for votes in southern West Virginia, said that Senator Byrd was one of the few politicians who never actually participated in the practice of supplying money to precinct captains. Chafin said that Byrd would attend political rallies and play his violin and meet and greet people. He said money was spent on behalf of Byrd to put him on their slates without his knowledge because people genuinely liked him.[582]

Senator Rockefeller makes no apologies for the amount of money he has spent on West Virginia elections. Following his only election loss in 1972, he has handily outspent any of his opponents in subsequent elections. I remember another occasion when I was speaking with Rockefeller at a small gathering of about thirty people in Keyser, West Virginia in early 2000 at former Congressman Harley O. Staggers, Jr.'s farm. Rockefeller and I were standing beside each other off to the side of the gathering and I was telling him about writing this book and how important I felt campaign finance reform was and asked him his thoughts. I told him I really wanted to know exactly where he stood on the issue and asked if he had ever thought about introducing any legislation in the Senate that dealt with money in politics. He put his hands on my shoulders and gave me a big smile and what appeared to me to be a forced concerned look and shook his head up and down as if he were listening intently to me. Even though I am six-foot-four inches in height, I was looking up to the six-foot-six Rockefeller as he changed the subject without uttering a single word on money in politics and instead told me how he likes to walk on a treadmill in the evenings to reduce stress. I quickly understood that this was not a topic of interest to him.

Senator Byrd, on the other hand, recognizes that as the amounts of money pumped into campaigns continue to grow to staggering sums, this elegant system of quasi-bribery–also known as campaign financing–proceeds to undermine political democracy. He has a much clearer philosophy on money in politics and says that unless you "win the lottery, or unless you strike oil in your backyard, or unless you are plugged into the political money machines, unless you actively compete to be part of the 'aristocracy of the money bag,' you are a long shot at best to win election to the United States Senate."[583]

Through the years, Senator Byrd, a modern election re-shaper, has co-sponsored a bill in the United States Senate on numerous occasions that would implement a constitutional amendment guaranteeing Congress' right to regulate campaign spending that would effectively overturn the United States Supreme Court precedent that currently restricts many legitimate campaign finance reforms by the state and federal governments.[584] The fact that he has often made clear his opposition to *any* amendment to the document that he loves so dearly–the Constitution of the United States–only underscores the critical nature and importance of campaign finance reform and his dedication to that issue.[585] To date, the proposed amendment has languished; however, if his amendment is ever successful, it would place caps on giving and spending in federal elections and empower states to set similar limits in state and local races.

Senator Byrd says that "out-of-control spending" prompted him to push for such a constitutional amendment and calls the record $975 million spent by United States House and Senate candidates in 2000 "outrageous." He also states that winning House candidates spent an average of $816,000 during the 2000 election while Senate candidates, on average, spent more than $7 million. He says that this figure represents 140 times the $50,000 he and Jennings Randolph spent together when they were first elected to the United States Senate in 1958.[586] Byrd states that the pressure to raise large sums of money detracts from the time he and other Senators could be spending on issues for their constituents by forcing them instead to focus on raising massive amounts of money for the high cost of television advertising. He has further declared that "[b]oth parties are enslaved to those who give campaign funds. We're beholden to the special interests when we go around the country holding out a tin cup, saying, 'Gimme, gimme, gimme.'"[587]

In 2002, the McCain/Feingold legislation passed Congress and was supposed to limit the amount of money pouring into campaigns through loopholes in existing laws. While Senators Byrd and Rockefeller voted for the reform legislation,[588] it was proven by the 2004 election cycle to be unsuccessful in stopping the hundreds of millions of dollars spent in elections as the so-called 527 groups successfully used an Internal Revenue Service loophole to bypass the Senate's reform efforts. I spoke with Senator John McCain (R-AZ) while he was in West Virginia for a couple of campaign stops in 2000. He has spent a career trying to make campaign finance reform a national issue. He told me Senator Byrd was a champion of election reform and that West Virginians should be proud of his efforts. When I read to Senator McCain some of Senator Byrd's comments on money in politics, he said he agrees with him and that: "As long as the wealthiest Americans and richest organized interests can make the six and seven figure donations to political parties and gain the special access to power that such generosity confers on the donor, most Americans will dismiss the most virtuous politician's claim of patriotism."[589]

As Senate Majority Leader in the late 1980s, Byrd pushed for a vote on legislation to overhaul the campaign finance system eight times, more than any other Senate leader. He believes raising money is "the most demeaning thing" he has had to do in his half-century of public service.[590] He says that candidates' hands are "manacled by the shackles of money."[591] Recalling his own experiences in campaigns, Byrd states:

> The current system is rotten, it is putrid, it stinks. The people of this country ought really to know what this system is giving to them and what it is taking from them. This system corrupts political discourse. It makes us slaves, makes us beholden to the almighty dollar rather than be the servants of the people we all aspire to serve. .
> . . It already costs tens of millions of dollars to run an effective campaign for the Senate in many States. What do we tell a poor kid from the hollows? What do we tell a poor kid from the coal camps? Forget it. Yet, that person may have the capacity and the drive to be a good Senator. A campaign for the Senate will be beyond his or her personal means and beyond the means of friends and associates.[592]

Byrd also says had he faced the same challenges that money in politics places on candidates today when he first ran for public office, he would not have been elected to office. He said,

> If 55 years ago, when I started out in politics, we had had the current system of funding campaigns, somebody else would be standing at this desk. It wouldn't be I. I came from the very bottom of the ladder. There were no lower rungs in my ladder. There weren't any bottom rungs in my ladder. I came out of a coal camp. What did I have? If I might, for a moment, tinker with grammar, 'I didn't have nothing,' as they would say. 'I ain't got nothing.' All I had was myself and my belief in our system. I believed in a system, then, in which a person who didn't have anything, a person who was poor, a person who came from lowly beginnings but who could pay his filing fee, could run for office. . . .[593]

For anyone in West Virginia those are powerful and alarming words. There is no one I am aware of in the history of this State who has had the impact of Senator Byrd. He is credited for massive funding of countless projects in a rural State with a small population. While nationally he is criticized for bringing so much to West Virginia, the people of his State look to him as a beacon of hope in desperate times. When someone is critical of West Virginia, he is ready to battle. I have heard him say on numerous occasions, "Hell has no fury like a Mountaineer scorned." He is seen as a man who has walked in their shoes and understands the struggles of putting food on the table. People know that he remembers what it was like to work in the coal company store and to live without electricity or running water. He is also seen as a man who has shown that the American dream is possible in spite of sometimes astronomical odds.

Indeed, both Senators Byrd and Rockefeller have lived very different lives, however, the lives they have led have been threaded with the commonality of serving the people of West Virginia.

# CHAPTER TEN

# The McGraw Brothers, Warren and Darrell

*Name recognition is one of the most important tools because you can't distin-guish yourself on the issues, so getting your name out by any means is one of the most important things in the election.*

State Senator John Yoder

This is a difficult story to tell as I have known both Darrell and Warren for many years and have been able to interact with them on a very personal level. I worked closely with Darrell in the Attorney General's Office and was able to get to know Warren during that same time period as well as during his service on the Supreme Court. I also developed relationships with many of their family members.[594]

As I have discussed throughout this book, personal relationships often temper our impressions of the actions of our acquaintances in politics. With that in mind, I have endeavored to remain completely neutral when discussing any of the State's politicians regardless of the status of my positive or negative person-al relationships with them and the McGraws are no exception. In working on this book, I believe I have stayed true to that principle with both political parties as I fully recognize that the quickest way to lose credibility would be to improperly and without objectivity show favoritism to one person or group over other peo-ple or groups. Accordingly, I wholeheartedly believe this book describes West Virginia's politics from a purely non-partisan manner.

Warren and Darrell McGraw have both been a part of West Virginia poli-tics on a prominent level since the early 1970s. Darrell, the more well-known of the two throughout the State, served as a Justice on the West Virginia Supreme Court from 1977 through 1988, and since his 1992 election, has served as the State's Attorney General. Warren, on the other hand, served in the State House of Delegates from 1969 through 1972 and in the State Senate from 1973 through 1984, but did not seek re-election to the Senate as he, instead, unsuccessfully ran for Governor. He was once the President of the State Senate, and most recently, from 1999 until his 2004 election defeat, was a Justice of the State Supreme Court. Both brothers also served as Chief Justice on the Supreme Court during their tenures with the Court.

Darrell appears to be a bit taller than Warren, but neither would break the six foot mark. Darrell also has what I would consider a larger build and probably weighs around 200 pounds compared to Warren's much smaller and skinnier frame. Warren wears gold wire-framed prescription glasses on a daily basis, while Darrell wears a pair of cheap store-bought plastic non-prescription magnifying glasses when he reads. Darrell has a silverish-white full head of hair, while Warren's hair is shorter, brown, and usually combed to one side of his head. Neither man has a mustache or beard. Warren speaks with more of a southern West Virginia twang in a relatively high voice, while Darrell speaks more slowly and in a much deeper voice as he strongly enunciates many of his letters such as the letter "S." They both have a colorful humor and street-corner smarts and both use anecdotes to keep audiences entertained.

Darrell, more so than Warren, is a highly guarded man who maintains a public fiction of openness in spite of his insecure and secretive nature, some of which stems from his 1988 re-election loss to the Supreme Court at the hands of Margaret Workman. I would have to describe Darrell, who is almost always addressed as "Judge," as a man with dual personalities. I had met him many years before I actually started working in the Attorney General's Office as I was a frequent attendant of political events throughout the State. Initially though, I was only able to get to know him from somewhat of a superficial standpoint as our dialogue was rarely anything too far removed from casual conversation. During those days I believe he wasn't sure how to converse with me since I had previously worked for Governor Gaston Caperton, whom he believed to be a political adversary.

It was during my final semester of law school in November of 1997 when I received a call from Darrell after a mutual friend had informed him I was soon going to be graduating. It was short and to the point. "Allen, I need you to work for me." I said, "I really don't know what I am going to do yet." He responded, "Well, I need you to work for me. When is your last day of law school?" I told him, "I am turning in my last final exam in on December 9th." He said, "Fine, you can start on the next day?" I honestly didn't know what to say because I knew I was going to have to begin studying for the bar exam which was in February of 1998 and I had my large educational loans to consider before accepting any position. I had also heard the stories about Darrell being an eccentric man who was difficult to work for and I was told by several friends not to take the job. In any case, I accepted the job and began working in December 1997.

It was an interesting situation because I was working directly for Darrell on "special projects" as he would call them. I was able to get to know him in a way many people will never have the opportunity. His perceived disloyalty by people was sometimes maddening. His management style was unlike anything I had ever witnessed. I remember my first week working for him when I put together a memorandum discussing my suggestions for improving press communications for the office and attempted to hand it to him. He refused it saying, "Allen, no memos. We don't put things in writing around here." I actually didn't mind that too much because I hated writing memos anyway, but it was another example of his unique style. I soon became very familiar with many of his peculiar behaviors. I began to learn his vulnerabilities and strengths–strengths I started to appreciate in spite of some of his often criticized actions.

I would have to say though that all-in-all, the years I worked as a Senior Assistant Attorney General was best described more than 100 years before I was even born. Charles Dickens, in *A Tale of Two Cities*, wrote:

> It was the best of times, it was the worst of times, it was the age of wisdom, it was the age of foolishness, it was the epoch of belief, it was the epoch of incredulity, it was the season of Light, it was the season of Darkness, it was the spring of hope, it was the winter of despair, we had everything before us, we had nothing before us. . . .

My work for Darrell was often "the best of times" because I was able to gain enormous professional experiences that I'll never forget including arguing more than twenty cases in front of the State Supreme Court. As part of my job I represented the State of West Virginia with oral arguments, appellate briefs, and other legal pleadings in the State Supreme Court as well as numerous circuit courts throughout the State and in various federal courts including the Southern and Northern Districts of West Virginia, the Southern District of Florida, the United States Court of Appeals for the Fourth Circuit, and the Supreme Court of the United States. I was even appointed to be a Special Prosecuting Attorney for specific litigation by several State circuit courts; I authored "Attorneys General Opinions" involving complex issues; worked directly with county prosecutors and various law enforcement personnel; and coordinated and implemented myriad special projects with the Attorney General. I am not trying to get my resume in print, I am merely pointing out that I was fortunate to have had such wonderful and valuable experiences as every day in the Attorney General's Office brought new challenges.

During my early years in the office, in addition to my legal duties, I acted as the Communications Director due to my prior background working with the press. I also met with constituents on behalf of Darrell and developed strategies to improve coverage in daily and weekly newspapers and broadcast media as well as coordinating press conferences, special events, and photo opportunities. I worked as the Attorney General's Office Federal Disaster Emergency Liaison; a liaison as a public information officer to the National Association of Attorneys General; served as the Idea Coordinator appointed to the State committee developed to reduce State government costs; served as a Legislative Liaison on behalf of Attorney General's Office; and worked with the Tobacco Litigation as one of two office employees who read, researched, recommended, and coordinated the signing of the Master Settlement Agreement which included more than $1.73 billion for West Virginia. I want to make perfectly clear, however, that it does not appear that I am taking credit for the settlement itself. Countless Attorney General's Office employees worked long and hard for many years against the odds on this lengthy and complex litigation, but were working in other employment by the time the case actually settled.

In my spare time (whatever that was), I traveled the State and spoke to many groups such as Kiwanis, Ruritan, Lions, other community service organizations, senior centers, and practically any group that I could think of where I could discuss consumer protection issues to warn people about the amount of fraud that occurs on a daily basis throughout the State. Then, as I learned more about consumer fraud and the number of scam artists who work overtime to bilk West Virginians out of their hard-earned money, I wanted to spend every spare moment I had trying to get the message out to as many people as possible. This part of my job was an extremely rewarding experience because I felt I could have some positive impact–even if small–on the lives of others. I must also say that I had the great fortune of working with some Attorney General's Office employees who are among the most capable people I've ever worked with, some of which have become lifelong friends. Darrell was also instrumental in strongly pushing me to continue pursuing higher legal education in spite of my busy work schedule.

As for "the worst of times" in the Attorney General's Office, they would have to circle around two people. One of whom I have attempted not to tax my mind with was probably the most insecure and conniving person I have ever known, but more or less just a day-in and day-out pain in the neck. The other I would describe as similar to Cruella Deville, the evil villainess character from Walt Disney's *101 Dalmatians*, who kidnapped Dalmatian puppies for their spotted fur to make a coat. Some of the shenanigans of the latter individual were so bizarre I often expected Alan Funt from the television show *Candid Camera* to appear and tell me it was all a joke. Funt never appeared. Working with this individual exposed me to the very worst side of politics imaginable. The individual even threatened to "ruin me" "both personally and professionally" if I ever "crossed" them in any way and explained that they knew "powerful people" who owed them favors. That person then laughed and told me that "it is amazing how you can twist a time sheet to make something look improper even when it isn't." I do not name those two individuals specifically because they are not elected public officials and most assuredly would sue me. Nonetheless, they are shining examples of what is wrong with West Virginia politics.

The worst of times for me also surrounded my struggles between Darrell's great qualities of taking on tough and sometimes politically unpopular issues versus his spending of State money on trinkets and other items. I admired the fact that he was not a man of great personal wealth serving in public office, but struggled with the constant theme surrounding his spending of State money for promotion of his name. Even though I was no longer working for Darrell at the time, a perfect example of this occurred less than a month before the November 2004 General Election when he spent nearly $8,000 of public funds to send 18,975 letters to people throughout the State promoting "McGraw." Both he and his brother Warren were running for re-election to their elected offices at the time. He sent the letters to people who had contacted his office's consumer protection division in recent years. The October 2004 letter began, "I want to take this opportunity to express my gratitude for you working with the consumer protection division in your quest for fairness. Together we worked hard to achieve fair and equitable treatment and we are pleased that your case was successful."[595] The letter went to everyone who contacted his office regardless of the actual result from their individual cases.

Darrell's Republican challenger, Hiram Lewis, IV, slammed the letters as thinly veiled campaign literature and said they were more evidence of Darrell's "disdain for the taxpayer." Lewis' concern followed the Attorney General's Office's purchase of more than $900,000 worth of State paid-for television advertising featuring Darrell during the year leading up to the election in addition to more than $141,000 in trinkets bought shortly before the election. Of course, just like the 18,975 letters mailed within weeks of the election, the television ads and the trinkets prominently featured the McGraw name. Darrell called Lewis' criticism "deplorable" and questioned his commitment to enforcing the State's consumer protection laws.[596] He said the letter was part of his office's consumer education efforts and added, "I think education, whether it is consumer education or whatever education, is very important. We wouldn't send any letter anywhere, anytime if it was not important."[597] The *Parkersburg News* wrote: "Attorney General Darrell McGraw is one of the most polarizing figures in West Virginia politics. While he is admired by his political constituency, he is at the same time loathed by an equal number of people for his self-promotion." The editorial expressed concern that the Attorney General was engaged in a "nearly transparent bit of electioneering for both himself and his brother."[598]

Prior to his May 2004 Primary and November 2004 General Election victories, Darrell, in addition to the criticism he received for mailing the letters, was denounced for spending, without the legislature's approval, $688,000 on advertising and public relations, including payments of $662,000 to a single Charleston lobbying firm from July 1, 2003 to February 17, 2004. The majority of that money was spent on television advertising under the guise of public service announcements which prominently featured Darrell. During the previous year, which was not an election year, Darrell's office only spent $17,000 on such television advertising. House of Delegates Finance Chairman Harold Michael (D-Hardy) said, "It indicates to me at least the appearance of the possible misuse of what I consider to be State funds [and there is] no office that I know of that can justify in one year spending $688,000 on what I assume is P.R." House Speaker Bob Kiss said, "They are not a private law firm [and] the monies that they use to pay their salaries, their benefits, their operations, come from several sources, a large one of which is the taxpayers of this State." Kiss further said this is the perfect example of why the Legislature should oversee the Attorney General's spending.[599] State Senator Andy McKenzie (R-Ohio) added that he did not believe the way McGraw was handing out money was legal because: "Any moneys that come in to the State of West Virginia belong to the taxpayers, and the Legislature is the only body that has the legal right to decide where that money is spent." McKenzie said such actions were a "systematic, fundamental, and blatant intrusion by the Attorney General upon the Constitutional powers and duties of the Senate.[600] In spite of such criticisms, the Legislature has done nothing to rein in such spending by the Attorney General's Office.

When Darrell's ad campaign was first criticized in August 2003, Fran Hughes said the Attorney General's Office was planning to spend "at least" $200,000 on television and radio commercials. Upon learning of the proposed $200,000 in spending, Steve Roberts, President of the State Chamber of Commerce, said, "This is another one of those cases where almost any person who cares about good government has to look at this and roll her eyes and say, 'there they go again.'"[601]  Roberts added,

> If we the public are to have confidence in our elected officials, particularly those who ask us to entrust them with powers related to the judiciary, they really should rise to a higher standard.  What he's proposing to do may be technically legal, but it does nothing to encourage the public's confidence that this is the right thing to do.

It wasn't until several months later, on March 5, 2004, that it was learned the Attorney General's Office had exceeded the $200,000 estimate by, in fact, spending a whopping $688,000 on advertising and public relations.  Then, just four days later, on March 9, 2004, it was further discovered the actual amount spent was nearly $900,000, with $873,224 going to Cheri Heflin & Company, a Charleston-based public relations and lobbying firm.[602]  At least one year prior to the public disclosure that the Office would be spending at least $200,000, one Attorney General's Office employee explained to me a plan which was already in place to raise more than $1 million through the Attorney General's Office's lawsuit settlements that were to be used to run television spots featuring Darrell during his election year to benefit both Darrell and Warren.  This individual called themself the "chief architect" of the so-called "brilliant plan" and said after spending that much money advertising the name McGraw, "no one will be able to touch us in this or any future campaign."

The *Charleston Daily Mail* wrote: "The Brothers McGraw should pay for their own ads" and asks:

> Who said West Virginia does not have publicly financed political campaigns?

> Attorney General Darrell McGraw is using the people's money to finance a series of ads that will raise his name recognition in a year both he and his brother seek re-election.

> This is an abuse of the office, and the Legislature should rein it in.[603]

The *Charleston Gazette* said, "it doesn't look right for a politician to blow such a large amount of State money on a project featuring his own image during an election year."  Saying that such spending invites scorn, the *Gazette* added,

MOST politicians use public funds to boost their re-election campaigns. Congress members bombard constituents with tax-paid newsletters designed to make themselves look good.

When the late A. James Manchin was Secretary of State, he spent thousands on certificates and medallions to present to potential voters. Former Governors Arch Moore and Cecil Underwood made personal appearances before news cameras to deliver State checks to communities. Putnam County Assessor D.W. 'Peachie' Arthur had peaches painted on his county cars [at taxpayers expense]. Etc., etc.

Attorney General Darrell McGraw is drawing fire because he commissioned $873,224 worth of TV commercials and other State-paid ads, many of them featuring himself.

They're public service announcements urging people to use his consumer protection office or file claims about prescription drugs, domestic violence and elder abuse.[604]

*Charleston Gazette* reporter Phil Kabler observed: "State GOP Executive Director Gary Abernathy spent much of last week trying to stir up a ruckus over the proliferation of public service advertisements featuring State elected officials, most of whom just happen to be up for election in 2004." Kabler explained:

You'll have to forgive Gary. He's from Ohio, and new to the State. He apparently doesn't realize that shameless self-promotion is practically a birthright of elected officials in West Virginia. . . . In some states, office-holders would consider it beneath their dignity to compete to see who could have the biggest, fanciest booth at the State Fair, manned by employees on State time, seeing who can give away the most pens, pencils, magnets and other paraphernalia featuring the official's name, paid for out of State coffers.

Kabler also said, "As for Abernathy's complaints, it's funny, but I don't remember Republicans complaining about then-Gov. Cecil Underwood's public service ads in 1999 and 2000 [when he was running for re-election in 2000]."[605]

Politicians spending millions of State dollars for their re-election campaigns is a practice that must end.  When the Attorney General's Office wins a
settlement, the money should be returned promptly to the public treasury.  No
Attorney General or any other office holder should be able to distribute millions
of dollars without full legislative approval.  It really is that simple.  The Attorney
General is the attorney for the State of West Virginia and is not the head of a private law office with completely independent domain.  The Attorney General is
elected by and completely accountable to the public.  I don't dispute that the
money sometimes goes toward worthy causes, but that doesn't make such
improper conduct proper.  It amounts to just another slush fund where politicians
hand out millions of dollars and trinkets just to get their pictures in the paper.
Elected officials should not be allowed to put themselves in place of the Governor
and the entire Legislature who have the authority with regard to State budget
matters.

As far as the argument that the money from these settlements is ordered
by a court to be spent on television settlements, that contention is similar to a
magician's slight of hand during a card trick.  More often than not these settlements are national settlements orchestrated by the National Association of
Attorneys General (NAAG), an organization consisting of Attorneys General of
the fifty states and the District of Columbia, the Commonwealths of Puerto Rico
(Secretary of Justice) and the Northern Mariana Islands, and the territories of
American Samoa, Guam, and the Virgin Islands.  The United States Attorney
General is an honorary member.  Pete Williams, NBC News Justice correspon-
dent and former Pentagon spokesman, has told me on a couple of occasions that
NAAG should really stand for the National Association of Aspiring Governors
since Attorneys General have historically used their offices to make a name for
themselves to eventually run for their respective state's Governor's Office.  I have
used that comment on several occasions because it is a pretty accurate observa-
tion, but now I will give proper credit for its source.

With regard to multi-state lawsuits, NAAG reaches a settlement with some
major company such as Phillip Morris or Microsoft after a cut and paste legal complaint has already been provided by NAAG to be filed in the courts of each participating state.  Lawyers at NAAG then hammer out the details, which usually include
a pre-determined amount of money to be set aside for each state.  The individual states
then decide how they want the lawsuit proceeds given to them and their proposals are
submitted to the court handling the settlement.  More often than not the state's request
is placed directly into a prepared court order and sent to a judge for his signature on
an order that all parties are then expected to follow.  Once the request is included in
the court order, the separate Attorneys General can then say they "don't have a choice

in how the money is spent." It is a great way for an Attorney General's Office to get substantial chunks of money and then be able to fend off political pressure for spending the money in an often highly political manner.

An example of this was a settlement reached by NAAG a few years ago whereby a significant amount of money was supposed to go to participating states to be used for domestic violence and elderly abuse victims. In West Virginia, even though the Attorney General's Office has no independent authority with regard to domestic violence, the State received between $200,000 and $300,000 as their share from the multi-state settlement. Many of the other states similarly situated chose to spend the money on domestic violence shelters or gave the money directly to the proper State agency who would best determine how to spend the money to assist victims in need. West Virginia, however, chose to spend *all* of the money on television advertisements that showed Darrell saying domestic violence is wrong while an elderly woman is then seen looking at herself in the mirror with bruises on her face as she begins to cry. The ads were aired during the year leading up to the election. My understanding from friends at NAAG as well as State Attorney General's Office employees is that West Virginia was the only State Attorney General's Office that spent the money on television advertisements when it could have gone directly to programs which supported and actually helped victims. Nobody really needs a television commercial to tell them that domestic violence or elderly abuse is wrong. The primary purpose of such advertisements was to promote Darrell's name even though his office had no statutory authority to do anything with regard to domestic violence.

Again, I *really* don't enjoy writing about an office where I once worked, but the incidents I have highlighted are all public record and precisely the types of situations that must be addressed, as they illustrate the much deeper problems within West Virginia's government. Politicians who are not independently wealthy or can't raise monumental amounts of money from wealthy donors must do something to stay in office. Thus, the constant cycle of campaigning ensues. I don't necessarily believe it is that Darrell loves to hand out magnets or run these types of commercials, I just think it is political survival and the fear that he may not be able to stay in office unless he can campaign on a twenty-four hour basis. And, don't get me wrong, it is *all* of West Virginia's elected statewide executive branch politicians who are in the business of using State money for self-promotion. Just as Arch Moore lived in constant fear of a wealthy challenger, politicians will often do whatever they have to do to stay in office regardless of the potential consequences for those actions.

Another area of controversial State spending surfaced in August of 2004 when one of Darrell's employees, Debra Whanger, was fired from her job. Whanger said the firing occurred after it was discovered by the press she was being asked by the office to work on Darrell's re-election as a part of her duties in the consumer protection division. Whanger said, "McGraw's office operates McGraw's re-election campaign on State time and with State money."[606]

A citizens' action group, West Virginia Wants to Know, filed a complaint with the Ethics Commission against McGraw, but Fran Hughes contended there was no merit to the charges. Hughes said, "Whanger is desperate after making a colossal mistake on her job" and claimed she fired Whanger because she went on a spending spree and purchased $141,814.61 worth of trinkets including pencils, pill boxes, keychains, crayons, and other items emblazoned with Attorney General Darrell McGraw's name on them.[607] Hughes said, "When I heard, it blew my mind. It's incomprehensible."[608] Attorney General McGraw, however, said, "Our people are out there doing what they are always doing, and that is educating the people." He added, "If one was of, say, a political mind, then one might make that charge. But this is what we always do to educate the people of the State."[609] The $141,814.61 purchased:

- 20,400 flag key chains
- 70,000 magnets
- 30,000 pill boxes
- 10,000 magnifiers
- 60,000 pens
- 50,000 crayon packs
- 30,000 whistles
- 50,000 pencils
- 10,238 highlighters
- 5,000 portfolios
- 50 briefcases
- 10,000 plastic banks shaped like houses
- 5,000 plastic bags
- a large quantity of coloring books.[610]

Whanger, who earned $35,000 a year working in the Attorney General's Office, argued she was simply ordering the materials with the full knowledge and approval of her supervisors and others in the office and she "would never risk [her] job for trinkets."[611] In fact, Whanger maintained she and several other employees were ordered by Hughes to organize Darrell's re-election and that she was supposed to concentrate the efforts of the consumer protection division in areas with the largest number of swing voters and in areas where Darrell may be "weak" with the voters.[612] She said these election efforts included using con-

sumer protection advocates, summer interns, and volunteers from other departments in the consumer protection division. She also said Darrell used his consumer protection division to coordinate his re-election campaign and that of his
brother, then-State Supreme Court Justice Warren McGraw by relying on Primary
Election returns to pinpoint where in the State it should focus consumer protection efforts and to distribute promotional items to those areas bearing McGraw's
name.[613]

Supreme Court Justice Warren McGraw denied any campaign coordination with his brother's office. Hughes also denied the charges and said the
Attorney General's Office "has no plans of slowing down the efforts of the division just because there's an election" but recognized that Darrell receives a "coin-
cidental benefit" at election time from the work of the consumer protection division.[614] Whanger was fired two days after Darrell's opponent Hiram Lewis filed
a Freedom of Information Act request for records of purchases of promotional
items. Whanger also said that after her firing, Hughes promised to find her a job
after the election if she "kept quiet about the re-election activities" and didn't
attack Darrell. Whanger said she was "shocked and sickened by the message."
She appeared on a campaign commercial just prior to the 2004 election explaining how Darrell fired her and she then directly accused him of campaigning at
taxpayer expense.[615]

With regard to 2003, which was not an election year, Hughes said the
Attorney General's Office spent about $30,000 on similar trinkets. She argued,
however, that the money spent on the trinkets was not taxpayer money as it came
from settlements the Attorney General made on behalf of consumers and that in
light of the controversy, the trinkets would not be distributed until after the 2004
General Election. "We don't want to taint the election and the campaign,"
Hughes said.[616]

The argument that the money is not State money is simply bogus. Even
though I was working at the Supreme Court at the time of the Whanger incident
I still had my Attorney General's Office contacts and friends. My first thought
with regard to the situation was that during the period when I worked in the
Attorney General's Office, my experience was that nothing happened there without Fran's approval. I even remember Fran announcing that the mere purchase
of a paper clip had to have her direct authorization. She ruled with an iron fist
and relished having such power and control over people. All I know for certain
is that it seems preposterous to think that a $35,000 employee decided to purchase
more than $141,000 in promotional items with her boss' name on them on her
own accord. It just doesn't make sense and it certainly doesn't conform to how
the office was being run when I was working there.

To act incredulous about State spending and then to hang one low-level employee out to dry when this has clearly been the office policy for years upsets me. I can't remember how many times Fran asked me for an opinion about the design of a key chain, a magnet, or a pillbox. I hated being put in that situation as her questions always surrounded the placement and prominence of the "McGraw" name. In addition, I remember a time in 1998, six years prior to Whanger's firing, when Randy Barton, a man who sold such items to the Attorney General's Office, told me he had already sold more than one million magnets with at least eight different designs to Darrell, not to mention countless key chains and other trinkets. He sold the magnets to Darrell in boxes which contained 50,000 magnets each.

The buying of magnets was a continuous endeavor year after year. I witnessed plenty of boxes being purchased while I was there. They were handed out by the hundreds of thousands by school children at countless parades and festivals throughout the State in exchange for cash payments of anywhere from fifty dollars to hundreds of dollars from the Attorney General's Office. Attorney General's Office employees also spent a considerable amount of time handing out magnets and other trinkets on State time at these events. I remember one Saturday when the office had employees in eleven different vehicles in eleven different areas of the State handing out such trinkets at parades. I remember another occasion when the office even rented a $3,000 float to ride through a Wheeling parade as State employees wore Santa hats and handed out magnets and key chains. Parades and special events are a major opportunity for State office holders to distribute millions of State paid-for trinkets. One question I often ask is: How can the average person who even considers running for office ever compete with a State office holder with seemingly endless coffers and a State paid-for staff whose sole job appears to be promoting a particular office holder's name?

State spending on trinkets is a huge problem which amounts to nothing more than pure campaigning with taxpayer dollars. It is time for everyone to truly be honest and recognize this ongoing problem and admit that no magnets, small plastic pill boxes for elderly people to use with their medication, key chains, pencils, pens, nor magnifying glasses, have anything to do with educating people about consumer fraud. In reality, the practice of such State expenditures on these trinkets should in itself be considered fraud. Taxpayers pay the bill for this junk and trash which is so blatantly used by incumbents to fund their statewide re-election campaigns. It has to stop. It has become so commonplace that even when newspapers write an occasional story dismissing such practices as wrong, they usually express that it is also expected behavior. It is particularly troubling though when the State's top law enforcement officer is one of the biggest violators of common sense and fundamental fairness with regard to the public purse.

During a budget presentation before the Senate Finance Committee on January 18, 2006, Hughes defended the use of trinkets bearing Attorney General McGraw's name. She said the Attorney General's Office produced numerous consumer-education materials, and that, "If we have to put it out anyway, I don't see–if they're elected by the people of West Virginia–why we can't put their names on the materials." Senate Finance Chairman Walt Helmick (D-Pocahontas) said the time had come for the Legislature to crack down on elected officials buying promotional trinkets. Helmick said, "There's been millions of dollars wasted, whatever you call them [and] the truth is, the taxpayers have paid millions over the years for promotional materials for a few politicians." Helmick added, "West Virginians are not stupid. They know what it's all about: It's political advertising."[617]

A few years ago in Indiana, a state with nearly four-and-one-half million more people than West Virginia, Attorney General Karen Freeman-Wilson faced relentless criticism for spending just $12,000 in Indiana's taxpayers' money on 12,000 promotional shopping bags imprinted with her name on them.[618] I discussed this situation with former Indiana Attorney General Jeff Modisett at a National Association of Attorney General's conference. Modisett was the Attorney General prior to Freeman-Wilson. He told me that people in Indiana were furious and even pushing for Freeman-Wilson's impeachment. Modisett said he couldn't believe the list of items we handed out in the West Virginia Attorney General's Office and said eventually the newspapers would make it a large issue and it would stop. I explained that it wasn't only one politician in West Virginia; it was most of them and that this practice had been going on for many years and had been reported *ad nauseam* by the press. I am not sure if he could fully comprehend how common it really is in West Virginia and how shameless many statewide politicians spend State money for self-promotion. In any case, in spite of Indiana's outrage over $12,000 in State funds for "shopping bags," West Virginia's spending of $900,000 in State money on blatant political announcements and $141,000 on plastic "shopping bags," whistles, magnets, and countless other items just before an election, warranted just a few stories in a few newspapers that didn't rise to the level of even a small slap on the wrist. Then, when Darrell sent 18,975 letters throughout the State just before the 2004 General Election, which were paid for with State money, the *Charleston Gazette*, in its endorsement of McGraw for re-election, simply said he probably shouldn't have done that.

The *Charleston Daily Mail* insists Darrell has been using public funds for personal promotion of himself and his family members for many years including the 1998 election, when his brother Warren McGraw was running to become a Justice on the State Supreme Court. The *Daily Mail* said during the 1998 campaign of his brother, Attorney General McGraw's "office spent in the five figures for 160,000 magnets that promoted 'Darrell "Judge" McGraw,' a slogan that benefits both brothers. He also had six 'mobile offices' [vans] emblazoned with the family name that cruised the State during the election cycle."[619] During the 1998 election, LUC Media handled Warren's Supreme Court campaign and sent his campaign television advertisements to various stations throughout the State. At the same time, LUC sent a letter to television and radio stations requesting separate television commercials featuring Darrell "Judge" McGraw be run as public service announcements from "Oct. 5 to Nov. 18 [1998]–coinciding with the campaign advertising frenzy leading up to Election Day." When some stations refused to run the Attorney General's so-called public service announcements, "the Attorney General decided to pay for them [with $50,000] from consumer protection funds."[620]

Willis Perry, treasurer for the campaign committee of Democratic candidate for State Supreme Court Joe Albright said, "This appears to be a very good example of just the kind of inappropriate coincidence and collaboration the public ought to fear if one McGraw is Attorney General and another McGraw is a Justice of the Supreme Court." John Yoder, another candidate for the Court said, "Name recognition is one of the most important tools because you can't distinguish yourself on the issues, so getting your name out by any means is one of the most important things in the election." Yoder said when Darrell placed his name on office handouts as "Judge" it created a confusion that benefitted his brother Warren as "voters don't know the difference between 'Judge' McGraw and 'Justice' McGraw."[621]

Throughout his many political elections, Darrell has been known for refusing debates with challengers and instead relying on his name recognition he gains from trinkets, State paid-for television announcements, and other Attorney General's Office communications. On one occasion when he refused to debate a challenger, he called a local chamber of commerce a "goofy, hateful outfit" and said participating in a chamber-sponsored candidates' forum would violate the principles of his church and the United Mine Workers.[622]

Darrell was criticized for these same behaviors years earlier while he was serving as a Justice to the State Supreme Court. In one instance, he was denounced for his treatment of Wanda Rea, his personal secretary at the Court. Rea was suffering from cancer which had spread through her lymph nodes and into her spine. She said Darrell had frequent outbursts especially when she scheduled a doctor's appointment.  On one occasion, after missing a few days of work, Darrell ordered her back to the office.  When she returned to the office, Darrell "went into a rage."  Rea said Darrell's tirades caused her constant stress which she feared led to her permanent health problems.  Supreme Court Administrator Paul Crabtree said "the staff was shocked by the treatment" of Rea.

According to Rea, Darrell became very angry on another occasion when she told him she needed to take time off to sit with her ill daughter.  She said it was after this incident that he tried to deny her a portion of her retirement benefits.  In spite of her health problems, Darrell even forced Rea to be on call twenty-four hours a day including weekends.  Crabtree said eventually Rea retired and "sought compensation for the unusual working conditions that had been imposed."[623]  She settled with the Court in April of 1992 for $14,280 for Darrell's alleged mistreatment and died the next month from her cancer illness.[624]  Darrell's attempt to deny Rea part of her benefits is ironic given the fact that he has spent every year since he left the Supreme Court in 1988 trying to finagle a way to qualify for the State's judicial retirement system.  He fell short of receiving the lucrative judicial retirement by one year of service with the Court.  Therefore, he falls under the regular State retirement system and will receive less money when he retires.  This is particularly troubling to Darrell since years earlier as Chief Justice he "wrote a legal opinion liberalizing retirement benefits for himself and other judges."[625]

Also as Chief Justice, Darrell was faulted for giving a lengthy interview to *Penthouse* Magazine.[626]  He later received further condemnation for being paid $3,700 in taxpayer money for a set of books he was given for free when he served on the Supreme Court.[627]  The *Charleston Daily Mail* also said he ordered dozens of expensive general interest books such as *A Guide to Orchestral Music* paid for at taxpayer expense while he was a Supreme Court Justice and for having the Court purchase cameras and related equipment at a cost of more than $2,000 that gathered dust in a cabinet, "or [were] given away to other government units."[628]  He also bought a substantial amount of stationery during the year he was up for re-election to the Court in 1988 as well as ordering 10,000 reprints of a favorable article written about him at a cost to the State of $3,614.[629]

According to the *Charleston Daily Mail*, "While Justice Darrell McGraw often portrays himself as a friend of the working person, those who work for him say he can be harsh, ruthless and overbearing."  The article cited the case of a Supreme Court librarian who Darrell asked to "photocopy pages dealing with conscience, loyalty, and ethics from three books."  When the librarian copied the information and placed it in a three-ring binder and handed it to Darrell, who thought the librarian "had leaked to a reporter information about his book orders through the library, he took the binder, shoved it back to the librarian and told her to read it."[630] On another occasion, while Chief Justice, Darrell wrote State Police Superintendent W.F. Donohoe saying he had received several harassing telephone calls from an *Associated Press* newspaper reporter. He alerted the press immediately about contacting the State Police Superintendent about the reporter's calls, but when the police contacted Darrell to investigate the matter he refused to be questioned.[631]

Similarly, years later as Attorney General, Darrell claimed that an Ohio business that his office sued was "harassing him and his family, following him, making threatening telephone calls to his home, and trespassing on his property."[632] This particular battle received an abundance of headlines for several years as a result of a sweepstakes operation by Suarez Corporation Industries owned by Ben Suarez. Suarez's business was just 1 of 106 out-of-state sweepstakes operations sued by Darrell's consumer protection division in 1994.[633] The company was once reprimanded by a United States District Court in Ohio following a complaint filed by the Postal Service alleging the Suarez mailings violated civil mail fraud statutes. Suarez blamed the Postal Service action on Attorney General McGraw and United States Senator Jay Rockefeller. Suarez spokesman Ron Sovik said, "We see the U.S. Postal Service action as retaliation as part of Suarez Corporation's exposure of the corruption process in West Virginia."[634] Suarez filed several legal actions against Darrell in West Virginia federal courts and in the Ohio state courts.[635] At one count, there were eleven separate legal suits filed by both Darrell and Suarez against each other in state and federal courts. Darrell said Suarez used a tactic of constant lawsuits against him in an attempt to drain the resources of the Attorney General's Office in hopes he would no longer pursue Suarez legally.

Suarez later spent $300,000 of his own money on television advertisements against McGraw in an unsuccessful attempt to defeat him in the 1996 election. He called West Virginia "one of the most corrupt states in the nation" and said the rulings against him were the result of decisions made by "McGraw's kangaroo courts" where the judges were friends of Darrell.[636] Conversely, Darrell called the Suarez tactics "a recent example of how the gamblers try to corrupt the governmental process in West Virginia."[637] That same year, Darrell criticized gambling in general when he spoke against West Virginia being involved in stock market investments. He told the *New York Times*, "West Virginia is a sordid, crooked state and pots of money are attractive to politicians. I don't believe government should be sitting on giant sums of money and playing the market."[638]

Another incident bringing negative press coverage occurred in 1992 when Darrell pled no contest to charges stemming from an incident in which he ran a West Virginia Turnpike blockade and brushed against the flag held by a highway workman. While at first blush this may not seem like a serious infraction, after having worked several summers during college with a private road construction company I can assure you this is extremely hazardous. The men and women who are working next to dangerous and loud equipment rely on the traffic control personnel to protect them. This is particularly so when dealing with asphalt which is typically pre-heated to 300 degrees and maintained at that temperature until it hits the ground. Darrell was charged with failing to obey instructions of a West Virginia Turnpike authority flagman, a misdemeanor, and was released on a $5,000 personal recognizance bond. He later issued a no contest plea in magistrate court and was only forced to pay a $10 fine and $56 in court costs.[639]

In 1995, in another controversial situation, impeachment was discussed in news stories with regard to an ethics charge filed against Darrell. It was alleged that he violated his duty to represent the Division of Environmental Protection in a lawsuit and violated the Rules of Professional Conduct for intentionally disclosing client information communicated at a meeting in which he had an ethical duty of confidentiality in the furtherance of their legal representation. After conducting hearings and investigating the incident, the Lawyer Disciplinary Board recommended that Darrell be publicly reprimanded; have his law license suspended for three months; and be forced to pay $4,430.55 for the costs incurred by the Office of Disciplinary Counsel in connection with the proceedings. The Supreme Court declined to adopt those recommendations and instead issued a public reprimand and reduced the amount he owed for the costs of the proceedings to $1,713.56.[640] Darrell called the situation political and said it "was an attempt by Governor Gaston Caperton's administration to muzzle him."[641] He even filed an unsuccessful petition with the Kanawha County Circuit Court trying to block the State Bar Ethics Committee from reviewing his conduct. He proudly displayed on his office wall a framed blown-up copy of the check he was forced to pay for his conduct.[642]

More recently, in 2001, Darrell was accused of stacking the deck in a lawsuit he filed seeking control over State and private attorneys hired by more than forty State agencies. Critics said Darrell was "seeking this legal control over State government through the judicial branch of government, currently headed by his brother, the Chief Justice."[643] The *Charleston Gazette* wrote: "McGraw's power grab is something that only someone with chutzpah and a brother on the high court would attempt. Unfortunately, McGraw has both."[644] Some legislators referred to Darrell's actions as "part of a continuing pattern of outrageous behavior." State Senate Minority Leader Vic Sprouse (R-Kanawha) said, "Here we have both McGraw brothers acting in concert to try to overcome the will of the Legislature to serve the Attorney General's personal interests. This is just more outrageous conduct from the Attorney General, but I'm stunned that he and his brother would do something so blatant."[645] The *Gazette* also noted:

> State Supreme Court Justice Warren McGraw still won't remove himself from a crucial case filed by his brother, Attorney General Darrell McGraw, who wants all State lawyers placed under control of his office. Meanwhile, the Attorney General has chosen an in-law of his justice brother as a special State lawyer to pursue an important lawsuit: the attempt to recover State damages from the Steptoe & Johnson law firm for the Fred Zain scandal. What a tangle. To follow State events, you need a family tree.[646]

Ironically, in 1984, while Darrell was a Supreme Court Justice, he authored a Court Opinion restricting the powers of the West Virginia Attorney General. He quoted an Iowa Justice who wrote: "To accord the Attorney General the power he claims would leave all branches and agencies of government deprived of access to the court except by his grace and with his consent." In 2001, however, as Attorney General, Darrell believed he should have the power he prevented the Attorney General's Office from having years earlier. Thus, he sued for control of more than 281 attorneys on the State's payroll that were not controlled by his office. Most agreed that the final outcome of the lawsuit could have shifted significant power from the Governor to the Attorney General. McGraw argued that several private law firms were at the public trough, and he was aware that it was costing the State $12 million to $15 million a year at a minimum.[647] He also contended that "the State [was] wasting resources and creating possible conflicts by not having a central clearinghouse for legal issues and [said] the State Constitution empowers only him and his deputies to represent the State."[648] McGraw said Governors don't want to relinquish the control of outside law firms as they are able to use their discretion to reward those who contributed to their campaign and who contribute to their future campaigns.

Steve Roberts, President of the West Virginia Chamber of Commerce, said: "Warren McGraw's continuing involvement in his brother Darrell's case could make West Virginia a laughingstock of the nation."[649] Roberts said Justice McGraw had placed himself "in a position to stack the deck among those who ultimately will decide the case." He noted that Justice Robin Davis removed herself from the case because of a potential conflict and then-Chief Justice McGraw chose her replacement. He said Warren's involvement tarnished the reputation of the legal system in West Virginia. Roberts said, "Employers want to operate in a State where good government is the norm, and there is nothing normal about this case. This attempted legal takeover by Darrell McGraw, already aided and abetted by his brother, must be recognized, identified and stopped."[650] John Rogers, a West Virginia lawyer, good friend to the McGraws, and former Governor of the State Bar, said Roberts' comments are representative of "[t]he people who are opposed to the petition [and] are basically those who for personal or ideological reasons do not like McGraw."[651]

In another situation, critics said Darrell retained private attorneys to assist the State with the tobacco litigation and those attorneys improperly received $33.5 million "for doing an undisclosed amount of work." Steve Roberts called the hiring of outside tobacco counsel "a deal that seems to have been kept a secret for two years."[652] Many of these same law firms contributed to Darrell's campaign for Attorney General. Conversely, Darrell said the lawyers were chosen because they had the expertise to handle such technical, high-powered cases.[653] House of Delegates Finance Chairman, Harold Michael, said, "I think what happened was that the money got diverted from the State's share before the State ever got its share. I don't think that's legal at all. It is being looked at. Obviously, the chief legal officer for the State needs to obey the law."[654]

During a March 7, 2006, speech on the floor of the House of Delegates Chamber, Delegate Bob Ashley (R-Roane) criticized Darrell's practice of hiring contingency fee lawyers to pursue litigation, and pleaded with his fellow Delegates to act immediately to pass legislation to stop such activity in the future. Specifically, Ashley said settlement proceeds from a recent OxyContin lawsuit filed by Darrell against Purdue Pharma did not go to the State agencies represented in the lawsuit.

It began in 2001 when Darrell filed a lawsuit on behalf of the Department of Health and Human Resources (DHHR), the Public Employees Insurance Agency (PEIA), and the Workers' Compensation Commission against Purdue Pharma over its potentially addictive painkiller, OxyContin. Darrell's legal complaint stated his office was seeking restitution and reimbursement for the losses sustained by the DHHR in the amount of $4.6 million, by the Workers' Compensation Division for $2.23 million, and by PEIA in the amount of $440,000.

Prior to the settlement, it was reported that State agencies spent $30.5 million in reimbursement claims for OxyContin. Nonetheless, Darrell reached a settlement for only $10 million with the company. The settlement provided that funds were to be delivered during a four-year period with the majority of the initial $2.5 million disbursement going to pay legal fees to the private attorneys Darrell retained to handle the case. The settlement also provided that all funds were to be deposited into the Attorney General's Consumer Protection Fund. After about $400,000 in expenses and $3.3 million in legal fees, the rest of the money was to go to programs within three categories of accredited continuing medical education programs and other prescription drug abuse and diversion programs.

According to the *State Journal*, other than a $250,000 award to the DHHR, none of the settlement money was sent to the government agencies that sued Purdue, "nor were the agencies made privy to the details of the settlement before it was signed, which violates a tenet in the State's Code of Professional Conduct for lawyers." The *Journal* also pointed out that Darrell's office gave a "$500,000 check to the University of Charleston's new pharmacy school, a private entity that will not be fully accredited for two years." Furthermore, the University of Charleston is not a State entity and was not a party to the lawsuit filed by the Attorney General on behalf of the State agencies.

Ashley said, "The real damage is that the people on whose behalf [Darrell] brought the Purdue Pharma case got nothing. And who are those people? They are all around us: Medicaid recipients under DHHR, injured workers and premium payers under workers' compensation and public employees and teachers under PEIA." He added, "The money that should have gone to them was sent instead to the Attorney General's Consumer Protection Fund which, by the way, has never been established by statute, and a healthy $3.3 million to his attorney friends. To add insult to injury, the attorneys are to be paid faster than the State."

Fran Hughes said the scrutiny could be attributed to politics and that the people elected Darrell and lawmakers should respect that, and added that the law firms she uses are not selected for political reasons. She said, "We can unequivocally state that who is selected doesn't have anything to do with campaign contributions. Have some of those attorneys given campaign contributions? They may have. I don't know." Hughes said the Attorney General's Office was simply doing what the court order stipulated. Ashley, however, countered, "It's very clear from Ms. Hughes' remarks that the court was simply doing what it was asked to do: give the money to the Attorney General and his lawyer friends. The court apparently had no way of knowing that the State agencies were unaware they were being sold down the river."

In Ashley's speech, he discussed a 1995 Kanawha County Circuit Court opinion by Judge Irene Berger, who ruled, "The Attorney General has no statutory or constitutional authority to retain private counsel under the contingent fee arrangement. Neither the Attorney General nor this court has statutory or constitutional authority to authorize payment of compensation to private counsel as contemplated under the contingent fee arrangement." Berger cited State Code, which states the Attorney General "may appoint such assistant attorneys general as may be necessary to perform the duties of his office" and those State appointees are to be compensated "within the limits of the amounts appropriated by the Legislature for personal services."[655]

Darrell's brother Warren has also received his share of newspaper headlines. On one instance, during the 2000 election, then-sitting-Justice Warren McGraw, whose term on the Supreme Court didn't end until 2004, attempted to run for another seat on the five-member Supreme Court that was vacated by retiring Justice Margaret Workman. Initially, Governor Cecil Underwood appointed House Speaker Bob Kiss in 1999 to fill Workman's seat, however, Warren authored an Opinion of the Supreme Court disallowing Kiss from taking the appointment. The Supreme Court said that since Speaker Kiss had voted on Legislation granting the Justices a pay raise during the 1999 legislative session, he was ineligible to be appointed to the Court because the Emoluments Clause contained in Article VI, § 15 of the West Virginia Constitution states that no Senator or Delegate shall be appointed to any office during the term he or she voted to give such office a raise. McGraw said, "To construe the exception language of Article VI, § 15 in the manner suggested by [Kiss] would thus require that we ignore the constitutional scheme intended by the Framers."[656]

Soon after declaring that Kiss could not take the position as Justice, Warren then filed for election seeking that very same open Justice seat on the Court. A Justice's elected term on the West Virginia Supreme Court is for twelve years. Warren was attempting to run for the open seat on the Court without vacating the seat he was already holding as a previously elected Justice on the Court even though he wasn't up for re-election until 2004. If successfully chosen by the voters, Warren would have had to resign his seat from the Court in order to accept a new seat on the Court and wouldn't have faced re-election until 2012. If Warren had lost the election, it would not have affected the term he was serving. After McGraw's name had already been placed on ballots throughout the State, a lawsuit was filed challenging Warren's candidacy and seeking his removal from the ballot claiming his candidacy was illegal due to the fact he was already an incumbent fulfilling a separate term on the Court to which he had already been elected. The Supreme Court denied their fellow Justice McGraw's candidacy and ordered his name to be removed from the ballots throughout the State.[657] Several county circuit clerks said removing Warren's name from the ballot was "time-consuming, expensive and problematic." For example, in Monongalia County, the change of the ballot cost $4,700, in Marion County it cost about $3,300, while in Boone County it cost an extra $3,000.[658]

When you say the names of either of these brothers, people are often confused as to who is Warren and who is Darrell. They generally don't know the difference and many actually believe they are the same person. The McGraw brothers have always been masterful in simply promoting the name McGraw throughout the State. They were successful at this tactic for many years partly because they rarely were on the ballot at the same time. One McGraw would campaign in one part of the State while the other would campaign in another area, thus getting maximum exposure of the McGraw name. Voters often knew they had met a McGraw and when they saw the name on the ballot they assumed it was the same person.

The many years of building their name recognition through trinkets and other means received its biggest test in 2004. During that year, Warren was running for re-election to the Supreme Court while Darrell was running for re-election as Attorney General. Darrell was narrowly re-elected while Warren was defeated. The 2004 State Supreme Court race between Justice Warren McGraw and opponent Brent Benjamin was an enormously contentious statewide race.[659] Much of the election surrounded a 2004 decision of the Court known as the *Arbaugh* case, and McGraw's "vote supporting a controversial decision to give a twenty-three-year-old sex offender another shot at probation." Benjamin called the Court's decision "an example of extreme judging" while his television ad said Warren's vote allowed Tony Dean Arbaugh Jr. to be assigned to a work release program that planned to place him in a school as a janitor.[660]

Warren said the negative ads against him "absolutely destroyed the life of a person who has been a responsible public servant in this State all his life."[661] Benjamin spokesperson Steve Cohen countered: "The victims of Tony Dean Arbaugh seem to be forgotten here, and Warren McGraw never once in his opinion addressed their plight."[662] The *Charleston Daily Mail* said millions of dollars were spent to run the kind of "attack ads that make parents want to cover their children's eyes."[663] Warren said he was "absolutely appalled" by Benjamin's use of Tony Arbaugh for political gain, a man who was sexually abused as a child and considered unlikely to commit another sex crime. Warren added, "When the time comes for me to determine whether or not I should continue to be a public servant or shall I destroy somebody's life then I willingly will walk away [and] I will no longer ask anybody to send me to perform public service if I must destroy somebody's life to do it."[664] Coming to Warren's defense, Justice Larry V. Starcher said the *Arbaugh* decision was a "bogus opinion" filed by Justice Robin Davis. Starcher said, "It is absolutely incorrect to say that we ordered that young man to be placed as a janitor in a school. That is absolutely incorrect."[665]

Justice Davis responded, "I continue to be falsely accused and harshly criticized by some political personnel and at least one of my colleagues for writing the Opinion [and I find such a] position and tactic offensive." Davis added, "Quite frankly, I feel drug into it by all sides [and] I'm not in this campaign [and] I'm not interested in being involved." Davis said "the Court's institutional integrity and procedures have been smeared–all in the name of politics [and that] this unfortunate situation is a perfect example of why there should be no politics in the judiciary."[666] In a commentary in the *Charleston Daily Mail*, Charleston attorney Charles McElwee defended Justice Davis and attacked the charges that the Opinion was a "bogus opinion." McElwee said, "In my view, Justices Starcher, McGraw, and Albright, in their actions in the *Arbaugh* case, have gone a long way towards diminishing the legitimacy of the Court."[667] McElwee, Benjamin's former boss, became a law clerk to Justice Benjamin after the election.

Tony Arbaugh, the subject of the onslaught of campaign commercials attacking Warren as being soft on crime, pled guilty, when he was fourteen-years-old, to sexually assaulting his younger brother and in exchange for his plea, prosecutors dropped other charges that he assaulted three siblings, two cousins, two nephews, and two other children.[668] Bill Sadler, Mercer County's elected prosecuting attorney and head of the West Virginia Prosecuting Attorneys' Association, disputed the allegations that Warren was soft on crime.[669] Sadler said, "I don't think he's a danger to law enforcement [and] as far as criminal decisions, I think he's in the middle of the road."[670] Warren's successor as Wyoming County Prosecutor, G. Todd Houck, who served under him before he was elected to the Supreme Court, said, "This has just been politicians foaming at the mouth without facts. It's just a smear campaign." Houck added, "I know what his priorities are [and he is] tough on crime."[671] Conversely, Wood County Prosecutor Ginny Conley said she was stunned by the news article that indicated other prosecutors believed Justice McGraw was tough on crime. Conley said, "I perceive McGraw as being a leader in the pro-defense decisions that are coming out of the Supreme Court."[672]

McGraw said the controversy with regard to the case was "masterminded by coal companies like Massey Energy Co. that want to control the high court but know he won't bow to them."[673] Just weeks prior to the election it was learned that Don Blankenship, the chief executive officer of Massey Energy Co., gave at least $1.7 million to a group called "And for the Sake of the Kids" designed to oust Warren from the Court. The group spent approximately $2.4 million on a series of ads calling McGraw soft on crime for voting to give Arbaugh another chance at probation. Blankenship said he financed the group because "without a change in the Supreme Court, businesses will continue to avoid West Virginia" and the State's job shortage would continue.[674]

The group collected $2.5 million from twelve donors between August 20, 2004 and September 30, 2004. Most of the donors were executives in coal operations, like Jenmar Corporation in Pennsylvania and Nelson Brothers in Alabama. Nearly a week after the election Blankenship said he ended up spending approximately $3.5 million of his own money to defeat McGraw.[675] It was also learned that And for the Sake of the Kids had raised more than $3.6 million by the end of the November election, with Blankenship contributing approximately $2.5 million; a group of physicians based in Wheeling, West Virginia, contributing $745,000; the West Virginia Coal Association contributing $223,000; with the remainder of contributions coming from eighteen smaller contributors, most of whom were tied to the coal industry.[676]

Steve White, the director of the Affiliated Construction Trades Foundation said, "People don't spend $5 million or $10 million for nothing, and they don't do it for altruistic reasons."[677] The campaign of McGraw's Republican challenger, Brent Benjamin, said Blankenship's huge contributions would not sway his decisions on the Court if he were elected. Campaign spokesman Steve Cohen said, "Brent Benjamin has been very clear that when he is on the Supreme Court, justice will not be for sale . . . he is running to bring an end to special interest justice on the Supreme Court."[678] Benjamin added, "I think it's unfortunate that our system has caused people to be so jaded as to believe that justices approach cases in a biased manner, and I think that's certainly something I'm looking forward to trying to change."[679]

According to the *Charleston Gazette*, "Under [Blankenship's] leadership, the company's mining subsidiaries have been cited repeatedly for dumping coal waste into streams and violating other environmental laws." The *Gazette* further said Massey was "fighting a number of lawsuits that could end up in front of the Supreme Court in the next few years, including workers' compensation claims, multimillion-dollar jury verdicts and a massive class-action suit accusing Massey of using mining practices that add to Southern West Virginia's flooding problems."[680] Specifically, *Gazette* reporter Paul J. Nyden said Massey Energy "may soon appeal to the State Supreme Court, asking it to review a $50 million verdict Hugh Caperton won in August 2002 in Boone Circuit Court stating that Massey illegally forced his coal companies out of business in Virginia. With interest, the verdict is now worth about $60 million."[681]

Conversely, Blankenship compared his political giving to a charitable enterprise and said, "Over the years, I and the companies for which I worked have donated millions to West Virginia charities, however, I decided this summer that the most productive donation I could make to my fellow West Virginians was to help defeat Warren McGraw."[682] At the time, Blankenship had already spent a dollar for every West Virginian in an effort to oust Warren. The *Charleston Daily Mail* illustrated that: "Put another way, that's an investment of about $142,000 for every year of the twelve-year court term. Or it's $388 for every day of every year of that term.[683] The figures discussed by the *Daily Mail* were based on the assumption that Blankenship would only spend $1.7 million instead of the $3.5 million he ended up spending by the end of the campaign.

Further defending the group's advertisements, Blankenship, a Williamson, West Virginia resident, said, "We just thought we'd give it a shot and see what happened. If you make the public aware of just how corrupt and deceitful [the McGraw Brothers have] been, maybe the public will vote for the alternative. I'm not sure they will." Blankenship said McGraw's campaign had been inconsistent in answering the claims against it. For instance, Blankenship said, "First, they said they released [Arbaugh] but didn't allow him to go into a high school. Then they went to the fact that he was a role model and started to say every young man deserves a chance. Then they said everyone, including McGraw, is allowed one mistake. Then they just said he didn't release him. [These are] the most incredible lies I've ever seen."[684]

Warren's campaign manager, Andy Gallagher, was quoted in *Roll Call* magazine as saying the television ads about the Justice's decision in the controversial case involving a child molester are a distraction as "[t]hey focus on one dumb shit issue, a sexy issue. They blew past everything and rely on that one case." With regard to Blankenship's then-$1.7 million expenditure against McGraw, Gallagher said, "I've been licking people's feet to get money, and then one guy spends $1.7 million dollars. It's disgraceful. They're unabashedly trying to tell West Virginians how to vote." The political ads that hammered McGraw from groups like And for the Sake of the Kids were countered by an organization funded by plaintiff's lawyers called West Virginia Consumers for Justice, which spent more than $1 million against Benjamin including ads painting him as a puppet of big business who was lying about McGraw's record.[685]

George Carenbauer, a lawyer with Steptoe and Johnson in Charleston, West Virginia, who was a former State Chairman of the West Virginia Democratic Party and former aide to both United States Senators Jay Rockefeller and Robert C. Byrd, was criticized by State Democrats for providing legal assistance to the group And for the Sake of the Kids. Carenbauer said, "As a West Virginian and a Democrat, I believe we need good judges in West Virginia as well." Carenbauer had tangled with McGraw years earlier when he filed the lawsuit to challenge Justice McGraw's 2000 candidacy for a vacancy on the Supreme Court even though his term of office didn't end until 2004. Carenbauer said McGraw was wrong and he challenged him after the State Supreme Court said "his attempted run had impaired the court's ability to function." Carenbauer explained: "I had brought that case entirely on my own and at my own expense, purely because Justice McGraw's actions threatened the integrity of the judiciary."[686]  Nearly a year after the election, an anonymous cartoon was sent to people who assisted the Benjamin campaign, such as campaign manager Rob Capehart, who called the cartoon a threat and sent it to the United States Attorney for the Northern District of West Virginia.  The picture portrayed Tony Arbaugh hanging on a cross with those associated with the campaign, including Capehart, Benjamin, Blankenship, and Carenbauer, taking part in the crucifixion.

In response to the charge against McGraw that he voted to make a convicted sex offender a janitor at a school, an ad surfaced accusing Benjamin's law office of handling a case involving a child sex offender from Fayette County, West Virginia.  Benjamin's employer at the time, Robinson & McElwee, was defending a Pennsylvania school system being sued by a plaintiff who alleged the school system hushed the resignation of a principal who had been accused of molesting children.  According to the *Charleston Gazette*, "the man later became a principal at a Fayette County school, where he was accused of drugging and molesting two children, one of whom died. The man is awaiting trial on murder charges. The surviving victim is suing over the incident."  Benjamin's campaign said he had no direct involvement in the case while Andy Gallagher said, "Benjamin is drawing a salary from the law firm that is defending far more despicable behavior than anything that occurred in the *Arbaugh* case. If he really stands for principle, let him resign the law firm and show us his ethics."[687]

Another political ad from the group West Virginia Consumers for Justice said Benjamin did not like it when politicians in courtrooms invoked the Bible. The advertisements focused on comments Benjamin made to a Beckley newspaper in response to Warren, who had quoted from scripture before the Beckley-Raleigh County Chamber of Commerce.  Benjamin said, "Personally, I have difficulty with politicians and with attorneys in courtrooms who quote the Bible. I don't think it's necessarily always a proper thing. In fact, generally it is never a proper thing to do. I think it's misusing the Bible."[688]  Warren's campaign also said Benjamin inappropriately handled a case in a class-action lawsuit over the diet drug cocktail fen-phen because Benjamin was listed as a plaintiff when the case was settled in 2002.  McGraw said, "I just find it inconceivable [and] frankly I want to tell you that being on both sides of a case would certainly cost most lawyers their license."[689]

Warren then questioned Benjamin's experience and qualifications to run for a seat on the Court where he hadn't even argued a case.  Benjamin responded that he had argued in front of the Supreme Court.  Benjamin later told the *Charleston*

*Gazette* editors in September 2004, as well as *MetroNews* radio commentator Hoppy Kercheval in October 2004, that he had argued one case before the West Virginia Supreme Court years earlier.[690] Following Benjamin's contention, the *Gazette* in October 2004 reviewed Court records and said Benjamin had not argued a single case before the Supreme Court in his twenty years of practicing law.[691] In response to the *Gazette* article, Benjamin, through a spokesman, Steve Cohen, said "if Benjamin says he argued one case before the High Court then that's gospel." Cohen asked, "Why would Benjamin have reason to lie about the issue?"[692] Benjamin later named a twenty-year-old case he said he had argued before the Court.[693]

Warren was also criticized for his comments in support of then-gubernatorial candidate Joe Manchin during the campaign. The *Logan Banner* reported that Warren spoke to political crowds and even cited the State Code of Judicial Conduct which says judicial candidates "shall not publicly endorse or publicly oppose another candidate for public office." Just after speaking those words in Williamson, West Virginia, Warren added, "If I were going to do so, I'd be endorsing Joe Manchin for Governor of West Virginia." During another political event in the City of Kermit, Warren told a crowd, "We know that this is a part of West Virginia which needs attention, and we know that Joe Manchin will give us that attention." Later, in the City of Delbarton, Warren referred to Manchin as "the next Governor." In response to the allegation that he endorsed Manchin for Governor, Warren's spokesman replied, "He obviously didn't endorse anybody. It's a ridiculous suggestion." The *Charleston Daily Mail* wrote: "This is conduct unbecoming a municipal court judge, let alone a Justice of the State Supreme Court. Once again, McGraw's actions have strained the judiciary. Judges are supposed to be referees, not players. It is time McGraw stopped acting like a Democratic ward heeler and began acting like a judge."[694]

Another campaign advertisement attacking Warren also focused on his brother, Attorney General Darrell McGraw. The advertisement featured cartoonish music and portraits of the McGraw brothers side by side while a narrator said,

> Brothers Warren and Darrell McGraw say they have family values. Their values? Justice McGraw refused to step down when the court heard a case benefitting his brother. Then Attorney General McGraw spent public money to promote the family name. Over $100,000 on pens and trinkets. . . another $600,000 on TV ads. That's your money they're wasting. The McGraws. Supporting their family values with your family's money.

Yet another campaign commercial attacking Warren described him as "too rad-ical for our families," while another commercial claimed that when a company wanted to fire "a cocaine-using safety director," Warren instead agreed to give the man eight years in salary.[695]

Warren argued that with regard to the negative advertisements against him, the group And for the Sake of the Kids was too closely tied to the cam-paign of his opponent Benjamin which would be a violation of election law. Andy Gallagher said, "You have to suspend disbelief to believe there is not coordination between the two [campaigns]." However, on the other side, Rob Capehart said, "Under the law, we're not allowed to comment on what [the independent campaign against McGraw] is doing. We can't even say that's good or that's bad. We're in a situation where the candidates don't have any control over what's said about themselves." Carl Hubbard, the organizer of And for the Sake of the Kids, said, "We have absolutely no connection to the Benjamin for Supreme Court committee or the Republican Party." Hubbard added, "Our efforts are not coordinated [and] we cannot nor do we wish to be authorized by Benjamin for Supreme Court." Nonetheless, both groups attacked Warren on the same issues while And for the Sake of the Kids bought billboards and distributed signs throughout the State asking: "Who is Brent Benjamin?"[696]

It was later reported that the organizer and founder of And for the Sake of the Kids, Carl Hubbard, had a criminal record of his own even though his group depicted McGraw as being "soft on crime" and a "radical" who did not support family values. Hubbard, the Vice President of a Beckley coal mining equipment company, had years earlier pled guilty to two counts of destruction of property, three counts of public intoxication, and two counts of battery dur-ing a period between 1977 and 1981 in the Mercer County Magistrate Court. McGraw's campaign manager Andy Gallagher said Hubbard had no business criticizing McGraw and, "We believe it is important for the public to know the criminal past of a man who sets himself up as a judge over the decency of Justice McGraw." Hubbard responded, saying, "While it is true I was rather rambunctious in my younger days, I quickly recognized the error of my ways and fortunately returned to the teachings of my upbringing. Those minor charges, dated some twenty-seven years ago, stemmed from my youthful zeal to defend my person and my family. They are long since yesterday's busi-ness."[697]

The Brennan Center for Justice at New York University School of Law named the 2004 race between McGraw and Benjamin the "nastiest in the nation." In an October 6, 2004, report, the Brennan Center explained:

"Benjamin has been running an ad that begins: 'According to the prosecutors, he sexually molested multiple West Virginia children.' It is not until well into the ad that it becomes clear that Benjamin is not talking about his opponent, but rather someone whose case was decided by the Supreme Court during McGraw's term."[698] The Brennan Center's report also said the McGraw-Benjamin race was the most expensive judicial campaign in the country.[699] In addition to the costly General Election, during the 2004 Democratic Primary, McGraw spent $599,060, compared to his opponent, Jim Rowe, a Greenbrier County circuit judge and former legislator, who spent $811,729.[700]

Perhaps with the Brennan Center's report in mind, nearly two weeks prior to the 2004 General Election, the West Virginia State Bar's Board of Governors unanimously passed a resolution reminding the candidates of the eth-ical rules that govern judicial campaigns. "The nature and tenor of some of the campaigning and advertising for both candidates neither enhances the status of the judiciary nor the credibility of our system with the public at large," the res-olution said. The resolution also explained that the rules governing lawyers bar them from making false or reckless statements "concerning the qualifications or integrity of a judge . . . or of a candidate for election or appointment to judicial or legal office." State Bar President Charles Love said, "The Bar generally was unhappy with the manner in which the race has been conducted [and] the con-cern was that both candidates were transgressing the strictures of the rules and canons."[701]

The millions of dollars spent against McGraw resulted in Benjamin receiving 376,691 votes compared to Warren's 329,822. With regard to the estimated $3.5 million spent by Blankenship on his behalf, Benjamin asserted, "I'm not bought by anybody." Those millions spent not only bought television and radio advertisements, but also paid for direct mail and recorded telephone calls to defeat Warren. Following his election night defeat, Warren's son Randolph gave a speech at the Charleston Marriott and said, "It's become impossible for ordinary people to compete against millions of dollars. Let a call go out for election reform. Without it, the people of West Virginia will be shut out."[702] Soon after the election, the *Charleston Gazette* reported that Justice Starcher posted a cartoon on the outside of his office door portraying Benjamin being delivered to the Supreme Court in a large box marked, "cour-tesy of $3.5 million from Massey Coal and other coal interests."[703]

A couple of weeks after the election, on November 22, 2004, Warren filed a lawsuit against Blankenship, George E. Carenbauer, and WOWK-TV, owned by West Virginia Media Holdings, headed by Bray Cary. McGraw's lawyer, former State Supreme Court Justice Richard Neely, said the lawsuit raised major national issues about the legality of airing libelous and false statements on television during political campaigns and added that television station owners must be held financially liable for airing ads they know are "patently false and/or misleading" and are aired with malice. Neely added, "There is a temptation in political campaigns. Money will always defeat quality. Whoever has the money can always find some issue to defeat quality officeholders." Neely said the use of the name And for the Sake of the Kids implied the people paying for the campaign ads "were parents concerned with the safety of their children rather than coal executives, business executives and their paid minions." Neely said, "The inference from the advertisement is absolutely wrong, and it was maliciously published with an evil, wicked intent to destroy Justice McGraw."[704]

The *Charleston Gazette* reported that "the Center for Public Integrity, a Washington, D.C. research group that studies political contributions and expenditures, ranked And for the Sake of the Kids as the nation's fifth-largest fundraiser among all political groups involved in State elections [in 2004]."[705] West Virginia Citizens Against Lawsuit Abuse director Bill Bissett said the libel suit was predictable saying, "The voters spoke loudly during this election, and Justice McGraw lost by a significant amount. This lawsuit seems to suggest sour grapes with the outcome. These types of personal injury lawyers–their first response seems to always be to sue someone. That's what they've done."

In June of 2005, Don Blankenship and Massey Coal Company struck back by filing their own lawsuit and asking for more than $300 million in damages. Blankenship and Massey sued the United Mine Workers of America; Cecil Roberts, President of UMWA; West Virginia Consumers for Justice, an independent political group that was active in the 2004 election season; and Kenneth Perdue, chairman of West Virginia Consumers for Justice and President of the AFL-CIO. Blankenship, independent from Massey, also sued the *Charleston Gazette*. According to the lawsuit, "the coordinated release of false and defamatory statements about Massey Energy and Blankenship by the defendants . . . was without justification and constituted a conspiracy to damage the plaintiffs in their business and profession." The complaint said the defamatory statements "were undisputedly false and were made with actual malice because the defendants made their false statements with knowledge or reckless disregard that the statements were false." Blankenship said he was looking for the media, the union, and others to be responsible in what they say or print publicly. The $300 million in damages requested in the complaint was based on the company's loss in productivity and other business damages due to the purportedly false statements.[706]

JFK and Jackie campaigning in Charleston. (*courtesy Charleston Gazette and Daily Mail*)

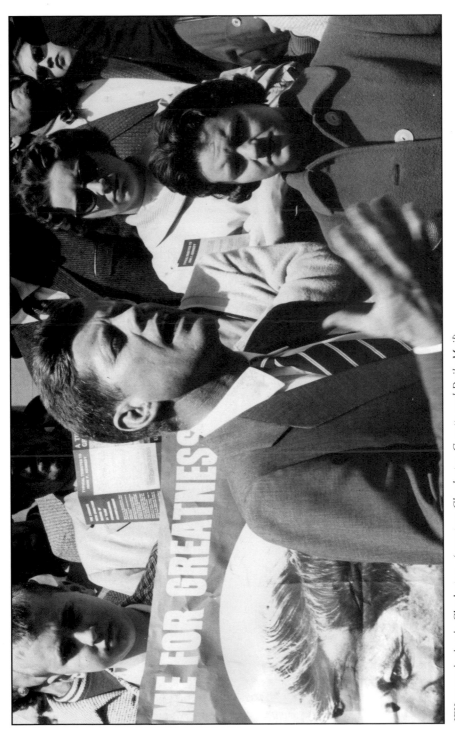

JFK campaigning in Charleston. *(courtesy Charleston Gazette and Daily Mail)*

Robert Kennedy campaigning for his brother in southern West Virginia in 1960. (*courtesy Charleston Gazette and Daily Mail*)

JFK campaigning in Logan County, West Virginia. Far left, U.S. Senator Jennings Randolph, center, State Democratic Chairman, later Governor, Hulett C. Smith. (*courtesy Charleston Gazette and Daily Mail*)

JFK campaigning in West Virginia. Far left, Charlie Peters, former West Virginia Delegate and current editor of *The Washington Monthly*. (*courtesy Charleston Gazette and Daily Mail*)

Campaigning in West Virginia on behalf of JFK, left to right: Governor Wally Barron, U.S. Senator Jennings Randolph, U.S. Senator Claiborne Pell (D-RI), the namesake for the Pell Grant, State Democratic Chairman Hulett C. Smith, U.S. Senator Robert C. Byrd, and future West Virginia Supreme Court Justice Jim Sprouse. (*courtesy Charleston Gazette and Daily Mail*)

Franklin D. Roosevelt, Jr. campaigning with JFK in West Virginia in 1960. In the center is State Senator Ward Wylie, Kennedy's West Virginia Campaign Chairman. (*courtesy Charleston Gazette and Daily Mail*)

JFK speaks to supporters at the Kanawha Hotel following his resounding victory in the May 10, 1960, West Virginia Primary. Kennedy told the crowd, "I am in debt to the people of West Virginia. I believe now that you have made it possible for me to be nominated for President." (*courtesy Charleston Gazette and Daily Mail*)

Kennedy family portrait, November 9, 1960–Standing from left, are, Robert Kennedy's wife Ethel, Steve Smith and wife Jean Kennedy, then President-elect Kennedy, Robert F. Kennedy, daughter Patricia Lawford, Sargent Shriver, Ted Kennedy's wife Joan, and Peter Lawford. In foreground, from left, are daughter Eunice Shriver, Joseph P. Kennedy with wife Rose seated in front of him, John Kennedy's wife Jackie, and Ted Kennedy. *(courtesy Charleston Gazette and Daily Mail/AP Wire)*

JFK's father, Joseph P. Kennedy.
(*courtesy Charleston Gazette and Daily Mail*)

President Harry S. Truman campaigns at the Charleston Municipal Auditorium in October 1948.
(*courtesy Charleston Gazette and Daily Mail*)

President JFK with Governor Wally Barron at the State Capitol, June 20, 1963, to celebrate the State's centennial. Five months later Kennedy was killed in Dallas, Texas. (*courtesy Charleston Gazette and Daily Mail*)

From left, U.S. Congressman Jennings Randolph, President Franklin D. Roosevelt, Governor H. Guy Kump, U.S. Senator Matthew M. Neely, and Attorney General and future Governor Homer A. Holt during Roosevelt's visit to Thomas, West Virginia on October 1, 1936. (*courtesy Charleston Gazette and Daily Mail*)

U.S. Senator Edward M. "Ted" Kennedy (D-MA) and Allen H. Loughry II in Logan County in 2000. (*photo by Justice Warren McGraw*)

Former U.S. Congressman Joseph Kennedy (D-MA), the eldest son of Robert F. Kennedy. (*courtesy Charleston Gazette and Daily Mail*)

Congressman Patrick Kennedy (D-RI), son of Senator Ted Kennedy, with Allen H. Loughry II in Charleston, West Virginia in 2000.

Claude "Big Daddy" Ellis, Logan County political king-pin, outside his Smoke House Restaurant on Stratton Street in downtown Logan in the 1970s. During the 1960 Primary Election, JFK's mother, Rose Kennedy, who campaigned for her son in southern West Virginia, frequently ate her meals at the Smoke House Restaurant. (*courtesy Logan Banner*)

Raymond "Cathead" Chafin, whose organization originally backed Hubert Humphrey for the 1960 Democratic Presidential Primary, switched its support to JFK after receiving $35,000 in cash from the Kennedy campaign to "buy" votes. (*courtesy Logan Banner*)

Francis H. Pierpont was the only Governor of the Reorganized Government of Virginia, which was initially located in Wheeling, present-day West Virginia. His government was recognized by President Lincoln as the "legitimate" government of Virginia during the Civil War following Virginia's decision to secede. Although he is known today as the "Father of West Virginia," Pierpont himself never actually became the Governor of his home State. In fact, after West Virginia's 1863 admission as a state to the Union, and its choice of Arthur I. Boreman as first Governor, Pierpont continued to serve as the Governor of the "Restored," or "Reorganized," Government of Virginia. Then, following the conclusion of the Civil War, he remained the Governor of Virginia until 1868, at which time he was replaced by a military commander. Following his stint as Virginia's Governor, Pierpont returned to his law practice in West Virginia and in 1870 served one term in the State Legislature. (*courtesy Charleston Gazette and Daily Mail*)

Arthur Ingram Boreman, the first Governor of West Virginia, 1863-1869. At the onset of the Civil War, Boreman presided over the Second Wheeling Convention, which formed the Reorganized Government of Virginia. While President of the Convention, Boreman declared, "We are deter- mined to live under a State Government in the United States of America and under the Constitution of the United States." (*courtesy Charleston Gazette and Daily Mail*)

Devil Anse Hatfield, patriarch of the Hatfield Clan. (*courtesy Charleston Gazette and Daily Mail*)

The Hatfield Clan. (*courtesy Charleston Gazette and Daily Mail*)

The Hatfields. In front, Tennis Hatfield and Willis Hatfield. Center, Devil Anse Hatfield. In back from left to right, Ock Damron, Elias Hatfield, Troy Hatfield, Joe Hatfield, Cap Hatfield, and W.B. Borden. In the doorway in back, Rose Hatfield and Louvicey Hatfield (Devil Anse's Wife). (*courtesy Charleston Gazette and Daily Mail*)

Devil Anse Hatfield proudly holding his gun. (*courtesy Charleston Gazette and Daily Mail*)

A young Randolph McCoy, patriarch of the McCoy Clan. (*courtesy Pikeville-Pike County Tourism Commission*)

An older Randolph McCoy. (*courtesy Pikeville-Pike County Tourism Commission*)

Asa Harmon McCoy. (*courtesy Pikeville-Pike County Tourism Commission*)

Roseanna McCoy, daughter of Randolph McCoy. (*courtesy Pikeville-Pike County Tourism Commission*)

Johnson "Johnse" Hatfield, son of Devil Anse Hatfield. (*courtesy Pikeville-Pike County Tourism Commission*)

"Big" Sam McCoy. (*courtesy Pikeville-Pike County Tourism Commission*)

Sheriff William Harmon Maynard and wife Arminta Rebecca Leslie. (*courtesy Vickie Lawrence Tryon*)

"Mother" Mary Harris Jones, an activist for labor union issues. This "Miners' Angel" was especially well-known for her work with, and as organizer for, the United Mine Workers. (*courtesy The Register-Herald*)

Mother Jones with President Calvin Coolidge. (*Library of Congress*)

Mother Jones. (*courtesy Logan Banner*)

Judge John Jay "Iron Judge" Jackson Jr. (1824-1907), who served as a Federal Judge appointed by President Abraham Lincoln. Among those most notable to appear in front of the "Iron Judge" were Devil Anse Hatfield and Mother Jones.

"Smiling" Sid Hatfield, who battled the Baldwin-Felts Detective Agency culminating in the bloody Matewan Massacre. (*courtesy Charleston Gazette and Daily Mail*)

Mother Jones, Sid Hatfield, and others. (*courtesy Charleston Gazette and Daily Mail*)

William Ellsworth Glasscock, West Virginia's 13th Governor who served from 1909-1913. (*courtesy Charleston Gazette and Daily Mail*)

Dr. Henry Drury Hatfield, "Devil Anse" Hatfield's nephew, who served from 1913-1917 as West Virginia's 14th Governor. Governor Hatfield, who was also a medical doctor, personally examined Mother Jones while she was under house arrest and suffering from pneumonia in 1913. (*courtesy Charleston Gazette and Daily Mail*)

A young Democratic Logan County
Sheriff Don Chafin, who ruled with an
iron fist during the mine wars in southern West Virginia. (*courtesy Logan
Banner*)

Nathan Goff, Republican candidate for
Governor in the infamous 1888 election.
Both Goff and Aretas Brooks Fleming separately took the Oath of Office claiming they
had been victorious in the election. The
election contest, however, wasn't resolved
for more than one year when Fleming was
chosen by the Legislature as the State's 8th
Governor. (*courtesy Charleston Gazette and
Daily Mail*)

Sheriff Don Chafin. (*courtesy Logan
Banner*)

Robert S. Carr, President of the West Virginia
Senate who, during the controversial election
of 1888, demanded from sitting Governor
Wilson, as well as petitioned the West
Virginia Supreme Court, that he be immediately declared Governor claiming it was his
right and duty under the West Virginia
Constitution to act as Governor until the dispute was resolved. His request was denied.

Emanuel Willis Wilson (1885-1890), the only Governor to serve a five-year term, which was the result of the election contest between Aretas Brooks Fleming and Nathan Goff, Jr.

Democratic Governor Aretas Brooks Fleming. Fleming, who was declared the winner of the controversial 1888 election by a Democratic Legislature, served only a three-year term from 1890-1893, due to the lingering dispute with the election results.

Jacob Beeson Jackson. Elected Governor of West Virginia in 1880 and served from 1881-1885.

William MacCorkle, who served as West Virginia's 9th Governor from 1893-1897.

General Thomas Jonathan "Stonewall" Jackson.  (*courtesy Charleston Gazette and Daily Mail*)

W. Bernard Smith (D-Logan), member of the West Virginia State Senate and the infamous "Logan Five." He is the only West Virginia lawmaker to ever be expelled from the State Legislature. (*courtesy Charleston Gazette and Daily Mail*)

November 1974–W. Bernard Smith and Ernest "Red" Hager, two members of the "Logan Five" being arrested. (*courtesy Charleston Gazette and Daily Mail*)

Lincoln County Circuit Clerk Greg Stowers, who pled guilty in December 2005 to vote-buying in southern West Virginia. (*courtesy Lincoln Journal*)

September 1988–House of Delegates member and Logan businessman Robert McCormick leaving the federal courthouse with his attorney, Rudy DiTrapano (left), after pleading not guilty to extortion and tax evasion charges. (*courtesy Charleston Gazette and Daily Mail*)

Earl Tomblin (left) with attorney, Joseph Farrell (right). Tomblin, a former Logan County Sheriff, served two different prison sentences, both dealing with election violations. He is father to the current State Senate President Earl Ray Tomblin. (*courtesy Charleston Gazette and Daily Mail*)

238

Kasey Warner, fired as U.S. Attorney for the Southern District of West Virginia in 2005 by President George Bush. (*courtesy Charleston Gazette and Daily Mail*)

2004 State Republican Chairman Kris Warner. (*courtesy Charleston Gazette and Daily Mail*)

2004 gubernatorial candidate Monty Warner. (*courtesy Charleston Gazette and Daily Mail*)

January 13, 1969–Inauguration of Arch Moore as the 28th Governor of West Virginia, serving from 1969-1977. Moore was elected again in 1984 and became the 30th Governor, serving from 1985-1989. (*courtesy Charleston Gazette and Daily Mail*)

A not-so-tall Governor Arch Moore standing on a platform during a State of the State speech in the House of Delegates Chamber. (*courtesy Charleston Gazette and Daily Mail*)

Governor Arch Moore. (*courtesy Charleston Gazette and Daily Mail*)

Governor Arch Moore with State Treasurer A. James Manchin at a sporting event in January 1987. (*courtesy Charleston Gazette and Daily Mail*)

Governor Arch Moore at a press conference in October 1993 following his release from federal prison where he served time for his conviction of mail fraud, extortion, filing false tax returns, and obstruction of justice. (*courtesy Charleston Gazette and Daily Mail*)

Robert C. Byrd "fiddling" while campaigning for the U.S. House of Representatives in 1952. (*courtesy Charleston Gazette and Daily Mail*)

U.S. Senator Robert C. Byrd with his wife Erma in 1973. When Byrd and his high school sweetheart, a coal miner's daughter, Erma Ora James, were married in 1937, he worked as a produce boy in a coal company store. Byrd has said he remembers the day he brought an empty orange crate home and nailed it to the wall outside the kitchen window, which served as the couple's first refrigerator. (*courtesy Charleston Gazette and Daily Mail*)

Byrd with fellow U.S.
Senator Jennings
Randolph in 1977.
(*courtesy Charleston
Gazette and Daily Mail*)

Byrd with Governor
Gaston Caperton.
(*courtesy Charleston
Gazette and Daily
Mail*)

A pensive Robert Byrd in 1982. (*courtesy Charleston Gazette and Daily Mail*)

Senator Byrd with Allen H. Loughry II and Kelly Swaim (now Loughry) at the Presidential Classroom in Washington, D.C., 1988.

Arch Moore and Jay Rockefeller at Jay's 1981 Inauguration. Former and future Governor Cecil Underwood seen in the background. (*courtesy Charleston Gazette and Daily Mail*)

248

John D. "Jay" Rockefeller IV, West Virginia's 29th Governor (1977-1985). Rockefeller is the great-grandson of oil tycoon John D. Rockefeller and the nephew of former New York Governor and United States Vice President Nelson Rockefeller. (*courtesy Charleston Gazette and Daily Mail*)

Washington, D.C., January 15, 1985–Senator Byrd meets with Senator-elect Jay Rockefeller prior to his swearing in ceremony on Capitol Hill. (*courtesy Charleston Gazette and Daily Mail*)

State Senator Bob Wise and State Senator Warren McGraw at Rockefeller's 1981 State of the State speech in the House of Delegates Chamber. (*courtesy Charleston Gazette and Daily Mail*)

In 1994, Senator Rockefeller with Gaston Caperton, West Virginia's 31st Governor who served from 1989-1997. Current U.S. District Judge, then-Speaker of the House, Chuck Chambers, is seen at the left of photo. (*courtesy Charleston Gazette and Daily Mail*)

Attorney General Darrell V. McGraw, Jr. *(courtesy Charleston Gazette and Daily Mail)*

Senate President Warren McGraw. *(courtesy Charleston Gazette and Daily Mail)*

West Virginia Supreme Court Justice Darrell McGraw. (*courtesy Charleston Gazette and Daily Mail*)

West Virginia Supreme Court Justice Warren McGraw. (*courtesy Charleston Gazette and Daily Mail*)

These magnets and hundreds of thousands like them are commonly handed out during numerous parades and public functions throughout the State. The Attorney General's Office frequently pays school children to distribute the magnets during parades.

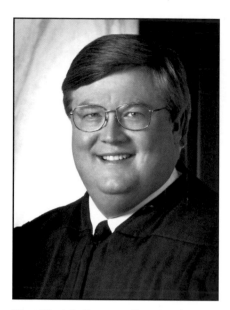

West Virginia Supreme Court Justice Brent Benjamin. (*courtesy West Virginia Supreme Court*)

Massey Energy Company Chairman and CEO, Don Blankinship. (*courtesy Don Blankenship*)

A newspaper comic charging that Massey Energy Company and special interest groups funded Brent Benjamin's 2004 State Supreme Court campaign. (*courtesy Roane County Reporter/Neil Grahame*)

Circuit Judge Joseph Troisi, the notorious nose-biting judge, answering reporters' questions as he left the federal courthouse in Clarksburg, West Virginia. (*courtesy Ritchie Gazette*)

Judge John Hey, Kanawha County Circuit Judge for seventeen years, who was prosecuted on sexual assault charges that led to his 1995 guilty plea to two counts of misdemeanor battery against two female court employees. (*courtesy Charleston Gazette and Daily Mail*)

254

West Virginia Supreme Court Justice Richard Neely, who served from 1973 until 1995. (*courtesy Charleston Gazette and Daily Mail*)

Circuit Judge James "Ned" Grubb, who was convicted in 1992 of criminal felonies for buying and selling the Logan County elections. (*courtesy Charleston Gazette and Daily Mail*)

West Virginia Supreme Court Justice Elliott "Spike" Maynard. Prior to his 1996 election to the Supreme Court, Maynard served as a circuit judge from 1981 until 1996, and a prosecuting attorney from 1974 until 1981, both in Mingo County. Years earlier, after joining the United States Air Force in 1961, Maynard was attached to a reconnaissance group during the Cuban Missile Crisis. (*courtesy West Virginia Supreme Court*)

2005 West Virginia Supreme Court. Seated, left to right, Justice Robin Davis, Chief Justice Joseph Albright, Justice Larry Starcher, standing, left to right, Justice Elliott Maynard and Justice Brent Benjamin. (*courtesy West Virginia Supreme Court*)

Governor William Wallace "Wally" Barron, who after serving as West Virginia's 26th Governor, was found guilty of jury tampering and sentenced to prison. The charges related to his 1968 trial in which he was indicted for bribery and found not guilty due to a $25,000 payment from Barron's wife, Opal, to the jury foreman's wife. (*courtesy Charleston Gazette and Daily Mail*)

February 15, 1961–Left, President John F. Kennedy, center, Governor Wally Barron, right, Barron Aide Curtis Trent, in the Oval Office. Both Barron and Trent later served prison sentences. (*JFK Library, Boston*)

President John F. Kennedy and Governor Wally Barron at the State Capitol during West Virginia's June 20, 1963, centennial celebration. (*courtesy Charleston Gazette and Daily Mail*)

Governor Wally Barron in the Governor's Office. (*courtesy Charleston Gazette and Daily Mail*)

The Governor with his wife Opal Barron. (*courtesy Charleston Gazette and Daily Mail*)

Governor Barron with his dog, Bozo, during his 1961 inaugural parade. (*courtesy Charleston Gazette and Daily Mail*)

Wally Barron with Cecil Underwood and his wife, Hovah Underwood. (*courtesy Charleston Gazette and Daily Mail*)

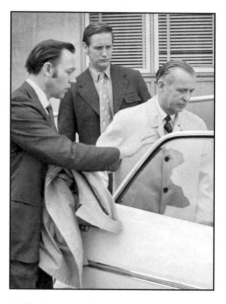

Governor Barron and Commissioner of Department of Commerce, later Governor, Hulett C. Smith. (*courtesy Charleston Gazette and Daily Mail*)

Wally Barron being arrested. (*courtesy Charleston Gazette and Daily Mail*)

Left, U.S. Congressman Ken Hechler, center, Governor Edmund G. "Pat" Brown (D-CA), right, Governor Wally Barron at a White House event. (*White House Official Photo*)

Attorney General C. Donald Robertson. (*courtesy Charleston Gazette and Daily Mail*)

State Treasurer John H. Kelly, who pled guilty to a mail fraud charge arising out of a bribery scheme to defraud the State. (*courtesy Charleston Gazette and Daily Mail*)

Attorney General C. Donald Robertson, who pled guilty to two of five federal charges involving bribes paid by a contractor who was bidding on public housing construction projects. (*courtesy Charleston Gazette and Daily Mail*)

State Senator Randy Schoonover, who was charged and later convicted of taking money from a prominent businessman who sought business on the West Virginia Turnpike. (*courtesy Clay County Free Press*)

Kanawha County Prosecuting Attorney Bill Charnock. (*courtesy Charleston Gazette and Daily Mail*)

Attorney General Charlie Brown was forced to resign in 1989 after allegations surfaced with regard to a plan to give a $50,000 payment to his pregnant secretary for an abortion and to keep the situation quiet. (*courtesy Charleston Gazette and Daily Mail*)

William Edward ReBrook, III, former attorney for the West Virginia Lottery Commission. (*courtesy Charleston Gazette and Daily Mail*)

Elton "Butch" Bryan, former Director of the West Virginia Lottery, convicted, along with William Edward ReBrook, III, then-attorney for the Lottery Commission, of corruption in their illegal activities involving the State Lottery. (*courtesy Charleston Gazette and Daily Mail*)

State Senator Majority Leader Si Boettner, convicted of tax evasion surrounding the slew of gambling-related convictions in the 1980s in the State Legislature. (*courtesy Charleston Gazette and Daily Mail*)

William "Bill" T. Ellis, a limited partner in Tri-State Greyhound Park Incorporated, a West Virginia corporation that conducted betting on greyhound races, was convicted in 1990 of extortion, conspiracy, racketeering, and obstruction of justice. He was sentenced to ninety months in federal prison and fined $50,000. (*courtesy Charleston Gazette and Daily Mail*)

January 14, 1988, Delegates Joe Ferrell, Bob McCormick, and Bill Anderson in the House of Delegates Chamber. Both Ferrell and McCormick pled guilty to various election crimes. In his 1992 signed sworn affidavit as a part of his federal plea bargain, Ferrell promised never to seek public office again. Nonetheless, he ran for and was elected to the House of Delegates in 1998, where he continues to serve today. Anderson was implicated during Lincoln County Assessor Jerry Weaver's December 2005 guilty plea for his part in the ring of politicos who bribed voters in southern West Virginia. Weaver told the federal judge that years earlier he received $5,000 from then-House Speaker Pro Tempore Bill Anderson to buy votes. (*courtesy Charleston Gazette and Daily Mail*)

Former West Virginia Senate President Dan Tonkovich, convicted of federal racketeering and extortion charges. On September 14, 1989, he pled guilty to taking a casino company payoff to help a legislative bill designed to legalize gambling. (*courtesy Charleston Gazette and Daily Mail*)

Charleston July, 1989–former Senate President Dan Tonkovich with attorney James Lees leaving the federal courthouse after initially pleading not guilty to a six-count federal indictment. (*courtesy Charleston Gazette and Daily Mail*)

West Virginia Senate President and banker Larry Tucker went to prison twice to serve sentences on separate charges of extortion, once for lying to a grand jury investigating corruption in State government, and once for obstruction of justice. Also in photo, his wife Jean and lawyer Gary Collias. (*courtesy Charleston Gazette and Daily Mail*)

This bumper sticker was distributed as campaign paraphernalia by Phillip "Icky" Frye after he announced his candidacy for Governor in 2004.

Robert "Bob" Ellsworth Wise, Governor of West Virginia from 2001-2005. *(courtesy Charleston Gazette and Daily Mail)*

December 1979–Delegate Clyde Richey found guilty of sexual assault of a minor by a Kanawha County Jury. Richey befriended the child through the Big Brothers Program. *(courtesy Charleston Gazette and Daily Mail)*

State Senate Minority Leader, Vic Sprouse (R-Kanawha). (*courtesy Charleston Gazette and Daily Mail*)

State Senate Majority Leader H. Truman Chafin (D-Mingo). (*courtesy Charleston Gazette and Daily Mail*)

Bob Graham, Wyoming County Council on Aging and All Care Home and Community Services Director, who was indicted on January 26, 2006, by a federal grand jury on twenty-one counts of embezzling, illegally transferring money, and filing false tax returns. Graham received compensation of $301,728 in 2002 and about $457,872 in 2003 even though the average senior director's salary in West Virginia was $42,000. (*courtesy The Register-Herald/Chuck Garvin*)

Delegate Jerry Mezzatesta (from right), lawyer Ben Bailey, and Mezzatesta's wife, Mary Lou, prior to the Mezzatestas entering their pleas of no contest to misdemeanor charges. (*courtesy Charleston Gazette and Daily Mail*)

August, 1990–Delegate Jerry Mezzatesta (D-Hampshire) was visited by nine year old Lenna Chambers as a morning session of the House of Delegates was about to begin. Lenna is the daughter of Chuck Chambers, then-House Speaker (D-Cabell). (*courtesy Charleston Gazette and Daily Mail*)

The Grim REAPer–A. James Manchin was appointed by Governor Arch Moore as head of the REAP (Rehabilitation Environmental Action Plan) program to help clear the State of junk cars, discarded appliances rolled over hills, illegal dumps, trashy creeks, and dilapidated buildings. Manchin was famous for saying, "Let us purge our proud peaks of the jumbled jungles of junkery." Manchin was posing as the Grim Reaper to symbolize the removal of the 31,000th junk car since the inception of the REAP program. (*courtesy Charleston Gazette and Daily Mail*)

"Hooray for Junk"–When the REAP program reached the 100,000th junk car collected, A. James Manchin sat atop the 1966 Pontiac convertible that had been painted blue and gold and hauled it through the streets of Charleston in a parade. (*courtesy Charleston Gazette and Daily Mail*)

A. James
Manchin.
(*courtesy
Charleston
Gazette and
Daily Mail*)

On July 9, 1989, Treasurer A. James Manchin, surrounded by family members, legal counsel, and employees, announces his decision to resign rather than face an impeachment trial after information surfaced about $279 million lost from a fund under his control. In spite of his impeachment, Manchin was elected in 1998 to the House of Delegates. (*courtesy Charleston Gazette and Daily Mail*)

272

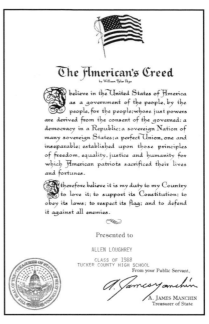

These certificates and others not pictured were presented to the author on separate occasions by A. James Manchin. During an eleven month period between 1981 and 1982, Secretary of State Manchin spent 42 percent of the total amount he was allotted by the West Virginia Legislature to run his entire office for the year on hundreds of thousands of trinkets. In doing research for this book, the author found that *every single person* he spoke with, who was similar in age and grew up in West Virginia, including his wife, had received multiple certificates or trinkets from A. James Manchin throughout the years, both while he was State Treasurer and Secretary of State.

This hat was mailed to the author by A. James Manchin at the State's expense.

All of West Virginia's governors are immediately placed on State maps as soon as they are inaugurated. Thousands of maps containing the former governor's pictures are then needlessly destroyed.

These are a few examples of trinkets given to the author's family members by West Virginia politicians.

Cecil Underwood being sworn in by James B. Riley, President of the State Supreme Court. (*courtesy Charleston Gazette and Daily Mail*)

Underwood and Arch Moore. (*courtesy Charleston Gazette and Daily Mail*)

September 1960 in Huntington, Governor Underwood and Attorney General Wally Barron at the West Virginia Press Association's Annual Convention. (*courtesy Charleston Gazette and Daily Mail*)

Governor Underwood greets New York Governor, later U.S. Vice President, Nelson Rockefeller, who was arriving by plane at White Sulphur Springs, West Virginia for a two-day meeting of the Council of State Governments. (*courtesy Charleston Gazette and Daily Mail*)

As temporary Chairman for the Republican Convention, Governor Underwood visits Chicago in July 1960 with his wife Hovah. (*courtesy Charleston Gazette and Daily Mail*)

The Underwood Family in the Governor's Mansion. (*courtesy Charleston Gazette and Daily Mail*)

Inauguration Day–Governor-elect Underwood with former Governor Bill Marland.
(*courtesy Charleston Gazette and Daily Mail*)

A Long Way from the Governor's Mansion–Bill Marland, Governor of West Virginia
from 1953-1957, seen here in 1965 working as a Chicago cabdriver. (*courtesy
Goldenseal/AP Wide World Photo*s)

March 1997 in Huntington, West Virginia–Vice President Al Gore meets with Governor Underwood, Congressman Bob Wise, Otis Cox of the Department of Public Safety, and others to discuss recent flooding in West Virginia. (*courtesy Charleston Gazette and Daily Mail*)

Governor Underwood and Allen H. Loughry II at the Governor's Mansion in 2000. (*courtesy West Virginia Governor's Office/Steven Rotsch*)

State Senate President Earl Ray Tomblin (D-Logan). *(courtesy Charleston Gazette and Daily Mail)*

Speaker of the House of Delegates Robert "Bob" Kiss (D-Raleigh). *(courtesy Charleston Gazette and Daily Mail)*

U.S. Congresswoman Shelley Moore Capito, daughter of former Governor Arch A. Moore, Jr. Capito and two-time-unsuccessful challenger Jim Humphreys, seen below, elevated spending in West Virginia's Congressional races to new heights. In 2000, the election between Capito and Humphreys was the third most expensive House of Representatives race in the country out of all 435 congressional elections that year. The 2002 Capito/Humphreys match-up continued the high-dollar trend and was the most expensive House race in the nation. Humphreys had the benefit of spending nearly $7 million of his personal wealth in the 2000 race and spending $7.7 million in 2002. (*courtesy Charleston Gazette and Daily Mail*)

State Senator Truman Chafin (D-Mingo) with State Senator Jim Humphreys (D-Kanawha) as they confer on a bill during the regular session of the Legislature in 1987. (*courtesy Charleston Gazette and Daily Mail*)

Current Governor Joe Manchin, III, West Virginia's 34th Governor. (*courtesy Charleston Gazette and Daily Mail*)

During an October 12, 1992, news conference, gubernatorial hopeful Charlotte Pritt announced her write-in campaign for Governor after being defeated in the Primary Election earlier that year by Governor Gaston Caperton. (*courtesy Charleston Gazette and Daily Mail*)

Former U.S. Congressman and Secretary of State Ken Hechler. (*courtesy Charleston Gazette and Daily Mail*)

Fred Zain, former head serologist of the State Police Crime Laboratory who falsified test results in as many as 134 cases from 1979 to 1989, resulting in several innocent people spending lengthy jail sentences for crimes they did not commit. (*courtesy Charleston Gazette and Daily Mail*)

March 1995, Marion County Courthouse, Fred Zain at trial. After two mistrials, the third trial of Zain was postponed indefinitely due to Zain's failing health. In spite of his false testimony in 134 criminal cases, he was never convicted of a crime. (*courtesy Charleston Gazette and Daily Mail*)

Governor Gaston Caperton "at home" in the Governor's Mansion in 1991, Communications Director Bob Brunner seen at right. (*courtesy Charleston Gazette and Daily Mail*)

Gaston Caperton before becoming Governor with the State Capitol in background as he sits at his office at McDonough Caperton Insurance Group (now Acordia). (*courtesy Charleston Gazette and Daily Mail*)

Scott Hovatter, grandfather of Allen H. Loughry II, talking with Governor Gaston Caperton during an event in Parsons, West Virginia. (*photo by Allen H. Loughry II*)

Governor Caperton and Allen H. Loughry II at a legislative bill signing ceremony in the Governor's reception room in 1992. (*courtesy West Virginia Governor's Office/Steven Rotsch*)

Governor Gaston Caperton in his office with Communications Director Bob Brunner (left) and Direct Aide Allen H. Loughry II (center). (*courtesy West Virginia Governor's Office/Steven Rotsch*)

Arnold Schwarzenegger, Allen H. Loughry II and Governor Caperton at a President's Council for Physical Fitness Event in Charleston, West Virginia. (*courtesy West Virginia Governor's Office/Steven Rotsch*)

President Bill Clinton and Allen H. Loughry II at the White House in 1996. (*White House Official Photo*)

Congressman Harley O. Staggers, Jr. and Special Assistant/Deputy Press Secretary Allen H. Loughry II at work in the U.S. Capitol.

U.S. Senator John McCain (R-AZ) in Barboursville, West Virginia speaking at a Veterans' Home in 2000. Governor Underwood seen to the right in the background. (*photo by Allen H. Loughry II*)

U.S. Senator John McCain and Allen H. Loughry II in Charleston, West Virginia in 2000.

Former Speaker of the West Virginia House of Delegates Lewis McManus, who served as a Delegate from 1965 until 1977, was Speaker from 1971 until 1977. He later served as President of the University of Charleston before becoming an Associate Vice President of Charles Ryan Associates in Charleston, West Virginia. Throughout his career, McManus demonstrated a long-time support of youth-oriented causes and a lifetime commitment to education and children. United States Senator Jay Rockefeller, who served one term in the House of Delegates with McManus, said Lew was "a giant in the political realm [and] a true statesman and a gentleman." (*courtesy Charleston Gazette and Daily Mail*)

State Senate President William Brotherton and State Speaker of the House of Delegates Lewis McManus in 1976. (*courtesy Charleston Gazette and Daily Mail*)

Allen H. Loughry II and wife, Kelly Loughry. This photo was taken in 2003 immediately after Loughry successfully completed the defense of his dissertation at The American University, Washington College of Law for the degree of Doctor of Juridical Science. His dissertation became the foundation for this book. (photo by *Linda Loughry*)

# CHAPTER ELEVEN

# "A Judicial Hellhole"

*Judge Grubb possessed substantial political power in Logan County and people
feared he might fabricate criminal charges or even attempt to have them killed.*

State Police Sergeant Marty Allen

Perhaps the most memorable controversy surrounding West Virginia's
judiciary is the so-called notorious nose-biting judge. It was June 26, 1997, when
Circuit Judge Joseph Troisi stepped down from the bench and bit off a piece of
the nose of William Witten, a twenty-nine-year-old defendant who was appearing
in the Circuit Court of Pleasants County. The incident began after Judge Troisi
denied Witten's request to reduce his post-conviction appeal bond following his
sentencing for two felony counts of breaking and entering.[707]  After Witten
uttered a derogatory remark about the judge to State Police Trooper Terry Nichols
as he was being led from the courtroom after the hearing, Troisi overheard the
remark and provoked the confrontation. "According to State Police spokesman
Captain Terry Snodgrass, the onlookers–including the trooper–were too shocked
to respond in time to stop the incident." After biting Witten, Troisi ordered him
to be sent for medical attention and began to adjudicate the next case before him
on the court's docket.

The *Ritchie Gazette* reported that the bite drew blood and removed a
piece of flesh from the tip of Witten's nose, which the judge then spat onto the
courtroom floor. "The incident occurred while a state trooper, a sheriff's deputy,
the prosecuting attorney and several lawyers and bystanders watched in shocked
disbelief as the incident unfolded."[708]  Moreover, "[n]o action was taken against
the judge following the attack, and witnesses stated that he calmly resumed court
while [Witten] was led bleeding from the courtroom. Police took Witten to get

medical treatment for the injury and then returned him to the Pleasants County Jail."

  According to Witten, he called the judge a "Fucking Asshole" as he was being led from the courtroom. Judge Troisi heard the remark and immediately stood and demanded that Witten return to the bench. Troisi yelled, "Bring Mr. Witten back here now!" Troisi then pointed to the area in front of the bench and ordered Witten, who assumed he was about to be found in contempt of court, to stand there. Troisi walked off the bench, unzipped his robe and "angrily" dropped it on the courtroom floor. The judge then taunted Witten, who said the judge "got in my face and backed me up against the bench." Then, "Troisi continued yelling at Witten, who said he stuffed his hands in his pockets and told the judge, 'You know I cannot touch you.'" Witten said Troisi then told him, "When you get out of the penitentiary, you look me up." Witten responded, "I'll make a point of it, Your Honor," as Troisi then "butted [him] two or three times with his chest, forcing [him] against the bench." Witten said Troisi "was trying to provoke me into hitting him." As Troisi snapped at him twice with his teeth, Witten "could hear his teeth clicking together." Witten said the bites "happened real fast [and] one of them caught my nose." "As Witten stood with blood running down his face, he heard the trooper say, 'Come on, Bill,'" and led Witten away from Troisi and the courtroom. After he bit Witten, Troisi told him twice to, "Do something about your nose," and then spat a piece of flesh from his mouth onto the courtroom floor. Witten said Judge Troisi then spat again, put on his robe, and returned to the bench. "On the bench, the judge spat yet a third time, and then called for the next case."[709]

  Troisi was first elected in 1992 to an eight-year term as judge of the Third Judicial Circuit serving Ritchie, Pleasants and Doddridge counties. Prior to the biting incident, he had been appointed by the State Supreme Court to handle a number of high-profile cases, including the embezzlement trial of Parkersburg Mayor Gene Knotts and the trial of Kanawha County Circuit Judge John Hey for sexual harassment. At the time of the biting, Troisi was a member of the Supreme Court's Judicial Investigation Commission, the panel which investigates charges of judicial misconduct.[710]

  Following the incident, Troisi *could have* faced a variety of charges stemming from the incident resulting in heavy monetary penalties and years in jail, including federal charges for violating the defendant's civil rights; state misdemeanor charges of assault and battery; a felony charge of malicious assault; administrative proceedings through the judicial investigation commission; and a civil suit for damages. On October 23, 1997, Troisi pleaded no contest to a misdemeanor battery charge and resigned from the bench. He also agreed to receive "psychological or psychiatric counseling and treatment for impulse and anger control."[711]

Prior to Troisi's sentencing, the Special Prosecutor against him was Kanawha County Prosecuting Attorney William Forbes, who argued Troisi should not lose his law license. Forbes said, "If they took the license away from every lawyer who committed a misdemeanor, none of us would have a license." Conversely, Disciplinary Counsel Sherri Goodman said Troisi's case was not that simple and added, "We're not talking about a traffic violation–this misdemeanor is a reflection on his ability to function properly in a court of law."[712] Troisi's personal attorney, Harry Deitzler, continued to defend his client's character stating, "Joe has never said that it was right, what he did. Regardless of what a small minority of lawyers have apparently said, this act was out of character for him." Goodman disagreed stating,

> My report outlining Judge Troisi's misconduct was not based on a small minority of lawyers. It was based on statements by lawyers from five counties, as well as court personnel, litigants, courthouse employees, and bystanders. It angers me that the judge continues to dismiss out of hand the seriousness of his conduct. If he doesn't see himself as having a problem other than that one incident (the Witten nose biting) then I question whether he will benefit from the required counseling.[713]

Following the disciplinary action against him, Troisi was allowed to keep his law license.[714] He agreed to accept a censure from the State Supreme Court and to pay more than $4,600 for the costs of the Judicial Hearing Board investigation and proceedings against him. The agreement did not place any restrictions on whether Troisi could be a candidate for political office in the future. After Troisi's agreement with the Judicial Hearing Board, Witten felt the punishment was not harsh enough and said, "I'm really disgusted. I still have a big mark on my nose. The doctors say it is permanent." Witten added, "If I had bitten the judge on the nose, they would have put me away for the rest of my life."[715]

On November 26, 1997, Troisi faced the charges against him in the circuit court. The former judge now stood as a defendant before Special Judge Arthur Recht, exactly five months after the incident, and was sentenced to just five days of confinement and one year of probation. He spent his five days in the Pleasants County Jail separated from the general jail population.[716] Judge Recht said, "This was the hardest part of the sentence. We cannot and we will not have two standards of justice." Recht then said he honestly didn't know if a five-day sentence was too much or too little, but "[i]t has to occur–to tell the community in which we live that we are a nation of laws." In response to the requirement of community service that was also part of the plea agreement, Recht told Troisi, "You are the type of man who will do community service without it being imposed. Your work with the Native American population was remarkable. The kind of work you must now do comes from within your own heart."[717]

Nonetheless, apparently five days behind bars for biting off part of Witten's nose, minimal fines imposed by the State Judicial Hearing Board, and the retention of his law license, was an insufficient deterrent to discourage Troisi from further hostility. After serving his five days in jail, Troisi confronted Pleasants County Deputy Circuit Clerk Ward Grose who had testified against him in the nose-biting incident. Troisi was then sent back to jail to finish a six-month suspended sentence after admitting he called Grose a liar and used other choice expletives in the St. Marys, West Virginia courthouse. Grose had filed a complaint claiming that Troisi insulted him, bumped his chest against him, and tried to keep him out of the courtroom. Troisi, however, was released from jail several weeks early and his lawyer, Harry Deitzler, said Troisi "was apparently a model prisoner and did everything he was told to do."[718]

With regard to criminals convicted of violent crimes, I always lean toward harsh sentences and strict punishment. It makes me sick when these criminal thugs, who often tie up the court docket wasting time and taxpayer money, walk away from the process with little to no punishment. Judge Troisi, however, was phenomenally out of bounds with his conduct. A judge in a courtroom is the voice of reason and the ultimate gatekeeper for justice. When judges break the law, the entire system fails. Moreover, when a judge bites the end off of a defendant's nose during court, scarring that person for a lifetime, and is only sentenced to five days in jail and even gets to keep his law license, there is something inherently wrong with that system. Even though Judge Recht said we can't have two standards of justice, unfortunately, West Virginia has always had two standards, one for politicians and another for the average person.

Troisi is just one more elected official whose outrageous conduct resulted in a jail sentence. Likewise, his five-day jail sentence was so minimal that it illustrates yet another example of no real accountability for a politician's actions. In fact, it was so lenient he immediately violated the conditions of his parole. Of all of the criminal politicians in West Virginia, the group that shatters the confidence of the people the most is a corrupt judiciary. It is essential that people have the absolute confidence in the integrity and impartiality of our system of justice. After all, they are the people elected to ensure that objectiveness and fairness prevails when other people break the law.  They are also the same people sending many of the executive and legislative branch elected officials to jail for their misgivings.  When the soundness of the judiciary is questioned, coupled with the corrupt activities of the other branches of government, how is the public ever to have any faith in State government?

Another intriguing figure in West Virginia's jurisprudence is former State Supreme Court Chief Justice Richard Neely.  Prior to being elected to the Court, Neely served as a law clerk to Richard Nixon in 1966 and also earned a Bronze Star for his service in Vietnam.  He was a member of the West Virginia House of Delegates in 1970 and served until his 1972 election to the Supreme Court.  During his twenty-two year tenure with the State Supreme Court, he received frequent headlines for his colorful language and sometimes questionable behavior.

On one occasion, Neely fired his government-paid Supreme Court secretary when she refused to continue babysitting his son.[719]  His secretary had babysat his infant son both in Neely's home and in her own home on at least eleven occasions, once for more than seven continuous days.  After telling Justice Neely she would be unable to continue babysitting "because it was affecting her health," he told her to look for another job because babysitting was a condition to her continued employment with the Court.[720]

A complaint was filed with the Judicial Hearing Board against Chief Justice Neely alleging he violated the Canons of the Judicial Code of Ethics by requiring his State-paid-for staff to perform personal services, including babysitting, as a condition of employment, and that he required his staff to be available on an around-the-clock basis.  After reviewing the case, the Board found that Justice Neely's "actions were not illegal, immoral, or unethical, as defined by the Judicial Code of Ethics."  On appeal, the State Supreme Court reversed the Board's decision and issued an admonition concerning Neely's conduct.[721]

Neely answered the charges against him by saying as a Justice of the Supreme Court he was on call twenty-four hours a day and it was necessary to have someone care for his son at times when he and his wife were away from the home.  "It is Justice Neely's position that utilization of a State-salaried secretary for this purpose promotes efficient administration of justice."  He also charged that his conduct was no different from previous Justices who assigned personal duties to their secretaries and staff, "including completing income tax returns and typing term papers for a Justice's children."  The Supreme Court, however, said, "No matter how arduous the duties of a Justice or judge may be, and how time-consuming, they must be performed with the help of the staff provided, and tasks of a personal nature remain personal responsibilities."  The admonition of Neely was the lightest sanction the Court could issue and amounted to nothing more than a warning.[722]

Aside from the babysitting issue, most of Neely's recognition stemmed from his eccentric comments. One such comment was in 1989 when he proclaimed that police cannot prevent crime and said, "It's time for citizens like you and me to go home and get out our baseball bats" to attack drug dealers. In 1990, Neely said, he "wouldn't work within 500 yards of a person with the AIDS virus," while in 1993, he told a group of teenage boys to "tape a rubber to your American Express card and don't leave home without it." Years earlier, in 1981, he compared the Supreme Court to the Ku Klux Klan, stating, "The Klan wears white robes and scares the hell out of black people, while the court wears black robes and scares the hell out of white people."[723] Another time when Justice Neely advertised in the *Virginia Law Weekly* for an open law clerk position, he wrote:

> West Virginia's infamous once and future Chief Justice Richard Neely, America's laziest and dumbest judge, seeks a bright person to keep him from looking stupid. Preference will be given to U.Va. Law students who studied interesting but useless subjects at snobby schools. If you are dead drunk and miss the interviews, send letters.[724]

He was also critical of federal prosecutors following the conviction of his friend Ed ReBrook, the former State Lottery attorney involved in the Lottery scandal of the early 1990s. Neely, with his typical flamboyant rhetoric, compared the actions of federal prosecutors to those who prepared the trains to go to Auschwitz and said the tragedy of the case was that ReBrook was convicted of a crime that didn't even exist. He said,

> His indictment, prosecution and conviction are monuments to Hannah Arendt's 'banality of evil.' Young, ambitious United States Attorneys salivate over high profile prosecutions; newspapers make money catering to the public's blood lust–a public remarkably reminiscent of nine-year-old children watching a spider suspended on a stick writhe in agony over an open campfire; and judges welcome something more prominent publicly than another lower class, street-level drug dealer or "ho-hum" diversity accident case. So, manned by the same type of high-principled family-valuing mechanics who fired the boil-

ers, coupled the cars, and controlled the switches for the trains that chugged relentlessly along to Auschwitz and Treblinka, the prosecutorial engine grinds resolutely on indifferent to anything but its own bureaucratic imperatives.[725]

Neely said with regard to the morality and the character of the people who staffed the United States Attorney's Office during that time period, "In my estimation, these were evil and immoral people and I called it exactly that way in the Law Review article [and] it is very dangerous to have evil and immoral people in high policy making positions."[726]

Perhaps many of his comments were a part of a well-planned strategy to keep him in the public eye. Neely, who has authored seven books on the law and social perplexities, said, "The trouble with politics is that you have to be terribly thick-skinned so that if somebody calls you a no-account, low-life, bottom-dwelling son-of-a-bitch, you don't take it personally." He explained that,

> in an elected office, you don't ever get any good publicity. All the good publicity you ever get as an elected official is limited to your obituary, and the only choice you have in politics is between bad publicity and no publicity. Well, I've won every election I've ever run in, in spite of the fact that I've gotten consistently bad publicity for twenty-five years. But, the people that I beat got no publicity. So essentially, being a politician is like being a whore or a bootlegger; you can't be very successful unless you advertise.[727]

The press coverage of Chief Justice Neely and the criminal behavior of Judge Troisi are certainly not the only situations that have brought attention to West Virginia's judiciary. For instance, a few years before Justice Neely's departure from the Supreme Court, former Logan County Circuit Judge James Ned Grubb had the dishonorable distinction of being West Virginia's first circuit judge to be convicted of corruption charges while still in office. Grubb, appropriately named, was convicted in 1992 of aiding and abetting the payment of a bribe, two counts of aiding and abetting mail fraud, conspiracy to commit fraud, tampering with a witness, obstruction of justice, and operating his judicial office as a racketeering enterprise. He had previously served as a member of the Logan County Democratic Executive Committee, the Logan County Board of Education, as a West Virginia State Senator, and as the Logan County Prosecuting Attorney.

Prior to his conviction, the Supreme Court of Appeals suspended him as "[h]is effectiveness as a judge and the integrity of the judiciary have been called into question."[728] The indictment against Grubb detailed his scheme to defraud as:

> one to 'obtain money and property by means of false and fraudulent pretenses'; 'to illegally fund the election campaign of the slate of candidates supported by' Grubb; and to 'defraud the citizens of Logan and Boone Counties in their rights to [a] fair and honest election [and] [t]he honest services of' Grubb as circuit judge and Burgess as state senator.[729]

In 1988, Circuit Judge Grubb personally gave $3,000 in cash to Oval Adams who was running for Logan County Sheriff.[730] Near this same time, Grubb's friend, Earl Tomblin, who was a former Sheriff of Logan County, met with Grubb in his judicial chambers and discussed Adams' race for county sheriff. When Grubb asked Tomblin if he was going to help Adams, Tomblin offered to give Adams $10,000 for his campaign in exchange for two years of part-time work if elected sheriff.[731] Tomblin, father of West Virginia's current State Senate President Earl Ray Tomblin, said he needed the two years of work to get his social security and State pension benefits. Grubb agreed to relay this offer to Adams and said he would "see what he could do."

Afterward, Grubb met with Adams and told him of Earl Tomblin's conditional offer, encouraging Adams to "think about it." Grubb later asked Adams if he had met with Tomblin and Adams told him he had met with him. On May 2, 1988, Tomblin gave Adams $10,000, with the understanding that he would hire Tomblin if elected or pay the money back if not elected. Adams won the election and in July 1989, Tomblin asked Grubb to "remind Oval [Adams] about my job." Grubb did so and Adams hired Tomblin as a part-time investigator for the Sheriff's Office. He received a salary, along with social security, retirement, and other benefits, but he did not "perform functions for the Sheriff's Office on a regular basis." For two years, the county clerk mailed to the West Virginia Public Employees Retirement System both the county and Tomblin's share of his pension contributions.[732]

Throughout the election, Grubb ignored the Canons of Judicial Conduct which clearly state that a judge who is not a candidate for re-election cannot be active politically. Specifically, judges are prohibited from making speeches for any political organization or candidate or from endorsing any candidate. Nonetheless, sitting Circuit Judge Grubb, who was not up for re-election until 1992, spoke on April 22, 1988, at a political rally in Chapmanville, West Virginia where he strongly supported Oval Adams in his race for Sheriff. Grubb told the large crowd,

> Now, Oval Adams was raised here. He has roots here. His family's here. Mine is, too. We're not going to come down here and bother you people. If he gets into office, no matter how much applause you give him tonight, he won't have helicopters and laws and policemen come in on you when there's no need to. If you all here tonight are like this judge is or like Oval Adams is going to be, we don't want justice, we want mercy, mercy, mercy.

> If you all believe in me, as I believe you do, because there's people in this room . . . most of you here in this room, I've touched your lives, one way or another . . . I have never closed my door on any of you. Lonnie, Barry, and Ron Dingess and Earl Tomblin . . . All of you can say I've been there when you needed me. I've never turned my back on you.

> But if you believe in me, which I believe you do, then believe in this ticket. I believe so strong in this ticket. If there's a daddy to this ticket, it's got to be me. It's getting close, but I don't want to lose it. And I want you all here tonight to make a commitment not only to me, I'm not running. Make a commitment to yourself for a better Logan County. Make a commitment to yourselves that you must have and will have better candidates to serve you and better officeholders to serve you.

> I'm not ashamed of my ticket. I'm for these gentlemen, and I want you to be. I want you to be able to come to me after this election and say, 'Judge, I did all I could.' If you do, I'll still have mercy. If you don't, it's justice.[733]

Grubb's political wheeling-and-dealing continued into the early 1990s when James Burgess, a candidate for State Senator in a district that included Logan County, sought Grubb's political support. Burgess testified he sought help from Grubb because "I needed some help in Logan County, and I figured he, being a circuit judge, he would have a lot of political clout and he would be very essential to my campaign." The two met at various places, including Grubb's judicial chambers. In April 1990, Grubb called Burgess and other candidates to a meeting at Grubb's house to discuss financing the upcoming election campaign. At that meeting, Grubb told Burgess that his contribution to the campaign expenses of the slate of candidates would be $10,000. Burgess agreed because "I knew [in] Logan County politics you had to get on the slate if you expect to win." Several days later, Burgess gave Grubb $10,000 in cash.[734]

In 1993, more of Judge Grubb's inauspicious escapades surfaced following the suspension of Logan County Prosecuting Attorney Mark Hobbs' law license for two years for failing to inform anyone of the extortion at the command of Grubb. Hobbs, who became Prosecuting Attorney in 1992, explained that the unethical conduct began in 1986 while he was a private attorney. He was representing Roy Dingess in a wrongful death action and Grubb, who was the circuit judge assigned to the case, met with Hobbs alone and asked: "Why don't you turn your two hundred and fifty thousand dollar case into a million?" Hobbs testified that Grubb wanted a share of Hobbs' collected fees to be given to the judge's wife. He said he complied because he feared retribution from the politically powerful Grubb, citing a time when Grubb jailed Hobbs for being late for a hearing.[735]

State Police Sergeant Marty Allen, who spent six years investigating Grubb, said, "Judge Grubb possessed substantial political power in Logan County and people feared he might fabricate criminal charges or even attempt to have them killed." Moreover, Logan County Circuit Clerk Alvis R. Porter said that on occasion Grubb would ask him to illegally fire or hire employees and had sought to impeach Porter when he failed to cooperate with the Judge's requests. In addition, Logan County Magistrate Leonard Codispoti testified that after reporting to the State Police the events surrounding Judge Grubb's attempts to coerce him into unethical conduct, Grubb filed "baseless ethics complaints" against him.[736]

Grubb's corrupt activities are incredible considering the fact that he and two other individuals presented a petition to the Department of Justice during the 1960 election in Logan County to express their outrage with the criminal activities that were rampant at that time. The *Pittsburgh Post Gazette* reported that the petition alleged:

> mass selling and buying of votes with money, whiskey, and moonshine; the entering of polling places by candidates and other persons; the forcible denial of voters to vote in privacy by some election officials, and the flagrant operation of the voting machines by some election officials without the consent of the voter and often against his overt protests.[737]

In 1992, Dan Fleming, Jr., noted historian and professor emeritus of Virginia Tech, published a book on the 1960 John F. Kennedy-Hubert Humphrey Presidential Primary in West Virginia. Fleming describes Grubb during and after the 1960 election as "someone who wanted to reform the whole corrupt system."[738] At the time of Fleming's book, Grubb had not been convicted for his laundry list of corrupt political activities. Soon afterward though, not only was he convicted, but he demonstrated his complete lack of remorse for his actions as well as his contempt for the judiciary and for the people of West Virginia. The *Charleston Gazette* wrote that "[d]uring and after the trial, Grubb laughed at the proceedings and, at one point, said he would die in prison and the government would be forced to pay for his funeral." He said, "I'm not as upset as everyone else is . . . really, I've got to live somewhere. (In prison) I don't have to pay no rent." He was sentenced on July 20, 1992, to five years and five months and fined $25,000.[739]

The Grubb situation once again highlights a member of West Virginia's elected class of politicians who committed scandalous crimes, but received minimal punishment. Moreover, his laughter about his conviction and imprisonment illustrates how commonplace such actions are in the world of West Virginia politics and how a slap-on-the-wrist sentence brought no justice for his actions. I really don't understand how aiding and abetting bribery, two counts of aiding and abetting mail fraud, conspiracy to commit fraud, tampering with a witness, obstruction of justice, and racketeering could become a badge of honor instead of an unrelenting source of embarrassment and shame.

In West Virginia, in addition to five State Supreme Court justices and 66 circuit court judges, there are 158 magistrates. Prior to the current magistrate system, which was created in 1974, counties utilized a system of Justices of the Peace.[740] That system was often criticized as being corrupt and out-of-control.[741] The magistrate court is by far the most common and familiar legal forum for the average West Virginian. It is usually the first and sometimes the only direct contact many people will ever have with an actual courtroom other than reading about one or seeing one on television. Unfortunately, however, many of the State's magistrates have operated their courts under their own set of questionable rules in violation of State law as well as in violation of the people's trust. A glaring example of this occurred on February 26, 2003, when ten-year Logan County Magistrate Danny Ray Wells was charged by the United States Attorney's Office for the Southern District of West Virginia for taking sexual favors, money, and labor, in exchange for freeing defendants from jail. After people were arrested and brought before Wells as Magistrate, he would often tell them they needed to pay a bond, usually hundreds of dollars, in order to be released from jail. Then, he pocketed the money and released the individuals on their own recognizance bonds. "In other cases, Wells allegedly let men out of jail in exchange for sex from their wives or girlfriends, or in exchange for work done on his property."[742]

Among Wells' accusers were: Charles Childer, of Verdunville, who claimed he gave Wells $100 to release him from jail; Richard "Rick" Lowe, of West Logan, who testified he gave Wells a "special bond" of $300 in order to secure his release from jail and onto home confinement; Michelle Cline, after having been charged with driving under the influence of a controlled substance and endangering a child, claimed Wells told her to give him $300 by the next day or he would have her re-arrested on the same charge and thrown in jail; Rodney Cooper, of Boone County, who claimed he gave Wells a load of fill dirt in exchange for releasing him from jail; and Wendy Toney, of Chapmanville, who claimed Wells forced her to have sex with him on two occasions in order to secure the release of her ex-husband. According to the *Logan Banner*,

> Toney said Wells let her in the magistrate court office and asked her if she was going to perform oral sex on him. She replied that she would. . . . Toney claims she and Wells left his office and went to the magistrate court's fax room/break room, when she performed oral sex on him and they had intercourse. After the alleged sexual encounter, Toney and Wells returned to his office when Wells completed the bond forms necessary for Adams' release.[743]

Wells was found guilty of racketeering on March 3, 2003, and sentenced to seven years and three months in federal prison. On March 27, 2003, he resigned from office. On January 10, 2005, former Logan Mayor Tom Esposito was charged by federal prosecutors with illegally concealing an extortion scheme surrounding Wells' activities. The federal information filed against Esposito said he paid Wells $500 to keep quiet about $6,000 worth of liquor that Esposito bought him at a country club on occasions between March 2001 and September 2002 in return for referring defendants to Esposito's legal practice.[744] On November 11, 2005, Esposito pled guilty to extortion charges admitting he paid Wells the money. After getting caught for his illegal activities, Esposito agreed to cooperate with federal investigators in 2003. In 2004, while working as a government informant, he filed to run for the House of Delegates in an agreement to help the federal investigators gather information with regard to election fraud in Logan and Lincoln counties. He withdrew as a candidate twenty-seven days before the election. According to the United States Attorney's Office, Esposito's undercover work helped provide information from several Logan County officials including: former Sheriff Johnny Mendez, who pled guilty to conspiring to buy votes; Logan attorney Mark Hrutkay, who pled guilty to mail fraud in relation to buying votes; former City of Logan Police Chief Alvin Ray "Chipper" Porter, who pled guilty to vote-buying; and Ernest Stapleton, a Logan Veterans of Foreign Wars post commander who admitted embezzling money from the post to be used for illegal campaign contributions.[745] On January 10, 2006, Esposito was sentenced to two years of probation on a charge of concealing a felony. United States District Judge David A. Faber said the sentence was "extremely lenient" and that while he in no way condoned Esposito's criminal conduct, he recognized that Esposito "wound up performing a significant public service."[746]

Wells was also arrested on January 22, 2003, and charged with domestic battery. Three State Police Troopers arrested him following a 911 domestic disturbance call at Wells' home on Crawley Creek. Upon entry into the residence, Trooper Sean Wolfe observed a female, Jonie F. Swims, with several facial injuries. According to the *Logan Banner*, Swims told the Troopers that "Wells forcibly threw her into the dining room floor and slapped her in the face and that when she had attempted to call 911, Wells ripped the phone off the wall to prevent her from calling." Two witnesses, one of whom was a child staying in the home, were subpoenaed by the Troopers to appear in the Logan County Magistrate Court. Wells then filed a criminal complaint against Swims for misdemeanor domestic battery and both Wells and Swims were held overnight before being released on a personal recognizance bond.[747]

In June 2004, while serving his seven-year and six-month 2003 prison sentence for running his magistrate office as a racketeering enterprise, Wells filed a lawsuit against police officers and the town of Chapmanville for allegedly "ruining his reputation" with an arrest after a traffic stop at 2:30 a.m. on December 1, 2001. Wells said the traffic stop was without probable cause and the arrest caused his reputation to be "irreparably harmed and in fact destroyed."[748] Also in June 2004, Wells sued four State Supreme Court Justices for their decision to suspend him from the magistrate bench without pay in October 2002 before he was actually convicted for racketeering. Wells sought $314,970.15 in compensation and damages from the Supreme Court for "effectively removing him from office before being convicted of a crime, a violation of State law."[749]

What can be said about Wells that isn't obvious? He seems to be a carbon copy of Judge Grubb from the respect that after his conviction he showed no remorse, but demonstrated plenty of contempt. Imagine being convicted of scurrilous racketeering activities and then suing the court from your jail cell for removing you from office because you hadn't actually been convicted at the time of removal because you hadn't officially been caught yet. Such actions take a great deal of arrogance. But wait, there's more. In spite of a laundry list of criminal activity, you sue the city and several police officers for pulling you over and irreparably harming your reputation. I wish this were fiction, but you just can't make up anything this preposterous.

In connection with Wells' activities, on June 2, 2005, thirty-one-year-old John W. Nagy, a former Logan County Court Marshal, was sentenced to six months in federal prison for lying to the FBI. He pled guilty to posing as a bondsman and helping Magistrate Wells collect bribes from the people who appeared in Wells' court. As a part of that guilty plea, Nagy had promised to tell the FBI about other people's criminal activities surrounding Wells. He also told investigators he had referred people needing legal services to a Logan attorney in return for cash payments. He later refused to assist investigators with the surrounding investigation.[750]

In September of 2003, in nearby Wayne County, Magistrate Tommy Toler was accused of sexually harassing a courthouse worker in August of 2003. According to State Police Sergeant K.S. Dickson, "It started off as just this one complaint and now there are several." Dickson said the additional complaints were not from courthouse employees; however, he did not further elaborate. The original ethics complaint was filed in the State Supreme Court, which oversees magistrates. Following much publicity, Toler was acquitted of sexual abuse and bribery charges even though several woman ended up testifying that he harassed them and subjected them to unauthorized sexual contact without their consent.[751]

In spite of his acquittal, the Supreme Court's Judicial Investigation Commission conducted its own investigation and found Toler's conduct to be reprehensible and in violation of the Rules of Judicial Conduct. Upon reviewing the findings of the Commission as well as the Judicial Hearing Board, the Supreme Court found that:

> These four victims went to the magistrate court to seek the court's help during times of stress and vulnerability. Imagine going to a magistrate's office to fill out a domestic violence petition after being beaten so badly that you required medical attention and then having the magistrate grab you and engage in revolting and inappropriate sexual contact. Such conduct cannot and will not be tolerated by this Court. On each of the four different occasions Mr. Toler engaged in improper touching of the women as well as grossly inappropriate talk about sex or sexual conduct. Moreover, on each occasion, Mr. Toler subjected each

individual to grossly inappropriate sexual misconduct while he was performing his official duties as magistrate.

The Judicial Hearing Board recommended various sanctions adopted by the Supreme Court including: that Magistrate Toler be publicly censured, suspended for one year without pay, fined $5,000, that he pay the costs of the proceedings before the Judicial Hearing Board, and that each of the sanctions be imposed consecutively for each of the four violations he committed against the four female victims the Court found to be "truthful and credible."[752]

In Morgan County, the State Judicial Investigation Commission recommended suspension for Magistrate Bonnie L. Riffle who scraped her own face, bruised her own body, and blamed it on a fictitious individual in hopes that she could claim workers' compensation benefits. On April 13, 1999, a Morgan County Grand Jury returned a seven-count indictment against Magistrate Riffle charging her with two counts of feloniously and fraudulently attempting to secure workers' compensation benefits. She was also charged with five misdemeanors, including three counts of providing false or misleading information to the Department of Public Safety [specifically, members of the West Virginia State Police], and two counts of falsely reporting an emergency incident.

Following the incident, the Judicial Hearing Board recommended a public censure of Riffle, suspension for one year as magistrate, and the imposition of a $5,000 fine. The Supreme Court agreed with the public censure and suspension; however, the Court "found no purpose for the additional penalty [of $5,000] and decline[d] to impose the recommended fine." The Court explained:

> As one Judicial Hearing Board member stated in a dissent to the Board's recommended disposition: 'This lady has been punished enough. There is no earthly reason to suspend a person from their position as magistrate for a year without pay when Ms. Riffle is not serving in that position. There is no reason to fine an indigent person $5000.00. I respectfully submit that the Circuit Judge of Morgan County who had the benefit of a pre-sentence investigation and the testing done by the Division of Corrections imposed the appropriate punishment of Ms. Riffle.' The same Board member further noted that sometimes 'a little mercy should be mixed with blind justice.'[753]

In another situation, on November 10, 1994, an eighteen-count indictment was returned against Wood County Magistrate Ira W. Atkinson, Jr. for various felony and misdemeanor offenses. Among the charges, Atkinson was accused of bribery and receiving gifts as a public official such as cash, an in-ground swimming pool, roofing work, and construction of a fish pond at his home.[754] Another Magistrate in McDowell County, David Hunt, was convicted in 1999 for the sale of cocaine and sentenced to six years in prison and a $25,000 fine.[755]

In 1985, in neighboring Logan County, Magistrate Johnny Mendez was publicly censured for a violation of the Judicial Code of Ethics when he suspend-ed the sentence of Mark Craddock without any authority to do so. Craddock, an eighteen-year-old student at Sharples High School, was arrested for shooting the moving vehicle of a teacher, Erskine T. Davis, who had disciplined Craddock for various transgressions of school rules.[756] Years later, in 1993, Mendez was con-victed of illegally paying poll workers $5,000 during his successful 1988 primary campaign for magistrate. Mendez had been a magistrate for twenty-two years when he pled guilty to the 1993 election-fraud charges. Even though he resigned as magistrate that year, he served as magistrate again from 1994 until his success-ful campaign for sheriff in 2000. As Sheriff, Mendez pled guilty on July 19, 2004, to two federal charges that he conspired with several other individuals to buy votes in the 2000 and 2004 Democratic Primaries. He was only sentenced to a short term of home confinement for his 2004 conviction.[757]

The conduct of many of these justices, judges, and magistrates acts to undermine the confidence in the judicial system that has already been eroded by years of reprehensible conduct. Another situation creating a perception of a lack of accountability for criminal behavior is when these convicted felon lawyers and politicians receive the return of their law licenses. The State Supreme Court attempted to rectify this and changed its rules for admission to the practice of law in West Virginia in December 2000. The change provided that people who were convicted of a felony or perjury could no longer be permitted to pursue law licenses in West Virginia. Justice George Scott, who proposed the rule change, called it "a step forward in the advancement and promotion of public trust."[758]

The change in the rule was short-lived, however, as the Supreme Court abandoned it in July 2001. In the Court's written comments, Justice Larry Starcher stated, "To exclude all persons with any sort of felony conviction from possible bar membership–without allowing for any hope of redemption and reha-bilitation–would be taking an extremist position." The rule change passed on a three-to-two vote with Justices Robin Davis and Elliott "Spike" Maynard dissent-ing. Critical of the Court's change in the rule, Justice Maynard stated, "Just think, in our State, if you are a convicted felon, you can't run a 'bar' and sell whiskey, but you can be a member of 'the bar' and practice law."[759]

The reversal in the rule change simply reinforced the perception of a lack of accountability for criminal behavior. Attorneys are officers of the Court and they have a responsibility to act trustworthily and to be held to standards above and beyond those of the general public. It really doesn't seem like too much to ask that attorneys be free from criminal backgrounds. In fact, that should be the minimum we should expect from them. This book is replete with examples of elected officials who committed felonies and lost their law licenses for only short periods of time. A lifetime ban from practicing law after committing a felony is warranted and necessary. The 2000 rule shouldn't have been changed. Sometimes extreme circumstances call for extreme measures as the overriding public interest in preserving the integrity of the judiciary demands that justices, judges, magistrates, and attorneys be accountable for their damaging behaviors.

In addition to the numerous judiciary indiscretions or "perceptions" of indiscretions, the integrity of the legal system of West Virginia has also been placed into question due to the influx of money pouring into political campaigns to elect the members of the judiciary. The most recent charges occurred in 2003, 2004, and 2005 when the American Tort Reform Association declared West Virginia a "judicial hellhole." The organizations's annual report gave a scathing review of the State's legal system, saying "pressure and politics played by powerful trial lawyers have turned the State's judicial system into a commodity business, akin to an ATM for claim filers." West Virginia was the only State to have its entire court system held up as a bad example.[760] Likewise, prior to the 2004 General Election, the *Charleston Daily Mail* declared that the atmosphere of the State Supreme Court "costs the State investment, jobs, doctors and insurers."[761]

Conversely, Marvin Masters, President of the West Virginia Trial Lawyers' Association, said the study was deeply flawed and was the work of a special interest group trying to protect its members from being accountable for their own wrongdoing. Masters said, "The people who are making these allegations are the same people who historically have killed, injured and robbed West Virginians of their savings." He added, "What these people want to do is change the law to protect themselves from what they did in the past and what I assume they will continue to do in the future."[762]

The 2004 Chief Justice of the West Virginia Supreme Court, Elliott E. Maynard, said the judiciary's reputation was being undermined by big-money campaigns largely financed by lawyers. Chief Justice Maynard said, "The appearance that justice is for sale is a really big problem." He said the large sums of money spent on judicial elections in West Virginia and other states give the impression of impropriety and explained that lawyers are the main contributors in judicial campaigns and that judges often hear cases from attorneys who have donated to their campaigns. With regard to lawyers contributing to the campaigns of judges, Maynard asked, "Does that influence your decision in a case? If you're the right man it doesn't but there's an appearance problem. It looks bad. And what counts is what it looks like." Former President of the West Virginia State Bar Tom Flaherty added, "Lawyers don't contribute to campaigns for altruistic reasons. They expect to gain influence."[763]

Justice Maynard warned that the problem is exacerbated by a system that uses partisan elections to select judges and noted that West Virginia is one of only eight states that elect judges in a partisan manner. Maynard supports non-partisan judicial elections similar to the system currently used in West Virginia to elect county school board members, saying "I don't think partisan politics have any place in the courtroom, just like it doesn't have any place in our schools."[764]

The *Charleston Daily Mail* says special interests "try to use the courts to get what they cannot win through the legislative process [as] it is much easier to persuade five judges to give you something than it is to get 134 legislators to agree that it's a good thing."[765] Moreover, "West Virginia is in trouble in part because its judiciary does not treat fairly all parties in every dispute. A trio of labor-backed liberals controls the State Supreme Court, and it regularly rewrites the law."[766] In announcing his bid for the West Virginia Supreme Court in 2004, Brent Benjamin said, "There is a perception that our highest court has been targeted by special interests, and that this has hurt our ability to keep doctors here, for people and businesses to find that insurance they need, and for West Virginia to maintain jobs." In endorsing Benjamin, the *Charleston Daily Mail* said,

> That is more than a perception. That is the truth. Too many businesses have given up trying to fight it out in biased courts and have simply invested their capital elsewhere.
>
> Rulings by the State Supreme Court are one major reason why insurance rates are so high and why doctors have had to leave the state. The court unraveled much of the hard-fought reforms of workers' compensation in 1995.[767]

In spite of Justice Benjamin's concern about special interest money affecting judicial elections, millions of dollars were spent on his behalf during the 2004 election. According to The Brennan Center for Justice at New York University School of Law, more than 5,000 television ads costing millions of dollars were aired during the 2004 judicial election. And, of those ads, four out of five of them were classified as negative attack ads. Moreover, of the nearly 10,000 attack ads that were run in 2004 in the fifteen states where judicial elections were held, 43 percent of all of those negative ads were used in the West Virginia election.[768]

The amount of money in politics is simply out of control and getting worse each election cycle. People are shutting down and becoming even more disinterested in the political process–if that is even possible. Apathy continues to grow year after year and something has to be done to stunt the growth and reverse the process to reestablish the public's faith in government. The money issues in judicial elections must be addressed well in advance of the 2008 election when two of the five State Supreme Court Justice seats, all 66 circuit court judge positions, and all 158 magistrate positions will be up for grabs. No special interest groups–whether I agree with their issues or not–should be able to buy justice in West Virginia.

This chapter is not to conclude that the entire court system in West Virginia is corrupt. I am proud and fortunate to work for the West Virginia Supreme Court and Justice Maynard, and hope to continue in my job long after this book. Moreover, I speak favorably about Justice Maynard not just because I want to keep my job or because I like him personally. I appreciate him on one level because he is exceptionally smart and particularly with criminal issues he speaks his mind and rules with a fair, but just hand. Mainly though, I like the fact that he comes from Mingo County, one of the southern West Virginia counties notorious for vote-buying and other shenanigans, and I have never heard a single comment or accusation about him buying votes during his lengthy career as a prosecutor, circuit judge, and now a Justice on the Supreme Court. I figure if he can survive unscathed in that environment without even a rumor of such corruption then that alone speaks volumes to me.

The current Court is composed of five very capable individuals who may have different opinions and interpretations of the law, but take their jobs seriously and do them to the best of their abilities. Moreover, their diverse backgrounds and interpretations only serve to bring new ideas to the table and consequently, better decisions from the Court. However, in spite of the collegiality of this particular Court, the numerous indiscretions of several members of the judicial branch as a whole have created a perception of systemic corruption. This perception is only furthered by the convictions of the countless public officials in the executive and legislative branches of government. To this end, when you ask the average person in the coffee shop or on the street about their opinions of the court system, if they say anything at all, they more often than not mention someone like Judge Grubb, Judge Troisi, or Magistrate Wells. Or, they mention something about the multi-million dollar negative ads they heard in the 2004 campaign for the open seat on the Supreme Court.

These negative ads are powerful and cannot be underestimated. I remember countless people during the 2004 election who told me about the ads they saw on television or heard on the radio. Others told me they believed the ads to be purely factual because they saw them on the 6:00 and 11:00 news, when in reality, what they saw were the paid political ads being run during the commercial breaks of the news. I have worked enough political campaigns to understand exactly why they run negative ads–because they work. Moreover, as much as people say they hate negative ads, when you hear five thousand times that a sitting justice is going to take a sex offender and place him in a school, it begins to weigh heavily on your mind.

Thus, while I personally understand that the perception of widespread judicial corruption is not completely accurate, perception, more often than not, becomes reality in the hearts and minds of the general public. This is precisely why West Virginia has to take measures step by step with each branch of government to repair a broken system in which people have lost all confidence. To begin this road to repair will require the people of West Virginia to push their elected representatives to enact the specific reforms outlined in my Contract With The Voter.

# CHAPTER TWELVE

# Bribery, Kickbacks, and Conspiracy

*During the Barron and Moore administrations, bribery investigations, indictments and convictions were so continuous, they were like a major state industry.*

*Charleston Gazette*

Throughout West Virginia, February 14, 1968, became known as the Valentine's Day Catastrophe as federal prosecutors indicted former Governor William Wallace "Wally" Barron and several of his colleagues on bribery and conspiracy charges involving kickbacks they had taken when Barron was Governor from 1961 through 1965. West Virginians were once again "saddened and disappointed by corruption in the state government [as] several high-ranking members of the Barron administration and the former governor, himself, were sentenced to prison terms for their part in some of the illegal practices."[769]

Then-State Attorney General Barron's problems began during his 1960 campaign for Governor as controversial stories surfaced with regard to his campaign. *The West Virginia Hillbilly* wrote that, "two damaging stories came out–one that he had used a gambler's private plane in the early days of his campaign and the other that he had offered State Treasurer Orel J. Skeen $65,000 to stay out of the Governor's race."[770] The proof of the latter was revealed after State Treasurer Skeen secretly recorded Barron offering him the illegal inducements. West Virginians, however, didn't heed the early warnings of Barron's illegal conduct as the Democrats pulled together bringing Barron a landslide victory in the General Election.

During his inaugural address, like most politicians, Barron proclaimed his honesty and pleaded for West Virginians to trust him in his endeavors to make the State a better place. He told the people that their involvement was essential as "the situation requires that we re-dedicate ourselves to principles apparently all but forsaken in the every-day commotion of our troublesome times. We must devote ourselves to unselfish service and exert unremitting energy to the purpose of regaining misplaced ideals." He then pledged to "give his all" and that, "as your Governor, I seek not personal power or prestige [and] I ask only that I be permitted to play my proper part in the building of a better West Virginia." Finally, Barron proclaimed that, "in the handclasp of mutual trust and toil, we shall advance to a brighter and more abundant future, not only for ourselves and our children, but for generations yet unborn."[771]

Shortly into his term as Governor, on July 2, 1962, Barron again touted his integrity as he announced that he had no plans to run for re-election even if the proposed Constitutional Amendment that would have allowed a Governor to serve more than one four-year term was passed by the voters. Barron proclaimed that his reasons for not seeking re-election were two-fold. First, he wanted the Constitutional Amendment to be successful and did not want the people of West Virginia to believe that he was supporting the Amendment for "selfish reasons." The second reason, Governor Barron proclaimed, was that he had two daughters to educate who were going to college and he wanted to get back to the private practice of law which would enable him to meet those financial responsibilities.[772]

In spite of Barron's attempted image shaping, he would not be able to escape his secretive and illegal political deeds as he and several of his administration officials were put on trial in 1968 for receiving kickbacks, bribery, and conspiracy charges related to Barron's term as Governor.[773] Barron was charged with taking two $25,000 payments from coal companies in exchange for supporting legislation that gave coal companies the right to condemn land for a coal slurry pipeline. Barron denied the charges against him and said the payments were given to him as attorney's fees he earned before he was Governor. Barron was acquitted while the other five men charged were found guilty. Among those convicted was Barron's chief of staff Bonn Brown, who was also a 1964 candidate for Governor.[774]

Following his acquittal, Barron and his wife moved to Florida; however, he soon faced a second indictment that was issued against him in 1970. This time, Barron and thirty-three other defendants were accused of rigging State purchasing contracts. After a few months, those indictments were thrown out by the State Supreme Court for technical reasons. The Charleston Gazette reported that a Kanawha County Grand Jury returned 107 purchasing indictments against Barron and other former State officials, "but most of the cases died after the State Supreme Court negated part of a law."[775] Thus, Barron successfully thwarted a second attempt by law enforcement to convict him of criminal behavior.

A few years later, however, it was learned that the jury acquitted Barron during his 1968 trial because of one holdout, the jury foreman named Ralph Buckalew. The jury foreman agreed to save Barron's hide in the jury room by securing his acquittal after the foreman's wife had received $25,000 in cash in a brown paper bag delivered by Governor Barron's wife, Opal Barron, with the instructions "not to spend large amounts of money." Joe Perry, Barron's attorney in his original trial, was forced to stand trial himself as he was accused of being the chief architect in the juror bribery scheme. Perry was acquitted; however, Barron, the jury foreman, and many other friends and colleagues of the Governor were convicted for various crimes and spent many years in prison. Perry later asserted that Barron stole more than $7 million during the course of his public service in West Virginia.[776]

On March 30, 1971, Barron pled guilty in federal court to conspiracy, bribery, and obstruction of justice for tampering with the jury.[777] Specifically, he pled guilty to "wilfully, unlawfully and knowingly combining, conspiring and confederating and agreeing with the other defendants and other unknown persons to commit bribery and of the commission of bribery of a juror in violation of Title 18, Sections 1503, 371, 201(b) and 2, United States Code, each of which offenses is a felony." After his sentence was later reconsidered, he was paroled in 1975 from the federal prison at Eglin, Florida. He served just forty-six months of his original twenty-five-year sentence.[778]

Governor Barron and Bonn Brown also lost the right to practice law in West Virginia. In calling their actions an attack on "one of the most vital areas of our legal structure," the West Virginia Supreme Court provided:

> It is clear beyond question that each of the crimes of conspiracy to commit bribery and bribing a juror is a crime which involves moral turpitude. It is difficult to consider an offense which is more destructive or corruptive of the legal system of West Virginia than bribery of a juror, especially when such crime is committed by an attorney who is an officer of the Court. Bribery of a juror is a perversion of justice and strikes at the foundation of the judicial system of this State.[779]

Barron never sought the return of his law license. Brown, however, later attempted to be reinstated to practice law in West Virginia. The Supreme Court denied his request "because of the extremely serious nature of [his] original offense of bribing a juror when coupled with the separate conviction of conspiring to bribe public officials." The Court wrote that his reinstatement would have a "justifiable and substantial adverse effect on the public confidence in the administration of justice [as] the nature of these crimes directed as they are to the core of the legal system and the integrity of governmental institutions demonstrates a profound lack of moral character on the part of the applicant."[780]

Barron's administration's shenanigans only reinforced West Virginia's already shaken confidence in State government. His actions were even discussed in the United States Congress by John R. Buckley, who had been granted immunity for his testimony against his former boss, President Richard Nixon. Buckley was a Republican political spy who worked on Nixon's 1972 re-election campaign with the infamous E. Howard Hunt, Jr., who was convicted for his role in the Watergate break-in. Buckley testified before the United States Senate Watergate Committee members in 1973 that his start in "political espionage" began while he was an investigator for Governor Cecil Underwood for several months during his unsuccessful 1964 bid for Governor. Buckley testified about the convictions of Governor Barron and many of his top aides for misuse of federal funds. He said, "We found out that $1.5 million [in] federal flood relief money was completely dissipated. We found out that there were kickbacks involved in dummy corporations purportedly designed to do this cleanup after the flood."[781]

Having lost a family business in Parsons, West Virginia to the devastating 1985 flood, I find Barron's conduct to be particularly despicable. How many struggling families didn't have enough money to eat or to repair their flood damaged properties because the Governor and his associates pilfered millions of dollars in federal aid? How many roads weren't rebuilt? How many water and sewer systems weren't repaired? It really was a sad and serious act which punished good people who were just trying to get their lives back in order after facing the many devastating flood-related problems.

A February 1968 *Charleston Gazette* article provided: "To date, 17 officials, confidants or business associates of the Barron administration have faced court action–although charges against five of them later were dropped."[782] *Charleston Daily Mail* columnist L.T. Anderson referred to the situation as "a continuing raid on the public treasury" and said, "It is a shameful fact that the federal government had to bring bribery-conspiracy cases against persons in West Virginia Government while West Virginia law and West Virginia government looked the other way and giggled nervously." He added, "It would dissipate a great deal of cynicism if the state would join in a federal effort to determine how much, if anything, was stolen, where it is and how it can be recovered."[783]

The *Charleston Gazette* said that Barron's administration resulted in the State being hit by wave after wave of scandal. It wrote that gubernatorial aide

Curtis Trent and Liquor Commissioner Clarence Elmore were convicted of income tax evasion; Motor Vehicles Commissioner Jack Nuckols was convicted of falsifying State travel expenses; Highways equipment supervisor Woodrow Yokum was convicted of stealing thousands of government items; Charleston businessman Alex Dandy and others were convicted of falsifying records in a State flood cleanup contract, but the verdict later was reversed.[784] The *Gazette* said of Dandy:

> Senior West Virginians may remember Alex Dandy, a 1960s Charleston appliance dealer who was entangled with the scandal-wracked Barron administration. Dandy was cleared in a Barron corruption trial, then he moved away–and entered bigger scandals. He pleaded guilty in a Cleveland bank fraud in 1979, and in 1992 he drew a 23-year prison term for bleeding a Michigan grocery chain. Dandy apparently still has Charleston holdings, because federal agents recently filed four liens totaling $9.5 million against his Kanawha County properties. The new filing updates previous liens seeking $14 million, which indicates that much of his past debt has been paid.[785]

Burl Allan Sawyers, the longest serving head of the State Road Commission was another member of the Barron administration to be convicted in a 1968 federal trial for bribery in fixing State contracts. It is believed that the convictions gave the State Road Commission such a bad reputation that it was later renamed the Division of Highways.[786]

The *Gazette* called the Barron era an "appalling shame and dishonor of that era."[787] Nonetheless, when Barron died in 2002, the front page headline depicted, *"'I remember how gracious he was . . .' Despite the scandals, former Gov. Barron described as a 'good, warm fella.'"*[788] In 1975, the year Barron was released from prison, he expressed sympathy for then-Governor Arch Moore, who was going through the first of his legal clashes after being charged by a federal court of accepting bribes from businessmen seeking a bank charter.

About the only things in common I had with Governor Barron were that we both became lawyers who were born in Elkins, West Virginia, and we both had dogs named Bozo. Apparently we both liked to take our Bozos for rides in vehicles as he even took his dog Bozo in the car with his family during his 1961 inaugural parade.[789] I called Governor Barron in early 2000 and told him that I was writing a book on West Virginia politics and wanted to discuss his scandal-ridden administration.

I told Governor Barron that I had read in his former Elkins, West Virginia hometown newspaper, the *Inter-Mountain*, that he once said, "You don't know what it's like in prison. I'd sit there and say, 'What have I done. What have I done to my State, to my family, to myself?'"[790] I asked him to elaborate on those comments. During our brief conversation, in a sad tone, he simply told me he was sentenced to prison, fined, stripped of his law license, and too embarrassed to go back to his hometown of Elkins where he so badly wanted to spend his dying years. He said he and his family lived at Pompano Beach, Florida after he served his four-year federal criminal sentence and later ended up in Charlotte, North Carolina, and "those places just weren't home" to him.

He told me that in years past he would sometimes quietly travel to West Virginia during the summer to camp at Bluestone Lake in the southern part of the State. He said he preferred to remain unnoticed when he came back to his home State because he had never forgiven himself for what he had done, but couldn't stay away because he "missed those West Virginia hills." I later confirmed this fact with my former colleague Bob Brunner, who once interviewed Barron for WSAZ television news during one of Barron's camping trips.

I asked Barron if he would like to discuss his gubernatorial years in detail so that he could share his experiences in a way that might be helpful to others who were entering public service. He said in a crackling voice that he might want to do that, but he would like to think about it. He then simply said, "I make no excuses for my actions." I gave him my telephone number, but that was the last conversation I had with the former Governor who died on November 12, 2002.

I have replayed that conversation several times in my mind. I wish that Governor Barron and I had spoken in more depth about his political days. After that brief conversation with him I do believe, however, he was truly sorry for his actions. I am in no way saying it excuses his criminal behavior; I am simply saying that I think a more detailed account of how his criminal actions had affected his personal life would serve as a good lesson to people entering politics. It would have also been helpful, had he truly been candid, to explore exactly how much money was actually stolen and where it all went because even though many of his colleagues served prison sentences, West Virginians will never know the full extent of the multi-million dollar schemes orchestrated by his administration.

Governor Barron's story would have been important because he was one of the few to have actually shown remorse for his actions. Most other convicted political West Virginia felons are often seen as people who commit crimes, serve short or even no jail sentences, and thumb their noses at authority with little or no remorse for their actions. When I think of his conduct following his conviction,

I can't help but compare how he handled himself versus how Governor Moore has acted during the years since his convictions.  Governor Barron served his time, left the State, did not request the return of his law license, and never denied his guilt once he was convicted.  Governor Moore, on the other hand, after serving time in a federal penitentiary based upon numerous criminal convictions, sought the return of his law license, sought reimbursement of legal fees for the State's charges against him, and continues to deny *any* guilt for any of his proven criminal actions.  Nonetheless, both Barron's and Moore's actions made them just two more convicted West Virginia politicians in a shameful list that continues to grow to this day.

Prior to being elected Governor, Barron was the State Attorney General.  He was succeeded by Attorney General Charles Donald Robertson, who served in that capacity from 1961 through 1969.  In 1968, Robertson ran for, but lost, the Democratic gubernatorial nomination to James Sprouse by a mere 5,000 votes.  Sprouse then lost the 1968 General Election in a close battle against Arch Moore.  Robertson wanted to run for Governor in 1964, however, much to his disappointment, Barron supported his chief of staff Bonn Brown's candidacy.

In 1972, four years after his failed gubernatorial bid, Attorney General Robertson, who had also served as a member of the State House of Delegates as well as a Harrison County Assistant Prosecuting Attorney, pled guilty to two of five federal charges involving bribes paid by a contractor who was bidding on public housing construction projects.  Specifically, he was found guilty of bribery of a public official and for violating interstate transportation in aid of racketeering enterprises.  He served only fourteen months of his two concurrent five-year terms in federal prison, was fined $15,000, and lost his law license.  Robertson's brother, Dana Robertson, also entered a plea of guilty for the same criminal endeavor and was fined $1,000 and sentenced to two years in prison.[791]

When Robertson's former Deputy Attorney General Philip J. Graziani was preparing to testify against him in the corruption and bribery case, he was shot twice in the head with a small-caliber gun in front of his Charleston home at 12:30 a.m. on April 9, 1972.  He survived the shooting as officials said the ammunition used against him may have been old and, thus, weaker than normal.  One bullet struck Graziani in the jaw, while the other bullet hit the base of his skull but somehow failed to penetrate the bone.

Graziani first testified on December 10, 1969, before a grand jury after the circuit court granted him a "full and complete immunity from prosecution under Federal or State law."  Even the grant of immunity, however, did not stop the State Supreme Court from annulling his law licence for his involvement in the bribery scheme.  Graziani, however, fought the annulment all the way to the

United States Supreme Court, but eventually lost his law license.[792]  In addition to being a Deputy Attorney General to Robertson, Graziani had previously served as a former member of the State House of Delegates from Randolph County, he had been the former owner of a steel fabrication plant, and was a Navy veteran of World War II.

On August 5, 1971, Graziani appeared before another grand jury.  This time Graziani testified in the United States District Court for the Southern District of West Virginia that C. Donald Robertson and his brother, Dana Aubrey Robertson, had conspired to bribe, and did bribe, James Frederick Haught.  Graziani's testimony revealed the connections between the president of Centurion Corporation (a construction company), Arthur J. Tarley, and Federal Housing Director James Frederick Haught, who entered into an illegal arrangement in which Tarley would pay Haught a $50 "finder's fee" for each apartment unit he ordered constructed by Centurion Corporation.  Tarley informed Graziani of this arrangement and it was agreed that Tarley would forward funds to Graziani for the so-called "finder's fee" and Graziani would pass the illegal funds on to Haught.  On six separate occasions over approximately sixteen months, Graziani gave Haught $18,700 in cash that had been sent to him by Tarley.  Graziani testified about another $12,500 that was given to Haught by Graziani's law partner, Dana Aubrey Robertson, drawn out of the partnership account of the law firm.

A suspect in the shooting of Graziani later said that Attorney General Robertson ordered Graziani's murder.[793]  Three men, Claude Weldon "Gene" Truslow, Bernard "Sticks" Brumfield, and George Davidson, Jr., were tried jointly and convicted by a jury on both counts of a two count indictment for (1) conspiracy to obstruct justice in violation of 18 U.S.C. § 371, and (2) obstruction of justice in violation of 18 U.S.C. § 1503 in the Graziani shooting in 1973.  Their convictions, however, were overturned by the United States Fourth Circuit Court of Appeals for issues related to hearsay evidence and the State's refusal to allow them to be tried separately.  The appeals court ordered a new trial, and the three were indicted a second time. The case ended when those indictments were dismissed in 1977.  Prosecutors said the sworn testimony of witnesses conflicted and the key witness had admitted lying to a grand jury.[794]

Attorney General Robertson became acquainted with Truslow years earlier.  On May 15, 1961, Truslow pled guilty to the offense of unarmed robbery and was committed to the custody of the West Virginia Board of Control for a period of from one to two years.  On August 9, 1962, he was placed on probation for a period of two years.  After violating the conditions of his probation, such probation was revoked and he was sentenced by the Intermediate Court of Kanawha County on March 13, 1964, to an indeterminate sentence of confine-

ment in the West Virginia State Penitentiary of five to eighteen years, with credit given for the time spent in the forestry camp which was under the jurisdiction
of the Board of Control.

On May 18, 1964, Truslow filed a writ of habeas corpus proceeding
arguing that he should be released from prison because the sentence against him
was too harsh and contrary to State law. Robertson, the State Attorney General
at the time, chose not to file an answer or brief on behalf of the State in opposition to Truslow's plea for release from prison. In fact, when the case was called
on the argument docket in front of the State Supreme Court, an attorney from the
Attorney General's Office announced that the State did not wish to contest the
matter. The case was submitted to the Court for decision based solely on
Truslow's brief and the Court granted his release from prison June 2, 1964.[795]

The Attorney Generals Office's decision not to file a brief or present
any argument in the case against Truslow is highly unusual. During my approximately six years as a Senior Assistant Attorney General briefing and arguing
cases before the State Supreme Court, I can't remember a single occasion when
any attorney in that office failed to file a brief or chose not to present oral argument. Even when the occasion arose where the Attorney General's Office confessed error on behalf of the State or agreed with a defendant's argument, the
case was always properly briefed and presented to the Supreme Court. In any
case, Truslow was released from prison, in part, due to Robertson's Office's
position on his case. Truslow was later killed by his wife Susan on February 4,
1979, two years after the Graziani indictments against him were dismissed.
Susan was convicted of voluntary manslaughter, but received a conditional par
don in December 1984 by then-Governor Jay Rockefeller.[796] Truslow and his
father, James H. Truslow, Sr., were notorious throughout the Kanawha Valley for
violent behavior. Truslow, Sr. was later killed by a bar owner while trying to force his
way inside.[797]

The United States Attorney asserted that Graziani was shot in an effort
to prevent his testifying in the pending criminal trial of C. Donald Robertson. As
stated, prior to the shooting, Graziani had testified before a federal grand jury that
was conducting an investigation of Robertson. He was then scheduled to testify
for the government in Robertson's pending criminal trial, which was scheduled to
begin in federal court on May 16, 1972, approximately one month after he was
shot in the head. The prosecution offered the testimony of James Haught to show
conversations between C. Donald Robertson, James Haught and Pete Haught
indicating Robertson's solicitation of their help in a plan to kill Graziani because
of his past and prospective testimony against Robertson, James Haught, and
Robertson's brother Dana.[798]

At trial, a Mr. Carr, a witness for the United States, testified that on April 10, 1972, the Monday after the shooting, that he had a conversation with Davidson in which Davidson stated that he had "'done a job for Mr. Truslow,' and that job was the shooting of the Assistant Attorney General." Davidson was also quoted as stating that he "received $3,000 for the commission of the crime" and that Davidson was nervous and upset during their conversation because Graziani was still alive.[799]

Mickey Vanater, another government witness, testified that Truslow had told him, "He put two bullets right in back of his head but even with Sticks with him he couldn't even kill him." "Sticks" is a nickname used by Brumfield, a fact that was known by the jury. Vanater said that there was no name used in connection with the "he" of the statement. He also quoted Truslow as saying of Brumfield, "Boy, if he rats on me he will hang me" and that Truslow had made similar remarks in regard to Davidson.[800]

Franklin Cox, another government witness, testified on direct examination as to a conversation with Brumfield: "I asked him if he had [seen] Davidson in town and he said Davidson had left town; he made some money and had left town. I asked him how and he said he knocked off a lawyer or tried to knock off a lawyer or something to that effect." Cox also testified as to a post-shooting conversation with Truslow: "Well, I asked him where Brumfield and Davidson [were] and he said he didn't care where they were, and I asked him why, and he said he paid them to do a job for him and they blew it." In response to a later question by the prosecution as to what kind of "job" he paid for, Cox replied, "Something to do with doing away with a snitching lawyer."[801]

On October 20, 1972, both Attorney General Robertson and Dana filed petitions in the West Virginia Supreme Court asking the Court to permit them to voluntarily resign from the West Virginia State Bar. The Court denied their petitions to voluntarily resign and annulled both law licenses writing that the Court had a mandatory duty "imposed upon it to annul the license of an attorney who has been convicted to any crime involving moral turpitude."[802] In 1978, with his conviction for defrauding West Virginians behind him, Attorney General Robertson was not without personal fortune as he sold his Clarion Coal Company for more than $1 million.[803]

Attorney General Robertson was also a part of the Lottery scandal years later involving former State Lottery Commission Lawyer Ed ReBrook and State Lottery Commissioner Butch Bryan. ReBrook was convicted in 1993 of insider trading for buying shares of stock based upon insider information and tipping off two of his friends, former Attorney General Robertson and businessman James Kay Thomas, to do the same. The three purchased a combined $90,000 of Video

Lottery Technologies (VLT) stock based upon the belief that the State would soon be expanding video lottery and awarding VLT a multi-million dollar contract.[804]

Robertson's successor, Chauncey Browning was also under significant investigation for corrupt activities. On one occasion, Browning pled the Fifth Amendment against self-incrimination and refused to testify before a 1972 grand jury investigating bribery and State purchasing abuse charges against him while he was in office. In spite of the investigations, he was not indicted and served another twelve years as Attorney General. The *Charleston Gazette* said that although Browning was never indicted, he was the subject of at least three investigations by state and federal agencies into his activities when he was Attorney General.[805]

Several years ago I studied for my legal bar exam five nights per week for approximately six weeks in a small room at the University of Charleston. At the time, I knew very little about Attorney General Robertson. There were usually only three or four of us studying together, one of whom I learned was Robertson's daughter and another was the son of one of Robertson's top Deputy Attorneys General. Soon afterward, the daughter of Joe Perry, Governor Barron's 1968 trial attorney, began working with me in the Attorney General's Office. I enjoyed working and studying with all of them and mention them only because it is an example of how small the State is and how in one way or another people inadvertently become acquainted with the numerous good and bad politicians and their families. They build relationships, both personal and professional, and those relationships necessarily become a factor in the excusing nature of West Virginians when these same people are convicted of crimes. Instead of the complete horror and outrage that people should feel, many West Virginians often express a mere disappointment as their personal relationships often temper their emotions.

Governor Barron and Attorney General Robertson were not the only statewide elected officials involved in corruption and bribery schemes during that time period. State Treasurer John H. Kelly, who served from 1961 through 1975, added additional color to an already picturesque scene of corruption. As he was being sworn into office to become West Virginia's State Treasurer in 1961, Kelly pledged, "I will administer the affairs of the office in an efficient and honest manner. I pledge to keep uppermost in mind the best interests of the people of this State."[806]

In spite of his earlier pledge, in 1976, Treasurer Kelly and Assistant State Treasurer Joseph F. Rykoskey, pled guilty to a mail fraud charge arising out of a bribery scheme. Part of Kelly's and Rykoskey's authority in the State Treasurer's Office was to designate depositories for the State's money and to determine the amount of State funds to be deposited in each depository. They were bribed to deposit the State's money in non-interest-bearing accounts creating huge profits for participating banks. These misapplied bank funds were then used in payment of bribes to them. The amount of money from the State's general account deposited in the bank was always substantial and normally maintained at several million dollars. In December of 1973, for example, the State's total deposits to this account exceeded $11 million.[807]

Basically, Kelly and Rykoskey agreed to make State money deposits in non-interest-bearing accounts at the bank of choice of the bribing bank officials in return for expense-free junkets, cash, and campaign contributions for Kelly's re-election. For example, at the bank's expense, both Kelly and Rykoskey, along with their wives, spent many nights at The Greenbrier, a five-star luxury resort located in White Sulphur Springs, West Virginia. No limitations were placed on the duration of their stays nor the expenses that could be incurred. Theodore J.S. Caldwell, Chairman of the Board of Directors of the First Huntington National Bank of Huntington, West Virginia, was convicted on each count of a twelve-count indictment for the scheme to defraud the State. Kelly and Rykoskey pled guilty to a single charge of mail fraud contained in the indictment naming Caldwell, and to various charges in other pending indictments and agreed to testify against Caldwell at his trial.[808]

Kelly's illegal behavior is appalling. At first it may seem a bit trivial in comparison to Governor Barron and Attorney General Robertson's corrupt activities, but in reality, it amounted to millions of dollars in lost State revenues. Just take a drive through some of West Virginia's former coal towns on the numerous roads in desperate need of repair or visit many of its decaying schools and the answer is clear where that stolen money could have been spent. As for The Greenbrier, it is a fabulous and luxurious resort. I spent one night of my life at The Greenbrier when I proposed to my wife. It was expensive and I had to save money for a while to afford just that one night. For State officials to use The Greenbrier as their own little playhouse any time they want, racking up thousands and thousands of dollars in expenses, in exchange for bilking the State out of millions of dollars, is an affront to every hard-working man and woman of the State who scrimps and saves in order to even take their families on a two or three day low budget vacation.

With bribery and kickback charges encompassing most of the executive branch of government, State Delegate Robert L. McCormick stepped up to make sure that the West Virginia House of Delegates was represented in the State's Hall of Shame. He was convicted for taking unreported campaign contributions in violation of the federal Hobbs Act. McCormick, a Delegate from Logan County, assisted foreign doctors in obtaining licenses to practice medicine, in exchange for cash. At the time, a temporary permit system allowed the doctors to practice, pending their completion of the formal requirements for a full license to practice, which included passing a particular test. McCormick assisted the doctors in 1984 by sponsoring a bill to extend the program. He also agreed to sponsor such a bill for the doctors during the 1985 legislative session.[809]

During his 1984 re-election campaign, McCormick told a lobbyist that he had not heard from the doctors. Subsequently, they provided him with several cash payments which were not recorded as campaign contributions, as required by law. His sponsorship of the 1985 legislation followed thereafter. Subsequent to the passage of the bill, McCormick received another cash payment from the doctors. In all, he received five cash payments that were not reported as campaign contributions or as income on his federal or state income tax reports.[810]

McCormick was sentenced to probation and given a fine of $50,000 for his conviction of extortion and income tax evasion. He was also forced to pay restitution of $900 to lobbyist John Vandergrift from whom he had extorted money.[811] After resigning his seat from the Legislature, McCormick said, "I hope my resignation in no way gives the people of West Virginia the impression that I am guilty of extortion. I am not guilty of the charges brought against me, and am confident that my appeal will completely vindicate me."[812] The United States Supreme Court did reverse his conviction based upon technical reasons dealing with the statute under which he was convicted. The United States Supreme Court wrote:

> To hold that legislators commit the federal crime of extortion when they act for their constituents' benefit or support legislation furthering their constituents' interests, shortly before or after they solicit or receive campaign contributions from those beneficiaries, is an unrealistic assessment of what Congress could have meant when it made obtaining property from another 'under color of official right' a crime.[813]

After the United States Supreme Court threw out McCormick's conviction, it was sent back to the circuit court for a new trial. He then pled guilty to five misdemeanor charges of accepting illegal campaign contributions from the foreign-educated doctors who were trying to obtain State medical licenses and agreed to pay $15,750 in fines.[814]

As the controversy continued with McCormick, another State Attorney General, Charlie Brown, who served from 1985 through 1989, reasserted for the people of West Virginia the lack of confidence in the State's highest legal office. Brown, a proud Yale graduate, left office in disgrace when he resigned on August 21, 1989. Kanawha County Prosecutor Bill Forbes ended the grand jury investigation of Brown after the Attorney General agreed to resign.[815] Brown defeated State Senator Si Boettner, and Danny Staggers, the son of United States Congressman Harley O. Staggers, Sr., in a close and costly 1984 Primary Election. Boettner, incidentally, was later convicted of tax evasion and lost his law license. Following Brown's first election as Attorney General in 1984, he was re-elected without opposition in 1988.[816]

In endorsing Brown, the *Charleston Gazette* said he was "a vast improvement over his three predecessors: W.W. Barron and C. Donald Robertson, both of whom went to prison, and Chauncey Browning, who was constantly under investigation."[817] Controversy, however, surrounded Brown during the years prior to his resignation. He survived one of his first political storms in 1986 when he was acquitted on the charge that he was leaning on his office staff for campaign contributions to pay off his campaign debts. He solicited the money in spite of a State law which prohibits the solicitation of money from State employees. Brown contended that he had solicited the contributions after his 1984 election to pay off his campaign debts, and as such, the State law prohibiting State officials from soliciting campaign funds from employees did not apply.[818]

Jay Arceneaux testified that he and other Deputy Attorneys General were solicited by Brown to buy $100 tickets to a fundraiser to help satisfy a $40,000 debt incurred in Brown's 1984 campaign. Arceneaux said Brown told him that in order to run for office in West Virginia "you practically had to be a Senator (Jay) Rockefeller, otherwise you'll be in debt." Another Deputy Attorney General, David Grubb, said he bought a ticket to Brown's fundraiser because he thought he would lose his job if he didn't buy a ticket.[819] Brown was charged with seven counts of illegally soliciting money for political purposes from State employees on State property, but maintained, "[a]s God is my witness, I do not believe I have violated any laws of the State of West Virginia."[820]

As Attorney General, Brown was forced to leave office in 1989 as part of an agreement to halt a separate grand jury investigation that involved a plan by Brown to pay $50,000 to a secretary who claimed to need an abortion saying she was carrying his child. In addition to that salacious charge, there was another investigation of the Attorney General's campaign financial records separate from the previous 1986 investigation.[821] The secretary, Brenda K. Simon, was later indicted on charges that she attempted to extort money from Brown in exchange for her silence about his alleged role in her pregnancy.[822] Some of the notes revealing the details of Brown's situation were exposed during a child custody battle between Brown and his ex-wife. He had written about himself that "[i]t's clogging my head so bad I can't move [and that he was] a sweet guy, morally committed, til I was in politics."[823]

A few years later, Brown's brother, former Secretary of State of Ohio, Sherrod Brown, also faced controversy in his public life. Just like Attorney General Brown, Sherrod went through a messy public divorce. Sherrod, however, dealt with issues such as alleged abuse of his wife and taking money from his children to finance his campaign. He also faced controversy for his travel and potential travel plans out of the United States.[824] Attorney General Brown told people that both he and his brother were climbing the political ladders in their respective states and would some day be Governors at the same time. Sherrod survived his negative headlines and later became a United States Congressman from Ohio, an office he holds to this day. Attorney General Brown, on the other hand, is a lawyer in Washington, D.C.

In 1998, former Deputy Attorney General Mark Kindt, who served under the Charlie Brown Administration, submitted an opinion editorial in the *Charleston Gazette* praising his former boss. Kindt said, "I asked myself whether I would ever have the chance again to work with an inspired, committed public servant like Charles G. Brown. No, I think not."[825] Without discussing or even alluding to any of former Attorney General Brown's numerous indiscretions, former Deputy Attorney General Kindt wrote:

> Attempting to rescue a faded political legacy is probably a fool's errand, but since the decade has faded even faster, maybe the future deserves an attempt to return some luster to a tarnished time. Attorney General Charles G. Brown was a greater public servant than we knew or, perhaps, cared to admit. It will be a long time before West Virginia ever sees another attorney general with the drive, leadership and inspiration of Charlie Brown.

Kindt added,

> A hard-working, unbelievably energetic, very effective and twice-elected public servant was forced from the political stage prematurely. The public has not been particularly well-served by the success of the detractors of Charlie Brown. Many fine young lawyers learned this terrible lesson—'Avoid public serv-

ice at all costs.' I know because that is what they tell me when
I talk with them about careers in government.[826]

Kindt's comments are outrageous and illustrate a perfect example of
how people allow their personal relationships to taint the reality surrounding a
corrupt elected official. His comments underscore the deeper problem of acceptance of corruption and subsequent blame that is shifted everywhere except where
it belongs, the politician. To say that Brown was "forced from the political stage
prematurely" begs the question, who forced him from the stage? Was it the media
that forced him to illegally solicit contributions from State employees or to cheat
on his campaign finance forms? Was it the media or his political opponents who
forced him to have sex with his secretary and then set the stage for a $50,000 pay-
ment to keep her quiet and to pay for an abortion so that the Attorney General's
wife wouldn't find out? And, what about Mr. Kindt's comments that "many fine
young lawyers learned this terrible lesson–'Avoid public service at all costs.'" If
they are paying attention, the lesson they will learn is that it is not enough to be
energetic and hardworking, but instead, elected officials also have to be honest,
not bribe their employees, and be faithful to their spouses. Is that really too much
to ask of a politician?

The Brown saga also reveals another major problem with West
Virginia's elections that I like to call the Rockefeller factor. As elected officials
watched Rockefeller spend $12 million for his re-election as Governor in 1980,
followed by spending another $12 million in 1984 for his United States Senate
seat, it becomes apparent to any non-wealthy elected official or potential candidate that a victory against a Rockefeller-like opponent is next to impossible. In
fact, many well-intentioned and exceptionally qualified individuals will never
become involved in politics because they either can't raise the preposterous
amounts of money or they fear that a multi-millionaire will run at the last second
and buy the office by flooding the television and radio airwaves with millions of
dollars in campaign ads. As a result, many politicians become so completely
focused on getting elected or re-elected that they will do almost anything to come
up with every possible penny they can beg, borrow, or steal, in order to run their
campaigns. Attorney General Brown's comments to Arceneaux about money in
politics and needing to be a Rockefeller to survive illustrate that point.

Another problem with Brown's resignation was yet another politician
going without punishment. Agreeing to call off the grand jury to allow an elected official to resign, in my opinion, is malfeasance in office on behalf of the prosecuting attorney. A prosecutor is granted wide discretion in how and when to
charge an individual and that decision is not always an easy choice. In some

cases, however, the facts are so blatant and so outrageous that no reasonable decision other than prosecution could be reached–this was such a case. I just don't
understand the decision not to prosecute Brown based on the argument of saving
the taxpayers money or embarrassment. When it comes to a State's highest elected officials, those are precisely the types of cases that demand prosecution and
accountability given the State's already lackluster faith in its political system.
From another standpoint, why are elected officials often placed in a much better
position than the average citizens? For example, what if shoplifters or murderers
simply promised the judge they would not commit those crimes again in
exchange for dropping the charges against them? Would that be fair? Of course
not. There is simply no justifiable or rational reason to ever allow a corrupt
politician who violates the trust of the entire State to merely walk away without
any accountability for his or her actions.

A few years after Brown's shameful departure from the State, almost
amazingly and in spite of a continuous number of corrupt politicians being
accused, charged, impeached, and convicted of numerous criminal offenses, a
December 10, 1998, *Charleston Gazette* editorial began, "KEEP your fingers
crossed, but corruption seems to be fading in West Virginia." The editorial pro-
fessed: "During the Barron and Moore administrations, bribery investigations,
indictments and convictions were so continuous, they were like a major state
industry."[827] The *Gazette* unfortunately only had to wait about nine months for a
return to normalcy as State Senator Randy Schoonover added to West Virginia's
rich history of political corruption by accepting a paltry $2,725 in exchange for
putting his influence up for sale.[828]

In September 1999, the United States Attorney's Office for the Southern
District of West Virginia charged Schoonover with accepting a bribe in three payments from a politically prominent wrecking service owner who sought business on
the West Virginia Turnpike.[829] Federal Public Defender Mary Lou Newberger, who
represented Senator Schoonover, said he was lured into the scheme by Steve
LaRose, who was a former Summersville mayor and former State Republican Party
chairman.[830] On January 25, 2000, West Virginians learned once again that one of
their elected officials would be spending time behind bars for bribery. Perhaps even
more unfortunate for Schoonover was the fact that after selling his influence for
$2,725, he discovered he really didn't have much influence as he was unable to help
the LaRose family-owned towing business obtain more business on the Turnpike.[831]

Schoonover was sentenced by a United States District Court Judge to a
year-and-a-half in prison with two years to follow on supervised release. On
January 4, 2001, he was released from a federal correctional institution in
Ashland, Kentucky and began living at the Bannum Place, a St. Albans halfway

house in Charleston, West Virginia. He was later released from all incarceration and returned to his home in Clay County and started a new business, Central West Virginia Outfitters.[832]

L.T. Anderson, a columnist for the *Charleston Daily Mail* said, "In West Virginia, crime-in-government is never of the great, soaring audacious variety from which Michael Caine pictures are wrought. Usually, it involves a greasy back alley scheme that would embarrass any self-respecting thief." He added, "The Randy Schoonover affair is an outstanding example of West Virginia corruption. In bush league sleaze, it equals any I have observed during my fifty years of watching the Legislature struggle against any appearance of public service."[833]

On the day that Schoonover began serving his sentence, State Senator Mike Oliverio (D-Monongalia) addressed the Senate and requested that Senators remember their former colleague. Oliverio was also critical of federal prosecutors for targeting Schoonover and stated, "While no one condones his activity, I question the way the U.S. Attorney's office has gone about this case. . . . They picked on the guy in the Senate with the least education and the least money. It seemed a bit heavy handed."[834] While I have known Senator Oliverio for many years, surprisingly, the latter portion of his comments are completely off base. Schoonover was smart enough to become elected as one of thirty-four State Senators and regardless of his income or educational levels, it doesn't take a rocket scientist to know that bribery is illegal. Moreover, Schoonover was not a political newcomer to West Virginia politics. He was first elected to the House of Delegates in 1988, re-elected in 1990 and 1992, and was appointed in 1993 to fill a vacancy in the State Senate. Thereafter, he was elected to his Senate seat in 1994 and re-elected in 1998.

As for the comment about a "heavy handed" investigation, it seems likely that Oliverio was simply reflecting the sadness felt by a colleague who liked Senator Schoonover personally and felt sorry for him. Nonetheless, it is enormously difficult for federal prosecutors to obtain enough information to convict a politician of corruption in the first place because those behaviors are often well hidden. When they actually do convict a corrupt politician, it doesn't make any sense to me to criticize them for arresting the ones who may not be the best at covering their tracks. Incidentally, on March 23, 2006, Schoonover was arrested on a felony charge of delivery of a narcotic substance.

Barron, Robertson, Kelly, McCormick, Brown, and Schoonover, as well as numerous other corrupt State elected officials, highlight an enormous problem with West Virginia politics–no accountability. There is such a lackadaisical attitude when statewide politicians commit crimes which necessarily trickles down to district, county, and city politicians. For instance, in an agreement to avoid prosecution similar to the situation of Attorney General Brown, Mingo County Clerk Tommy Diamond resigned amid allegations that he overcharged the county for expenses; sold computers that were donated to the Young Marines and kept the proceeds; attempted extortion of his employees; received a $2,000 advance payment to attend a meeting that he later did not attend and did not return the money to the county coffers; and paid various people listed as employees who didn't actually work for the office.[835]

Diamond contended that he was resigning for personal health reasons, declaring he had done nothing wrong and that the prosecutor's office had a "personal vendetta" against him. Another charge was that he used a county credit card assigned to him, as well as another county credit card belonging to another county officeholder, for his personal use without reimbursing the county. In addition, Diamond was accused of altering birth records for a doctor under federal indictment and accepting payment from the City of Williamson for holding Primary Elections in 1989, 1993, 1997, and 2001, and then pocketing the money for himself.[836]

This was not his first brush with controversy. A few years earlier, in June 2000, Diamond pled guilty to a misdemeanor battery charge for striking Mingo County convicted felon Johnnie Owens. Owens, incidentally, was the Sheriff of Mingo County who sold his office in 1982 for $100,000. Following his conviction, Owens returned to Mingo County where he is said to still possess considerable political influence in county politics.[837] Nonetheless, the accusations against Diamond were serious and he simply retired and walked away. Criminal politicians should be prosecuted to the fullest extent of the law, stripped of their retirement, and sentenced to the longest possible jail sentences. Otherwise, the only lesson that is learned by other current and prospective county elected officials is to steal all that they possibly can while they're in office in hopes that they don't get caught. Then, if they do get caught, they can simply resign or retire and maybe even run for election again a few years later as many of West Virginia's scoundrels have done.

Another example of a lack of enforcement at the county level occurred following the December 10, 2004, resignation of Randolph County Clerk Rosezetta Lloyd, who left her post of eighteen years and entered a plea of no contest to a misdemeanor embezzlement charge on December 13, 2004. She entered the plea just eleven days after search warrants were issued based on discrepancies found during an audit. The plea also occurred prior to a full investigation of how much money was actually stolen. Lloyd agreed to be charged with the misdemeanor and to pay restitution to the county in the amount of $48,000 over a five-year period, without interest. Circuit Judge John Henning sentenced Rosezetta

Lloyd to one year in the regional jail and ordered her to pay a $2,500 fine and court costs.

After serving only eight months of her one-year sentence, Lloyd was released for good behavior. Under her plea deal, she can't be prosecuted for any additional missing funds even though further audits of the Randolph County Clerks Office revealed that more than $198,000 dollars was unaccounted for during her final five-years as County Clerk. On September 27, 2005, the Randolph County Commission voted two-to-one to proceed with a forensic audit of the records in the County Clerk's Office to try to ascertain how much money was actually stolen throughout the years. Regardless of their results and even if it is determined that she was able to take more than $1 million, Lloyd will never be forced to pay another dime that she pilfered from the unsuspecting taxpayers. Moreover, the $48,000 penalty, which was paid in full by Lloyd in January 2006, was already earmarked by county commissioners to pay for forensic audits on four additional years of records kept while Lloyd served as county clerk. Thus, in actuality, the citizens were unable to recover a single dime of the stolen money![838]

In Marshall County, Assessor Alfred "Pinky" Clark, who served as assessor for twenty-six years, was indicted in 1992 on fifteen racketeering charges of extorting money, land, and groceries from companies in exchange for lower tax rates. In spite of the indictment against him, Clark ran for re-election in 1992 and was narrowly defeated during the Primary Election. He then announced a couple of weeks prior to the General Election that he was running as a write-in candidate. Clark lost but still received nearly 20 percent of the total votes which is a significant number of votes for a write-in campaign. Clark called the charges against him a personal vendetta by the federal prosecutor.[839]

In July 1995, however, Clark, described by *Charleston Gazette* editor James Haught as "West Virginia's worst demagogue," was sentenced to three years of probation and ordered to pay an $8,000 fine to Housing Showcase Mobile Homes, Inc.[840] Clark pled guilty in federal court to one felony count of tampering with a witness and agreed not to seek political office for at least three years.[841] Just months before the indictment against Clark, Marshall County Prosecuting Attorney Thomas E. White pled guilty on January 3, 1992, to three misdemeanor drug charges for possession of cocaine, marijuana and Percocet, and resigned from office. According to the West Virginia Supreme Court, "White became involved in a physical relationship with a woman and, during the course of this relationship, he began to use marijuana and cocaine." White also admitted forging the name of his dentist on a prescription form and using it to obtain Percocet.[842] White was sentenced to six months in a federal correctional facility, followed by four months of home detention, and three years of probation. A $3,000 fine was also imposed in addition to a two year suspension of his law license.

Assessor Clark and Prosecutor White received statewide news coverage throughout the years when they became entwined in a conflict with what may be the most famous Hare Krishna temple in North America. Everybody has heard of the Hare Krishnas or perhaps watched them in an airport proudly dancing in their robes with their shaved heads as they aggressively solicit cash for their group. I remember seeing large numbers of the group in a Los Angeles airport years ago as they chanted loudly, danced and hopped up and down in an almost trance-like gathering. I remember one Hare Krishna member dancing around me as I was trying to maneuver my two pieces of luggage and had to keep stepping around him. He had a pair of kartals, the finger cymbals used during their worship ceremonies, and used them right next to my ear. Another Krishna member was beating a tabla drum. As they chanted the Hare Krishna maha-mantra: "Hare Krishna, Hare Krishna Krishna Krishna, Hare Hare Hare Rama, Hare Rama Rama Rama, Hare Hare," I found myself feeling very out of place.

Little did I know, however, that was the Krishna group that had actually developed a large 4,000 acre New Vrindaban compound in the Northern Panhandle of West Virginia. It was that compound where Assessor Clark battled the Krishnas and attempted to raise the property taxes on the compound which contains the ornate "Palace of Gold," which has become a huge tourist attraction in West Virginia. Clark challenged the group's tax-exempt status as a church and sought to appraise the Krishnas' property for millions of dollars.[843]

During the 1980s, however, as Clark sought to raise taxes on the Krishna compound, this supposed place of peace and spiritual enlightenment had also become tainted by charges of child abuse, malicious wounding, drug trafficking, vandalism, and murder. Even the community's founder, Kirtananda Swami Bhaktipada, was sentenced to twenty years in a federal prison for racketeering and was accused of being involved in the murder of two Hare Krishna dissidents. He was also charged with arson surrounding the burning of an apartment building near the New Vrindaban commune to collect $40,000 in insurance money. He was found not guilty of arson, but a federal court did find Hare Krishna devotee Thomas Drescher guilty of the arson and of the murder of Steve Bryant, a thirty-three-year-old disenchanted Hare Krishna devotee who exposed some of the group's wrongdoings.

Following the murder of Bryant and the numerous rumors of other transgressions within the New Vrindaban compound, Clark requested a concealed weapon's permit and began carrying a pistol. Clark said a worker at the compound told him that after Bryant's death, plans were in the works to seek revenge against Clark for the tax assessments which cost the compound a lot of money. Clark only lives within three miles of New Vrindaban.[844]

Even though Clark was convicted in federal court in 1995, he continued to seek political office. In 2004, he ran for the House of Delegates and lost by only 284 votes.[845] He is another example of how personal relationships seem to excuse the criminal behavior of elected officials. I met Clark prior to his 1992 indictment. He was a former President of the Association of West Virginia Assessors at the same time my father was the Tucker County Assessor. I often traveled with my father and attended the association's meetings. I would describe Clark as a person who enjoyed the spotlight and seemed to always be campaigning. I could only imagine that he acted the same way within his county by constantly shaking hands and promising favors. Clark bragged to me about his 300 mile walk to Charleston, West Virginia with 20,000 signatures in protest of the Legislature's re-appraisal legislation that resulted in higher taxes. He laughed as he told me how some newspapers criticized him harshly, but how the people in his county saw him as a great fighter against higher taxes even though he was the assessor. I thought of his comments in 2004 when, in spite of his earlier guilty plea in federal court, many of his county's residents placed an "X" next to his name on the ballot for his run for Delegate. To me, however, it is another example of a convicted criminal who was never truly held accountable for his actions.

Once again, I am left wondering why West Virginia doesn't have a lifetime ban on people who have been convicted of corruption-related felonies preventing their election to another public office. Moreover, Clark's indiscretions, as well as other corrupt assessors, have led me to another conclusion that the position of county assessor simply should not be an elected political office. Paying taxes is not popular in any place in the world and what incentive is there for an elected county assessor to actually do his or her job? As taxes increase, the likelihood of an assessor keeping his job decreases. It also creates a situation ripe for fraud as wealthy companies and individuals are sometimes able to bribe some of the fifty-five county assessors who have the power to affect the tax amount these companies or individuals will have to pay. The result is that people throughout the State are not treated equally. Personally, I feel that property taxes in general are regressive taxes and the State should review other options to raise revenues. Nonetheless, if the State does continue to operate under this system, then serious reform is necessary. When I pay my tax bill each year, it is only fair that large companies and wealthy landowners also pay their fair share.

Another example on the county level of a lack of accountability occurred when Kanawha County's Prosecuting Attorney, Bill Charnock, who was elected on an anti-corruption platform in 2004, was charged in May 2005 by the State Legislative Auditor's Office with making at least $345 worth of personal calls on his State-owned cell phone while working in his previous job as head of the State Prosecuting Attorney's Institute. The auditors said they could not tell whether another $588 in calls were personal or work related. How did Charnock respond to the charges against him? Obviously he was embarrassed by his lack of judgment and illegal use of taxpayer money and apologized profusely, right? Well, not exactly. Charnock said, "I admitted error. I accepted responsibility. I've got more important things to do." He then told a *Charleston Daily Mail* reporter, "I was preparing to try a murder case today. I've got work to do. I don't have the time to go through a cell phone bill."[846]

Charnock was also under investigation with regard to falsified time sheets used to maximize federal grant funding.[847] The audit also alleged that time sheets may have been doctored during 2004 so that the salary of Fred Giggenbach, an assistant prosecutor assigned to the Institute, would be fully covered by a federal grant from the United States Department of Justice which required him to spend at least 90 percent of his time related to the grant. Giggenbach initially submitted time sheets indicating that he spent approximately 25 percent of his time working on cases covered by the grant. Charnock signed and approved those time sheets.

On November 4, 2004, a conference call between the Division of Criminal Justice staff and Charnock and Giggenbach was held wherein the Division reiterated that Giggenbach needed to spend 90 percent of his time on cases related to the grant. The following day, Giggenbach submitted two amended time sheets where he changed his hours from the 85 listed on his first set of time sheets to reflect 352 hours on grant-related work on the amended time sheets. Charnock signed and approved the amended time sheets. Normally, such an investigation would be turned over by the Legislature to the Kanawha County Prosecutor; however, since Charnock is the Kanawha County Prosecutor, he cannot be assigned to investigate himself. Speaker of the House Bob Kiss and Senate President Earl Ray Tomblin were reluctant to get the Legislature's Commission of Special Investigations involved in the matter because they have to cooperate with Charnock on other cases.

My question to Prosecutor Charnock is simple: Are you really too busy to explain to the taxpayers how you bilked them out of their money? If so, I can say unequivocally to him that since illegally using State property is a trivial matter, I will be "too busy" to check the box next to his name during the next election. I find this very troubling because I had spoken with him on many occasions while I was a Senior Assistant Attorney General during the same period when he was leading the Prosecuting Attorney's Institute. I rarely had disagreements with him and was excited about his candidacy. Once again, my initial excitement about a political candidate has turned to disappointment.

Several months after the time sheet and cell phone controversy, Charnock again faced heavy criticism for additional actions while he was the head of the Prosecuting Attorney's Institute. The charges surrounded whether he used State employees and resources to help him win the election as Kanawha County Prosecuting Attorney in 2004. Charnock immediately denied any wrongdoing and called the legislative audit a "political witch-hunt." When asked if he would stay in office, Charnock said, "Why would I resign? The only thing more absurd would be for me to change my registration to Democrat."[848]  John Charnock, Sr., a former State Ethics Commission Chairman and former Charleston municipal judge, echoed his son's comments saying, "What we have here is a witch hunt. Period." Charnock, Sr. added, "Some people get carried away with their own importance" saying auditors were "overzealous" and simply trying to "embarrass someone."[849]

The audit charged that Charnock was frequently absent from work for the two months before the election; he printed and copied thousands of campaign letters on office equipment; he generated an estimated 700 campaign-related emails on his office computer in the fourteen months before his election; a State-paid technician created a website for Charnock and his family members' campaigns; that he had State workers helping him put on political fundraisers; and that he used State employees, phones, printers, copiers, and other supplies for his campaign and the campaigns of his brother, City of Charleston employee John Charnock, and sister, Kanawha Family Court Judge Jane Charnock Smallridge. The audit said Charnock may have violated ethics and election laws, and may have committed five different felonies, ranging from destruction of public records to embezzlement.[850]

Prosecuting Attorney's Institute Chairwoman Ginny Conley said Charnock promised her several times in 2003 and 2004 that he would not use the resources of the office to further his campaign. Tom Susman, then-Secretary of Administration, said he also warned Charnock "not to use his office's resources during the campaign." In an email from his State account sent to his campaign manager Les Milam, Charnock said, "Got a call from the asshole in the state-house (Tom Susman–he is my agency's cabinet secretary) who told me there is talk at the statehouse wondering how I can be a candidate and a state employee–not from a legal standpoint but an ethical standpoint. My response to asshole was I told my board, they support me so be it."[851]

The audit revealed Charnock complained that a State employee was keeping him from copying campaign materials on a State-owned copy machine.

He said, "I am trying to get a bunch of stuff printed, but Amy is hogging the copier so I am having a hard time." The audit also quotes the State agency's database coordinator as saying Charnock "asked me to clear out his computer so that nothing could be found." Charnock said the auditor's review of his State computer was "just like placing an eavesdropping device in my bedroom [and that] the tactics used during this two-and-a-half-year audit were despicable, disgusting and no other person should have to endure it."[852]

The Charnock audit also revealed emails where he and former United States Attorney Kasey Warner discussed how to circumvent State campaign finance laws. In an email to Charnock, Warner asked, "Can you tell me whether contributors to your campaign are reported by name?" When Charnock replied that "anonymous contributions are verboten," Warner said, "Let me try to steer some contributions your way (gently) and perhaps use a family member with a different last name to make my contribution." In June of 2005, the State auditors sent the emails between Charnock and Warner to the Department of Justice. On July 5, 2005, the Department replied that it was opening a formal investigation. On August 1, 2005, it announced that Warner was no longer a United States Attorney. Warner said, "I worked at [the President's] will and pleasure. At some point, he decided my service was no longer needed [and that] I was given a letter saying that my services were no longer needed." As the *Charleston Gazette* explained,

> Here's an irony in the uproar over Kanawha prosecutor Bill Charnock: At the same time former U.S. Attorney Kasey Warner was bringing election charges against Democratic politicos in southern county courthouses, Warner sent an email offering to violate election laws by funneling money surreptitiously into the campaign of fellow Republican Charnock. No wonder the Justice Department ousted Warner.[853]

Investigations of Charnock were instituted by the Secretary of State's Office as well as the State Police. Kanawha County Chief Circuit Judge Paul Zakaib then appointed Dwane Tinsley as a special prosecutor to examine the evidence collected by the State Police. In spite of the charges against him and the fact that he openly admitted he used State resources for his campaign and the campaigns of his family members, Charnock said, "The audit reveals absolutely no violation of the criminal law." He called his use of State resources for electioneering "incidental and de minimus." He also called the audit and investigation against him "wasted countless hours of government time and countless dollars on taxpayers' time and expense trying to discredit me" and said that the audit was "a distraction to my doing my job I was elected to do."[854]

In addition to the many other negative newspaper headlines involving Charnock, on December 16, 2005, the *Charleston Gazette*, reported that the prosecutor had left the scene of a brawl with a man accused of breaking a beer bottle over someone's head at a West Virginia University football game in October 2005. According to the *Gazette*, as well as a criminal complaint filed in Monongalia County, Jeffery L. Johns, Jr. broke a beer bottle over the head of Joseph Wickline and punched him in the face. The fight took place next to Charnock's silver Volvo, which was parked in a prime tailgating area. After the alleged assault, Johns climbed into the Volvo and Charnock drove him away. Charnock was not accused of a crime with regard to this incident.[855]

In another situation involving a Legislative Audit, the State's General Services Division, which maintains the Capitol Complex grounds and buildings, demonstrated its ability to participate in the State's history of corruption. On January 18, 2006, the *Associated Press* broke the story that an office in the State Capitol labeled "electric shop" in a high-traffic area located beside the cafeteria and just one floor beneath the Governor's Office, had been illegally operating a pirating studio on State time and with State computers. I personally have walked by that office countless times on my way to lunch. Just one week earlier, on January 11, 2006, Governor Joe Manchin, III unveiled the twenty-six new West Virginia signs that would soon thereafter be appearing at all of the State's border entrances. Manchin proudly touted his slogan "Open For Business" which he ordered be included on all of the new signs. Little did he know that it would be discovered the very next week that some members of his General Services Division had been operating under that mantra already.

Investigators stumbled onto the office, which was outfitted with computers, video and audio gear, and software used to pirate movies and music recordings. "Specifically, one hard drive contained approximately 40 full-length motion videos [and] two other hard drives contained over 3,500 MP3 music files consuming more than 14 [gigabytes] of hard drive space." The office also contained hundreds of blank DVDs, CDs and jacket covers along with software "commonly used to crack header codes on copyrighted materials such as movies and music to allow duplication." It was also learned that someone in the General Services Division sidestepped State purchasing rules to buy more than $88,000 worth of computers and related equipment during the preceding three year period, while much of that computer-related equipment could not be located. The FBI and the Legislature's Commission of Special Investigations immediately began investigating the matter.[856]

The Capitol recording studio scandal fell on the heals of the firing of two other General Services staffers, Gary McClanahan and Gary Bryant, after they claimed they had worked 18-hour days 119 times during the course of two-and-one-half years when in reality they didn't actually work those hours. In fact, former health and safety manager Bryant admitted that he sometimes exercised along Kanawha Boulevard when he was supposed to be supervising asbestos removal projects. According to one contractor, Bryant also forced contractors to slow down their work so he could jack up his overtime. A Legislative Audit found that, "[the contractor's] representative was instructed not to run any clearance samples prior to 21:30 hours even if the asbestos removal had been completed much earlier as this would further justify . . . overtime."

The Audit further revealed that General Services did not keep any inventory of its tools, so there was no way of knowing where their tools were located or if any were missing. The Division also used the asbestos cleanup money improperly to pay for cell phones, car rental, and the salary of an employee who did minimal asbestos work. If that's not bad enough, a previous Audit, completed just one month earlier, revealed that General Services employees may have rigged the asbestos contract bids to benefit two asbestos-removal companies, including one owned by former Division of Motor Vehicles Commissioner Roger Pritt, the brother to former gubernatorial candidate Charlotte Pritt. General Services personnel split large jobs into several small contracts, apparently to evade competitive-bidding procedures. Pritt, whose company, Astar Abatement, received 27 of the 32 asbestos-removal contracts, denied any wrongdoing. According to the Audit, in one instance, what should have been one asbestos-removal project was split into nine separate contracts, one for each heating and air-conditioning unit in the basement, even though the units were just a few feet from one another. Each of the nine contracts were worth slightly less than $10,000, the limit that would have triggered statewide competitive bidding.[857]

The people of West Virginia only had to wait a couple of more weeks before the next disappointment with their State government. On February 9, 2006, newspapers throughout the State reported that more than $1 million was missing from RESA 1, one of the eight State Department of Education's Regional Education Service Agencies. The Legislature created the regional agencies in 1972 to equalize and extend educational opportunities for public school students. Each of the eight RESA agencies are made up of the county superintendents, a school board member from each participating county, a teacher, a principal, and a representative for the State Schools Superintendent. RESA 1 serves McDowell, Mercer, Monroe, Raleigh, Summers and Wyoming counties.

Soon after learning that the money was missing, the RESA 1 Advisory Board accepted the resignation of Deborah Calhoun Mitchell, executive secretary of RESA 1 for more than twenty years. Advisory Board member and McDowell County Superintendent Mark A. Manchin, brother to current Governor Joe Manchin, III, said that more than $1 million was unaccounted for over the past five years. "It appears some corporations were created, invoices were generated, [Post Office boxes] were generated and checks were sent to them [and that] obviously, it gives us great concern."[858]

In a matter-of-fact statement, one member of the Advisory Board said, "It has been determined that financial irregularities have occurred at RESA 1." "Financial irregularities" to me sounds like a very minor problem, when in reality, this was a very serious situation. What I saw with this latest debacle was the same lack of outrage by public officials that I have become accustomed to throughout the years. Consider that more than $1 million in educational funds cannot be accounted for during the past five years which were set aside for some of the poorest counties in most need of assistance. Then, consider that the RESA 1 accounts were audited each year by the State Auditor's Office, but the "irregularities" weren't found during any of those audits. This is precisely the type of situation where West Virginians yearn to hear politicians screaming for immediate action, and then taking that action. Instead, the stolen money amounted to a one-or-two-day story in the newspapers. If history repeats itself in West Virginia, someone will eventually be sent to jail for a short period of time and be forced to pay a small fine, while few questions will be asked and few, if any, safeguards will be put in place to prevent this type of scandal in the future.

Just weeks later, on March 9, 2006, it was learned that the State Legislature's Commission on Special Investigations launched a probe into more than $5.8 million in misspent homeland security funds. According to State Military Affairs and Public Safety Secretary James Spears, "almost every single" county misspent some of the money. This came on the heals of the April 2005 resignation of Neal Sharp, who headed the department's regional response team program. Sharp resigned amid an investigation into emergency equipment purchases, his use of State credit cards, and flights he took on the State's airplane and helicopter. Soon afterward, two more homeland security officials, Lee Gray, the former budget director, and Steve Rogers, a coordinator with the regional response team, resigned. Around that same time, Steve Kappa, who headed the State Office of Emergency Services, and who reported Sharp's alleged wrongdoing, was fired.[859]

As this cycle of corruption continues, how can any West Virginian have any confidence in a system when they watch their governors and attorneys general, those responsible for the execution and enforcement of State laws, being convicted of seedy and sometimes salacious activities. Those feelings are only further bolstered when they witness these same people serving little or no prison sentences followed by little or no remorse for their actions. In some cases, these individuals don't even seem to lose any of their political clout in State government.

Additionally, political corruption has become so commonplace that many people expect such behavior as an accepted result of politics. In many instances people don't even get upset and don't seem to understand why others take political corruption so seriously. For example, even after Governor Barron was accused of stealing millions of dollars which was supposed to go to flood cleanup, and even after he admitted bribing jurors to secure his acquittal, people were quick to defend his tenure in office. Likewise, after Attorney General Robertson was convicted for bribery and was later accused of putting a professional hit on a former employee who planned to testify against him, many people were quick to forgive and forget those actions. In fact, one *Charleston Gazette* reader criticized the paper for mentioning some of Robertson's indiscretions in his obituary. The reader wrote a letter to the editor saying he believed it was wrong to bring out the details of Robertson's conviction and prison time because, "[t]he man has served his term. Why bring up the sordid facts and embarrass his family again?"[860]

The reason you bring up the sordid facts is to show that his actions were wrong. I want to know when the bar for political indiscretions was dropped to such an unbelievably low level. Instead of being held to a much higher standard as should be the case, we hold politicians to a much lower standard than we would accept from kindergartners. A more appropriate sanction for convicted politicians, in addition to lengthy sentences with steep financial penalties, would be to force them to wear large letters on their shirts, coats, or suits indicating their crimes. They could wear a large "B" for bribery or a large "C" for conspiracy, just as Hester Prynne wore her "A" in Nathaniel Hawthorne's *The Scarlet Letter*. Better yet, we could even require their license plate on their vehicle be bright Red with the initial letter of their license indicating the crime they committed. Moreover, these political criminals should be sentenced to walk the streets for eight hours per day with large sandwich placards around their necks explaining their criminal actions followed by hours on end speaking to school children and service organizations about the consequences of their criminal behaviors.

When did it become politically incorrect to actually be embarrassed by a criminal conviction? These people should be embarrassed. Even if the law has been violated countless times with impunity, as is the case with many West Virginia politicians, that doesn't mean that subsequent violations should be considered legal or acceptable. Just as an armed robber may steal your wallet, these criminal politicians who engage in bribery are stealing your democracy.

# CHAPTER THIRTEEN

# Gambling

*It is time to take the 'For Sale' sign off the Capitol building.*

Assistant United States Attorney Joe Savage

West Virginia politics has been surrounded by controversy and corruption and one contributing factor has undoubtedly been the gambling industry. An example of this is Elton "Butch" Bryan, a former Director of the West Virginia Lottery and William Edward ReBrook, III, then-attorney for the Lottery Commission. Both were convicted in the early 1990s of corruption for their illegal activities surrounding the State Lottery.[861]

In September 1993, after a jury trial in federal District Court, Bryan was convicted of two counts of mail fraud, one count of wire fraud, one count of securities fraud, and perjury. He was convicted of forcing his subordinates to lie and produce false documents to award the lottery's 1991 advertising contract to Fahlgren Martin Inc., of Parkersburg, West Virginia. He also rigged bids in a failed attempt to grant a video lottery contract to Video Lottery Technologies (VLT) of Bozeman, Montana, in exchange for promises of a job with the company. Bryan resigned as Lottery Director and was sentenced to four years and three months incarceration for bid-rigging and attempting to steer the $2.8 million advertising contract to a company that did not have the best rating for the job. He was also convicted of perjury for giving false testimony before a grand jury.[862]

I first met Bryan in 1992 when I was working for Governor Caperton. I remember one occasion on a Wednesday during the early part of that year when I was in charge of a day of legislative bill signing and photograph opportunities, known simply as "photo ops." Such events were usually held weekly in the Governor's Reception Room for just about any group who requested a picture with the Governor whether it was signing a particular piece of legislation or simply posing for a picture with a county fair queen or a winner of that year's soap box derby. Those events usually included an eclectic group of people and this day was no exception. I remember waiting for the Governor to arrive from the Mansion that morning as I was trying to coordinate the more than 200 people who filled the room.

On this particular day, Bryan approached me and instead of saying hello, he abruptly said, "I am Butch Bryan and I have to speak with Gaston prior to the bill signing." I told him that I didn't "believe it would be possible because. . ." as he cut me off and said, "Don't you know who I am?" "I am Butch Bryan," he said in a condescending tone stressing the "I." "I am the Director of the Lottery. Now, young man, I want to talk with Gaston now." Keeping my cool, I calmly said, "I know who you are and it's just not possible this morning."

As I continued to prepare for the morning event with the many others who were there to see the Governor, Bryan began shaking a lengthy speech printed on note cards in my face and said, "You will give this to Gaston and he will read it." As I think of that day, I can't remember exactly which photo op Bryan was even there for because there were so many people waiting and quite frankly I didn't see any one of them as more important than the other. The one thing I did know was that I had had enough of his arrogance and had too many other people to worry about getting ready for the event. I turned to him, handed him back the speech, and said, "I work for Governor Caperton, not for Butch Bryan. This speech will not be read. And, in the future, if you have any press suggestions or speech suggestions then submit them in advance and in writing to Bob Brunner or George Manahan in the press office. Are we clear?" Bryan turned so red that I thought he was going to burst a vain in his balding forehead. I am quite certain that he didn't appreciate this coming from a twenty-one-year-old kid.

In any case, I had no idea that a controversy would soon surround this man and the State Lottery. In fact, it wasn't until months later, while I was working for Congressman Harley O. Staggers, Jr., that I began to hear rumors of potential corruption surrounding the Lottery. People assumed since I worked with the Governor that I must have known everything that occurred in the Governor's Office and had some new or secret information to share on the brewing scandal. The fact was that I knew nothing about the Lottery at the time and found the stories in the newspapers confusing as they talked of insider-trading, bid-rigging, and even questions of sexual improprieties surrounding Lottery attorney Ed ReBrook. Even as the story unfolded throughout the years, I wasn't sure exactly where all of the pieces fit. Some of the facts I believe will never be known.

In April 1990, Ed ReBrook was hired as Lottery counsel by Director Bryan. ReBrook, a 1992 candidate for Attorney General, was later sentenced to two years and three months in jail for buying stock in the Montana gaming company and telling others to do so based upon inside information that Governor Caperton planned to expand video lottery immediately following the General Election. Among those ReBrook provided information to was former State Attorney General C. Donald Robertson, who years earlier was convicted of bribery of a public official, and businessmen James Kay Thomas. ReBrook, Robertson, and Thomas purchased a combined $90,000 worth of VLT stock based upon the belief that the State would soon be expanding video lottery and awarding VLT a multi-million dollar contract.[863]

ReBrook was convicted on November 5, 1993, of wire fraud and insider trading. During that same period, he faced other problems unrelated to the Lottery scandal as he lost his law license amid allegations that he exchanged legal services for sexual favors with several women. Although he admitted having sex with two of his clients, in addition to the federal conviction against him surrounding the State Lottery, the West Virginia Supreme Court returned ReBrook's law license to him in May of 2001.[864] He currently practices law in Charleston, West Virginia.

The gambling issue is not new to West Virginia. In January 1931, Governor William G. Conley, Attorney General Howard B. Lee, and Logan County Circuit Judge Naaman Jackson met to discuss the illegal gaming activity and conditions existing in Logan County. Circuit Judge Jackson said: "Since Don Chafin began his reign in Logan County in 1913, the county has had a tradition of lawlessness, and much of that criminal activity has been traceable directly to the Sheriff's Office."[865]

Circuit Judge Jackson reported that gambling was widespread in Logan County and operated within the protection of the Sheriff. It was noted that then-Sheriff Joe Hatfield installed an estimated 200 slot machines in the county to pay for the money he had to borrow in order to win the election. "The machines [were] designed to accommodate all classes of gamblers–dime, quarter, half dollar, and dollar" including "some school children gambl[ing] away their lunch money."[866] Joe Hatfield was the son of Devil Anse Hatfield (Hatfield-McCoy feud) and a cousin to West Virginia Governor Henry D. Hatfield (1913-1917).

Attorney General Lee said the Logan City Council was opposed to the gambling machines and ordered the Chief of Police, Lon Browning, to arrest "all persons who have such gambling devices on their premises." The Chief of Police quickly resigned, stating that he was not ready to die. A new Chief, Roy Knotts, was hired. Upon his appointment, Knotts entered a local pool hall to purchase cigarettes and was shot five times in the back. The warrants for the arrest of slot machine operators were later found in his pocket soaked with his blood. The Logan County Prosecutor would not enforce the gambling laws as he feared that he would suffer the same fate as Chief Knotts. According to Judge Jackson, the Prosecutor was "grossly incompetent and drunk most of his waking hours."[867]

Such problems surrounding gambling have occurred throughout the years and were not limited to specific locations of the State. For instance, West Virginia's Northern Panhandle has not been immune to the problem of illegal gambling. In Dan Fleming's book *Kennedy vs. Humphrey, West Virginia 1960*, he interviewed Harry Hamm, long-time editor of the *Wheeling News-Register*. Hamm described the Northern Panhandle of West Virginia as a "political snakepit." He explained that "racketeers" and even the Mafia played a role in the State's elections due to the prevalent gambling activities. Hamm explains:

> Ohio County, where Wheeling is located, for many years was a forbidden zone to the Mafia because of the dominance by local crime overlord 'Big' Bill Lias, who operated the Wheeling Downs racetrack and according to Hamm, all of the remaining forms of crime, including the 'numbers' and slot machines. However, Hamm said the Pittsburgh Mafia considered nearby Hancock and Brooke Counties part of their territory. In these two counties, particularly Hancock, the Mafia was 'always active in every political campaign' from governor on down. He added that most of the statewide political figures in West Virginia over the years would negotiate with the racket leaders such as Bill Lias to secure their support in elections in that area of West Virginia.[868]

Fleming said that during the 1960 Primary Election a strong Hancock County organization well-financed by "local rackets that controlled illegal slot machines, the numbers, track betting, and other forms of gambling" dominated local elections. In addition, he describes a close relationship between gaming interests and some State officials. He said that one State figure received $15,000 per year for several years to insure that the State Police would leave slot-machine gambling alone.[869]

The Northern Panhandle's gambling problems didn't end with the Kennedy election. In 1979, the Hancock County Prosecuting Attorney, Robert G. Altomare, was found guilty for his involvement in illegal gambling activities. As a result, he was indicted on three counts for violating, and conspiring to violate, in 1977 through 1979, the federal Racketeer Influenced and Corrupt Organizations Act (RICO) and for violating, on January 31, 1979, the Obstruction of Justice Act, by attempting to induce a witness before a grand jury to testify falsely. During the same time, he stood trial for conspiring to obstruct the enforcement of the criminal laws of West Virginia "with the intent to facilitate an illegal gambling business." Altomare was convicted of all charges on May 2, 1979.[870]

Altomare's situation was similar to Marion County Sheriff Charles H. Dodd's, who served in various public positions including Deputy Sheriff and Circuit Court Clerk. Dodd resigned as Sheriff in 1985, and was later convicted for receiving illegal payments in exchange for failure to enforce anti-gambling laws against a certain gambling establishment operating illegally in Marion County. He was fined $3,000, placed on probation for three years, and lost his State pension for "less than honorable service."[871] While I agree with the fact that Sheriff Dodd should have lost his pension because of his illegal activities, such action when a West Virginia politician leaves office due to corruption usually doesn't occur. More often than not, these law violating politicians are simply asked to resign or plead guilty to a lesser crime and pay a small fine resulting in little to no accountability for their actions.

In another case of gambling impropriety, in May 1990, William T. Ellis was convicted of extortion, conspiracy, racketeering, and obstruction of justice.[872] When I first read the federal criminal case against Ellis, I thought that his name seemed familiar. I soon realized that he was a former landlord of mine. It is just one more example of how small West Virginia is and how people unknowingly become intertwined during their everyday lives with the actors in this unscrupulous play of political corruption misfits.

The conviction of Ellis was another case involving a race track and politicians. He was a limited partner in Tri-State Greyhound Park Incorporated, a West Virginia corporation that conducted pari-mutual betting on greyhound races. Under West Virginia statutes, Tri-State was permitted to retain a specific percentage of the revenue generated by public betting. Because of unexpected financial shortfalls in 1986, the owners supported a bill that would have given dog track owners a larger percentage from the bets. Although the bill passed both houses of the West Virginia Legislature, it was vetoed by the Governor. The owners endeavored to get a similar bill passed again in 1987. To support its efforts, Tri-State promised to pay Ellis $500,000 if the bill became law. Ellis, working through lobbyist Samuel D'Annunzio, allegedly provided cash and amenities to various State legislators.[873] This time, the bill passed the Legislature and was signed by then-Governor Arch A. Moore, Jr.

A subsequent corruption investigation led to a plea agreement from D'Annunzio, who detailed the corruption scheme and his relationship with Ellis. D'Annunzio also gave the government tapes, which he had secretly recorded, of conversations with Ellis and other participants in the scheme. Consequently, in December 1988, in the midst of the continuing investigation, D'Annunzio committed suicide. At Ellis' trial where he faced charges of mail fraud, racketeering, and obstruction of justice, the government sought to admit statements of the deceased D'Annunzio which implicated Ellis. D'Annunzio's statements provided information to United States Attorneys on the corrupt activities of Ellis, former State Senate Presidents Dan Tonkovich and Larry Tucker, State Senate Majority Leader Si Boettner, and Governor Arch Moore, Jr. Ellis was sentenced to ninety months in federal prison and fined $50,000.[874]

Thus, Ellis' corrupt practices helped to bring down two back-to-back State Senate Presidents and a third soon-to-be Senate President (then-State Senate Majority Leader), all of whom were sentenced to prison for taking money from gambling interests. One Senate President was charged with soliciting $15,000 from a casino company to help pass a bill that would have allowed casinos in the State. The other Senate President was convicted for accepting an illegal $10,000 payment from gambling interests.[875] The *Charleston Gazette* referred to the State Senate during the mid 1980s as a time "when the institution was gaining a reputation for freewheeling business dealings and partying that resulted in the convictions of former Senate Presidents Dan Tonkovich and Larry Tucker."[876]

Former West Virginia Senate President and banker Larry Tucker went to prison twice to serve sentences on separate charges of extortion, once for lying to a grand jury and once for obstruction of justice. In 1991, Tucker was sentenced to thirty-seven months in federal prison for lying to a federal grand jury investigating corruption in State government and was fined $45,000.[877] At his sentencing hearing, Assistant United States Attorney Joe Savage pleaded with the Court for a stiff sentence. Savage said, "It is time for this court to say to Larry Tucker and his colleagues who might consider doing the same thing in the future–enough. It is time to take the 'For Sale' sign off the Capitol building."[878]

West Virginia Senate President Dan Tonkovich, Tucker's successor, was soon to follow in the footsteps of his predecessor as he became the next West Virginia politician to become a resident of the Ashland, Kentucky federal prison. Tonkovich, the sixteen-year legislator who unsuccessfully ran for Governor in 1988, was soon afterward convicted of federal racketeering and extortion charges. On September 14, 1989, Tonkovich pled guilty to taking a $5,000 payoff from a casino company to help in passage of a bill legalizing gambling.[879]

Tonkovich had been charged with three counts of extortion, two of attempted extortion, and one of racketeering. He pled guilty to one count of extortion and
faced a possible sentence of twenty years in prison and $250,000 in fines.[880] United
States Attorney Michael Carey told Tonkovich at his sentencing hearing: "Your misconduct, along with others, has quaked the very foundation of our public institutions
and has left the citizens of the State shaken in their confidence and trust of the legislative process."[881] He was later sentenced to five years in jail.

Also in 1989, Senate Majority Leader Si Boettner was sentenced to five
years of probation and 200 hours of community service after pleading guilty to
tax evasion. He also had his law license suspended for three years and was compelled to resign his position with the West Virginia Senate. Prior to becoming a
Senator, Boettner was a former member of the House of Delegates and was one
of three candidates who ran for the Office of Attorney General in 1984. He was
narrowly defeated by Charlie Brown, who himself was forced to resign as
Attorney General in 1989 following issues surrounding allegations of a plan to
give a $50,000 payment to his pregnant secretary for an abortion and to keep the
situation quiet. Although Boettner entered into a 1989 guilty plea agreement with
the United States, he later challenged his conviction in various courts with his
final unsuccessful challenge occurring in 1998.[882]

Boettner's violation occurred when two individuals made interest payments totaling approximately $4,000 due on a bank loan he obtained. His con-
viction in the Federal District Court for the Southern District of West Virginia was
for willfully evading the payment of federal income taxes under 26 U.S.C. §
7201. He was charged with supporting dog track legislation in return for a promise from William Ellis that Tonkovich would be paid $10,000 and, or, receive
property of substantial value. Boettner told the federal judge that the charge
against him stems from a $25,000 loan he obtained to help finance his unsuccess-
ful 1984 campaign for State Attorney General. He explained that the interest on
the loan was paid by other people and that he failed to report that on his 1985
income tax return.[883]

Boettner was initially under investigation in 1987 for the manner in
which his $13,000 campaign debt was paid. Beer lobbyist, Samuel D'Annunzio's
corporation, S&J Inc., had borrowed $13,000 more for a house it was purchasing
for Boettner to lease. His $13,000 campaign debt was then paid. Nonetheless,
even as the allegations surfaced against him, Boettner was named to the Senate
Ethics Panel and said that he would fight to pass a bill to set up a State Ethics
Commission.[884]

The problems of gambling did not end with the slew of gambling-related convictions in the 1980s surrounding corruption in the State Legislature. Even

current Senate President Earl Ray Tomblin from Logan County has been a source of controversy with his connections to the gaming industry. When Tomblin began his reign as the Senate President in 1994 there was much pressure on him to serve in the Senate's top spot in a corrupt-free manner, given the fact that two of his three predecessors had served federal prison sentences.

Moreover, President Tomblin's father, Earl Tomblin, a former Logan County Sheriff, served two different federal prison sentences, both dealing with election violations. The senior Tomblin's latest conviction in 1992 stemmed from the same election scheme where Logan County Circuit Judge Ned Grubb was convicted on several counts of corruption. Earl Tomblin offered a $10,000 bribe in 1988 to Oval Adams, who was a candidate for Sheriff. Tomblin gave Adams the money in exchange for a job after the election so that he would qualify for a State pension. While he did get the job, the elder Tomblin ended up going to jail for bribing a public official.[885]

As a Senator, in 1995, controversy surrounded Senate President Tomblin's successful push of the State Racing Commission to change its rules to prohibit non-residents who owned and raced West Virginia bred greyhounds from sharing the money from a breeders' fund that was set up by the Legislature. The potential conflict existed because Freda Tomblin, the Senator's mother, was then and is currently the recipient of a majority of the money and changing the rules ensured it remained that way. For instance, in 2001, Senate President Tomblin's mother and brother received $623,057 from the legislatively-created fund.[886]

Following the change in the rules, Jeannie Hampton, an Ohio resident who had invested thousands of dollars in West Virginia-born dogs, was not able to receive money from the West Virginia Greyhound Breeding Development Fund. Hampton, in referring to the situation as "more dirty politics," said most of the Development Fund money was already going to Freda Tomblin anyway and the change just kept it that way. Freda Tomblin has a large puppy farm at Harts in Lincoln County and a kennel in her name. Freda's dogs race at both Tri-State and at Wheeling Downs, a dog track in Wheeling, West Virginia.[887]

Until 1995, the Tomblin family also owned Southern Amusement, a company that installed video lottery machines around the State. The problem with the video lottery machines at that time was that it was illegal for the machines to issue pay-outs. A few years earlier, in a push to legalize the machines, Tomblin's father reportedly met with then-Governor Gaston Caperton to discuss a plan that would have expanded video lottery statewide where Tomblin's company would have been among twenty companies that could have shared $58 million a year by replacing Tomblin's video machines with video lottery terminals. The plan was stopped by Governor Caperton amid political corruption investigations that led to ex-Lottery Director Butch Bryan and Lottery counsel Edward ReBrook serving sentences in federal prison.[888]

These video lottery machines, however, remained unregulated until the 2001 session of the West Virginia Legislature and have been a source of much controversy before and after their legalization. In 1994, in reference to the video lottery machines, House Speaker Chuck Chambers said, "[b]asically we have illegal gambling going on in every community." The video gambling machines were located throughout West Virginia in bars, convenience stores, gasoline stations, coffee shops, and exotic dancing strip clubs.[889]

These so-called "gray machines" owned by the Senate President's family were stamped "for amusement only;" however, it was one of the worst kept secrets in the State that the machines openly paid cash winnings in violation of West Virginia law. In 1995, Tomblin's friend, Joe Ferrell, who is also a family business associate, convicted felon, and current State Delegate, purchased Southern Amusement in what was believed to be an attempt by Tomblin to divert criticism of his stance against State regulated casino gambling "to protect the family business, which had its own gray (poker) machines."[890]

The *Charleston Gazette* discussed Tomblin's gambling connections at the time as follows:

> What does it say about West Virginia that one of the state's highest officers, the Senate President–first in line to succeed the governor–makes his living from those 'millions of dollars in untaxed revenue'?
>
> How can Tomblin work on the state budget, knowing that he's part of the untaxed, unregulated operation?

The *Gazette* further asked:

> Other questions hang over him: Why did he kill riverboat gambling in the 1995 session? To prevent competition to his machines? Why did an amendment slip through giving his family a still-bigger share of greyhound racing money? The Tomblin political family is the state's biggest greyhound breeder, although the senator's father's name was removed after two corruption convictions.

Fellow senators support Tomblin. The Ethics Commission does nothing. Yet this dubious situation clouds the Legislature.[891]

Delegate Ferrell, who also served for two years as Logan County Clerk, bought Southern Amusement Company from Senate President Tomblin's family for an amount that has never been disclosed. It was one of the State's largest providers of amusement devices, such as pool tables, jukeboxes and the video poker gray machines. Ferrell was able to buy Southern Amusement Co. in spite of filing for bankruptcy a few years earlier with his mining company PayBra that owed approximately $31 million in debts.[892]

In June of 2001, thirty of Delegate Ferrell's illegal machines were confiscated by the State Police. Logan County Democratic Prosecuting Attorney Brian Abraham, however, did not prosecute Ferrell saying he "had better things to do right now than prosecute gray machine cases." Incidentally, Abraham's father and brother own Nidie & Bill's, a convenient store and grocery store that, at the time, had fourteen to sixteen gray machines. Abraham was re-elected in 2004 in spite of his open defiance for enforcing the State's gambling laws. Moreover, even though Ferrell showed his open defiance of the gaming laws, he was issued a video gambling operator's license by the State to operate legal gaming machines in September of 2001.[893]

Ferrell first served in the House of Delegates from 1983-84 and 1987-92. In 1992, he pled guilty to illegally spending $58,000 in Logan, Lincoln, and Boone counties during the elections of 1986, 1988, 1990, and 1992 to help buy his seat in the State House of Delegates. This included a $10,000 cash payment to then-Logan County Circuit Judge Ned Grubb. Ferrell explained, "I delivered the cash to [Judge] Grubb in Grubb's judicial chambers in the Logan County Courthouse." He gave Judge Grubb another $1,500 during a political rally in April 1988, just prior to the Primary Election. Grubb was later convicted for accepting illegal campaign cash and was sent to federal prison.[894]

As a part of his federal plea bargain, Ferrell signed a sworn affidavit promising never to seek public office again and paid a fine of $174,000. His written affidavit with Kanawha County Circuit Court Judge Charles King stated: "I know that it was illegal to use cash in the elections and that in doing so I participated in depriving the citizens of Logan, Boone and Lincoln counties of honest elections. I never intend to run for, or hold, public office again." Ferrell, however, changed his mind. During a 1998 interview by the *Charleston Gazette*, he maintained that he merely agreed that he "had no intention of running" when he signed the plea agreement. Ferrell said, "But my mind changed. You change your mind on things."[895] Despite many newspaper stories and editorials, Ferrell's election to the West Virginia House of Delegates was not challenged by any law enforcement agency. In fact, then-United States Attorney Rebecca Betts said she was "unable to comment on the case [because she] was a partner in the firm that defended Mr. Ferrell" years earlier. She simply said, "I'm out of this one."[896]

In 1998, Ferrell was once again elected to the West Virginia House of Delegates. When he arrived in Charleston for the legislative session, he was immediately placed on the House Judiciary Committee. According to the *Charleston Gazette*, he was elected because "[t]he people of Logan County, who apparently have a high tolerance for crooked politicians, elected him."[897] Ferrell, apparently not satisfied with being a member of the House, announced that he would "throw his hat in the ring" to run for the State Senate during the 2002 West Virginia election for the seat vacated by Senator Lloyd Jackson, II. Ferrell indicated that he already had the support of political faction leaders in Logan and Lincoln counties.[898]

A *Charleston Gazette* editorial pronounced: "Liar: Ferrell breaks promise." It continues: "So the people in [retiring Senator Lloyd] Jackson's district will get a chance to vote for a politician who breaks his promises and who has made a living in a highly suspect business. Sadly, chances are good they'll elect him."[899] Ferrell later decided not to run for the Senate seat and currently remains a member of the House of Delegates.

On June 28, 2005, federal authorities armed with search warrants roped off the area surrounding Ferrell's Southern Amusement business and conducted a search. They didn't reveal whether the search was linked to his business or to the ongoing southern West Virginia vote-buying investigation. Delegate Ferrell has long been linked with the Stowers political faction in Lincoln County. Lincoln County Circuit Clerk Greg Stowers was convicted in 2005 for buying votes in Lincoln County elections from 1990 through 2004.[900] Federal prosecutors later revealed that Ferrell was, in fact, listed as a co-conspirator in the ongoing investigation of election fraud in southern West Virginia.

When the issue of legalizing the video lottery terminals was debated in 2001, State Delegate Paul Prunty declared, "We have a cancer in this State, and that cancer is gambling." Then-Delegate and formerly impeached State Treasurer A. James Manchin countered, "Don't be too concerned that we're going to corrupt the people of West Virginia. We're a strong people."[901] Within a year of Delegate Prunty's comments, West Virginia's Racing Commission chairman was forced to resign for what Governor Bob Wise's Administration called "unethical betting activities."[902]

Just two years earlier, in 1999, the State Legislature passed a bill authorizing a referendum in Greenbrier County for citizens to vote on whether The

Greenbrier could open a casino in its former congressional fallout shelter. The Greenbrier Casino Bill, sponsored in the State Senate by Senator Randy Schoonover, was the subject of investigation by the United States Attorney's Office for the Southern District of West Virginia. A spokeswoman for The Greenbrier confirmed that the United States Attorney's Office had contacted the hotel, however, she would not confirm what information had been requested. During this same time period, Senator Schoonover resigned his seat in the State Senate after being charged with taking $2,725 from a "prominent wrecking service owner who sought business on the West Virginia Turnpike."[903] The gambling referendum at the famous and historical resort failed as Greenbrier County voters defeated it during the 2000 General Election.[904]

A few years before Schoonover's conviction, then-Congressman Bob Wise expressed his views on gambling and the negative effects of State involvement as the topic of corrupt gambling practices was debated in the United States Congress in 1995. During the discussion, United States Congressman Frank Wolf (R-VA) testified that: "In 1990, a former West Virginia Governor pleaded guilty to taking a bribe from racing interests. In 1994, a West Virginia Lottery director was sentenced to federal prison for rigging a video lottery contract."[905] Then-Congressman Wise joined Congressman Wolf to co-sponsor a bill to create a National Gambling Impact and Policy Commission. Wise called gambling "a quick fix" and said that states and municipalities may base their decisions on faulty information. Wolf said, "Government is supposed to be the protector of society, not the sponsor of its ruin," while Wise concurred beholding that "over time, gambling doesn't contribute a lot to the moral climate." Wise also declared: "I am not wild about gambling. Too many people see it as a panacea, which isn't there. I want to see some empirical evidence."[906]

Despite then-Congressman Wise's 1995 negative statements with regard to the gambling industry as well as West Virginia's poor track record with gambling interests, the topic dominated the 2001 West Virginia Legislative Session. Governor Wise, who had spoken against the expansion of gambling, was now open to the idea of legalizing the gaming machines in order to increase revenue for a struggling state budget and to fund his Promise Scholarship plan. Wise proposed to reduce the video lottery enterprise to 9,000 machines, limit them to adult establishments, and believed the State could then collect as much as $100 million in State revenue from them. A *Charleston Gazette* editorial asked:

> Will Gov. Bob Wise's effort to clean up the scummy, illicit,
> video poker racket succeed? Or will legislators do what they've
> done repeatedly in past years–let the criminal enterprise contin-

ue running wide-open, bleeding hundreds of millions of dollars from West Virginians and paying no taxes on the loot?

The *Gazette* further elaborated:

> Incredibly, at Wednesday's public hearing on the so-called "gray machines," most of the witnesses were lawbreakers begging to be allowed to continue operating illicitly. Amazing.

> When the session ends April 14, if the Legislature once again has left the racket untouched, West Virginians will be justified in asking whether some lawmakers obstructed reform to assist the illegal operators now raking in fortunes.[907]

During the 2001 debates on legalizing the video terminals, individuals who had been openly housing and providing illegal pay-outs on thousands of video poker machines (so-called gray machines) in convenience stores, bars, and even supermarkets, argued against enforcement of their illegal activities. These video gambling machines often allowed easy access to children and had been virtually ignored by law enforcement officials, however, the perpetrators pleaded that enforcement of the laws would put them out of business. A column by *Charleston Gazette* news editor, Dan Radmacher, describes the preposterous position of the owners of the machines who were operating them illegally throughout the State. Radmacher explains:

> IMAGINE a crack dealer getting up before a legislative committee and complaining that the state would put him out of business if it enforced drug laws. Legislators would probably tell the crack dealer he has no right to make a living engaging in illegal activity, and they might well call in troopers to have the idiot arrested.

> But Wednesday at the Capitol, criminal after criminal got up to tell legislators that they could not stay in business unless they were allowed to continue engaging in illegal activity. . . .

> Of course, the criminal activity I'm talking about isn't selling crack cocaine. It's paying off on "amusement only" video poker machines. And, of course, the Legislature isn't talking

about enforcing laws against this; it's talking about regulating the machines so state government gets its cut. . . .

What's happening now in this state is shameful. The wide-spread flagrant lawbreaking is sucking hundreds of millions of dollars out of the economy. It's making many gray machine owners and operators wealthy at the expense of thousands of poor West Virginians.[908]

It was fitting that the speaker for the Legislative Breakfast on the opening day of the 2001 West Virginia Legislative Session was former South Carolina Governor David Beasley. South Carolina had just declared their video lottery machines to be illegal. He called the video poker industry corrupt and explained that all efforts to regulate poker machines in his State failed. To further explain his opposition, Beasley said the video poker industry was "powerful, corrupt, and unregulatable."[909] He stated that the gaming industry is "so corrupt . . . they'll end up owning part of your political machine. They do it in every state."[910] He asserted:

> They get their tentacles into certain members of the House and the Senate, and they end up owning, I mean owning, some of your political machine. And I mean that in the most corrupt way. I saw it in South Carolina. If I hadn't taken them on when I did, they would have been forever in our state.[911]

In spite of Governor Beasley's warnings, the West Virginia Legislature legalized video lottery. Then, soon after the passage of the new gambling legislation, the controversy continued. The *Charleston Gazette* declared:

> Political connections by former operators of the "video poker" racket are amazing. Everyone knows that Senate President Earl Ray Tomblin and Delegate Joe Ferrell, both D-Logan, are veterans of the illicit business. Now columnist Fanny Seiler has revealed that Eastern Panhandle "gray machine" operator Lee Wesson, who had cocaine and tax convictions in the past, is partners with three powerful Steptoe & Johnson lawyers in a new legal gambling firm, Advanced Lottery Technologies. His partners are George Carenbauer, former state Democratic chairman; Pat Kelly, who was Gov. Underwood's legal coun-

sel; and Ralph Bean, chairman of the Council for Community and Economic Development.[912]

West Virginia's history with the gambling industry is nauseating when considering the numerous convictions of many of West Virginia's political officials due to gambling links. As one small example, it was the bribes from a single racetrack owner that led to the convictions of former Governor Arch Moore, two Senate Presidents, and a Senate Majority Leader.[913] While some State politicians have recognized the bad associated with expanded and/or unregulated gambling, the majority seem to have heavily embraced the gaming industry. Moreover, the warnings against expansion were illustrated by those just mentioned and the many other gambling-related convictions of State politicians.

A few years ago the *Charleston Daily Mail* held a strong position against expanded gambling that began with forceful opposition to a 1995 casino gambling debate in the West Virginia Legislature. Calling expanded gambling a "bad roll of the dice for West Virginia," the *Daily Mail* commented: "First, I've had an uneasiness from the very beginning that the massive amounts of money involved in casinos will be too big a temptation to some of our public officials. Unfortunately, West Virginia has a dismal record when it comes to public corruption." The editorial continued: "You read it here first: If riverboat gambling happens in West Virginia you'll see public officials in jail within three years." The *Daily Mail* even intimated that their anti-gambling position may not be shared by other newspapers as "[t]he talk I hear at newspaper publisher meetings is that casinos have quickly become significant advertisers for the newspapers in those communities."[914] In another editorial, the *Charleston Daily Mail* opined:

> West Virginia's track record on corrupt politicians is poor. The state couldn't even handle its own lottery without sending a lottery director and a lottery attorney to prison. In the past ten years, federal prosecutors have bagged a governor, two state Senate presidents and a host of lesser officials on various charges related to using a public office for private gain. But even if official corruption does not materialize with so many dollars floating around–which is a poor bet–the riverboats could still wind up running the Legislature.[915]

With the writing on the wall surrounding the negative effects of gambling, State government has moved full steam ahead. During each of the 2003, 2004, and 2005 fiscal years, State Lottery sales exceeded $1 billion. The proceeds from those sales are relied on so heavily that it would be nearly impossible for the State to operate without them, especially considering the fact that the $3.19 billion State budget for the 2005 fiscal year was only about three times as large as the actual Lottery sales.

My problem with relying on gambling so heavily is not based largely upon a personal moral judgment as I have bought my share of Powerball Lottery tickets. I just believe that it is an extremely dangerous fiscal policy for any state to rely so heavily on gambling revenues. As the revenues increase, instead of paying off the State's massive pension and workers' compensation debts, the State will immediately earmark the money for long-term projects requiring yearly funding.

States like West Virginia are going to learn, however, that the gambling revenues will not remain constant. As the gaming industry pushes for expansion in every market possible, state after state will oblige by legalizing the machines with promises of buckets of cash. Eventually, when the well goes dry after West Virginia's surrounding states begin to place gambling machines on every corner to try and fix their state's revenue problems, the number of people dropping coins in West Virginia machines will necessarily decrease. In fact, Pennsylvania's installation of its own video lottery terminals in 2006 is expected to lessen West Virginia's yearly proceeds significantly.

Gambling proponents correctly assert that the legalization of state-sponsored gambling creates a potential source of revenue, it draws tourism, and it may reduce illegal gambling by creating better enforcement mechanisms. It is also argued (although it seems like a silly argument to me) that legalization of gambling may even help potential gamblers, who will gamble regardless of the laws, from being scammed by "fixed" machines. Nonetheless, those same gambling proponents often ignore the increase in crime, the potential of a renewed focus of income for organized crime, gambling addictions, increased bankruptcies, the likelihood of political corruption, and the resulting demands for arrests, prosecution, and incarceration that follow an increase in gambling.

Initially, the promises of countless jobs and staggering increases in state revenues is exciting for a lot of people. Years down the road, however, when the problems that surround gambling begin to surface in neighborhood after neighborhood, people may begin to question whether gambling has actually produced more economic benefit than actual harm. Then, as revenues decrease, West Virginia's politicians will finally be forced to address the pressing need to restructure State government and rein in State spending. Moreover, someone will have to foot the bill for the increased costs that arise to incarcerate the additional politicians who will eventually be convicted for selling their influence surrounding future gambling legislation. The question that can only be answered by time is whether the social costs to West Virginia have outweighed the gamble of relying so heavily on video lottery.

# CHAPTER FOURTEEN

# Sex Scandals

*It's Wednesday, or as the people of West Virginia know it, hump day. . . . Good thing [Wise] was just governor and not the football coach of Alabama. . . . He could have lost his job. Wise said he was sorry for letting his wife down, his children down . . . and his pants down.*

Jay Leno
*The Tonight Show*

"That little weasel-faced bastard. . . . Typical Democrat" were the words of Philip "Icky" Frye on the front page of the *Charleston Daily Mail* on May 12, 2003, describing Governor Bob Wise as Frye proclaimed that Wise and Fryc's wife, Angela Mascia-Frye, had been having a lengthy love affair. Soon after Frye's assertion, Governor Wise released a statement saying he was "not faithful to [his] family."[916] Several months later, Icky Frye entered the 2004 race for Governor and handed out political buttons and bumper stickers saying, "Vote for Icky Frye. He'll do his job and not his staff." Frye said, "I had private detectives all over this thing. I've got pictures and documents–all kinds of hard evidence."

Even though thirty-five-year-old Angela Mascia-Frye, who oversaw European operations for the West Virginia Development Office, was Wise's subordinate, clearly making the affair a public issue, Wise stated, "I apologize deeply to the people of our State for my actions. In my private life, I have let many people down."[917] Mascia-Frye accompanied Governor Wise on State-paid trips to Spain, Italy, and Germany in 2002. Travel records also indicate the two of them were in several other cities for overnight stays during the same time periods including: Detroit, Michigan; Huntington, Clarksburg, and Lewisburg, West Virginia; and Windsor, Ontario.[918] Following a freedom of information request, many of the email messages between Wise and Mascia-Frye were released for public consumption.

Wise's 2003 feelings on adultery committed by a public official differed drastically from his sentiments a few years earlier, in 1998, when Wise was still a United States Congressman from West Virginia's Second Congressional District. In fact, during the impeachment proceedings against President Clinton, Wise said it was important for Congress to recognize that the President was wrong when he lied about having sex with Monica Lewinsky "and take some action of punishment" against him.[919] Wise called Clinton's actions "indefensible personal conduct."[920] When Wise became Governor, he continued to stress the importance of family. During his first inauguration on January 15, 2001, he said, "My fellow West Virginians. Sacred to every West Virginian is the concept of home and the home place. The word 'home' is more than just a place. . . . It also means caring about and caring for each other."[921]

Upon learning of Wise's admission of adultery, Senator Robert C. Byrd said he was "saddened," while Senator John D. Rockefeller, IV, said, "I'm disappointed. . . . I'm shocked, because it's wrong."[922] The *Charleston Daily Mail* asserted:

> Make no mistake: Wise's actions were wrong. The hurt goes beyond the injury to his family, which includes his children. American society is built on trust. This affair undermines the public's faith in the governor.
>
> West Virginians have far more serious problems than Wise's personal life. They deserve a government that focuses on and solves those problems.
>
> Wise has taken the focus off those problems.[923]

The story of the affair was not confined to the border of West Virginia as Jay Leno, during his monologue on NBC's *The Tonight Show*, discussed Wise's unfaithfulness with his millions of viewers. Leno said, "It's Wednesday, or as the people of West Virginia know it, hump day." Leno then referenced former University of Alabama football coach Mike Price, who was fired after reports surfaced about him spending hundreds of dollars at a Pensacola, Florida, topless bar. Leno declared, "Good thing [Wise] was just Governor and not the football coach of Alabama. . . . He could have lost his job." Leno then remarked, "Wise said he was sorry for letting his wife down, his children down . . . and his pants down."[924]

Soon after Wisc's admission he had been unfaithful in his marriage, a parody of the 1966 Beach Boys hit "Barbara Ann" quickly surfaced and subsequently spread throughout West Virginia like wildfire as an anonymous singer started out the lyrics "Bob, Bob, Bob–looks like you're done" and "Oh, Bobby Wise, you were so unwise, a-courtin' Missus Frye." The nearly two-minute song played first on WQBE, a local Charleston radio station, and the station's Internet website had more than 120,000 hits that same day by people downloading the song. By the end of the first week, the website, which normally had about 6,000 visits per week, had more than 1 million.

The anonymous singer was apparently a State of West Virginia government employee who declined to identify himself due to possible retribution. The lyrics of the parody are as follows:

> Bob, Bob, Bob–looks like you're done, Bob, Bob, Bob–looks like you're done.

> Oh, Bobby Wise, that was not your wife, I saw you with last night. It was a little foreign cutie wigglin' her booty. Now you're done. Bob, Bob–looks like you're done.

> You climbed on a plane, flew off to Spain, hot for a tryst with your little Swiss miss. Bob Wise, tell me why oh why, you spent the whole trade mission tryin' new positions. Now you're done. Bob, Bob–looks like you're done.

> Bob, Bob, Bob–looks like you're done, Bob, Bob, Bob–looks like you're done.

> Oh, Bobby Wise, were you mesmerized, by her tight Levis What the lady was concealin' must have been appealin' Now you're done. Bob, Bob–looks like you're done.

> Can you explain, why you entertained, some hot little ho on taxpayer dough, Bob Wise, what's your alibi, Don't you know there's a danger havin' sex with strangers, Now you're done. Bob, Bob–looks like you're done.

> Bob, Bob, Bob–looks like you're done. Bob, Bob, Bob–looks like you're done.

Oh, Bobby Wise, you were so unwise, a-courtin' Missus Frye. After rollin' in the clover, your career is over,  Now you're done.

Bob, Bob–looks like you're done. Bob, Bob, Bob–looks like you're done.[925]

Hoppy Kercheval, host of *MetroNews Talkline*, argued that Wise should not have been able to duck questions about the incident because "as taxpayers, the ones who hired Wise and pay him and pay Mascia-Frye, we're entitled to know a few more details of the 'when' and 'where' of this relationship." Kercheval said, "Wise was involved with a State employee, someone who works for him. Travel records place Wise and Angela Mascia-Frye from the Development Office together on trips four times over the last year [and] that prompts several questions that the Governor should answer." Kercheval, whose show is the largest West Virginia radio talk show, asked,

Was any of the travel engineered for a convenient rendezvous for Wise and Mascia-Frye?

Were they together conducting personal business on state time?

Has Mascia-Frye benefitted at all from her relationship with Wise?

Was their relationship known about in the Development Office and did it affect the working climate there?

Can she continue to work for that office and be effective given what is now known?

Did she ever meet him at the Governor's Mansion?[926]

Kercheval further said that if those questions seemed too harsh, then consider the following: "If a county school board learned that a married school principal was having an affair with a married teacher of the same school during recess, do you think the school board might want some answers? Do you think the principal and teacher might be in trouble? The answer, of course, is yes." Citing another example, he then asked, "Let's say a company executive attended a business conference and met at the conference an underling of the same company. Both are married. They hook up. The company finds out. Again, it's likely somebody is going to be in trouble, not just at home but also at work."[927]

Just prior to Wise's 2005 departure from the Governor's Office, I interviewed him in depth about West Virginia politics. I asked him specifically whether he felt that events in a politician's personal life, which create negative attention to State politics and amount to violations of the public trust, create further apathy among voters. I have to admit that I am glad this was my last interview question for Governor Wise because his tone changed dramatically. He said, "Quite frankly, I think that's bullshit!" He said, "Nobody has come up to me in a year-and-a-half and said anything other than sympathy. But what they're mostly concerned about is am I getting the job done." He then said, "If that's the situation then talk to Bill Clinton, talk to Rudy Giuliani, talk to a whole bunch of people. I had the press on me a lot more than I had voters. That's not to in anyway soft-pedal what I did, it was wrong on a personal basis, but in terms of voter apathy, I think that's crap."[928]

I thanked him for his time, but I thought to myself, "Are you really that naive?" The reason nobody may have approached Governor Wise and expressed anything other than sympathy is simple, he was still Governor at the time. Would a State employee approach the Governor, their boss, and criticize him to his face? Would a business interested in doing business with the State openly criticize Wise? Would any State citizen in need of the Governor's help for any possible reason criticize him and then ask for a favor? The answers to those questions are obvious. Governor Wise did a good job from a public relations standpoint of shaping the issue as a purely private one in spite of Kercheval's questions to the contrary.

I guess what bothers me about this situation most is that once again people didn't seem to be overly outraged by an elected official's inappropriate conduct. Given the years of corruption and questionable behaviors of West Virginia's many politicians, I believe that many people simply expect their elected officials to disappoint them. That way, instead of being sick to their stomachs when another State official commits some act that places them on the brink of resignation or impeachment, then the average person simply concedes that it was only a matter of time before the politician of the moment let them down.

The fact is that people should have been upset with Wise's behavior because his affair involved one of his subordinates and questions surfaced about their use of State money and the State plane to facilitate the affair. This is yet another example of the bar being lowered for those holding the State's highest positions. Had it become known that a Governor's Office employee had an affair with a subordinate with whom the employee had the power to fire, assign tasks, or control the subordinate's salary, the Governor would have assuredly fired that employee. Why should the rules be any different for the boss?

Moreover, what if a member of the Governor's staff faced scrutiny for his sexual misconduct which actually did occur purely within his personal life, how would the Governor react toward such an individual? When Bradford Keller, an assistant to Governor Wise's Chief of Staff Mike Garrison, was arrested on a solicitation of prostitution charge in 2002, the year before Wise's affair, Governor Wise called the charges "incredibly disappointing" while gubernatorial spokesman Bill Case said, "The Governor expects all of his staff to conduct themselves in a way that reflects the trust placed in them by the people of West Virginia."[929] While Keller was forced to resign from his State employment for his inappropriate conduct in his personal life, Wise, who faced negative headlines for his improper conduct, was able to simply issue an apology and keep his job.

When the fifty-six-year-old Wise left office, his departure was met with little fanfare. Wise's relationship with the Legislature was described by Hoppy Kercheval as follows:

> Wise was never their kind of guy. Arch Moore was a guy law-
> makers could fear and fight. Gaston Caperton was their buddy
> who shared a beer with them. Cecil Underwood was a guy they
> would work with or run over top of, depending on the need.
> Bob? He was none of the above.

Wise's farewell address to a joint session of the State Legislature on January 12, 2005, was described by Kercheval as "polite but not warm, respectful but not enthusiastic."[930] I attended the Governor's speech and Kercheval's description is certainly accurate. The people I spoke with that day attended the speech with the main intention of seeing other politicians instead of Wise, and any excitement toward the Governor's speech I would describe as lackluster at best. In fact, of the two standing ovations received by Wise during his speech, one of them was when he introduced Governor-elect Joe Manchin, III.[931] Following the speech, Governor Wise, the Legislators, and those of us who were watching from the House Gallery, left the House Chamber and mingled in the hallway. Governor Wise spoke with a couple of people, I briefly wished him well in Washington, D.C., and he left unnoticed.

There have been many different kinds of sex-related scandals that have plagued West Virginia politics and not all of them include a man cheating on his wife with another woman. One such example was Delegate Clyde H. Richey, who was serving as a member of the West Virginia House of Delegates in 1979 when he was convicted of sexual assault in the third degree for sexually molesting his fourteen-year-old legislative page. Richey developed a relationship with his young legislative page through the Big Brothers Program.[932]

Delegate Richey arranged for the victim to accompany him from Morgantown, West Virginia, and stay with him for several days in a hotel room he was renting during the legislative session in Charleston.[933] The crime occurred on February 22, 1979, in a Charleston hotel. Richey was later convicted of having anal intercourse with his young legislative page. After convicted, he was not sent to jail. Instead, he received just five years of probation.[934]

Evidence presented during Richey's trial indicated that after he learned of the indictment against him, he had consulted with a lawyer and was advised of the date set for his arraignment. He then left the State. An arrest warrant was issued for Richey, but he returned and answered the indictment before he was located and arrested. During his trial, prosecutors attempted to use evidence of a novel that was written by Richey several years earlier which contained "incidents of sexual interplay between adult and consenting juvenile males."[935] Richey's book, *Near Fatal Attraction*, has been described as "the 'hunter and prey' game played in secret by youthful members of Boy Scout Troop 44 [which] resulted in a series of gruesome tragedies."[936]

In 2004, twenty-five years after his conviction, Richey filed an original jurisdiction writ of mandamus in the West Virginia Supreme Court seeking to have the proper authorities "either conduct DNA tests on certain evidence used in [his] 1979 trial for third-degree sexual assault or to release such evidence so that he can arrange his own testing." At his 1979 trial, the State introduced three-pairs of the victim's underwear that were tested by State Police Serologist Robert Murphy. He performed testing on all three pairs of the underwear and found semen on two of them, but determined that there was an insufficient amount to identify the blood type of the semen. During his 2004 court case, Richey claimed that new DNA testing would prove his innocence. His argument is confusing considering the fact that he was convicted even though the State Police testimony during his 1979 trial did not conclude that any of the semen on the underwear belonged to Richey. The West Virginia Supreme Court denied Richey's request for judicial relief and dismissed the case.[937]

Parents are told to experience the magic of involving their children in the community and school based Big Brothers mentor program. Imagine being the parent of a child who was fortunate enough to befriend a State Delegate through the program as his Big Brother. Then imagine the joy of the parent as he or she learns that this same Delegate decided to take a special interest in their child by finding the time to involve him or her in the enormously educational experience of acting as a legislative page during a session of the West Virginia Legislature. Then imagine being that same parent finding out that this generous Delegate, who was chosen by the majority of the voters to represent his region in the State Legislature, was having anal intercourse with their son. Then, instead of serving a lengthy sentence and being strongly reprimanded for such conduct, the Delegate simply received a few years of probation. Richey's conviction solidified the view that State politicians could escape accountability or incarceration even after being convicted of such an atrocious crime involving a young child.

If a Governor's affair with another member of the executive branch, or a State House of Delegate's member having anal intercourse with his legislative page isn't bad enough, West Virginians have also witnessed the sexual indiscretions of the judicial branch. Circuit Judge John Hey, who served as a Kanawha County Circuit Judge for seventeen years, was prosecuted on sexual assault charges that led to his 1995 guilty plea to two counts of misdemeanor battery on two female court employees.[938] His plea came after he had retired "for medical reasons" and amid allegations that he had sexually harassed women throughout his career and was often drunk while acting as circuit judge on the bench during trials and hearings in court.[939]

Governor Caperton approved Hey's application for an $80,000-a-year disability pension "the same day the Judicial Investigation Commission was bringing charges against him for excessive drinking and sexual harassment–including an accusation that he opened his judicial robe to give an astonished woman visitor an up-close and personal demonstration that, like a Scotsman in kilts, he wore nothing underneath." Former West Virginia Supreme Court Chief Justice Margaret Workman called Caperton's action, which prevented the possibility of Hey being fired and losing his pension, "a sordid chapter in the history of the judicial system of West Virginia."[940]

Following Hey's conviction, he served five days in a regional jail, was fined $500, and was discharged from probation in 1998. Judge Hey now receives his full judicial retirement despite his conduct that led to his early retirement. Upon entering the guilty plea, Judge Hey agreed to surrender his law license, but while it was supposed to have been annulled, it was instead placed on inactive status. Hey later began a battle to have his license returned and on October 10, 2003, the State Supreme Court returned Hey's law license.[941]

Justice Robin Davis and Warren McGraw voted not to reinstate the license. Davis wrote in her Dissenting Opinion that Hey "failed, repeatedly, to comply with conditions placed upon him, either completely or until some additional action was taken." She also explained that he did not make any payments toward his fine for more than a year and, "[a]bove all, the record does not demonstrate that Petitioner Hey has accepted responsibility for his actions [as] by his own admission, he pled guilty to the criminal charges only to preserve his pension."[942] In agreement with Davis' comments, the *Charleston Daily Mail* sarcastically remarked:

> Why should [Hey demonstrate that he has accepted responsibility for his actions]? The State Supreme Court will not make him. 'Egregious and deplorable' conduct is eventually forgotten.' This is not about Hey and his license. This is about respect for the law. Routinely giving lawyers their law licenses back simply because it has been a few years since they committed their crimes is a recipe for more bad behavior by lawyers.[943]

Former Kanawha County Prosecuting Attorney Bill Forbes, who led the original charges against Hey, said that he should not have had his law license returned to him until he fully apologized for his misconduct on the bench. Forbes said, "At the heart of the judicial system is the integrity of judges, and Judge Hey never addressed any of the issues that were levied against him. In my mind, he has never apologized for the things he did."[944] As a part of his 1994 agreement with the State Judicial Hearing Board, the judge agreed to refrain from ever again seeking public office. Nonetheless, in 2006, he ran for the State Democratic Executive Committee.

Judge Hey also made the news in 2001 for allegedly making job threats against Kanawha County Assistant Prosecutor Don Morris after Hey's friend and political supporter, Mike Clifford, successfully defeated Forbes during the May 2000 Democratic Primary. Morris had given sworn statements in the earlier investigation that helped cost Hey his position as Judge. Consequently, Hey allegedly sent word to Morris that he would "have his job" once his friend Clifford took office.[945] West Virginia law makes it a felony to take or threaten to take someone's job because they gave testimony in a court proceeding. Not surprisingly, Clifford supported the return of Hey's license saying he "had his license suspended for long enough" since he had only been convicted of a misdemeanor.[946]

In a separate matter, in 1992, the State Supreme Court publicly censured Judge Hey for his 1989 appearance on the nationwide television CNN program *Crossfire*.[947] He appeared on the program and discussed specific facts and issues of a case in which he had been the presiding circuit judge while the case was still pending on appeal in the State Supreme Court.[948] During the program, Judge Hey made negative comments relating to the case about the child's educational performance, the same child's church attendance, and cast aspersions on the fitness and character of the child's mother, Judith Erlewine, as a custodial parent.

Erlewine, known at the time as Judith Roush, was the subject of Judge Hey's public comments following a hearing with regard to a dispute she and her ex-husband were having over alimony. During the hearing, Hey told Erlewine that she would lose custody of her thirteen-year-old daughter if she did not marry her live-in boyfriend or move out. He said of his appearance on *Crossfire* that, "[i]t gave me an opportunity, number one, to get exposure and name recognition [as] there's not a judge in West Virginia who doesn't want as much favorable recognition as they can get, because they have to run for elective office."[949] The State Supreme Court found that Hey violated Canon 3A(6) of the Judicial Code of Ethics and found that it merited a public censure; however, the Court declined to adopt the recommended sanction of the Judicial Hearing Board which advocated that Hey be required to pay the costs of the proceeding.[950]

Soon afterward, Erlewine sued Judge Hey for his comments. It was not until 2004, however, that Hey was forced to testify in front of a jury to answer allegations that he slandered Erlewine by implying to a national television audience that she was sexually promiscuous. After spending three days as a defendant in his old Charleston courtroom where he previously presided, former Judge Hey agreed to pay Erlewine $125,000 to end her defamation lawsuit against him.[951]

Another politician, current State Senate Majority Leader Truman Chafin, has also faced scrutiny for his private divorce that became a public episode. During his political days, Chafin has been indicted, but not convicted, on two occasions. His earlier brush with the law surrounded the accusation that he accepted a bribe when he was a county commissioner to help Charles Edward Hilbert "buy the [sheriff's] office from [Mingo County Sheriff] Johnnie Owens for $100,000." Owens said he gave $50,000 to the Mingo County Commission as part of the deal and Chafin was president of the county commission at that time.[952] He was charged with,

> unlawfully and feloniously accept[ing] or agree[ing] to accept, directly or indirectly, from Charles Edward Hilbert to Johnnie M. Owens on his behalf and upon behalf of Steve Adkins and Rastie Runyon, a pecuniary benefit as consideration for the acceptance of the resignation of Johnnie M. Owens and the appointment of Charles Edward Hilbert as Sheriff of Mingo County in that he agreed not to render official action against the approval of the resignation of Johnnie M. Owens as Sheriff, the

approval of Charles Edward Hilbert as Sheriff, and the creation of the position of Administrative Assistant for the Sheriff's Department, and the subsequent appointment of Johnnie M. Owens thereto, against the peace and dignity of the State.[953]

While a grand jury indicted Chafin, the charge was dropped because the grand jury was improperly empaneled. Not only were no additional charges filed against Chafin, but he also forced the county to pay his legal bills in the amount of $91,600. Sitting as a special judge in the case and approving of Chafin's award of legal fees was Circuit Judge Ned Grubb, who was later convicted of criminal felonies for buying and selling the Logan County elections. The *Charleston Daily Mail* described Chafin as "a politician who proudly has no convictions despite being indicted on two different occasions."[954]

In 1995, in a separate matter, Chafin faced a potential twenty years in prison and $1 million in fines after being charged with "one count of conspiracy to violate federal wiretapping laws and three counts of procuring others to illegally wiretap." Chafin, in the process of a "lengthy, bitter divorce," was charged with paying two men to record the telephone conversations of his former wife Gretchen Lewis who was at the time the State Secretary of Health and Human Resources.[955] He pled not guilty to the charges. Mark McMillian, however, a private detective who was hired by Chafin to investigate the Senator's wife, was sentenced to two months in prison and fined $2,500 for installing a wiretap in what a federal judge called "reprehensible" conduct.[956] Chafin was acquitted after a jury trial and continues to serve as the State Senate's Majority Leader.

Chafin denied involvement with the wiretap and said he received one tape from McMillian and said he was "shocked" to learn the investigator had been using a wiretap on his ex-wife.[957] Years earlier, McMillian had been fired as a Deputy in the Kanawha County Sheriff's Department in 1987 for taking an unauthorized civilian on a trip to Florida to retrieve a prisoner. The unauthorized civilian was Tina Means, a secretary in the Sheriff's Office. Deputy McMillian was married at the time, but not to Ms. Means.

While in Florida, McMillian and Means spent the night at the Don Ce Sar Beach Resort, a luxury resort in St. Petersburg. The two of them spent the following night at a Holiday Inn in Sebring, Florida. Upon his return, McMillian sought reimbursement for his personal expenses; however, within those expenses were the costs he incurred in paying for Ms. Means' meals, as well as the additional costs he incurred due to double occupancy lodging. McMillian was also charged with misconduct relating to a May 1985 extradition trip to New Mexico to retrieve another prisoner and charged with misconduct while serving as bailiff during a night session of the Kanawha County Magistrate Court. The firing of McMillian was found by the State Supreme Court to be justified as his "actions herein cast aspersions and doubt as to his honesty and integrity."[958] In spite of his firing as a deputy sheriff and his conviction of wiretapping in the Chafin situation, on June 21, 2005, the State Supreme Court granted his admission to the West Virginia Bar.[959]

With regard to Chafin, according to court records, his divorce proceedings began in 1993 after his wife twice caught him in bed with another woman. As of 2006, the issues surrounding their divorce were still being challenged in the courts. The *Charleston Daily Mail* reported: "Lawyers for State Senator Truman Chafin are trying to use changes to divorce laws he may have helped pass four years ago to help him in his decade-old divorce case." The *Daily Mail* added: "If his lawyers are successful, Chafin (D-Mingo) could pocket an estimated $167,500 in interest the Supreme Court ordered him to pay his ex-wife . . . in 1998."[960]

Incidentally, two years after Senator Chafin was accused of illegally taping his wife's conversations, Kanawha County Circuit Court Judge Lynn Ranson stepped down as a judge after taking responsibility for two tape recorders found in her husband's law office. Judge Ranson signed an agreement with the United States Attorney's Office that if she resigned she would not be prosecuted for the illegal bugging incident. Prior to becoming a circuit judge, Ranson herself was an Assistant United States Attorney as well as a State Ethics Commission attorney.[961]

In addition to Majority Leader Chafin's public divorce, the current State Senate Minority Leader Vic Sprouse (R-Kanawha) has also had his share of unfavorable headlines surrounding his family life. Sprouse, who commonly ran his elections on family values, announced in 2005 that he was filing for a divorce from his third wife, Amy McKinley-Sprouse, who was four months pregnant at the time. McKinley Sprouse is the daughter of former GOP gubernatorial candidate David McKinley, Sprouse's former employer. McKinley, Sprouse's father-in-law, a former House Minority Leader, former State Republican Party Chairman, and former candidate for Governor, said the thirty-four-year-old Sprouse should step down as Minority Leader. McKinley said Sprouse's actions were "shameful" and that Sprouse needed help because: "This is the third time he's caused anguish and ripped a family apart."[962] Sprouse said his divorce was a personal matter and shouldn't affect his leadership of the Senate Republicans. State newspapers reported that rumors circulated saying Sprouse left his pregnant wife for another woman, believed to be a well-known Charleston television news reporter.[963]

During the 2005 legislative session, Sprouse successfully amended the bill to grant higher pay to Family Court Judges. Even though his divorce would eventually wind up before a Family Court Judge, Sprouse said he saw no conflict in pushing for $26,000 raises for the judges. The bill was quickly approved in the Senate.[964] The bill also raised State Circuit Court Judges and Supreme Court Justices by $26,000. Appellate issues surrounding Sprouse's divorce could have been heard in both of those courts. In 1999, he also amended a bill to give non-custodial parents legal recourse to challenge in court the right of a custodial parent's ability to relocate from the area.[965] Sprouse at the time was a non-custodial parent.

During his 2004 campaign, a deposition from Sprouse's earlier 2002 divorce surfaced containing salacious details of his extramarital relationship. Sprouse divorced his first wife in 1993, remarried in 1996, and filed for divorce again in 2001.[966] Prior to his second marriage, neighbors heard a woman's screams coming from Sprouse's house so loudly that they feared someone was being hurt. It turned out that Sprouse was having sex with an acquaintance of his. The screams were also heard by the police when they arrived, along with a camera crew who had been traveling with them from the *Real Stories of the Highway Patrol* television show.[967]

As sexual indiscretions have surrounded all three branches of State government, in May of 2003, the West Virginia State Police, the people who most often arrest people for sexual misconduct, began conducting an internal investigation into a trooper who described his own position as the person who "polices the police." Questions surfaced around Major B.D. Gore after three female employees filed sexual harassment complaints against him. The employees alleged that he sexually harassed them and created a hostile work environment. Ironically, Gore, who was chief of executive services for the State Police, headed the agency's Professional Standards Unit, which conducted all internal inquiries of troopers' actions including sexual harassment charges. According to the *Charleston Gazette*:

> One of the women complained to Gore's superiors about him last year. She and the other two say he has left sexually harassing messages for them, including email and text messages, made telephone calls to them and indicated that he wanted to have sexual relations with them. One has said she had a short affair with him. Gore is one of the highest-ranking members of the State Police, with only lieutenant colonels and the superintendent above him. He is considered a finalist for the deputy superintendent's post, the No. 2 position with State Police.[968]

According to the *Charleston Gazette*: "Lawsuits and other allegations of wrongdoing against the West Virginia State Police have cost the State nearly $5 million the past five years." Among some of the cases settled against the State Police included claims of sexual harassment within the State Police offices; an officer who killed his girlfriend and then killed himself; alleged beatings by officers resulting in hospitalization of the victim; and federal and state charges against another State Police officer.[969] One such incident was State Trooper Gary Messenger who was sent to federal prison after he beat a Welch resident who had called 911 to complain about a drunken party and gunfire by other State Police officers who were attending the party. The *Charleston Gazette* wrote: "Subsequent investigations found that troopers were drinking and having sex with young women inside the Welch detachment. Even Messenger's attorney likened the barracks to a fraternity house."[970]

The perception of county officials involved in sexual escapades and inappropriate conduct is just as appalling as the perception of statewide officials. On January 17, 2003, Kanawha County Commissioner Dave Hardy publicly pushed for the resignation of Kanawha County Prosecutor, Mike Clifford. Hardy cited $83,500 in settlements covered with taxpayer and county insurance money to resolve two sexual harassment complaints against Clifford by former employees in his office.[971] The *Charleston Gazette* editorialized:

> Altogether, counting lawyer fees, Kanawha County taxpayers probably must shell out more than $100,000 to pay for the vulgar, lowbrow, trashy, sex obsession of Prosecuting Attorney Mike Clifford.
>
> It's disgusting that tax revenue from Kanawha families and businesses will be consumed resolving Clifford's obscene sexual harassment of two former female employees. Allegations against him described crudity so gross that it was astounding.
>
> Further, if the prosecutor drove away from a Putnam County service station Friday without paying for gasoline, as state troopers suspect, that's one more straw on the camel's back.[972]

In 2003, more than 130 Kanawha County residents sought Clifford's removal from office in a case brought in front of a three-judge panel. The panel later ruled that the allegations brought against Clifford did not warrant his removal from Office.[973] The panel, however, did say that his sexual banter with office employees was "tactless" and called the information he used to launch investigations against political opponents "questionable" including allegations from a convict "too preposterous to even dignify." It further said that Clifford "stretched the limits of his authority to its outermost boundaries."[974] Charleston Mayor Danny Jones said the ruling hurts the legal community's credibility and added, "It's why people don't have faith in the legal profession, and it's why lawyers are held in such low esteem."[975]

Following the panel's decision, the *Charleston Gazette* said:

> THREE judges decided that Kanawha County prosecutor Mike Clifford is somewhat loathsome, but the evidence against him isn't quite enough to justify his removal.

> The conclusion is rather like a *New Yorker* cartoon in which a judge, glowering at a defendant, said: 'You're not guilty, but you're very, very close.'

The *Gazette* also wrote:

> The judges also found that the prosecutor was 'mean-spirited' and 'vindictive' when he distributed a letter making baseless allegations against County Commissioner Dave Hardy. . . .

> When Clifford defeated former prosecutor Bill Forbes in the 2000 primary election, we felt that Kanawha County was rid of an oddball, difficult public figure. But Clifford's behavior subsequently has made Forbes seem like King Solomon.[976]

In response to Hardy's actions, Clifford pressed for an investigation of Hardy for sending campaign solicitations to people with the heading "Re-elect Dave Hardy Commissioner" when, in actuality, Hardy had been appointed to fill a vacant seat on the commission and had not been elected at that time. Clifford also complained that Hardy illegally used county vendor lists to solicit campaign contributions for his election. Clifford was later criticized for his prosecution of a criminal when a Kanawha County Circuit Judge barred Clifford's office from working on a convicted murderer's attempt to be released from jail, "saying it showed questionable judgment by supporting a deal that could spring him from jail in two years."[977]

Sexual allegations have also been prevalent on the city level of West Virginia politics. On December 20, 2002, in Elkins, West Virginia, the *Inter-Mountain* reported: "Mayor, Clerk Accuse Each Other of Sexual Misconduct." During the city council meeting, Elkins City Clerk Phil Graziani, Jr. read an accusatory statement which also was reprinted and boldly displayed on the front page of the local newspaper. The following is merely the introduction of that statement:

> Three different female employees of the city have been sexually harassed by Mayor Virgil P. Broughton. One of the sexually harassed females was under my supervision; the other two were under the mayor's supervision. The mayor sexually harassed my employee in December 2001. He sexually harassed his receptionist in April 2002, and, as a direct result of that harassment, she left her employment with the city. The receptionist who replaced her was sexually harassed in September 2002.[978]

Broughton, in turn, accused Graziani of also engaging in sexual impropriety. He said that Graziani told him: "Cover for me. Cover for me while I'm at deer camp. Cover for me while I'm out of town."[979] The day before this public display, the *Inter-Mountain* published a front page article that included a patriotic color picture with fireworks and an American flag serving notice of the upcoming city council meeting.[980] Little did the newspaper know when the article was printed that there would actually be fireworks at the meeting.

Broughton was eventually censured and placed on leave until his term ended. He lost his re-election bid in March 2003 and settled a sexual harassment complaint filed by city employees Angela Broschart and Angela Simmons and issued a public apology. The terms of the settlement remained private. Broughton then sued the City of Elkins to recover his attorney fees saying the city should have represented him. The city countersued to recover money it spent on the case. The city and Broughton settled their suit in March 2005.[981]

During the controversy, Graziani filed a complaint against Broughton with the Human Rights Commission. He claimed that Broughton retaliated against him by announcing his concerns about Graziani's job performance as city clerk as soon as he became aware of Graziani's knowledge of the sexual harassment allegations against the mayor. In February of 2006, however, the claims against Broughton were dismissed.

In her ruling, Administrative Law Judge Elizabeth Blair described Graziani's motivation to bring to light Broughton's alleged incidents of sexual harassment as an attempt to deflect attention away from his own disservice to the citizens of Elkins. She labeled Graziani's inability to perform certain duties as "mis and malfeasance." The ALJ asked: "Was his motive really to embarrass the mayor, his family and have him removed from office?" Blair then said: "Perhaps Mr. Graziani thought the mayor and Mrs. Broughton did not do enough to help him get elected to the House of Delegates, blamed them for his defeat and by having the mayor out of office, Mr. Graziani felt his position and reappointment as city clerk would be secure and a given, despite his failure to perform his duties." The ALJ further said: "Attempting to hide his disservice to the citizens of Elkins appears to be the city clerk's motivation for deflecting attention away from himself and onto Mayor Broughton's alleged incidents of sexual harassment. Fortunately for Mr. Graziani, instead of being removed by the City Council for his failure to perform his duties and cause the city to violate state laws, possibly incurring fines and suffer embarrassment, he was reappointed to another two-year term and given a $3,400 pay raise."

Finally, the ALJ found that, "This case is not about sexual harassment, discrimination or retaliation. It is a political power play whose casualties are the three women who were used by the city clerk to embarrass the mayor and his family and have him removed from office. The true victims in this case are the citizens of the City of Elkins, who deserve better appointed and elected officials who take their duties seriously, sufficiently performing them and ensuring that their character is beyond reproach and always remembering that they are representing the citizens of Elkins." Graziani responded to the ALJ's report by saying, "The judge's opinion is replete with speculation about matters that do not involve the true issues, and the conclusions which were reached by the judge during her speculative ramblings are invariably wrong."[982]

Once again, even at the smallest levels of city government, because of West Virginia's small size, people either know the people involved in the negative headlines personally or they know something about their families. For example, Graziani is well-known to some because his father was Phil Graziani, Sr., the Assistant Attorney General involved in the bribery scandal with Attorney General C. Donald Robertson during the 1960s and 1970s. Broughton, on the other hand, is the owner of Broughton's Sports and Trophy World and sells shoes, trophies, and other sports related items to people throughout Randolph County as well in the surrounding counties. In fact, until I graduated high school, every pair of tennis shoes I ever owned was purchased from Mr. Broughton or one of his sons working at the store. It wasn't out of loyalty to his store, it was just the better deal on shoes during that time period. Again, this is just another example of how connected in one way or another people become with these individuals whether they want to or not.  When a political scandal occurs, chances are that the people involved in the scandal often become more than just names in a newspaper surrounded by stories about distant and unknown people.  They are people whom we know or have known about for many years of our lives.

Another West Virginia municipality, the now dissolved Town of Jefferson, has faced more than its share of problems.  For example, in 2004, Town police officer Corporal William H. Gritt pleaded no contest to making harassing phone calls to the home of a local woman named Rebecca Parsons.  He was charged with the misdemeanor after making thirty-nine calls to Parsons within an hour-and-a-half after a St. Albans Patrolman, R.A. Thomas, investigated Parsons' complaint.  On one occasion after Thomas answered Parsons' telephone, Gritt became irate "and threatened to whip [Thomas'] ass."  When Thomas explained that he was a St. Albans police officer, Corporal Gritt didn't seem to mind as he continued to call Parsons several more times during the period when Thomas was filling out his police report on the harassing calls.[983]

The former Town of Jefferson, however, has been in constant controversy since its inception.  Former Mayor Kathy Wolfe was indicted and charged with twenty-one counts ranging from tax evasion to embezzlement on October 25, 2001.  As soon as many of those charges were dropped, several new charges surfaced against Wolfe dealing with how she handled the town's money.  In 2002, Wolfe pled guilty to a felony charge of filing false accounts and was sentenced to five years probation for placing the town's money in an unauthorized bank.[984] She later resigned from office.

In 2005, Jefferson's final mayor, Thomas Lewis, along with councilman James Lynch, and Recorder Kathy Miller, were the subject of a lawsuit filed by councilman William Meadows seeking their removal from office.  Following an investigation by a three-judge panel, Jefferson Town Recorder Kathy Miller was removed from office for failing to keep and certify proper minutes and town records.  The panel wrote: "Due to Miller's incompetence, she successfully covered up Mayor Lewis' actions, yet clearly revealed her own. . . . Mayor Lewis is saved from removal due to the incompetence and uselessness of the town's record keeping.  It is a conundrum that is disturbing."[985]  The panel further said, "It cannot be made more clear that Mayor Lewis is providing a disservice to the citizens of Jefferson.  By sheer dumb luck, Mayor Lewis was able to hide behind the recorder's cloak of disorganization and chaotic mess, yet still managed to be unveiled as an unremovable official."[986]

Jefferson, also know as "the Badlands," was incorporated in 1997 and had a reputation for its many bars, strip clubs filled to the brink with exotic dancers, and constant reports of prostitution.[987]  According to the three-judge panel investigating the mayor and council, "If this court did not know better, the Town of Jefferson may very well pass as a typical ghost town that existed in the 1700 to 1800s, which included the buzzards, stray dogs and pigs and of course the ubiquitous tumbleweeds." Kanawha County Commissioner Dave Hardy referred to Jefferson as "an outlaw government" as he and fellow Commissioner Kent Carper fought for the town's dissolution.[988] The county commission voted to dissolve the town on March 8, 2005, and the Circuit Court of Kanawha County upheld that decision on June 29, 2005. On November 18, 2005, the West Virginia Supreme Court refused to hear an appeal of the circuit court's decision. Even though the town had been dissolved, they continued to meet to discuss town business such as the difference between the town's debts and assets which were nearly $100,000.[989] During one such meeting at the Jefferson Town Hall on May 6, 2005, Councilman Lynch was arrested and charged with battery for punching Councilman William Meadows twice, punching Councilman Thomas Williamson, and grabbing Town Recorder Thomas Whaley's shirt.[990] On November 16, 2005, Lynch pled guilty to battery surrounding the fight.[991] The Kanawha County Commission appointed a special receiver to oversee the town's financial and legal matters which included liquidating town property such as police weapons, vehicles, and even a former strip club that was seized by federal prosecutors in a money laundering and tax evasion bust and later provided to the Town of Jefferson to become its town hall.

The incidents surrounding sexual misconduct of West Virginia's politicians has the same effect as much of the other inappropriate conduct exhibited by the State's elected officials. The violators more often than not receive little or no punishment for their actions leaving voters with the impression that elected officials' actions are above any recourse. When it becomes politically incorrect to question a Governor about an affair with a State employee, when a State Legislator simply receives probation for having anal intercourse with his teenage legislative page, when a circuit judge is surrounded by sexual harassment allegations against many of his employees yet receives his full judicial pension and has his law license returned to him, what are people supposed to conclude? They conclude that those in high political positions rarely are held accountable for their actions.

# CHAPTER FIFTEEN

# Stealing Our Children's Futures and Confiscating Our Seniors' Golden Years

*Sometimes things leave a bad taste in your mouth that you have to do, but as long as it is for something good, it's O.K. to do so.*

Delegate Jerry Mezzatesta

Many West Virginia politicians have failed the youth and the senior citizens of the State. Most recently, West Virginia went through a saga with former Chairman of the House of Delegates Education Committee, Delegate Jerry Mezzatesta. "Mezz," as he is often called, began many years ago as a history teacher with the Hampshire County Schools. In fact, when I worked for United States Congressman Harley O. Staggers, Jr. in 1992, I brought the Congressman to Mezzatesta's classroom to speak with his students. Mezzatesta is a short skinny man who has black curly hair with a few noticeable streaks of white running through it. He is known for his never-ending energy and sometimes intense temperament.

Since early 2004, numerous investigations have surrounded Delegate Mezzatesta which has resulted in hundreds of statewide newspaper articles. Among them was an investigation by the Ethics Commission on whether Mezzatesta improperly used his legislative position to solicit State education grants; another investigation by the Legislature's Commission on Special Investigations looking into whether he fabricated letters to fend off ethics complaints (bolstered by the fact that the stationery didn't exist when the letters were dated); as well as other investigations by the Kanawha County and Hampshire

County Prosecuting Attorneys who were pursuing numerous criminal charges against him.[992]

The well-publicized situation with Mezzatesta, the nine-term Democrat from Hampshire County, intensified on September 23, 2004, when Speaker of the West Virginia House of Delegates Bob Kiss (D-Raleigh) held a press conference in the State Capitol rotunda and released an eighty-plus-page report. The report detailed a House of Delegates investigation that concluded that a letter produced by Mezzatesta was fabricated in an attempt to clear himself during an ongoing investigation being conducted by the State Ethics Commission.[993]

Speaker Kiss said, "I have been here for 16 years, and I feel very strongly about this: this is an aberration, not a norm but, if it happens once in 16 years or once in 100 years, that's too often."[994] House Finance Chairman Harold Michael (D-Hardy) said, "I think it very well could affect how the public perceives the entire House of Delegates [as] everybody in the Legislature gets painted with the same brush. It's not something I would condone or any member of the House could condone."[995]

Kiss explained that Mezzatesta's fabricated letter was actually delivered to State Schools Superintendent David Stewart and Ethics Commission Director Lewis Brewer in early July 2004. The letter, erroneously dated January 13, 2003, focused on a conversation Mezzatesta had with Stewart about grant money he wished to procure for his employer, the Hampshire County School System. Kiss said the letter was not written in January of 2003, but instead, it was actually written on July 1, 2004.[996] The day before Speaker Kiss' press conference, Mezzatesta issued a press release announcing that he was diagnosed with early stage prostate cancer and soon would have surgery.[997]

The back-dated January 13, 2003, letter was hand delivered by House of Delegates lawyer Richard Lindroth, who also acted as Mezzatesta's personal lawyer, to both the Ethics Commission and the Kanawha County Prosecutor after the Commission was asked to reopen a complaint alleging Mezzatesta violated a 1999 agreement with the Commission. The earlier agreement between Mezzatesta and the Commission provided that he could accept the position of "community specialist" with the Hampshire County Schools as long as he agreed to never use his legislative position as Chairman of the House of Delegates Education Committee to request State Department of Education grants for them. Any such requests would clearly be unethical and a conflict of interest between his legislative duties and those of his employer, the Hampshire County Schools. Soon after the 1999 agreement, Mezzatesta moved from being a history teacher into a newly created position of community specialist paying $60,000-per-year.[998]

The fake letter was crafted to appear as a reply from Mezzatesta to State Superintendent Stewart, and said, "I hope you realized that I was not soliciting monies for my specific school district."[999]   The letter was in reference to Stewart directing a $100,000 strategic "staff development" grant to Hampshire County at Mezzatesta's earlier request.  The $100,000 went to Hampshire County even though the Legislature had only allocated $500,000 for "strategic development" for the entire State.  As such, Hampshire County received 20 percent of the funds, while its students made up only 1.3 percent of West Virginia's public school enrollment.  In addition, Superintendent Stewart sent the $100,000 to Hampshire County Schools just two months after the Department of Education's special education director, Stewart's subordinate, rejected Mezzatesta's initial request for a grant in the same amount.[1000]

The Ethics Commission dismissed the first complaint against Mezzatesta in June of 2004.  It based its decision, in part, on Mezzatesta's affidavit, along with similar sworn statements provided by Hampshire County Schools Superintendent David Friend and State Schools Superintendent Stewart.  Following the April 2004 ethics investigation, Stewart said in a sworn statement that he had never been solicited by Mezzatesta for funds.[1001]  After his deposition, however, it was discovered that Stewart had written a January 2, 2003, letter to Mezzatesta to "confirm our telephone conversation of this morning concerning your request for additional funding for Hampshire County Schools."[1002]  When presented with the January 2, 2003, letter, Stewart then admitted that his memory had been wrong when he testified on behalf of Mezzatesta to the Ethics Commission.[1003]

In spite of his conflicting statements, on January 6, 2005, the Ethics Commission found there was no evidence to support the claim that Stewart had filed a false affidavit with the Commission.  Perhaps coincidentally, prior to Stewart's initial testimony stating that Mezzatesta had not solicited funds from him, Mezzatesta pushed hard to raise Stewart's salary to $200,000 during the 2004 legislative session.  Stewart stood to become the fifth-highest-paid State Schools Chief in the nation; however, even though the House of Delegates passed the $60,000-a-year pay hike, the Senate Finance Committee rejected it.[1004]

Due to much public outcry and constant negative press coverage, the Ethics Commission, for the first time in its fifteen-year history, decided to reopen its investigation into Mezzatesta's alleged grant requests.  In addition to the fabrication of the letter, it was also determined that Mezzatesta, his wife Mary Lou Mezzatesta, who also served as his House of Delegates office assistant, and Richard Lindroth, sought ways to delete or obscure files on computer hard drives to hide them from investigators and the media.[1005]  Investigators ultimately searched computers assigned to six of their probe's witnesses in an unsuccessful search for the letter. Delegate Mezzatesta's secretary, Melinda Swagger, told investigators that he told her to overwrite hard drives with entire sections of the West Virginia Code. Swagger said that the pressure from both Mezzatesta and Mary Lou was so intense that she "had been spitting up blood."[1006] Mezzatesta reportedly told House Education staff members, "Sometimes things leave a bad taste in your mouth that you have to do, but as long as it is for something good, it's O.K. to do so."[1007]

During the investigation, more than eighty nude photographs were found on Lindroth's State computer hard drive of which Lindroth said he had "no clue" how the images wound up there. He said he occasionally received unsolicited computer pop-up ads, but would immediately delete them. Kanawha County Prosecuting Attorney Mike Clifford said, "It was clearly inappropriate, but I couldn't find a statute that was sufficiently descriptive to warrant prosecution." According to the *Charleston Gazette*, many of the images on Lindroth's computer were "accessed while Lindroth was on State time and collecting pay, according to a comparison of Lindroth's time sheets and dates attached to the computer files." Clifford said that with regard to the Mezzatesta letter scandal, he asked Lindroth to take a polygraph test, but Lindroth refused and declined to cooperate with prosecutors throughout their inquiry.[1008]

In August 2004, just prior to Speaker Kiss' scathing report on the Education Chairman, Delegate Mezzatesta sent out a press release saying that the January 13, 2003, letter was authentic. He further denied soliciting money for Hampshire County Schools and called media reports about him "negligent" and "wrong" and declared, "I don't mind the scrutiny. Just bring it on. There's nothing to hide."[1009] The House report included Mezzatesta's statement to investigators where he said, "At no time did I fabricate either of these letters, nor did I ever order or instruct anyone to do so." Mary Lou later admitted dictating the deceptively dated January 13, 2003, letter on July 1, 2004.[1010]

Mezzatesta's office assistant, Shelda Howard, told House Education Committee lawyer Candace Kraus that, "[Delegate] Mezzatesta wanted Howard to re-create the letter." Howard told State investigators that Mezzatesta ordered her to file the phony letter in Delegate Larry Williams' office shortly after she finished typing it on July 1, 2004. Howard said for the next few weeks she received frantic phone calls and visits from both Mezzatestas as they urged her to go along with the story. Conversely, Mezzatesta denied giving directions to Howard or anyone else regarding the January 13, 2003, letter. He said, "I gradually learned more details, but was not fully aware of my wife's actions in this matter until reading her statement she made for the investigation [and that he] still [did] not know all of the events surrounding the fabrication of the letter." Wanda Carney, co-director of the watchdog group West Virginia Wants to Know, said, "This speaks volumes about Jerry Mezzatesta's character [as] there's a tractor-trailer of an investigation, and here he wants to throw his wife under the wheels of the truck."[1011]

Carney herself faced controversy when she and a former Kanawha County School Board member, Betty Jarvis, were charged on August 4, 2005, with burglary, petit larceny, and conspiracy to commit those crimes upon entering the residence of a murder suspect. Jarvis said the pair did nothing wrong and that, "They're trying to discredit us, because we're getting too close to the truth in Mingo County." The pair were trying to conduct their own investigation into the murder of drug informant Carla Collins. Jarvis' nephew, Walter Harmon, Jr., was facing charges with regard to the murder.[1012] Just a few months before that, in an unrelated matter, Nitro City Councilman Bill Clark sued Carney saying she "offered to drop an investigation of the City of Nitro . . . in exchange for oral sex." Carney hired former Kanawha County Prosecuting Attorney Mike Clifford and countersued Clark for $20 million claiming he "knowingly, recklessly, willfully, wantonly and maliciously" slandered her with his comments. Clark alleged that Carney said, "I understand you are a player" saying she could be his "political advocate or largest adversary" if he played ball with "casual sex, oral sex, short fun time, wherever you would like, whenever you can, we will work well together."[1013]

My problem with lawsuits like the one against Carney is that anyone can file them. Carney and her co-founder in West Virginia Wants to Know have been successful in bringing to light several instances of misconduct by public officials. In fact, had the pair not pressed the Mezzatesta situation so hard it is more than likely that the case would not have been re-opened and nothing would have been done. Are the charges against Carney true? My guess is no, but I don't know either of the parties involved so my comments are purely speculation. However, this situation illustrates precisely the legitimate fear that I sometimes feel with regard to the publication of this book because an effective tool in politics is to call a person nuts or crazy or discredit them in some other manner when they are trying to uncover fraud and push for reforms. Moreover, once such a preposterous and scandalous charge is publically made against you, it's hard to erase it from people's minds regardless of its veracity.

As far as Mezzatesta, then-Kanawha County Prosecutor Mike Clifford initiated an investigation of him and four State employees in November 2004. Clifford later turned over part of his investigation to Hampshire County Prosecuting Attorney Stephen Moreland to determine whether Mezzatesta lied to the State Ethics Commission and turned another part of the investigation over to incoming Kanawha County Prosecutor Bill Charnock. With regard to the remainder of his investigation, on November 16, 2004, Clifford accepted a plea of no contest to a misdemeanor from both Mezzatesta and Mary Lou for crimes committed in Kanawha County which still left Delegate Mezzatesta subject to prosecution in Hampshire County. Mezzatesta and his wife were both ordered to pay a $500 fine and sentenced to ninety days probation for pleading no contest to a charge that he deleted or altered legislative computer records.[1014]

     Clifford said his decision to strike a plea bargain with Delegate Mezzatesta was based on several factors including "the facts of the case, the available evidence, the veteran Delegate's defeat in the General Election and his battle with prostate cancer." Clifford also decided not to pursue charges against the other workers in the education committee office. He said, "the two women who were ordered to do certain things by the Mezzatestas have cooperated fully with investigators and are to be commended." He added, "A lot of people are going to say I dealt with this case too mildly, [but,] I'm prepared to accept that criticism. I felt this was the proper culmination of this case." Conversely, Tifney Terry, the other co-director of West Virginia Wants to Know, the group that filed a separate ethics complaint on another matter against Mezzatesta, said, "This is another example of a corrupt, unethical West Virginia politician who got a slap on the wrist, and the taxpayers again take it on the chin."[1015]

     Following his conviction in Kanawha County, Mezzatesta sought reimbursement for travel and expenses from the State in the amount of nearly $1,000 for driving from his home in Hampshire County to Kanawha County "during which he cleaned out his office, said goodbye to friends, and pled no contest to a criminal charge in Kanawha County Magistrate Court."[1016] Mezzatesta turned in an expense tab for $450 extra duty pay, $345 for hotel and food costs, plus $192 in mileage. The *Charleston Gazette* said, "The former House Education Chairman long has been notorious for his arrogance–but this obscene gesture to the West Virginia public takes the cake. Previously, he collected $265 compensation for time he and his wife spent in his Statehouse office, purging computer files in an apparent attempt to conceal evidence as investigators closed in on him."[1017] During the same time period, the State Ethics Commission also began an investigation into whether Mary Lou ran Viking Vending Services, her Hampshire County video poker machine company, from the House Education Committee offices at the Capitol. A complaint filed by a citizens group alleged that she used a House Education office computer and fax machine to operate her private company.[1018]

     In early December 2004, after Clifford accepted the Mezzatestas' guilty pleas, he urged Hampshire County Prosecuting Attorney Steve Moreland to investigate whether Delegate Mezzatesta filed a false affidavit with the Ethics

Commission. Clifford said he didn't pursue that charge in Kanawha County since Mezzatesta signed the affidavit in Hampshire County. Moreland then disqualified himself, citing a conflict of interest and Clifford was appointed Special Prosecutor to handle the Hampshire County charges by Bill Charnock, who was then the director of the West Virginia Prosecuting Attorney's Institute. Clifford, however, who had not been re-elected to his position as prosecutor, went on vacation in late December and did not bring additional charges against Mezzatesta. This automatically made Charnock the Special Prosecutor, as he was elected to the Kanawha County Prosecutor position and took office in January 2005.

Charnock, whose father served as a chairman of the Ethics Commission, said that the plea agreement orchestrated by Clifford provided immunity to Mezzatesta for the Hampshire County charges so he declined to bring any additional charges. Clifford, however, flatly disagreed with Charnock's interpretation of the plea agreement and said, "To imply that because of the plea agreement that Mr. Mezzatesta can't be charged in Hampshire County is wrong. It was clear that the plea agreement applies only to Kanawha County offenses." The original plea agreement states, "The parties agree that this agreement only applies to Kanawha County and does not bind any other governmental entity." Nonetheless, Charnock sent a letter to Hampshire County Circuit Judge Donald Cookman omitting the Kanawha County reference when quoting from the plea agreement. Clifford said that Charnock "strategically omitted that [and] it's clear to me, if Mr. Charnock wants to present this case, he can."[1019] Clifford added, "To say what I did would bar any further prosecution against Mr. Mezzatesta in Hampshire County was just plain erroneous."[1020]

The *Charleston Gazette* wrote that: "Mezzatesta's critics alleged Monday that Charnock sent the letter to [Judge] Cookman as a special favor to Mezzatesta's attorney, Ben Bailey, who contributed $1,000 to Charnock's campaign and hosted a $3,600 fundraiser for the Republican prosecutor at his Charleston law firm." Charnock, who promised to crack down on political corruption throughout his campaign, acknowledged that he had spoken with Bailey about the letter to Cookman, but said Bailey did not help him write it and that he made his decision "based upon what was the right thing to do."[1021] Judge Cookman disregarded Charnock's letter and appointed a special prosecutor to determine whether Mezzatesta lied in an affidavit that he gave to the State Ethics Commission in 2004. Subsequently, in April 2005, a special grand jury returned an indictment against Mezzatesta. In July 2005, Judge Cookman asked to be recused from further involvement in the criminal and ethics cases against Mezzatesta and retired Judge C. Reeves Taylor was appointed as his replacement. On July 29, 2005, Judge Taylor dismissed the false swearing charge.[1022]

In a matter separate from the Hampshire County charges against Mezzatesta, in March 2005, the Ethics Commission and Mezzatesta agreed to settle the ethics complaints against him with a public reprimand and a $2,000 fine. He was given a deadline of April 10, 2005, to pay the fine. His lawyer, Ben Bailey, later faxed a letter to the Ethics Commission saying that Mezzatesta did not agree to the fine when he signed the "conciliation agreement" with the Commission. Bailey said Mezzatesta hadn't admitted to any wrongdoing and that the Ethics Commission had "insufficient proof" he had "violated the State Ethics Act in any way." On May 6, 2005, the Ethics Commission unanimously authorized a lawsuit against Mezzatesta for his failure to pay the fines. It was the first time in the Commission's history that it had to file an enforcement action.[1023] Even so, Mezzatesta still refused to pay the fine.

It was just days later, on May 15, 2005, when Charnock faced problems of his own as the State Legislative Auditor's Office revealed that he was being investigated for his actions prior to January 2005, when he worked as the head of the State Prosecuting Attorney's Institute. The audit revealed that nearly 60 percent of the calls made by Charnock between August 2002 and April 2004 on his State issued cell phone were personal. Charnock called the cell phone probe "petty" and called the Legislature's actions "payback" because he had formed a political corruption unit.[1024]

The saga with Mezzatesta did not end with the letter investigation and the controversy surrounding Charnock's attempt to end the investigation of the former Delegate. He also faced criticism for taking paid professional leave during regular and special legislative sessions and collecting double payments from his $24,000 per-year job as a State Delegate and as his $60,000 per-year job with the Hampshire County Schools. In April 2004, the State Republican Party filed an ethics complaint against Mezzatesta alleging he broke State law by collecting both salaries at the same time.[1025] The Ethics Commission, however, found no problem with his two simultaneous government salaries.

Mezzatesta claimed that he worked eight-to-ten hours every night and twelve-to-sixteen hours on weekends during legislative sessions. Hampshire County Schools Superintendent David Friend called Mezzatesta a "workaholic" and someone who worked sixteen hours a day and deserved every penny of his $60,000-per-year salary.[1026] While nineteen other State lawmakers also worked for county school boards during this same time period, Mezzatesta was the only one who collected his school board salary while also getting paid to be a State legislator. The other eighteen legislator-school board employees all asked for unpaid leave from their education posts while serving in the Legislature.[1027] Moreover, while Mezzatesta contended that he performed the duties of both jobs at the same time which justified his dual pay, later-discovered records indicated he actually received "paid professional leave" during each legislative session.[1028] The *Charleston Daily Mail* called Mezzatesta's dual salaries "an outrageous abuse of the taxpayer."[1029]

State Senator Roman Prezioso, who in addition to his legislative position oversees an alternative school and adult education center in Marion County, said for the sixteen years he had been with the Legislature, he had always taken an unpaid leave of absence from his school board administrator job during the legislative session since he collects legislative pay during that time. Prezioso said he will continue to shun his school pay while serving in the Legislature in spite of the Ethics Commission's apparent green light for school employees/legislators to collect dual pay. Prezioso said, "I'll continue to do the work and take an unpaid leave of absence [as] I don't intend on being paid twice. I'm being compensated for the job I'm doing in Charleston." Prezioso said it was a shame the Ethics Commission even had to address the issue in the first place because the voters elect their leaders and hold them to a higher standard–a standard that agrees double-dipping is wrong. He said that unfortunately a few legislators have brought the many under the microscope; however, he believed it could actually be a good thing because it will be made clear that lawmakers cannot make their own rules while expecting their constituents to follow another set of rules. State Delegate Dale Manuel (D-Jefferson), who teaches fifth grade at Wright Denny Elementary School, agreed saying, "It's not the right thing to do, regardless of the Ethics Commission's [decision]."[1030]

Due to the constant controversy, myriad groups and individuals urged action with regard to Mezzatesta. Candy Canan, a Hampshire County teacher and Vice President of the Hampshire County Education Association, pushed the State Board of Education to investigate "questionable practices" by top Hampshire central office administrators." Canan alleged that funds were misappropriated, including the bulk of a $75,000 State Department of Education grant that Mezzatesta steered to volunteer fire departments in Hampshire County. She maintained that the money was earmarked for a sheltered workshop in Romney, West Virginia, that serves some Hampshire County special education students.[1031] In October of 2005, the United States Department of Education Office of Inspector General "sent out a flurry of subpoenas to Hampshire County fire departments, the county's Office of Emergency Services, and the Capon Bridge Library . . . asking for documents that detail how the agencies spent their share of the $75,000 State Department of Education grant."[1032]

Canan was so concerned with Mezzatesta's conduct that she campaigned door-to-door prior to the 2004 General Election in an attempt to defeat him. She said that in spite of his alleged misconduct, local residents heavily supported his re-election due to the millions of dollars he had brought to the county through the Budget Digest.[1033] Canan said, "People are saying, 'Look what Jerry has done for Hampshire County. I'm not going to vote him out over a bunch of letters.'" Canan added, "The bottom line is everyone in Hampshire County knows that the things Mr. Mezzatesta has done are wrong [and while] some try to do something about it, others will still vote for him on Election Day based solely on what he has done for them in the past. The only thing we can hope for is that conscience supercedes greed." *Charleston Gazette* reporter Eric Eyre explains:

> They tell Canan about Mezzatesta, the former basketball coach and high school teacher who gave them an 'A.' They talk about the $5,000 he secured through the state Budget Digest to save an old church and turn it into a much-needed community center in Green Spring. They talk about the state money–$1,000 here, $10,000 there–he has steered to volunteer fire departments, the sheriff's office, the local Ruritan Club.[1034]

As the investigation progressed, Tom Lange, then-President of the West Virginia Education Association, called for Mezzatesta to resign. He said the situation involving Mezzatesta "has cast a dark cloud over the entire House of Delegates."[1035] Mezzatesta was removed from his Education Chairman's position during the middle of the investigation on August 17, 2004. The *Charleston Gazette* said that during his tenure as Education Chairman "he had behaved like a petty tyrant" and pushed the various investigatory agencies to continue the probes against him notwithstanding his committee removal.[1036] Nonetheless, Lange said removing him as House Education Chairman was not going far enough as he was still a member of the House Finance Committee which "as it is, has a hand in how all of the money for the State's schools is allocated."[1037] Several county boards of education also passed resolutions expressing their desire to have Mezzatesta resign from the House of Delegates including the Boards of Education in Kanawha, Lincoln, Braxton, and Monroe counties.[1038]

On November 2, 2004, Mezzatesta was narrowly defeated by Republican opponent Ruth Rowan. After the election, Mezzatesta filed a Freedom of Information request with the Hampshire County Board of Education seeking tape recordings of school board meetings during which people talked about him.[1039] Soon afterward, as public pressure mounted for the firing of Mezzatesta, Hampshire County School Board attorney Norwood Bentley dug in his heels during a March 2005 regularly scheduled meeting of the Board. As more than 100 people, who had previously signed a required list to speak at the board meeting, began speaking about Mezzatesta, they were quickly muzzled. After the first speaker, Robert Lee, finished only a few sentences, which included calling for Mezzatesta and Hampshire County Superintendent David Friend's firing, Bentley intervened and instructed Lee that neither he nor any of the speakers could mention specific people in their comments about problems in the school district. Bentley told the *Associated Press*, "You can't take an employee of a school board to task in an open session. It's not the public's meeting. It's the school board's meeting."[1040]

This may be the first time I have heard a public official instructing the public they can't complain about public officials. That is simply absurd. Governmental bodies need to be informed that they work for the people and not the reverse. It is the public who owns the school system and elects the board members. Telling the public–who in reality pays the bills–that they can't speak about employees at a public meeting just reeks of arrogance. Perhaps citizens should have brought a copy of the United States Constitution with them to the meeting. It reminds me of a day in December 2004 following my second interview of Governor Wise when I went to his press office and asked his Press Secretary for the official State photo of the Governor for possible inclusion in my book. The photo is not copyrighted and is available to *anyone* upon request. In fact, when I worked for Governor Caperton stacks of such photos were readily available and given to anyone who wanted one. Nonetheless, I was refused a photo unless I allowed this person to read and approve the content of my book before it was published. Of course I refused, but so much for the First Amendment. This person later told me that she and "senior staff" had discussed the issue and they stood by her decision. Such arrogance is just another example of how some elected officials and their staff members have forgotten that politicians are actually elected by the people to serve and not anointed to the throne to rule.

In any case, on February 10, 2005, the State Board of Education declared a "state of emergency" in the Hampshire County Schools, stripped the school board of its accreditation, and threatened a complete State takeover. This action followed an audit which revealed that top Hampshire County Schools administrators hired employees illegally and misspent State grants solicited by the former Delegate. Superintendent Friend and Mezzatesta were named throughout the audit report which also revealed claims by Hampshire County School Board office employees that Friend and Mezzatesta "threatened, verbally abused and intimidated them," and ordered them to do things that were "highly irregular." Then-State School Superintendent David Stewart, who had defended Mezzatesta during the initial ethics investigation, called the situation "a breakdown of leadership at all levels."[1041]

The team of auditors from the State Office of Education Performance Audits inspected the Hampshire County School Board's central office in January 2005 and found State grants secured by Mezzatesta that weren't spent as intended. The audit also revealed that in 2003, the school board illegally hired Mezzatesta's sister, Tammy Moreland, as Hampshire County High School's principal after Mezzatesta sat on a committee that interviewed three qualified and certified applicants for the job, but chose not to hire them.

Moreland wasn't even a candidate at the time of the first interviews, but Superintendent Friend re-advertised the position on Mezzatesta's recommendation following a memo that said, "The three applicants are knowledgeable, but I feel we may have to re-advertise for a broader base." After the second round of interviews, Moreland was hired, even though she wasn't certified as a principal, while the other candidates had the appropriate certification and more experience. Moreland even privately negotiated her salary with the school board, which according to the audit team, was a highly unusual practice. She was paid $72,000 a year, $4,300 more than she would have received if the board followed the school system's administrative salary schedule.[1042]

State school officials concluded that illegal personnel practices were widespread in Hampshire County and wrote: "In almost all the cases, the people with the highest qualifications weren't hired." The auditors further raised questions about Mezzatesta's $60,000-a-year "community specialist" job saying he was hired under suspicious circumstances, and that the school board had repeatedly changed his job title and duties without advertising or re-advertising the position.

The audit team also found that Friend's son, D.J. Friend, was hired illegally for a job that was never posted in Hampshire County. He worked for Hampshire County Schools, but received his paycheck through the regional education service agency in Martinsburg, in Berkeley County. He was working as an alternative education aide at the Hampshire County High School without a proper license and was paid for three weeks in July 2004, even though the alternative program wasn't open in July 2004.

Following the damaging State schools audit report, the Hampshire County Board announced they would be eliminating Mezzatesta's created job of "community specialist" and reassigning him as transportation director. The bus drivers were immediately angry by the Board's decision.[1043] On April 22, 2005, due to enormous pressure, the Hampshire County Board of Education voted unanimously to fire Mezzatesta. According to the *Charleston Gazette*, "two school board members wiped tears from their eyes as they cast their votes to fire Mezzatesta." Larry Schultz, a lawyer for the Board, said, "The Board was quite clear that he was not to solicit grants, and he did it anyway."[1044]  In September of 2005, Mezzatesta appealed his firing to the Circuit Court of Hampshire County. On January 11, 2006, the State Board of Education seized control of the Hampshire County School System saying it needed to get the lack of leadership problem corrected quickly and that it would focus on personnel and finances. The director of the audit, Kenna Seal, said, "Overall, there is a climate of distrust, and there's a climate of explosive behavior in the central office."[1045]

The Board's actions in firing Mezzatesta were disingenuous. Should Mezzatesta have been fired? Yes. Should he have been hired in the first place as a "community specialist?" No. Let's be perfectly honest about what happened here. The Hampshire County School System took a good history teacher out of his classroom based upon his position in the Legislature and created a job specifically for him in hopes he would bring big money to the county. He did this for years and nobody complained. His main job duty was to write grant proposals, even though he wasn't allowed to solicit grants from the State. Then, it was the worst kept secret in Hampshire County that he didn't even write a single grant proposal during his five years as a board office administrator.

I believe the Board members knew exactly what Mezzatesta was doing from day one. As long as he was bringing buckets of money to Hampshire County they were his biggest supporters. Moreover, the creation of Mezzatesta's community specialist position was no secret in Hampshire County and when public pressure mounted after weeks of negative press coverage, the Board members finally threw Mezzatesta to the wolves even though they had plenty of blood on their own hands. Again, he should have been fired. However, the about-face by Board members after at least five years of going along with the problem–and maybe even creating some of it–and then accepting no responsibility for their actions is difficult to fathom. Each and every member of the Board should have voted to fire Mezzatesta and Superintendent Friend. Then, directly after making those decisions, all of the members who supported the creation of the community specialist position and remained silent throughout the years of controversy should have tendered their resignations effective immediately. This is the type of situation where temporary State control of the school system was warranted in order to make sure that all of the snakes were removed from the woodpile.

On Janaury 3, 2006, Superintendent Friend resigned saying he could no longer work in a "hostile environment of ill will, animosity, anxiety and stress." Friend, who was paid more than $133,000 while out of the office on sick leave during the fifteen months leading up to his resignation, denied any wrongdoing and filed a lawsuit against the school board in the Circuit Court of Hampshire County alleging defamation of character. According to the lawsuit, Friend said the board members and board office employees made "false and groundless" accusations against him.[1046]

Even though State School Superintendent Stewart's conduct surrounding the Mezzatesta situation was questionable at best, several other recent State superintendents and top State education officials have faced their share of scrutiny. For instance, former West Virginia State School Superintendent Hank Marockie was investigated for his use of a little-known expense account called the "Superintendent's Discretionary Fund." Marockie, who signed off on his own travel expenses, accepted more than $99,000 between 1989 and 1999 from an organization whose contributors included private foundations and some of the largest corporations in the State. It was also reported that businesses sometimes paid other travel expenses of the Superintendent including hotel rooms and airline tickets not included in the totals reported on the Fund expenses.[1047]

Then, in January 2005, another top State Schools official, former West Virginia Assistant Superintendent of Schools G.A. McClung was charged with extortion and defrauding the State for his role in awarding a $2.4 million furniture deal and other contracts to his longtime friend, Phillip "Pork Chop" Booth, after floods ravaged schools in McDowell and Wyoming counties in 2001. In exchange, Booth gave McClung cash, checks, tickets for a Bahamas cruise, and tickets to the Kentucky Derby. Booth also forgave substantial loans that he had previously given to McClung.[1048]

Following the floods, Federal Emergency Management Agency (FEMA) officials estimated that it would cost $3 million to repair the flood damaged schools; however, McClung ordered the Wyoming and McDowell County School Boards to spend $12 million. Also, in 2001, after the State School Board seized control of the failing McDowell school system, McClung served as acting county superintendent for about a month. According to current McDowell County Schools Superintendent Mark Manchin, first cousin to current Governor Joe Manchin, III and son of former impeached State Treasurer A. James Manchin, during the month McClung was in charge, he ordered school employees to hand deliver checks to Booth in a scheme that cost the county schools more than $700,000. One of the checks ordered by McClung included a fake invoice for $68,000 for classroom furniture that was never delivered. Booth was convicted of wire fraud and engaging in a monetary transaction involving "criminally derived property." He faced a possible sentence of fifteen years in prison and a $250,000 fine and was scheduled to be sentenced on August 29, 2005, but died of a heart attack on June 19, 2005.

McClung pled guilty to one charge of extortion and to filing a false tax return on May 23, 2005, in exchange for federal prosecutors dropping twenty-two additional federal counts against him. He faced a maximum penalty of twenty-three years in prison and a $250,000 fine.[1049]  On August 29, 2005, McClung was sentenced to seven years in federal prison and ordered to pay back $68,000 to the McDowell County School Board and $37,500 to the State School Building Authority.  In sentencing McClung, United States District Court Judge Joseph Goodwin said, "You were a high-ranking public official entrusted with important decision-making [and] honesty and respect for the law are paramount for any public official."[1050]  In spite of the jail term and financial penalties, McClung had already successfully cashed out his State retirement (on the day of his resignation) thereby preventing the State from denying him a pension.  On October 19, 2005, instead of seeking any penalties against McClung, the State Consolidated Public Retirement Board voted to send him a "less than honorable service" letter which would prevent him from being able to participate in the State retirement system in the future.[1051]  If they weren't going to go after his pension and file a lawsuit against him to recover the money, I am not sure why they wasted the ink and a stamp to send him a "stern letter."  Such a letter only highlights the fact that the Board didn't do anything, as usual, in recognition of his illegal activities.

The *Charleston Gazette* maintains that given the fact that "West Virginians rank 49th in per capita income and high on taxation per $1,000 of personal income, it is particularly galling when people elected or appointed to exercise power on their behalf use that power to rack up reimbursements from the State."  The editorial particularly focused on the expenditures of some members of the State Board of Education who "have relentlessly milked the State for 'expenses' involved in serving the public."  The State reimburses Board members for regular meetings and travel expenses, while State law also allows Board members to claim $100 in expenses for any day or part thereof spent on public business as "some board members have abused this shamelessly."[1052]

The editorial maintained that West Virginia reimbursed State Board of Education members $247,000 in per diem payments during a four-and-a-half-year period and cited examples including the following: former Board member Jim McKnight, who charged $200 for attending a conference on waste in schools, and $400 for spending four days inspecting potential sites for educational forums (He billed for when he attended the forums, too); the former President of the Board and disgraced banker J.D. Morris, who billed the State $100 when he attended a funeral (for the first wife of House Education Chairman Jerry Mezzatesta) in addition to receiving money from the State seven times, at $100 each, for attending the boys and girls high school basketball tournaments; Sandra Chapman, who asked for reimbursement sixty-six times during three years for doing "research, emails, and preparation for [State Board] meetings" for total reimbursement of $6,600; Paul Morris, who was reimbursed $100 for attending a Christmas party at the State Department of Education; another former State School Board member, Cleo Mathews, who charged the State after being interviewed by FBI agents during an investigation of former State Schools Superintendent Hank Marockie; and several Board members who received $100 when they met with education leaders like West Virginia Education Association President Tom Lange. The *Gazette* wrote: "This is simply outrageous conduct. If legislators understood what damage this kind of abuse does to public sympathy for higher taxes or fees, they would end it immediately."[1053]

With regard to former State School Board President J.D. Morris' actions in accepting payment from the State for attending a funeral, Delegate Mezzatesta vowed to sponsor legislation to restrict per diem pay and said he was unaware that Morris collected taxpayer money while attending the June 1999 funeral. Morris also charged mileage to the State for the drive from his house in Clay County to the funeral home in Hampshire County. Mezzatesta added, "That offends me. That offends me quite a bit. That far exceeds any quality of taste."[1054]  Morris resigned amid federal charges that he embezzled $172,000 when he was President of the Clay County Bank. He was sentenced to eighteen months in federal prison after being found guilty of embezzling $135,000.[1055]

The West Virginia Constitution mandates that, "the legislature shall provide by general law, for a thorough and efficient system of free schools."[1056] Several bad apples have ensured that West Virginia has failed in that regard. Teachers badly in need of raises sitting in classrooms requiring repair should be outraged. In reality, all West Virginians should be furious and demand action as the future of every West Virginia child is being compromised by the millions of dollars in wasted and often corrupt spending.

West Virginia's children are not the only ones getting hurt though. In addition to stealing from the futures of the State's youth, other bad actors have made a living profiting to a point even beyond extravagance with regard to the State's growing elderly population. These unscrupulous individuals take money from federal and state programs designed to help the seniors during their golden years as they squander it for their own personal pleasures. Perhaps the most glaring example is Wyoming County Council on Aging and All Care Home and Community Services Director, Bob Graham, who arranged compensation for himself of $301,728 in 2002 and about $457,872 in 2003 even though the average senior director's salary in West Virginia was $42,000 according to a report of the State Bureau of Senior Services. Graham, the former aide to former United States Congressman Ken Hechler in the 1970s, is currently the director of both agencies which have the same board of directors and perform the same function of providing case management and in-home care for seniors.[1057]

Graham's agencies' money came from both the federal and state government and funded a $50,000 Lincoln Navigator that he used as his personal vehicle, as well as an apartment at the senior center that contained a hot tub, a tanning bed, a thirty-seven-inch television, and a paid satellite service that included every single National Football League (NFL) game available for broadcast. He and his family members also went on all-expense-paid trips to Hawaii; Florida; Pigeon Forge, Tennessee; Nashville, Tennessee; Lancaster, Pennsylvania; Asheville, North Carolina; and Las Vegas, Nevada.[1058]

Graham's $457,872 state and federal compensation in 2003 included: base pay of $185,001; time-and-a-half pay for approximately 330 hours of overtime at a rate of $133.41 per hour for a total of $44,180; a Christmas bonus of $34,000; $34,598 for cashed-in personal leave; and $160,093 for cashed-in sick leave.[1059] In addition to Graham's salary, he also receives: 54 days of paid vacation, three personal days, and 24 sick leave days, all of which may be converted to cash if not used; 18 paid holidays; 100 percent paid health insurance coverage for life under the Public Employees Insurance Agency; $100,000 worth of life insurance, an Individual Retirement Account paid to Peoples Bank at 15 percent of gross wages; Jefferson Pilot Disability Insurance; Concord Heritage Life Insurance; AFLAC Intensive Care and Cancer Insurance; and dental and eye care; and full reimbursement for a minimum of two out-of-state trips per year.[1060] Graham's salary increased significantly throughout the years as indicated below by the year followed by the actual compensation received for that year.

- 1989 salary of $22,825
- 1993 salary of $50,127
- 1999 salary of $152,761
- 2001 salary of $217,175
- 2002 salary of $301,728
- 2003 salary of $457,872

To put it into perspective, in 2003, Graham's $457,872 compensation was more than the salary of the President of the United States, more money than any member of Congress, and more money than any West Virginia statewide elected official. In fact, if you combine the salaries of every single statewide elected West Virginia executive branch constitutional officer, you would only slightly exceed Graham's salary.

| Governor | $95,000 + |
| Attorney General | $80,000 + |
| Auditor | $75,000 + |
| Agriculture Commissioner | $75,000 + |
| Secretary of State | $70,000 + |
| State Treasurer | $75,000 + |

(Total combined salaries) = $470,000 v. Graham's $457,872

A quick glance at the above list would deceptively make it appear that the salaries of all of those elected officials combined are slightly higher than Graham's salary, however, it must be kept in mind that the $457,872 received did not include the free trips to exotic locations, free use of vehicles, use of an extravagant apartment with a hot tub, a generous retirement, and myriad insurance policies. Perhaps equally incredible, his 2003 salary was more than thirty-times that of a West Virginia State Senator or House of Delegate's $15,000-a-year-salary.[1061] Graham even made more than the combined salaries of United States Senators Robert C. Byrd and Jay Rockefeller as well as more than the total salaries of all of West Virginia's members of the United States House of Representatives!

Graham's agencies' budget was $5.3 million a year, with approximately 80 percent of that coming from federal funds and 20 percent coming from State funding. Most of the money comes from Medicaid funds intended to help elderly and poor people. He said the agencies are able to use Medicaid reimbursement funds in any way they want after the required services are provided to seniors. From that budget, Graham, who is active in the Princeton High School athletic boosters club and announces Princeton football and basketball games on a local radio station, provided money from his seniors' agencies for his "pet sports projects–including paying for out-of-state private school teams to come to Princeton to play exhibition basketball games."[1062]

Graham allowed the Princeton High School football and basketball teams to use senior center vans, which were intended to shuttle senior citizens to "nutrition sites, medical appointments, shopping, banking and recreational activities," to instead, haul equipment to sporting events across the State from at least 1999 to 2004. He has denied any wrongdoing and said his salary was justified because of his twenty-five years of service and the agencies' success.[1063]

Graham's salary and benefits are determined by his agencies' board. In November 2003, a State report investigation into the matter revealed that Graham had the agencies' bylaws changed so that no one under the age of sixty could serve on its board of directors. The amendment also removed the board's secretary and treasurer from responsibility for financial reports. At the time of the inflated salary discovery, it was learned that all of Graham's board members were elderly women who also went to the agencies' senior center. While one board member resigned because she had not attended any meetings, others said they had no idea how much money Graham made and never voted on his salary.[1064]  Wyoming County resident, sixty-eight-year-old Francis Bailey, said she has known Graham for years and thinks he is just doing his job. Bailey said, "When you work, don't you go for however much you can get paid? That's what we all do. He's a nice man, and knowing him, knowing how smart he is, I'm sure he wouldn't be making that much money if that's not exactly how much he deserves."[1065]  Amid calls for his resignation, Graham said, "I'm not going anywhere. It'll just be another headline, and it will draw the directors' association into [the controversy]."[1066]

It was later learned that Graham's live-in girlfriend since 2000, who later became his wife in 2004, was also well paid by his nonprofit Wyoming County Council on Aging.  Carol Graham initially earned $3.35 an hour for six hours per day as a bus driver and typist for Graham's agency.  When questioned by the State Attorney General's Office, Carol admitted that her pay increased from $3.35 per hour to $52,000 a year, plus a $14,000 bonus as well as other benefits.  Even though Carol admitted to the Attorney General's Office that she made $66,000 in 2003, the Form 990 disclosure report required of all nonprofit groups showed that her 2003 compensation was actually $81,537.[1067]  It was also discovered that in addition to her salary, she receives thirty days of vacation, twelve sick days, three personal days, an independent retirement account, and 100 percent of her health benefits paid by the agency.  The agency even paid for a transmission for her personal vehicle.  Carol was also a frequent traveling companion to Graham and had taken several out-of-state trips at the expense of the nonprofit agency.[1068]  On January 26, 2006, perhaps due to the onslaught of negative media coverage, a federal grand jury indicted Graham on twenty-one counts of embezzling, illegally transferring money, and filing false tax returns.  Following the indictment, Congresswoman Shelly Moore Capito said, "These are taxpayer dollars and they're not to be messed with.  We just can't allow this to happen.  This guy was serving needy people and that has to be the priority."[1069]

Just one day before he was indicted, Graham filed a lawsuit against former Governor Bob Wise, former Bureau of Senior Services Commissioner Ann Stottlemyer, and former acting Administration Secretary Tom Susman, claiming they inappropriately targeted him because he exposed misconduct.  Graham said he was retaliated against because he revealed wrongdoing in a statewide program and criticized Stottlemyer's former employer, the West Virginia Medical Institute. He said Stottlemyer then "intentionally twisted information" and made "false and misleading" allegations against him. Wise, who now serves as president of the nonprofit Alliance for Excellent Education in Washington, D.C., called Graham's lawsuit "totally ridiculous" and explained that: "The fact there was a separate independent investigation that resulted in a sweeping indictment of Bob Graham shows how absurd these allegations are [and that Graham's] problems weren't caused by my administration. His problems were caused by himself." Graham is represented by Mike Carey, a former United States Attorney who was instrumental in bringing down countless southern West Virginia corrupt politicians in the mid 1980s to early 1990s.[1070]

On February 7, 2006, Graham was given paid temporary personal leave by his board of directors. Graham's chief financial officer, Jennifer Gibson, was appointed interim executive director with a temporary annual salary of $65,000, until resolution of the charges against Graham. The board's resolution said, in part, "Due to adverse publicity and to allow Graham time to prepare his defense, the board of directors has determined that Graham should be placed on temporary personal leave pending resolution of these matters."[1071]

Another issue with regard to Bob Graham resulted from the fact that State Senator Billy Wayne Bailey (D-Wyoming) receives a salary from Graham's Wyoming County Council on Aging even though Senator Bailey also secures State funding for the agency. Bailey blamed the media and the State Republican Party for "dragging his name through the mud" after revelations that he was a "contract employee" with the Council on Aging at the same time he used his position in the State Senate to direct State Budget Digest money to that agency. Bailey also said he was "stupefied" by the indictment against Graham. He said, "It's time to set the record straight. I've answered their questions, I've endured their mud slinging, and I don't plan to take it anymore."[1072] Bailey admitted that he had directed nearly $415,000 to the Wyoming County Council on Aging through the Budget Digest from 1998 to 2003. In 2004, in spite of the investigations and controversy surrounding Bailey's employment, he requested an additional $55,000 of Budget Digest funds for Graham's agency. Bailey, who made $25,000 as a contract employee for Graham, said while he considered Graham a good friend and a boss, he had no idea the amount of money received by Graham and said, "Probably we need a little bit of oversight."[1073] Bailey's $25,000 salary from the agency was based on his $25 to $28 per hour fee to help cook and serve meals for a catering service organized by Graham's agency used to help pay for senior programs.

On August 25, 2005, Wanda Carney, vice president of West Virginia Wants to Know, filed a complaint with the State Ethics Commission with regard to Bailey securing funds for his employer resulting in using his public office for private gain.[1074]  On December 22, 2005, the Ethics Commission dismissed the complaint without comment.  Senator Bailey said, "This is a Christmas present. I thank God for helping me get through this."  The *Charleston Daily Mail* responded, "Celebrating such an awful decision would be like cheering bubonic plague."[1075]  The *Charleston Gazette* asked, "Just out of curiosity, we wonder what kind of outrage a politician would have to commit, to draw reproach from the commission?"[1076]

State Republican Party Chairman Kris Warner said, "Unfortunately for Bailey, he is a victim not of the media or the GOP, but rather of the mind set that has ruled the Legislature for years, a mind set that too often puts a low premium on ethical behavior and a high premium on getting a cut of the action."  Warner added that, "the people of West Virginia have a right to know whether any of the State money generated by their elected representatives goes into the pockets of their Delegates or Senators" and urged the Legislature to immediately pass a law prohibiting an elected official from directing money to an agency for which he or she works.[1077]

Following the exposure of the Bob Graham situation, it was learned that the director of the neighboring Lincoln County Opportunity Council on Aging, Alice Tomblin, received a $136,694 salary per year.  Additionally, in March of 2005, it was revealed that Northern Panhandle behavioral health center, Northwood Health Systems agency's executive director, Pete Radakovich, earned $482,517 in 2003.  When Senator Ed Bowman, who served as a member of the agency's board, learned of the astronomical salary he said he would serve his term on the board, but would not accept reappointment to another term. Bowman, who didn't know about the salary, said, "I'm not going to defend it, I never have attempted to defend it."[1078]

Other State senior centers have made the news including: the Mercer County Commission on Aging who asked the State for a $358,000 bailout to pay its debts and its mortgage on its $1 million senior center; the Putnam County aging program that ran up a $300,000 annual budget deficit; and the Marion County aging program that "spent thousands on billboards that featured its director, who then ran for office and [was elected to serve] in the Legislature."[1079]

The Marion County Delegate who was featured on the billboard advertisements was Donna Reid Renner.  In 2004, Renner made $71,500 from senior citizen programs in her region, even though she only reported on a survey of senior center directors that she made $41,000.  Also in 2004, Renner was criticized for taking an unreported trip to the Yucatan peninsula of Mexico at the expense of a local television station, WBOY, after her county's non-profit aging organization spent thousands of dollars on television ads that could have been run for free as public service announcements. According to the *Charleston Gazette*, if she had not taken the trip, the media company would have given free advertising to the senior program instead. Renner, however, said she thought the free trip to Mexico was a reward for the $2,100 she spent in television advertising for her 2002 campaign for the House of Delegates. After the story ran in various newspapers, she agreed to repay the value of the free trip she and the former Marion County Commission President, who serves on Renner's senior center board, had already taken.[1080]

When I think about today's children in West Virginia, I often reflect upon my own experiences growing up and learning in State schools. I particularly remember my junior and senior years of high school when I was fortunate enough to play in the Football State Championship games. It was a dream for a young boy from a very rural part of West Virginia. My first State Championship game was in 1986, the same year that Gene Hackman stared in the movie *Hoosiers*, where a small-time high school basketball team from a rural area became the top contender for that State's championship game. It was an inspirational film because our game was the first time a Tucker County football team had ever played in a State Championship game in any sport and it almost didn't seem real at the time.

I remember that night well. The game was in Charleston, on Laidley Field, a football field located by the State Capitol. As I was standing on the field just before the first kick-off, I looked through the eastern side of the football stadium's open-ended end-zone. What I remember most about that moment was seeing the awesome presence of the State Capitol as it filled the skyline. It is a beautiful building designed by the famous architect Cass Gilbert, the skyscraper pioneer who also designed the United States Supreme Court. I just stared at that brightly illuminated building. Its dome, modeled after the 1671 Hotel des Invalides in Paris, was inspiring. I actually remember smiling as I thought that it had to be one of the best places in the State to work.

I do work in that building today and still find it inspiring and feel very fortunate to work within its marbled walls. I previously worked in the West Wing of the Capitol in the Governor's Office, the East Wing of the Capitol in the Attorney General's Office, and today in the East Wing in the State Supreme Court. As I walk to my office in the mornings and look at the majestic building, I often get disgusted when I think of the countless money-grubbing, self-interested, and all-out corrupt individuals who have openly and without shame ignored the futures of West Virginians of all ages as they traveled down a path of self enrichment. I think of the taint attached to the beautifully golden gilded dome. I try to picture a day in the future when all West Virginians are able to walk into this magnificent building without those same feelings of disgust due to the many corrupt politicians and the special interest groups who launder their dirty money buying favors. So many initially well-meaning politicians have eventually fallen to the allure of money.

Children who grow up in West Virginia learn in school that one vote equals one voice. Later in life, however, they learn the harsh reality–the reality that money-corrupt politicians speak louder and have tainted the State's system of politics. Moreover, that same child who is told that he or she can be anything, that their future and their happiness is theirs to pursue, also learns that unless they come from a family of wealth, win the lottery or "sell out" to the highest bidder, their dream to make a change in government and their State is limited or may be quieted forever by the stronger voices of lobbying groups, corporations, and wealthy individuals and self-serving politicians. The next lesson learned is that the corrupt and unseemly actions of many political actors have left the impression that there are virtually no consequences and therefore no accountability for such lawless individuals. When children read or hear about elected officials who continually commit crimes and walk away with a slap on the wrist, when they hear a crowd cheer for a former Governor who has been convicted for numerous felonies, when they read that local officials whom they are told to respect have enriched themselves with hundreds of thousands or millions of State tax dollars earmarked to educate the children or provide for the care of the poor or elderly, or when they read that many of their trusted politicians have been convicted for DUI, bribery, fraud, extortion, and even obstruction of justice, how can we expect them to believe they will be held responsible for their own wrongdoings?

To educate our children, to empower them with the dream and desire that they can one day make a difference and then to force them to inherit such an outrageous history of corruption may be the greatest injustice. But therein lies the possible beginnings to a true reform at the most basic level–to educate, to hold those we elect to the highest of standards, to hold individuals accountable for their actions, to enforce the laws, and to implant and nurture the desire to influence and improve our government. Such actions affect the very nature of the State and its citizens' futures within it.

The late 1980s witnessed an era of accelerated electronic and technological advancement. Children in West Virginia were being left in the dust of other states' school systems. West Virginians have always had to deal with the stereotype of being less advanced or even "backwoods," fighting images of having no shoes, bad grammar, and less education. Students who did go to college soon realized how much it would have helped to have had more knowledge of computers, foreign language, advanced math, science and writing skills, and fewer State paid-for certificates, pens, combs and key chains emblazoned with a State politician's name. While school budgets did not allow some children to go on educational field trips, thousands of tax dollars were available for chartered flights, awards, certificates, key chains, magnets, billboards, hot tubs, satellite television, and trips to exotic locations for many State officials. Just as the coal companies kept the miners isolated out of greed during the early 1900s, the improper and illegal use of State money has kept generations of West Virginia children less educated, less advantaged, and less prepared for the world they were about to enter.

We raise our children in a nation which encourages the pursuit of happiness and teach them of an extremely poor and underprivileged young man named Abraham Lincoln who grew up to be President and affect the minds of people and therefore changed a nation. Unless we reform our system of elections and weed out the corrupt politicians, the cost to our states, our country, and even our world could be incomprehensible, for imagine if young Abraham would have been told that he was too poor to ever be President. Imagine the great minds, the innovative thinkers, and the historical leaders who have been ignored, or worse, jaded by the very process that could have changed their life or the lives of others. Then evaluate the cost of the lack of serious political reform.

# CHAPTER SIXTEEN

# Follow the Money

*And, like the proverbial ostrich who sticks his head in the sand to avoid seeing the obvious, the majority of this Court has refused to recognize the blatantly unlawful nature of the present Budget Digest preparation practice by actually allowing one of the biggest legal fictions in West Virginia history to continue unchecked ad infinitum.*

West Virginia Supreme Court Chief Justice Robin Davis

A. James Manchin, sometimes referred to as "the most potent political force in West Virginia in the 20th century," was so popular during the 1980s that Governor Jay Rockefeller offered him a $60,000-per-year job in 1984 just to work under him, thus, helping to improve Rockefeller's own reputation among West Virginians. Manchin's reputation was tarnished, however, when bad investments were made under his watch as State Treasurer resulting in the loss of nearly $300 million from the Consolidated Fund which he managed.[1081]

On March 29, 1989, the West Virginia House of Delegates adopted House Resolution nineteen which contained seventeen Articles of Impeachment against Manchin. It charged that Manchin knew of the multi-million dollar losses of State money for at least a year and hid them. Legislative auditors also concluded that the massive losses were not uncovered sooner "because records in the Treasurer's Office were falsified and some employees in the office failed to supply them accurate records."[1082] According to Jim Lees, special prosecutor against Manchin: "My conclusion is that Mr. Manchin would have had to be blind, deaf and dumb not to have been aware in April of 1987 of precisely what was transpiring with the Consolidated Fund."[1083]

Arnold Margolin, Assistant State Treasurer under Manchin, went to prison in 1990 for lying about and covering up the losses. Margolin initially pled not guilty to a twenty-six count indictment of charges of perjury and federal securities law violations, but later changed his plea to guilty to two felonies and was sentenced to one year in prison and a $10,000 fine. The State operating funds were being placed in high-risk securities and by early 1987, trades of $7 billion a month were being made by the Treasurer's Office, which amounted to more than triple the amount of money actually in the Fund. At Manchin's impeachment hearing, it was discovered the State's losses totaled $279 million.[1084]

Manchin, who said his staff hadn't told him of the State's losses, said, "Sometimes I don't always have the knowledge" and indicated he was unfamiliar with several of the investment terms.[1085] He even testified that he didn't know that the number inside the parentheses on his Treasurer's Office's accounting books indicated a loss. Manchin said he "left office with [his] head up" and "[he] was a victim of the system itself." He further proclaimed, "I've never hurt anyone, but I didn't realize I had so many solid enemies."[1086] On July 9, 1989, Manchin released his unapologetic statement before resigning. He said:

> Dear Governor Caperton,
>
> The time of my departure is at hand. I have fought a good fight, I have finished my course and I have kept the faith. Accordingly, I will enter into retirement on my last day of service as Treasurer of the State of West Virginia at 5 o'clock p.m. on July 9, 1989. I will seek the strength and guidance of Almighty God as I prepare to embark upon a new journey and to open new doors of public service which will enable me to continue loving and serving the people of this State until they lay me away on top of the hill at my beloved Farmington. May the bright morning star be a lamp unto our feet and being with sentiments and respect, I'm your public servant,
>
> A. James Manchin

Manchin's political career stretched fifty-five years, with highs that included four elections to statewide public office, and lows that included his forced resignation as State Treasurer. Manchin used money from the Consolidated Fund to travel under the guise of "Official Duties of the Treasurer of State" for engagements that had little or nothing to do with the Fund.[1087] Money from the Fund was permitted to be spent to cover all costs and expenses of the board including: "fees of professional consultants, advisers and auditors, brokerage commissions and all other necessary expenses of the board incurred in the performance of its functions shall be proper charges against, and payable on a pro rata basis from the earnings of the various funds managed by the board."[1088]

From July 1986 to June 1987, Manchin spent more than $27,000 on chartered airplanes and helicopters while he spent an additional $18,872 for air travel from July 1987 to June 1988 from the Consolidated Fund. During just the months of August and September 1988, he spent $5,123 for aircraft charter. Moreover, on many of the same days Manchin chartered planes for travel, he also turned in expense sheets and received payment for mileage where he claimed he had also driven to various destinations.[1089]

Money from the Fund described by the special prosecutor as "an abuse of office" was spent to the tune of $62,323.90 from August 4, 1987, until June 26, 1988, on 765,000 trinkets which proudly promoted his name. That really is incredible considering there were only about 688,000 households in West Virginia at the time. Those items for that ten month period alone included:

- 75,000 Constitution of U.S. certificates, $1,440
- 50,000 State flag certificates, $2,000
- 50,000 U.S. Constitution certificates, $960
- 2,000 proclamations, $96
- 50,000 souvenir cards of the Treasurer's seal, $4,400
- 25,000 Pledge of Allegiance sheets, $3,750
- 1,000 associate Treasurer certificates, $95
- 30,000 American's creed sheets, $2,568
- 500 Boys State and 500 Girls State certificates, $77.65 each
- 65,000 'Public Friend' certificates, $9,945
- 150,000 State flag certificates, $6,000
- 125,000 Pledge of Allegiance sheets, $18,750
- 141,000 American's Creed, $12,069[1090]

In 1985, Manchin was criticized for the same practices as he handed out hundreds of thousands of certificates to school children, volunteer firemen, hospital volunteers, and senior citizens. He said, "There will always be a cynic who thinks it's a waste of taxpayers' money. There is so much money wasted, but this is not a waste [and that his office would] make more money in twenty minutes in interest on our investments than what it costs for a whole year to hand out our certificates."[1091] Manchin also said, "I have made more innovations in State government than any treasurer in 100 years. I bring happiness into the lives of the people."[1092] During his tenure as State Treasurer from January 1985 until his resignation on July 9, 1989, Manchin's expenses for charter flights, certificates, photographs and awards totaled $209,682. His resignation was one day before his impeachment trial was to begin in the State Senate.[1093]

Even though a State investigation found Treasurer Manchin was siphoning from the Fund for his own political operations, and his office had lost $279 million of the State's money, the voters from his home district in Marion County elected him in 1998 to the House of Delegates where he served until his 2004 death. Due to his mismanagement of the State's Investment Management Board, the State Treasurer's Office was stripped of its independent power to manage those funds. It was not until 2002 that the State Legislature even discussed returning to the State Treasurer's Office the power over the $1.9 billion managed by the Investment Management Board.[1094]

Manchin was also criticized for settling a $1 million federal lawsuit involving fifteen former State Treasurer employees who claimed he fired them for political reasons after he became Treasurer in 1985. Initially, he provided notice that he would be firing thirty-five employees in the Treasurer's Office on the Friday before the Monday he was sworn into office. Manchin sought to have half of the settlement paid from the Treasurer's budget while the other half was to be paid by the State insurance company; however, the insurance policy did not cover back wages for employees. Eventually, he settled the lawsuit for $120,000 without the requisite approval of the Attorney General. The employees claimed they were fired for supporting Manchin's election opponent. Incidentally, Manchin's friend Governor Arch A. Moore, Jr.'s administration was also forced to pay $150,000 to eight county highway supervisors who had been fired simply because they were Democrats.[1095]

Years earlier, while Manchin was serving as Secretary of State, "he perfected the art of using public office as a continuous campaign platform [as] it was the rare West Virginian from the mid-1970s to the late 1980s who didn't receive some medallion, citation or certificate of recognition from [him]."[1096] He was criticized for spending $66,800 during an eleven month period in 1981 and 1982 that could not be identified as legitimate office expenses according to the Legislature's Commission on Special Investigations. The $66,800 amounted to 42 percent of the total amount Manchin was allotted by the West Virginia Legislature to run his entire office for the year.[1097] The money was spent on various items such as $12,821 for State flags, while another $20,204 was spent for about 720,000 pieces of printed matter including "honorary certificates, patriotic and historical brochures, souvenir and informational literature pertaining to the State and its heritage, and the State seal." In addition, more than $10,000 was spent on photographic prints, while nearly $6,000 was spent for such items as "specially engraved plaques and trophies, State pins, pendants, medallions and other honorary symbols and the purchase of more than 7,500 yards of assorted ribbon material, apparently used for ceremonial occasions and honorary awards."[1098] Manchin called the expenditures "a proper function of the Office of Secretary of State."[1099]

Manchin was known for his florid oratory. In the mid 1970s, when Governor Arch Moore found out that his old college friend needed a job, he put Manchin in charge of the REAP (Rehabilitation Environmental Action Plan) program to help cleanup the State hillsides of junk cars, discarded appliances rolled over hillsides, illegal dumps, trashy creeks, and dilapidated buildings. Governor Moore said, "I don't know anybody who ever fell in love with a junked car, but he did [and] we cleaned up the State." Manchin was famous for saying, "Let us purge our proud peaks of the jumbled jungles of junkery." In just his first year he helped rid the State of more than 31,000 old cars, 77,900 rusted and rolled appliances, 17 shacks, and 31 unlawful roadside dumps.

He referred to himself as the Grim REAPer and bestowed awards like his Oscars for Junk Collectors or Grand REAPer Awards on those who made an effort to haul the most junked cars and refrigerators out of their communities. Once, Manchin even dressed his twelve-member REAP crew in Revolutionary War uniforms and fired a cannonball into a junk car full of trash to kick off a litter cleanup. When his program reached the 100,000th junk car collected, he had the 1966 Pontiac convertible painted blue and gold and hauled through the streets of Charleston in a parade that included bands, veterans, and school children.

On another occasion, Governor Moore said he received a call from Manchin who was engaged in a face-off with an elderly woman on her porch. Moore said Manchin "had chains attached to the pillars of the porch, ready to tear the house down, but he said the woman had a shotgun. I asked him if he was sure he had the right house and he said he'd check." Manchin called Governor Moore again and informed him "he had made a mistake and his target was actually a vacant eyesore four doors up the street." During his first State of the State speech in 2005, Governor Joe Manchin, nephew to A. James, announced that he would resurrect the REAP program in honor of his uncle.[1100]

Moore recalled another instance when Manchin spoke at an otherwise uneventful groundbreaking. Moore said, "He pulled a pistol out of his pocket, fired into the air, and proclaimed, 'Let the bulldozers roll!'" Former Secretary of State and United States Congressman Ken Hechler recalled a time when Manchin was accompanied by twelve trumpeters for a sewage treatment plant dedication ceremony. Hechler said, "He made that sewage plant seem like the biggest thing in the world."

After his death, and in spite of his failings with regard to the misman-agement of State funds and his gross expenditures of State money on millions of trinkets, newspapers and public officials touted Manchin's praise. The *Charleston Daily Mail* called him "one of the State's most clever and interesting politicians." It said, "Above all, Manchin changed attitudes about the State. He injected in West Virginians more than a little pride and enthusiasm. His 'Captain of the Ship of State' certificates reminded people of what a pleasure and honor it is to live in Wild, Wonderful West Virginia."[1101]  *Daily Mail* Managing Editor Bob Kelly said every West Virginian knew Manchin because he either "handed them a pin or certificate, declared them a member of the Order of the 35th Star, shaken their hands, kissed them or taken off his hat and bowed majestically upon greeting them."[1102]  West Virginia Speaker of the House Bob Kiss said, "There were probably three things that were important to [Manchin]–God, his family, and the people of the State of West Virginia."[1103]  Even United States Senator Edward M. Kennedy said, "Jim Manchin helped Jack become President. He was one of the original foot soldiers in the West Virginia Primary, and his strong and loyal support for President Kennedy was the same kind of devotion he gave to his beloved West Virginia."[1104]

I knew A. James for many years. On one occasion when I was in high school I was talking with him at a public event and made a few comments about his hat. I told him it looked like a gangster hat atop his pin-striped suit. About a week later he sent me a hat with the Treasurer's seal on it. He also mailed or pre-sented to me–and many others in West Virginia–countless other certificates for everything from playing football, participating in a science or social studies fair, to simply graduating from high school. When A. James returned to the Legislature in 1999, I talked with him on many occasions at the State Capitol. He was easy to find–particularly if there was free food involved. I have yet to meet a man who could eat more food and I don't say that in a disrespectful way. It was just another facet of his colorful character. On one occasion I saw him with five entree plates in front of him at the same time in Fazio's, a Charleston Italian restaurant. He was a man who never knew a stranger. Even if he had never met you or simply had no idea who you were, by the end of a conversation with him he would convince you that he had been a lifelong friend of yours and your fam-ily. He told me on one occasion that when he was a statewide elected politician, he often went to funerals of people he didn't know and greeted the grieving spouse. From my recollection he explained it to me like this:

> If I were in a county for a meeting I would always pick up the
> local newspaper and read the obituary and funeral notices. I

would read the name of the individual who died and see who his or her surviving spouse was. I then went to the viewing area at the funeral home and it was always obvious who the surviving spouse was standing by the casket. I would approach them and greet them by name. I would tell them that their loved one, regurgitating his or her name as well as some fact from the newspaper's obituary, was a great friend of mine and a great West Virginian. It would bring them joy.

He campaigned every waking moment of his life and people remembered him for that. In spite of his impeachment he remained popular. The problem, however–and I can hear the jeers already because so many people liked A. James on a personal level–is that his unprecedented spending of State money on these trinkets was simply wrong. It really is irrelevant if it made people feel good, it is still wrong, and it continues today without shame by most statewide politicians. If he had raised the money as campaign contributions instead of using hundreds of thousands of State dollars to distribute millions of these poorly disguised campaign trinkets, then that is one thing. Nonetheless, I am amazed at how people often try to justify some of his actions because they received something from A. James at some point during their lives, and in spite of the evidence to the contrary, they still feel as if he knew them and personally recognized them with the trinket or certificate. Others, however, like me, are outraged, but really have no power to stop it. I wonder though how anyone can justify spending 42 percent of the entire budget for the Secretary of State's Office on such junk.[1105] For a man who got his start on a statewide stage by cleaning up junk in West Virginia, he certainly bought his share of it throughout the years.

Moreover, his spending wasn't limited to a single statewide elected office as he continued his pattern of excessive spending of taxpayer money as well as the amount of time wasted by him and his employees to order, prepare, address, and distribute these office souvenirs, when he served as both Secretary of State and State Treasurer.[1106] Perhaps if more time had been spent on the actual duties for which he was elected, $279 million would not have been lost in State investment funds.[1107] The sense of outrage is clearly missing when a public official commits bad acts–particularly if the politician is a widely-known individual who campaigned well. In fact, most of the time politicians are even rewarded for their bad behavior by getting re-elected or serving minimal sentences when they are convicted of a crime. This is because this corruptive practice has become so ingrained in West Virginia politics and no one has had the courage to address the problem.

Another example of excessive spending of taxpayer money for re-election is Governor Cecil H. Underwood. Governor Underwood's 1996 election victory made him the oldest Governor while his gubernatorial 1956 victory solidified his place as the State's youngest. During his farewell address in 1961 for his first term as Governor, Underwood stressed the importance of government honesty. He proclaimed:

> In reviewing the last four years, four concerns appear with overriding importance. The first is honesty in Government.
>
> In recent months, the pressing nature of other problems has abated the intensity with which this issue was paramount in 1956. I believe that my administration established and has maintained fair practices, honest dealings and personal integrity in Government as a matter of course. The very lack of this issue in 1960, in spite of petty recriminations, is evidence of our success.
>
> These qualities of public honesty and personal integrity are little recognized when we have them, slowly realized when they are going, and missed only when they are gone. I hope that the standards which have been set will be maintained.[1108]

Winding the clock forward to the year 2000, as the State's oldest elected Governor, Underwood left office under a cloud of controversy. For instance, just prior to his departure from office, the road that dead-ends at his Tyler County farm was covered with 100 tons of gravel.[1109] A spokesman for the Division of Highways said thirty tons would have been adequate for the 1.6 mile road named Governor's Road.[1110] Nonetheless, similar to the response following the many questionable actions of other West Virginia political figures, nothing became of the situation other than a few small newspaper articles.

On a personal level I have always gotten along well with Governor Underwood. In fact, he awarded my father a Distinguished West Virginian Award for his service in cleaning up the Tucker County Assessor's Office during his years of service. My grandfather, however, has never been a big fan of the Governor because he was one of a long list of Democrats who lost their jobs with the State Road (Department of Highways) soon after Underwood's election in 1956. This was a common practice during those days by both parties as the State Road was a highly political entity. Nonetheless, Underwood has never been anything but kind to me. In fact, when I was working as a Senior Assistant Attorney General, some of his staff members would communicate to me messages they wanted relayed to Attorney General McGraw. There was clearly a lack of trust and cordiality between the two offices and I guess Underwood's staff spoke with me because they knew I would be honest with them even if they didn't like what I had to say and would provide accurate information without a political agenda.

When I think of Governor Underwood's years in office though, a couple of instances come to mind that reinforce my disillusionment with West Virginia politics. I immediately remember January 12, 2001, his last day as Governor, when he signed an order commuting the sentence of former Grant County Deputy Sheriff Paul Ferrell, a convicted kidnapper, murderer, and arsonist, making him eligible for immediate parole.[1111] Deputy Ferrell, who was convicted in 1989 by the Circuit Court of Grant County for the above mentioned crimes, appealed his case and lost in the West Virginia Supreme Court as well as the United States Supreme Court. Ferrell's counsel then filed briefs in the Circuit Court of Grant County, the West Virginia Supreme Court, the Federal District Court in Elkins, West Virginia, and the Fourth Circuit Court of Appeals in Richmond, Virginia, requesting relief in the form of a writ of habeas corpus. Ferrell was denied relief by all of those courts and the final order from the Fourth Circuit was entered September 12, 2000.[1112]

Nonetheless, in spite of the complete denials of his claims by courts at every level of the judicial process, Governor Underwood issued an order commuting the sentence of Ferrell stating simply, "There was no evidence to convict him."[1113] The appearance of corruption and abuse of power was due to the fact that Underwood did not follow the regular process of hearing both sides of the case before commuting or pardoning a murderer. In fact, he didn't contact the county prosecutor, the State Attorney General's Office, the parole board, any of the victim's family members, or any of the law enforcement officials involved with the case.[1114] Top Governor's Office employees, who would only speak on a condition of anonymity for fear of reprisal, conceded to me that commuting Ferrell's sentence was nothing more than "a political payoff that had absolutely nothing to do with the merits of the case."[1115] Specifically, I was told that one high ranking State official pleaded for Ferrell's release, "because his daddy was a fine fellow originally from Logan County who saved someone's life years ago." I still can't figure out what the good deed of a father has to do with releasing a murderer from jail.

I am uniquely familiar with this case because I was the Senior Assistant Attorney General, along with Managing Deputy Attorney General Barbara Allen, who filed the briefs on behalf of the State of West Virginia in the Federal District Court as well as the Fourth Circuit Court of Appeals. I always took my job in the

Attorney General's Office seriously–particularly when dealing with the criminal appeals of dangerous individuals. Barbara and I worked countless hours reviewing literally boxes and boxes of evidence and to say there was no evidence is infuriating to me. In fact, 75 witnesses testified on behalf of the State while 141 items of documentary evidence, all of which pointed to Ferrell's guilt, were introduced during his trial. The individual strands of evidence introduced against Ferrell wove a fine mesh net of evidence that proved beyond a reasonable doubt to twelve jurors that he was guilty of murder. For any Governor–regardless of political affiliation–to completely disregard a jury verdict as well as every federal and State court who upheld this verdict, in my opinion amounts to an enormous abuse of office. To return a murderer to the streets is reckless and endangers every person in the State–not to mention me and my family because I filed legal briefs to keep him in jail. Politics should never be used to circumvent the criminal system of justice. Just as I told the *Charleston Gazette* after Underwood's decision, it is troubling to me that the Governor thought he was in a better position to make factual determinations than twelve jurors, the circuit court, the State Supreme Court, the Federal District Court, the Fourth Circuit Court of Appeals, and the United States Supreme Court. His decision amounted to a circumvention of the process and set poor precedent for future Governors.[1116]

Ironically, when pressed about being soft on crime during the 1996 election, Underwood's campaign officials stated that he always followed proper procedures before making a decision. Underwood stated in 1997 that in order to get a pardon a criminal must contribute "extraordinary service" to the prison that housed him, demonstrate motivation toward rehabilitation, or face a life-threatening illness.[1117] Unfortunately, Governor Underwood failed to follow his own prescribed procedures when he commuted Paul Ferrell's sentence. Ferrell was subsequently granted parole by Governor Bob Wise and released from prison. The last minute decision to change this convicted killer's sentence was referred to as "a terrible miscarriage of justice" by Grant County Prosecuting Attorney Dennis DiBenedetto, who tried the case against Ferrell.[1118] Had Underwood followed the process of hearing both sides he would have at least created the appearance of a proper exercise of the Governor's power. Similarly, newspaper reports surfaced during the 1996 election disclosing that Underwood had used his pardon power often during his first term in office from 1957 through 1961 when he pardoned ninety individuals, while forty of those individuals were convicted murderers. He didn't deny the reports, nor did he attempt to explain them.[1119] I asked Governor Underwood about this and he simply said he did nothing improper and would not further elaborate.

Another last minute questionable act by Governor Underwood was in leaving a balance of $20,000 in the Governor's Contingency Fund that had a balance of $22.36 million just six months earlier. He was accused of using the fund to illegitimately hand out millions of dollars in Contingency Fund grants to cities, counties, and civic groups throughout the State during the months leading up to the November 7, 2000, election where he faced challenger and then-United States Congressman Bob Wise. A senior deputy in the Auditor's Office said, "I've never seen a fund get so mangled in my life as the Governor's Contingency Fund."[1120]

The *Charleston Gazette* declared Underwood's use of the Contingency Fund as "shameless campaigning with taxpayer money–giving government funds to get votes. There's no other way to describe it." The editorial suggested the Governor could have used thirty-three cent stamps to deliver the more than $20 million to recipients instead of "day after day . . . visits [to] courthouses, senior centers and other local facilities to hand State checks to smiling recipients, while news cameras record the happy event." State Auditor Glen Gainer, III, said it was "insanity" for Underwood to distribute millions of dollars from the Contingency Fund while State tax collections were running below estimates. Wise, who defeated Underwood in the 2004 election, exclaimed that his office would not operate the Contingency Fund like a "candy store" or use it to make "one of the largest publicly funded campaigns." Mike Plante of the Wise campaign quipped: "Governor Underwood may be the first Republican to support public financing of campaigns."[1121]

Underwood said, "Faced with Democratic majorities in the Legislature, he was forced to split the funds in thirds among his office, the House of Delegates, and the Senate." He continued: "Except for emergency relief funds, the Legislature influenced and directed the spending of most of the taxpayer dollars earmarked for the Governor's Contingency Fund. As legislative leaders made numerous demands for these funds, they assured us that any shortfall would be corrected during the next legislative session." In response to newly elected Wise's criticism of his Administration, he added, "I think it's destructive and confusing to the public. It displays a negative image and reflects on the morale of State employees."[1122]

Before leaving office, Underwood also depleted a $1.76 million budget item intended to cover personnel salaries for the Governor's Office through June 30, 2001, leaving a gaping hole forcing newly elected Governor Wise to calculate how to pay his employees for the first six months in office. As a result, Wise had to have a special supplement from the Legislature just to pay his staff. Moreover, even though Underwood's payroll had averaged $70,000 per pay period during the months of July to October 2000, the amount for November following his failed re-election bid, increased to $192,000 per pay period and ballooned to $286,000 per pay period in December while the final payroll for half of a month in January 2001 dropped to $167,000.[1123]

One of the reasons leading to this problem was that just prior to leaving office, top officials in Governor Underwood's office cashed in more than 5,400 hours of compensatory time totaling more than $208,626. It was later discovered that his employees were overpaid a total of $186,749, of which $169,553 was overpaid as compensation time while $12,782 was overpaid for unused annual leave, or vacation time. Governor Wise said it is common sense that as "a senior executive working for the people of West Virginia, you don't ask for comp time."[1124]    The payments staff members received ranged from $39 to $25,866. After much negative press coverage of the payment of compensatory time to senior administrative staff members, many of those payments were returned to the State. However, of the twenty-four members of Underwood's staff who received the payments, several of those individuals never returned the money.[1125]    State Auditor Glen Gainer called the payment "unprecedented" saying it warranted an investigation.[1126]    Underwood called the charges against his administration a "continuous barrage of blame" and argued that Wise's financial problems derived from his increase in staff payroll."[1127]

Underwood was also criticized for his decision not to pursue lawsuits against major coal companies–who donated heavily to his campaign–for unpaid premiums owed by contractors in the amount of more than $200 million even though the State had spent more than $3 million on legal fees to prepare the cases for trial.    William Vieweg, Commissioner of the Bureau of Employment Programs for the Underwood administration, "made secret deals with at least eight coal companies" just prior to leaving office according to Commissioner Robert Smith, Vieweg's predecessor.  Smith told members of the Performance Council the deals "could cost the agency millions of dollars and be spread out among all the other employers in the State."  Smith said, "Vieweg violated agency rules by not asking the Performance Council for its approval before making the agreements, which allow companies to change from being self-insured to regular subscribers."[1128]    Smith called Vieweg's sworn statements "deceptive, misleading, and false" tactics to attempt to get rid of lawsuits for $400 million worth of workers' compensation premiums.[1129]    It was later determined the amount was actually closer to $450 million.

Smith said Vieweg, who previously worked as an executive for Island Creek Coal Company between 1976 and 1986, allowed the coal companies, including Island Creek Coal, to pay between $35 million and $40 million to buy out their future liabilities as self-insured companies.  Similar to Governor Underwood's ballooning payroll after his November 7, 2000, election defeat, Vieweg apparently approved most of the deals with the coal companies after the results of the election were finalized.  He filed a motion to have his testimony in his depositions remain confidential. The *Charleston Gazette* said, "Vieweg–a former coal executive–seemed to spend most of his time helping coal mine owners escape part of their State obligations."[1130]   In addition to that settlement, Governor Underwood wrote off as uncollectible, $41 million in unpaid fines for coal mine environmental violations.  The money would have gone into a fund that is currently millions of dollars in the hole, which is supposed to be used to cleanup abandoned strip mine sites including hundreds of polluted and untreated streams.  According to the Department of Environmental Protection, the write-offs involved more than 300 mining operators.[1131]

Underwood also left office in a manner similar to his Republican predecessor, Governor Arch Moore, with regard to the State's bills.  Newly elected Governor Wise found the State owed millions of dollars in unpaid telephone bills though the exact amount owed to Verizon, AT&T, and Citizens Communications was not readily agreed upon but believed to be $10.28 million.  Verizon officials alone claimed the State owed them as much as $5.3 million.  It was not until November 2003, that the State settled the dispute agreeing to pay $6.36 million in unpaid bills for 1997-2000, $1.66 million for 2001, and $625,000 for 2002.[1132]

Governor Underwood is yet another example of a State politician using millions of dollars in State money to campaign for re-election.  On December 8, 2004, his successor Governor Wise sent $850,000 by mail to a Hardy County cabinet manufacturer from his Sunny Day Fund, a fund he created in 2002 to help create and retain jobs.[1133]  The answer as to why Wise didn't deliver the check in person and hold a large event touting his contribution and commitment to the creation of jobs like Underwood and almost every other politician, regardless of their political party affiliation, is simple–Wise decided not to run for re-election due to his marital affair.  Had he been running for re-election, I can guarantee that a check of such a large amount would have been hand delivered with great fanfare that included a stage, speeches, and a lot of television cameras.  Underwood clearly is not alone in taxpayer spending as demonstrated by Secretary of State and State Treasurer A. James Manchin who mastered the process of spending State money for self-promotion, followed closely by current Attorney General Darrell McGraw, whose magnets–prominently displaying his name–are on just about every refrigerator in the State while his key chains are in thousands and thousands of the pockets of State citizens.

It is so commonplace that some of the State's office holders don't even realize their offices so freely buy and hand out these trinkets.  For instance, when I was discussing this matter with then-Governor Wise, I asked him whether his office handed out such political trinkets and whether or not the practice should be specifically regulated or prohibited by the Legislature.  "I think that they should be fully disclosed and the voters will decide," he said. Wise added, "That may have been a factor in the Attorney General's election results. I think that was clearly a factor." Wise was referring to the fact that Attorney General Darrell McGraw only won the 2004 election by approximately 5,000 votes. Wise then said, "People judge us. We don't hand them out, we don't have refrigerator magnets, and things like that, we do have pens, we may have some cufflinks out there, but I think once again, the voter is pretty smart concerning what it is that is relevant and what isn't." With regard to whether or not there should be more restrictions on the use of State paid-for trinkets, thousands of keychains, magnets, and the countless other items, Wise said, "My guess is that the more that information gets out there, the more the voters are aware, and they'll speak about whether they approve or not."

I was so surprised by Wise's declaration that his office didn't have magnets with his name on them given the fact that it is so brazenly done by so many other West Virginia politicians that I went to his press office after the interview and asked, "Do you have any of the Governor's magnets that are handed out?" Without pause I was handed a stack full of Capitol dome shaped magnets that say, "Call Gov. Bob Wise." When I said, "What else do you have?" I was given a bag full of pens, pencils, rulers, bookmarks, and other items.

The well-entrenched practice of spending State tax money to fund future re-election campaigns or campaigns for a higher elected office is not limited to the statewide elected officials. In fact, the West Virginia Legislature has developed a nearly $35 million "slush fund for local projects that help incumbents get re-elected" year after year.[1134] The Budget Digest, often referred to as a "corrosive charity," is money set aside by the Legislature to fund special projects chosen by legislators. It allocates millions of dollars for home-district fairs, festivals, athletic fields, economic development projects, and other such programs. The allocations occur *after* the Legislature is out of session and without open debate.

The Budget Digest guarantees poor policy as millions of dollars go to projects that the entire Legislature would never pass if they had to do it under the light of day. It is also quite clear that Delegates and Senators get a lot of photo opportunities in their local newspapers for bringing back hundreds of thousands of dollars, one project at a time from the Budget Digest. It is a re-election tool that most challengers simply cannot compete against. It is also a tool of coercion used by House leaders to keep Delegates in line by controlling how they vote due to the fact that funding decisions are not made until all of the votes are recorded during the regular legislative session. Thus, various Delegates either vote a certain way on the leadership's bills or they are left out of the divvying up of millions of Budget Digest dollars.[1135] It is also a slick way to bypass a Governor's veto. For instance, in April 2005, Governor Manchin vetoed $8.7 million from line items in the State's budget bill. When the Budget Digest was approved by the ten-member legislative conference committee on July 25, 2005, it re-inserted the $8.7 million into their directive to State agencies.[1136]

The *Charleston Daily Mail* argues: "Legislators should stop playing Santa Claus with taxpayers' money. Local causes should be supported locally" and "Legislators should be ashamed and voters should demand better."[1137] A *Charleston Sunday Gazette-Mail* editorial declared, "It's too bad the public doesn't see through this charade," and specifically cited four State legislators who spent an entire day in 2004 driving through their election district in Pocahontas County delivering State checks to local officials totaling $180,000. Instead of mailing the checks at the cost of a thirty-nine cent stamp, the legislators bolstered their chances of re-election by delivering the checks in person and posing for newspaper photographs. It identified a Pocahontas County resident who sarcastically remarked that the State Budget Digest should be renamed, "The Taxpayers Campaign Fund to Re-elect Legislators." The editorial further proclaimed:

> Of course, many elected officials have used this same campaign gimmick for generations. Various governors landed dramatically in the state helicopter at local festivals to hand out taxpayer money, as crowds cheered and news cameras clicked. And we assume that the Pocahontas exercise was replayed in West Virginia's 54 other counties.[1138]

The 2003-2004 Budget Digest was roughly $28 million, while the 2002-2003 amount topped $35 million. The total amount given away statewide during the 2001-2002 fiscal year was $37.33 million, up from $37.15 million in 2000-2001, and down from the $38.6 million allocated in 1999-2000.[1139] Among the highlights from the 2003-2004 Budget Digest were $2 million for more than 350 fairs and festivals across the State including $105,000 for the YMCA's summer camp and $80,000 for Wheeling's annual Festival of Lights.[1140]

The $105,000 allocation was sent to the Ohio-West Virginia YMCA camp near St. George which is located in my home county. The allocation is sent in approximately the same amount each year from the Senate's portion of the Budget Digest and is secured by Senator Sarah Minear (R-Tucker), who currently serves as the President of the YMCA's Board. Without the money the program would be forced to make drastic cuts. In high school I was a participant with the YMCA's Youth in Government Leadership Program. I was also a frequent volunteer to the program during the weekends that it spends each year at the State Capitol with students from throughout the State as they exercise a mock Legislature and Supreme Court. I even volunteered with the program during my years in law school in Ohio and set up several events for the group when I was working for Governor Caperton.

The YMCA is a great organization and I wish it many years of continued success. My volunteering days ended, however, following a couple of newspaper articles which appeared in the *Charleston Gazette* quoting former United States Congressman Harley O. Staggers, Jr. as saying I was rumored to be a potential challenger to Senator Minear during a future election.[1141] While I didn't run for election against Senator Minear, I have never been asked to volunteer again since those articles appeared even though my office is just about twenty feet from the Supreme Court courtroom where a large part of the program takes place. Prior to the articles, I had very close relationships with the people with the YMCA and frequently met them for lunch when they were visiting the Capitol. This situation, to me, illustrates a good example of how the Budget Digest wields so much power for those in control of the purse, while at the same time creating a paranoia for those who desperately need the money and don't want to do the slightest thing–however trivial–to upset their benefactor to the State treasury.

Due to financial constraints of the projected multi-million dollar deficit for the State's 2005-2006 Budget, the 2004-2005 Budget Digest amount of $27 million was lower than previous years, including the 1997-1998 $39 million Budget Digest. The allocations from the 2004-2005 Budget Digest ranged from $500 appropriations for an American Legion Post in Braxton County and for the Lewis County Story Telling Festival, to appropriations for nearly two dozen Fourth of July celebrations around the State including $10,000 for Hardy County, which is within the House District of Finance Chairman Harold Michaels.[1142] The *Gazette* wrote:

> The distribution of $38 million or more in public funds by a handful of legislators is hardly a simple political matter. The Budget Digest subverts the democratic process in countless ways. It usurps executive spending authority established by the state constitution. It concentrates power in too few hands. It shuts the public out of the decision-making process.[1143]

*Charleston Gazette* Reporter Phil Kabler illustrates one example of the process and reasons behind the Budget Digest as follows:

> The Budget Digest mentality? That's finding the easiest, most expeditious means to reach the desired end, even if it bends the letter or the spirit of the law.

Example: Let's say a legislator wants $10,000 to fund repairs to a municipal swimming pool in his district.

The standard, 'how-a-bill-becomes-law' route would be to submit an appropriations bill for the $10,000. Of course, that avenue is full of pitfalls: Other legislators might question whether the project is the highest and best use of taxpayer dollars, and could kill the bill. Or the finance chairman might decide a municipal pool in his district needs some fixing up, too, and amend the bill to divert half of that $10,000 allocation to his district.

The Budget Digest process is a subterfuge that lets the legislator avoid those problems entirely. He simply submits the $10,000 among his digest requests, bends the ear of a friendly budget conferee, and voila, the Budget Digest.[1144]

One such example of funding outside of the legislative process was the creation of a new community college in House Finance Chairman Harold Michael's home district even though the Legislature did not decide that West Virginia needed another community college. The *Charleston Gazette* argues that it "isn't right" and "certainly can't be legal" when "one legislator [can] appropriate $2 million to his pet college without a single vote being taken?"[1145] In addition to the amount of money Michael has received for his District through the Budget Digest, "Michael [also] funneled more millions to his turf through the Governor's Contingency Fund . . . and a mysterious $8 million account at the State Department of Education." The *Gazette* said even though the "Governor's Contingency Fund supposedly is designed for rush assistance during floods, forest fires and the like–it's used as a goodie bag for lucky districts." It cited several examples of funds obtained by Delegate Michael including:

The Moorefield High School golf team got a $30,000 van. The school's football team got $19,500 worth of digital video gear, plus a $3,000 "turf aerator." More than $108,000 went to a Moorefield cemetery. The Hardy County Rod and Gun Club (where Michael and his wife belong) got $25,000. Another $16,000 went to a bowling alley. Etc., etc. . . .

The *Gazette* explained that "thanks to the House finance chief, people in his district reaped a bonanza from the Governor's fund. Hardy got $528 per-capita–compared to a State average of just $40. Doddridge county got only $11 per-capita."[1146] The *Charleston Daily Mail* said, "Michael has shaken $6.7 million from the Governor's Contingency Fund to act like a sugar daddy for his district." The *Daily Mail* also reported, "On top of that, $8 million was set aside in the State education budget that can be released only with Michael's signature. Surely this has to be unconstitutional, for Michael was elected as a Delegate, not as a King."[1147] With regard to the $8 million placed in two special State Department of Education accounts, named "Collaborative Resource Allocation" and "Educational Achievement Incentives," State School Superintendent David Stewart said he didn't have a clue what the money was for and "we didn't ask for it." Stewart explained the caveat to the additional $8 million in the Education Department accounts was "that it can be released only on orders from Harold K. Michael, chairman of the House of Delegates Finance Committee." More than 80 percent of the money from the two accounts went to items such as $30,000 for a meat smoker at a high school in Michael's District.[1148]

The confusion with all of these secret accounts and mismanaged accounts was highlighted in 2001, when Delegate Stan Shaver (D-Preston) sent a letter to Delegate Michael and asked for $5,000 from the "House of Delegates Contingency Fund" for a Preston County sportsman association to stock the Cheat River with fish. "One problem: The West Virginia House of Delegates doesn't have a contingency fund. Shaver actually meant the 'Governor's Contingency Fund.' But it's easy to understand Shaver's mistake. West Virginia lawmakers have increasingly become accustomed to tapping the Governor's dis-cretionary fund for pet projects for their home districts."[1149]

Another example of improper allocations funded by the Budget Digest was the $2,950 sent to the City of Davis in 1995, 1998, and 1999, for a Blackwater 100 festival. The problem is that the Blackwater 100 was a motor-cycle-ATV race that was last run in 1992.[1150] Nonetheless, the City of Davis knowingly cashed the "Blackwater 100" checks and used the money for other purposes. I know about this specific situation because it was brought to my attention when I was working in the Attorney General's Office during a time when I was conducting an investigation for the Attorney General. Through a Freedom of Information request I obtained copies of all of the contracts from the Department of Education and the Arts which were signed by the mayor and recorder of Davis and used to deceptively receive the money for the non-exis-tent event. The contracts were one page and were clear and concise documents that included "Blackwater 100" in bold on several occasions as the stated pur-pose for which the State was giving the money and for which the City of Davis was accepting it.

When I reported this illegal expenditure to the proper authority at the Department of Education and the Arts who oversaw the distribution of Budget Digest money to various festivals, she simply told me, "I just hope the press doesn't find out about this or we'll get questions." I said, "I don't care about the press, what about the improper use of State money during at least three different years?" She responded, "Well, I'll make sure they don't get any additional Budget Digest money for the race." I told her that was not good enough and discussed it with the Attorney General, but our office had no independent prosecutorial power to go after these lawbreakers. The way West Virginia law works, the Attorney General's Office could only act upon such an impropriety if another State Agency with jurisdiction over the infraction–in this case the Department of Education and the Arts or the State Legislature officially requested the Attorney General's Office to prosecute the matter. In spite of my efforts, I was unable to convince any State agency to investigate this matter because they were not interested in prosecuting anybody as they feared the negative press coverage that would follow would only highlight many of the blatant problems with the Budget Digest. So, once again, no one was held accountable. Another indiscretion was swept under the rug.

In 2001, former Delegate Arley Johnson from Cabell County joined several civic and citizens' action groups in a lawsuit challenging the constitutionality of the Budget Digest process. Johnson argued that House of Delegate leaders used the Budget Digest as a strong-arm tactic controlling rank-and-file Delegates with the threat of withholding digest funds.[1151] The case was heard by the State Supreme Court and a decision rendered said the process is constitutional so long as the procedures set forth by the Supreme Court are followed such as open discussion and debate of the Budget Digest.[1152] In her Dissenting Opinion, Justice Robin Davis said, "And, like the proverbial ostrich who sticks his head in the sand to avoid seeing the obvious, the majority of this Court has refused to recognize the blatantly unlawful nature of the present Budget Digest preparation practice by actually allowing one of the biggest legal fictions in West Virginia history to continue unchecked *ad infinitum*."[1153]

West Virginia Supreme Court Justice Larry V. Starcher referred to the Budget Digest as "a mechanism whereby millions of dollars for local projects and jobs are annually passed out like holiday gifts by the West Virginia legislative leadership."[1154] When the Court first considered a challenge to the Budget Digest in 1991, dissenting Justice Thomas Miller wrote:

> What a true laboratory of horrors the majority has concocted with
> this lineage of back-room documents that will transform what was
> originally pronounced as dead and having no force and effect of

law into something alive. The Igors of the world may rejoice at the majority's concoction. I do not, because it takes the legislative process out of the clear light of day where matters are voted on by the entire legislature and condemns it to that subterranean realm where memoranda of negotiations, compromises, and agreements exist and discussions in committee are used to validate the specific expenditure of funds through the Budget Digest.[1155]

The Supreme Court held that the Budget Digest must be the result of "discussion, debate, and decision" by the budget conferees. After the West Virginia Supreme Court's 2001 Decision, the House and Senate budget conferees met for "a total of 11 minutes" to fully debate and approve the 241-page 2001-2002 Budget Digest that totaled $37.33 million. In reference to the eleven-minute meeting, Senate Finance Chairman Oshel Craigo (D-Putnam) said, "We're here a little bit because of the Supreme Court."[1156]

In 2005, the House and Senate budget conferees spent less than three minutes to approve the $26.5 million Digest in spite of the fact there was a case pending for the third time in the State Supreme Court dealing with the validity of the Budget Digest process. The Supreme Court agreed to hear arguments during its Fall 2004 Term of Court. The argument in the case, filed by Charleston lawyer Dan Hedges, was that the process of setting the Budget Digest is illegal because it is done in secret by legislative leaders and is unconstitutionally approved outside of other budget appropriations. During the hearing in front of the Supreme Court, legislative attorneys admitted that the Legislature wasn't following the procedures for preparing the annual Budget Digest that were set down in the Court's 2001 Opinion. In fact, they argued they weren't obligated to follow those rules.[1157]

The case was sent to the Kanawha County Circuit Court to consider the legal challenges. The Legislature argued that legislative employees could not be forced to testify about proceedings of the Legislature. In 2005, the circuit court ruled that the State Constitution did not protect legislative staffers from testifying about how they helped put together the Budget Digest. Perhaps in reaction to Circuit Judge Jim Stucky's decision which would have allowed legislative staffers to be questioned under oath, the Legislature introduced and passed a bill during the 2006 Legislative Session proclaiming they eliminated the controversial Budget Digest in its entirety. Unfortunately though, the Legislature's actions amounted to nothing more than smoke and mirrors. What actually occurred is that they simply moved up the date for including these items in the budget, whereby creating the appearance that the entire Legislature fully debated and carefully considered these items.

In West Virginia, the Legislature meets once per year for a sixty day legislative session.  At midnight on the sixtieth day the gavels in the House and Senate bang their respective podiums and the session is declared concluded for that year.  Unbeknownst to most people in the State, however, the real politics begins during the very next week when the top ranking members of the Senate and House meet to put together the budget.  It is during this time period when the new and improved Budget Digest will be included in the budget.  Upon the completion of the budget by the select members of the Legislature, legislators return from their home districts to the State Capitol for the ceremonial vote on it.  The result being that even though the Budget Digest items are included in the budget, this occurs without a full and fair discussion from the entire Legislature.  In years past, unlike today, when the gavels struck at midnight on the sixtieth day, the entire session, including all budgetary items, were concluded.  The 2006 change in the Budget Digest was simply a way for legislators and staff members to avoid testifying in court about how the secretive process worked and did absolutely nothing to change the corruptive nature of handing out millions of dollars to constituents to secure re-election.

The problem of financing campaigns with taxpayer money is not just that the practice is preposterous and wrong, it also creates a situation where other governmental agencies and actors tend to follow the lead of the examples set for them by higher State governmental actors.  A perfect example of this is what I call the mini-Budget Digest at a county level.  In West Virginia, county sheriffs collect fees for issuing concealed-weapons permits, often referred to as the "pistol fund," and can use that money in any way they choose as long as they cover the office expenses of issuing the permits—which are minimal.  In one example, the Putnam County Sheriff's Office pistol fund generates about $30,000 per year.  Putnam County Sheriff Stan Farley has spent thousands from that fund on scholarships, donations, and floral arrangements.  The *Charleston Gazette* reports:

> The pistol permit fund is a nugget for county sheriffs.  By law,
> gun permit fees must be used to cover a sheriff's expenses in
> administering concealed-weapons permits.  But anything left
> over can be spent on other operating needs of the department as
> the sheriff sees fit, with very little outside oversight.[1158]

Farley provided $1,000 scholarships to students at four high schools, donations to 4-H groups, donations to a softball team, a donation to a deputy's sister who had cancer, money for a middle school science lab, and a donation to another person facing a liver transplant.  The *Gazette* asked, "Are sheriffs supposed to give public funds to sickness victims and sports groups? [to which] Farley said he didn't see anything wrong with helping out some needy people and some kids." The *Gazette* responded: "Doubtlessly, he also sees no wrong in the grateful feelings such donations buy for him among voters."[1159]

In November 2004, in neighboring Kanawha County, Sheriff Dave Tucker used his pistol fund for purchases including a $2,000 expenditure for new shoulder patches he designed for his deputies even though he only had one month left before the new sheriff was sworn into office. With regard to the patches, Tucker said, "I'm real tickled to death. I just wish I had more time to enjoy them." Sheriff-elect Mike Rutherford called spending money on the new patches and shields an "outlandish" waste of public funds, especially when Tucker was in the final weeks of his eight years in office. Kanawha County Commissioner Dave Hardy said, "It's totally in character with past performance and one last assault on the taxpayers, while fellow Commissioner Kent Carper called it "just an obscene waste of funds." Tucker had previously redesigned the department's badges after he took office in 1997 and had the new badges replace the old ones in 1998 and 1999 at a reported cost of about $10,000, while in 1971, he designed the logo for the Charleston Police Department, where he worked at the time.[1160]

Tucker also used thousands of dollars from the pistol fund to purchase costumes, shirts, jackets, and pictures of himself and his deputies. Many of the expenditures were made public due to a Freedom of Information request filed by Kanawha County Commissioner Kent Carper, which revealed that Tucker even bought two native American style teepees in May 2003 and had them shipped overnight.[1161] Tucker says his use of pistol fund money to buy teepees and costumes was worthwhile because it helped educate children. Commissioner Hardy said it was hard to understand how Tucker could spend money on such things when he claimed he couldn't afford mobile data terminals for cruisers and bulletproof vests and shotguns for deputies.[1162] Tucker also spent $2,249 on oxford shirts, polo shirts and sixty-eight tax deputy polo shirts bought from Dynamic Graphics on August 28, 2003. Other expenditures included $1,361 on January 6, 2004, to Martin Marietta Material for what was listed as "unidentifiable materials," while there were also thirty-nine checks of which information was missing with regard to the dates the checks were issued, the parties they were issued to, and the purposes for which the checks were actually written.[1163]

The solution to the pistol fund seems obvious. If they are taking in so much money that it is creating huge slush funds, then reduce the fees. It is not simply a matter of oversight or putting the funds in the control of the county commissioners. Why collect thousands of extra dollars simply to blow them on pet projects? It certainly doesn't seem to me like a proper duty for a county sheriff. The State of West Virginia has to get out of the business of creating re-election slush funds whereby politicians can give money to any private interest group or individual they want. A lot of people in this State have low incomes and they work hard every day in honest jobs just to make ends meet. Yet with the stroke of a pen a county sheriff can spend more money on pictures, costumes, teepees, donations, and flowers, in amounts higher than the average yearly income of most West Virginians. It really is a no-brainer. Cut the fund and start the end to the cycle of waste.

Another example of questionable activity with regard to State money, was a so-called "secret account" known as the 098 account, created wherein surplus funds from House of Delegates accounts were moved to an account in the Governor's Contingency Fund. While the Governor's Contingency Fund is a set of accounts to be used for emergencies or other projects the Governor deems worthwhile, the money in these newly created accounts was actually controlled by Speaker of the House Bob Kiss.[1164] When details of the fund began to surface, Speaker Kiss denied any connection saying, "It's the Governor's Civil Contingent Fund."[1165] In fact, when a lawsuit challenged the constitutionality of the account in 2000 in the State Supreme Court, Speaker Kiss said he "didn't even know what the 098 account was until this summer."[1166] Conversely, then-Governor Underwood said, "We don't move any funds from that account without a written request from the Speaker or from House leadership."[1167]

In the 1997-98 budget, the speaker transferred surplus money from two House accounts to the Contingency Fund for a total of $1.85 million,[1168] During the summer of 1998, Kiss asked the Governor for $1.25 million to be transferred, while a few months later he requested that an additional $600,000 be transferred for grants to projects in various Delegate districts.[1169] The 098 account was eliminated by the State Legislature just days after the challenge was filed in the Supreme Court. Former West Virginia Supreme Court Chief Justice Margaret Workman called the account another example of "legislative leadership doing an end-run around the lawful procedure" for appropriating State revenue. This was yet another account that Underwood "zeroed-out" just prior to leaving office. This time, however, he had the help of the Legislature.

In addition to spending State money so irresponsibly, Governors are able to spend private donations following their gubernatorial inaugurations. Even though corporations are not allowed to donate to candidates, they are free to donate to inauguration festivities and contributions traditionally reach high limits in West Virginia. For example, Governor Underwood raised $1.07 million for his inauguration and spent $801,624 for his January 1997 festivities. He used the remaining $225,000 from his inauguration to establish "Mission West Virginia," his church-based charity.[1170]  In 2001, Governor Wise had $440,000 remaining from his inaugural funds and donated that amount to finance 100 students to attend the Governor's Honors School for Math and Science.  He raised nearly $952,000, while $690,000 of that came from 138 corporate sponsors who bought $5,000 tables at the inaugural ball.[1171]

In 2005, according to Governor Manchin's spokesperson, Manchin raised nearly $900,000 and spent between $600,000 and $700,000 for his inauguration.  In actuality, it was later discovered there was nearly $500,000 remaining from his inaugural funds which he used for upgrades and renovations to the Governor's Mansion.[1172]  Speaking of the Mansion, Governor Manchin began the unprecedented policy in 2005 of renting out the Governor's Mansion for $350 per party to State Delegates, Senators, and the Governor's Staff.  Several State officials and staff took advantage of this new program and rented it for anniversaries, birthday parties, and wedding receptions.[1173]  As I look back to my days working with Governor Caperton in 1992, it is impossible for me to ever imagine him renting out the Governor's Mansion.  There is just something unsettling about it.

As there are few restrictions on how the surplus inaugural funds can be spent, it is clear that this is yet another way to circumvent campaign finance laws as candidates are able to take large sums of money from corporations and wealthy people and contribute to causes in their names or to individuals who will most certainly remember them during the next election cycle.  And, it is yet another example of how the wealthy are able to buy access that the average person cannot.  For example, Governor Manchin and his wife Gayle hosted a private party at the Clay Center in Charleston the night before his inauguration for those who contributed money to the inaugural events.  The black-tie reception was not open to the public or the media.[1174]  Once again money buys access that is unavailable to the average person.  While large contributors were able to have an intimate evening with the Governor, the average person who attended the Governor's Ball on the evening of the inauguration did so along with more than 8,000 individuals.  And, although more than a million dollars was raised from a list of donors that looked like a Who's Who Among West Virginia Businesses, and $500,000 remained as unspent inaugural money that would later be used on pet projects, each of the 8,000 attendees of the inaugural ball had to pay $50 for a ticket.

The State should set aside a specific amount of money for inaugural ceremonies every four years and prohibit these private donations which clearly buy favor with an incoming Governor.  This would limit the appearance of impropriety and special access to wealthy contributors.  And, it would stop the practice of politicians being able to donate the remaining and often massive amounts of funds to charities in their names in yet another way to circumvent elections laws.  When

Governors Underwood and Wise donated a combined $665,000 to their causes, which were certainly worthwhile causes, they had the benefit of taking corporate money and spending it in any way they chose to spend it. Likewise, the 2005 left-over inaugural funds used to renovate the Governor's Mansion created an impression of impropriety. Since incoming Governors are allowed to do whatever they want with the second-and third-floor portions of the Mansion–where they live during their term as Governor, the Manchins will be able to renovate their new home with money from wealthy West Virginia businesses.[1175] People who make the argument that such donations don't buy access are either extremely disingenuous or naive. If the donations don't buy access, then why don't Governors set up a system whereby the large contributors remain completely anonymous? The answer is because the businesses want the Governor to know they gave him $5,000 because that buys access and they wouldn't contribute otherwise.

The longer an elected official is in office, the longer he or she is able to amass a more visible name recognition with a State's citizens, thus, significantly improving the chances of re-election. The *Charleston Daily Mail* quipped: "Who says West Virginia doesn't have public financing for political candidates?" referring to incumbents in statewide-elected offices who "turn their offices into taxpayer-funded political strongholds."[1176] The *Charleston Gazette* writes: "Campaign money is an American disgrace–and it's distressing to see tax funds being used, as well as special-interest money." The *Gazette* continued:

> The brazen nature of the giveaways was illustrated . . . when Sen. Vic Sprouse, R-Kanawha, stupidly left a recorded telephone message at the Quick Community Center, saying an $18,000 gift to fix the center's roof might be withheld because a photo of Democratic gubernatorial nominee Wise was on a center wall. If the center's leaders renounced support for Wise, Sprouse implied, Underwood would give them $18,000 of taxpayer money for their roof.[1177]

In addition to the actual cash given to groups and individuals by Legislators and Governors for various projects, the distribution of so-called trinkets has "started to get somewhat out of control for the last couple of years," according to Speaker of the House of Delegates Bob Kiss. The *Charleston Daily Mail* reports: "As common as the items are, the personalized pens, pencils, key chains and other trinkets offered for free by various State officers–but paid for with taxpayer funds–are considered by some to be an important public relations tool that constituents have come to expect."[1178]

In a 1998 editorial, the *Charleston Daily Mail* noted: "West Virginians are the second-poorest people in the nation. They devote a higher percentage of their meager incomes to State government than people in twenty-seven other states. What do they get for their money?" The editorial listed numerous other taxpayer paid-for trinkets distributed by various elected officials–all of which prominently display the name of the elected official–that are commonly provided to the citizenry. The editorial called the giveaways "self-promotional nonsense [that] is an assault on taxpayers' wallets and an affront to common decency." It also asks: "How dare these politicians have their next campaign subsidized by taxpayers?"[1179] While many of the State constitutional officers differ in their "giveaways," they *all* distribute trinkets and brochures that contain their names. The *Charleston Daily Mail* wrote that the number one problem in West Virginia is poverty,

> yet Auditor Glen Gainer, Treasurer John Perdue, Attorney General Darrell McGraw used the money at their disposal to promote themselves – to further their own interests.

> Voters should by all means commit those names to memory. These guys play West Virginians for fools–funding their constant campaigns for public office with money obtained from or for some of the poorest people in the nation.

> Disgusting.[1180]

The spending of money by a State politician does not only benefit that politician, it is generational and directly benefits their family members who share their surname. This name recognition that is garnered by spending years in an elected office and providing trinkets proudly displaying their name is invaluable and is analogous to the same way people know what Proctor & Gamble is when they go to the grocery store. For example, two of West Virginia's three United States House of Representatives members, Shelly Moore Capito and Alan Mollohan, both had fathers in the House of Representatives, while Harley O. Staggers, Jr., who served in Congress from 1983 to 1993 succeeded the late Harley O. Staggers, Sr., who served in Congress from 1949 until he retired in 1981. State Auditor Glen Gainer, III succeeded his father in 1993, Glen Gainer, Jr., who served from 1977 until 1993 and succeeded a distant cousin Denzil Gainer, who served from 1960 until his death in 1972. Even current Governor Joe Manchin, III is a nephew to one of the State's most colorful politicians, A.

James Manchin, who served as a House of Delegates member, Secretary of State, and State Treasurer. Moreover, Attorney General and former Chief Justice of the West Virginia Supreme Court Darrell McGraw, Jr., is brother to former Supreme Court Justice Warren McGraw, who was a former State Senate President and county prosecutor. Warren is also the father to former House of Delegates member Randolph McGraw and current Family Court Judge Suzanne McGraw. State Senate President Earl Ray Tomblin's father, Earl Tomblin, was a former Logan County Sheriff, while former State Senator Lloyd Jackson, II, who spent more than $3 million of his own money in his unsuccessful bid for Governor in 2004, is the son of former State Senate President Lloyd Jackson, Sr. Further, former Chief Justice of the West Virginia Supreme Court Richard Neely is the grandson of former Governor and United States Senator Matthew Neely.[1181] This certainly is not an inclusive list but it illustrates the benefit of having a father or close relative in office gaining name recognition on a daily basis.

This continued self-promotion at the expense of the taxpayers must end without haste. The problem, however, is that legislators would have to pass legislation prohibiting such activity and they are some of the biggest offenders. It happens from top to bottom and even the so-called smaller examples are really not small considering that it is so commonplace by so many State actors. Thus, even a low budget race for State Delegate allows for incumbents to use the State to fund their campaigns in numerous ways.

Delegate Greg Butcher is an example of this as the *Charleston Gazette* reported:

> Delegate Greg Butcher, D-Logan, is stapling his campaign card to free official Division of Highways' road maps and putting them out for campaign material. A patron at a Lincoln County restaurant picked up one of the maps that were on a counter with other candidates' campaign material. DOH gives the maps away to anyone who asks for them. A DOH source said during legislative sessions lawmakers often ask for three boxes of maps at a time. Each box has 300 maps. DOH doesn't keep a list of whom they give the maps to, said Bill Wood, a supervisor in the planning section. Wood said the maps cost about 11 cents each.[1182]

This, keep in mind, is in addition to any Budget Digest money that he was able to hand out to constituents while posing for pictures, or for any additional money he may have been able to secure through the Governor's Contingency Fund. For anyone who says "big deal, it was just a few boxes of maps," I ask, what if all 100 Delegates and all 34 Senators, as well as all statewide elected officials did the exact same thing? This situation and other like it must be considered in the aggregate. What if all State employees–and there are thousands of them–spend hundreds of dollars illegally and don't get caught?

In reality, there are no small indiscretions when considered in conjunction with the massive amounts of taxpayer money wasted by the Budget Digest, Contingency Fund, secret accounts, and millions of worthless trinkets that are handed out so freely on a daily basis by statewide elected officials. Perhaps equally important–and I never hear anyone mention this destructive consequence–but generations of honest, hard-working, and well-meaning people have been, and continue to be, completely shut out of the political process because they can't afford to run against an entrenched politician who has the State Treasury at his or her disposal and isn't afraid to use it.

# CHAPTER SEVENTEEN

# Legally Buying Elections and Perceptions

*Money! It is money! Money! Money! Not ideas, nor principles, but money that reigns supreme in American politics.*

United States Senator Robert C. Byrd

West Virginians who try to choose candidates during elections are usually bombarded with millions of dollars worth of television advertisements–most of which are usually slanderous and negative. In describing the period just prior to the November 2002 election in West Virginia, the *Charleston Gazette* wrote: "Traditionally, this is the time when candidates squander great sums on mean-spirited, distorted, over-expensive, TV 'attack ads' designed to make their opponents seem repulsive. 'Going negative' is the common label for it." Additionally, "[t]his unseemly process disgusts many Americans. No wonder vast numbers of adults don't bother to vote." Exactly one year prior to that editorial, the *Gazette* proclaimed: "Political attack ads during election campaigns are so dishonest they make millions of Americans contemptuous of politicians in general. The TV and radio spots twist facts to make opponents seem unpatriotic, immoral, corrupt or worse."[1183] The *Charleston Daily Mail* wrote:

> Politicians wouldn't run these ads if they didn't think a dumbed-down electorate would fall for them. Here's hoping voters who do nothing to inform themselves except watch television ads will stay home on May 11. They, as well as the politicians

who pander to them, are responsible for what's wrong with
West Virginia.[1184]

For a small and financially destitute State, West Virginia spends a lot of
money electing those who represent them. In fact, "[o]nly three other states spent
as large a share of their Gross State Product on candidates, Political Action
Committees, and parties as the Mountain State did in 2000." Even though it's
known widely as a Democratic stronghold, West Virginia donated large amounts
to President Bush during his 2000 Presidential Campaign as more than 400 West
Virginians contributed a total of $277,363 to Bush, while Democratic challenger
Al Gore amassed less than $53,000 from one-fourth as many voters.[1185] Given
the disparity in fundraising, it was not surprising that Bush was victorious in West
Virginia.

With regard to running for office in West Virginia as a statewide or congressional candidate, elections have become a multi-million dollar endeavor.
Good examples of this surround the 2000, 2002, and 2004 elections in the Second
Congressional District, one of West Virginia's three congressional districts. In
2000, Democratic candidate Jim Humphreys spent approximately $7 million dur-
ing the election contest, while Shelly Moore Capito, along with others spending
money on her behalf, may have actually spent more money overall during the
final critical months of the campaign. Humphreys spent the majority of his
money during a crowded May 2000 Primary, while Capito was able to save the
$1.29 million she had on hand for the General Election.[1186]

The election was the third most expensive House of Representatives
race in the country out of the 435 congressional elections during the 2000 election cycle.[1187] Former legislator and current lobbyist Michael Queen wrote a
commentary in *West Virginia Executive* magazine titled: "Political campaigns are
BIG business in West Virginia–and the future looks even better." The article said
$10.3 million was spent by six different candidates–most of which was spent by
Capito and Humphreys–in seeking the congressional seat vacated by Bob Wise's
decision to run for Governor.[1188]

During the 2000 election, even though Capito raised $1.3 million, the
help she received from the National Republican Campaign Committee assisted
her in achieving a narrow victory of approximately 5,000 votes. It is almost
impossible to accurately quantify the exact amount that national Republicans
spent on Capito's behalf, but some estimates reach as high as $2.5 million for tel-
evision announcements, mailings, and other get-out-the-vote activities.
Moreover, the millions of dollars spent on thirty-second television advertisements
were plenty to plaster the broadcast and cable airwaves with a constant affront of

negative advertising. Capito's spots communicated Humphreys' connections to a racetrack scandal, illegal campaign contributions during the 1992 Presidential Campaign, and stated that no less than eighteen ethics complaints were filed against him.[1189]

Another Capito campaign ad featured a former employee of Humphreys who alleged that someone in his office attempted to wrongfully obtain her medical records. Capito explained that her campaign advertisements simply documented "the truth about Jim Humphreys' questionable conduct, deceit, and repeated violations of personal and professional trust." One of the ads went so far as to state that Humphreys "demanded immunity under the Organized Crimes Act" before testifying in "a political corruption case" and that he had "made illegal campaign contributions in violation of federal law."[1190]

During the 2000 campaign, United States Senator John McCain made two campaign stops in West Virginia on behalf of Capito.[1191] After the United States Senate passed the McCain/Feingold campaign finance reform bill, attention quickly turned to the House and to freshman Representative Capito whose vote would become critical to whether or not the bill would survive a House vote. In an editorial, the *Charleston Gazette* asked: "Campaign finance–What will Capito do?" It questioned how Capito would vote, noting contributions of $10,000 to Capito's campaign by House Majority Leader Tom DeLay who promised to do anything he could to stop the campaign reform legislation.[1192] The *Gazette* also noted that House Speaker Dennis Hastert's political action committee (PAC) donated $9,999 to Capito, while about 40 percent of the PAC money Capito received came from GOP groups. It posed the question: "Capito needs to decide who she will side with: A man who gave her moral and political support by appearing on campaign stages with her, or the Republican leadership who showered her with cash."[1193]

Despite being unsuccessful in the 2000 race, Humphreys decided to challenge Capito again in 2002. The 2002 Capito/Humphreys match-up continued the high-dollar trend and was the most expensive House race in the nation among all 435 congressional elections. By June 30, 2001, just six months into her first term as a member of Congress, Representative Capito had already raised nearly $500,000 in campaign contributions preparing for her 2002 re-election. Of the contributions, $305,650 came from PACs while $160,040 was from individual donors. In fact, during 2001, Capito raised more cash than 419 of her fellow 434 members of the House of Representatives.[1194] According to the *Charleston Gazette*, Capito "gathered three times the typical amount of PAC contributions raised by House members in 2001, and two-and-a-half times the typical amount of overall contributions."[1195] Nearly a year before the re-election challenge,

Capito had already raised $733,155. On June 30, 2002, just six months later, Capito and Humphreys had raised $5.29 million and had spent $3.94 million.[1196]

Capito was also successful at using the power of the presidency to benefit her 2002 re-election campaign. On April 12, 2002, Vice President Dick Cheney held a $500 per ticket fundraiser for Capito in Charleston. During the event, Cheney's speech accounted for $250,000 of Capito's re-election war chest. In fact, some of the attendees even payed an extra $500 to get their picture taken with Vice President Cheney.[1197] Capito also had the help of the Office of the President as George W. Bush made eight trips to West Virginia between 2000 and her 2002 re-election–including five trips once elected President and a large July 4th Celebration in Ripley, West Virginia, a critical vote-rich Capito area. President Bush's last trip to West Virginia during that election cycle was just days prior to the General Election and received live extended coverage from all of the surrounding television stations as well as front page news coverage.[1198] He has continued making frequent trips to West Virginia, including a July 4, 2004, appearance at the State Capitol, and a July 4, 2005, appearance at West Virginia University in Morgantown. Incidentally, during the 2005 appearance, television cameras showed President Bush speaking to the crowd as Congresswoman Capito and her father, convicted felon and former Governor Arch A. Moore, Jr., stood directly beside him on the stage. At the same time of Bush's appearance with former Governor Moore, rumors were already prevalent that Congresswoman Capito had been seeking a Presidential pardon for her disgraced father.

During the early part of the 2002 election, Jim Humphreys, whose personal worth is estimated at between $50 and $200 million, criticized his Primary Election opponent, former State Supreme Court Chief Justice Margaret Workman, for loaning her campaign $500,000 from joint accounts between her and her husband Ty Gardner. Workman's financial disclosure listed family assets between $13 million and $35 million. Workman called it "hugely ironic" that Humphreys would be complaining about her contributions when he made his own personal contribution of $785,000 to the 2002 campaign and $6 million to his unsuccessful 2000 campaign.[1199]

Big money flooded the campaign from both sides of the political aisle during the 2000 and 2002 congressional campaign. Moreover, while Capito raised large sums of money from individual contributions and PACs, it is clear that she benefitted from independent expenditures during both the 2000 and 2002 races. Although by federal law the Capito campaign and the National Republican Committee were not permitted to work in tandem, the television spots with a $750,000 total television buy from the Republican Committee endorsing Capito were extraordinarily similar to the footage and language contained in the Capito campaign spots paid for by her campaign.[1200]  Humphreys had the benefit of spending nearly $7 million of his personal money in the 2000 race, but had more difficulty than Capito in raising money from outside sources.[1201]  During his second unsuccessful attempt to unseat Capito in 2002, Humphreys ended up spending $7.7 million, most of it from his personal finances.[1202]

Capito's third consecutive election contest was also costly.  After her 2004 Primary Election victory, she had already raised more than $1 million for her re-election campaign for her congressional seat.  She found herself in the unusual position of having more money than her opponent, Erik Wells, who had only raised $14,000 at the time, of which $8,000 were from personal funds he loaned his campaign.[1203]  State Republican Party Chairman Kris Warner cited a subsequent visit by Vice President Dick Cheney on September 15, 2003, for a packed Capito fundraiser luncheon in Charleston as the kind of move that would make Capito a tough incumbent to beat in 2004.  The *Charleston Daily Mail* reported, "With deep pockets and high-profile support from Washington, Warner said Capito is ready to face any of the possible candidates who have been mentioned [as possible challengers]."[1204]

In response to the large amounts of money raised by Congresswoman Capito during her 2004 election, then-State Democratic Party Chair Mike Callahan said he believed a self-funded candidate able to put his own personal wealth into a campaign may be the best choice for a future Democratic challenger.  Callahan said, "We don't have the kind of money that the national Republican Party is able to raise, so that will be the foremost concern [and] we don't want to get blown away by the Republican machine."[1205]  His comments illuminate the fact that money is the most important part of any election.  They also demonstrate that money is unquestionably a significant deciding factor with regard to even which candidates are supported or not supported by their respective political parties.

In West Virginia, money in State politics has reached staggering amounts which more often than not prevents average citizens from participating as serious candidates for any statewide political office.  For instance, State Treasurer John Perdue's decision not to run for Governor in 2004 was due to his unsuccessful attempts to raise $1 million, which he believed was the minimum amount necessary to wage a successful campaign.  Perdue said, "I'm not a millionaire [and] I don't have great personal wealth.  It all comes down to money.  It's as simple as that."[1206]  His spokesman, Nelson Sorah, said, "[Perdue] is extremely frustrated by the ability of people with their own resources to be the only people to run for office."  Sorah added, "[Perdue] feels like the common man needs a voice." Following Perdue's announcement, then-Secretary of State and gubernatorial candidate Joe Manchin, III said, "A lot of people have the desire and a lot of people have the ability, but the money situation makes it difficult for a lot of people to get involved." He said due to the amount of money necessary to run for Governor, that publicly financed elections "level the playing field a little bit more [and] campaign finance reforms have to be looked into."[1207]

Many of the candidates who ran during the 2004 gubernatorial Primary were able to spend large amounts of their own money on their campaigns. For example, of the $3,411,339 former Democratic State Senator Lloyd Jackson, II spent on his campaign, $3,043,420 of that amount came from his own pocket through personal loans he made to his campaign. Fellow Democrat Jim Lees spent $462,370 of which he loaned his campaign $190,000 from his personal bank accounts.[1208] Conversely, Manchin raised $2.6 million while he only had to loan his campaign $3,200. Much of Manchin's fundraising success was due to his front-runner status since he was the sitting Secretary of State at the time, as well as his significant name recognition due in part to his Uncle A. James Manchin's flooding of the State with millions of trinkets emblazoned with the Manchin name.[1209] Meanwhile, GOP contender, retired banker and car dealer, Dan Moore, spent more than $1.8 million on his campaign of which $825,000 was from personal funds. Other GOP contenders such as Monty Warner loaned his campaign more than $400,000, while fellow candidate Dr. Doug McKinney, who spent a total of $247,308 in his unsuccessful bid, loaned his campaign $109,719.[1210]

During the 2004 gubernatorial General Election, and almost immediately after pressing his opponent Democrat Joe Manchin to come to a "gentleman's agreement" with regard to negative campaigning, Republican candidate Monty Warner began making negative allegations against Manchin. He accused Manchin of being a career politician of appeasement unable to deal with the cancer of corruption and cronyism in West Virginia. He then incriminated more than a dozen Lincoln County residents for vote-buying and attempted to link many of those individuals with the Manchin campaign. Among those individuals, Warner included Logan County Sheriff Johnny Mendez and lawyer Mark Hrutkay, both of whom were, in fact, later convicted in an ongoing federal probe of vote-buying in southern West Virginia being conducted by Monty Warner's brother, United States Attorney for the Southern District of West Virginia, Kasey Warner.[1211]

Monty Warner said Manchin failed as the State's chief elections officer and declared, "vote-buying in the 2004 General Election has already begun." Manchin spokeswoman Lara Ramsburg called Warner's assertions "outrageous . . . and baseless allegations."[1212] Manchin had used Hrutkay's helicopter to attend the 2003 Labor Day rally in Racine, West Virginia, and traveled with Sheriff

Mendez during campaign appearances in 2003 and early 2004 in Logan County. The Manchin campaign received contributions from both men, which were returned when the allegations against them surfaced.[1213] Monty Warner said when Manchin became Secretary of State in 2000, he turned over to federal prosecutors information about ongoing investigations, including those involving Hrutkay and Mendez. When Warner asked Manchin why he would have ridden in Hrutkay's helicopter or Mendez's car if he knew they had been part of a vote-buying operation, Manchin said, "Monty, you know we can't talk about ongoing investigations."[1214] After the election, additional charges were brought by United States Attorney Kasey Warner against numerous Lincoln County individuals including the county's circuit clerk Greg Stowers who was convicted for buying and selling the Lincoln County elections every two years from 1990 through 2004.

In 2003, former Secretary of State's Office Chief Investigator Damon Sloan filed a lawsuit against then-Secretary of State Joe Manchin and his chief of staff, Larry Puccio, alleging he was fired from the criminal investigator's position in order to stop investigations he was conducting into political corruption in Logan and Boone counties. Puccio maintained Sloan was fired as a part of a reorganization of the Secretary of State's Office. The *Logan Banner* reported that "after Sloan's dismissal, Manchin's office made absolutely no effort to follow-up on Sloan's investigations, or refer them to the West Virginia State Police, or any other investigative agency."[1215]

Sloan added that prior to his firing, he had started the Boone and Logan County investigations following the 2000 Primary Election after receiving a request from the prosecuting attorney of Boone County to investigate the possible fraudulent use of as many as 500 absentee ballots. The *Logan Banner* reported: "Sloan was examining allegations of absentee ballot fraud, vote-buying, influence peddling, and exchanging tax breaks for political support, among other things." The *Banner* wrote:

> Sources say that, upon assuming office, Puccio asked Sloan for a list of the targets of the investigations in Boone and Logan counties. It was shortly thereafter when Sloan received the termination letter.

> The sources also say Puccio specifically asked if one particular Logan County politician was a target–and he was. That politician then received a gubernatorial appointment.

> According to the confidential sources, the Logan County Investigation reached up to State-level politicians.[1216]

The complaint filed in the lawsuit stated, "[Manchin and Puccio] promised politicians being investigated that when Manchin took office, the investigations would stop and Mr. Sloan would be fired before he could report his findings to the proper authorities. Thus, any threat of prosecution would be eliminated." On January 15, 2004, United States District Judge Elizabeth Hallanan dismissed Sloan's case.[1217]

With regard to Monty Warner, his candidacy was not without controversy. It was reported just days before the 2004 Primary Election, he, and his brothers, Mac Warner, Ben Warner, and State GOP Chairman Kris Warner, were all delinquent in local property taxes in three different counties by more than $75,000.[1218] Nonetheless, Monty Warner was able to come up with more than $400,000 of his own money to loan his campaign in order to win the Primary Election. Then, just prior to the General Election, he spent at least another $100,000 in personal funds to launch television and radio ads.[1219]

The Warners were also criticized for buying a building valued at more than $1 million for just $10,000 in exchange for a promise to bring employment to "job-starved" Barbour County, and then placing that same building on the market for $795,000. Joe Mattaliano, then-Director of the Barbour County Economic Development Authority, said the Warners did not fulfill their promise and "[w]e got suckered." Additional condemnation surfaced when it was learned the Warners were only paying a $5.57 tax bill on the $1 million building. Current Barbour County Assessor Sandra Sipe said because her predecessor, Loring Phillips, "never put the property on the books, the Warner property was assessed at the default rate, $100." Sipe was also critical of the Warners for being delinquent on $5.57 in property taxes they were charged for the $1 million building.[1220] Incidentally, Assessor Phillips was accused of using taxpayer money on personal building supplies and consequently resigned in December 2002 after paying the money back to avoid prosecution.

More controversy swirled around Monty and his family both before and after his defeat to Manchin. One major flap surrounded campaign signs that were produced prior to the General Election bearing the names "Bush-Warner" in an attempt to demonstrate support from President George Bush who was also running for re-election. The Bush-Cheney campaign, however, sent a cease-and-desist order to the Warner campaign telling them to stop using the signs as it was a violation of election law to mingle state and federal candidates. The Warner campaign not only ignored the cease-and-desist order, they denied any knowledge of the signs and claimed no responsibility for them saying they were paid for by a political action committee and not the Warner campaign. One day following Warner's denial of any connection to the signs, Manchin's campaign produced a photograph of Monty Warner's vehicle with Bush-Warner campaign signs stacked against it.[1221]

Warner campaign workers also disputed the Warner brothers' denials and claimed Kris Warner was behind a plan to funnel private donations through a defunct political action committee, the Northeast Conservative Political Action Committee, to pay for the signs in order that Monty Warner would not be blamed, and could claim he had nothing to do with them. The treasurer of the Northeast PAC was the ex-girlfriend of Monty Warner staffer Sam Pimm.[1222] It wasn't until after the election that it was learned Kris had signed over a $3,002.28 check to the PAC that was written to him from his brother's campaign (he initially denied that he signed over that check to the PAC), and that Kris' wife sent a $4,000 check, as well as a $2,000 check sent from Mac Warner, Kris and Monty's brother, and a $1,000 check sent from their father, George "Brud" Warner, to the PAC responsible for the signs. On January 6, 2005, Charles Bolen, the chairman of the State Young Republicans sent a complaint to the Federal Election Commission requesting an investigation into the Bush-Warner signs stating Kris and Monty Warner "may have engaged in activities that skirted or broke laws in regard to the creation of signs."[1223]

Warner's former campaign manager Dick Leggitt said, "Kris Warner conceived the plan for the Bush-Warner signs, which he and Monty have both denied knowing anything about."[1224] He added that Kris created and paid for the signs, and that he knew prior to the actual production of the signs that Kris had received an email with the sign design, and then came into the Warner campaign headquarters holding checks from himself and others to pay for them.[1225] Leggitt further explained, "Kris Warner said, 'We need to pay for the Alabama signs.' I said, 'What signs?' He said the printer wouldn't finish the work until he'd been paid." Leggitt said Kris then returned to the Warner campaign within twenty-four hours and requested reimbursement from his brother's campaign for the Bush-Warner signs and even requested the reimbursement check be made in "an odd number" to avoid scrutiny. Kris did receive a $3,002.28 reimbursement check from his brother's campaign on September 28, 2004, but he says it was not for the signs, but for postage and gas receipts he spent on his brother's campaign.[1226]

Kris Warner responded that Leggett "looted" his brother's campaign and said he was "trying to extort money from my brother Monty [and] I relate this to the act of a terrorist [and] Monty was in the military too long [and] he's not going to deal with a terrorist."[1227] The Warner campaign ended with $753,312 in campaign debts including: $400,326 that Monty loaned his campaign; $18,767 to campaign manager Dick Leggitt; $55,814 to Sam Pimm, the campaign's deputy manager; $7,050 to Leggitt's wife, a campaign staffer; a debt of $7,535 to campaign spokeswoman Kristina Grabosky; and a debt of $65,060 owed to McCarthy Marcus Hennings, a leading national GOP consulting firm that produced the campaign's last minute television ads.[1228] Pimm later filed a lawsuit seeking damages for breach of contract for nearly $65,000.[1229] Leggitt also said Kris and his brother Mac Warner bragged about hiring a private investigator to dig up dirt on Manchin and that they "talked openly about it around the campaign and laughed about the video footage."[1230] In January 2006, Kris sent a letter to the State Republican Party threatening to sue if it didn't pay him $24,000 he claimed it owed him.

Perhaps the largest blow to the Warner political dynasty came in July 2005, when it was reported that the United States Justice Department in Washington, D.C., asked Kasey Warner to resign as United States Attorney. Warner refused to resign and would not comment on the speculation surrounding his departure stating he serves "at the will and pleasure of the President."[1231] He was subsequently fired for what was believed to be violating the State's election laws. When I called the United States Attorney's Office for the Southern District of West Virginia, they refused to comment on Warner's firing and directed me to their superiors in Washington, D.C. Thereafter, I called Michael Battle, Director of the Executive Office for the United States Attorneys, Department of Justice. Mr. Battle refused to accept my call, and two of his employees, during two separate telephone occasions, refused to identify themselves, told me that they do "not speak to the public," and slammed the phone in my ear. I even sent a federal Freedom of Information Act request seeking a copy of the letter sent to Warner, but I did not receive a response from Mr. Battle's office even though the Department of Justice regulations require his office to respond to such a request within twenty days. I guess the United States Attorneys' Offices feel that they only need to enforce the laws and not follow them.

Gubernatorial elections in West Virginia have consistently been costly and controversial well before the 2004 election. For example, prior to the May 2000 West Virginia Primary Election, the leading Republican and Democratic candidates had already raised more than $1 million. Then-sitting Governor Cecil H. Underwood, who faced minor Primary opposition, had collected $1.2 million, while eighteen-year West Virginia Congressman Bob Wise had amassed $1.1 million.[1232] Both Underwood and Wise easily won their Primary races.

After Wise won the General Election, he immediately began gearing up for the 2004 gubernatorial election. By April 2003, he had already raised $1.087 million for his re-election campaign. His 2000 campaign political consultant Mike Plante said, "There is no such thing as too early for fundraising in politics." Plante added, "The Governor has laid down a marker to any would-be challenger and has elevated the bar by raising and not spending a significant amount of money this early in the game." The *Charleston Daily Mail* points out:

> By this time before the 2000 election, incumbent Republican Gov. Cecil Underwood had raised about $693,000 and had about $560,000 in his war chest. Wise's report suggests that not only has the incumbent amassed more this time around, but he has raised it from some of the same people who supported the man he beat.[1233]

Soon afterward, however, following Governor Bob Wise's announcement that he had an extramarital affair, his wife, First Lady Sandy Wise, moved back to Washington, D.C. Consequently, Wise later decided not to run for re-election even though he had already raised $1.2 million. He issued nearly $825,000 in refund checks to people who contributed to his campaign, while the remaining funds were used to pay leftover bills and campaign expenses.[1234] Incidentally, with regard to Wise's former congressional seat he held for eighteen years prior to running for Governor, which is currently held by Shelly Moore Capito, Wise told me that because of the steady increases in campaign spending, "I know in looking at the congressional races in my district, since I left my district, I couldn't afford to run" for that seat today.[1235]

Wise's 2000 challenger, Governor Cecil H. Underwood said during his first campaign for Governor in 1956, he spent $19,000. After being elected again as Governor in 1996, Underwood, both the youngest and oldest person to serve in the State's Governor's Office, said that amount "wouldn't even get you out of the starting gate."[1236] The 1996 election was surrounded by controversy and millions of dollars buying negative political advertisements by both the Republican and Democratic candidates.

During the 1996 Democratic Primary, Joe Manchin, III spent $2.2 million in his first attempt at the Governor's Office, but was narrowly defeated by Charlotte Pritt. The total spent by candidates during the 1996 Primary Election was $4.7 million.[1237] In that very contentious election, Pritt's campaign charged that C. MacClain Haddow, who was previously convicted of federal corruption charges, "played a key role in [Manchin's] campaign." Manchin, however, explained that Haddow was simply one of thousands of volunteers involved with his campaign. Manchin said he "does not do background checks on unpaid volunteers or quiz them about their political party affiliation" and he did not screen or scrutinize everyone who offered to help because he was extremely pleased "when people want to volunteer for us."[1238] Despite his explanation with regard to his association with Haddow, the *Charleston Gazette* criticized his campaign for the association. The *Gazette* wrote:

> IT HAS COME to light that Joe Manchin's Democratic campaign for governor was guided partly by C. MacClain Haddow, a former Reagan administration official who went to prison for corruption in the 1980s. After getting out of jail, Haddow became a Washington lobbyist for Mylan Laboratories of Morgantown, headed by Milan Puskar, Manchin's chief backer. Frankly, we wish crooked Reagan Republicans would stay in their own party–West Virginia Democratic ranks already contain enough tarnished characters.[1239]

The *Gazette* also stated that during the previous year, Manchin was picked up at the airport for a campaign stop in Huntington "by a man convicted of bank robbery and a woman convicted on drug charges and income tax evasion." Manchin said he "had no idea about their backgrounds."[1240]

Pritt defeated Manchin in the Democratic Primary, but was the subject of negative campaigning during the General Election against Underwood. In fact, Pritt even filed a libel suit against Republican officials in 1997 based upon television advertisements sponsored by several Republican organizations that aired throughout the State during the 1996 General Election. Some of the campaign spots claimed Pritt voted as a State Senator to permit the sale of pornographic videos to children, to teach first-graders about condoms, voted to allow convicted drug abusers to work in public schools, wanted to allow burning of the American flag, and opposed honoring Gulf War veterans.[1241] Pritt sued the Republican National Committee, the National Republican Senatorial Committee, the West Virginia State Victory Committee, a group named the RNSC temporarily formed for the 1996 gubernatorial election, and others, stating she did not cast votes for anything resembling the subjects in the campaign advertisements, and those groups "committed common-law libel, slander and defamation by publishing false and injurious statements against her."[1242] More specifically, Pritt alleged the GOP groups damaged her campaign with the false radio and television spots in the final weeks of the race causing her to lose to Underwood. She sought $2 million in compensatory damages and $10 million in punitive damages.[1243] The *Gazette* cited several examples of advertisements used against her. For instance:

> Because then-Democratic nominee Charlotte Pritt previously had voted in the state Senate for 'human growth and develop-

ment' classes in public schools, the GOP ads said she 'proposed teaching first-graders about condoms.' What a distortion. Such sex-education courses merely teach boys and girls at the grade-school level to be nice to each other.

Because Pritt had supported the right of adults to choose any movies they wanted, the ads declared that she 'voted to permit the sale of pornographic videos to children.' Another gross distortion.[1244]

The Circuit Court of Fayette County initially dismissed Pritt's lawsuit; however, a unanimous Opinion by the West Virginia Supreme Court reversed the dismissal and sent the case back to the circuit court for a trial. Former West Virginia Supreme Court Chief Justice Margaret Workman, who represented Pritt with her lawsuit, called the political advertisements outrageous and said maybe this case could help to reform campaigning in West Virginia elections. During oral argument before the Supreme Court, the GOP attorney against Pritt said, "America's freedom of speech is so open that erroneous information may be published out of ignorance." He then added that "[i]n a political campaign, the adverse party is going to try to inflict damage."[1245]  Pritt also chastised Underwood for running similar campaign spots against her. The Underwood advertisements accused Pritt "of publicly supporting the legalization of marijuana, voting to allow the sale of drug paraphernalia to children and voting to pay workers' compensation benefits to jailed convicts."[1246]

The Pritt case returned to the West Virginia Supreme Court in 2003 when she said Judge Charles Vickers improperly limited her case by disallowing the testimony of six expert witnesses. The State Supreme Court again ruled in Pritt's favor ordering the circuit judge to allow Pritt's experts to testify and for the case to "proceed promptly to a trial on the merits and be finally resolved."[1247] The case finally went to trial in March 2006, nearly ten years after it was first filed. Pritt told jurors that by filing suit "we can stop this from happening in the future." She also explained that she hoped her reputation and integrity could be restored. She specifically disputed the ads which said, among other things, that she wanted to dishonor West Virginia veterans, teach first-graders how to use condoms, prevent the saying of the Pledge of Allegiance, and allow flag burning. With regard to the ad saying she wanted to dishonor West Virginia's Gulf War veterans, Pritt told jurors, "I was a Marine Corps wife. My high school sweetheart came back in a body bag." She explained that she voted to give veterans a bonus, but voted against a resolution to authorize the President to send people to war. She said her idea of supporting veterans was to give money and support to them and their families, not to send them off to be killed.

Pritt, a former school teacher, cried when she began to talk about the ad stating that parents could not entrust their children to her. She said, "The whole reason I ran was to help children. This is the one that really struck to my very heart." She said at the Legislature that she had developed a reputation that when there was an issue involving children, people would say, "You might want to talk to Charlotte." In discussing another ad showing three large "X's" and Pritt's face, she said, "It makes me sick to my stomach." She explained that contrary to the blatantly false assertions included in the ad, she never voted to allow children to see "triple-X videos. If you are thinking logically, I don't know of a single legislator who would."[1248] Even her 1996 opponent, former Governor Underwood, testified on behalf of Pritt saying it had been a hallmark of his decades-long political career to distance himself from conducting negative advertising. He described false advertising in general as very distasteful and said the ads against Pritt bothered him so much that he asked the sponsors to stop airing them.[1249] On March 13, 2005, jurors found in favor of the Republican groups and against Pritt.

Pritt's first attempt at obtaining the Governor's Office was in 1992. While she was unsuccessful during her 1992 gubernatorial bid, she did, however, pull 35 percent of the vote in the Primary Election despite her low-budget campaign that spent a mere $115,000. Her loss set up the challenge between two millionaires in the General Election as: "[sitting Governor] Caperton, who comes from a wealthy coal and insurance family, will be challenged by Republican Agriculture Commissioner Cleve Benedict, a 'gentleman farmer' who is heir to much of the Procter & Gamble fortune."[1250] Caperton was re-elected by a wide margin.

In 1988, Gaston Caperton, who was a newcomer to politics, spent $4.5 million to secure his election as Governor. The amount of money spent by all of the candidates running for Governor that year was "more than $9.4 million, or nearly $15 million in today's dollars."[1251] Caperton spent $2.15 million in the 1988 Democratic Primary, most of which was his own money. Former Caperton Communications Director Bob Brunner said, "Caperton would have probably been considered an amusing sidelight to the campaign story fifteen years ago. But now, with the money and skills of media people, he can become in the public's eye a viable candidate for Governor in a matter of a couple of months—from nowhere."[1252]

While the millions of dollars spent during the 1988, 1992, 1996, 2000, and 2004 gubernatorial elections are staggering and unimaginable amounts to most people, they are dwarfed by Jay Rockefeller's $12 million in personal money spent for his re-election as Governor in 1980 and his $12 million spent for his election to the United States Senate in 1984. In 1976, Rockefeller spent $2.8 million to win the Governor's Office by defeating former Governor Cecil Underwood, while four years earlier, in 1972, Rockefeller spent approximately $1.5 million (a State record) in his loss to incumbent opponent Arch A. Moore, Jr., who spent about $700,000.[1253] In 1980, Moore spent another $1.1 million on his challenge of Rockefeller during that election.

State gubernatorial elections are not the only costly political races in West Virginia. During the 2002 election, $6 million was raised by State legislative candidates with nearly $4 million of that raised by the winning candidates and $2 million going to losing candidates. Of the total amount raised, 14 percent, $475,650, came from physicians, hospital executives and other health-care providers, while personal funds and family contributions accounted for 20 percent of all the money spent. Other major donors to 2002 legislative races included: "lawyers, who donated 10 percent; labor unions, 8 percent; coal executives, 7 percent; real estate and construction, 5 percent; gambling interests, 4 percent; banking and finance executives, 4 percent." Another 19 percent of identifiable donations came from a variety of other business interests, including: pharmaceuticals, railroads, timber, oil and gas, tobacco, chemicals, beverage distributors and electric utilities.[1254] A report compiled by the West Virginia People's Election Reform Coalition, stated, "In most legislative races, the candidate who was able to raise and spent the most money won. . . ." The report also found that the "typical Senate winner's contributions increased by 86 percent, from $51,159 to $95,372, between 1986 and 2002" and that "the average House of Delegates winner raised 46 percent more last year than six years earlier, up from $17,486 in 1996 to $25,589 in 2002."

During the 2002 State Senate campaigns, Senate Finance Chairman Oshel Craigo (D-Putnam) spent $408,587 against challenger Lisa Smith (R-Putnam), who spent $294,000, of which she loaned her campaign $258,000. A total of $666,587 was spent by the two candidates in spite of the fact that both State Senate and House of Delegates positions only pay $15,000 per year. A *Charleston Gazette* editorial, "Cash, Political Bonanza," stated that people think "politics is a sleazy business, tainted by special-interest money. We wonder where they got such an idea." The editorial said after Smith defeated Craigo she held an illegal fundraiser to attempt to erase her $258,000 campaign debt she loaned herself. The newspaper further said newly appointed Republican United States Attorney Kasey Warner was uninterested in investigating this incident "although he previously probed a different campaign finance problem involving Democrat Craigo."[1255]

With regard to the probe against Craigo, two weeks before the election against Smith, he was called before a federal grand jury in Beckley to discuss allegations that he failed to properly report a campaign contribution. The grand jury never returned an indictment, but Craigo said rumors about the indictment led to his defeat. On January 10, 2006, Smith and her husband were indicted on federal charges of tax evasion, mail fraud, and not withholding about $1 million in employee taxes while she allegedly schemed to use some of that money to fund her 2002 State Senate campaign against Craigo. According to the indictment against Smith,

> The object and purpose of the scheme and artifice was to enrich
> defendant Lisa D. Smith by fraudulently securing the funds used
> in her campaign and fraudulently securing the election of defen-
> dant Lisa D. Smith as a member of the West Virginia State Senate
> and thereby obtaining the compensation paid to members of the
> Senate and the emoluments pertaining to that office."[1256]

Also during the 2002 election, the State Senate race between Jesse Guills (R-Greenbrier) and Mary Pearl Compton (D-Monroe) cost nearly $285,594. Lagging close behind was the Senate race between Evan Jenkins and Dr. Tom Scott who spent $273,347. Even Senator Ed Bowman raised $122,952 despite the fact that he was unopposed in the election.[1257] One race that received a lot of coverage that year was the State Senate contest in Mingo County. The *Gazette* wrote: "If ever the adage that elections are about choosing the lesser of the two evils rang true, the 6th Senatorial District Primary is proof." The *Gazette* wrote:

> Incumbent Sen. Truman Chafin's political career includes
> dodging two indictments: One State charge, over a scheme to
> 'sell' the Mingo County sheriff's seat. (It was dismissed on a
> technicality). The other was federal, over wiretapping the
> phone of ex-wife Gretchen Lewis, former state Health and
> Human Resources Secretary.

Moreover,

> Chafin's challenger: Dr. Diane Shafer has a rap sheet of her
> own, including a conviction in Kentucky for bribery (later
> overturned), and the suspensions of licenses to practice medi-
> cine in Kentucky and West Virginia for workers' compensation

fraud. (She got her West Virginia license back in 2000, when the state Supreme Court overturned the revocation.)[1258]

Dr. Shafer came to West Virginia after her Kentucky medical license was revoked due to the fact that she tried to influence a probe looking into her billing practices by secretly marrying the investigator and giving him money. Armando Acosta, Shafer's partner in her Williamson, West Virginia medical practice, was sentenced to serve four years in federal prison for tax evasion and trading OxyContin for sex. Shafer's manager of the Williamson medical practice from 1999 to 2001, Henry W. Vinson, pled guilty to helping Acosta shield about $1 million of his income from a $209,000 federal tax lien. Vinson, a former Mingo County coroner,

> also had a checkered past. In 1986, he resigned as Mingo County coroner after getting convicted of making harassing phone calls and leaving a coal miner's remains in an unrefrigerated vault for seven weeks. In 1991, he was convicted of racketeering and fraud related to a Washington male-prostitution ring, operating under names such as 'Man to Man,' that catered to socialites and lobbyists.[1259]

In addition to the high cost of State Senate seats, West Virginia's House of Delegates races, where single district delegates represent only 17,500 people, are unreasonably expensive. For example, Carrie Webster (D-Kanawha) spent $40,481 by June 2, 2000, to garner just 616 votes to win the Primary against challenger Perry Bryant, who after spending $24,894, finished second with 568 votes.[1260] Webster spent about $65.72 per vote. In her 2002 re-election campaign, Webster increased her spending to $84,000 in defeating opponent Mark Sadd who spent $40,890.[1261]

Also in 2002, newcomer Dan Foster (D-Kanawha) spent more than $118,000 to win his House seat. Foster said he spent the money wisely and "that much money is not appealing." That same election, House Majority Leader Rick Staton, who also ran unopposed in the General Election, spent $41,183 of the $61,840 he raised.[1262] During the 2004 House of Delegates Primary Election, Doug Reynolds, a Huntington attorney, spent nearly $59,000 in the 16th House District; Mark Hunt spent about $49,000 in the 30th District; House Majority Leader Rick Staton (D-Wyoming) spent about $36,000; Sally Susman (D-Raleigh), and House Speaker Bob Kiss (D-Raleigh) spent $28,000 and $26,000, respectively.[1263]

Even the mayors' elections are becoming more and more expensive and out of reach for the average West Virginian. For instance, in 2003, millionaire Danny Jones spent $188,776 to become the Mayor of the City of Charleston, which has a population of just 50,000. Jones poured $130,000 of his own money into the campaign, including a $30,000 check for last-minute advertising and a final get-out-the-vote push. Jones' opponent, Chris Smith, spent approximately $150,000 on his unsuccessful bid. In 1999, then-mayor Jay Goldman spent $189,356 to become Charleston's Mayor.[1264]

As more and more millions are spent on West Virginia's elections, even politicians who have spent their careers speaking against money in State politics have succumbed to high priced campaigns in an attempt just to continue to participate in West Virginia politics. In Charles Moffet's book, *Ken Hechler: Maverick Public Servant*, he explained that Hechler, a longtime West Virginia politician, was often critical of the amount of money involved in West Virginia elections. He wrote:

> 'The system of politics in the Appalachian region was probably the most corrupt in the nation.' What disgusted [Hechler] even more was that it was tolerated so blithely by the people. He said that the only newspaper in the region that dared to sound the tocsin against the 'establishment' was the *Charleston Gazette*. [Hechler] felt that college professors were entirely too reticent and passive, but even more appalling, the churches, he said, were apathetic toward political corruption. Hechler considered it downright 'obscene' that a candidate is allowed to spend nearly three million dollars to capture the governorship of a State of fewer than two million people. (Of course he was four times as exercised when John D. 'Jay' Rockefeller IV spent $12 million dollars in 1984 to capture a Senatorial berth.)[1265]

Hechler claimed to deplore, "the increasing number of millionaires and candidates financed by privilege-seeking special interest groups who cynically expend their money to buy elections" and said it "pollutes the very well-springs of democracy."[1266]

Amazingly though, during the 2004 Secretary of State's race, Ken Hechler, the former United States Congressman and Secretary of State, spent $553,907 to win the Primary Election. Of that amount, $550,000 was from Hechler's personal funds.[1267] By the General Election, Hechler's spending increased to $1.084 million.[1268] In endorsing his opposition in the General Election, the *Charleston Daily Mail* noted his distinguished political career, but said, "Hechler's expenditure of almost $1 million in this campaign is a case of wretched excess."[1269]   In spite of his astronomical expenditure to gain the $70,000-a-year job as Secretary of State, Hechler said he supports so-called clean-election bills because, "[t]he legislative winners all testified that they could concentrate on the issues instead of wasting time raising campaign funds."[1270]

Ironically, in 1995, while Secretary of State, Hechler lobbied for the passage of the Code of Fair Campaign Practices which includes a provision whereby candidates for constitutional offices, other than Governor, who sign the voluntary code, agree to limit spending to $150,000 for each Primary and General Election campaign.  During his 2004 campaign for Secretary of State, Hechler, who had long favored making the voluntary spending limits mandatory, signed the Code of Fair Campaign Practices and wrote in a qualification at the bottom of the page saying he would not abide by the spending limits because he needed to overcome criticism of his age.[1271]  As for attacks on his age, when the ninety-year-old Hechler was fifty-seven, he sponsored a bill in Congress to limit the terms of office holders at age seventy.[1272]

The idea of the Voluntary Code of Fair Campaign Practices is admirable, but the key word to keep in mind is "voluntary."  Even though candidates sign the pledge that they will only spend within defined limits they constantly break their pledge.  For example, during the 1996 Democratic Primary, gubernatorial candidate Charlotte Pritt exceeded the $1 million limit as her opponent Joe Manchin spent approximately $2 million.  During the General Election, Republican Cecil Underwood broke his pledge to follow the spending limits because he claimed Pritt broke the pledge in the Primary.  Another example was State Senator Sarah Minear who spent nearly $75,000 in spite of her signed pledge to spend just $25,000 in her first election in 1994.  In order for the Voluntary Code to have any teeth, the legislature must draft legislation making the limits mandatory.[1273]

Hechler's signature on the Code in 2004 was invalidated by the State Elections Commission because he wrote on the form "with exception of the outdated expenditure limits."  Hechler, who actually wrote the spending limits, did not attempt to increase the limits during his sixteen years as Secretary of State from 1985 to 2001.[1274]  He said, "I have to get my message out, and it costs money to get that message out."  In an attempt to further justify his spending of nearly $1 million on a campaign that he himself believed that no candidate should ever spend more than $150,000, Hechler said his money comes from royalties on three books he authored, his congressional and military pensions and that "[i]t is not from lobbyists."  He added that he would rather spend it on the race than "on the beach in Acapulco or something like that."[1275]

Prior to the 2004 Democratic Primary, Hechler sent a "Letter to the Editor" to newspapers throughout the State. He proclaimed:

> My April 2 campaign spending report confirms that I am spending over $400,000 for the primary nomination for secretary of state. Questions have been raised as to why, with name recognition, I am spending so much. In 1976, I left a safe seat in Congress because I wanted to shine a searchlight on the big spending of Jay Rockefeller in his race for governor. Rockefeller rolled over me like an Army tank. I finished a dismal third, and completely lost the opportunity to advocate campaign finance reform, which I had been championing in Congress. Then in 2000, I was way ahead in all polls in a race for Congress until Jim Humphreys unleashed his TV ads. Despite wide name recognition, I finished a dismal third.
>
> At the age of 89–17 years older than George Daugherty, more than twice the age of Natalie Tennant and Mike Oliverio, and 41 years older than Roger Pritt, I face a serious handicap. I must advertise to prove I am mentally and physically capable of handling the job.
>
> I have signed the Code of Fair Campaign Practices, which I designed as secretary of state, and included a spending limit of $150,000 for the secretary of state's office. In signing the code, I have noted "except for the spending limits."
>
> I have been labeled a 'hypocrite' for this action while I walked over 530 miles on behalf of campaign finance reform. I strongly support the state Clean Elections bill providing for public financing of elections. Like Sen. Russ Feingold, co-author of the McCain-Feingold campaign reform bill, who is raising more than $2 million for his re-election campaign, I believe that we can serve the cause of future campaign finance reform if we succeed in getting elected in 2004.[1276]

Hechler's Republican challenger, Betty Ireland, criticized him for spending more on his campaign than the spending limits he championed as Secretary of State. Ireland said, "You championed the fair campaign practices act . . . and it's almost as if you're saying, 'Do as I say, not as I do.' I have a real problem with the reformer attacking the reforms instead of seeing them through."[1277] Ironically, Ireland, who also criticized election officials for using taxpayer-paid-for trinkets for self-promotion, was admonished for that same behavior in 2006.

One area where Hechler has been given credit was his support in 1985 in getting a 300 foot limitation on how close campaigning can be to the voting precincts. The distance had previously been 60 feet and he argued that expanding the distance would reduce election fraud on the election grounds, would allow voters to vote freely without being harassed by paid campaign staffers, and would generally improve the entire election process. Following the May 13, 1986, Primary Election, he was given great praise for pushing for such a change in the election law as candidates, people campaigning for candidates, precinct captains, leafletters, or any campaign literature were prohibited to be within 300 feet of a polling place.[1278]

Limitations were also placed on the amount of money that is permitted to be paid to campaign workers such as drivers or volunteers and better defined which voters could be "assisted" at the voting booth, as well as who could "assist" them.[1279] Raymond Chafin, a former Logan County political boss, criticized the changes in the election process saying Hechler "took the fun out of [elections]." He explained that the 300 foot restriction made it more difficult to control the precincts which was the key to winning any race. The precinct captains were used to make sure voters were paid for their votes after election officers confirmed that those selling their votes filled out their ballots for the candidates for which they were paid to vote.[1280]

As United States Senator Robert C. Byrd has often said, "Money! It is money! Money! Money! Not ideas, nor principles, but money that reigns supreme in American politics." The fact is that without it you can't participate in West Virginia politics. And, there are only two ways to get it legally, spending your personal wealth or raising it by soliciting countless contributions in an attempt to challenge a potentially wealthy self-financed competitor.

If a non-wealthy candidate faces a multi-millionaire challenger who isn't afraid to spend his or her money then another problem necessarily exists. The problem is that the non-wealthy candidate is forced to spend countless hours on the telephone begging wealthy people to give them money in $1,000 increments–the State contribution limit–in order to simply compete. This, in turn, creates a bond with the wealthy donors that supersedes those of individuals who are unable to contribute to political campaigns. The result is that most West Virginia citizens are completely shut out of the political process. Then, even if elected, fundraising becomes a time thief as politicians spend many hours each day raising as much money as possible just to stay in office. Senator Byrd has said that legislators have become part-time legislators and part-time fundraisers and the lack of money weeds out good people and good talent from even getting involved in politics. It is a pay-to-play system in which principles and payments go hand in hand with donors' wishes.[1281]  Moreover, as much as major donors complain they hate the system, they like even less the possibility of losing their powerful voice in governmental decisions.

For instance, Charleston Attorney Thomas Potter, President Bush's co-finance chairman for West Virginia, felt he had a voice in State political appointments since he raised $200,000 for Bush's 2000 Presidential campaign. He called the choices for the United States Attorneys for the Northern and Southern Districts of West Virginia by the White House "outrageous." Potter believed his daughter, who worked as an Assistant United States Attorney in the Northern District, "was clearly the best candidate."[1282]  Can we reasonably assume that Potter felt his daughter should have been given the position since he raised so much money for the Republican Party?

In West Virginia, the people shouldn't feel they have to contribute large sums of money in order to participate in their system of government. The situation of money flowing into campaigns at a level equivalent to alcohol flowing to pubs after the repeal of prohibition in 1933 has made West Virginia elections a millionaires playground. No candidate for Governor should ever be put into a position where they are asking for millions of dollars in contributions for a job that pays $95,000. Furthermore, it is difficult to legitimize the actions of a candidate for the West Virginia State Senate spending more than $400,000 or a candidate for the West Virginia House of Delegates spending more than $100,000 in an election when both positions pay $15,000 per year.[1283]

By its very nature, democracy, despite all of its flaws, has the ability of self-correction. Unfortunately though, young people are becoming more and more distant from the system as they realize you cannot run and win without buckets of cash. Whether it is money buying influence from an elected official, buying votes or buying elections, or whether elected officials are buying votes and elections, money is the common theme. The influx of massive amounts of money into campaigns only discourages voters, candidates, and clean elections. Even former Governor Arch Moore was raking in illegal campaign donations presumably because he knew he faced a Rockefeller who could spend–and later did spend on two occasions–$12 million to win those elections. Wealthier people should not have a louder voice simply because they have more money.

When people talk about the power of the pen, they typically are referring to a newspaper's ability to effectuate change with its coverage of a story or through its editorials; however, to a politician in West Virginia, the power of the pen stands for the number of $1,000 checks that can be procured from wealthy individuals toward their campaign. Money is the conduit to votes. Groups contribute hundreds of thousands of dollars to garner favorable results with issues important to their interests. For instance, a chief executive officer of a large company cannot go to the board of directors to solicit hundreds of thousands of dollars and suggest that it be funneled through political action committees and given to specific candidates merely out of the benevolence of their nature.

The nexus between campaign contributions and public policy must be disengaged. If a lawyer handed each justice a $1,000 check just prior to an argument before the West Virginia Supreme Court, it summarily would be called a bribe. Nonetheless, when a lobbyist hands a key State legislator a check for $1,000 just prior to a big vote, that act is euphemistically considered a legitimate campaign contribution. Understandably, an average citizen may believe the message is that money buys elections, influence after the election, and, in some cases, that the entire office is sold or up for bid.

Equally true, the average West Virginia citizen–who has among the lowest average income in the country–would have to attend countless county fairs and festivals and wear out several pairs of tennis shoes to attempt to reach the same number of individuals as that of an opponent who can buy millions of dollars worth of television advertising. This lack of personal wealth or the existence of a large campaign account filled with high-dollar campaign contributions places a burden on a potential challenger that is more often than not insurmountable. Such realities further disenfranchise voters and potential candidates as many well-qualified potential candidates will never get involved in a system where they have to amass a fortune only for the *chance* to participate.

Moreover, this practice of buying elections through legal contributions and multi-million dollar personal expenditures is another reason entrenched incumbent politicians are so willing to spend millions of dollars from the State treasury from the Governor's Contingency Fund, the Budget Digest, and secret accounts to bolster their chances of getting re-elected even against a wealthy potential challenger. It is also precisely why these same incumbents freely distribute to voters millions of trinkets paid for with State money that prominently promote their names. Elected officials must stop spending people's hard-earned tax dollars on trinkets and wasted projects from State accounts solely for the purpose of re-election.

Kanawha County Circuit Judge and former Kanawha County Prosecuting Attorney Charlie King has been critical of elected officials using their office for personal gain to the detriment of West Virginia citizens. In reference to the large amounts of money spent by former Treasurer A. James Manchin on flags and other trinkets, King proclaimed: "You will find a lot of outrages in State government that the criminal code does not cover. The Legislature has failed to fill in the gaps. The only remedy the public has is when they go to the polls." When questioned as to why he didn't stop some of these payments for incumbent political expenditures, then-Commissioner of Finance and Administration and former West Virginia Supreme Court Justice John McCuskey said, "[Manchin] is elected by the people and you get what you *vote* for."[1284] More accurately, McCuskey should have simply said you get what you "*pay* for."

Obviously in West Virginia the For Sale sign is still posted, it is just that the price has gone up. Votes continue to be for sale to the highest bidder, but now, in addition to a pint of whiskey in some of the southern counties, it also takes millions of dollars raised from individual donors or simply spent by self-financed wealthy individuals for petty and superficial television advertising to buy someone's vote. This, of course, is in conjunction with millions of dollars of wasteful spending by State politicians on blatantly political expenditures of State money. The political system, because of the very nature of human beings, will be fallible. Nonetheless, it is time that West Virginians demand that the government be returned to the people as government should be available to all citizens and not simply to those who can pay for it.

# PART THREE

## THE ROAD TO REFORM

# CHAPTER EIGHTEEN

# Attempts and Obstacles to Reform

# The Ethics Commission and Statewide Prosecutorial Power

*The Ethics Commission is a sham. It has no teeth. It has no guts. It has become a rubber stamp of approval for unethical behavior. If the Legislature is not going to be serious about ethics, it should get rid of the agency.*

Charleston Daily Mail

In spite of corruption that has flourished since the State's very inception, the first Ethics Act in West Virginia's history didn't occur until 1989. It was my former boss, Governor Gaston Caperton, who successfully pushed the Legislature almost immediately after his inauguration to pass an Ethics Act due to "a string of legislators, governors and State administrators [who were] sent to prison."[1285] Caperton, who campaigned as a government outsider, appealed to voters "to recommit ourselves to ensuring that we never go back. The back-room, slipshod politics of the past must forever remain in the past."[1286] Caperton commandeered a courageous step against the establishment which it seemed had turned a blind eye to reform.

The *Charleston Gazette* said, "legislators had little choice but to pass the legislation, especially with new scandals in the news almost daily."[1287] The *Gazette* further explained:

> Several prominent corruption cases in the late 1980s helped lead to the passage of the 1989 ethics bill, according to Robert "Chuck" Chambers, the bill's sponsor and former Speaker of the House.

Two successive presidents of the state Senate were convicted on federal corruption charges for accepting money from lobbyists.

Former Senate President Larry Tucker pleaded guilty to accepting $10,000 from lobbyist Sammy D'Annunzio of Clarksburg. He reportedly tried to return the money, but D'Annunzio was cooperating with federal investigators and wore a tape recording device during the meeting.

Tucker's predecessor as Senate President, Dan Tonkovich, also pleaded guilty to extorting money from gambling and insurance interests.

In 1988, former Gov. Arch Moore was already accused of extortion, mail fraud and tax evasion, charges that would earn him a prison term in 1990. At the trial, Assistant U.S. Attorney Joseph Savage said, 'Let there be no mistake. Arch Moore is a criminal.'[1288]

Governor Caperton signed the historic ethics bill into law as State Senate President Larry Tucker stood beside him and posed for cameras. The *Charleston Daily Mail* explained later that, "For real sleaze, one must turn to former State Senate President Larry Tucker" who stood beside Caperton in support of reform even though within the year of the ethics bill signing he entered a plea with the United States Attorneys on a charge of extorting $10,000 from dog-track lobbyist William Ellis.[1289]

At the time of the Ethics Act's 1989 creation, the Ethics Commission had been granted powers of independent investigation and a $400,000 budget. From 1990 through 2005, however, the Ethics Commission could only rule on complaints it received, all at the same time being forced to operate on a reduced $290,000 budget. The Ethics Act was weakened almost immediately with a 1990 change in the law that made West Virginia and Florida the only States with an ethics panel lacking the power to initiate investigations or use anonymous tips to investigate wrongdoings. Not surprisingly, given the number of State Senators sent to jail during that time period, the 1990 weakening of the Ethics Commission's powers passed the Senate by a vote of 34-0. Moreover, due to its reduced budget, the Commission staff dropped from four full-time employees to two full-time staffers and one part-time assistant.[1290]

Specifically, the change in the Ethics Act, which successfully passed during the closing minutes of the 1990 legislative session, provided that the Commission was allowed to institute investigations *only* upon a verified complaint where a person was willing to openly sign his or her name to the complaint. Another stumbling block provided that if the allegations of any such complaint were found to be false, sanctions could be imposed upon the person filing the complaint. While the goal of this provision may have been to prevent vindictive filings, it clearly discouraged legitimate complaints because people fear retribution for their veracity from corrupt politicians who are rarely held accountable for their rotten behaviors.

The *Charleston Gazette* called the Commission "effectively hogtied" and said it had virtually turned into a "rubber stamp, approving almost every questionable action that comes before it."[1291] A legislative survey conducted in 1995 showed that 44 percent of the West Virginia Legislators favored legislation that would restore the Ethics Commission's power to initiate investigations of possible ethics violations. The poll revealed that 29 percent opposed the change in the ethics laws, with some of the legislators fearing political "witch hunts" while 27 percent of the legislators were undecided.[1292]

In 2005, following years of negative press coverage on the issue of West Virginia's weak and ineffectual ethics laws, Governor Joe Manchin, III proposed changes to the Ethics Act by introducing a bill during a special session that he called almost immediately after his inauguration. Manchin announced, "Working together with the Legislature, we will put in place a new code of ethics that will hold our officeholders, and all those entrusted to do the people's work, as well as all those receiving public funds, to the highest rules of professional conduct."[1293]

The bill passed both houses of the Legislature, but was amended to include a "gag order" making it illegal for people who submitted ethics complaints against public officials to talk about the complaint or even acknowledge they filed a complaint with the Ethics Commission. Even though the provision blatantly violated both the Constitutions of West Virginia and of the United States, Governor Manchin signed the bill on February 11, 2005, but pledged to introduce a new bill to remove the gag provision.[1294]

The gag order provision subjected violators to fines of up to $5,000 and even included a provision for dismissal of their complaint regardless of its validity. One Delegate, Charles Trump, IV (R-Morgan), told me he avidly supported ethics reform, but felt so strongly against the gag order provision that he voted against the bill. "This puts a muzzle on the citizens who have the right of free speech," he said. I agree completely with him. As far as the gag provision, you can't pass a law that says you can't speak to the press. I remember a certain State

Senator who, while in her first term in office, pushed for a law to force newspapers not only to print her press releases, but to print them verbatim regardless of length or content. It begs the question as to how some of the people making the laws can write legislation when they don't understand the basis for such legislation, the Constitution. Apparently some legislators have never understood that "Congress shall make no law . . . abridging the freedom of speech, or of the press."[1295]

Instead of signing a defective ethics bill, the Governor should have simply vetoed it. The only possible reason for not vetoing it–and I mean this with complete sarcasm–is that the Governor must have thought I needed more information for this book. What other possible reason could there have been to sign a clearly flawed and unconstitutional bill when legislators were beginning the regular session of the Legislature the following week and could have passed a constitutional bill? The bill restricted anyone who even had knowledge that a complaint had been filed, including the news media, from commenting on it publicly. West Virginia University Law School Professor Bob Bastrass, who specializes in First Amendment issues, called the gag order, "patently and incredibly unconstitutional."[1296]

The Legislature weakened Manchin's 2005 original ethics reform legislation in other ways, including removing a section from the bill that would have made it illegal for people to lie to the Ethics Commission. This provision was removed even though no action was taken against Delegate Jerry Mezzatesta for lying to the Commission in a well-publicized saga. In that case, the Commission said it was unable to do anything about lying under the Ethics Act because no such provision prevented lying to the Commission. The new bill did restore the Commission's power to launch an investigation without first receiving a citizen's sworn, signed complaint; however, it could only do so after the majority of a twelve-member commission *and* a unanimous vote from a newly created three-member Probable Cause Review Board agreed that a complaint warranted the filing of a formal ethics charge.

Day after day of negative publicity forced the Legislature to remove the gag order from the Ethics Act and instead, reinsert a provision making it illegal to provide false information to the Commission. Conversely though, the Legislature did reduce Governor Manchin's $1 million budget request for the West Virginia Ethics Commission to $700,000, leaving the Commission underfunded once again to properly carry out its powers. Initially, however, the House of Delegates had only agreed to a $500,000 budget for the Commission.

Ethics Commission Executive Director Lewis Brewer said that absent legislative action to increase the budget of the Commission by 2006, it "will have shrunk to the point where the agency will not be functional." The lack of funding for the Commission in the 2005 legislation amounted to nothing more than a systematic effort to weaken it. Conversely, House Judiciary Chairman Jon Amores (D-Kanawha) believes the Commission is fulfilling its duties and argues that success cannot be measured by the number of "scalps it gathers."[1297] In addition to money constraints, the revised ethics legislation didn't include any provision forcing legislators to reveal their real estate holdings or their spouses' assets making it sometimes impossible to determine when a conflict of interest exists surrounding legislation introduced or voted on by the individual legislators.[1298]

No changes in the Ethics Act, regardless of how they might appear on paper, will have any effect whatsoever when people are scared to actually bring a complaint. And, adding extra cumbersome layers of review before a complaint even gets to a point of any significant review is not helpful. The bottom line is that the public should be given all of the information available as soon as possible. The perfect example of why this is important surrounds the initial complaint against Delegate Mezzatesta. In spite of the overwhelming evidence that he violated the Ethics Act, the complaint against him was dropped by the Ethics Commission in 2004. It wasn't until constant scrutiny by newspapers regarding the situation that the Commission agreed to reopen the case and eventually found that Mezzatesta did violate the ethics laws. In fact, this was the *only* time in the Commission's history that it reopened a case.

Shutting down the voices of people and the media will only help an organization, which is funded and controlled by the Legislature, to sweep under the rug many viable complaints and indiscretions. In addition, a person who files a legitimate complaint that is later dismissed by the Commission, knows that given West Virginia's history of corruption it is conceivable that the person who was the subject of the complaint could seek retribution against them. I don't know of anybody, except maybe the actual members of the Commission, who has any faith in the Ethics Act or its enforcement.

The 2005 changes to the Act once again left a toothless tiger in place to enforce ethics violations by public officials. The debate itself highlighted the need for immediate and worthwhile reform particularly in consideration of the Legislature's tactic to hamper legitimate reform efforts by adding the gag order provision that included a fine of $5,000. Even though that specific provision was later changed it shows that some legislators obviously have something to hide and fear serious ethics investigations. Further evidence of this was the failure to include proper disclosure of assets as a requirement for elected officials. It is unbelievable that legislators don't have to disclose such financial information when doing so is a common practice in just about every democratic system in the world. The only reason to fight such disclosures so vehemently is because there must be numerous conflicts of interest by legislators unknown to the public.

The West Virginia Ethics Commission has become a joke throughout the country. A few years ago, the Washington-based Center for Public Integrity found that after nearly five years of existence, the Commission had not cited a single legislator for any ethical infraction. The group said that this "defie[d] imagination." The lapse in activity made the West Virginia Ethics Commission the "only such body in the nation that had not cited a legislator in the past five years."[1299] Unless the Legislature and Governor are serious about legitimate ethics enforcement, the entire Ethics Commission should be disbanded. It is disingenuous to the people of West Virginia to continue this charade.

The Governor should call a special session of the Legislature as soon as possible to deal with nothing but ethics reform. Everything should be placed on the table and openly debated. Among the changes should be the end to the practice of the free parties paid for by special interest groups during the legislative session. I have attended many of these functions during my years of working for various elected officials. I remember when I began working for Governor Caperton and within days of my employment a fellow employee handed me a list of legislative receptions and told me I needed to go to as many of them as possible to mingle with the legislators. As I befriended several veteran legislators that session, they ranked the receptions for me and told me which ones I had to attend because of the shrimp or some other food being served and which receptions I could miss if I had some-thing else to do that evening. The receptions are a well-entrenched part of the leg-islative session and seemed harmless to me at the time. After years of reflection and experience, however, the practice is clearly wrong and must be changed.

What happens, unbeknownst to most people in the public, is that after a day of legislative work, special interest groups provide large parties, usually at one of several Charleston hotels, where they often serve plenty of free food, drinks, provide entertainment, and sometimes furnish small gifts. The top ten receptions that occurred during the 2004 legislative session followed by the num-ber of legislative/government officials in attendance were as follows:

- West Virginia AFL-CIO, cost $22,300, attended 113
- West Virginia Business and Industry Council, cost $17,773, attended 150
- West Virginia Municipal League, cost $15,624, attended, 120
- West Virginia Coal Association, cost $15,076, attended 254
- West Virginia Hospitality and Travel Association, cost $11,515, attended 200
- Affiliated Construction and Trades Foundation, cost $8,085, attended 120
- West Virginia Beer Wholesalers, cost $4,813, attended 135

- West Virginia Home Builders Association, cost $6,310, attended 101
- West Virginia Insurance Federation, cost $6,237, attended 85
- West Virginia Trial Lawyers Association, cost $3,448, attended 70.[1300]

The problem is that these are closed door events put on solely by special interest groups and are only open to legislators, their staff members, and other high-ranking State officials and their employees. The result is that once again the average person is left out of a very influential part of the political process because they cannot afford to pay for an expensive reception to wine and dine legislators.

During the flawed ethics legislation debate in 2005, Senators Walt Helmick (D-Pocahontas) and Shirley Love (D-Fayette) introduced an amendment to outlaw these receptions hosted by lobbyists. Helmick said, "It takes on the appearance of a conflict of interest [and we] can do without the meals," while Senator Love asked, "If the bankers or Mountaineer Racetrack have receptions, don't you think they are trying to influence us? Why be hypocritical?" Conversely, Senator Truman Chafin (D-Mingo) said the amendment went too far in prohibiting a lawmaker from accepting dinner bought by a lobbyist. Chafin said, "This is a big economy for the State of West Virginia and the City of Charleston in particular [and] if you can be bought for a dinner, gee whiz. I don't see anything wrong in having dinner."[1301] The amendment failed and the receptions continue. If legislators are going to limit the appearance of impropriety then the policy of freebies must be strengthened. In that same light, even though legislators are given a daily meal allowance, many of their evening meals, separate from the food provided at the receptions, are actually paid for by lobbyists which amounts to double-dipping by collecting money from the State for a meal which is actually paid for by a lobbyist.

Even the Legislature's interim meetings are subject to public questions due to the legislative perks provided at all non-Charleston interim meetings which are sponsored by businesses and special interest groups. For example, in August 2003, the Legislature held its three-day interim session at the Glade Springs Resort in Raleigh County. According to the *Charleston Daily Mail*: "Attending lawmakers and guests each received a gift bag brimming with trinkets and promotions from local establishments."[1302] During a three-day legislative meeting, Glade Springs Resort, near Beckley, West Virginia, spent nearly $50,000 for meals, receptions and entertainment for the legislative attendees. Of the $50,000 spent to entertain and feed legislators, about $45,000 of that was provided by thirty-one sponsors, including major lobbying groups. The sponsorships, which included $5,000 for "Gold Sponsors," $2,500 for "Silver Sponsors," $1,000 for "Bronze Sponsors," and $500 for "Contributing Sponsors," were defended by Jim Holthaus, executive director of the Southern West Virginia Convention and Visitors Bureau. Holthaus said that without the sponsorships, the Beckley area could not have hosted the interim meetings on such an elaborate scale as "[i]t meant we were able to have barbecue ribs at the cookout instead of pinto beans." Holthaus added, "We really feel we showed them a good time, and gave them a good idea of what's going on here in southern West Virginia."[1303]

According to *Charleston Gazette* Reporter Phil Kabler:

> For sponsors, the contributions bought access to legislative breakfasts, lunches and dinners, receptions and other events that were off-limits to those without the proper identification tags. Name-badge-required events included a dinner and welcome reception Sunday at the Glade Springs clubhouse, a Theatre West Virginia presentation Sunday, a barbecue cookout at Winterplace Ski Resort on Monday, as well as breakfast and lunch Monday and Tuesday at the Glade Springs conference center, and a hospitality tent open until 2 a.m. each night.

Nelson Robinson, a long-time legislative lobbyist with various clients, objected to the Glade Springs interim organizers soliciting sponsorships from lobbyists and lobbying organizations, and restricting access to those who did not contribute. Robinson said, "I just think it's wrong [and] I was adamantly opposed to any of my clients supporting any interim events." He added, "It was clear if you weren't a sponsor you weren't going to be a participant." Ethics Commission Executive Director Lew Brewer said nothing in the State ethics law prohibited the "sponsors of the Beckley interims from soliciting contributions from lobbyists, or from restricting access at receptions and other events to legislators, legislative staff and official sponsors."[1304]

During the time period surrounding the first ethics legislation in 1989, the *Charleston Daily Mail* wrote: "The TV show, 'I Love The 80s,' may be popular on VH-1, but when West Virginians look back upon that decade, they wince. Elected officials rented themselves to the highest bidder. Federal prosecutors finally succeeded in putting away a Governor, two State Senate Presidents and several lesser officials." The *Daily Mail* also said, "Since its inception, the Commission has devolved into a group that offers the Good Housekeeping Seal of Approval to behavior that is not only unethical, but should be illegal."

In fact, between its formation in 1989 and June 21, 2004, the Ethics Commission had received nearly 250 complaints. Nonetheless, in only twenty-five cases did the Commission reprimand or fine a public official for a violation as it ruled more than 90 percent of the time in favor of the public official.[1305]  To put it another way "in its fifteen-year existence, the State Ethics Commission has meted out punishment to small town mayors and courthouse politicians, handing offenders small fines and slaps on the wrist."[1306]  The *Daily Mail* further wrote: "The Ethics Commission is a sham.  It has no teeth.  It has no guts.  It has become a rubber stamp of approval for unethical behavior.  If the Legislature is not going to be serious about ethics, it should get rid of the agency."[1307]  Delegate Mitch Carmichael (R-Jackson) agreed saying, "We need to just get rid of that Ethics Commission.  Just get rid of it."[1308]

Kanawha County Commissioner Kent Carper, who brought two ethics complaints against fellow county officials only to have both dismissed without any action, said, "I want to say something nice about the Ethics Commission.  I'm trying to think here.  Maybe it's not their fault.  Maybe it could be that the Legislature just doesn't want anybody to police them.  Maybe their authority is watered down.  Nah.  I just think they're useless."  Kanawha County School Board member Pete Thaw expressed his disagreement with an ethics ruling that allowed fellow board member Becky Jordon to cast the deciding vote giving a contract to a company in which her family owned stock.  Thaw said, "That Ethics Commission has never seen a violation, have they?  Thank goodness they didn't take the Abraham Lincoln assassination."[1309]

While the twelve-member ethics panel did prohibit the Mayor of Charles Town from using city employees to pave his driveway, the Mayor of Richwood from making long-distance personal calls on city phones, and the Mayor of Anmoore from owning a business that sold items to the town, the *only* State law-makers the Commission rebuked as of the date of this publication, were former Delegate Ray Keener, who in 2002 mentioned his position in the Legislature on advertising for his law practice, and Delegate Mezzatesta, who solicited money for his employer in spite of an agreement with the Commission not to do so.[1310]

It is equally clear that many of the decisions of the Ethics Commission have been the subject of statewide discussion and frustration.  For example, State Republicans argued that a 2001 Ethics Opinion improperly allowed Senate Education Chairman Robert Plymale (D-Wayne) to become director of the Nick Joe Rahall, II Appalachian Transportation Institute at Marshall University.  The underlying issue was that the West Virginia Constitution prohibits employees of the state, federal government, or any foreign government from serving in the Legislature.  Then-State GOP Executive Director Gary Abernathy said Plymale's position was a clear violation because Plymale was either a state employee since he reported directly to Marshall University President Dan Angel, or a federal employee because the Institute draws about half of its funding from the United States Department of Transportation.[1311]

Nonetheless, the 2001 Ethics Opinion concluded that nothing in the State ethics law prevented Plymale from serving as the Institute's director, as long as he made "every effort to avoid taking official legislative action on matters which uniquely affected the university." In spite of the Commission's ruling, Senate Health and Human Resources Chairman Roman Prezioso (D-Marion) inquired as to whether politics influenced the way the Higher Education Policy Commission distributed an additional $9 million of higher education bond funds in 2004. Prezioso was critical of Plymale's dual roles stating, "He answers to Dan Angel [the President of Marshall University]. That's who sets his schedule, who approves his leave [and] that's where he gets his paycheck."[1312]

More recently, the Commission was heavily criticized for its June 4, 2004, ruling dismissing two ethics complaints against Delegate Jerry Mezzatesta (D-Hampshire). In one complaint Mezzatesta, then-House of Delegates Education Chairman, accepted pay for his legislative work while at the same time he accepted his salary for his position as a community specialist for the Hampshire County Schools. The second complaint alleged he used his power to steer a $70,000 grant to his home county even though he promised the Commission in 1999 he would not use his job in the Legislature to solicit funding for his position with the Hampshire County Board of Education. The *Charleston Gazette* maintained: "This fiasco shows that the Commission is useless, and should be abolished."[1313] The problems of the Ethics Act are further illustrated by Ethics Commission Executive Director Lewis Brewer's comment that "it would not be a violation of anything under the Ethics Act to lie to the Commission under oath."[1314]

Another incident untouched by the Ethics Commission occurred in 2003 when State House of Delegates Finance Chairman Harold Michael (D-Hardy) owned 4,756 shares of Summit Financial Group stock worth $168,000 that gained in value due to an act of the Legislature. In September 2003, the *Charleston Gazette* asserted, "It's troublesome that a bank in which Michael owns stock stands to benefit from a $1 million State economic development grant." The *Gazette* was referring to the fact that Summit Financial wanted to sell its old Moorefield, West Virginia building and move into a new headquarters. Then, instead of selling the old property through the private market, the Hardy County Rural Development Authority bought Summit's former office building for $1 million, paying half the price with its own funds and borrowing the other half from Summit. Then, it sought a $1 million State grant to recoup all of its investment. The *Gazette* wrote:

Is it worth $1 million to West Virginia taxpayers to prevent seven federal jobs from moving across a county line? Because of Delegate Michael and Hardy [County's] appointee to the State grant committee, Mallie Combs-Snider, this deal smacks of home cooking.

Maybe Michael had no direct involvement in funneling State funds to the bank in which he owns stock. However, it reinforces the cynical public view that those with political connections always win.[1315]

In February 2006, Michael resigned as a member of Summit's Board after his fellow Board members refused to investigate fraud allegations against the contractor who built their new headquarters as well as Michael's new six-bay garage. Michael sent the Board a letter in August 2005 asking for an independent investigation of Hinzman Construction because he suspected the construction company was using materials bought by Summit to build his personal garage project. On February 10, 2006, following Michael's push for an investigation, Summit's Board of Directors did not nominate Michael for re-election to the Board. That same day, Michael resigned saying he hoped the Board members would seek answers to questions that were "potentially real problems to the integrity of Summit Bank itself." Conversely, Summit officials said it declined to keep Michael on the Board because he did not support its decision to enter the insurance business due to the fact that Michael is an insurance agent and the competition could hurt his business. While Michael said he did not think it was right for a bank to try to sell insurance to its customers, he believed the real reason he wasn't asked to stay on the Board was due to his questioning of Hinzman Construction.[1316]

Michael was also criticized for the creation of Eastern West Virginia Community and Technical College (hereinafter "Eastern College") in his home county. The *Gazette* said:

In 1999, he started the State Eastern West Virginia Community and Technical College in his home county–with Budget Digest money without a vote in the Legislature, and despite the presence of college campuses in nearby Petersburg, Keyser and Shepherdstown. Thus he created a new headache for West Virginia taxpayers to support–while the State's legitimate higher education institutions are being ordered to make drastic budget cuts.[1317]

In creating Eastern College, Michael used $4 million from the State Budget Digest "to launch an unneeded community college in Hardy County–just 10 miles from a Shepherd University branch and not far from Potomac State." The *Gazette* said, "Michael's school–just minutes away from two long-established colleges, Shepherd and Potomac State–wasn't needed in the first place. Now it is gobbling a lion's share of State funds. This isn't higher education, it's higher politics." The editorial was referring to the fact that even though Eastern College had only 400 students, it was going to receive $8 million from a $172 million higher education bond issue, while West Virginia State University, which had 5,000 students, was going to receive $1.35 million.[1318]

More recently, in August 2004, then-State Senator Mike Ross (D-Randolph) was under investigation for voting on legislation that benefitted a golf course with State money after he personally financed its purchase in 2001.[1319] The main issue was that Senator Ross failed to disclose his financial interests in the Pete Dye Golf Course before voting for a $750,000 State grant for a golf tournament to be held there. He helped pass the bill in March 2004 providing the $750,000 to help promote the July 2004 Inaugural Pete Dye West Virginia Classic in Bridgeport, West Virginia. The money provided by the Legislature also funded tournament prizes and television coverage for the four-day golf tournament.[1320] According to the *Charleston Daily Mail*:

> Through his oil and gas company, Ross and a friend helped the family of Clarksburg coal operator James D. LaRosa buy the golf course in 2001 by loaning them $7.69 million.

> In exchange, Ross and I.L. Morris enjoy free and unlimited access to the golf course and club, including its restaurant, bar and pro shop. Ross also received eight free club memberships, each worth about $15,000.[1321]

The Ethics Act requires disclosure of most loans greater than $12,500 and requires disclosure of gifts worth more than $500 from non-family members. Ross, however, did not list the loan on his annual financial disclosure form. The Ethics Commission's investigative panel found probable cause that he violated ethics law and announced that it would set a full hearing on the charges. In finding probable cause, the panel held that he should not have voted on the bill because a "corporation in which he is the principal shareholder, Mike Ross, Inc., has a $7.7 million loan outstanding to the owners of the golf course property. The company also owns about 170 acres of property adjacent to the course."[1322]

Ethics Commission lawyer Teresa Kirk said Ross' interest in the club stands out because of his loan, land, and perks. She said the exposure from the tournament brought prestige and name recognition to the Pete Dye Golf Club which, in turn, should help the club financially and benefit Ross.[1323]

The August 5, 2004, ethics charge filed by West Virginia Citizen Action Group (CAG) also stated that Ross' company owns land along or near the golf course. Scott Finn, a reporter for the *Charleston Gazette*, said, "Property records show Mike Ross, Inc. and Glenville businessman Ike Morris together own almost 150 acres at the resort, which includes the golf course, a county club, and land for vacation homes."[1324] CAG Executive Director Norm Steenstra said, "Ross deceived his colleagues [as] most of the people did not know when they voted for that bill, the interest he had in this."[1325] Steenstra said West Virginia has an ethics crisis in the Legislature and due to the weakness of the ethics law, "[t]he worst that can happen to [Senator Ross] for protecting an $8 million investment is a $1,000 fine."[1326] In fact, according to the Ethics Commission, if Ross would have been found guilty of a violation, the most he could have received was a public reprimand from the Commission and fine of up to $1,000. Steenstra added, "The Legislature has got to clean itself up. No one else can do it, outside of perhaps the U.S. Attorney."[1327]

Then-State Republican Party Chairman Kris Warner called Ross' vote on the tournament "shocking" and said, "There is a continuing pattern of this behavior by our legislators. To use your public office for public gain is the height of arrogance." Ross, who owns and operates an oil and gas business, said he saw no conflict of interest in voting for the money for the tournament. He said, "It's no more than teachers voting on a salary increase, or me voting on an oil or gas interest. It's a class interest, not a personal interest." The *Charleston Gazette* responded: "Exactly. All those conflicts by legislators are undesirable."[1328] Ross also said, "I've already apologized to everybody in the State for voting for it, not because it's a bad project, but because it created the presumption I was going to make a lot of money and that's not true at all," adding, "It's just part of the political game and I've been through it before. . . . We'll weather the storm and keep on going."[1329] Ross told the Ethics Commission hearing that he did not benefit from the $800,000 in State money ($750,000 from the State Tourism Promotion Fund and $50,000 from the Governor's Contingency Fund) that went to the July tournament, which received nationwide exposure on the Golf Channel. "Mike Ross didn't benefit from the tournament. West Virginia did," he said.[1330]

The financial disclosure of the State's contribution to help underwrite the tournament shows the biggest chunks of State funding went toward the tournament purse ($335,000 of the $600,000 in total prizes) and to underwrite the costs of broadcasting the tournament on the Golf Channel ($132,000). Other expenses paid through State grants included:

> Advertising: television advertising, $14,300; radio advertising, $10,666; print advertising, $45,967; media day, $446 (obviously, only a portion of the total cost, since any sportswriters worth their salt would go through more than $446 of food and beverages in one sitting); and Board of Parks & Recreation, $1,500. Operating expenses: Administrative staff salaries, $43,582; sponsorship development and marketing, $2,339; equipment/furniture, $6,456; postage, $2,227; and telephone, $375. Tournament operating expenses: Tournament sponsor implementation (pro-am tournament), $58,202; tenting–JV Chujko, $78,596; roping–T-Works, $9,000; portable office–Pac-Van, $2,907; Fibernet, $4,876; Waste Management, $6,000; Central Cab tours, $7,420; copier rental, $1,691; and electrical set-up, $461; Printing, $19,143; and tournament signage, $16,841.[1331]

On April 7, 2005, after completing its investigation, the Ethics Commission, ignoring its investigative panel's finding of probable cause, dismissed the complaint and found that Senator Ross didn't "directly or indirectly gain" from his vote to give a State allocation of $750,000 to the golf course in spite of his clear financial ties to the course. With regard to Ross' adjoining property, Administrative Law Judge Katherine Dooley said, "It was the position of the Commission that as a result of the golf tournament coming to the Pete Dye course, the property in close proximity to the course would increase in value and perhaps developers might become interested in the property and as a result Mike Ross, Inc. and others might reap a financial windfall. . . . These arguments are speculative and full of supposition."[1332]

I know Mike Ross personally and have been to his house for his annual picnic on a couple of occasions. He has treated me with nothing but kindness and respect throughout the years. I have even worked with or formed friendships with other members of his family and have valued those friendships. A situation like this one illustrates the difficulty in writing a book about West Virginia politics. It is a small State with a finite number of politicians and politically involved people. The result is that everybody knows everybody in one way or another if they are involved in State politics to any degree.

Nonetheless, when I think about this situation and others like it, it makes me believe that the bar has been dropped so low, and politicians have operated under these same virtually non-existent rules for so many years, that many politicians truly don't see any conflicts with their actions even when they appear blatantly obvious to the average person. In this case, as hard as it may be to believe, I guess it is possible that Mike may not have seen a conflict in this particular vote because this is just normal West Virginia politics. Politicians routinely vote on laws that affect them personally and in most cases, since West Virginia doesn't have adequate requirements in place to report the financial assets of politicians or their spouses, the public rarely even knows about most of the actual or perceptive conflicts. Under these specific facts though, any non-West Virginia politician operating under real world rules with real world consequences would look at this case and determine there was something clearly amiss. This ruling, coupled with its handling of Delegate Mezzatesta's case, are glaring examples of the uselessness of the Ethics Commission and why its very existence should be thoroughly examined unless significant changes are enacted.

Another example occurred in 2005 when Senator Karen Facemyer (R-Jackson) was charged with wrongly reporting her mileage from her home to the State Capitol, allowing her to avoid paying federal taxes on more than $99,000 in reimbursed expenses when she attends legislative meetings in Charleston. She also received approximately $2,000 more than she was entitled to by exaggerating the distance of her commute to the Capitol. In 1995, Facemyer, even though her residence hadn't changed, increased her mileage on expense forms from 45 miles to 52 miles, to take advantage of a little-known section of the federal tax code that exempts State legislators from paying taxes on reimbursed expenses as long as they live more than fifty miles from a State's Capitol building.

When a *Charleston Gazette* reporter drove to and from Facemyer's home, it was recorded as a distance of forty miles. Delegate Mitch Carmichael, also from Jackson County, lives forty-six miles from the Capitol and reports his reimbursements as income on his taxes. He said, "It adds up. You have to pay taxes if you're under fifty miles. That's the rules. We all ought to play by the same rules." Facemyer, however, even though she admits overstating the mileage and shorting the IRS, said, "We're pushing five, ten miles here tops, we're swallowing a camel and gagging on a gnat. I can't help but believe this is a witch-hunt on somebody's part. You can ask three-fourths of the people out here [in the senate]. Lying's not my thing."[1333] Facemyer admitted that she misreported her mileage, however she said it wasn't intentional. She further said she was unsure whether or not she took advantage of the tax exemption which was available to legislators. Nonetheless, records from the Senate payroll office showed that she signed and submitted five forms requesting the tax break each year since 2001. Senate Minority Leader Vic Sprouse said, "You're talking about seven miles. That's pretty ridiculous."[1334]

Apparently the Ethics Commission agreed that the situation was "pretty ridiculous" and "gagging on a gnat" because it dismissed an ethics complaint filed against Senator Facemyer. The Commission found that Facemyer didn't violate the ethics rules by wrongly reporting her mileage and failing to pay income tax on $99,000 in income and receiving additional money she wasn't entitled to from the State coffers due to her incorrect reporting of that income. Wanda Carney, who filed the complaint against Facemyer in April 2005, said the Ethics Commission was outrageous and has given a green light to State employees to exaggerate mileage. Carney said, "If exaggerating your mileage is not wrong, then I need to stop filing ethics complaints."[1335] What a mockery the Commission has become on the citizens of West Virginia. It is nothing more than a joke.

With those and many of the other occurrences in mind, it is easy to conclude that stronger State laws regulating elected officials must be enacted. For example, with regard to financial disclosure laws making basic information public with regard to legislators' income, assets, and potential conflicts of interest, West Virginia ranked forty-third in the nation according to a September 2004 report by the non-profit, non-partisan, Center for Public Integrity. The report gave West Virginia a grade of "F" for disclosing lawmakers' outside ties. The report also found that West Virginia had nearly twice the national average of legislators who were employed by other governmental entities and that 42 percent of lawmakers served on committees that oversaw their personal business interests.[1336]

The report concluded that West Virginia had weak mechanisms for disclosing potential conflicts such as legislators' clients, real estate holdings, positions on corporate boards, or their spouses' investments. In turn, the lack of disclosure offers many opportunities for legislators to boost their own fortunes or those of their employers. Disclosure laws require lawmakers to disclose information to the public regarding employment income and financial assets. Charles Lewis, the Center for Public Integrity's Director, said, "You've just let the fox into the henhouse, potentially. I'm not saying it always happens that way. We have an entrenched class of legislators at the State level that is often forgotten. Occasionally checking the landscape is healthy to a democracy."[1337]

The slippery slope of ethics in West Virginia politics has also extended to the constant need to raise money for election or re-election. The *Charleston Gazette* asks "whether the corruption that permeated the Statehouse [in the past] remains now, cloaked in legality. Have bags of cash merely been replaced with legal donations, fundraisers, receptions and other methods of gaining favor with politicians?" It added that the current structure of funding campaigns may be every bit as corrupting and damaging to the political system as the bags of cash carried to the Legislature in 1974 when a group of mine inspectors wanted a raise. It continues:

> Today they host a reception for lawmakers. They contribute generously to a campaign. They use money to build relationships with lawmakers that give them access to influence legislation–often in ways detrimental to the general good. Ordinary citizens, or citizen group lobbyists who lack deep pockets, are left out in the cold.[1338]

According to the *Gazette*, the mine inspectors gave a brown paper bag filled with cash in 1974 to the chairman of the House Finance Committee and asked him to deliver it to Delegate T.J. Scott, who sponsored legislation to increase their salaries.[1339] Instead, the money was given to then-House Speaker Lewis McManus, who, in turn, demanded a meeting with the mine inspectors.[1340] The mine inspectors admitted that the payment was intended for Delegate Scott and didn't think they had done anything wrong. In fact, even after Speaker McManus admonished the group for their actions, at the end of the meeting they asked, "What about our raise?" The House of Delegates Rules Committee reprimanded Delegate Scott for "irresponsible actions." Nonetheless, Delegate Scott remained in office for another six years and was never charged with any violation of law.[1341]

The passage of the Ethics Act in 1989, however, didn't put an end to situations like that of the mine inspectors. Moreover, while the Ethics Commission exists today, it operates without significant authority and even places limits on its own power. For instance, in 2002, it reversed itself on a decision that had originally made a provision of the ethics law stronger. Initially, it had issued an Opinion that would have prevented a member of a public body from seeking business from that body until at least six months after the person is no longer a member. The Commission later reversed itself yet again, saying, "It was difficult to determine lawmakers' intentions."[1342]

Weak and ineffectual responses to ethical complaints seem to be the norm rather than the exception with regard to the Commission's actions in enforcing the Ethics Act. In 2001, the Putnam County Assessor was fined $1,000 for placing a peach logo on official county vehicles, publications, and uniforms of staff members. The Commission found that Assessor D.W. "Peachie" Arthur violated the Ethics Act by including the logos, which parodied his campaign signs, on the Assessor's Office property.

The Commission's order, however, found that the employees could continue to wear the uniforms with the peach logo but that any replacement uniforms should not be purchased with the peach logo. The complaint filed with the Commission alleged that Arthur used the peach logos for private gain in an attempt to promote his re-election. Lewis Brewer, lawyer for the Ethics Commission, said, "When you put the peaches on all of these things that are subsidized by the taxpayers, and then use it on campaign signs, it's all part of a grand scheme to benefit yourself." In turn, Arthur said his logo is not any different from governors putting their pictures on State road maps and added, "I don't feel I did anything unethical." In 2004, "Peachie" Arthur was easily re-elected.[1343]

Arthur may actually be correct that his actions weren't much different from those of other State and county officials; however, they were still clearly inappropriate. His situation highlights two glaring problems with West Virginia politics. The first surrounds yet another flawed Ethics Commission response to a clear violation of State law. I guess I should jump for joy that they even did anything, but the result of their limited action leaves me once again disappointed. While the Commission did fine Arthur, it still allowed his employees to wear the blatantly political uniforms until they "wear them out" which could take years. That really doesn't make a bit of sense to me. The convoluted result is that, "yes, it's wrong and clearly in violation of West Virginia law, but go ahead and do it anyway, day after day, year after year, until the clothing wears beyond repair. Then, just don't do it again."

I have worked enough political campaigns to know that the only person who benefitted from this decision was Peachy Arthur because his minuscule $1,000 fine allowed him to continue to advertise his name at the taxpayers' expense possibly for several more years in spite of the Commission's finding that such conduct was unethical. Clearly, $1,000 for years of advertising his name on employee uniforms is a better rate than he would have received had he bought even one billboard in one location of the county which could have cost more than $1,000 for just a single month. Peachy Arthur wins and once again West Virginians lose. And, even the fine imposed on Arthur was less than the $1,354 in taxpayer money spent to buy the "peachy" uniforms. That doesn't include the taxpayers' cost for the peaches that turned ordinary vehicles into giant moving billboards or county stationery with no other purpose than garnering name recognition.

The second major problem surrounding the Arthur situation is akin to so many other West Virginia politicians' blatantly corrupt behaviors, highlighting the everybody else does it so why are you picking on me attitude. My taxes are high enough without the tax assessor spending my tax money on self-promotional items just so that I might remember his name during the next election. Again, my dad was the Tucker County Assessor years ago, and when I told him about Arthur's conduct, he just shook his head and said, "Are you really surprised? He is just another example of what is wrong with this State's politics." He added, "It is difficult to get mad at one outrageous situation anymore because he is just one in a long list of bad actors who have and continue to corrupt West Virginia's politics. Having been elected by the people of my county to do a job for them, a job which I took very seriously, it saddens me to learn about other assessors and county and State officials who have spit in the faces of the people who placed their trust in them."

Arthur should have been fined, but the action against him shouldn't have stopped there. He should have also been investigated for the misappropriation of State and county money. Then, if convicted, instead of a small fine, he should have been forced to pay for the costs of replacing all of the improper and unethical logos on the shirts, vehicles, and publications. He should have then been removed from office and placed in jail. How else will elected officials realize that there are consequences for their actions?

In addition to significant reform to the Ethics Commission, efforts to criminally prosecute public officials for violating the State's laws must be significantly improved. One of the most predominant factors impeding effective State prosecution of corruption is that the West Virginia State Attorney General, along with the fifty-five county prosecuting attorneys, lack statewide prosecutorial authority. The primary function of the Attorney General is to render Opinions, provide advice, and represent the State in all criminal appeals and civil suits, thus, criminal prosecutions are left to the individual county prosecutors who are elected in county elections to four-year terms and are not equipped to handle such prosecutions.[1344] Thus, as the law stands today, virtually the only way a criminal state politician gets indicted, arrested, or convicted of a crime, is through the United States Attorney's enforcement of federal criminal laws.

Former Speaker of the West Virginia House of Delegates and current Federal District Judge for the Southern District Court of West Virginia, Chuck Chambers, believes the State Attorney General's Office should be given criminal prosecutorial powers. Chambers cites the lack of such power in the Attorney General's Office as a reason that State corruption prosecutions have been limited.[1345] Moreover, former West Virginia Congressman and Secretary of State Ken Hechler is a proponent of delegating prosecutorial power to the Attorney General in vote fraud and corruption cases. Hechler said the county prosecuting attorneys can't be counted on to enforce election laws because they are frequently "a part of the system."[1346] During a campaign stop in Williamson in 1984, he announced that he intended to enforce the voting laws "without fear or favor" to which he and Mingo County Democratic Chairman Johnnie Owens, who was later convicted for election fraud violations, entered into an altercation. Owens, who had considerable control over Mingo County elections, was openly upset with Hechler's attempts of reform.

The *Charleston Gazette* has also recognized the need for the Attorney General to have prosecutorial powers. It criticized a 1982 West Virginia Supreme Court Opinion which limited the Attorney General's power to review contracts "as to form" even it suspects criminal wrongdoing. The *Gazette* maintains:

> The attorney general should be able to question a contract that may be unconstitutional or have been illegally awarded. He or she should be able to blow the whistle on a bureaucrat who is betraying the trust of the citizens. The attorney general should be able to initiate investigations into corruption in the Statehouse. West Virginia's attorney general can do none of these, and the State suffers because of it.[1347]

Both the Attorney General and prosecuting attorneys would face fiscal considerations even if they had authority. The Attorney General must survive within the confines of a budget set by the West Virginia Legislature, while a county prosecuting attorney must live within the restrains of a budget set by their county commission. With constant financial difficulties at both the State and county levels, it is easy to imagine how investigations would become nonexistent. Moreover, corrupt politicians controlling the budget of the person who could use that money to investigate them creates a separate problem. Thus, any newly created enforcement efforts must be adequately funded by the State Legislature.

Realistic enforcement efforts by county prosecutors are necessarily limited with regard to statewide elected officials violating the law. A county prosecuting attorney is responsible for the prosecution of all crimes committed within the boundaries of their county including murder, kidnapping, arson, rape, robbery, sexual assault, and intoxication offenses. In addition, many of the county prosecutors in West Virginia only work part-time and thus, they supplement their incomes by maintaining a private civil practice on the side. Moreover, corruption investigations are both costly and time consuming and it is unrealistic that a prosecuting attorney could sacrifice the necessary amount of time to develop the expertise to pursue public corruption investigations or that he or she could get approval from their respective county commissions to fund such a prosecution. County prosecuting attorneys also face additional procedural limitations as many of the crimes occur in multiple counties and even beyond the State's border.

It is therefore the Attorney General's Office which must be given specific legal authority, as well as provided sufficient funding, to investigate and prosecute political corruption charges. Perhaps the largest hurdle to prosecutorial authority has been a long line of questionable behaviors, resignations, and even convictions of past Attorneys General. For instance, only four people served as Attorney General from 1957 through 1989 in West Virginia. Two of the four were convicted on bribery related scandals, a third resigned in disgrace to avoid prosecution, and the fourth pleaded his Fifth Amendment right to remain silent in front of a federal grand jury investigating bribery in State government.

Thus, the grant of prosecutorial power to the Attorney General will not curb corrupt activity overnight. Instead, such a grant will only be truly effective when combined with the many other reforms necessary to cleanup West Virginia elections that I set forth in my reform chapter. For instance, prosecutorial authority is useless without stronger laws sending the message that illicit behavior will no longer be tolerated. Moreover, realistic reform of the police and prosecutors is imperative to any successful reform because increasing the authority of the Attorney General and other state, federal, and local law enforcement authorities is not always popular since people often don't trust those in power to be ethical.

Perhaps a major stumbling block to granting such prosecutorial power is that people in West Virginia have read story after story about corrupt government actors including the prosecutors and cops who enforce the laws. For instance, newspaper stories have covered the significant impact of the United States Attorney's role in cracking down on election violators since the State Attorney General is without authority to do so. Then, however, they read about someone like Paul A. Billups, an Assistant United States Attorney from 1989 to 1996 who allegedly seduced a witness, Kelly Jones, to influence her testimony in an accident case while he was in private practice representing an insurance company. In that case, Billups made a confidential settlement with Jones after she learned that Billups, who posed as a divorced man, was actually married.[1348] In a separate situation, the firing of United States Attorney Kasey Warner in 2005 was another example of the shattered trust West Virginians feel toward those enforcing the laws. Equally troubling was the March 2006 arrest of John Canterberry, Secretary of State Betty Ireland's former chief election fraud investigator, who was charged with embezzling $10,650 from a Christian television station.

In another example, John A. Field, III, a former United States Attorney for the Southern District of West Virginia from 1972 to 1977 and top enforcement officer of the Commodity Futures Trading Commission from 1977 to 1980, pled guilty to racketeering and conspiracy charges in a telemarketing plot that bilked so-called investors out of more than $80 million. Field had been highly regard-ed as a prosecutor, "who won national attention and a reputation for integrity in 1975 when he obtained an indictment of Arch A. Moore, Jr., the Governor of West Virginia on conspiracy and corruption charges."[1349]

With regard to the State's highest law enforcement officials, in 1993, the Supreme Court of Appeals of West Virginia discovered that a forensic serologist for the West Virginia State Police systematically falsified his reports. As a result, the Court ordered new trials in all cases in which his testimony had a material effect on the verdict. It held that the misconduct was so pervasive that on appeal, the corrupt officer's testimony could be treated as false in each prior case.[1350]

The former head serologist of the State Police Crime Laboratory who falsified the test results in as many as 134 cases from 1979 to 1989 was Fred Zain. Several wrongly convicted people, often for rape or murder, later exonerated, were sentenced to long prison terms based upon Zain's false testimony. The Court held that "as a matter of law, any testimonial or documentary evidence offered by Zain at any time in any criminal prosecution should be deemed invalid, unreliable, and inadmissi-ble." It also cited in its findings that these were "shocking and egregious viola-tions," and that his actions were a "corruption of our legal system."[1351] The *Charleston Gazette* professes:

> NOTHING is more sacred than the principle of trustworthy jus-tice. Lives are at stake. When society sends a criminal suspect to prison, the public needs to feel sure that the evidence was accurate and the outcome was as fair as possible.
>
> That's why the Fred Zain scandal was so horrifying. The for-mer State Police crime lab chief falsified test results to help obtain convictions, putting innocent men in prison on rape charges. When DNA tests proved their innocence, taxpayers coughed up millions to pay for false imprisonment.[1352]

The Zain saga produced numerous cases in which individuals were con-victed of violent crimes and were sent to prison based on Zain's testimony regard-ing scientific evidence. One such individual successfully sued and received a $1 million settlement from the State of West Virginia for incorrectly sending him to prison.[1353] Another inmate released was Bernard Wallace, who was convicted in 1983 for attempted aggravated robbery largely based on testimony from Zain. On September 12, 2003, McDowell County Circuit Judge Booker Stephens set aside Wallace's conviction. McDowell County Prosecutor Sid Bell did not oppose Wallace's petition to set aside the verdict after reading a transcript of Zain's testimony in the trial. Wallace said, "It's been twenty years that I've been fighting this [and] I'm not angry at the prosecutor or the judge[,] I'm bitter that the system took so long."[1354]

Questions surfaced whether a private law firm, Steptoe & Johnson, helped cover up Zain's miscarriage of justice in an attempt to hide it from ever being discovered. Trooper Ted A. Smith testified that Steptoe lawyer Steve McGowen told select people that he "was going to bury this thing so deep that no one could find it." A member of the West Virginia House of Delegates, Larry Faircloth, sent a letter to United States Attorney General John Ashcroft to investigate the actions of Steptoe lawyers for complaints of police brutality and civil rights violations.[1355] In 2002, Attorney General McGraw filed a lawsuit against Steptoe & Johnson declaring "[t]he misconduct proximately caused the State to pay considerably more money in settlement of those claims than would have been necessary but for the defendants' actions." McGraw also alleged the law firm conspired to conceal the misconduct of Zain's falsified test results and deceptive testimony, which were blamed in at least six wrongful convictions. Two of those wrongfully imprisoned individuals sued Steptoe & Johnson, alleging they spent extra years in prison because of McGowen's silence.[1356]

One wrongfully imprisoned man due to Zain's testimony was Glen Dale Woodall who was sentenced to between 203 years to 335 years in prison for numerous felony convictions. When Woodall sued the State of West Virginia, it was learned that Zain "apparently perjured himself" by testifying "that he performed laboratory tests on seminal fluid that the laboratory was incapable of performing at that time." A letter written by McGowan and sent to the State's insurer recommended settling the Woodall case "as quickly and quietly as possible, as the potential exposure [for more lawsuits] is catastrophic."[1357] Despite McGowan's recognition that the Zain situation was "catastrophic," three months later, McGowan drafted a letter for Superintendent Jack Buckalew that was sent to Kanawha County Prosecuting Attorney Bill Forbes, assuring him that the investigation had concluded and "there was no need to take any further action with respect to any of Fred Zain's cases."[1358]

In 2002, after much of this information implicating Steptoe & Johnson attorneys surfaced, the firm began asserting that former West Virginia Attorney General Mario Palumbo, who was suffering and later died from Lou Gehrig's disease and was unable to defend himself against the allegations, knew about Zain's deceptions even before McGowan knew about them.[1359] Conversely, Palumbo's former Chief Deputy disagreed with Steptoe's assertions stating that Palumbo "sought answers from Superintendent Buckalew and was assured that nothing was amiss."[1360] Even though then-State Police Superintendent Jack Buckalew pleaded the Fifth Amendment and refused to testify during the disgraceful Fred

Zain miscarriage of justice, he was still elected to the State Senate in 1994. He currently serves as a member of the State Ethics Commission.

The *Charleston Gazette* illustrates the glaring problem that seems to follow many of West Virginia's unfortunate corrupt misgivings–the lack of accountability. The *Gazette* asks: "Did the Legislature's Commission on Special Investigations recommend action? Did United States prosecutors consider civil rights charges on behalf of the men who were wrongly imprisoned? Has the State Bar examined the lawyer conduct in the sorry affair? Not as far as anyone knows."[1361]

After leaving West Virginia in 1989 to take a similar position in Texas, Zain continued to return to West Virginia to testify in criminal cases against alleged offenders. By 1999, it was learned that six men in both West Virginia and Texas had spent a combined forty years in prison for crimes they didn't commit as a result of Zain's false and damaging testimony. After two mistrials in the West Virginia circuit courts, the third trial was postponed indefinitely due to Zain's failing health. On December 3, 2002, the fifty-two-year-old Zain, who was never convicted for his egregious behavior, died as a result of colon cancer.[1362]

The West Virginia State Crime Lab's problems did not end with the discovery and death of Fred Zain. Many years later, another one of the lab's chemists, Todd McDaniel, pled guilty to falsifying test results on marijuana. Moreover, in March of 2002, two more lab officers were suspended and the FBI was asked to conduct an independent probe, while an outside lab was hired to retest evidence from narcotics prosecutions. In May 2006, Kanawha County Public Defender George Castelle argued before the State Supreme Court that: "The problem identified in the [lab's] serology division may be more widespread and may include analysts in other divisions who may still be committing much of the same misconduct that was committed by Tropper [Fred] Zain and his assistants."[1363] The problem of having a State crime lab directly connected to the State Police is obvious. As Richard Grimes of the *Charleston Daily Mail* maintained: "Common sense tells us that any laboratory assigned to a police agency is going to have pressure on it to come up with strong evidence. But that, in turn, could mean that what is presented to a jury in the courtroom could be tainted." Grimes added,

> Under this kind of arrangement, the laboratory's incentive would be to conduct the best crime test results available from a scientific standpoint. The judgment of its presentation in the courtroom would be the medical thoroughness and accuracy of its work, rather than whether the jury finds the person on trial guilty.[1364]

Just below United States Attorneys and State Police are county prosecutors and sheriffs. People depend on these individuals to keep them safe and enforce the State's laws. In 1989, the State Supreme Court suspended the law license of James E. Roark, the former Kanawha County Prosecutor and then-City of Charleston Mayor, for three years based upon his plea of guilty to six counts of the federal misdemeanor offense of possession of cocaine. The guilty pleas were made pursuant to a plea agreement in which twenty-four other counts in the indictment were dismissed. Roark was sentenced to serve a period of 179 days in the federal prison at Petersburg, Virginia and was placed on probation for three years and resigned from the position of Mayor of Charleston. Even though Roark admitted he committed the crimes, he argued that a three year suspension of his law license was not warranted because his crime was not a crime involving moral turpitude.[1365]

Conversely, in expressing his displeasure that a three year suspension was simply insufficient, West Virginia Supreme Court Chief Justice William Brotherton wrote:

> James E. Roark corrupted the office of prosecuting attorney in violation of the statute. Mr. Roark obtained cocaine from known drug dealers and obligingly turned a blind eye to their criminal activities. He socialized with drug dealers at a time when our schools and community were being inundated with drugs. This behavior was all the more unfortunate because citizens relied on Mr. Roark for prosecution and protection without realizing that his office had been compromised. Mr. Roark's lack of moral accountability was further evidenced by his indignant protests to the voters, to the press, and to anyone who would listen, that he had never used drugs, all the while maintaining, consistent with his 'mad dog' image, that he was out to clean up crime in Kanawha County.

Chief Justice Brotherton further said:

> Mr. Roark breached the trust which exists between an office holder and the citizens whom he represents. Such a violation is not only a breach of the public trust, but is also a tear in the fabric of our form of government. What value is government if we cannot trust our elected officials?[1366]

The Kanawha County Sheriff during then-Mayor Roark's criminal drug behavior was Danny Jones, who, according to the *Charleston Gazette*, met with federal agents in 1986 and detailed his own use of marijuana and cocaine, naming nearly fifty individuals who either supplied the illegal drugs or used them with him. The documents containing Jones' interviews with federal agents were leaked to the media and contained an outline of his alleged marijuana use for several years in the early 1970s and his alleged cocaine use from 1978 to 1983. Following reports of Jones' cocaine use, he told reporters, "You've got to understand, in 1980 and '81, cocaine flooded this valley."[1367]  Roark said his drug use "never influenced [his] job performance," while Jones claimed that he "quit [using] when [he] was elected sheriff."[1368]  Jones is currently the Mayor of Charleston, West Virginia.

The image of more bad actors on the city level is more of the same misguided behavior. The result is the shaping of the opinions of the average people about those chosen to enforce the laws. For instance, with regard to city police in Mingo County, an editorial in the *Charleston Gazette* asks, "Mingo: Trust the police?"  It provides:

> Former Delbarton Police Chief Robert Justice has pleaded guilty to demanding a $1,000 bribe from an arrested man, and bilking Mingo County residents out of $5,600 through a phony charity appeal.  In return for his guilty plea, prosecutors dropped charges that he burned his sister's car to get insurance money, and that he helped steal money from a Delbarton restaurant cash register.
>
> Meanwhile, former Mingo Sheriff's Deputy William Evans has been charged with pretending that his all-terrain vehicle was stolen, and collecting $6,349 insurance money.
>
> Good lord–it must be terrible for Mingo residents to live with an uneasy sense that some police officers, supposedly their protectors, can't be trusted.[1369]

The Mingo chronicles continued as David Ramey, a former Kermit police chief, was convicted of drug conspiracy (pharmaceutical drugs, marijuana and cocaine) and tax evasion.  He was sentenced to fifteen years in prison, a $115,000 fine, and a $1,150 special assessment, while Clark Belcher, the former McDowell County Sheriff, was convicted of extortion from gambling operations and sentenced to eight years in prison and ordered to pay a $15,000 fine.[1370]  By October 15, 1986, a total of seven individuals, including Ramey's wife, Deborah

Preece Ramey, and Kermit Fire Chief Wilbur Preece, pled guilty in the drug ring.[1371] As discussed earlier, former southern West Virginia Assistant United States Attorney Joseph F. Savage said that in West Virginia, "the corruption was systemic." He said he was quickly introduced to the crooked ways of Mingo County when "Wig Preece, his wife, Cooney, and several of their thirteen children sold drugs from a trailer parked across from the police chief's office."[1372]

The one thing that non-politicians in West Virginia agree on is that the system is in need of drastic reform. The problem, however, is that most people have such little confidence in a system that has let them down so many times that talk of reform sometimes seems like an exercise in futility. The lack of confidence in State government and elected officials is precisely why a massive overhaul of the entire system is necessary to restore integrity to the idea of public service.

West Virginia has an Ethics Commission that doesn't seem to recognize anything as an ethics violation. Likewise, the State itself lacks significant statewide prosecutorial power to enforce current laws, but even when an elected violator is prosecuted, the result is often little to no accountability. Then, we see several corrupt actors within West Virginia's police force who have tainted the many fine, upstanding, and capable officers who do care about West Virginia and fight against corruption. A continuous cycle of corruption, perception of corruption, lack of accountability, and lack of trust, have left people hopeless as to how to break this generational trend.

People are often left wondering in whom they can believe. They often shut down and become completely disengaged from a political system in which as a young boy or girl, they once had faith. Friends of mine have told me it is easier to just give up on West Virginia politics than to be disappointed one more time. I will readily admit that during the years I spent writing this book, my emotions fluctuated drastically. I would find myself getting frustrated and angry one minute, but then becoming amazed by the audacity of some of these criminal political schemers. I often felt helpless, powerless, and even enraged by the non-sensical unscrupulous villains who have tainted what should be one of the most noble professions in the world–public service. Ultimately though, those same feelings of disappointment, frustration, and disgust were precisely why I decided to come up with simple, but comprehensive, avenues to reform the numerous problems of the State's corrupt political system, and have outlined fifty specific reforms to change West Virginia's government forever.

# CHAPTER NINETEEN

# Reforming West Virginia Politics

*Cautious, careful people, always casting about to preserve their reputation and social standing, never can bring about a reform. Those who are really in earnest must be willing to be anything or nothing in the world's estimation, and publicly and privately, in season and out, avow their sympathy with despised and persecuted ideas and their advocates, and bear the consequences.*

Susan B. Anthony

West Virginia, known for its age-old corruption-plagued politics, must implement significant changes to revitalize and cleanup its system of government and elections. Unfortunately, in a state where corrupt practices have been ingrained in the culture, such attitudes can't be changed overnight, just as generation after generation of corruption can't be cured with a single reform or magic pill. Likewise, with so many corrupt practices, simply concentrating on fixing just one or two of the State's political problems would allow the many other corrupt and destructive practices to flourish unbridled. Thus, the only cure for West Virginia politics is a sweeping and comprehensive reform not to be implemented in a piecemeal fashion, but all at once. It is similar to a jigsaw puzzle that can't be completed without all of the pieces.

Due to West Virginia's laundry list of political problems, I have outlined numerous avenues to reform the State's politics and I have included at the end of this chapter a contract for reform to be used by individual voters. The Contract represents a written agreement and commitment by a candidate to a voter to support specific reforms to cleanup West Virginia politics. Voters will now have the ammunition to help them make better choices during elections by taking a copy of the Contract With The Voter and having political candidates sign it, thereby agreeing to do everything possible to achieve such reforms or to agree not to run for re-election. If a candidate refuses to sign the Contract because he or she disagrees with one or two of the reforms, then voters should simply cross out those particular sections and ask the candidate to agree to the remainder of the Contract. If the candidate refuses to commit to any of the reforms, then voters shouldn't vote for or waste any of their time with that candidate and should consider the other candidates in the race. It really is that simple. It is time to hold politicians accountable for turning a blind eye to these blatant, but correctable problems in State politics.

Moreover, these reforms are not just for statewide and legislative candidates. Voters must also ask local mayors and city council members to agree to such reforms even if they don't appear to be in a position to directly effect such change at a statewide level. In the first place, mayors and other city and county officials often seek higher political offices such as becoming members of the Legislature. Secondly, these reforms reflect sound government principles which also apply to government at the State's smallest level. Thirdly, reform is more likely to start from the bottom up instead of from the top down due to the fact that many statewide politicians have already become a part of the corrupt system in order to survive in politics.

Changing West Virginia's politics is similar to the popular movie *Field of Dreams* where voices told actor Kevin Costner, "If you build it, he will come." In this case, however, if West Virginians build a good, honest, credible, and responsible government, business and prosperity will come. I have often wondered how many businesses and positive opportunities West Virginians have missed out on because of corruption in State politics. I also wonder how many millions or possibly billions of dollars have been squandered by politicians spending State money on worthless trinkets and other blatantly political State-funded projects. Rebuilding the State's image will help attract sorely needed industry while at the same time it will promote sound fiscal policy.

With any avenue to reform, it is necessary to view the relationship between the problems of the past and the present. In West Virginia, for example, the State's political culture of corruption is a problem of present-day politics which can't be discussed intelligently without a clear understanding of the past. In addition, every culture has its own particular customs and West Virginia is no exception. Such customs include structure and function of the family, patterns of written and spoken language, different beliefs and attitudes toward religious worship, death, literacy and learning, patterns of education, ways of dressing, attitudes toward wealth, and authority and power. This unprecedented look at West Virginia politics from its inception until present day provides precisely such a thorough and complete consideration of West Virginia's background. Thus, these reforms are not suggested in light of just a few years of bad actions or a couple of high level indiscretions by public officials leading to a public outcry for change as is often the case with reform movements. Instead, these reforms are specifically designed to fix longstanding problems which have significantly hindered the State's advancement in areas such as education, healthcare, and basic infrastructure.

Quite frankly, some of these ideas are just common sense. However, many West Virginia elected officials have proven that if a specific conduct is not expressly spelled out as a violation of the law then it must be acceptable conduct no matter what good old-fashioned common sense says to the contrary. Moreover, West Virginia politicians are often nervous about election innovation and slow to change, and reformers aren't exactly encouraged to strive for such change. Nonetheless, West Virginia needs more smart, politically savvy, courageous men and women who are willing to risk their careers all for the sake of having a shot at making their ideas for reform stick.

This culture of corruption in State politics has provided a setting in which corruption flourishes and has become expected behavior. Cracking down on these political lawbreakers is the only way to show West Virginia is genuine in its efforts to reform a corrupt system. These political abusers must be punished fairly, but strictly, or no reform will ever occur as violators must fear punishment or they will continue to break the laws. Thus, with the inclusion of firm language in West Virginia's laws and rigid enforcement, including long prison sentences and exorbitant fines, offenders will understand there are finally consequences for their actions.

Given the fact that State politicians have ignored attempts at any significant reform, cleaning up West Virginia politics is a job for the individual West Virginia voter. The public has become immune and apathetic to election violations following year after year of crooked politicians and resigned to the belief that, "everybody does it." It is not necessarily that people feel so disengaged from the issues, but rather that they simply feel they have no control and their votes have nothing to do with changing the system. Therefore, people are not going to become completely engaged in politics until the system is changed. This is precisely why forming a contract with politicians will return that sorely needed voice to the individual while at the same time provide for accountability of the politician.

If a government, a corporation, or a single person continues to hold a group of people under thumb, then it is only time that holds those people in oppression. For one day, it happens–a strike, a massacre, or a strong-willed person emerges to change minds and champion an effort that soon becomes a movement. The oppressed cannot continually be subjected to seeing convicted political felons held in the highest esteem and they cannot be continually threatened at the local polling places to vote against their conscience. Equally important, they cannot continually see back-alley payoffs and greater financial exchanges from corporation to candidate not only go unpunished, but also be accepted and even expected as the cost of doing business in West Virginia.

Furthermore, apathy escalates when voters watch self-proclaimed, "honest" candidates promise to change the system and speak against injustice and corruption, yet see these very same people become, not only elected officials, but also as corrupt as the individuals they had initially set out to replace. Such unrestrained behaviors create social norms and unrestrained and unregulated activity, such as the influx of the large amounts of money that donors provide, creates the "belief" that everything is for sale. Of course, it naturally follows that such an attitude carries over to actions of elected officials after the election and while they are holding the office. A history of political factions, intimidation, vote-buying, vote-stealing, and limited regulation have bred this culture surrounding West Virginia elections while the social norms created by the constant violations of state and federal law without adequate consequences, perpetuates an ongoing and escalating level of apathy and indifference. As such, West Virginia's current system of elections discourages individuals from entering politics unless they are willing to compromise their ethics while at the same time raise massive amounts of money. This is further perpetuated by West Virginians watching this continuous cycle of money pouring into each election contest followed by relentless negative campaign advertisements. I have often wondered what chance an honest politician even has with people standing on the sidelines with millions of dollars ready to destroy reputations in deceitful and slanderous ways.

West Virginians have also–sadly–read headline after headline describing a substantial number of State politicians who have been convicted or accused of seemingly endless corrupt practices in both their personal and professional lives. Moreover, these tainted politicians are often the same individuals making the decisions affecting the day-to-day lives of the people due to the fact that the government acts as the functional arm tasked with implementing State policies formulated by the three branches of State government, the executive, the legislative and the judiciary. Further, both perceived and actual corruption is prevalent at all levels of the governmental hierarchy in West Virginia. Consequently, West Virginians need to elect leaders willing to step forward and unselfishly fight for real change. This is the only way real change can occur. Otherwise, we will continue to be mired in a corrupt system that only gets worse as time progresses.

There is the perception by many that an honest politician cannot survive in politics and that fighting for some reforms will not leave a lasting effect on State politics due to the amount of corruption within the system. As Shakespeare observed, "The evil that men do lives after them, the good is oft interred with their bones."[1373] With that in mind, the very first item on the Contract With The Voter is that a candidate for office must support a constitutional convention and a special session of the State Legislature to deal solely with the comprehensive reforms set forth in my Contract to cure West Virginia's problems of election fraud and corrupt politicians.

The Legislature must take several immediate steps to address the lack of accountability for those who violate the laws of the State and enact new laws to achieve the goals set forth in my Contract. Those intent on corrupting the process have never feared the consequences as many of the offenses of these violators are well-known, but rarely prosecuted, in spite of the scale of some abuses. Remember the Attorney General accused of extorting money from his employees to pay for his campaign debts and then attempting to pay a secretary $50,000 in hush money to remain quiet about the allegation that he was the father of her unborn child? Again, the Kanawha County Prosecuting Attorney agreed not to prosecute as long as the Attorney General agreed to resign from office. The result was that he simply resigned and became a successful and wealthy Washington, D.C. lawyer. This is just one of countless examples of an offender being handed no sanctions or fines and serving no jail time. Even when violators are actually brought to court, the message from the so-called prosecutions of elected officials is that there is usually no threat of jail time or any serious consequences for those who break election laws or violate the public trust.

Is it really too much to ask to have honest public officials? Some of the reforms I have set forth are strict, but honest politicians shouldn't be concerned. Accordingly, the first actual reform must be prohibiting felons from being candidates for office or serving as public officials. Similar to the three strikes and you're out rule many states have with regard to criminal felony convictions, West Virginia must enact a one strike and you're out rule for State politicians convicted of election-related or fraud-related felonies. Yes, I said a lifetime ban from State politics. Politicians in West Virginia are like the children you tell "no" to 100 times, but never actually see any follow through of punishment. There is rarely any negative reinforcement for their corrupt and corrosive behaviors, and it is time that changed. Besides, West Virginia's extreme and relentless history of corruption requires such strict consequences. In fact, even though it is mind-boggling, the State currently has a felon serving in the State Legislature who was convicted of election fraud. He even proudly serves on the House of

Delegates Judiciary Committee even though he was listed as a co-conspirator in the United States Attorney's 2006 investigations surrounding several Lincoln County officials and residents who were convicted of buying votes during more than a dozen past elections.[1374]

One of my law degrees is from the University of London with a concentration of study in Criminology and Criminal Justice. I have read many articles and books from criminologists and know that many of them argue back and forth about the purpose of having stern laws. Some argue laws are strictly for punishment of individuals while others contend that laws are primarily for deterrent purposes. It is clear to me, however, that laws serve both purposes. Officials who have violated the public trust should be punished, while at the same time, that punishment should be severe and should send a clear message to other politicians that such conduct will not be tolerated under any circumstances.

With that in mind, politicians and individuals convicted and sent to prison for defrauding the State for election or other fraud-related felonies must pay for their entire stay in jail. These villains, particularly those involved in bribery schemes with State money, have already cost the State enough and therefore, upon their release from prison, they should be forced to pay for the cost of their prosecution and incarceration. For anyone concerned this could be a substantial amount of money and may be difficult for an individual to pay immediately, the solution is simple. These ex-con politicians will have debt accounts set up much like government student loan accounts. They will have specific interest rates and the "loans" can be paid off throughout an extended period of time.

West Virginia has had two standards of justice since its inception. One standard of accountability and justice is set much lower for politicians, while the other for non-politicians is often more strict. Since West Virginians are familiar with such a system of justice, we should continue to have two standards, only we must shift the scales in the other direction to adequately and more severely punish criminal politicians. Thus, just as any convicted felon must have a lifetime ban from participating in West Virginia politics, any public official convicted of a felony who is also an attorney or may become an attorney, must never again be given the privilege of practicing law in West Virginia. Just as Chief Justice Maynard has observed, it doesn't make sense that a felon would be prohibited from operating a bar in West Virginia, but still be able to practice with the State's legal bar? Felons shouldn't waste the Court's time or the State's money as perception is as good as reality and the perception of felons serving as public officials does nothing to restore confidence in State politics. Another necessary step toward reform is that public officials who commit felonies related to their publicly paid-for jobs must lose their entire State pension. Why on earth should these felons receive money from the State when they spent a lifetime pilfering from it and stealing our children's futures?

Another problem is that there must be truth in sentencing for corrupt politicians. For example, when a State Treasurer shafts the State out of interest on millions of dollars in an intentional bribery scheme, there must be a dollar for dollar penalty to recover the money lost. It seems egregious to consider that someone be allowed to intentionally scam the State out of millions of dollars only to face a small fine. The State should prosecute these felons to the fullest extent of the law and recover the money in any manner possible, including taking the individual's personal property, house, and vehicles and selling them at public auction. Likewise, if a prosecutor falsifies time sheets to obtain a federal grant, he or she should have to pay back the grant out of his or her personal bank accounts. If a magistrate uses his or her office as a racketeering enterprise, the State should immediately sue that magistrate to recover all lost revenues as well as any monies received from the criminal endeavor. It is that simple.

The goal will be to get every last dime back that was scammed from the State. Someone has to come up with these lost State and county revenues and it is wrong that the burden always gets shifted to the honest and hardworking West Virginians who time and time again are forced to account for these shady criminals. Moreover, if a county assessor deliberately lowers the taxes of someone in exchange for a favor or a bribe, that assessor must be personally responsible for the lost taxes, interest, and penalties for late tax payments. Further, an assessor who takes his campaign logo and uses State money to place it on county vehicles, office stationery, and employee uniforms, must be removed from office and the State must be reimbursed dollar for dollar to replace these materials with appropriate non-political ones. Speaking of assessors, and again, my father was one, these positions really shouldn't be elected offices in the first place. Think about it, everyone hates taxes. I hate taxes. An election of a county assessor really is contrary to the purpose of having an election in the first place, i.e., the better job an assessor does assessing people's property, the more likely he or she will be defeated at the polls.

There are countless other examples of these types of frauds, but the consequences should always be that the State of West Virginia, without exception, should do everything possible to recover every penny from these scurrilous felons. When someone like Attorney General Charlie Brown is allowed to walk away without a trial, an admonition, or any recourse, there is something seriously wrong with the system. It infuriates me when politicians try to explain away the weak enforcement system saying that allowing politicians to resign without charging them with a crime often spares the State the great expense of a trial and embarrassment. The technical term for that is hogwash! I wonder who will spare the State the expense of not having a trial as the constant lack of enforcement of the State's laws just sends the continued message that there are no consequences to any West Virginia politician's illegal actions.

Another problem still alive and well in West Virginia is vote-buying with alcohol, cash, college tuition payments, and just about anything else imaginable. West Virginia laws must specifically provide that vote-buying is a felony and that a conviction will result in a lifetime ban from politics, jail time, and provide for stiff monetary fines. I say this in a tongue-and-cheek manner, but it is too bad that public flogging isn't an option for these villains. Likewise, vote-selling must immediately become a State felony and any conviction of such would carry a lifetime ban from voting or running for office in West Virginia. While West Virginia Code § 3-9-13 (a) and (b) currently provide that buying votes is a felony and selling votes is a misdemeanor, neither penalty for either of those offenses provides for a ban from politics or the strict penalties necessary to deter future vote-buying or vote-selling. Thus, those laws must be significantly strengthened. If these people care so little about their State that they buy or sell their votes then they shouldn't have a say in how it's run. Along those same lines, any election poll worker, circuit clerk, county clerk, or any other public or private individual who has anything to do with the performance of an election, and who violates the election laws causing any election fraud, must also be banned from participation in State politics for life.

Moreover, anyone convicted of any felonious election violation, whereby it is proven that their fraud led to an alternative result in the election, will be responsible for paying for the costs of an election contest filed by any candidate and there will be no statute of limitations on this law. For example, if it is not learned until 2010 that felon "A" bought enough votes during the 2008 election to sway the election results, and candidate "X" filed an election contest in 2008, felon "A" would be responsible for those election contest costs whenever it was determined that such a fraud was actually committed. Thus, specific State laws against vote-buying and vote-selling or the conspiracy to commit any election fraud must be enacted making any such violations felonies with severe penalties in addition to the lifetime ban from State politics. The effect of the corruptive cash for votes politics causes candidates who don't want to participate in such a corrupt system to feel pressured to buy a slot on slates because they fear they could lose the election if their challenger buys a position on the slate and gets those votes. It is a disgusting cycle of corruption that must end. The underlying theme for any vote-related reform must be whether votes are being recorded, whether those votes are being counted accurately, and whether all voters are treated fairly in a bipartisan manner. Republicans, Democrats, and other political parties only stand to benefit from clean elections and must work together to improve elections for all voters.

Along those same lines, specific legislation must be enacted outlawing any candidate from paying to be listed on any political slate which is used to buy votes and any violation of such will result in a felony conviction, significant jail time, and a lifetime ban from participation in State politics. We tolerate the conduct of these misfits because it's just the way it has always been, but slates have been synonymous with political corruption in West Virginia. Moreover, "voting the dead" must become a memory of the past–and any individual who knowingly casts a false ballot should be guilty of a felony and immediately banned for life from participating in West Virginia politics. While some steps have been taken on both federal and state levels to cleanse the voters registration rolls, much more must be done to rid West Virginia of this disgusting practice. Thus, cleaning up the voters' registration rolls in the county offices must be a priority in preventing the time-honored dead person voters.

Laws should also be enacted allowing prosecutors charging politicians with election or other political fraud violations to make it easier to secure change of venue motions. Many people who sit on juries in some counties are fearful of convicting local election violators or political bosses because they fear retribution against them due to the amount of influence exerted by many of these powerful individuals. Thus, jury trials in the same county where many of these powerful people live or where those in charge of the prosecution may even be involved with the same criminal enterprise, makes it less likely that these violators will be convicted. Perhaps legitimately, people fear that even if these political individuals are actually convicted, they still wield a significant amount of power and influence. One need not look further than the investigator against Judge Ned Grubb who said people feared the judge might make up false charges against them or might even have them killed.

Additionally, just as people who commit crimes against law enforcement officers and other public officials should receive more severe criminal sentences, it is equally important for police officers, prosecutors, magistrates, judges, and justices who violate the law to receive tougher penalties for their corrupt actions. These are the people we count on in our everyday lives to protect us from the common criminals. When these governmental actors turn bad, it destroys the entire system of justice. In addition to sentencing enhancement laws for these public safety officials, mandatory sentencing laws should be in place for politicians who commit election violations and commit fraud on the State while in public office. No longer should a judge receive a five-day sentence for biting off the end of a defendant's nose. It's outrageous! These people who violate the public's trust must be held accountable. In this same light, there should be no statute of limitations for any fraud-related election violation by public officials. These political hacks should not escape prosecution simply because a few years have passed without getting caught for their fraudulent acts.

One significant problem with enforcement of the State's election and fraud laws with regard to elected politicians is that the State must rely on the United States Attorney's Office to cleanup most of the political filth, sludge, and statewide corruption. And that system, while it has been just about West Virginia's only enforcement body, is not without its problems as demonstrated by the United States Attorney in Southern West Virginia who was fired by President Bush in 2005. His firing was allegedly for, among other things, violating State election laws, even though as United States Attorney, he was successful in convicting several politicians for their election frauds. Thus, prosecutorial power for the State Attorney General and expanded enforcement mechanisms for the Secretary of State's Office must be enacted and adequately funded. While the current Secretary of State has created a larger election fraud unit than her predecessors, only so much can get accomplished on a limited office budget. The Secretary of State's Office must have an election fraud division funded well enough so that it is actually capable of thoroughly investigating and prosecuting election fraud throughout the State.

It is equally important that any candidate for office must declare to the voter that he or she will do everything within their constitutional powers to enforce the State's laws. For instance, a legislator would agree to introduce impeachment proceedings immediately for any public official at any level of State politics who misuses his or her office funds to purchase magnets, pill boxes, key chains, or any other blatantly political trinket which will soon be illegal once the reforms from my Contract are enacted. Peer pressure can sometimes be a valuable tool so candidates must also commit to publicly denouncing a fellow politician convicted of corrupt behavior or known to be engaged in corrupt activities.

Thus, the problem of wasted tax money used to put names on vans, key chains, magnets, and millions of other trinkets, letters, television and radio commercials under the guise of public service announcements and constituent education, must immediately be stopped. It is not good enough to regulate or limit this corruptive and wasteful practice, it must be ended entirely and any violations of this new law must result in a felony for misuse of State funds and violators should immediately be removed from office. If the State is going to have public financing of campaigns it should be a legitimate system open to all candidates.

Likewise, Governors' Contingency Funds, the Budget Digest (or its equivalency), and any secret accounts containing hidden State tax dollars must be reined in and individual politicians must be held accountable. These corrosive charities have no place in State government as State money should be given to groups *only* after legislative approval following a full and open debate or by the Governor during a time of crisis. In like manner, county sheriff slush funds from their pistol permit fees must be ended. Sheriffs should only collect the amount necessary for administrative costs of issuing the pistol permits and should not be allowed to create a yearly State paid-for re-election fund. These really are no-brainer reforms, but unless the people step up and make them a reality, such indiscretions will continue in perpetuity.

In addition to spending State money so irresponsibly, Governors should be prohibited from spending private corporate donations from their gubernatorial inauguration funds. Corporations are prohibited from contributing to a candidate's campaign; however, they are permitted to contribute to inauguration fundraising. Spending corporate money is completely outside the spirit of campaign financing, and Governors have begun the practice of intentionally raising much more money than is necessary for their inaugural activities just so they will be able to spend massive amounts of money later in just about any way they want. Thus, inaugural funds should be limited to contributions by individuals, not corporations, and any excess money not used for inaugural activities must be returned pro rata to inaugural donors. Moreover, the Governor's Mansion should not be rented to any individual for any purpose regardless of whether it is an anniversary, birthday, or wedding reception. It is a trashy idea that carries with it the stigma of impropriety. It is also another way of using State property to influence legislators and individuals for favors. It is bad enough that the Governor's Office is for sale every four years as millions of dollars pour into each election, but renting the Governor's Mansion is just too much.

Specific legislation is also necessary to prohibit legislators or other politicians from voting on legislation or directing State money to any entity in which they work, own, own an interest in, or simply receive a benefit. It is another one of those areas where legislation shouldn't be necessary, but politicians have proven that in actuality such a written law is completely necessary. It is a practice which is blatantly wrong even though the State Ethics Commission doesn't see a problem with such conduct. Speaking of the State's Ethics Commission, this joke on the State taxpayers should either be completely revised or completely dismantled. When a State Senator can vote on $750,000 in funding benefitting his investment and surrounding property, while another can alter her travel records and benefit from $99,000 tax free, all with the stamp of approval from the

Ethics Commission, this sham of a public entity is beyond simple change. The Legislature must start from scratch and revisit this toothless tiger and begin anew with publicly debated laws and a completely new group of people running the Commission for they have lost all credibility as an enforcement agency. When an Ethics Commission says it has no authority to do anything against someone who lies to them during an investigation, the problems are obvious.

Money in State politics–both legal and non-legal–must also be fully addressed if any reform is going to be successful. Millions of dollars are spent each election cycle to buy State elections and currently a 1976 United States Supreme Court case called *Buckley v. Valeo*[1375] limits a state's ability to restrict spending in political elections. Nonetheless, the key word is *limits* as politicians often inaccurately cite the *Buckley* case as an all-out prohibition to any election reform which is simply disingenuous. Countless State politicians have thrown their hands in the air and told me, "I would love to do something about money in politics, but the Supreme Court won't let me." It amounts to just an easy way out of addressing an issue that would end many of the incumbents' fundraising advantages.

For one thing, *Buckley* dealt with federal elections such as the United States Senate or the United States House of Representatives. States, on the other hand, have more rights to enact laws to control the elections for their state-created political offices such as Governor, Attorney General, or State Legislator. In fact, in February 2005, the Second United States Circuit Court of Appeals in New York upheld a decision by a three-judge panel which concluded that Vermont's reform laws limiting spending in State elections were constitutional. The decision was the first in the nation to rule that such spending limits were constitutional and didn't violate a candidate's First Amendment right to free speech. Vermont's law limits its State's gubernatorial campaign spending to $300,000, lieutenant governor spending to $100,000 and other statewide races like Secretary of State and Auditor to $45,000. The law also limits spending on Vermont House and Senate races. The Court said Vermont can limit campaign spending for two reasons: to stem the corruptive influence that money can have on politics, and to relieve candidates of the time burden necessary to raise large sums of money.[1376]

Thus, just like Vermont, West Virginia must enact expenditure limits compatible with each elective office. Currently, West Virginia's Voluntary Code of Fair Campaign practices prescribe limits of $1 million for gubernatorial races; $150,000 for all other executive officials and Supreme Court Justices; $50,000 for circuit judge elections; $50,000 for State Senate candidates; and $25,000 for House of Delegates candidates. While those limits are probably too high, a full debate on expenditure limits must be held and the Voluntary Code must be replaced with the adoption of appropriate and *mandatory* expenditure limits. Additional limits must also be adopted for Family Court Judge elections as well as all county and city elected officials and board of education candidates. While the concept was certainly admirable, the voluntary code in reality amounts to nothing more than a joke. Even when candidates sign it they often exceed the voluntary limits which is precisely why the Code must become mandatory.

Another enactment which tackles the money in politics issue will be passing legislation limiting contributions to candidates located within the district where a contributor lives. For instance, an individual who lives in California will be prohibited from donating to a candidate for Governor in West Virginia, while any West Virginia resident will be able to donate to any West Virginia candidate for Governor. Likewise, if a person lives in the State's fourteenth senatorial district, he or she will be permitted to contribute to fourteenth senatorial district Senate candidates, but will not be permitted to contribute to any other Senate candidates from other senatorial districts. People will be able to contribute to candidates who directly represent them, thereby significantly reducing the ability of outside influences buying elections.

Ask yourself, who is the first person to receive a returned call from a politician, the person who raised $150,000 during the past election, or the average person who votes regularly, but cannot afford to donate money to campaigns? The answer is obvious and an insult to democracy. This system of legalized bribery has to stop as it simply increases citizen alienation from democratic government. Further, the buying of elections has become a cancer on democracy as average citizens making $25,000 per year cannot spend millions of dollars on a political campaign just for the *chance* to procure an office and, therefore, generally do not become involved in the system. This influx of massive amounts of money into campaigns only discourages voters, candidates, and clean elections. Wealthier people should not have a louder voice simply because they have more money as campaigns have become so expensive that non-wealthy men and women of excellence are priced out of running for office. Another necessity is to agree to support state and federal constitutional amendments making it easier to control spending in state elections. Senator Byrd introduces such an amendment in Congress nearly every year, but so far has been unsuccessful in gaining its passage. The amendment will allow even more significant monetary restrictions which are currently prohibited by United States Supreme Court precedent.

Another problem with State campaigns is that millions of dollars are spent by politicians and wealthy individuals on misleading political advertisements such as the ads saying gubernatorial candidate Charlotte Pritt supported giving condoms to school children. While that ad was ridiculous and false, it still effectively turns voters against a candidate. There is a clear difference between factual ads that represent and educate voters with regard to the negative or corrupt actions of a candidate versus blatant lies used to mislead voters and often destroy the reputations of good men and women. This type of dirty, scummy campaigning should not be tolerated and one way to bring some accountability to a politician's deceitful actions is to place "None of the Above" as a choice on all ballots for all candidates for State political offices during all West Virginia General Elections.

If None of the Above is actually chosen by the voters, then another election must be held within forty-five days, with none of the original candidates allowed to participate during that election except None of the Above. New candidates would be chosen by the respective political parties and write-in candidates would also be allowed to participate in the subsequent election. Inserting None of the Above on the ballot will serve to make candidates accountable for their campaign actions. Many times during elections both candidates have thrown so much mud and conducted themselves in such a poor manner that neither deserve a place on the ballot, but voters feel compelled to hold their noses and choose the lesser of two bad candidates. I can't imagine anything more effective to keep a politician less rotten and more honest than adding this choice to the ballot, for the ultimate political embarrassment would be losing an election to "None of the Above." And, I have trust in the voters of West Virginia to use such a measure only when the circumstances truly merit the choice of None of the Above.

Along those same lines, West Virginia must have a strong truth in campaigning law wherein if an individual knowingly uses a false statement about a candidate in a campaign advertisement, then such an infraction should become a felony under State law and should include strict penalties making potential violators think twice before they spread destructive lies about a candidate.[1377] Surprisingly, a court in the State of Washington recently overruled a similar law saying candidates have a constitutional right to lie. That, however, is simply ludicrous and I can't imagine any scenario where the West Virginia Supreme Court would form the same conclusion as that of the court in Washington. For too long, West Virginians have witnessed lying about candidates as a matter of tradition and expected behavior. The result, however, is that lying during a campaign erodes democracy, defames good people, and discourages others from even considering entering politics. There is simply no justification and no First Amendment right to lie and destroy someone's reputation and life. It amounts to obtaining a public office through stealth and deception and by robbing every voter of a fair election.

Among the reforms must also be the end to the practice of the free, private and well-catered parties paid for by special interest groups during the legislative session. These parties are wrong. Enough said. In addition, the sponsorship of the Legislature's interim meetings and the gifts provided by special interest groups must immediately be stopped. Whoever thought that major lobbying groups would so openly sponsor legislative meetings and even label the highest to lowest contributors as gold, silver, bronze, and contributing sponsors? I guess nothing should be a surprise, but this is another example of one of those situations where you really would think common sense would prevail and a law would not be necessary. Unfortunately though, that is not the case. As well-known *Charleston Daily Mail* reporter L.T. Anderson said, State legislators would "take hemorrhoids if they were being given away."[1378]

Similarly, there needs to be a limit on the power of money from lobbying groups, corporations, associations, and individuals because these entities have the wealth and power to control who comes into an office and who remains. Whoever sits on the throne makes the laws so these major players both navigate and drive us into the future. During the May 2002 Primary Election, eighty-seven candidates for the West Virginia Legislature had no opponents. Part of this resulted in entrenched incumbents who raised the most campaign cash from big money lobbying groups seeking legislative favors. With such large campaign war chests it renders incumbents all but invincible as well as being perpetually perceived to be owned by special interests.

For example, prior to the 2000 General Election, a cartoon in the *Charleston Daily Mail* depicted the prevailing views of the average voter with regard to elections. The cartoon was entitled "Special Interests 2000" and illustrated a huge trough that was overflowing with cash. A donkey and an elephant are submerged in the cash while the "special interest men" are standing in the background proclaiming "We've already won!"[1379] Without such political action committee (PAC) money in elections, newspapers are more likely to question a candidate or an elected individual with substantive questions about issues and votes instead of whether or not their stance on an issue is based upon a large campaign contribution from a special interest group or individual donor. Thus, West Virginia must immediately eliminate all contributions from PACs. While there are many well-intentioned PACs, others have simply become avenues for corporations to illegally funnel money into funds to get around the prohibition against corporate donations. Moreover, while some good honest groups might feel punished by this move, a much better system of elections will prevail. And, individuals from legitimate groups will still be able to contribute, but they will just have to do it openly and with individual political contributions just like every other West Virginian.

With regard to judicial elections, two possible ways to reduce the influence of money in Supreme Court elections are to extend the terms of Justices to sixteen years as well as increase the number of Justices from five to seven. The focus of most individuals critical of the judicial selection process in West Virginia is usually centered around the debate on election of judges versus the appointment of judges. When asked, "What is your opinion of the Judicial Selection Process that West Virginia now maintains?" former Chief Justice Neely said:

> The Judicial Selection process is exactly like the two restaurants in a small WV town. I once had business affairs in a small West Virginia town and when I was a boy, I first went into that town about lunch time and I asked a constable where to eat. He said, "Oh son, there are two restaurants here, X and Y and they're both about the same, you could eat at either one of them." And I said, "Well, which one do you think is better." And he said, "Oh, they're just exactly the same, I'd go to whatever one is closer." And I said, "Well, if you were going to eat at one, which one would you pick." He said, "It wouldn't make a bit of difference to me, but," he said, "I'll tell you one thing boy–which ever one you pick, you'll wish to hell you'd picked the other one." And that's the system of judicial selection.[1380]

While I favor the election of judicial candidates, I certainly agree with Justice Neely that both the election and appointment selection of judges have their pitfalls. For instance, a system of appointed judges chosen by the Governor is problematic because wealthy individuals who have considerable influence with a Governor would have influence in choosing all five justices, all sixty-six circuit judges, and all thirty-five family court judges, versus the voters making those decisions in a system of judicial elections.

One aspect of the State judicial retirement system is that a justice must have sixteen years of service in order to retire. With the current term of a justice being twelve years, unless he or she has previous years on the bench as a circuit judge, that justice will have to run for re-election in order to qualify for judicial retirement. Increasing the term to sixteen years will remove the fear of losing an election with just four years left before retirement. Thus, justices will have a shield in their decision making much like federal judges who receive lifetime appointments. With regard to the argument that the election of justices will continue to result in millions of dollars pouring into judicial campaigns, expanding their terms to sixteen years will ensue that justices are not truly beholden to anyone since they won't have to run for re-election. It also addresses the fact that it is rare for a justice to actually serve two full twelve-year terms anyway and thus eliminates the likelihood of a justice retiring early during a second term and having his or her successor appointed by a governor creating a distinct advantage in the next election for the appointee. Moreover, electing seven State Supreme Court Justices will reduce the amount of influence that one individual justice actually has on the Court and will create more stability in Court Opinions. Additionally, as the costs of elections continue to consistently increase dramatically, the idea or perception of purchasing Supreme Court decisions will be much more difficult with seven justices on the Court. Thus, the better solution to judicial reform would be to continue electing justices, but to change their terms to sixteen years and to expand the Court from five to seven members.

The State's political parties must also take responsibility and denounce members of their own parties who commit election violations or other egregious crimes. Nothing infuriates me more than the head of one political party answering a question about one of its members who committed an election violation by saying, "Well, the other party has been doing this for years" followed by a list of examples. My response is, "so what?" The argument is akin to a three year old saying he shouldn't have to take a nap because his little brother didn't have to take a nap the previous day. It is time for politicians and political parties to take responsibility for the acts of their members as corruption is not a party based infraction. It is individually based and Republicans should never invite convicted Governor Arch A. Moore, Jr. to be a keynote speaker for any event just as Democrats shouldn't invite the many convicted State Senate Presidents and Attorneys General. In this light, candidates must agree to condemn participation in their campaigns or political party events by these criminal politicians.

Other ideas needed immediately in West Virginia are initiative, referendum, and recall. The initiative is a process that enables citizens to bypass their state Legislatures by placing proposed statutes and, in some cases, constitutional amendments on the ballot. Referendum, on the other hand, is a device which allows voters to approve or repeal an act of the Legislature. For instance, if the Legislature passes a law that voters do not approve of, they may gather an appropriate number of signatures on a petition to demand a popular vote on the law. Such enactments would promote grassroots democracy. Referendum and initiative are already available in twenty-four states and have been successful in bringing a voice directly to the people. For instance, if these provisions were available to West Virginians right now, and the Legislature failed to enact the reforms provided herein, the citizens could have my Contract With The Voter reforms placed directly on the ballot to be voted upon during the next election. The other necessary tool for West Virginia citizens is a process known as recall. This provision provides a procedure whereby a public official, such as a governor, an attorney general, or a state senator or delegate, could be removed from office before the end of his or her term by a vote of the people. Such action could be taken only after the filing of a petition signed by a required number or percentage of qualified voters. These provisions should be used in circumstances when a Legislature ignores the constant will of the people or the cry for such political reforms. Moreover, the requirements for initiative, referendum, and recall should be somewhat rigorous as these tools are certainly necessary, but should not be enacted in such a manner that radical groups can abuse the process. Thus, the requirements for such procedures should be high enough to demonstrate that a significant number of State citizens have expressly indicated with their signature that such action is necessary or deserves more consideration. Citizens need a way to bypass an unresponsive and corrupt body of government.

In addition, not only must West Virginia enact better Sunshine laws providing for better access to government meetings, but also Freedom of Information Act laws ensuring better public access to most government documents. As United States Supreme Court Justice Louis Brandeis said, "Publicity is justly commended as a remedy for social and industrial diseases. Sunlight is said to be the best of disinfectants; electric light the most efficient policeman."[1381] And, along with openness must come affordability. I remember once when I was getting a copy of something from Secretary of State Ken Hechler, who was a down-to-earth politician who allowed more access to himself than most other elected politicians I have known. Even so, he explained to me that his office charged $5 for a single copy and $5 for subsequent copies of information requested by the public. I told him that was outrageous and he replied that it cut down drastically on the number of requests for information, adding that he just didn't have enough employees to fulfill all of the requests he would receive if he only charged 10 cents per copy. My response was "too bad, this is wrong." Politicians need to go to the Legislature if it truly does become a problem providing access to the public for government information and explain why they need more people or more money. The average person must have access, and cost restrictive measures certainly limit such access.

Speaking of the Secretary of State's Office, the State's election laws are convoluted and confusing. They should be written in clear and concise language making it easy for the average person to understand without a lawyer. Thus, the Legislature, with the advice of the Secretary of State, must study, revise, and completely overhaul the laws by clearly spelling out specific penalties for election-related violations. They must also take the numerous misdemeanor election violations and make many of those crimes felonies. Moreover, the requirements for running for office should be easy for anyone to understand. The labyrinth of requirements for filing papers and campaign finance reports must not be the reason preventing any potential West Virginia candidate from running for office. Running for office in West Virginia should be easy, without hassle, and accessible to anyone. With this in mind, the State must also enact legislation allowing potential candidates to secure a place on the ballot by obtaining a set number of voter signatures in lieu of paying the set filing fee, as costly filing fees often prevent potential candidates from seeking political office.

There is also much discussion about new types of voting machines. West Virginia currently has several different types of voting machines throughout the State and that must end. Why should one county's faulty voting system affect the entire election throughout the State? If one county's system is defective and causes 5,000 votes to go to one candidate rather than another candidate, or its system is easy to defraud and an equal number of votes are transferred to another candidate, then the entire statewide election results can easily be affected. For example, if during one election cycle in West Virginia, the elections of candidates for the United States Senate, the Governor, and the Attorney General's offices were all decided by between 1,000 and 4,000 votes, a political boss who fraudulently controls 5,000 votes in his region suddenly has a significant amount of influence. Moreover, an illegal shifting of votes could even have national ramifications and alter the electoral college votes and improperly lead to a candidate becoming President of the United States based upon a handful of corrupt votes. If such a scenario seems unlikely, consider the fact that George Bush won the Presidency in 2000 by just three electoral votes while West Virginia provided five electoral votes securing his victory. During that same election, as evidenced by the arrests and convictions of county sheriffs, county clerks, circuit clerks, chiefs of police, and several other individuals for their election violations, vote-buying was rampant in southern West Virginia and those illegal votes bought and sold necessarily swayed the results in one direction or the other during that statewide election.

Thus, the Governor, the Secretary of State, and the Legislature need to seriously study this issue and find a uniform system of voting with the most safeguards in place to prevent fraud. Such a system must be sufficiently accountable and provide a legitimate paper trail. Likewise, the voting machines must be owned by the people, not by private companies who could ultimately manipulate elections. There are some great county officials in this State who want nothing more than to have clean elections, but dirty politicians in even a few counties can potentially change both statewide and national results in any election.

Other ideas often mentioned with regard to election reforms consist of ways that make it easier for people to vote and register to vote, such as permitting online voting and enabling voter registration as late as election day. Others include curbside voting, voting by mail, phone-in voting, or holding a two or three day election. West Virginia has an early voting period, referred to as no-excuse voting, a system different from most other states which often just have an absentee voting system whereby a voter must have a valid excuse for not being able to vote on election day. No-excuse voting allows people to vote during a fifteen day period prior to the election without a reason.

Initially I was very much in favor of the idea of early voting as it makes voting much easier and seems to have improved voter turnout. However, several circuit clerks and county clerks, who are in charge of those early ballots, have been arrested, convicted, and sentenced throughout the years for buying and selling West Virginia elections. That causes great concern for the legitimacy of the entire process. Giving criminal politicians more time to handle people's ballots and to commit fraud doesn't seem like the direction to go with any reforms. These suggested reforms, as well as the no-excuse voting period, do nothing to address the causes of corruption or low voter turnout and really aren't helpful to improving the problems with West Virginia politics. After all, how does having more votes cast, when the validity of many of those votes are in question, help improve a broken system? And, many of these new ideas for voting seem to create the potential for much more election fraud in a system which has already proven that, even with so-called safeguards in place, it can't be trusted.

Nonetheless, I am not advocating eliminating the no-excuse voting period in West Virginia because the enactment of my Contract With The Voter will alleviate many of my concerns with early voting. However, election reform is much more than access to voting, and restoring trust in the system will be the best solution to voter turnout. With that being said, every possible accommodation must be made for military personnel who wish to vote in any election. Men and women fighting for the freedom of this nation should have full access with as many obstacles removed as possible.

Another necessity to reforming West Virginia politics is providing an adequate whistleblower statute so workers don't commit illegal acts just because they want to keep their jobs. People are often placed in enormously unethical situations by employers mainly because they know they can get away with such behavior due to West Virginia's weak enforcement of its laws. Such an enactment will also act as a deterrent for those who push employees to commit illegal acts as the fear of reprisal against an employee will be removed. Many West Virginians struggle to make ends meet and the thought of reporting a violator under current State laws and then facing the real possibility of losing their job and health benefits is not very alluring.

Finally, so-called Clean Money reform is also something that must receive more discussion in West Virginia politics. I don't propose the implementation of a Clean Money system for a couple of reasons and that shouldn't be a sign that I question its legitimacy for some states. First, people don't know enough about Clean Money elections, and opponents are able to easily put a negative spin on the issue in a public perception campaign. Telling people the government is going to pay for campaigning is one of those ideas that at first blush just sounds bad. I'll admit that when the idea was initially mentioned to me I was extremely skeptical. I had read articles in papers like the *Charleston Daily Mail* saying, "Some legislators seriously propose that West Virginia create an entitlement program to subsidize politicians. It's called the 'clean elections' bill, and it is one terrible idea." The *Daily Mail* added, "Backers of this measure see nothing wrong in giving fringe candidates money earned in the overwhelming majority of cases by people who would not support those candidates voluntarily [and] people who are 49th in per capita income should not be forced to subsidize candidates they may or may not support."[1382]

The idea of Clean Money may one day have its place in West Virginia politics, but today is not that day. This will be an uphill battle for proponents and should not become a poison pill for the other reforms which must be enacted immediately. Moreover, Clean Money elections will become more effective after the other reforms from my Contract are steadily in place. Then, the issue can be better addressed at that time. In the interim, candidates must pledge to seriously consider this issue and to seek a legislative committee assigned specifically with investigating and making recommendations to the entire Legislature about the positives and negatives of such an enactment and the potential of such a reform on West Virginia elections.

Under Clean Money systems, candidates renounce special interest donations and large donations from wealthy individuals. Instead, candidates agree to strict spending limits with fixed and equal sums of money from a publicly financed election fund. A system of publicly funded state elections fosters a healthier democracy by increasing the number of candidates who run for office and thus, increases voter choices. Clean Money reform also addresses the imbalance in campaign funds available to incumbents and challengers. In addition, candidates participating in a Clean Money system have the advantage of actually being able to listen to the voters on important issues instead of spending the majority of their time fundraising in order to become elected or achieve re-election. As such, candidates become candidates instead of full-time fundraisers. In order to qualify for public funding in a Clean Election, a candidate must collect and remit a fixed number of small donations from a set number of registered voters. This process requires candidates to connect with voters early in the campaign season, rather than with special interest groups and multi-millionaires. Candidates selecting a Clean Money option must also agree not to raise private money for their campaign and not to spend any of their own money.

Maine's Clean Money system is the prime example of an effective model and could serve as a model for West Virginia in the future. It provides in part:

> Candidates can opt not to accept or spend private funds for their campaigns. They must demonstrate credible public support by raising a minimum number of $5 individual contributions.

> That money is transferred to a state Clean Elections Fund, which then gives each candidate 75 percent of the average spent in recent elections for that office. (With no need to spend money on fundraising, available funds go further).

> If candidates running with private money outspend set levels, opponents playing under the clean-elections rules are entitled to extra public funding.[1383]

I spoke with State Delegate Boyd Marley of Maine who was successfully elected as a Clean Money candidate and who campaigned with slogans such as "your special interest free candidate" and "voter owned elections." Marley said Maine's Clean Money system works and should become the norm for all states. He said during the 2002 General Election in Maine, 59 percent of the victorious Maine Legislators were clean election candidates and that prior to becoming a Clean Money candidate he spent 70 percent of his time raising money and not nearly enough time actually going to community based functions. He also said legislators are able to vote their conscience when they do not have to rely on special interest money as they can vote without fear of losing future campaign donations.[1384]

West Virginia State Senator Mike Oliverio says that public financing of elections is probably a good idea, but not a practical idea for the State. Oliverio stated that West Virginia could not afford a Clean Money system because, "We're a state that can't pay our health insurance premiums for our employees."[1385]

Oliverio's argument, however, is precisely the reason West Virginia should consider implementing Clean Money reform. The reason the State cannot pay health insurance premiums is a result of the influence already yielded by special interest groups. So, with regard to Clean Money reforms, this issue deserves more study and more consideration.

The reforms provided herein and outlined by my Contract With The Voter will force candidates to return to "old-fashioned" politics where candidates campaigned door-to-door, attended editorial meetings, frequented local political functions, and answered questionnaires from politically active organizations. Former Logan County political boss Raymond Chafin recalls past elections in southern West Virginia when political candidates, "came out to where you lived [and] found you in your cornfield and told you what they stood for."[1386] Today, those images are figments of the imagination. During typical statewide campaigns of recent years in West Virginia, campaigning has transformed into an all out battle for television time, while face-to-face politics has become a faded memory.

Just as former West Virginia Supreme Court Chief Justice Richard Neely has said, "In yesteryear, the average voter–a person unable to make political campaign contributions, unable to entertain lavishly, and unable even to flatter convincingly–had at least one weapon in his never ending battle with government–his vote!" These days though, "[t]he wealthy classes–particularly those in commerce, industry and the professions who do business with the government–are amply represented in the political process because they have money [and] politicians have become simple commodities to be flogged on the television like soap or toothpaste." Neely added, "MONEY and MORE MONEY are now the only requirements for winning elections."[1387]

Many of the unfortunate events that have played out in the history of West Virginia demonstrate how the corruptive influence on the election process transcends the simple campaign donation; however, the one common thread with election corruption is that money in one way or another is almost invariably the mechanism behind such corruption. People have lost faith in their system of government and the reforms provided herein will revitalize the State's government in a manner which will promote involvement with confidence in the system. The Contract With The Voter must be taken by every State voter during each election contest and presented to potential candidates ensuring that West Virginia politicians who play by the rules and who don't proudly and shamelessly violate the law will someday become the norm rather than the exception.

In discussing these reforms with a few of my close friends, a couple of them indicated to me that while they agreed that these changes were certainly necessary and long-overdue, that fifty separate reforms was just too ambitious. They suggested that I reduce the Contract to just ten or fifteen reforms. After considering their suggestions, however, I concluded that the specific reforms in the Contract were not something that could be carved away at like a Thanksgiving turkey. For too long, West Virginians have accepted too little from their government and each and every reform on the Contract is specifically designed to address some corrosive activity which has been ignored and/or tolerated. Thus, I firmly believe that only comprehensive reforms will begin to heal the tissues of betrayal felt by many West Virginians due to year after year of the corruption and questionable behaviors of some State politicians.

# THE LOUGHRY PLAN TO REFORM WEST VIRGINIA POLITICS

## A CONTRACT WITH THE VOTER*

I, _____, a candidate for political office in West Virginia, do hereby form this contract with _____, a voter, as well as all other citizens eligible to vote for this political office in the upcoming election. I fully recognize that West Virginia has had an unseemly history of political corruption and I promise to be a part of the solution and not a part of the problem. As such, I will do everything in my power to seek the implementation, introduction, and passage of the following reforms or I agree not to seek re-election.

1.      I will support a constitutional convention as well as a special session of the State Legislature to deal exclusively with enacting comprehensive and fundamental reforms designed to overhaul West Virginia's political system.

2.      I will support legislation providing that a public official who knowingly uses his or her office in a corrupt manner shall lose all of his or her State pension benefits.

3.      I will agree to support specific legislation prohibiting any public official from purchasing or distributing thinly veiled campaign re-election State paid-for trinkets, such as magnets, key chains, cups, pens and pencils, or by placing his or her name on State

---

* A free printable copy of the Contract With The Voter is available at www.reformwv.com.

vehicles, and believe that such action should constitute a felony and result in removal from office for misuse of State funds.

4.        I will support legislation placing restrictions on the Governor's Contingency Fund preventing millions of dollars from being spent for shameless political purposes and require that the monies set aside in that fund be used only during times of State disasters or as otherwise specifically prescribed by the State Legislature.

5.        I agree to support legislation providing for a complete audit of the annual Budget Digest or its equivalency, as well as providing that the passage of the Digest occur *during* the sixty-day legislative session and only after a full and fair debate by the entire Senate and House of Delegates.

6.        I agree to support legislation prohibiting any secret legislative accounts and any such violation shall be punishable as a felony.

7.        I will support a law providing for a lifetime ban from running for office in West Virginia for individuals who have been convicted of a felony.

8.        I will support a law providing for a lifetime ban on the return of a law license or admittance to the State Bar of any public official who commits a felony.

9.        I will support state and federal constitutional amendments making it easier for the State of West Virginia to control spending in political elections.

10.      I will support serious reform of the State's Ethics Commission allowing for a complete overhaul of the Ethics Act or will vote to disband the current and ineffective agency.

11.      I will support changing West Virginia's multiple types of voting machines and will seek legislation providing for a uniform system of voting with sufficient safeguards put in place to prevent fraud.

12.     I will support legislation making vote-buying and vote-selling punishable as felonies which include imprisonment, a significant fine, and a lifetime ban from voting or participating in West Virginia politics.

13.     I will support legislation strengthening truth in campaigning laws providing that any individual who knowingly uses false statements about a candidate in a campaign advertisement would be guilty of a felony punishable by strict penalties.

14.     I will support legislation making any election fraud committed by any public or private individual a felony punishable by imprisonment, fines, and a lifetime ban from voting or participating in West Virginia politics.

15.     I will support specific legislation outlawing any individual or group from paying money to be listed on political slates which are used to buy votes and make any such violations a felony punishable by imprisonment, fines, and a lifetime ban from voting or participating in West Virginia politics.

16.     I will support legislation making any act of voting the dead, voting more than once, or knowingly casting any false ballot, a felony punishable by imprisonment, fines, and a lifetime ban from voting or participating in West Virginia politics.

17.     I will support legislation to further purge the county voters' registration rolls in hopes of ending West Virginia's sad tradition of dead people voting.

18.     I will agree to a "one strike and you're out" rule for felony-election or political-related violations of West Virginia's laws.

19.     I will support legislation providing that individuals convicted of election or political felonies for defrauding the State shall be forced to pay the full cost of their incarceration and prosecution against them.

20.    I will push for the enactment of a law granting the Attorney General of the State of West Virginia independent prosecutorial power to enforce the election laws of the State and to pursue public officials who commit frauds related to their public office.

21.    I will push for the enactment of laws granting expanded enforcement mechanisms to the West Virginia Secretary of State to handle election-fraud investigations and will make sure that the office is adequately funded to pursue such political criminals.

22.    I will agree to support immediate impeachment proceedings against any public official who is convicted of a felony.

23.    I fully support reducing the sheriffs' pistol permit fees to amounts strictly sufficient to cover administrative costs and provide that any such excess money collected shall immediately be transferred to the county commission to be placed in its general revenue fund thereby prohibiting slush funds for county sheriffs which are used as campaign re-election tools.

24.    I will support legislation providing that inaugural contributions shall be prohibited from corporations; that such contributors must follow the same rules that candidates follow in political campaigns; that such contributions must be used specifically for inaugural festivities; and that all excess inaugural funds must be returned pro rata to the contributors of that money and cannot be spent by governors in any other manner.

25.    I will support legislation prohibiting the renting of the Governor's Mansion.

26.    I will support legislation extending a State Supreme Court Justice's term of office from twelve to sixteen years.

27.    I will support expanding the State Supreme Court from five to seven Justices.

28.     I will support legislation banning special interest groups from financial sponsorship of legislative interim meetings or any other legislative meetings.

29.     I will support legislation banning the private legislative receptions provided by special interest groups during the legislative session.

30.     I will support legislation that prevents State Senators and Delegates from voting on or directly providing for State funding that goes to their employer, or to an event, property, or anything in which they receive a direct or indirect benefit.

31.     I will support legislation ensuring that all military personnel shall receive every accommodation in casting a ballot and that any obstacles making it difficult for a service member to vote absentee shall be immediately removed.

32.     I will support legislation providing sentencing enhancement penalties for law enforcement officers, prosecutors, and all members of the elected judicial branch.

33.     I will support a law making change of venue motions easier to obtain for prosecution in politician-related criminal trials.

34.     I will support legislation providing for mandatory sentencing laws for public officials who violate any law punishable as a felony.

35.     I will support laws mandating limits on campaign expenditures for all candidates in State elections, including those of state, county, city, and boards of education.

36.     I will support legislation placing limitations on campaign contributions whereby individuals will only be permitted to finan-

cially support candidates located within their own election district for a particular office on the ballot.

37.  I will support legislation completely eliminating all political action committee contributions in West Virginia elections.

38.  I will support a study of Clean Money reform legislation and seek a legislative committee investigation and report of the potential positives and negatives on West Virginia elections.

39.  I will agree not to support convicted felons from my political party who are chosen as keynote speakers at political events and will denounce any political party or group that supports such an activity.

40.  I will support legislation requiring "None of the Above" to be included as a choice for every office on every West Virginia General Election ballot.

41.  I will support legislation making public officials accountable for every penny from which they have bilked the State due to their fraudulent behaviors.

42.  I will support legislation providing for stronger Sunshine Laws.

43.  I will support legislation providing for more lenient Freedom of Information Act laws as well as making sure all necessary affordability safeguards are in place allowing people to truly have access to government documents.

44.  I will strongly support legislation providing for the enactment of Initiative, Referendum, and Recall.

45.  I will support legislation to overhaul the State's election laws eliminating confusion for individuals wishing to run for political office as well as prescribing clear and concise laws setting forth clear and specific penalties for potential violations of such laws.

46.     I will support legislation eliminating any statute of limitations on any law dealing with election violations or fraudulent behavior by a public official.

47.     I will support legislation whereby election contest expenses shall be paid in full by any individual convicted of election fraud surrounding the particular contested election.

48.     I will support legislation providing for the appointment of county assessors by the State Tax Department as opposed to the partisan election of those positions.

49.     I will support legislation allowing potential candidates for elective office in West Virginia to have the option of supplying a petition containing the signatures of a set number of registered voters in lieu of paying the filing fee for an office in which he or she wishes to seek election.

50.     I will support legislation providing for stronger whistleblower laws in order to allow for greater protection of workers who risk their careers to expose criminal activity of corrupt public officials.

# CHAPTER TWENTY

# Final Thoughts

*Our government rests in public opinion. . . . Whoever can change public opinion, can change the government, practically just so much.*

President Abraham Lincoln

West Virginia's official State Motto is *Montani Semper Liberi*, Latin for "Mountaineers Are Always Free."[1388] While it may stand for the pride of its people, it does not accurately represent its system of elections. To this end, the State Motto has become a cruel joke on West Virginians who have witnessed outrageous and disgraceful election conduct throughout the years coupled with the consistently rising costs of campaigns. On a scale of corruption, West Virginia ranks at the top of the list with Mayor Richard J. Daley's Chicago and Boss Tweed's Tammany Hall running somewhere close behind.

West Virginia's political history is the stuff of legend and mythology and unfortunately continues to create plenty of new fables on a seemingly daily basis. Ask yourself this: In how many states in 2006 was vote-buying for cash and liquor still a significant problem followed by the state's sheriffs, chiefs of police, county clerks, circuit clerks, and countless other elected officials being hauled into federal district court in shackles to answer for their crimes? I can think of only one and I live there. West Virginians have allowed the elite few to run their lives from their thrones by controlling their money, their time, and their freedom. While it certainly doesn't justify the extreme corruption that has existed, it does at least help to explain the culture which allows it to breed. This unprecedented look at the State's politics, followed by my proposed reforms, will eventually demonstrate to a nation that reform is possible anywhere.

People cite incidents of corruption that have occurred in their states and say, "Corruption in politics happens everywhere and West Virginia is just another corrupt State." If corruption truly is as prevalent in every state to the extent it is in West Virginia then there is no hope for democracy to survive. Clearly, it is not as bad in other states and my book shows the outrageousness of West Virginia's political corruption, an area in which the State, unfortunately, is unrivaled! For instance, some of the charges against West Virginia's elected officials during merely the last two decades include:

- stealing
- cheating
- gambling
- bribery
- ballot box/poll tampering
- corrupt real estate transactions
- insurance sales fraud
- tax evasion
- extortion
- mail fraud
- filing false tax returns
- obstruction of justice
- fraud
- accepting illegal cash contributions
- illegally distributing cash to influence elections
- making illegal campaign promises
- failing to report income
- receiving money through illegal actions
- lying
- covering up unlawful acts
- countless campaign violations
- selling political offices
- selling cocaine
- failing to pay State bills
- concealing State bills
- violating the public trust
- numerous sex offenses
- falsifying documents
- defrauding the government
- drug racketeering
- judicial nose biting

- jury tampering
- threatening witnesses
- soliciting prostitution
- liquor sales racketeering
- perjury
- federal securities law violations
- illegal withdrawal of public funds
- embezzlement
- forgery
- larceny
- assault
- battery
- public drunkenness
- police brutality
- civil rights violations
- falsifying State Police laboratory test results
- "election-rigging"
- blackmail
- illegal gambling
- illegal wiretapping
- sexual harassment
- robbery
- arson
- drug usage
- child abuse

As illustrated in earlier chapters, West Virginia's colorful history was tumultuous even before its actual statehood. From the Civil War, with a divided loyalty pitting brother against brother, to the $27,000 in stolen gold coins used to finance the makeshift government that voted to secede from Virginia, the State's birth was unlike any other. Constitutional scholars even today debate the very legality of West Virginia's statehood, which is not an argument with any other state. West Virginians were also equally divided between loyalty to Virginia (the Confederacy) and loyalty to the Union which became a problem early on as ex-Confederates were not allowed to vote or run for office during the early years. Then, as the new State continued to struggle to find its footing, the Capitol see-sawed back and forth several times between Wheeling and Charleston during a twenty-two year period. Moreover, as West Virginia was trying to find its independence during those early years, its actual border remained in limbo, while at the same time, its debt to Virginia for forming its own state wasn't paid off until seventy-six years later in 1939.

The early years of statehood included the Hatfield and McCoy feud adding to the State's unique history with the bloody and tragic events becoming a part of national folklore. That era was closely followed by the age of the "Miners' Angel," Mother Jones, whose confrontations with the coal companies defied reality. Events such as The Battle of Blair Mountain and the Sid Hatfield-Baldwin-Felts Detective Agency battles that culminated in the bloody Matewan Massacre were such astonishing events that most would believe they were elaborate fictional tales if they weren't such well-documented truths. Just imagine living in southern West Virginia in 1921. You are a part of the largest uprising since the Civil War as federal troops are sent following the declaration of martial law by the President of the United States to fight you; martial law was ordered many more times by several Governors during the 1900s; and the creation of military courts that completely suspended the "guaranteed" United States and West Virginia constitutional rights of the citizens were set up throughout the region. Keep in mind this wasn't the old West–it was just the former western part of Virginia.

The State's early election battles were also unique to West Virginia such as the time when four individuals separately staked their claim to the Governor's Office while hundreds of armed men guarded the Office prohibiting anyone from entering. When the sitting-Governor, whose term was supposed to have already ended, called the National Guard and stationed them around the Capitol to prevent a takeover by the other individuals who claimed the office, it is probably a miracle that a massacre didn't ensue. Then, the constant elections plagued with fraud resulted in continuous contests, some of which had to be settled by the United States Congress and the United States Supreme Court. Unlike other states, West Virginia's tempestuous and corrupt election charges were nonstop as city, county, state, and federal election contests went back and forth like a painful never-ending ping-pong match with the results of the elections often taking more than two years to determine the actual winner.

The early years that included complete control of southern West Virginia by coal companies as well as the iron fist of the infamous Logan County Sheriff Don Chafin, who received his substantial salary from these companies in addition to his government salary, shows how upholding the law was not without conflict for many elected officials. By running elections at gunpoint, with intimidation, burning ballots or just filling them out for voters, not allowing voters to vote in secrecy, not opening certain districts, arresting ballot commissioners, and determining the winners year after year regardless of the actual results, the stage was set for corrupt and nasty election day practices which still exist even today. In

2005 alone, in addition to just about every year before, several election officials were arrested, and later convicted, for election-related criminal activities. Several years earlier, between 1984 and 1991, seventy-seven public officials in southern West Virginia were convicted of offenses involving corruption such as extortion, fraud, arson, drugs, tax evasion, and various other revolting crimes. In one county alone, just about every elected official was convicted. In 1988, readers of the *Chicago Tribune* learned about Mingo County and southern West Virginia politics. The *Tribune* reported:

> The sheriff in corruption-plagued Mingo County pleaded guilty Monday to buying his job for $100,000, while the man who sold the post was sentenced to fourteen years in federal prison for conspiracy and tax evasion. . . .

> Fifteen [Mingo] county officials were charged last week with conspiring to control the county elections of 1984 with Owens, who was county Democratic Chairman at the time.

> Nearly fifty public officials or employees in southern West Virginia have been charged or convicted in corruption or drug cases over the past three years.[1389]

Again, does it really happen in every state to this extent? Has any other state convicted seventy-seven politicians during any seven year period at any point in their history? The answer is no. The problem is serious in West Virginia, and without a massive overhaul of the system the cancer only continues to spread to the next generation of politicians. Even during the 2004 election, the Republican candidate for Governor and the State Republican Chairman, who were brothers to the United States Attorney, were targets of death threats they believed came from people perturbed by the Republican Party's pledge to root out voter fraud in the southern part of the State. In 2005, the Lincoln County Circuit Clerk, who is actually in charge of that county's elections, was arrested for buying and selling votes to control every election during a fourteen year period in order to obtain the power to direct millions of State and county funds to himself, as well as to his family and friends.

West Virginia's politics is unparalleled. Only in West Virginia can a Governor attempt to reform State politics only to find himself years later broke and driving a cab in Chicago. No other state in the country has such a time-honored tradition of "voting the dead" coupled with the constant flow of county and

State officials who continually violate the law. The 1960 John F. Kennedy campaign was a great example of West Virginia's unique system of elections. Most scholars agree West Virginia was the key to Kennedy winning the Presidential Primary nomination. Had Kennedy lost West Virginia, there quite possibly would have been another President in 1961. Money flowed openly, and people today, like Raymond Chafin and Claude Ellis, speak bluntly and with pride about buying votes during those days of the so-called "fist-and-skull" elections. Those were dangerous days. Imagine millions of dollars in cash directly buying votes for a potential President and every State and county official on the ballot. It was so commonplace it was even joked about by Kennedy himself who told crowds that his dad told him to only buy enough votes to win the election and not to buy a landslide victory. That election also highlighted people like Ned Grubb who complained to the FBI about corrupt Logan County elections even though he was later convicted for some of the same corrupt activities while serving as a circuit judge in Logan County.

It is rare to hear about any state's Governor resigning from office and being convicted for corruption, but here, of course, we had two in recent history and another whose sexual indiscretions were even talked about on *The Tonight Show* by host Jay Leno. Thanks to former Governors Arch Moore and Wally Barron, West Virginia can boast having leadership that not only went to jail, but took many of those in their administrations with them. After being convicted of mail fraud, extortion, filing false tax returns, and obstruction of justice, coupled with his hiding of millions of dollars in State bills owed by his campaign contributors and secretly absolving them from liability, Moore has to be the most corrupt Governor ever to lead any state. His shakedowns of business leaders and individuals for cash he later used to buy votes in West Virginia was bad enough, but his lurking behind garbage dumpsters and hiding in the back of a political boss' car begging him to buy votes for him somehow seems like a story you would read about describing an election in a corrupt country in South America. And, like a rebellious, childish gang being expelled from school, he and/or his staff members left the Governor's Office in major disarray by plugging toilets, removing light bulbs and typewriter ribbons, disabling the telephones, jamming electrical outlets, and countless other criminal and destructive actions. I have never heard of any Governor in any state leaving office in such a disgraceful way.

Not only did Moore plead guilty to a laundry list of crimes, later deny his guilt, and even sue the State's insurer for not paying his legal fees, he was even able to gather more than sixty prominent West Virginians, including former Supreme Court Justices, statewide officials, religious leaders, heads of State universities and university law professors, who ironically taught criminal law and ethics courses, in support of his petition for the return of his law license. And, as he proudly stood on stage with President George W. Bush at a public July 4th celebration in 2005 in Morgantown, the home of West Virginia University, the crowd cheered. Moore hopes a Presidential pardon for his crimes is in his future, but until then the invitations requesting him to be a headline speaker at countless events throughout the State will have to do.

Wally Barron, who set up dummy corporations to funnel millions from federal money set aside for flood cleanup and who later bribed the jury foreman with $25,000 that his own wife delivered in a brown paper bag, ran a close race only to finish as possibly the second most corrupt Governor any state has ever seen. More than twenty of his administration employees were also charged with crimes. Is the picture becoming clearer? It's not just one rotten apple, it is nearly the entire tree that has gone bad. Then, the 2004 extra-marital affair involving Governor Wise and a female State employee became national news as the pair traveled to Spain, Italy, and other exotic locations all on the State's dime. Of course there was no investigation of Wise for misuse of State money conducted by any governmental agency and no charges were brought against anyone.

How about a State Delegate getting convicted of sexual assault for sexually molesting his fourteen-year-old legislative page he developed a relationship with through the Big Brothers Program, or the charges against a sitting judge for excessive drinking and sexual harassment while on the bench—including an accusation that he "opened his judicial robe to give an astonished woman visitor an up-close and personal demonstration that, like a Scotsman in kilts, he wore nothing underneath?" I guess the only thing worse than that would be a sitting Attorney General's plan to pay his secretary, who said she was carrying his child, $50,000 for an abortion.

Much like a traveling circus with its unique and colorful characters, West Virginia has the distinction of having the nation's only nose-biting judge. I have never heard of anything like this situation anywhere in the country. I haven't even seen or read anything in books or movies about a judge acting in such a manner. I guess it just wouldn't be believable enough to write in a work of fiction about a judge biting off and spitting out the end of a defendant's nose and then returning to the bench and calling the next case on the court's docket.

Other law-related circumstances include the countless prosecuting attorneys pleading guilty to drug charges for possession of cocaine, marijuana and other drugs, just as magistrates have demonstrated their complete disrespect for the State by running racketeering businesses from their office and exchanging sex for lighter sentences. It just boggles the mind. Situations like the magistrate who scratched her face and blamed it on a fictitious individual in hopes of collecting workers' compensation benefits, the other magistrates who accepted cash and other gifts such as an in-ground swimming pool, roofing work, and construction of a fish pond in exchange for favorable treatment, and the magistrate who was in the business of selling cocaine, are all deafening screams for reform.

Where else does the United States Justice Department in Washington, D.C., ask for the resignation of its own United States Attorney from southern West Virginia due to his alleged election violations when he ironically made his name by prosecuting politicians for none other than election violations? Where else does the Secretary of State spend a lifetime in politics fighting the amount of money in State politics only to spend more than $1 million running for Secretary of State? This, of course, was the same Secretary of State who authored the Code of Fair Campaign Practices which includes a provision restricting candidates for Secretary of State who sign the voluntary code to agree to limit their spending to $150,000. While he did sign the Code during his last election for Secretary of State, he included a notation in the corner of the document saying he agreed with the Code except for the outdated monetary limits. Curiously, the monetary limits were the purpose he wrote the Code in the first place and even though he had actually been the Secretary of State for sixteen years, he did nothing to change his written limits.

Still not enough? How about testimony from several individuals that an Attorney General hired a professional hit on his former Deputy Attorney General resulting in him being shot in the back of the head twice? What about a State Treasurer living it up at the luxurious Greenbrier Resort, receiving cash and gifts in exchange for shafting the State out of millions of its dollars in interest only to receive a minimal sentence and fine? Still yet, another State Treasurer who lost $279 million in State dollars and then testified during the impeachment proceedings against him that he didn't know that the numbers inside of the parentheses on his Treasurer's Office accounting books indicated a loss. That same politician handed out anywhere from 750,000 to more than 1,000,000 State paid-for trinkets every year while in office proudly promoting his name even though there were only 688,000 households in West Virginia at the time. And, while his actions were unique to the actions of treasurers in other states, they are just more of the norm for West Virginia politics. Year after year, elected officials in the State proudly and prominently display their names on vans, hand out millions of trinkets, send countless letters, and spend enormous sums of State money on newspaper, television, and radio advertisements under the guise of public service announcements–all of which are blatantly political and paid for by the State taxpayers. One elected official, "Peachy" Arthur, even placed a peach logo parodying his campaign material on official government vehicles, publications, and uniforms of his staff members.

Staggering amounts of money, impossible now to calculate, have been squandered by West Virginia's elected officials throughout the years on taxpayer paid-for trinkets. Sure, to some extent in every state, politicians feed from the trough of public money to promote their names, but I challenge anyone in America to find even one state politician from outside of West Virginia who wastes more money on trinkets of which their *only* purpose is to ensure re-election. The result is that once again West Virginia remains fiftieth in every important category but first in corruption and wasteful categories. A partial list of some of the more recent fleecing of the people through trinkets paid for with State money, which prominently display a particular elected official's name, include *millions* of the following items:

- banners
- State flag certificates
- United States Constitution certificates
- proclamations
- souvenir cards of the treasurer's seal
- gubernatorial collector cards
- State seal stickers
- highlighters
- nail files
- Pledge of Allegiance sheets
- associate treasurer certificates
- American's Creed sheets
- Boys' State certificates
- Girls' State certificates
- "Public Friend" certificates
- engraved plaques
- trophies
- letter openers
- pencil sharpeners
- money clips
- notepads
- calendars
- State pins
- pendants
- medallions
- Blenko glass vases
- hats

- patches
- "honorary" awards and certificates
- patriotic brochures
- historical brochures
- souvenir literature
- souvenir dinner plates
- Ambassadors of Communications certificates
- pens
- pencils
- litter bags
- key chains
- magnets
- flags
- paperweights
- coffee cups
- yardsticks
- coin purses
- fans
- bumper stickers
- pill boxes
- magnifying rulers
- "financial literacy" kits

If that's still not enough to convince you the State is unmatched in political corruption and election tomfoolery, maybe a Governor leaving a balance of $20,000 in the Governor's Contingency Fund just prior to his re-election which had a balance of $22.36 million just six months earlier will be the final straw. If not, then consider that the West Virginia Legislature created a Budget Digest, which is a financial fiasco unlike any fund established by any other state's legislature in the country. This multi-million dollar slush fund is used by State legislators to fund their re-elections as the money is given to just about every fair, festival, athletic field, and private club or organization in the State. Incredibly, this fund has never been audited, occurs outside of the sixty-day legislative process, and has even funded non-existent private projects such as the checks that were sent in 1995, 1998, and 1999 to the Blackwater 100 motorcycle race. The mayor and city employees in Davis gladly cashed the State checks even though the Blackwater 100's final race was in 1992.

With many of West Virginia's citizens having low incomes and working hard every day in honest jobs just to make ends meet, this State-funded re-election tool is used to give away money to any private interest group or individual that the legislators want without any accountability. If that's not bad enough, other "secret accounts" are created from time to time wherein surplus funds from House of Delegates accounts are moved to hidden accounts allowing certain legislators to give away millions of dollars completely outside of the legislative process. Another example unique to West Virginia allows all fifty-five county sheriffs each year in office to spend government money on pictures, costumes, native American teepees, donations, flowers, or anything else they choose, more often than not in amounts higher than the average yearly income of most West Virginians.

It's everywhere in the State. It's not just in the executive, legislative, and judicial branches with the elected officials. It is also their high level employees who have used their offices for crime and personal gain. The State's Lottery Director who was convicted of bid-rigging and perjury, the State's Lottery attorney who was convicted of insider trading and later accused of trading sex for legal fees in his private law practice, the operation of an illegal movie, music, and DVD piracy studio for more than three years in the State Capitol just one floor below the Governor's Office, the State Police Crime Lab Serologist who falsely testified in at least 134 trials putting innocent people behind bars for many years for crimes they didn't commit–it's all inexcusable! Imagine spending twenty years in jail for a murder you didn't commit as you left your spouse and children behind to grow up without you as that same criminal serologist who lied to put you behind bars didn't spend a single day in jail because he wasn't even convicted of a crime. In 1999, the *Chicago Sun-Times*, in discussing one of the innocent men who spent time in prison because of that serologist, wrote:

> Wilbert Thomas is now a famous man in West Virginia. His is the latest case connected to widespread corruption in the State Police crime lab there, including evidence tampering, officers falsifying test results, lying on the witness stand and generally tampering with evidence in whatever way would guarantee a conviction. Even if all signs pointed to a suspect's innocence.[1390]

It's a state where several county senior service directors openly fleeced the government to the tune of millions of dollars. Why do we reward, for example, a person who arranged compensation for himself of $301,728 in 2002 and about $457,872 in 2003, used taxpayer money to buy a $50,000 Lincoln Navigator, as well as an apartment at the senior center that contained a hot tub, a tanning bed, a thirty-seven-inch television, and a paid satellite service that included every single NFL game available for broadcast? That, of course, was on top of his unbelievable health benefits, sick and annual leave, every type of life and health insurance possible, and government all-expense-paid trips to Hawaii and other exotic locations in spite of the fact the per capita income for that particular county is just $14,220 with 25.10 percent of the population living below the poverty line. After significant negative coverage of that director's outrageous pay appeared in newspapers on nearly a daily basis, his salary was only reduced to $200,000, while he kept his job and benefits and wasn't prosecuted and certainly not punished. And, the decrease in salary probably won't be too hard on his family as he employs his wife at his agency and pays her more than $80,000 per year which is an increase from the $3.35 per hour she originally made at the agency when she was just his girlfriend. The fact that one State Senator even sent State money to the director's agency from the Budget Digest, even though he was also employed by the agency, further shows that those who push the ethical limits continue to take care of those who have paved the way.

In addition to the outright slime exhibited by many of the State's office holders and high-level employees, its sparsely populated border has been the home to some of the most costly elections in the nation. Imagine a Governor spending nearly half as much on his re-election in West Virginia as the sitting President of the United States spent on his re-election campaign throughout the entire country that same year. That is precisely what happened in 1980 when Jay Rockefeller spent $12 million to narrowly defeat Arch Moore. Rockefeller's $12 million spent on his Governor's seat, followed by another $12 million spent to obtain his United States Senate seat, was succeeded by one West Virginia politician after another spending millions to get elected to public offices. For instance, gubernatorial candidates have spent millions of dollars in every election, often from personal wealth, in order to buy that office. Then, imagine this small and financially struggling State having the most expensive congressional race of all 435 congressional races in the nation. It even had the most expensive Supreme Court election in the nation in 2004. Outrageous!

Most people hear the multi-million dollar numbers and realize it is a lot of money, but they never consider the additional fact that due to West Virginia's rural nature, it is much cheaper to buy television, radio, newspaper, and billboard advertisements than it is in more metropolitan areas. Thus, running for office in West Virginia should be much less expensive because these political advertisements are purchased for just a fraction of the cost of advertising in someplace like New York. It is so out of control that candidates even spend hundreds of thousands of dollars for State Senate and Delegate positions that only pay $15,000 per year.

West Virginia's history of corruption and problems with money in politics have been reported throughout the country and beyond during the years. In discussing the enormous amounts of corruption in West Virginia politics, the *Los Angeles Times* wrote: "There have been eighteen months of scandals in high places, a fireworks of sex, stupidity and greed extraordinary even for this notoriously corrupt state" and "[i]t seems there has been a for-sale sign up at the Legislature for some time. And at the governor's office the sign was a blinking neon." The front page article, with regard to the staggering number of convictions, stated, "It is as if a conveyor belt has been installed to carry slag from the Capitol building itself, hauling off the Treasurer, the Attorney General, two State Representatives, the Senate Majority Leader and two Senate Presidents."[1391]

In his recent book, *At Home in the Heart of Appalachia*, John O'Brien writes, "Since the 1880s, coal companies have been financing political campaigns and then rewarding elected officials after their terms. This has created an atmosphere in which corruption flourishes."[1392] A *Charleston Gazette* editorial said, "During the Barron and Moore administrations, bribery investigations, indictments and convictions were so continuous they were like a major State industry."[1393] Likewise, Pulitzer Prize winning author Theodore White, in his prominent book, *The Making of the President, 1960*, depicts West Virginia politics as "sordid" and among "the most squalid, corrupt and despicable in the nation,"[1394] while the *Logan Banner*, after the 1960 Presidential Primary, described West Virginia politicians and the surrounding election circumstances with regard to the amount of money being spent buying votes as "[l]ike hungry hogs going to the trough."[1395]

Even Harold L. Ickes, the Secretary of Interior during President Franklin D. Roosevelt's Administration, included on February 14, 1937, an entry in his secret diaries regarding West Virginia. During a particular entry that day, Ickes recalls a discussion he had with the President concerning Roosevelt's proposed constitutional amendment that would have increased the number of United States Supreme Court Justices. Roosevelt, in recognizing that it only takes thirteen states to block a Constitutional Amendment, said he believed there were enough purchasable legislatures available to equal thirteen. Ickes said, "[t]he President told me the other day that Senator [Matthew] Neely of West Virginia, had said that $25,000 would do the trick in his State."[1396]

In recent years, Dick Morris, Fox News television consultant and former political consultant to President Bill Clinton, said West Virginia was among six states that are "completely and thoroughly corrupt." Morris explained that to survive in politics in West Virginia, an honest person has to at least tolerate corruption.[1397] In 1988, the front page of the *Wall Street Journal* depicted West Virginia as a "state of despair" and "a poor and politically corrupt state with scant hope for its shrinking population."[1398] West Virginia even gained an international reputation of political corruption in 1992 when a London, England newspaper, *The Sunday Telegraph*, said,

> West Virginia is easily the poorest and probably the most corrupt of the country's non-southern states, with a recent governor currently behind bars, an attorney general, state treasurer and former state president disgraced, and scores of local officials indicted.   The state's senior senator, Robert Byrd (Democrat), was briefly a Klan member.[1399]

Similarly, a large spread in the *Sunday Magazine* from the *Washington Post* advanced the negative depiction of West Virginia politics.   In describing West Virginia, it noted that corrupt politics was a part of the State's system of government.  It provides:

> West Virginia is only an hour's drive from the Beltway, but not much news from the Mountain State reaches Washington.  And what does can usually be classified as grim or Gothic.  Bloody coal mine accidents and bloody coal mine strikes.  Floods of near-biblical proportions.  Towns with air so badly polluted that it rots out screens and peels the paint off cars.  A governor and two former state Senate presidents convicted in corruption cases.  A coal county that the *Reader's Digest* recently called "the most corrupt place in America."  A millionaire who hears God tell him to erect clusters of crosses along the highways of America.  A feud between two families, over a woman who'd dated members of both, that erupts in a shootout that leaves one dead and nine wounded.  A fundamentalist Christian who dies after being bitten by a three-foot-long rattlesnake during a snake-handling ceremony.[1400]

On another occasion, the *Washington Post* wrote:

> Shortly after he left office early last year, it became widely known that Moore was again under investigation as part of a wide-ranging federal probe of corruption of state and local offi-

cials that began in 1984. As part of the plea arrangement, Moore agreed to help federal prosecutors in the investigation. Two Democratic legislators, presidents of the State Senate, the State's No. 2 political office, were among the more than fifty officials who had pleaded guilty to various corruption charges in the probe.[1401]

Even within a national article discussing radio shock jock Howard Stern, who announced his candidacy for Governor of New York, West Virginia's reputation was highlighted. The *USA Today* article said a Stern candidacy may not be that far fetched in light of some of the other Governors who have served in various states. It said,

> We've had governors who've done everything from taking kickbacks to fathering illegitimate children, to selling pardons to jailed mafia leaders. Arch Moore, West Virginia's corrupt three-term governor who was sentenced to more than five years in prison, nearly got re-elected while under indictment.[1402]

West Virginia's reputation for a history of corrupt politicians is well-documented and well-deserved. In a light-hearted column in the *Charleston Gazette,* reporter Rick Steelhammer sarcastically suggested that West Virginia should take advantage of its troublesome corrupt past by building a shrine flaunting the events that have shaped the State's political image. Steelhammer says the State should open "The West Virginia Politics Hall of Shame," a museum that "would feature prison garb worn by the State's convict-governors, replays of the federal wiretaps used to send them to prison, and the cheap, government-issue tennis rackets they were forced to use when doing their time."[1403]

One of the problems in fighting for election and government reforms is the lack of attention given to the issue on the national level and that's why reform at the State level is so important. Nevertheless, for a short period of time, one citizen, Doris Haddock, attained her fifteen minutes of fame and national attention. Haddock, who is known as "Granny D," embodies the yearning of average citizens who recognize the problems with the present-day system and the need for change. During her 89th and 90th year, Granny D walked 3,200 miles from Pasadena, California to Washington, D.C. to carry the message that campaign finance reform was a major issue of concern to the people of this country. Rain or shine, she walked ten miles a day.[1404] I spoke to Granny D in Charleston, West Virginia. As she held a bologna and cheese sandwich in one hand and my tape recorder in the other, she said,

Campaign finance reform is the answer to solve our problems, the fact that we have no longer access to our Representatives or to our Senators because they have been bought by corporations, by unions, and by special rich men. Today a man has to sell his soul in order to run for office if he is poor or he has to be a multi-millionaire and that is not a Democracy and we have got to change it.

Campaign finance reform is the answer because it gives everybody a level playing field, you don't spend your money, you don't spend anybody else's money, you spend the taxes or some of the taxes that have been now given to corporations to make them rich while we are getting poorer and poorer.[1405]

To reform the system in West Virginia, other states, and on a national level, individuals must lead grass-roots efforts, for to facilitate change from the national level down or from the highest state officials down, is to ask the people who are already part of the problem to fix the problem. Therefore, it not only matters which box you mark for President of this country, but also who you support for offices such as Sheriff, Mayor, Delegate, and State Senator. President Abraham Lincoln, who signed the April 20, 1863, proclamation creating the State of West Virginia, understood the critical importance of public sentiment in a democracy. Lincoln said, "Our government rests in public opinion. . . . Whoever can change public opinion, can change the government, practically just so much."[1406] During a speech in 1839 about the existence of corruption, future President Lincoln said,

I know that the volcano at Washington, aroused and directed by the evil spirit that reigns there, is belching forth the lava of political corruption in a current broad and deep, which is sweeping with frightful velocity over the whole length and breadth of the land, bidding fair to leave unscathed no green spot of living thing; while on its bosom are riding, like demons on the waves of hell, the imps of that evil spirit, and fiendishly taunting all those who dare resist its destroying course with the hopelessness of their effort.[1407]

President Lincoln's comments represent that reform is not just about simply supporting and fighting for an individual, but it is also about fighting for an idea or principle. In Maine, for example, legislation for Clean Money reform passed through a referendum by the people because they were unsuccessful in getting the sitting Legislature to act. In the case of West Virginia, the State Constitution doesn't even allow for such a referendum by the people. However, after the reforms from my Contract With The Voter are implemented, that situation will change.

West Virginians cannot continue to accept the status quo from their elected officials. They must stand up and make scurrilous politicians, who taint the reputations of well-intentioned elected officials, pay for their crimes. Citizens must hold these law breakers accountable for their actions and vote against them during each election cycle. Notions must strongly be dispelled that only corrupt politicians can be successful and that people must accept their bad behaviors in order to receive jobs, education reforms, healthcare benefits, or even to get a local road paved. Such a change in attitudes will not be easy because people continually read story after story in the newspapers of one politician after another committing some questionable act. Even former West Virginia Supreme Court Chief Justice Richard Neely has said:

> Counter-intuitive as it may seem, the means invariably overwhelm the ends in the world of practical politics. Political battlefields are perennially littered with the mangled corpses of officials who believed government could be run like a business. But government and business run on completely different principles: business thrives on efficiency; government thrives on patronage. Business always lowers costs as a means to an end, while in government the means are the end. That's why the back-slapping, log-rolling, pork-barreling, job-giving, vote-buying and deal-making M.M. Neelys, [Justice Neely's grandfather] of this world are so wildly successful in politics, while the narrow, clean-cut, honest, technocratic, humorless [other elected officials] are such stupendous failures.[1408]

Clearly West Virginia has been a hotbed of political corruption since its untidy birth, and that is precisely why it can become a laboratory for making politics honest throughout the nation. Massive reform of the nation's most corrupt system of government will show how the lessons of West Virginia can transform the way politics is practiced in every state in the country. West Virginia has bred corruption in the past, but can now become a model for how politics should be practiced throughout the United States. Thus, because of West Virginia's notorious history of corruption, it actually provides the potential for nationwide reform. The national implications for successful reform in West Virginia are that if reform can work in this State, it can work anywhere.

The first step to reforming this system is the realization that it will not occur overnight, for it is a system that has been corrupt since its inception. West Virginians must see their enslaved past with open eyes and understand that they can only be victimized and forced silent by their elected officials if that is what they allow. Reform will not be without effort, it will not be without controversy, but most importantly, it must not be without success. It is time for West Virginians to finally bring truth to their official State Motto and prove that indeed, Mountaineers Are Always Free.

# Acknowledgments

In the many books I have read throughout the years, I have noticed that more often than not, that authors mention their spouses in the final paragraphs of their acknowledgments. I guess this is their attempt to save the most important "thank you" for last. With this book, however, I wish to begin by expressing my deep and heartfelt gratitude to my beloved wife Kelly. This has been an enormous undertaking requiring years of research and writing, and Kelly has been with me every step of the way. She has had to put up with my strange writing hours and endure countless discussions on election and political corruption reform. She is my sounding board and the brightest and most talented person I know. She has read, edited, criticized, and praised, in an open, honest, and unabashed manner. She is my constant check and balance and makes sure that I always consider every side of an issue, and she has done these things without complaint. Her contributions to this book were immeasurable.

I have been fortunate to have so many other extraordinary people during my long journey of completing this book who have provided invaluable guidance and assistance. My father, Allen H. Loughry, Sr., and my mother, Linda Loughry, have always been there for me in innumerable ways. My father, along with my grandfather, Scott Hovatter, a former Tucker County Democrat Party Chairman, really pushed my political interests during my early years. Uunbeknownst to me at the time, the foundations for this book were indeed being formed at an early age. I remember being six years old sitting beside my grandmother, Mary Hovatter, as we watched the Presidential General Election Results with the rest of my family. I was confused with much of what I was watching, but realized, for some reason, that politics was important to my life. Year after year and election after election I became more and more interested and curious about government. As I watched countless politicians on a state and national level, I began to form my own opinions about which ones were "good and bad" and what I thought was "right and wrong" with politics.

My father's 1988 campaign and subsequent campaigns for Tucker County Assessor were my first introductions to real down-to-earth politics as I knocked on just about every door in the entire county on his behalf. Standing on the porch steps and sometimes sitting in the living rooms of both friends and strangers, we discussed my father, but also discussed politics in general. I learned so much about what issues were truly important to people. More often than not, those I spoke with had a very unpopular view of politics and politicians. I wanted to change these opinions, but didn't know how. I found myself trying to defend politicians in general, but years of disappointment by many corrupt public officials made sure that such arguments fell upon deaf ears. And, the more I began to learn about the true extent of the corruption in West Virginia politics, such arguments simply became impossible to make with a straight face. I just knew that my father was as good and honest a man as I had ever met and I didn't like to think that he was being painted with the same brush as the politicians who tainted the idea of honesty in public service. Perhaps that was one of the stronger early driving forces for me. From that moment on, I wanted to change the face of politics in West Virginia and do what I could to help get rid of the rotten individuals who consistently abuse the trust of all West Virginians.

High school was also an important time for me in continuing my political interest. Mrs. Carol Roy, who taught numerous civics courses, was an inspiration in many ways. Being from different sides of the political aisle, she and I argued politics on nearly a daily basis. In the end though, she was more concerned that I retained my interest in government than whether I voted for her candidates. She was also the person who nominated me to go to Presidential Classroom in Washington, D.C. It was that conference which impacted my life in numerous ways including introducing me to the woman I would marry many years later. It was also during that week in D.C. that life's challenges suddenly seemed more achievable for an average boy from a rural area as the experiences and individuals from the conference opened my eyes to a new way of thinking.

Another high school teacher who impacted my life more than he probably knows was Mr. Jared Parsons. During my junior and senior years, Mr. Parsons taught me building construction for three hours per day as he explained the ins and outs of the construction trade. He demanded perfection each and every day. If a board was cut even one-sixteenth of an inch too short, it couldn't be used for that particular project and another board would have to be cut. At the time he seemed like a perfectionist, but it was that same quality that pushed me throughout my life to never take the "it's good enough" attitude with anything I have attempted. It was also those same ingrained convictions which caused me to become so frustrated with West Virginia's corruption and year-after-year fiscal irresponsibility as schools struggled without adequate funding while there always seemed to be enough money to give each child a refrigerator magnet with a West Virginia politician's name prominently displayed.

Another teacher who became a friend during my adult life is Mrs. Eileen Poling. As I have told her on many occasions, she was my favorite fourth grade teacher. She was certainly a wonderful teacher, but the fact that she kept up with me throughout the years and was always available if I needed anything is what I appreciate even more. She would often take the time to send me a note (now an email) to wish me well or congratulate me for something she had read about me in the local newspaper. Her helpful nature and our political conversations also sent the message to me to fight for change because that was important, but to do so by retaining the small-town values I learned in rural Tucker County.

My high school years also began my interest in journalism and writing, which in turn, inspired a deeper interest in politics. I was playing football for the Tucker County Mountain Lions and our team made the playoffs for the first time in the school's history. I remember criticizing Mariwyn Smith, the editor of the local newspaper, the *Parsons Advocate*, by telling her that I thought she should have covered the team more in the newspaper during the season and the playoffs. She immediately shot back, "Then, you write it!" It quickly put me in my place because I had difficulty stringing two sentences together at the time. She later called me at Tucker County High School and asked me again to write the sports articles for the paper. I agreed, but only with the understanding that I needed a lot of assistance from her. Soon afterward, it was every Sunday night when I showed up at her house to drop off my sports articles for that week's paper. I would sit quietly while she took her red pen and made numerous corrections and suggestions. Sometimes there were so many red marks that my article looked like a battlefield. I appreciated and respected every one of the changes and learned so much from her. I soon branched out to news articles which prompted my awareness of the community around me. It helped me see the bigger picture with state and local issues and began taking me down a road of thinking how to address many of those that interested or concerned me. On those evenings at their home, Mariwyn's husband George and I often stayed up late into the night with our political discussions (even though I had school the next day). Those thought-provoking talks were important not only to my political development and continued interest in the system, but also my drive to seek reform. Both George and Mariwyn have been enormously helpful throughout the years. In fact, Mariwyn even edited one earlier version of this book and compiled a part of the index to the final version. I am sincerely thankful for all of her help.

After high school I attended West Virginia University. When I first arrived on campus as a freshman, I remember running into an upperclassman and discussing the possibilities of running for a student government office in the future, perhaps during my junior or senior year. He was running for student body President himself that particular year. That discussion opened my eyes to something in politics prevalent no matter what level of elected office in which you are interested—the importance of money. He told me that in order to be competitive in a run for any student body office, I had to spend a lot of money buying posters and many other items. Having come from an average West Virginia family and making just enough money through summer employment of road and building construction, writing for two newspapers, and mowing lawns, running for a student government seat was no longer an option for me. I quickly gave up the idea of competing with rich, out-of-state kids who could easily write checks for thousands of dollars without giving it a second thought.

I have been so fortunate throughout my lifetime to have been surrounded with such supportive friends and family members. With regard to editing some version of this book, I want to specifically thank my wife Kelly Loughry, who as I said earlier, has stood beside me throughout this lengthy process. My mother Linda Loughry and mother-in-law Ann Swaim, both of whom possess phenomenal proofreading skills and who thoroughly read at least a couple of versions of this book were absolutely priceless and I treasure and appreciate them more than they know. Also, for editing I want to specifically thank Jed Drenning, who read more than one version and has had to put up with late night emails, telephone conversations, and lengthy discussions about sentence structure and countless other editing questions; Mariwyn Smith for her constant apostrophe instruction; Marsha Francis-Booth, who also read several versions of this book with her keen eye to find typographical errors; Dan Kimble for reviewing several different versions and who was perhaps only second to my wife as far as listening and engaging in *ad nauseam* political conversations and debates about this book; Greg and Diana Noone, whose comments and suggestions were invaluable; Professor Jamin Raskin, Professor Thomas Sargentich, Professor Stephen Wermiel, and Charlie Peters, who served on my dissertation committee and offered extremely valuable critiques leading to a better final product; Bill Bissett, who provided critical analysis for final versions of my book on a very short notice and who has always been available to help in any way I have asked; and George Manahan, CEO of The Manahan Group, who has had to endure many discussions with regard to this book and whose suggested edits kept me in check, making sure that I had considered all of the arguments both pro and con for each chapter and/or issue presented in the book. Both George and his creative director, Alex Morgado, were responsible for designing the cover for this book. George is not only the most talented and creative PR/Marketing person I know, he is genuinely a good friend and a good person. All of these people did so much with only a thank you in return for their time. I am so truly appreciative to all of them, but also enormously grateful to have such thoughtful, talented, and loyal friends and family members from a political melting pot of backgrounds. I must point out, however, that none of these people is responsible, of course, for any flaws in this work, and that from my point of view, the book is incomparably better than it would have been without them. There are others who have been so unbelievably helpful during the years, but I am afraid to single some of them out specifically because I fear that certain politicians will seek retribution against them. You know who you are and I sincerely thank you!

There have been several professors along the way who have been overly helpful. West Virginia University Professor Jim Paty and WVU Journalism Dean Emery Sasser became my close friends, confidants, and motivators. Dr. Paty always had a moment for me even when I am sure he really didn't have the time. The same goes for Dean Sasser, who unfortunately died a few years ago (and regretfully will not see this book). Another former WVU Journalism Dean and Professor was Christine Martin who also challenged me in ways that other professors had not up until that point. In spite of the fact that I had written stories for newspapers for several years, her critiques of my work in her classes clearly reminded me that I had much more to learn. WVU Journalism Assistant Dean Ivan Pinnell also has always provided unselfish aid whenever I have contacted him. Three other WVU professors in political science of whom I would like to acknowledge are Dean Allan Hammock, Dr. Robert DeClerico, and Dr. James Whisker. Dean Hammock and Dr. DeClerico were always available for political discussions and helped me in many ways during those critical college years when I believe students are more likely to either gravitate toward politics or away from it. Dr. Whisker and I seemed to agree on just about nothing at the time as we had countless lengthy political debates from opposite views. Those discussions, however, were helpful as he showed me different viewpoints which, in turn, pushed me to more critically consider every side of a particular issue. While at Capital University School of Law, Shirley Mays was an inspiration. Her course on State and Local Government was informative, challenging, and helped to provide a foundation for me for learning the ins and outs of state government. Former Capital University School of Law Dean, Dr. Rodney K. Smith, was also a genuinely caring person who readily made himself available to discuss politics and government and helped in numerous other ways.

While I mentioned them earlier with regard to critiquing my 2003 doctoral dissertation, Professors Jamin Raskin and Thomas Sargentich have been with me throughout this entire process. Professor Sargentich was the head of the LL.M. program at American University, The Washington College of Law, and pushed me to pursue my passion for clean politics. He was such a genuine person and unfortunately he died in 2005. I very much wish I could have given him this book in print and thanked him again for all of his help. He was the one who introduced me to Professor Jamie Raskin, who later became my dissertation advisor. Professor Raskin opened my mind to being able to push for real reform instead of just having a case study pointing out all of the problems with West Virginia's politics. He is brilliant. Enough said.

I am also grateful to have worked with some amazing people in the Governor's Office, the Attorney General's Office, the Supreme Courts of Ohio and West Virginia, and the Congressman's Office. There really are too many to mention, but I have been very fortunate with my life's experiences and the people I have met along the way. I do, however, want to say that Governor Caperton was a real pleasure to work for and I appreciate the time he spent helping me to learn about politics when I was a young man fresh out of college. Likewise, my current position working for Justice Maynard has been equally rewarding. While he has said on occasion that he is probably difficult to work for, he couldn't be further from reality. He is kind, intelligent, and an all-around extraordinary person.

I am thankful to Senator Byrd and Senator McCain for their efforts in providing forewords to this book. Their courage in attaching their names to a project like this demonstrates their true yearnings for reform. Their recognition that money dominance and corruption-related activities are non-partisan issues will lead to other politicians from both sides of the aisle taking similar stances. Their staff members, Senator Byrd's Press Secretary Tom Gavin, Senator McCain's Chief of Staff Mark Salter, and Mark's Executive Assistant Katie Fox, were instrumental in making the Senators' involvements a reality.

The pages herein and my opinions expressed in the book have been shaped in one way or another by the  politicians who hired me, by the many friends and relatives who have talked with me incessantly about the need for reform, and by the newspapers I worked for like the *Dominion Post* and *Parsons Advocate*. Moreover, you don't complete a project like this without a plethora of people along the way who have helped or inspired you in one way or another throughout your lifetime. Even throughout the years as I met thousands of West Virginians, I realize now that those conversations had a larger impact on me than I contemplated at the time. I believe that, contrary to what some politicians and members of the media might say, people really do care about corruption in government issues. People from all walks of life have shared with me their disgust and disappointment with elected officials. In fact, most of them believed that all politicians were corrupt, regardless of their political affiliation. It showed me that these same people yearned for change, but had been disappointed so many times before by slick-talking candidates who forgot their political platforms as soon as they were elected and took office. Many of these people inspired me to write this book. It was their frustration, as well as my own frustration, that pushed me to create my Contract With The Voter, a roadmap to reforming West Virginia's corrupt politics.

Equally important, I have to strongly acknowledge McClain Printing Company President Ken Smith and Vice President of Publishing Shelly Mullenax-McKinnie. I am so pleased that this book was able to be published by a West Virginia publisher who has had a long and distinguished reputation of preserving the State's history. Both Ken and Shelly have been extraordinarily easy to work with, professional, and remarkably helpful throughout this entire process. I couldn't have chosen a better publisher for this book. Moreover, I want to thank Asim Islam, McClain's Graphic Designer for all of his hard work on this book.

Additionally, while one State agency was impossible in trying to work with in obtaining information and photographs for this book, numerous others in the private sector were exceptionally supportive. For example, the *Charleston Gazette* was very helpful in providing me with pictures for this book. In particular, I would like to thank President/Publisher Betty Chilton, Editor James Haught, Design Editor Charles Reilly, Librarian Ron Miller, and *Charleston Newspapers* Administration General Manager Craig Selby. I believe that the pictures included in this book from the *Gazette* help to bring many of the stories to life. I also would like to thank the following individuals, newspapers, and organizations for providing pictures with little notice and without a second thought. Keith Davis, the Managing Editor of the *Logan Banner*, was not just helpful in providing photographs, he also spent a lot of time talking with me about his own published books and was always available if I had a question of any kind. Moreover, I would like to thank: Laurie Austin and James Hill at the John Fitzgerald Kennedy Library; Butch Antolini, Executive Director, *The Register-Herald*; Thomas Robinson and Lee Arnold, *Lincoln County Journal*; John Lilly, *Goldenseal*; Denise Shiflet and Jay Cronin, *Ritchie Gazette*; Phyllis Hunt, Executive Director, Pikeville-Pike County Tourism Commission; Betty Howard, Hatfield/McCoy historian; Clinton Nichols, *Clay County Free Press*; Neil Grahame, *Roane County Reporter*; Mary Ison, Library of Congress; Don Blankenship, Massey Energy Company; and Kandi Greter, Information Services Specialist, the Supreme Court of Appeals of West Virginia.

This book was published in June 2006 as my wife and I were expecting our first child in August 2006. The thought of raising a child in West Virginia certainly has been another justification in my desire for reforming its politics. It is my sincerest hope that many years from now, our child will have the opportunity, if he so chooses, to participate in a much cleaner system of government where scandal is a faint memory discussed only by the "old-timers" who remember the salacious days of vote-buying, vote-selling, constant convictions, and countless negative newspaper stories surrounding the State's elected officials.

# Notes

1.     Editorial, *Bribery–World cleanup effort*, Charleston Gazette, Dec. 10, 1998, at A4.

2.     *See* Chapter Nineteen, Reforming West Virginia Politics.

3.     *Jack's W. Va. Jack Returned Hundred Fold*, The West Virginia Hillbilly, Jan. 16, 1961, at 11; Meg Vaillancort, *JFK campaign allegations W. va. politician writes of buying votes for candidate in '60*, The Boston Globe, July 17, 1994, at A9; Leslie Phillips, *W. Va.: Local elections hold sway on voters*, USA Today, May 10, 1988, at A6; Mary Wade Burnside, *Talking about the politics of picking presidents*, Charleston Gazette, May 7, 2000, at F1 (West Virginia University Professor Robert E. DiClerico said that Kennedy "needed to demonstrate his viability to the party elites, who had some doubt whether or not a Catholic could be elected President."); Theodore White, *The Making of the President, 1960* 100-106 (Atheneum Publishers: New York 1961)(Theodore White proclaims that in December of 1959 Kennedy held a 70 to 30 percent lead in the polls against challenger Hubert Humphrey; however, once people learned that he was a Catholic, he actually trailed Humphrey in April 1960 by a margin of 60 to 40 percent.).

4.     White, *surpra* note 3, at 103; *see also* Nellie Bly, *The Kennedy Men: Three Generations Of Sex, Scandal And Secrets* 106 (New York, NY: Kennsington Publishing Corp. 1996) ("Jack and Bobby identified the West Virginia Primary as key to winning the nomination. The State's nomination was ninety-five percent Protestant and a win there would convince convention delegates that Jack's Catholicism would not be an issue in the presidential election."); F. Keith Davis, *West Virginia Tough Boys, Vote Buying, Fist Fighting, And A President Named JFK* 161 (Chapmanville, WV: Woodland Press 2003).

5.     Charles Kenney, *John F. Kennedy: The Presidential Portfolio: History as told through the collection of the John F. Kennedy Library and Museum* 38 (Public Affairs 2000).

6.     *Id.*

7.     Bob Miller, *Looking Back: 1960 primary turned nation's eyes toward state*, Charleston Gazette, May 29, 2001, at A5.

8.     Kenneth P. O'Donnell and David Powers, *Johnny, We Hardly Knew Ye* 162 (Little, Brown and Company: Boston, Toronto 1970).

9.     *Id.* at 160, 161, and 163.

10.     J. Howard Myers, *West Virginia Bluebook* 721 (Jarrett Printing: Charleston, West Virginia 1960).

11.     A slate is a printed list of candidates that a political faction group provides to an individual–in many cases with money–so that the individual will support and cast their ballot for the slate of candidates. The slate, often printed on index-style cards, could contain names for every office on the ballot or simply the names of a few candidates that the specific faction would choose to support. Slates often determined the winner of the election.

12.     Dan B. Fleming, Jr., *Kennedy vs. Humphrey, West Virginia, 1960: The Pivotal Battle for the Democratic Presidential Nomination* 109 (McFarland 1992).

13.     Angela Charlton, Associated Press, *Dan Fleming is confounded by a book that . . .*, Charleston Gazette, Nov. 11, 1997, at C1.

14.     Seymour M. Hersh, *The Dark Side Of Camelot* 35, 36, 37 (Canada: Little, Brown & Company 1997) (In 1919, Fitzgerald was "investigated in the House of Representatives for months before being unseated for vote fraud." Nonetheless, in her best-selling biography *The Fitzgeralds and the Kennedys*, Doris Kearns Goodwin observed that in spite of being ousted from the House, he "remained as exuberant as ever, emerging once again from disgrace like a duck from water, and the local newspapers still considered him the leading citizen of Boston.").

15.     Bob Miller, *Looking back: 1960 primary turned nation's eyes toward state*, Charleston Gazette, May 29, 2001, at A5.

16.     *Id*; White, *surpra* note 3, at 100; *see also* Richard Reeves, *President Kennedy, Profile of Power* 28 (Simon & Schuster: New York 1993) ("'Do you know how I won the West Virginia Primary? What he did for me there?' Kennedy had thought he might lose in West Virginia, and probably be knocked out of the race, until Franklin Roosevelt's son had come down to campaign for him. It was as if the son of God had come to give the Protestants permission to vote for this Catholic.").

17.     Davis, *supra* note 4, at 145.

18.     Charles H. Moffat, *Ken Hechler: Maverick Public Servant* 270 (Mountain State Press: Charleston, WV, 1987).

19.     Rusty Marks, *A look at the rough-and-tumble, vote-buying*, Charleston Sunday Gazette-Mail, Mar. 21, 2004, at F10.

20.     Staff Reports, *County Machines helped to Swell Vote for Kennedy in Primary*, Baltimore Sun, May 11, 1960, at A1.

21.     Staff Reports, *Plenty of Votes Bought in W. Virginia Primary*, Pittsburgh Post-Gazette, June 1, 1960, at A1.

22.     Staff Reports, *Votes Bought and Sold Openly on Streets*, Baltimore Sun, May 11, 1960, at A1.

23.     Dickson Preston, *Votes bought in West Virginia Primary*, New York World-Telegram and Sun, May 26, 1960, at A1.

24.     Ronald Kessler, *The Sins of the Father: Joseph P. Kennedy and the Dynasty He Founded* 352 (New York, NY: Warner Books 1996).

25.     Fleming, *supra* note 12, at 109.

26.     *Id.*

27.     *Id.* at 111, 117 (July 12, 1960 announcement by the Justice Department that its probe failed to show any federal election-law violations and that there was no federal law specifically covering ballot-box stuffing.).

28.     Associated Press, *Ex-Judge Grubb Dies*, Charleston Gazette, Apr. 17, 1997, at C1 (At the time of his arrest, James Ned Grubb was an elected circuit judge of the Seventh Judicial Circuit of West Virginia, located in Logan County.).

29.     United States v. Grubb, 11 F.3d 426, 430 (4th Cir. 1993).

30.     Fleming, *supra* note 12, at 116.

31.     State ex rel. Brown v. Thompson, 149 W.Va. 649, 142 S.E.2d 711 (1965).

32.     Fleming, *supra* note 12, at 101.

33.     Joe Savage, *Just Good Politics: The Life of Raymond Chafin, Appalachian Boss*, Washington Monthly, Vol. 26, No. 12, Dec. 1, 1994, at 56.

34.     Kessler, *supra* note 24, at 349-350.

35.     Don Wilson, *The Half-Pint Vote, Slating and the Lever Brothers*, Life, May 9, 1960, at 26, 27.

36.     Fleming, *supra* note 12, at 101.

37.     White, *surpra* note 3, at 100.

38.     *Id.* at 97-100; *see also* D. Wilson, *A Small State Takes the Limelight—In Logan County, the Half-Pint Vote—Slating and 'Lever Brothers*,' Life, May 9, 1960, at 24-29; State v. Hobbs, 168 W.Va. 13, 282 S.E.2d 258 (1981).

39.     Leslie Phillips, *W. Va.: Local elections hold sway on voters*, USA Today, May 10, 1988, at A6.

40.     *Id.*

41.     Davis, *supra* note 4, at 2.

42.     *Id.* at 154.

43.     Raymond Chafin & Topper Sherwood, *Just Good Politics, The life of Raymond Chafin, Appalachian Boss* 149 (Univ. of Pittsburgh Press 1994).

44.     Jennifer Bundy, Associated Press, *Logan Politics Hits the Light in Boss' Book*, Charleston Sunday Gazette-Mail, July 17, 1994, C1.

45.     Davis, *supra* note 4, at 152, 155.

46.     Jennifer Bundy, Associated Press, *Logan Politics Hits the Light in Boss' Book*, Charleston Sunday Gazette-Mail, July 17, 1994, at C1.

47.     Chafin, *supra* note 43, at 115, 137, 141, 143; Fleming, *supra* note 12, at 104; Meg

Vaillancort, *JFK campaign allegations W. Va. politician writes of buying votes for candidate in '60*, The Boston Globe, July 17, 1994, at A9; Rusty Marks, *A look at the rough-and-tumble, vote-buying*, Charleston Sunday Gazette-Mail, Mar. 21, 2004, at F10; Charlie Peters, *Buying votes hurts W.Va.*, Charleston Sunday Gazette-Mail, Oct. 3, 2004, at E3 (Peters' column was reprinted from *The Washington Monthly* where he is the founding editor.)(Peters, the former West Virginia House of Delegates member, said, "I assure you [the Logan County story] is not apocryphal."); Davis, *supra* note 4, at 139.

48.  Davis, *supra* note 4, at 153, 155.

49.  Chafin, *supra* note 43, at 149.

50.  Davis, *supra* note 4, at 140, 141.

51.  *Id*; *see also* Lester "Bus" Perry, *Forty "40"Years, Mountain Politics, 1930-1970* (Parsons, WV: McClain Printing 1971).

52.  Chafin, *supra* note 43, at 149.

53.  Davis, *supra* note 4, at 141.

54.  Fleming, *supra* note 12, at 104.

55.  Davis, *supra* note 4, at 154.

56.  Chafin, *supra* note 43, at 149.

57.  Davis, *supra* note 4, at 150, 154; *see also* Chafin, *supra* note 43, at 149.

58.  *Id*. at 151, 248.

59.  Chafin, *supra* note 43, at 149; Meg Vaillancort, *JFK campaign allegations W. Va. politician writes of buying votes for candidate in '60*, The Boston Globe, July 17, 1994, at A9; Davis, *supra* note 4, at 60.

60.  Chafin, *supra* note 43, at 53, 54, 136.

61.  *Id*. at 47; Meg Vaillancort, *JFK campaign allegations W. Va. politician writes of buying votes for candidate in '60*, The Boston Globe, July 17, 1994, at A9.

62.  Chafin, *supra* note 43, at 99.

63.  Jennifer Bundy, Associated Press, *Logan Politics Hits the Light in Boss' Book*, Charleston Sunday Gazette-Mail, July 17, 1994, at C1.

64.  Rusty Marks, *A look at the rough-and-tumble, vote-buying*, Charleston Sunday Gazette-Mail, Mar. 21, 2004, at F10.

65.  Davis, *supra* note 4, at 168.

66.  Chris Stirewalt, *Probes are talk of town, political corruption, vote-buying are hot topics of conversation*, Charleston Daily Mail, July 30, 2004, at A1.

67.  Davis, *supra* note 4, at 149, 171.

68.  Chris Stirewalt, *Probes are talk of town, political corruption, vote-buying are hot topics of conversation*, Charleston Daily Mail, July 30, 2004, at A1.

69.  Davis, *supra* note 4, at 170, 171.

70.  *Id*. at 244, 248.

71.  Chafin, *supra* note 43, at 52, 123 n. 2, 136 (Chafin said that around 1960 it usually cost about $100,000 gathered from candidates and interest groups (like coal companies) to run a campaign in Logan County.).

72.  *Id*. at 53, 54.

73.  *Id*. at 54, 55.

74.  *Id*. at 27.

75.  Fanny Seiler, *Logan neighbors wrangle over paving of road*, Charleston Sunday Gazette-Mail, June 24, 2001 at C3.

76.  Chafin, *supra* note 43, at 189, 190.

77.  Fleming, *supra* note 12, at 105.

78.  Chafin, *supra* note 43, at 190.

79.  *Id*. at 175.

80.  Joe Savage, *Just Good Politics: The Life of Raymond Chafin, Appalachian Boss*, Washington Monthly, Vol. 26, No. 12, Dec. 1, 1994, at 56.

81.  Chafin, *supra* note 43, at 68.

82.  *Id*. at 85.

83.        Fleming, *supra* note 12, at 68, 69.

84.        *Id.* at 83, 129 (interview of Harry Pauley by Dan B. Fleming, Jr., at Bluefield, West
           Virginia, Apr. 26, 1985).

85.        *Id.* at 87 (Edward W. Hiserman, interview with Roscoe Born, Wall Street Journal reporter,
           Charleston, West Virginia, May 25, 1960.).

86.        Tom Searls, *"The Dark Side of Camelot" casts West Virginia in bad light*, Charleston
           Gazette, Nov. 12, 1997, at A3.

87.        Hersh, *supra* note 14, at 96. On March 1, 2005, Hersh lectured in Charleston, West
           Virginia on "The Road from 9/11 to Abu Graib" as a part of the *Charleston Gazette*-West
           Virginia University Festival of Ideas. After Hersh's lecture I briefly discussed his book
           *The Dark Side Of Camelot*. I found his book to be very well-written and accurate based
           upon my own investigations and interviews with regard to the events surrounding the 1960
           election.

88.        *Id.* at 98.

89.        *Id.* at 91, 92, 93, 95.

90.        Fleming, *supra* note 12, at 87.

91.        Davis, *supra* note 4, at 169.

92.        Merle Miller, *Plain Speaking* 199 (Medallion Books 1974).

93.        Kessler, *supra* note 24, at 376.

94.        David Lieber, *Kennedy didn't buy W. Va., he just rented it, ex-aide says*, Charleston
           Gazette, Nov. 24, 1983, at A1.

95.        Angela Charlton, *Dan Fleming is confounded by a book that . . .*, Associated Press Political
           Wire Service, Nov. 11, 1997.

96.        Jean Stein, ed. George Plimpton, *American Journey: The Times of Robert Kennedy* 71
           (Brace Jovanovich 1970) (Roosevelt stated that, "[i]t was quite clear to everybody that the
           Kennedy family spent an enormous amount of money on television, radio, newspaper ads;
           a very large and expensive staff . . . as compared with Hubert's campaign which really was
           poorly financed.").

97.        109 CONG. REC. 198, Dec. 5, 1963 (Statement of Congressman Hechler).

98.        Chafin, *supra* note 43, at x, xi (*citing* Dan B. Fleming, Jr. *Kennedy vs. Humphrey, 1960:
           The Pivotal Battle for the Democratic Presidential Nomination* at 145 (McFarland &
           Company, Inc., 1992).).

99.        Dawn Miller, *Sheriffs Given Money to Help Kennedy, Salinger Confirms*, Charleston
           Gazette, May 13, 1995, A3.

100.       John H. Davis, *The Kennedys: Dynasty and Disaster* 286 (McGraw-Hill 1984).

101.       L.A. Times-Washington Post News Service, *Sinatra asked crime boss to aid JFK, daugh-
           ter says*, The Dallas Morning News, Oct. 7, 2000, at A1; *see also* Associated
           Press, *Daughter Says Frank Sinatra Got Mob Boss to Help With JFK Election*, The Inter-
           Mountain (Elkins, West Virginia), Oct. 7, 2000, at A3. Again, this is another example of
           perception of corruption. The author is simply providing an example of newspaper and
           television stories that were far-reaching in the public realm.

102.       Fleming, *supra* note 12, at 69.

103.       Hugh Davies, *Sinatra told me about links with the Mob: Daughter Tina claims that singer
           secured Mafia help for Kennedy*, Daily Telegraph (London), Oct. 7, 2000, at A14; *Don
           Cheadle Stars In 'The Rat Pack'*, Los Angeles Sentenel, Aug. 20, 1998, at A4; The Dallas
           Morning News, *Sinatra asked crime boss to aid JFK*, daughter says, Oct. 7, 2000, at A4;
           Verne Gay, *Daughter: Sinatra's mob ties helped JFK*, South Bend Tribune (Ind.), Oct. 7,
           2000, at A1; Stephen Salisbury, *Robert F. Kennedy's reputation has negotiated flak around
           publication of 'The DarSide of Camelot'*, Philadelphia Inquirer, Dec. 10, 1997, at A1.

104.       Nellie Bly, *The Kennedy Men: Three Generations Of Sex, Scandal And Secrets* 107, 123
           (New York, NY: Kennsington Publishing Corp. 1996).

105.       Jules Witcover, *Officials probe N.J. campaign Boast that votes were suppressed puts advi-
           sor Rollins in hot seat*, The Baltimore Sun, Nov. 13, 1993, at A2.

106.       *Barron Meets With Kennedy*, Charleston Gazette, Mar. 16, 1962, at A1; Fleming, *supra*
           note 12, at 167, 168; Chafin, *supra* note 43, at 157.

107.       Bob Kittle, *Pomp and circumstance*, Charleston Daily Mail, Dec. 9, 1976, at A1.

108.       *What Was The First Inagural Day in 1863 Like?*, The West Virginia Hillbilly, Jan. 16, 1961,
           at 5; *see also* Phil Conley, *A.I. Boreman named first State Chief*, Grafton News (Grafton,
           WV), Dec. 16, 1938, at A1.

109.    Virgil A. Lewis, *History of Government: West Virginia* 48 (New York: American Book Company 1913); On August 18, 1747, George Washington surveyed lands for Lord Fairfax on the Upper Potomac River. Washington not only surveyed much of the West Virginia Lands, he also owned a 2,233-tract of land in the Eastern Panhandle. In fact, Charles Town was named for Washington's brother Charles Washington. He also owned land in Wood County.

110.    Otis K. Rice, *West Virginia: The State and Its People* 108 (Parsons: McClain Printing Company, 1971); UPI, *Blennerhassett letter reminder of family's last days*, Charleston Gazette, Dec. 9, 1985, at A3; Mary Cobb, *Island history, Ruins hold view of past Blennerhassett culture*, Charleston Sunday Gazette-Mail, Sept. 20, 1981, at H1; Forrest Hull, *Hamilton Lost Duel, Won In Long Stretch Over Burr*, Charleston Daily Mail, Feb. 17, 1957, at A1. (Although Burr was found not guilty, his political life was ruined. Blennerhassett was arrested, but after Burr was cleared of the charges, Blennerhassett was not prosecuted.).

111.    *Id.* at 156, 160-161; Charles Shelter & Michael M. Reynolds, *Milestones of West Virginia History* (Parsons: McClain Printing Company 1963).

112.    V.B. Harris, *Great Kanawha: An Historical Outline* 112 (Jarrett: Charleston, WV 1974) (Abraham Lincoln became the 16th President of the United States on March 4, 1861).

113.    *Id.* at 111 (Virginia voters approved the Virginia Ordinance of Secession by a vote of 137,911 to 23,607).

114.    Arthur C. Prichard, *An Appalachian Legacy: Mannington Life and Spirit* 24 (McClain; Parsons, WV 1983); Rice, *supra* note 110, at 174.

115.    Rice, *supra* note 110, at 173.

116.    Harris, *supra* note 112, at 112, 113; Virginia v. West Virginia, 78 U.S. 39, 43 (1870); Rice, *supra* note 110, at 193, 194; Elizabeth Cometti & Festus P. Summers, *The Thirty-Fifth State* 654 (Morgantown: West Virginia University Library, 1966).

117.    Harris, *supra* note 112, at 114, 116 (The 1863 Constitution was mostly patterned after the Commonwealth of Virginia Constitution and thus a second Constitution was approved in 1872.); Rice, *supra* note 110, at 206.

118.    Staff Reports, *MAC Loved The State To Mushiness*, The West Virginia Hillbilly, Jan. 16, 1961, at 16. MacCorkle was elected West Virginia's ninth Governor in 1892.

119.    Staff Reports, *Governor Championed Our Mountains*, The West Virginia Hillbilly, Jan. 16, 1961, at 16.

120.    Staff Reports, *Two Presidents Help Construct Fort Here, Hays and McKinley Officers With Army*, Charleston Gazette, Nov. 22, 1925, at A1.

121.    John C. Nicolay, *Abe Lincoln, ed.* Vol. II at 286 (New York: The Century Co., 1894).

122.    Dr. Thomas Camden, *My Recollections and Experiences of the Civil War* (McClain Printing Co.: Parsons, West Virginia 2000); Rick Steelhammer, *Seized coins helped fund our wartime government*, Charleston Gazette, June 20, 2001, at A1 (The coins were of assorted denominations of quarter eagles ($2.50), half eagles ($5), eagles ($10), and double eagles ($20); *see also* (<http://westongoldrobbery.com>) (William Arnold Letters Dated January 1860 and March 25, 1861);(<http://www.hackerscreek.com/WVgold.htm>). The $600,000 figure is based upon the United States Department of Labor's Consumer Price Index as well as various college and university studies. Of course the collector's value of $27,000 in rare pre-civil war gold coins in today's value could easily be hundreds of millions of dollars.

123.    Rice, *supra* note 110, at 147.

124.    Virginia v. West Virginia, 78 U.S. 39 (1870).

125.    The various litigations of *Virginia v. West Virginia* are to be found in 206 U.S. 290 (1907); 209 U.S. 514 (1908); 220 U.S. 1 (1911); 222 U.S. 17 (1911); 231 U.S. 89 (1913); 234 U.S. 117 (1914); 238 U.S. 202 (1915); 241 U.S.C. § 531 (1916); 246 U.S. 565 (1918); Rice, *supra* note 110, at 210; Comett, *supra* note 116, at 654.

126.    William A. MacCorkle, *The Recollections of Fifty Years of West Virginia* 540-541 (The Knickerbocker Press: New York 1928).

127.    Slack v. Jacob, 8 W.Va. 612 (1875) (1875 WL3439 (W.Va.)) (This case involved a bill of injunction to prohibit the Capitol from being moved back to Wheeling.); Harris, *supra* note 112, at 173.

128.    Harris, *supra* note 112, at 173 (According to Harris, there was much "fanfare" in receiving the physical transfer of office paraphernalia and records which was made by boat from Wheeling to Charleston.); Rice, *supra* note 110, at 215.

129.    Harris, *supra* note 112, at 173; Slack v. Jacob, 8 W.Va. 612 (1875) (1875 WL3439 (W.Va.)).

130. Harris, *supra* note 112, at 175; *see also* Phil Conley, *West Virginia Encyclopedia* (Charleston: West Virginia Publishing Company, 1929) (An act was passed providing for a referendum on the permanent location of West Virginia's Capital.); Lewis, *supra* note 109, at 258; Charles Shelter & Michael M. Reynolds, *Milestones of West Virginia History* (Parsons: McClain Printing Company 1963); Rice, *supra* note 110, at 215, 302.

131. *Id.*

132. Tom Searls, *Manchin revives parade tradition, Today's is first since Moore's in 1973*, Charleston Gazette, Jan. 17, 2005, at A1.

133. *Mathew's Telegram Relates History*, The West Virginia Hillbilly, Jan. 16, 1961, at 16 (Later, in 1880, Governor Mathews sent troops to Hawks Nest in southern West Virginia to stop the States first major coal strike.).

134. Lawrence Messina, *W. Va. not a state: Maybe, law article opines*, Charleston Gazette, May 22, 2002, at A1.

135. John C. Nicolay, *Abe Lincoln, ed.* Vol. II at 286 (New York: The Century Co., 1894).

136. U.S. Congressional Globe, 38th Cong., 1st Sess., 1863, Part 1, p. 1 (Senator Davis died in office in 1872 the same year in which West Virginia approved its present-day Constitution.).

137. Jefferson Davis, *The Rise & Fall of the Confederate Government*, 2 vols., Vol. II at 306 (New York: D. Appleton and Co., 1881).

138. Article IV, Section 3, of the United States Constitution, in part, provides:

> New States may be admitted by the Congress into this Union; but no new State shall be formed or erected within the Jurisdiction of any other State; nor any State be formed by the Junction of two or more States, or Parts of States, without the Consent of the Legislatures of the States concerned as well as of the Congress.

139. Theron Clark Crawford, *An American Vendetta; a Story of Barbarism in the United States* (New York: Belford, Clarke and Co., 1888); Richard Kyle Fox, *Devil Anse, or the Hatfield-McCoy Outlaws, a Full and Complete History of the Deadly Feud Existing Between the Hatfields and McCoy Clans*, (New York: R.K. Fox, 1889); G. Elliott Hatfield, *The Hatfields*, (Stanville, KY: Big Sandy Valley Historical Society, 1974); Lawrence D. Hatfield, *The True Story of the Hatfield-McCoy Feud* (Charleston: Jarrett Printing Co., 1944); Virgil Carrington Jones, *The Hatfields and the McCoys* (Chapel Hill: University of North Carolina Press, 1948); Harry Harrison Kroll, *Their Ancient Grudge* (Bobbs-Merrill, 1946); Otis K. Rice, *The Hatfields and McCoys* (Lexington: University Press of Kentucky, 1978); John L. Spivak, *The Devil's Brigade; the Story of the Hatfield-McCoy Feud* (Brewer and Warren, 1930); Paul Curry Steele, *Anse on Island Creek, and Other Poems* (Mountain State Press, 1981): George Thomas Swain, *The True Facts About the Famous Hatfield-McCoy Feud* (Ace Enterprises, 1962); Jean Thomas, *Big Sandy* (New York: Henry Holt and Co., 1940); Altina Laura Walker, *Feud: Hatfields, McCoys, and Social Change in Appalachia, 1860-1900* (Chapel Hill: University of North Carolina Press, 1988); Charles H. Ambler and Festus P. Summers, *West Virginia: The Mountain State* (Englewood Cliffs, New Jersey: Prentice-Hall, Inc. 1940); Charles H. Ambler, *A History of Education in West Virginia* (Huntington, West Virginia: Standard Printing and Publishing Company 1951); James M. Callahan, *A Semi-Centennial History of West Virginia* (The Semi-Centennial Commission of West Virginia 1913); Ann Rinaldi, *The Coffin Quilt. The Feud Between the Hatfields and the McCoys* (Orlando, Florida: Gulliver Books 2001); Coleman C. Hatfield and Robert Y. Spence, *The Tale of the Devil, The Biography of Devil Anse Hatfield* (Chapmanville, West Virginia: Woodland Press LLC 2003).

140. Altina Walker, *Feud: Hatfields, McCoys, and Social Change in Appalachia, 1860-1900* 16 (University of North Carolina Press 1988); Don Seagle, '*They've Said Too Much Already,' Son Of Devil Anse Hatfield Refuses to Talk About Clash With McCoys in Late 1800's*, Charleston Daily Mail, Feb. 10, 1952, at A8.

141. Boone was captured on several occasions by the Indians, but each time either managed to escape or was released. Colonel Daniel Boone (1734-1820), the former Virginia legislator (due to the fact that the present-day Kentucky region was still a part of Virginia at the time), American pioneer, and folk hero, called the area a hunter's paradise as he roamed the woods that were then occupied by elk, bison, cougars, and wolves. In fact, Boone County, present-day West Virginia, was formed from an act of the Virginia General Assembly on March 11, 1847, from Cabell, Kanawha, and Logan counties in honor of Daniel Boone.

142. Coleman C. Hatfield and Robert Y. Spence, *The Tale of the Devil, The Biography of Devil Anse Hatfield* 20 (Chapmanville, West Virginia: Woodland Press LLC 2003).

143. *Id.* at 82.

144. Walker, *supra* note 140, at 16; *see also* Virgil Carrington Jones, *The Hatfields and the McCoys*, (Chapel Hill, NC: The University of North Carolina Press, 1948); Clarence Shirley Donnelly, *The Hatfield-McCoy Feud Reader* (Parsons, WV: McClain Printing Company, 1971).

145. *Id*; Byron Crawford, *Niece trembled when visiting Devil Anse*, The Courier-Journal (Louisville, KY), Aug. 19, 1988, at B1; Rice, *supra* note 110, at 324.

146. Hatfield, *supra* note 142, at 116.

147. Hatfield v. Commonwealth, 11 Ky.L.Rptr. 468, 12 S.W. 309 (1889).

148. 11 Ky.L.Rptr. at 469, 12 S.W. at 310.

149. Byron Crawford, *Niece trembled when visiting Devil Anse*, The Courier-Journal (Louisville, KY), Aug. 19, 1988, at B1; Rice, *supra* note 110, at 324.

150. 11 Ky.L.Rptr. at 469, 470, 12 S.W. at 310, 311.

151. Staff Reports, *McCoys Take Cemetery Feud with a Hatfield to Ky. Court*, Charleston Gazette, Jan. 27, 2003, at A2; Staff Reports, *Hatfields, McCoys Claim Victory in Cemetery Dispute*, Charleston Gazette, Apr. 19, 2003, at A2; Staff Reports, *Hatfields, McCoys Take Feud into 2003*, Dec. 28, 2002, at A2; Staff Reports, *McCoy v. Hatfield*, The Washington Times, Apr. 12, 2002, at A2.

152. *See* Ellison v. Torpin, 44 W.Va. 414, 30 S.E. 183 (1898).

153. Hatfield, *supra* note 142, at 138.

154. In re Mahon, 34 F. 525, 526 (D.C. Ky. 1888).

155. *Id*; 127 U.S. 700, 703; Rice, *supra* note 110, at 324.

156. 34 F. at 527; Rice, *supra* note 110, at 324.

157. *See* Commonwealth of Kentucky Department of Military Affairs, Office of the Adjutant General (<http://www.military.state.ky.us/kyngemus/what_in_sam_hill.htm>).

158. Mahon v. Justice, 127 U.S. 700, 706 (1888); *see also* In re Mahon, 34 F. 525 (D.C. Ky. 1888); Hatfield v. Commonwealth, 11 Ky.L.Rptr. 468, 12 S.W. 309, Ky. (1889); Hatfield v. Commonwealth, 21 Ky.L.Rptr. 1461, 55 S.W. 679, Ky. (1900); Rice, *supra* note 110, at 324.

159. Hatfield v. Commonwealth, 21 Ky.L.Rptr. 1461, 1462, 55 S.W. 679, 680 (1900).

160. *Id*.

161. *Id.* at 1463, 55 S.W. at 681.

162. Hatfield, *supra* note 142, at 251-253.

163. *Id.* at 251.

164. *Id*.

165. State v. Hatfield, 48 W.Va. 561, 37 S.E. 626 (1900); *see also* State v. Hawk, 47 W.Va. 434, 34 S.E. 918 (1900).

166. Staff Reports, *More Hatfield troubles*, Charleston Gazette, August 30, 1899, at A1.

167. *See* Runyon v. Rutherford, 55 W.Va. 436, 47 S.E. 150 (1904).

168. Hatfield, *supra* note 142, at 253.

169. Hatfield v. Scaggs, 101 W.Va. 425, 133 S.E. 109 (1926); Conley v. Thompson, 99 W.Va. 622, 129 S.E. 397 (1925); State ex rel. Hatfield v. Farley, 97 W.Va. 695, 126 S.E. 413 (1924); State v. Board of Canvassers of Mingo County, 98 W.Va. 41, 126 S.E. 708 (1925).

170. Hatfield v. Hatfield, 113 W.Va. 135, 167 S.E. 89 (1932).

171. Hatfield, *supra* note 142, at 129, 183-186.

172. Jane Gibson, *Feud researchers find few poor, dumb hillbillies*, Charleston Sunday Gazette -Mail, Sept. 15, 1991, at A3.

173. Hatfield, *supra* note 142, at 272.

174. Political advertisement, Charleston Daily Mail, Nov. 1, 1912, at A2.

175. Bob Kittle, *Pomp and circumstance*, Charleston Daily Mail, Dec. 9, 1976, at A1.

176. The "county court" is known today as the "county commission" and hereinafter will be referred to as "county commission" so that it is not confused with a county "circuit court." *See* McClure v. McClure, 184 W.Va. 649, 655 n.1, 403 S.E.2d 197, 203 n.1 (1991)("In 1974, Article IX, Section 9 of the West Virginia Constitution was adopted, and the county court is now designated as the county commission.").

177. Webster's Revised Unabridged Dictionary Version published 1913 by the C. & G.

Merriam Co. Springfield, Mass (<www.dictionary.reference.com>)("Martial law, the law administered by the military power of a government when it has superseded the civil authority in time of war, or when the civil authorities are unable to enforce the laws. It is distinguished from military law, the latter being the code of rules for the regulation of the army and navy alone, either in peace or in war.").

178.    Howard B. Lee, *Bloodletting in Appalachia* 31, 32, 35 (Parsons: McClain Printing Company, 1969).

179.    *Id.* at 35; *see also* Richard D. Lunt, *Law and Order vs the Miners–West Virginia 1907-1933* (Hamden, Conn.: Archon books, 1979).

180.    Latin for "You have the body." Most often, a writ of habeas corpus is a judicial order forcing law enforcement authorities to produce a prisoner they are holding, and to justify the prisoner's continued confinement. A petition for a writ of habeas corpus often is filed in federal courts by state prison inmates who say their state prosecutions violated federally protected rights in some way.

181.    Lee, *supra* note 176, at 41.

182.    W.Va. Const., Art. III, § 4, § 12 (1872).

183.    Lee, *supra* note 176, at 77.

184.    *Id.* at 40; *see also* West Virginia State Archives (<http://www.wvculture.org/history/glass-coc.html>).

185.    Hatfield v. Graham, 73 W.Va. 759, 81 S.E. 533 (1914); *see also* Rice, *supra* note 110, at 239.

186.    Mary Harris Jones, *Autobiography of Mother Jones* (New York: Arno Press, Inc., and the New York Times, 1969); Rice, *supra* note 110, at 237; Dale Fetherling, *Mother Jones, the Miners' Angel* (Carbondale: southern Illinois University Press, 1974); Linda Atkinson, *Mother Jones: The Most Dangerous Woman in America* (New York: Crown Publishers, 1978); Philip S. Foner, *Mother Jones Speaks: Collected Writings and Speeches* (New York: Monad Press, 1983); Edward Steel, *The Correspondence of Mother Jones* (Pittsburgh: University of Pittsburgh Press, 1985); Edward Steel, *The Speeches and Writings of Mother Jones* (Pittsburgh: University of Pittsburgh Press, 1988); Judith Pinkerton Josephson, *Mother Jones: Fierce Fighter for Workers' Rights* (Minneapolis: Lerner Publications Company, 1997); Elliott Gorn, *Mother Jones: The Most Dangerous Woman In America*, (New York: Hill and Wang, 2001).

187.    Mother Jones states that she was born in 1830; however, numerous scholars speculate that her date of birth was anywhere from 1830-1844. Some scholars believe that she may have exaggerated her age to better fit her maternal image in the labor movement.

188.    Judith Pinkerton Josephson, *Mother Jones: Fierce Fighter for Workers' Rights* 16 (Minneapolis: Lerner Publications Company, 1997).

189.    Jones, *supra* note 186, at 136.

190.    *Id.* at 184.

191.    *Id.* at 185.

192.    *Id.* at 189, 194.

193.    *Id.* at 194, 201-203.

194.    *Id.* at 202-203, 204.

195.    *Id.* at 40-41.

196.    *Id.* at 49.

197.    *Id.* at. 50-53.

198.    Rice, *supra* note 110, at 239; *see also* (<http://www.wvculture.org/history/glasscoc.html>); Staff Reports, *"Mother" Jones Under Arrest*, Charleston Daily Mail, Feb. 13, 1913, at A1; Staff Reports, *"Mother Jones" Will Tell 'Em When and Where to Use Arms*, Charleston Daily Mail, Feb. 13. 1913, at A1.

199.    Staff Reports, *"Mother Jones" Will Tell 'Em When and Where to Use Arms*, Charleston Daily Mail, Feb. 13. 1913, at A1.

200.    Jones, *supra* note 186, at 148-150.

201.    *Id.*

202.    *Id.* at 151.

203.    *Id.*

204.    *Id.* at 156, 160.

205.   Staff Reports, *"Mother" Jones Arrested in City*, Charleston Gazette, Feb. 14, 1913, at A1.

206.   Edwin D. Hoffman, *Miners at War*, Sunday Gazette-Mail, Mar. 5, 1978, at M2.

207.   Jones, *supra* note 186, at 163.

208.   *Id.* at 168.

209.   Lee, *supra* note 176, at 27.

210.   *Id.* at 171.

211.   Harris, *supra* note 112, at 239.

212.   Jones, *supra* note 186, at 234-235, 237.

213.   *Id.* at 63.

214.   John C. Nicolay, *Abe Lincoln, ed.* Vol. II at 286 (New York: The Century Co., 1894).

215.   Jones, *supra* note 186, at 232-233.

216.   *Id.* at 237.

217.   Lee, *supra* note 176, at ix.

218.   *Id.* at 6.

219.   Topper Sherwood, *Protected politics: Insulation of politicians isn't new to West Virginians'*, Charleston Gazette, Sept. 7, 2004, at A5.

220.   *Id.*

221.   One such contract of employment provided:

> I am employed by and work for the _____ Company, of _____, West Virginia, with the express understanding that I am not a member of the United Mine Workers of America, and will not become so while an employee of said _____ Company; that said Company agrees to run an "Open Shop" while I am employed by said _____ Company. If at any time I want to join or become connected with the United Mine Workers of America, or any affiliated organization, I agree to withdraw from the employment of said Company, and I further agree that while I am in the employ of said Company that I will not make any efforts amongst its employees to bring about the unionization of said employees against the Company's wishes. I have either read the above or it has been read to me.
>
> Dated this the_____day of _____, 19___.
> (Signed)
> _____

> *See* Republic Steel Corp. v. United Mine Workers of America, 570 F.2d 467 (3rd Cir. 1978); Lee, *supra*, note 176, at 78.

222.   *Id.*

223.   *Id.*

224.   John J. Cornwell, *A Mountain Trail: To the Schoolroom, the Editor's Chair, the Lawyer's Office, and the Governorship of West Virginia* 59-60 (Philadelphia: Dorrance and Company, 1939).

225.   Rice, *supra* note 110, at 240; *see also* West Virginia State Archives (<http://www.wvculture.org/history/minewars.html.>).

226.   Dallas H. Jude, *Eyewitness: Marie Robinette of Matewan*, Goldenseal, Winter 2004, Vol. 30, No. 4, at 24-29.

227.   Lon Savage, *Thunder in the Mountains: The West Virginia Mine War, 1920-21* 56 (Univ. Of Pittsburgh Press 1990); Lee, *supra* note 176, at 68-71; *see also* State ex rel. Lively v. Strother, 89 W.Va. 352, 109 S.E. 337 (1921).

228.   Savage, *supra* note 227, at 56.

229.   *Id.* at 23.

230.   Rice, *supra* note 110, at 240; Charlotte Sanders, *Man recalls Matewan Massacre*, Williamson Daily News, Sept. 20, 1996, at C10; Grant Parsons, *Lost Case: Discovery of Tom Felts' records provide new view of 'massacre,'* Sunday Gazette-Mail, Aug. 11, 1991, at C1; Associated Press, *Matewan Massacre was 70 years ago Saturday*, Clarksburg Telegram, May 18, 1990, at B1.

231. Lee, *supra* note 176, at 74, 96 (The United Mine Workers Union was not able to organize the coalfields until the early 1930s when President Roosevelt came to power); *see also* Rice, *supra* note 110, at 240-241; Joseph E. Finley, *The Corrupt Kingdom, the Rise and Fall of the United Mine Workers* (New York: Simon and Schuster, 1972); Heber Blankenhorn, *The Strike for Union* (New York: H. W. Wilson Company, 1924).

232. Savage, *supra* note 227, at 39, 43.

233. *Id.* at 102.

234. *Id.* at 107, 135.

235. *Id.* at 143.

236. Jerry Bruce Thomas, *An Appalachian New Deal* 6, 19 (University Press of Kentucky 1988).

237. *Id.* at 37.

238. James C. McGregor, *The Disruption of Virginia* 268-269 (New York, NY: Macmillon Company 1922).

239. Otis K. Rice & Stephen W. Brown, *West Virginia, A History* 140-141 (Lexington: The University Press of Kentucky 1993).

240. McGregor, *supra* note 238, at 258.

241. Richard Orr Curry, *The Virginia Background for the History of the Civil War and Reconstruction Era in West Virginia: An Analytical Commentary*, 20 W.Va. History 215, 244 (State Department of Archives and History, Charleston, West Virginia: 1959). The 1865 W.Va. Acts ch. 56, provided the required oath as follows:

> I, A.B. (Name of affiant) do solemnly swear that I have never voluntarily borne arms against the United States, the reorganized government of Virginia, or the State of West Virginia; that I have never voluntarily given aid, comfort or assistance to persons engaged in armed hostility against the United States, the reorganized government of Virginia, or the State of West Virginia; that I have not at any time sought, accepted, exercised, or attempted to exercise any office of appointment whatever under any authority or pretended authority, hostile or inimical to the United States, the reorganized government of Virginia, or the State of West Virginia; that I have not at any time yielded a voluntary support to any government or pretended government, power or Constitution within the United States, hostile or inimical thereto, or hostile or inimical to the reorganized government of Virginia, or the State of West Virginia; that I will support the constitution of the United States and the constitution of the State of West Virginia; and I take this oath freely without any mental reservation or purpose of evasion.

242. Milton Gerofsky, *Reconstruction in West Virginia*, 6 W.Va. History 295, 302 (State Department of Archives and History, Charleston, West Virginia: 1945) (quoting Charles H. Ambler, *Disfranchisement in West Virginia*, 14 Yale Rev. 38 (1905)).

243. Ex. parte William Stratton, 1 W.Va. 304, 305-6 (1866). The Supreme Court also upheld the oaths for jurors, *Lively v. Ballard*, 2 W.Va. 496 (1868); lawyers, *Ex parte Hunter*, 2 W.Va. 122 (1867); *Ex parte Quarrier*, 4 W.Va. 210 (1870); *Ex parte Charles James Faulkner*, 1 W.Va. 269 (1866); litigants or potential litigants, *Higginbotham v. Gaselden*, 3 W.Va. 17 (1868); and even voters in public elections, *Randolph v. Good*, 3 W.Va. 551 (1869).

244. *Journal of the House of Delegates of the State of West Virginia*, 7th Sess., 46-47 (1869).

245. Rist v. Underwood, 206 W.Va. 258, 268, 287 n.17, 524 S.E.2d 179, 189, 208 n.17 (1999).

246. *Id*; *see also Journal of the House of Delegates of the State of West Virginia*, 4th Sess., 115 (1866).

247. Loomis v. Jackson, 6 W.Va. 613 (1873) (1873 WL 2836 (W.Va.)); At the time, the 5th Judicial Circuit was composed of the counties of Tyler, Pleasants, Ritchie, Wood, Wirt, and Calhoun.

248. *Id.*

249. 61 CONG. REC. H948 (Remarks in the House Jan. 29, 1890) (Statement of Speaker of the House Thomas B. Reed).

250. In *United States v. Ballin*, 144 U.S. 1 (1892), the United States Supreme Court held the practice of counting those not voting as present for purposes of a quorum as constitutional.

251. Staff Reports, *The Bond Case in Retrospect*, Charleston Gazette, Oct. 21, 1926, at A1;

Staff Reports, *Unexplained facts caused Gore to order removal of Auditor*, Charleston Gazette, Oct. 26, 1926, at A1.

252. Daniel Bice, *Past impeachments have variety of outcomes*, Charleston Daily Mail, Mar. 8, 1989, at A1; Staff Reports, *The Bond Case in Retrospect*, Charleston Gazette, Oct. 21, 1926, at A1; Staff Reports, *Unexplained facts caused Gore to order removal of Auditor*, Charleston Gazette, Oct. 26, 1926, at A1.

253. State v. Miller, 24 W.Va. 802 (1884), (1884 WL 2829 (W.Va.)).

254. Brazie v. Fayette County Commissioners, 25 W.Va. 213 (1884), (1884 WL 2706 (W.Va.)).

255. Halstead v. Rader, 27 W.Va. 806 (1886), (1886 WL 1888 (W.Va.)).

256. Richards v. Town of Clarksburg, 4 S.E. 774, 775 (1887).

257. The Seventeenth Amendment to the United States Constitution, in part, provides: "The Senate of the United States shall be composed of two Senators from each State, elected by the people thereof, for six years." Prior to the Amendment, Article I, § 3 of the United States Constitution was applicable and provided that "[t]he Senate of the United States shall be composed of two Senators from each State chosen by the Legislature thereof."

258. Wise v. Chandler, 270 KY 1, 8-10, 108 S.W.2d 1024, 1031-1033 (1937).

259. *Id.* at 1032-1033.

260. Todd C. Willis, Editor, West Virginia Blue Book, Vol. 64 at 267 (1980).

261. Carr v. Wilson, 32 W.Va. 419, 9 S.E. 31 (1889); Goff v. Wilson, 32 W.Va. 393, 9 S.E. 26 (1889); Fleming v. Commissioners, 31 W.Va. 608, 8 S.E. 267 (1888); MacCorkle, *supra* note 126, at 431-444.

262. Shirley Donnelly, *Four Claimed Governorship In 1889*, Beckley-Post Herald, Oct. 1, 1970, at A4; *see also* Shirley Donnelly, *When State had Four Governors, Part I*, Beckley-Post Herald, Dec. 14, 1957, at A4; Shirley Donnelly, *When State had Four Governors, Part II*, Beckley-Post Herald, Dec. 14, 1957, at A4; George W. Summers, *West Virginia Delayed, Wilson held post 5 years*, Charleston Daily Mail, Sept. 11, 1938, at A1.

263. Goff v. Wilson, 32 W.Va. 393, 9 S.E. 26 (1889).

264. Fleming v. Commissioners, 8 S.E. 267, 268 (1888); MacCorkle, *supra* note 126, at 435.

265. Staff Reports, *Fleming to contest election*, Wheeling Register, December 27, 1888, at 1.

266. Goff v. Wilson, 32 W.Va. at 394, 9 S.E. at 27.

267. MacCorkle, *supra* note 126, at 437.

268. *Id.*

269. Shirley Donnelly, *Four Claimed Governorship In 1889*, Beckley-Post Herald, Oct. 1, 1970, at A4.

270. *Id.*

271. Goff v. Wilson, 32 W.Va. 393, 394, 9 S.E. 26, 27 (1889).

272. Carr v. Wilson, 32 W.Va. 419, 9 S.E. 31 (1889).

273. *Id.* at 31, 36.

274. Rice, *supra* note 110, at 309.

275. Carr v. Wilson, 32 W.Va. 419, 9 S.E. 31, 36 (1889).

276. Fleming v. Guthrie, 32 W.Va. 1, 2, 9 S.E. 23, 24 (1889).

277. *House Journal*, 1889 at 99.

278. *Id.* at 47-93, 184-308.

279. Associated Press, *One Governor of State Had 5-Year Term*, Clarksburg Exponent, Apr. 9, 1939, at A24.

280. Atkinson and Gibbens, *op. cit.*, at 226; *House Journal*, 1889, at 557-558.

281. *House Journal*, 1889 at 560-561.

282. Associated Press, *One Governor of State Had 5-Year Term*, Clarksburg Exponent, Apr. 9, 1939, at A24.

283. MacCorkle, *supra* note 126, at 442-444..

284. *Id.* at 438, 444.

285. Todd C. Willis, Editor, West Virginia Blue Book, Vol. 64 at 267 (1980); Staff Reports, *One Governor of State had 5-year term*, Clarksburg Exponent, Apr. 9, 1939, at A24.

286. *House Journal*, 1889 at 148, 581, 585-606. The actual term of his Senate seat was to com-

mence March 4, 1913, but Goff did not immediately take his seat, preferring to remain on the federal bench until April 1, 1913.

287.  *Id.* at 11-22, 23-30, 32-38, 42-46, and 96-97.

288.  *Id.* at 392, 893, 396, 426-428; Staff Reports, *Contested Senate Seats*, The Preston County Journal, January 24, 1889, at A1.

289.  *House Journal*, 1889 at 11-30, 32-38, 42-46, 47-93, 184-308, and 319-320.

290.  State v. Cunningham, 33 W.Va. 607, 11 S.E. 76 (1890).

291.  *Id*; Alderson v. Commissioners, 32 W.Va. 454, 9 S.E. 863 (1889); Alderson v. Commissioners, 32 W.Va. 640, 9 S.E. 868 (1889); Alderson v. Commissioners, 31 W.Va. 633, 8 S.E. 274 (1888).

292.  State v. McClaugherty, 33 W.Va. 250, 251, 10 S.E. 407, 408 (1889).

293.  State v. Griggs, 34 W.Va. 78, 11 S.E. 740 (1890).

294.  Dial v. Hollandsworth, 39 W.Va. 1, 3, 4, 19 S.E. 557, 559, 560 (1894).

295.  Hamilton v. Tucker County Court, 38 W.Va. 71, 18 S.E. 8 (1893); Minear v. Tucker County Court, 20 S.E. 659 (W.Va. 1894).

296.  Special Dispatch, *County Seat War Down in Tucker County Has An Unique Ending, Records Moved in Night Time*, Wheeling Intelligencer, August 3, 1893, at 1.

297.  *Id.*

298.  Special Dispatch, *Blood May Flow, Armed Men Guarding the Courthouse at Parsons*, Wheeling Intelligencer, August 8, 1893, at 1.

299.  Minear v. Tucker County Court, 20 S.E. 659 (W.Va. 1894).

300.  Moore v. Strickling, 46 W.Va. 515, 33 S.E. 274 (1899).

301.  *Id.* at 279.

302.  State v. Young, 173 W.Va. 1, n.7, 311 S.E.2d 118, n.7 (1983).

303.  Rice, *supra* note 110, at 141.

304.  Doll v. Bender, 55 W.Va. 404, 408, 47 S.E. 293, 297 (1904).

305.  Kirkpatrick v. Board of Canvassers, 53 W.Va. 275, 44 S.E. 465 (1903); *see also* Morris v. Board of Canvassers, 49 W.Va. 251, 38 S.E. 500 (1901); Daniel v. Simms, 49 W.Va. 554, 39 S.E. 690 (1901); Dunlevy v. County Court, 47 W.Va. 513, 35 S.E. 956 (1900); Marcum v. Ballot Commissioners, 42 W.Va. 263, 26 S.E. 281 (1896); Snodgrass v. County Court, 44 W.Va. 56, 29 S.E. 1035 (1897).

306.  McWhorter v. Dorr, 57 W.Va. 608, 50 S.E. 838 (1905); Morrison v. McWhorter, 57 W.Va. 614, 615, 52 S.E. 394, 395 (Special Court of W.Va., Twelfth Judicial Circuit 1905).

307.  Williamson v. Musick, 60 W.Va. 59, 61-62, 65, 53 S.E. 706, 708-709, 712 (1906).

308.  Ex. parte Caldwell, 138 F. 487, 491 (Circuit Court, N.D. W.Va. 1905).

309.  *Id.* at 491, 492, 495.

310.  W.S. Laidley, *History of Charleston and Kanawha County* 163 (Chicago, Illinois: Richmond-Arnold Pub. Co. 1911).

311.  *See* United States Senate's Internet website, listed under "Direct election of Senators," (<http://www.senate.gov/artandhistory/history/common/briefing/Direct_Election_Senators.htm>)("Voters have elected their senators in the privacy of the voting booth since 1914. The framers of the Constitution, however, did not intend senators to be elected in this way, and included in Article I, section 3, 'The Senate of the United States shall be composed of two Senators from each state, chosen by the legislature thereof for six Years; and each Senator shall have one Vote.' The election of delegates to the Constitutional Convention established the precedent for state selection. The framers believed that in electing senators, state legislatures would cement their tie with the national government, which would increase the chances for ratifying the Constitution. They also expected that senators elected by state legislatures would be able to concentrate on the business at hand without pressure from the populace.").

312.  West Virginia State Archives, *Time Trail West Virginia, Death of U.S. Senator Stephen B. Elkins* (< http://www.wvculture.org/history/timetrl/ttfeb.html>).

313.  *Id.*

314.  Stacey Ruckle, *Real characters have held court at the Capitol, State has had many memorable governors*, Charleston Daily Mail, Aug. 4, 1999, at A1; *see also* West Virginia State Archives, *Time Trail West Virginia, Death of U.S. Senator Stephen B. Elkins*, (< http://www.wvculture.org/history/timetrl/ttfeb.html>).

315.    Hatfield, *supra* note 142, at 266; West Virginia State Archives, *Time Trail West Virginia, Death of U.S. Senator Stephen B. Elkins*, (< http://www.wvculture.org/history/timetrl/ttfeb.html>).

316.    From 1893-1897 Chilton served as West Virginia Secretary of State. In a 1901 Opinion by the State Supreme Court, Chilton was charged to have "sold books of the State, and failed to account for their proceeds, to the amount of $7,000, and had received taxes upon State seals amounting to $3,000, and failed to account therefor." Chilton said he did not owe the sums alleged and paid the State $6,490, however the State refused the amount and sued Chilton for more money. Initially a circuit judge found the $6,490 as sufficient payment. The State Supreme Court, however, reversed the circuit court and ordered a new trial. *State v. Chilton*, 49 W.Va. 453, 39 S.E. 612 (1901).

317.    *See* John Alexander Williams, *New York's First Senator from West Virginia: How Stephen B. Elkins Found a New Political Home*, West Virginia History 31 (January 1970) 73- 87.

318.    County Court v. Duty, 77 W.Va. 17, 87 S.E. 256 (1915).

319.    Love v. McCoy, 81 W.Va. 478, 94 S.E. 954 (1918).

320.    United States v. Gradwell, 243 U.S. 476 (1917); *see also* United States v. O'Toole, 236 F. 993, 994 (1916).

321.    *Id.* The defendants charged with conspiracy were Edward O'Toole, Guy C. Mace, John M. Tully, Abner N. Harris, William P. Kearns, Neil Friel, Willis W. Harding, Jesse H. Petty, Everett Woodson, Andrew T. Robertson, Roy E. Lee, John Young, John M. Davidson, Earl D. Strohecker, and Emmett Conner, and I. H. Dunn, E. V. Albert, J. D. Jennings, A. E. Riley, and W. G. Martin.

322.    Sutherland v. Miller, 91 S.E. 993 (W.Va. 1917).

323.    *Id.* at 998.

324.    Associated Press, *Impeachment of Sturgiss recommended*, New Dominion (Morgantown, WV), Feb. 18, 1919, at A1.

325.    Staff Reports, *Judge Sturgiss Asks Public to Suspend Judgment on Petition for Impeachment*, New Dominion, Jan. 15, 1919, at A1; Staff Reports, *Evidence on Sturgiss Case is Being Taken*, Charleston Daily Mail, Feb. 1, 1919, at A3; Staff Reports, *Judge Sturgiss goes on stand in defense*, Charleston Daily Mail, Feb. 8, 1919, at A1; Associated Press, *Judge Sturgiss says he wants no compromise*, New Dominion, Feb. 10, 1919, at A1; Staff Reports, *House Refuses to impeach judge on Committe Report*, Charleston Daily Mail, Feb. 19, 1919, at A1; Associated Press, *Defeat of Majority Report in House of Delegates Definitely Ends Impeachment proceedings Against Judge Sturgiss*, New Dominion, Feb. 20, 1919, at A1.

326.    Lee, *supra* note 176, at 91, 92.

327.    *Id.* at 90; Staff Reports, *Chafin to run for delegate to Convention*, Charleston Gazette, Jan. 4, 1924, at 7.

328.    Lee, *supra* note 176, at 102-103.

329.    *Id.* at 9.

330.    State ex. rel. Thompson v. Logan County Court, 97 W.Va. 210, 124 S.E. 664 (1924).

331.    A writ of mandamus is an order issued by a court of superior jurisdiction commanding performance of a particular act by an inferior court or public official.

332.    97 W.Va. at 211, 124 S.E. at 665.

333.    Hatfield v. Scaggs, 101 W.Va. 425, 133 S.E. 109, 113 (1926.); State ex. rel. Thompson v. Logan County Court, 97 W.Va. 210, 124 S.E. 664 (1924).

334.    *See* Hatfield v. Scaggs, 101 W.Va. 425, 133 S.E. 109 (1926); Conley v. Thompson, 99 W.Va. 622, 129 S.E. 397 (1925); State ex rel. Hatfield v. Farley, 97 W.Va. 695, 126 S.E. 413 (1924); State v. Board of Canvassers of Mingo County, 98 W.Va. 41, 126 S.E. 708 (1925).

335.    George T. Swain, *The Incomparable Don Chafin* 10, 37 (Jones Printing Co: Charleston, WV 1962).

336.    *Id.*

337.    Hatfield v. Scaggs, 101 W.Va. 425, 428, 133 S.E. 109, 112 (1926).

338.    *Id.* at 109, 111, 113.

339.    Lee, *supra* note 176, at 89.

340.    *Id.* at 90.

341.    *Id.* at 118; *see also* Chafin v. United States, 269 U.S. 552 (1925); Chafin v. United States, 5 F.2d 592 (1925).

342. Lee, *supra* note 176, at 9, 10, 11.

343. State ex rel. Banks, 98, W.Va. 332, 333,128 S.E. 301, 302 (1925).

344. Lee, *supra* note 176, at 51.

345. Daniel Bice, *Past impeachments have variety of outcomes*, Charleston Daily Mail, Mar. 8, 1989, at A1.

346. Associated Press, *Many were paid but few did work, trio of state clerks tell Gore Probe*, Charleston Gazette, Oct. 4, 1926, at A1.

347. Staff Reports, *Bond found insane, going to hospital*, Charleston Daily Mail, May 15, 1927, at A1; Staff Reports, *Bond's impeachment is ordered by House*, Charleston Daily Mail, January 20, 1927, at A1; Staff Reports, *Senate Committee is ready to set trial date for Bond*, Charleston Daily Mail, January 25, 1927, at A1; Staff Reports, *Bond attacks authority of Gore to remove him*, Charleston Daily Mail, Mar. 8, 1927, at A1; Staff Reports, *Hallanan upheld by senate; Bond impeachment Dropped*, Charleston Daily Mail, Mar. 16, 1927, at A1; Staff Reports, *Governor appoints Mallison to succeed Bond as Auditor*, Charleston Daily Mail, Mar. 18, 1927, at A1.

348. West Virginia State Archives (<www.wvculture.org/history/timetrl/ttoct.html/:1020>) (visited February 18, 2005.).

349. Stacey Ruckle, *Real characters have held court at the Capitol*, Charleston Daily Mail, Aug. 4, 1999, at A1.

350. *See* Paul F. Lutz, *From Governor To Cabby: The Political Career and Tragic Death of West Virginia's William Casey Marland 1950-1965* 3 (Marshall University Library Associates; Huntington, West Virginia 1966); Stacey Ruckle, *Real characters have held court at the Capitol*, Charleston Daily Mail, Aug. 4, 1999, at A1.

351. Stacey Ruckle, *Real characters have held court at the Capitol*, Charleston Daily Mail, Aug. 4, 1999, at A1.

352. Staff Reports, *Few to attend Marland Rites at Pinch Ridge*, Charleston Daily Mail, Nov. 30, 1965, at A6.

353. Paul J. Nyden, *Workers' Comp deal blasted*, Charleston Gazette, Jan. 11, 2002, at A1; *see also* Editorial, *$50 million Coal contractor mess*, Charleston Gazette, Jan. 11, 2002, at A4.

354. Editorial, *Giveaways, Are they worth it?*, Charleston Gazette, Nov. 16, 2001, at A4.

355. Payne v. Staunton, 55 W.Va. 202, 210, 46 S.E. 927, 935 (1904)(J. Dent, Dissenting).

356. Michael W. Carey, Larry R. Ellis, Joseph F. Savage, Jr., *Federal Prosecution of State and Local Public Officials: The Obstacles To Punishing Breaches of the Public Turst And A Proposal For Reform, Part One*, 94 W.Va. L. Rev. 301, 302-303 (1992).

357. Editorial, *Maybe we need to name sellers, Going after vote-buyers doesn't seem to have been very effective*, Charleston Daily Mail, July 27, 2004, at A4.

358. Editorial, *It's time to put a stop to this, Here's to federal prosecutors hitting much pay dirt*, Charleston Daily Mail, Aug. 30, 2004, at A4.

359. Scott Finn, *Logan sheriff withdraws from race, Delegate denies involvement in vote-buying scheme*, Charleston Gazette, May 11, 2004, at A1.

360. Staff Reports, *Statehouse Notebook, Republicans duel over secretary of state candidates*, Charleston Daily Mail, Sept. 6, 2004, at A4.

361. Associated Press, *Judge sends election fraud case to grand jury, Pair in Lincoln case charged with trying to intimidate witnesses*, Charleston Daily Mail, Oct. 8, 2004, at A1; Staff Reports, *Witness Threats Connected With Vote Buying*, MetroNews Talkline, (Sept. 29, 2004, <www.wvmetronews.com.>).

362. Associated Press, *Judge sends election fraud case to grand jury, Pair in Lincoln case charged with trying to intimidate witnesses*, Charleston Daily Mail, Oct. 8, 2004, at A1; *see also* Staff, *Witness Threats Connected With Vote Buying*, MetroNews Talkline, (Sept. 29, 2004, <www.wvmetronews.com.>); Staff, *Men Allegedly Attacked Federal Witnesses*, MetroNews Talkline, (Sept. 28, 2004, <www.wvmetronews.com.>).

363. Associated Press, *Federal charges dropped in probe of vote-buying*, Charleston Gazette, Dec. 8, 2004, at A1.

364. Editorial, *Charleston Daily Mail: Purge 'em*, Charleston Saturday Gazette-Mail, May 14, 2005, at A4.

365. Chris Wetterich, *Logan lawyer says he paid to buy votes, Mark Hrutkay says he is cooperating in election fraud case*, Charleston Gazette, Aug. 11, 2004, at A1.

366. Tom Searls, *Ex-football star sentenced in assault, figure in Lincoln vote case convicted on firearms charge*, Charleston Gazette, Oct. 19, 2005, at A1.

367. Chris Stratton, *Feds say Stowers controlled Lincoln elections*, The Logan Banner, May 9, 2005, at 1; *see also* Tom Searls, *Lincoln circuit clerk hires N.C. attorney*, Nov. 16, 2005, at A1; Associated Press, *New lawyer ordered in vote-buying case*, Charleston Gazette, Nov. 4, 2005, at A1; Tom Searls, *Judge considers dismissing attorney is vote fraud case*, Oct. 29, 2005, at A1.

368. Lawrence Messina, Associated Press, *Fraud charges*, Charleston Daily Mail, May 6, 2005, at A1; Tom Sears, *Stowers faction controlled political climate in Lincoln*, Charleston Gazette, May 6, 2005, at A1; Toby Coleman, *Lincoln circuit clerk arrested, Stowers accused of buying votes for politicians with cash, liquor*, Charleston Gazette, May 6, 2005, at A1; Jennifer Bundy, Associated Press, *Lincoln circuit clerk accused of vote buying*, Charleston Daily Mail, May 6, 2005, at A5; Toby Coleman, *Manchin denies knowing of Lincoln vote buying, State GOP chief wants ex-secretaries of state, new governor included, grilled on accountability*, Charleston Saturday Gazette-Mail, May 6, 2005, at A1; Chris Stratton, *Feds say Stowers controlled Lincoln elections*, The Logan Banner, May 9, 2005, at 1; Toby Coleman, *Lincoln circuit clerk to fight vote buying charge*, Charleston Gazette, May 6, 2005, at A1.

369. Toby Coleman, *Manchin denies knowing of Lincoln vote buying, State GOP chief wants ex-secretaries of state, new governor included, grilled on accountability*, Charleston Saturday Gazette-Mail, May 6, 2005, at A1.

370. Therese Smith Cox, *Low license numbers up for grabs*, Charleston Daily Mail, May 9, 2005, at A1.

371. Chris Stratton, *Lincoln Woman guilty in vote probe*, The Logan Banner, Oct. 7, 2004, at 1.

372. Associated Press, *Another Person charged in vote-buying probe*, Charleston Daily Mail, Nov. 19, 2004, at A1.

373. Associated Press, *Voting probe tactics at issue*, Charleston Gazette, June 1, 2005, at A1.

374. *Id*; Tom Searls, *Lincoln loaded with property tax disparities, Feds have subpoenaed all real estate and other tax records from '90 on*, Charleston Sunday Gazette-Mail, July 10, 2005, at A1.

375. Tom Searls, *Two more charged in Lincoln vote probe*, Charleston Gazette, Aug. 4, 2005, at A1.

376. Lawrence Messina, Associated Press, *Lincoln pleads guilty*, Charleston Gazette, Dec. 28, 2005, at A1.

377. Associated Press, *U.S. attorneys score guilty plea in Lincoln election fraud probe*, Charleston Daily Mail, Dec. 29, 2005, at A1.

378. Lawrence Messina, Associated Press, *Lincoln clerk, two others plead guilty to election fraud*, Charleston Daily Mail, Dec. 30, 2005, at A1.

379. Associated Press, *Final Lincoln suspect pleads*, Charleston Saturday Gazette-Mail, Dec. 31, 2005, at A1.

380. Editorial, *Elections, A clean process is to the benefit of every person in West Virginia*, Charleston Daily Mail, May 18, 2004, at A4.

381. Tara Tuckwiller, *'Early voting' fraud alleged for second time in two days*, Charleston Gazette, May 12, 2004, at A1.

382. Staff Reports, *Ballot Official in Mingo accused of election fraud*, Charleston Gazette, May 11, 2004, at A2.

383. Tara Tuckwiller, *'Early voting' fraud alleged for second time in two days*, Charleston Gazette, May 12, 2004, at A1.

384. Editorial, *It is southern West Virginians who must make the change*, Charleston Daily Mail, Oct. 14, 2004, at A4.

385. Editorial, *Selling votes sold Logan out, Logan voters need to set higher standards for leadership*, Charleston Daily Mail, Sept. 13, 2004, at A4.

386. Editorial, *It is southern West Virginians who must make the change*, Charleston Daily Mail, Oct. 14, 2004, at A4; *see also* Toby Coleman, *Worker charged in vote scheme, Division of Highways employee allegedly paid four people for votes*, Charleston Daily Mail, Aug. 27, 2004, at A1; Editorial, *It's time to put a stop to this, Here's to federal prosecutors hitting much pay dirt*, Charleston Daily Mail, Aug. 30, 2004, at A4; Associated Press, *Judge sends election fraud case to grand jury, Pair in Lincoln case charged with trying to intimidate witnesses*, Charleston Daily Mail, Oct. 8, 2004, at A1; Chris Stratton, *Lincoln Woman guilty in vote probe*, The Logan Banner, Oct. 7, 2004, at 1; Chris Stirewalt, *Man faces fraud charges, Logan resident allegedly skimmed funds from VFW Post to give to political campaign*, Charleston Daily Mail, Sept. 10, 2004, at A1; Toby Coleman, *Hrutkay's motives still a mystery, Millionaire workers' comp lawyer faces prison sentence after buying votes,*

Charleston Daily Mail, Sept. 9, 2004, at A1; Associated Press, *Voter fraud probes could end up affecting election, Officials fear scandals may discourage faithful from going to the polls*, Charleston Daily Mail, Sept. 13, 2004, at A1; Associated Press, *Another Person charged in vote-buying probe*, Charleston Daily Mail, Nov. 19, 2004, at A1; Staff Reports, *Men plead no*t guilty to vote-buy charges, Charleston Gazette, Nov. 30, 2004, at A2; Associated Press, *Men plead innocent to fraud, Lincoln men had been charged with vote buying in May primary election*, Nov. 30, 2004, at A1.

387.    Associated Press, *Logan County sheriff charged again, John Mendez implicated in two cases of vote buying*, Charleston Sunday Gazette-Mail, May 9, 2004, at A1; State Briefs, *State doesn't want ex-sheriff to get pension*, Charleston Daily Mail, Oct. 14, 2004, at A7; Chris Wetterich, *Logan Sheriff pleads guilty, Mendez resigns, will cooperate in vote-buying investigation*, Charleston Gazette, July 20, 2004, at A1.

388.    Chris Wetterich, *Logan Sheriff pleads guilty, Mendez resigns, will cooperate in vote-buying investigation*, Charleston Gazette, July 20, 2004, at A1.

389.    State Briefs, *State doesn't want ex-sheriff to get pension*, Charleston Daily Mail, Oct. 14, 2004, at A7; Chris Wetterich, *Logan Sheriff pleads guilty, Mendez resigns, will cooperate in vote-buying investigation*, Charleston Gazette, July 20, 2004, at A1.

390.    Associated Press, *Logan County sheriff charged again, John Mendez implicated in two cases of vote buying*, Charleston Sunday Gazette-Mail, May 9, 2004, at A1.

391.    Chris Wetterich, *Logan Sheriff pleads guilty, Mendez resigns, will cooperate in vote-buying investigation*, Charleston Gazette, July 20, 2004, at A1; Associated Press, *Logan County sheriff charged again, John Mendez implicated in two cases of vote buying*, Charleston Sunday Gazette-Mail, May 9, 2004, at A1.

392.    Scott Finn, *Logan sheriff withdraws from race, Delegate denies involvement in vote-buying scheme*, Charleston Gazette, May 11, 2004, at A1.

393.    Lawrence Messina, Associated Press, *Delegate named a co-conspirator*, Charleston Daily Mail, Oct. 20, 2005, at A1.

394.    Scott Finn, *Logan sheriff withdraws from race, Delegate denies involvement in vote-buying scheme*, Charleston Gazette, May 11, 2004, at A1.

395.    Associated Press, *Another Person charged in vote-buying probe*, Charleston Daily Mail, Nov. 19, 2004, at A1; Tom Searls, *Lawyer pleads guilty to fraud*, Charleston Gazette, January 8, 2005, at A1.

396.    Chris Wetterich, *Logan lawyer says he paid to buy votes, Mark Hrutkay says he is cooperating in election fraud case*, Charleston Gazette, Aug. 11, 2004, at A1; Chris Stratton, *Lincoln Woman guilty in vote probe*, The Logan Banner, Oct. 7, 2004, at 1.

397.    Chris Stratton, *Lincoln Woman guilty in vote probe*, The Logan Banner, Oct. 7, 2004, at 1; Chris Stirewalt, *Man faces fraud charges, Logan resident allegedly skimmed funds from VFW Post to give to political campaign*, Charleston Daily Mail, Sept. 10, 2004, at A1; Chris Wetterich, *Logan lawyer says he paid to buy votes, Mark Hrutkay says he is cooperating in election fraud case*, Charleston Gazette, Aug. 11, 2004, at A1.

398.    Chris Wetterich, *Logan lawyer says he paid to buy votes, Mark Hrutkay says he is cooperating in election fraud case*, Charleston Gazette, Aug. 11, 2004, at A1.

399.    Toby Coleman, *Hrutkay's motives still a mystery, Millionaire workers' comp lawyer faces prison sentence after buying votes*, Charleston Daily Mail, Sept. 9, 2004, at A1.

400.    Chris Wetterich, *Logan lawyer says he paid to buy votes, Mark Hrutkay says he is cooperating in election fraud case*, Charleston Gazette, Aug. 11, 2004, at A1.

401.    Staff Reports, *Delegate's Former Husband Pleads Guilty*, MetroNews Talkline, (Jan. 7, 2005, <www.wvmetronews.com.>).

402.    Chris Wetterich, *Logan lawyer says he paid to buy votes, Mark Hrutkay says he is cooperating in election fraud case*, Charleston Gazette, Aug. 11, 2004, at A1; Toby Coleman, *Hrutkay's motives still a mystery, Millionaire workers' comp lawyer faces prison sentence after buying votes*, Charleston Daily Mail, Sept. 9, 2004, at A1.

403.    Toby Coleman, *Hrutkay's motives still a mystery, Millionaire workers' comp lawyer faces prison sentence after buying votes*, Charleston Daily Mail, Sept. 9, 2004, at A1.

404.    *Id.*

405.    Associated Press, *Logan lawyer must spend year in jail, pay fine and restitution*, Charleston Daily Mail, Apr. 5, 2005, at A1; Toby Coleman, *Logan lawyer gets year*, Charleston Gazette, Apr. 5, 2005, at A1. Hrutkay's law license was annulled on June 24, 2005, by the State Supreme Court. *See* Tom Searls, *Logan lawyer loses license for at least 5 years in vote case*, Charleston Gazette, June 25, 2005, at A2.

406.    Toby Coleman, *Prosecutor says Logan police chief tainted 2002 primary*, Charleston

*Daily Mail*, Aug. 3, 2004, at A1; Chris Wetterich, *Logan lawyer says he paid to buy votes, Mark Hrutkay says he is cooperating in election fraud case*, Charleston Gazette, Aug. 11, 2004, at A1.

407.    Toby Coleman, *Former Logan police chief pleads guilty in federal vote-buying case*, Charleston Gazette, Dec. 8, 2004, at A1; Associated Press, *Ex-police chief pleads guilty to vote buying*, Charleston Gazette, Dec. 8, 2004, at A1.

408.    Toby Coleman, *Ex-police chief gets lesson in civics*, Charleston Gazette, Feb. 16, 2005, at A1.

409.    Editorial, *Supply and demand in Logan County*, Charleston Daily Mail, Sept. 14, 2004, at A4; Chris Stirewalt, *Man faces fraud charges, Logan resident allegedly skimmed funds from VFW Post to give to political campaign*, Charleston Daily Mail, Sept. 10, 2004, at A1.

410.    Chris Stirewalt, *Man faces fraud charges, Logan resident allegedly skimmed funds from VFW Post to give to political campaign*, Charleston Daily Mail, Sept. 10, 2004, at A1.

411.    Editorial, *Potpourri*, Charleston Gazette, Jan. 2, 2006, at A4.

412.    Editorial, *Vote fraud hurts all West Virginians*, Charleston Gazette, Dec. 30, 2005, at A4.

413.    Tom Searls, *Two plead guilty to vote fraud*, Charleston Gazette, Dec. 14, 2005, at A1; Eric Eyre, *Logan man gets probation in vote-fraud scandal*, Charleston Gazette, Mar. 1, 2006, at A1; Staff Reports, *Logan man receives fine, probation for role in vote-buying conspiracy*, Charleston Daily Mail, Mar. 1, 2006, at A1.

414.    Chris Stirewalt, *Probes are talk of town, political corruption, vote-buying are hot topics of conversation*, Charleston Daily Mail, July 30, 2004, at A1.

415.    West Virginia Code of State Rules § 146-4-5.1, provides: "An election worker's pay, including direct or indirect payments for expenses, shall not exceed six dollars ($6.00) per hour up to a maximum of fifty dollars ($50.00) per day. . . ." Moreover, West Virginia Code of State Rules § 146-4-8.1, in part, provides: "Each candidate or candidate's authorized committee, but not both, may employ paid election workers solely for the candidate's personal campaign: Provided, however, That within the limits of one (1) election worker per precinct. . . ." During the 2004 election, West Virginia had 1,960 precincts statewide.

416.    Phil Kabler, *Statehouse beat, Mezzatesta could have put positive spin on case*, Charleston Gazette, Aug. 23, 2004, at A4.

417.    Hoppy Kercheval, *Hoppy's Commentary For Tuesday*, MetroNews Talkline, (July 20, 2004, <www.wvmetronews.com.>).

418.    Editorial, *Every vote counts . . . you hope, Elections will make interesting politics in W.Va. this year*, Charleston Daily Mail, May 21, 2004, at A4.

419.    K.W. Lee, *Revolt in the Mountains*, Sunday Gazette-Mail, Apr. 19, 1969, at M3.

420.    Editorial, *Plan for Honest Elections*, Charleston Gazette, July 16, 1966, at A4.

421.    Paul F. Lutz, *From Governor To Cabby: The Political Career and Tragic Death of West Virginia's William Casey Marland 1950-1965* 2 (Marshall University Library Associates; Huntington, West Virginia 1966).

422.    *Id.* at 3.

423.    *Id.* at 19.

424.    Staff Reports, *Former Governor Marland Dies In Barrington, Ill.*, Charleston Daily Mail, Nov. 26, 1965, at A1; Staff Reports, *Few to attend Marland Rites at Pinch Ridge*, Charleston Daily Mail, Nov. 30, 1965, at A6 (the six pall bearers at his funeral were members of the Barrington Chapter of Alcoholics Anonymous.); William C. Marland, Associated Press, *Marland Tells own Story*, Charleston Gazette, Mar. 18, 1965, at A1.

425.    Donald Wilson, *Slating and 'Lever Brothers,'* Life, May 9, 1960, at 26.

426.    *Id.*

427.    United States v. Ramey, 336 F.2d 512 (4th Cir. 1964).

428.    Charlie Connor, *Outright Forgeries*, Charleston Daily Mail, July 18, 1966, at A3.

429.    *Id*; *see e.g.*, Charlie Connor, *Who Voted As Mrs. Logan?*, Charleston Daily Mail, July 8, 1966, at A17; Staff Reports, *3 More Dead Voters Turned Up*, Charleston Gazette, July 30, 1966, at A11; K.W. Lee, *They Swear Dead Voted*, Charleston Gazette, Apr. 30, 1968, at A2; Jack Greene, *21 In Precinct 47 Deny They Voted; Secrecy Step Fails*, Charleston Daily Mail, Sept. 21, 1966, at A1; Don Marsh, *38 Testify to Vote Wrongs*, Charleston Gazette, Sept. 22, 1966, at A1; Don Marsh, *Phony Signatures, Preacher Vote-Paying Found*, Charleston Gazette, Sept. 30, 1966, at A1.

430.    K.W. Lee, *Test of Power*, Sunday Gazette-Mail, Apr. 27, 1969, at M2.

431.   *Id.*

432.   United States v. Townsley, 843 F.2d 1070, 1079 (8th Cir. 1988).

433.   Stacey Ruckle, *Southern West Virginia's history of voting corruption is a long tale,* *Charleston Daily Mail*, Aug. 5, 1999, at A1.

434.   *See* 54 Ops. Att'y Gen. 128 (W.Va. 1971) (The Attorney General's Opinion held that the Federal conviction did not automatically result in the removal from office for Smith. It charged that the Senate had the authority to expel Smith or any other member by a two thirds vote of the members of that elected body.); In re Bernard Smith, 166 W.Va. 22, 25, 270 S.E.2d 768, 771 (1980); Staff Reports, *"Logan Five" Defendant Dead at 64,* Charleston Gazette, Apr. 17, 1995, at A1; In re W. Bernard Smith, 158 W.Va. 13, 206 S.E.2d 920 (1974).

435.   Staff Reports, *"Logan Five" Defendant Dead at 64*, Charleston Gazette, Apr. 17, 1995, at A1.

436.   In re W. Bernard Smith, 158 W.Va. 13, 16, 206 S.E.2d 920, 922 (1974).

437.   *Id; see also* Anderson v. United States, 417 U.S. 211 (1974); In re Bernard Smith, 166 W.Va. 22, 23, 270 S.E.2d 768, 769 (1980); United States v. Anderson, 481 F.2d 685 (4th Cir. 1973); Staff Reports, *Logan Five Defendant Dead at 64*, Charleston Gazette, Apr. 17, 1995, at A1.

438.   *Id*; Tom Searls, *Week in Review,* Sunday Charleston Gazette-Mail, Apr. 23, 1995, at B4.

439.   Stacey Ruckle, *Southern West Virginia's history of voting corruption is a long tale,* *Charleston Daily Mail*, Aug. 5, 1999, at A1.

440.   In re Bernard Smith, 166 W.Va. at 25, 270 S.E.2d at 771; United States v. Anderson, 481 F.2d 685 (4th Cir. 1973); Anderson v. United States, 417 U.S. 211 (1974); Committee on Legal Ethics of the West Virginia State Bar v. Smith, 184 W.Va. 6, 399 S.E.2d 36 (1990).

441.   54 Ops. Atty Gen. 128 (January 25, 1972, West Virginia); *see also* Staff Reports, *Majority Leader's Job In Hand Of Legislature: Senate To Vote On Employment If Chafin Convicted Of Charges,* Charleston Daily Mail, Mar. 21, 1995, at A1; *see also* Richard Grimes, *Bernard Smith's Fate as Senator Faces Lawmakers,* Charleston Daily Mail, Jan. 12, 1972, at A1.

442.   Staff Reports, *Brown Indicted for Soliciting Contributions,* Charleston Gazette, Feb. 11, 1986, at A1; Staff Reports, *Brown Pleads Innocent to Election Law Charge,* Charleston Daily Mail, Feb. 22, 1986, at A1; Editorial, *Brown Endorsed,* Charleston Gazette, Apr. 28, 1988, at A4.

443.   In re Bernard Smith, 166 W.Va. at 28, 270 S.E.2d at 774; Staff Reports, *Logan Five Defendant Dead at 64,* Charleston Gazette, Apr. 17, 1995, at A1; Staff Reports, *Majority Leader's Job In Hand Of Legislature: Senate To Vote On Employment If Chafin Convicted Of Charges,* Charleston Daily Mail, Mar. 21, 1995, at A1.

444.   Committee on Legal Ethics v. W. Bernard Smith, 156 W.Va. 471, 194 S.E.2d 665 (1973); In re Smith, 158 W.Va. 13, 206 S.E.2d 920 (1974).

445.   In re Smith, 166 W.Va. 22, 25, 28, 270 S.E.2d 768, 771, 774 (1980); Staff Reports, *Logan Five Defendant Dead at 64,* Charleston Gazette, Apr. 17, 1995, at A1.

446.   Anderson v. United States, 417 U.S. 211, 225 (1974).

447.   Committee on Legal Ethics of the West Virginia State Bar v. Smith, 184 W.Va. 6, 399 S.E.2d 36 (1990); Associated Press, *Ousted State Senator William Smith Dies,* Charleston Daily Mail, Apr. 17, 1995, at A1; Staff Reports, *"Logan Five" Defendant Dead at 64,* Charleston Gazette, Apr. 17, 1995, at A1.

448.   *Id.*

449.   State v. Hobbs, 168 W.Va. 13, 282 S.E.2d 258 (1981); Whitman v. Fox, 160 W.Va. 633, 236 S.E.2d 565 (1977).

450.   Hobbs, at 17, 282 S.E.2d at 262.

451.   *Id.* at 17, 18, 282 S.E.2d at 262, 263.

452.   Stacey Ruckle, *Southern West Virginia's history of voting corruption is a long tale,* *Charleston Daily Mail*, Aug. 5, 1999, at A1.

453.   Associated Press, *Grand jury to see NBC videotape,* Charleston Gazette, Jan. 8, 1981, at A1.

454.   UPI, *Miffed Manchin vows to meet NBC officials,* Charleston Gazette, Nov. 28, 1980, at A1.

455.   Associated Press, *Marion Man Faces Ballot Charge,* Charleston Gazette, June 4, 1980, at A1; UPI, *4 indicted for alleged vote fraud,* Charleston Gazette, Jan. 8, 1981, at A1;

Associated Press, *Boone election OK'd, despite prosecutor's plea*, Charleston Gazette, Nov. 21, 1980, at A1; Fanny Seiler, *Grand juries may investigate Logan, Mingo election charges*, Charleston Gazette, Nov. 6, 1980, at A1, UPI, *Witness list leaked*, Charleston Gazette, Oct. 2, 1980, at A1; Associated Press, *McDowell vote complaint prompts investigation*, Charleston Gazette, June 6, 1980, at A1.

456.    Associated Press, *Boone officials' evidence may show election fraud*, Charleston Gazette, Nov. 20, 1980, at A1.

457.    *Id*; Associated Press, *Voting error or rigging suspected*, Charleston Gazette, Nov. 13, 1980, at A1; Associated Press, *Boone election OK'd, despite prosecutor's plea*, Charleston Gazette, Nov. 21, 1980, at A1.

458.    Hutchinson v. Miller, 797 F.2d 1279 (4th Cir. 1986); Hutchinson v. Staton, 994 F.2d 1076 (4th Cir. 1993).

459.    State ex rel. Underwood v. Silverstein, 167 W.Va. 121, 278 S.E.2d 886 (1981).

460.    Hutchinson v. Miller, 797 F.2d at 1279, 1280, 1281; Hutchinson v. Staton, 994 F.2d 1076 (4th Cir. 1993).

461.    A modem is a device that enables a computer to send and receive information over a telephone line.

462.    *Miller*, F.2d at 1281.

463.    Tom Searls, *Ex-county GOP chairman pleads guilty to tax evasion*, Charleston Gazette, Jan. 12, 2006, at A1.

464.    Kay Michael, *County Willing to Pay Miller Defense Costs*, Charleston Daily Mail, Aug. 25, 1983, at A1; Kay Michael, *Jury Clears Miller of all charges*, Charleston Daily Mail, June 2, 1983, at A1; Chris Knap, *Miller reflects on unsuccessful 'witch hunt,'* Charleston Gazette, June 4, 1983, at A1.

465.    Chicago Tribune wires, *Sentencing, Guilty Plea Latest In A County's Corruption Saga*, Chicago Tribune, Apr. 19, 1988, at C14; *see also* State ex rel. Owens v. Brown, 177 W.Va. 225, 351 S.E.2d 412 (1986); Staff Reports, *Arrests in Mingo County, West Virginia, exemplify state actions to control public corruption*, Des Moines Register, Apr. 8, 1988, at 3 (The article said that in Mingo County, prosecutors indicted fifteen public officials for bribery, false accounting procedures, illegal contributions, illegal expenditures, and even drug dealing.).

466.    State ex rel. Owens v. Brown, 177 W.Va. 225, 351 S.E.2d 412 (1986); Associated Press, *15 Charged With Buying Spots on Ballot; Action Called Blow to Corruption in West Virginia county Elections*, The Washington Post, Apr. 9, 1988, at A5 (The article quoted special prosecutor James Colburn as saying the practice of slating candidates and encouraging citizens to vote straight tickets contributed to the conditions alleged in the 15 indictments.); *see also* Fanny Seiler, *Ex-sheriff files counter complaint in Mingo County tiff*, Charleston Gazette, Oct. 3, 2001, at A9 (In 2001, Owens filed a complaint against a former political collaborator for what he called "terroristic threatening." George Williamson said the dispute began after he recently put up a campaign sign over his driveway for State Senator Truman Chafin and Owens threatened to kill him. Owens claimed that the commission received half of the $100,000 he received for the sheriff's office and Chafin was then president of the county commission in 1981-82.).

467.    Patricia Nealon, *Prosecutor ends a job of conviction*, The Boston Globe, Nov. 23, 1996, at B1.

468.    Associated Press, *Special Prosecutor sought for Mingo investigation*, Charleston Daily Mail, Mar. 20, 2002, at A11.

469.    Rochelle Olson, Associated Press, *'Bloody Mingo' West Virginia county writes long, eventful–and troubled–history*, Bluefield Daily Telegraph, Nov. 13, 1995, at A5.

470.    Staff Reports, *Around The Nation*, The Washington Post, Sept. 15, 1989, at A18.

471.    Aviva L. Brandt, Associated Press, *State ranked 42nd in voter turnout for 1992 election*, Charleston Gazette, Jan. 12, 1993, at C3.

472.    Kay Michael, *Disgraced politicians becoming state's stereotype*, Charleston Daily Mail, Aug. 28, 1989, at A1.

473.    This fact was confirmed anonymously by several campaign members of a particular 2002 congressional campaign in West Virginia. One such campaign worker said that "it was a disgusting process, but we felt compelled to participate for fear of losing critical votes."

474.    Chris Knap, *Kanawha political slates cost as much as $7,000*, Charleston Gazette, Sept. 26, 1984, at A1.

475.    Editorial, *Vote Fraud*, Charleston Daily Mail, May 13, 2002, at A4.

476.    George Gannon, *Kasey Warner is no longer U.S. attorney*, Charleston Daily Mail, Aug. 1, 2005, at A1; Matthew Thompson, *Charnock calling jabs partisan*, Charleston Daily Mail, Aug. 3, 2005, at A1.

477.    For a discussion on the so-called public choice theory, *see, e.g.*, Kenneth Arrow, *Social Choices and Individual Values* (John Wiley & Sons: New York, 1951); James Buchanan, *Essays on the Political Economy* (University of Hawaii Press: Honolulu, 1989).

478.    White, *surpra* note 3, at 99.

479.    In his book, *The Selling Of The President 1968*, Joe McGinnis writes: "The American voter, insisting upon his belief in a higher order, clings to his religion, which promises another, better life; and defends passionately the illusion that the men he chooses to lead him are of finer nature than he." Joe McGinnis, *The Selling Of The President 1968* (Trident Press, New York: 1969).

480.    Sam Tranum, *Deceased's vote counted in Mingo: Many counties fail to update rolls of registered voters*, Charleston Daily Mail, Apr. 25, 2002, at A1.

481.    Editorial, *W.Va. Voting, The state needs to concentrate on clean voting, not more voting*, Charleston Daily Mail, Mar. 10, 2001, at A4.

482.    Stacey Ruckle, *Southern West Virginia's history of voting corruption is a long tale*, Charleston Daily Mail, at A4.

483.    Associated Press, *More than 125,000 people cast ballots prior to Nov. 2*, Charleston Daily Mail, Jan. 13, 2005, at A1.

484.    I obtained this information from the West Virginia Secretary of State's Office. Dan Kimble, Chief Counsel to the Secretary of State, assisted me and confirmed the information.

485.    Sandy Wells, *'My adviser said to take the job in West Virginia,'* Charleston Gazette, Jan. 10, 1997, at C1.

486.    One such road map is located in the "Governor Moore Clippings File" held by the State Archives and History in the Cultural Center at the State Capitol Complex in Charleston, West Virginia. A copy of it appears in the photograph section of this book.

487.    Tom Miller, *Moore's legacy one of highs and lows*, Charleston Gazette, Aug. 1, 1999, at C1.

488.    Sprouse v. Clay Communications, Inc., 158 W.Va. 427, 211 S.E.2d 674 (1975).

489.    *Id.* at 699.

490.    *Id.* at 687.

491.    *Id.* at 685, 687, 699-705; *see also* Staff Reports, *James Marshall Sprouse dies at 80*, Sunday Charleston Gazette-Mail, July 4, 2004, at A1. James Marshall Sprouse died July 3, 2004. He served as a State Supreme Court Justice until his appointment by President Jimmy Carter to the Fourth Circuit Court of Appeals in 1979, three years after he had staged his second unsuccessful attempt to become West Virginia's Governor.

492.    Bob Kittle, *Pomp and Circumstance*, Charleston Daily Mail, Dec. 9, 1976, at A1.

493.    West Virginia State Archives and History, (Visited Mar. 16, 2003 <http://www.wvculture.org/history/mooreia1.html>.) A portion of Moore's address stated:

>      The oath prescribed by law and to which I have submitted signifies, in my judgment, the commencement of a new beginning for all West Virginians.
>
>      The people of West Virginia have now committed to one of their fellow citizens a supreme trust, and I here and now, dedicate myself to their service. I firmly believe that he who takes this oath only assumes in public ceremony the solemn obligation which every West Virginian must share with him.
>
>      The Constitution which prescribes the oath of office is your constitution. The government which you have chosen one to administer is your government. The laws which your elected representatives enact and I must enforce are your laws. So it should be emphasized that every citizen owes to his State a vigilant watch over the fidelity of its public servants. When this is done, the will of the people is impressed upon the function of government. . . .
>
>      Furthermore, when the people have bestowed their confidence upon a chief executive, they have a right to expect the type of leadership and action which will make the man and the office effective instruments of their government. This leadership–this action, I shall provide.

> We must make integrity in state government a tradition in West Virginia, and the time to begin to build such respect is now. Like an individual, a state can have no asset more valuable than a reputation for honesty. West Virginians deserve honorable government, and I will demand it.
>
> Through public trust, we must provide a fresh stimulus for improved government. Society is built upon trust, and without trust, there can be little more than discouragement. Without trust, hope is small and we must understand distrust and progress are incompatible.

494.    By 1973, John S. Knight owned fifteen newspapers, including the *Tallahassee Democrat*, the *Springfield Sun*, the *Philadelphia Inquirer* and the *Philadelphia Daily News*. In 1974, the Knight Newspapers merged with the California-based Ridder Publications and became Knight-Ridder Newspapers, Inc. By 1981, Knight-Ridder consisted of thirty-two newspapers in seventeen states, employed 15,000 workers and boasted a circulation of 3.6 million daily. *See* The University of Akron's Biography of John S. Knight (<http://www3.uakron.edu/library/jsknight/bio.html>).

495.    Editorial, *Nobody Knows Damage Caused By Knight Story On Governor*, Charleston Daily Mail, Apr. 11, 1970, at A4.

496.    Bob Mellace, *State Robbed Of More Than $100 Million By Political Chicanery, Governor Avers*, Charleston Daily Mail, July 28, 1970, at A1; *see also* William Barrett, *Wild, Wonderful West Virginia Has Charmed-Gov. Arch Moore*, Mineral County News-Tribune, Nov. 26, 1971, at 5; *3rd Time Moore Back As Governor*, Mineral County News-Tribune, Jan. 14, 1985, at 8.

497.    Barry Bearak, *Corruption in West Virginia: Scandals as Thick as Coal Dust*, Los Angeles Times, July 8, 1990, at A1; Associated Press, *Moore sentenced to 5 years, 10 months*, Times-West Virginian (Fairmont, WV), July 11, 1990, at A1.

498.    State ex rel. Maloney v. McCartney, 159 W.Va. 513, 517, 223 S.E.2d 607, 611 (1976); *see also* Richard Grimes, *Old Money, New Politics* 77 (1984). W.Va. Const. Art. 7 § 4 provides:

> None of the executive officers mentioned in this article shall hold any other office during the term of his service. A person who has been elected or who has served as governor during all or any part of two consecutive terms shall be ineligible for the office of governor during any part of the term immediately following the second of the two consecutive terms. The person holding the office of governor when this section is ratified shall not be prevented from holding the office of governor during the term immediately following the term he is then serving.

499.    *Id.*

500.    Barry Bearak, *Corruption in West Virginia: Scandals as Thick as Coal Dust*, Los Angeles Times, July 8, 1990, at A1.

501.    Jill Wilson, Associated Press, *W. Virginia indicts former governor*, The Phoenix Gazette, Apr. 13, 1990, at C2; *see also Ex-West Virginia Governor Admits Corruption Schemes*, New York Times, Apr. 13, 1990, Abstracts at 8; Bill McAllister, *Ex-Gov. Moore Agrees to Plead Guilty; W. Virginian Charged With Fraud, Extortion*, The Washington Post, Apr. 13, 1990, at A1.

502.    United States v. Moore, 931 F.2d 245 (4th Cir.1991) (rejecting challenge to guilty plea entered by Arch A. Moore to charges that he committed bribery and extortion while Governor of WestVirginia); *see also* Staff Reports, *Former West Virginia Governor Is Sentenced to 5 Years for Graft*, N.Y. Times, July 11, 1990, at A10, col. 4 (describing case, noting that Moore had been tried and acquitted on extortion charges while serving previous term as Governor); Editorial, *Arch Moore*, Charleston Daily Mail, Dec. 28, 1998, at A4.

503.    Associated Press, *Ex-Gov. Moore Faces 36-Year Term, Fines*, The Washington Post, May 9, 1990, at A11; Maryclaire Dale, *Kizer Will Testify Against Moore In State*, Charleston Gazette, July 29, 1995, at A1.

504.    Barry Bearak, *Corruption in West Virginia: Scandals as Thick as Coal Dust*, Los Angeles Times, July 8, 1990, at A1; *see also* Cheryl Caswell, *Ex Politicos Rebound after Fall from Grace*, Charleston Daily Mail, Sept. 6, 1994, at A1.

505.    Barry Bearak, *Corruption–with a Capitol 'C'*, Newsday, July 8, 1990, at 13 (The article proclaimed that the public thought Moore was a better Governor than then Governor Gaston Caperton even though eighty-one percent believed Moore belonged in jail.); Maryclaire Dale, *Kizer Will Testify Against Moore In State*, Charleston Gazette, July 29, 1995, at A1.

506.     Associated Press, *Ex-Gox. Moore Faces 36-Year Term, Fines*, The Washington Post, May
         9, 1990, at A11; Maryclaire Dale, *Kizer Will Testify Against Moore In State*, Charleston
         Gazette, July 29, 1995, at A1; Associated Press, *Moore answers suit, denies defrauding
         state*, The Herald-Dispatch (Huntington, WV), June 23, 1995, at B3; Associated Press,
         *Taylor: Moore records may be blocked by court*, Bluefield Daily Telegraph, Aug. 16, 1995,
         at A1; Lawyer Disciplinary Bd. v. Moore, 214 W.Va. 780, 591 S.E.2d 338 (2003); Cheryl
         Caswell, *Ex Politicos Rebound after Fall from Grace*, Charleston Daily Mail, Sept. 6,
         1994, at A1; Lawrence Messina, *Moore wants his law license back, files secrecy motion:
         Questionnaire should be public, lawyer says*, Charleston Gazette, Dec. 23, 1998, at A1; *see
         also* Indictment, *United States of America v. Arch A. Moore, Jr.*, Criminal Action Number
         2:90-00078, United States District Court for the Southern District Court of West Virginia,
         Charleston Division, filed April 12, 1990; Plea, *United States of America v. Arch A. Moore,
         Jr.*, Criminal Action Number 2:90-00078, United States District Court for the Southern
         District Court of West Virginia, Charleston Division, filed May 8, 1990; State v. Moore,
         895 F.Supp. 864 (S.D. W.Va. 1995).

507.     *Murder in the Appalachians*, The Nation, Mar. 20, 1972, Vol. 214, Issue 12, at 357.

508.     George Gannon, *Well-known local newsman makes his way back home to W.Va.*,
         Charleston Daily Mail, May 5, 2005, at A1; *see also* Staff Reports, *Decisions on Disaster
         Puzzling*, Charleston Gazette, Mar. 1, 1997, at A1.

509.     Staff Reports, *Decisions on Disaster Puzzling*, Charleston Gazette, Mar. 1, 1997, at A1.

510.     Robert Morris, *Brotherton Raps Moore, Calls Bentley Incapable*, Charleston Gazette, Feb.
         15, 1980, at A1.

511.     Jennifer Bundy, Associated Press, *If negotiations fail, Moore goes on trial: Case sched-
         uled for Tuesday as state seeks money back from convicted ex-governor*, The Dominion
         Post (Morgantown, WV), July 30, 1995, at B5; *see also* Associated Press, *Moore answers
         suit, denies defrauding state*, The Herald-Dispatch (Huntington, WV), June 23, 1995, at
         B3; Associated Press, *Moore set to face state suit*, Bluefield Daily Telegraph, July 30,
         1995; Complaint, *State of West Virginia v. Arch A. Moore, Jr.*, Civil Action Number 2:90-
         0747, United States District Court for the Southern District Court of West Virginia,
         Charleston Division, August 2, 1995; Amended Complaint, *State of West Virginia v. Arch
         A. Moore, Jr.*, Civil Action Number 2:90-0747, United States District Court for the
         Southern District Court of West Virginia, Charleston Division; Order, *State of West
         Virginia v. Arch A. Moore, Jr.*, Civil Action Number 2:90-0747, United States District
         Court for the Southern District Court of West Virginia, Charleston Division, July 20, 1995.

512.     Associated Press, *Moore answers suit, denies defrauding state*, The Herald-Dispatch
         (Huntington, WV), June 23, 1995, at B3.

513.     Jennifer Bundy, Associated Press, *Moore settles lawsuit: Agrees to give back $750,000*,
         The Dominion Post (Morgantown, WV), July 31, 1995, at A1; Associated Press, *Moore
         must pay up: State settles ex-governor's lawsuit*, Bluefield Daily Telegraph, Aug. 1, 1995,
         at B1.

514.     Jack McCarthy, *Records in Moore corruption case remain closed to the public*, Charleston
         Gazette, Aug. 2, 1995, at A1.

515.     Committee on Legal Ethics v. Moore, 411 S.E.2d at 456; *see also* A.V. Gallagher,
         Associated Press, *High court annuls Moore's law licence*, Charleston Gazette, November
         1, 1991, at D5; Jim Cochran, *Arch Honored to Honor the Fallen: Ex-governor much dec-
         orated WWII vet*, Wheeling Intelligencer, May 27, 1997, at A1 ("Gov. Moore has received
         the Bronze Star Medal, Military Order of Public Heart, Combat Infantry Badge with three
         battle stars, and the Grand Cross of Homage, the Military Order of Ardennes in recogni-
         tion of his service to his country.").

516.     Committee On Legal Ethics Of The West Virginia State Bar v. Craig, 187 W.Va 14, 15, 22,
         415 S.E.2d 255, 256, 263 (1992); Paul J. Nyden, *Failed Bank Linked To Beer
         Distributorship*, Charleston Sunday Gazette-Mail, July 28, 1996, at A11; *see also* Gillespie v. Wood,
         154 W.Va. 422, 175 S.E.2d 497 (1970) (Ed Gillespie was accused of bribing Governor
         Moore employee Dale Curry, a buyer in the Purchasing Division of the Department of
         Finance. The so-called bribe was an attempt to gain "favor and award business to the Debs
         Hospital Supplies, Inc." Gillespie convinced the West Virginia Supreme Court that
         although Curry was working in State government that he was a mere employee and not "an
         executive and ministerial officer of the State" as contemplated by the statute. Gillespie
         was successful and the indictment was declared void." ).

517.     Eric Eyre, *Manchin brings 54-foot yacht to state: Governor and friends took state plane
         to pick up boat in Alabama*, Charleston Sunday Gazette-Mail, May 15, 2005, at B1.

518.     Eric Eyre *Bankruptcy bluffer now Manchin aide*, Charleston Sunday Gazette-Mail, Mar.
         05, 2006, at A1.

519.     Peter Carlson, *The Magic and the Misery*, The Washington Post Sunday-magazine, Nov.

22, 1992, at W9; Toby Coleman, *Moore's lawyers call on court to return law license*, Charleston Daily Mail, Nov. 18, 2003, at A1.

520.  Lawrence Messina, *Moore wants his law license back, files secrecy motion: Questionnaire should be public, lawyer says*, Charleston Gazette, Dec. 23, 1998, at A1.

521.  Editorial, *Arch Moore*, Charleston Daily Mail, Dec. 28, 1998, at A4.

522.  Lawrence Messina, *Moore wants his law license back, files secrecy motion: Questionnaire should be public, lawyer says*, Charleston Gazette, Dec. 23, 1998, at A1.

523.  Editorial, *Arch Moore*, Charleston Daily Mail, Dec. 28, 1998, at A4.

524.  Martha Bryson Hodel, Associated Press, *Counsel recounts former governor's past, Charges allege Moore used cash for personal gain*, Charleston Daily Mail, June 30, 2003, at A1.

525.  Ken Ward Jr., *Moore's lawyers defend his consulting*, Charleston Gazette, Sept. 30, 2003, at A1.

526.  Associated Press, *Bar panel recommends denying reinstatement for former governor*, Martinsburg Journal, Aug. 21, 2003, at A1; Associated Press, *No license, panel tells Arch Moore*, Weirton Daily Times, Aug. 21, 2003, at A1; Associated Press, *Bar panel won't move to reinstate Moore*, Bluefield Daily Telegraph, Aug. 21, 2003, at A1; Associated Press, *W.Va. Bar panel refuses to reinstate former governor*, The Logan Banner, Aug. 21, 2003, at 1; Editorial, *Moore's license fight disgracing state once again*, Herald-Dispatch, Aug. 23, 2003, at A1. The Hearing Panel Subcommittee of the Supreme Court of Appeals of West Virginia ("Hearing Panel") concluded:

> While Moore asks the Panel to conclude that he can now be trusted to abide by the law and the Rules of Professional Conduct in the future, he has failed to offer any evidence that he has personally addressed the reasons for his misconduct, expressed contrition for what he did, or even recognized that he did much wrong in the first place. Yet, without some acknowledgment from Moore that he has consciously dealt with the personal failings that led to his history of misconduct, there is no assurance that he will act in accordance with the Rules of Professional Conduct in the future. To the contrary, Moore's attitude toward backdating documents and his less than candid testimony under oath before this Panel, about both the reasons for his plea and his complicity in the underlying crimes, is inconsistent with his claim of rehabilitation. As a result, the Panel concludes that Moore has yet to recognize and accept responsibility for the gravity of his actions or to realistically address the character traits that led to his wrongful acts in the first place.

214 W.Va. at 795, 591 S.E.2d at 353. The Hearing Panel explained that Moore's conduct embodied a pattern of behavior that had existed throughout his many years of public service. The Hearing Panel provided:

> To appreciate the severity of Moore's offenses, it is important to understand that Moore's offenses did not just involve the taking of unreported cash on an isolated occasion. Rather, Moore demonstrated a pattern of accepting cash payments for political and personal use over a period of many years without reporting the payments as income on his income tax returns or as political contributions in his campaign finance reports. His explanations for this conduct are unconvincing. For example, his claim that he thought there was no duty to report the contributions until the campaign expended the money defies credulity in light of both Moore's sophistication and his claim that he believed Craig would report the funds despite the fact that Moore never even told Craig where the money came from.

*Id.* at 790, 791, 591 S.E.2d at 348, 349. The Hearing Panel further conveyed:

> Moreover, Moore's attitude toward the cash "gifts" that he received demonstrated, in both his past testimony and his testimony before the Panel, an insensitivity to the high standards expected of an attorney, let alone a public official entrusted with the highest political office within the State. For example, Moore's testimony to the Government in 1990 that he told a donor that he would only accept an $8,000.00 gift during the 1984 campaign in cash because to accept a check "would have an indication that it was politically arrayed" is hardly consistent with the integrity and moral character expected of an attorney in West Virginia.

Not only did Moore profit personally and politically from large cash gifts over a period of many years, but there is also compelling evidence that Moore led others to think that they would benefit from these undisclosed and unreported "gifts" through his influence and power as Governor. This is apparent from the history of gifts to Moore from D'Annunzio and others as well as the Kizer transactions and Moore's intervention with the Department of Natural Resources on behalf of Kizer, an intervention that he admitted in 1990, but denied, under oath before this Panel.

The Hearing Panel also recognized that Moore's questionable conduct had even continued throughout his cooperation with the Hearing Panel's investigation of whether or not to return Moore's law license.

Worse, particularly from someone who wishes to return to the practice of law, Moore actively engaged in an attempt to obstruct the investigation against him in 1990 by testifying falsely to federal investigators and by encouraging others to join him in doing so. While Moore denied, in his testimony before this Panel, that his conversation with Leaberry was an attempt to obstruct justice, his denial is not credible. Comparing the transcript of Moore's tape recorded conversations with Leaberry with Moore's explanation of those conversations in his testimony before the Panel demonstrates that Moore was not only willing to conspire to fabricate testimony when facing indictment in 1990, but, sadly, that he was just as willing to provide disingenuous testimony in this proceeding in the hope of reinstating his law license.

*Id.*

527.  Editorial, *Moore, Amazing arrogance*, Charleston Gazette, Nov. 18, 2003, at A4.

528.  *Id.*

529.  Lawyer Disciplinary Bd. v. Moore, 214 W.Va. 780, 591 S.E.2d 338 (2003); Toby Coleman, *State's chief justice angry over ruling's release*, Charleston Daily Mail, Dec. 5, 2003, at A1; Toby Coleman, *High Court denies Moore's license*, Charleston Daily Mail, Dec. 4, 2003, at A1; Ken Ward Jr., *High court rejects Moore's plea, Disgraced former governor won't get law license back*, Charleston Gazette, Dec. 5, 2003, at A1.

530.  In re Smith, 214 W.Va. 83, 585 S.E.2d 602 (1980); Staff Reports, *Bernard Smith's law license restored*, Oct. 8, 1980, at A1.

531.  *Id.* (The eight Barron associates were gubernatorial aide Curtis Trent, Attorney General C. Donald Robertson, his brother Dana Robertson, Deputy Attorney General Phillip Graziani, Assistant Attorney General Marshall West, Barron business partner Joseph Berzito, and Barron law partner Bonn Brown.).

532.  The *Hey* decision was disposed of by a memorandum order in the recent case of *Lawyer Disciplinary Board v. Hey* (No. 28239, October 10, 2003). In Justice Davis' dissent in *Lawyer Disciplinary Bd. v. Moore*, 214 W.Va. 780, 591 S.E.2d 338 (2003), she stated:

Both Mr. Hey and Mr. Moore pled guilty to criminal charges and both petitioners refused, in reinstatement proceedings, to acknowledge their role in committing the crimes to which they pled guilty. I believe it is this Court's duty to the public and the bar to deny reinstatement of a law license when there is no admission and acceptance of responsibility for the conduct which caused disbarment.

Chris Stirewalt, *Pick for Hey prosecutor questioned, former judge may face witness intimidation charge*, Charleston Daily Mail, Mar. 28, 2001, at A1.

533.  214 W.Va. at 790, 798, 799, 591 S.E.2d at 348, 356, 357; Toby Coleman, *Ruling shows justices will be tougher*, Charleston Daily Mail, Dec. 13, 2003, at A1.

534.  *Id.*

535.  214 W.Va. at 790, 798 n.2, 591 S.E.2d at 348, 356 n.2; Associated Press, *Moore's lawyers cite 'fairness' of Hey ruling*, Charleston Daily Mail, Nov. 1, 2003, at A1.

536.  Moore v. CNA Insurance, 215 W.Va. 286, 599 S.E.2d 709 (2004); *see also* Chris Wetterich, *Ex-governor seeks $1 million*, Charleston Gazette, Apr. 29, 2004, at A1; Chris Wetterich, *State Supreme Court refuses Moore legal fees, Justices rule that former insurer does not have to pay ex-governor $1 million*, Charleston Gazette, July 1, 2004, at A1; United States v. Moore, 931 F.2d 245 (4th Cir.1991) (rejecting challenge to guilty plea entered by Arch A. Moore to charges that he committed bribery and extortion while Governor of West Virginia); West Virginia v. Moore, 897 F.Supp. 276 (S.D. W.Va. 1995)

(detailing facts that Governor Moore's guilty plea established his guilt and estopped him denying the essential elements of his guilt); and 895 F.Supp. 864 (S.D. W.Va. 1995).

537.     Chris Wetterich, *State Supreme Court refuses Moore legal fees, Justices rule that former insurer does not have to pay ex-governor $1 million*, Charleston Gazette, July 1, 2004, at A1; West Virginia has a ten year statute of limitations for suits alleging a breach of contract. *See* W.Va.Code § 55-2-6 (1923); *McKenzie v. Cherry River Coal & Coke Co.*, 195 W.Va. 742, 466 S.E.2d 810 (1995) (per curiam); Moore v. CNA Insurance, 215 W.Va. 286, 599 S.E.2d 709 (2004). In denying Moore's claim, the State Supreme Court held:

> In this case, the allegations against Governor Moore were set forth clearly by the State's complaint and were undeniably predicated solely upon Governor Moore's guilty plea. . . . Additionally, it is important to recognize that Governor Moore pled guilty to every count of the federal criminal indictment against him. To this end, his guilty plea to the criminal charges was the sole foundation for the State's subsequent civil action. Consequently, it is clear that the claim against Governor Moore does not fall within the coverage of the liability insurance policy and therefore, CNA had no duty to defend Governor Moore.

538.     Barry Bearak, *Corruption—with a Capitol 'C'*, Newsday, July 8, 1990, at 13.

539.     Staff Reports, *Minear, Moore, Sprouse to speak at Lincoln Day Dinner*, Parsons Advocate, Apr. 23, 2003, at 1.

540.     L.T. Anderson, *Honoring our governors of the past*, Charleston Daily Mail, March 8, 2002, at A4.

541.     Editorial, *An honest governor*, Charleston Gazette, Oct. 27, 1980, at A4.

542.     Bill McAllister, *W. Virginia Politics Gets 'Soap Opera' Spin*, The Washington Post, Mar. 25, 1990, at A1.

543.     Barry Bearak, *Corruption—with a Capitol 'C'*, Newsday, July 8, 1990, at 13; Barry Bearak, *Corruption in West Virginia: Scandals as Thick as Coal Dust*, Los Angeles Times, July 8, 1990, at A1.

544.     Bill McAllister, *W. Virginia Politics Gets 'Soap Opera' Spin*, The Washington Post, Mar. 25, 1990, at A1.

545.     Paul J. Nyden, *Ex-coal operator Kizer backs Moore's bid for law license*, Charleston Gazette, Dec. 10, 2002, at A1.

546.     Fanny Seiler, *Jay's Desk Doesn't fit, Moore Pays $13,606 for Furniture*, Charleston Gazette, Jan. 19, 1977, at A1.

547.     According to the Federal Election Commission, President Carter received $29.44 million in August of 1980 and $21.82 million in public funds in July of 1976 for his general election campaigns during those respective years. *See* (<http://www.fec.gov/info/appone.htm>).

548.     Lunch interview at Shoney's in (Kanawha City) Charleston, West Virginia between Allen H. Loughry II and Bob Brunner on April 7, 2005, confirming the previous discussions of this occurrence. Bob also worked as a reporter for WCHS television and later accepted a position in Montgomery, Alabama. He then served as spokesman for the Red Cross in Mobile, Alabama before accepting a position at a television station in Knoxville, Tennessee. He is currently the news director for WOAY television in Oak Hill, West Virginia.

549.     Rockefeller's daughter Valerie was named for Sharon's twin sister Valerie, who was brutally murdered in 1966 in her bed at Senator Percy's home in what still remains an unsolved murder. David J. Krajicek, *Killed without a clue*, New York Daily News, Aug. 1, 2004. (<http://www.nydailynews.com/news/crime_file/story/217714p-187324c.html>).

550.     Senator Robert C. Byrd, Cong. Rec. Sen. Daily Ed. May 10, 2002, at S4193.

551.     *Id.*

552.     Eric Pianin, *A Senator's Shame*, The Washington Post, June 19, 2005, at A1.

553.     Senator Byrd was President Pro Tempore of the Senate from January 3, 1989-January 2, 1991; from January 3, 1991-January 4, 1993; from January 5, 1993-January 3, 1995; from January 3, 2001-January 20, 2001, and from June 6, 2001-January 3, 2003.

554.     Paul J. Nyden, *Byrd to run in 2006*, Charleston Gazette, Feb. 6, 2005, at A1.

555.     *See* Unites States Senator Robert C. Byrd's Senate website (<www.byrd.senate.gov>).

556.     Just some of the named buildings, roads, and institutions include:

> Robert C. Byrd Drive, from Beckley to Sophia (Byrd's hometown);
> Robert C. Byrd Health Sciences Center of West Virginia University,

Morgantown; Robert C. Byrd Cancer Research Labratory of West Virginia University, Morgantown; Robert C. Byrd Technology Center at Alderson-Broaddus College, Philippi; Robert C. Byrd Hardwood Technologies Center, Princeton; Robert C. Byrd Bridge, between Huntington and Chesapeake, Ohio; Robert C. Byrd Addition to the Lodge at Oglebay Park, Wheeling; Robert C. Byrd Community Center, Pine Grove; Robert C. Byrd Expressway, U.S. 52, near Weirton; Robert C. Byrd Institute, Charleston; Robert C. Byrd Institute for Advanced Flexible Manufacturing; Huntington, Charleston, Bridgeport & Short Gap; Robert C. Byrd Visitor Center at Harpers Ferry National Historic Park, Harpers Ferry; Robert C. Byrd Federal Building & Courthouse, Charleston; Robert C. Byrd Federal Building & Courthouse, Beckley; Robert C. Byrd Academic and Technology Center at Marshall University, Huntington; Robert C. Byrd National Technology Transfer Center at Wheeling Jesuit University, Wheeling; Robert C. Byrd United Technical Center; Robert C. Byrd Hilltop Office Complex, Short Gap (near Keyser); Robert C. Byrd Library & Robert C. Byrd Learning Resource Center at Mountain State University, Beckley; Robert C. Byrd Rural Health Center at Marshall University, Huntington; Robert C. Byrd Clinical Addition to Veteran's Hospital, Huntington; Robert C. Byrd Industrial Park, Moorefield; Robert C. Byrd Locks & Dam, Gallipolis Ferry; Robert C. Byrd Green Bank Telescope, Green Bank; Robert C. Byrd Science and Technology Center at Shepherd College, Shepherdstown; Robert C. Byrd High School, Clarksburg; Robert C. Byrd Biotechnology Science Center at Marshall University, Huntington; Robert C. Byrd Conference Center at Davis & Elkins College, Elkins; Robert C. Byrd Health and Wellness Center of Bethany College, Bethany; Robert C. Byrd National Aerospace Education Center, Bridgeport; Robert C. Byrd Appalachian Highway System; (For Byrd's Wife) Erma Ora Byrd Center for Educational Technologies at Wheeling Jesuit University, Wheeling.

557.   Jack Deutsch, *Jay moves closer to presidential bid*, Charleston Daily Mail, July 5, 1991, at A1.

558.   Phil Kabler, *Bush not unbeatable, Rockefeller says*, Charleston Gazette, May 9, 1991, at A1.

559.   Robin Toner, *Rockefeller's presidential ambitions inevitable*, New York Times Magazine, July 21, 1991, at B1.

560.   Richard Grimes, *Jay Rockefeller, Old Money, New Politics* 111, 120, 155 (McClain: 1984) (Moore received 423,817 votes while Rockefeller received 350,462.).

561.   *Id.* at 12, 16 (McClain: 1984); *see also* West Virginia State Archives and History (<http://www.wvculture.org/history/jayrock.html>) (Visited Mar. 16, 2003)).

562.   Richard Grimes, *No communication between Moore, Jay*, Charleston Daily Mail, Nov. 11, 1976, at A1; Associated Press, *Transition Effort Said Nonexistent*, Charleston Gazette, Nov. 12, 1976, at A1; Associated Press, *Moore Won't Meet with Rockefeller*, Clarksburg Exponent, Nov. 13, 1976, at A1.

563.   Grimes, *supra* note 560, at 173.

564.   *Id; see also* Bob Kittle, *First Day..., some Awkward Moments Confront Newest Governor*, Charleston Daily Mail, Jan. 19, 1977, at C1.

565.   Bob Kittle, *First Day..., some Awkward Moments Confront Newest Governor*, Charleston Daily Mail, Jan. 19, 1977, at C1; Fanny Seiler, *Jay's Desk Doesn't Fit, Moore Pays $13,606 for Furniture*, Charleston Gazette, Jan. 19, 1977, at A1.

566.   Grimes, *supra* note 560, at 17, 69 (After the 1968 Valentine's Day indictments for bribery and conspiracy by a grand jury of former Governor Wally Barron and five other democratic officials Rockefeller went on record for the first time proclaiming that he was too rich to steal.).

567.   Bruce J. Shulman, Politics; *Anyone can be President, but it helps to be rich*, Los Angeles Times, Oct. 12, 1997, at M1; Bruce J. Shulman, *President Moneybags; the wealthy have long occupied command posts in American government*, Pittsburgh Post-Gazette, Oct. 26, 1997, at E4; Bruce J. Shulman, *Today's breed just pretenders to historically noble throne*, Arizona Republic, Oct. 19, 1997, at H5.

568.   Editorial, *The myth of low voter turnout, Don't be fooled; despite numbers, W.Va. Is voting*, Charleston Daily Mail, June 29, 2004, at A4.

569.    Chris Wetterich, *State last in 2002 vote count*, Charleston Gazette, July 29, 2004, at A1.

570.    Associated Press, *AP survey: W.Va. voters don't know, don't care*, Charleston Sunday Gazette-Mail, May 9, 2004, at A1. Tim McGraw is a country music singer and son of baseball hall-of-fame pitcher Tug McGraw.

571.    Susan Leffler, *Cash flow in politics targeted, Reformers try to persuade candidates to reduce spending*, Charleston Sunday Gazette-Mail, Aug. 30, 1992, at B1.

572.    Grimes, *supra* note 560, at 243.

573.    *Id.* at 40, 42, 241, 244; Jim Ragsdale, *Jay spending to hit $12 million?*, Charleston Gazette, Nov. 1, 1980, at A2; Rosalie Earle, *$11.6 million spent in Jay's campaign*, Charleston Gazette, Dec. 5, 1980, at A1; Robert Morris, *$7.5 million spent by Jay since primary*, Oct. 31, 1980, at A1.

574.    Susan Leffler, *Cash flow in politics targeted, Reformers try to persuade candidates to reduce spending*, Charleston Sunday Gazette-Mail, Aug. 30, 1992, at B1.

575.    *Id.* at 42, 53; Robert Morris, *Election buying charge is an 'insult to state,' Jay says*, Charleston Gazette, Nov. 1, 1980, at A1.

576.    Grimes, *supra* note 560, at 248.

577.    *Id.* at 83.

578.    *Id.*

579.    *Id.* at 97.

580.    *Id.* at 70, 180, 181, 243.

581.    *Id.* at 71.

582.    Davis, *supra* note 4, at 155.

583.    Karin Fischer, *Sen. Byrd Pushes Campaign Finance Reform, Champion of The Constitution Backs New Amendment*, Charleston Daily Mail, Feb. 14, 2001, at A1.

584.    *Id*; In 1976, the United States Supreme Court proclaimed that giving money to a politician was in effect a form of expression and thus granted protection under the First Amendment to the Constitution. It is known as *Buckley v. Valeo*, however, it is poorly understood. The Court did not end all efforts toward reforming campaigns. While the Court was extensively restrictive on direct expenditures by candidates or individuals, they did say that Congress could limit contributions to campaigns to reduce the risk and reality of corruption. The Court also noted that a voluntary system of public financing of campaigns is legitimate so long as it does not forbid private expenditures. The laws regulating campaign financing prior to 1971 were generally ineffective and largely ignored. The early campaign regulations were designed to prevent flagrant abuses by restricting spending and limiting contributions. Nevertheless, the early laws were riddled with loosely enforced loopholes that resulted in little more than candidates avoiding both the regulation and the reporting of campaign dollars. An antiquated system of political finance that was simply no longer effective frustrated reformers who witnessed years of congressional neglect and inaction. *See, eg.,* Herbert E. Alexander & Brian A Haggerty, *The Federal Election Campaign Act: After A Decade Of Political Reform*, at 13, 19 (Joyce J. Bartell, ed., 1981).

585.    147 CONG. REC. S2853 (daily ed. Mar. 26, 2001) (statement of Sen. Hollings); (visited Mar. 14, 2001 <http://thomas.loc.gov/cgi-bin/query>.) (introduced by Senator Hollings and co-sponsored by, Senators Specter (R-PA), Cleland (D-GA), and Byrd.) (As an amendment to the Constitution, the article must be passed by two-thirds of each House and then it must be ratified by the legislatures of three-fourths of the several states within seven years after the date of final passage by Congress.).

586.    Lawrence Messina, *Spending 'obscene,' Byrd says*, Charleston Gazette, Mar. 13, 2001, at A1.

587.    Associate Press, *Senate helps candidates facing wealthy foes*, Charleston Gazette, Mar. 21, 2001, at A1; 147 CONG. REC. S2541 (daily ed. Mar. 20, 2001) (statement of Sen. Byrd).

588.    Byrd and Rockefeller's Democratic counterparts in the United States House–Nick Rahall and Alan Mollohan–were two of only a dozen Democrats to vote against the Bill. Conversely, West Virginia's sole Republican Representative Shelley Moore Capito, in a courageous move, voted in support of the campaign finance legislation and against the heavy pressure applied by Republican House Leadership. *See* Editorial Roundup, *Capito* (The Herald-Dispatch, Huntington, WV), Charleston Daily Mail, Feb. 23, 2002, at A4. ("Capito successfully inserted an amendment in the bill that would raise contribution ceilings for candidates running against wealthy opponents spending their own money. Her concern is understandable given her bitter 2000 election battle with Charleston attorney Jim Humphreys, who spent $6 million of his own money in his unsuccessful race for the House seat she won.").

589.    Interview of John McCain by Allen H. Loughry II, August 5, 2000, Barboursville Veterans Home, Barboursville, West Virginia.

590.    Karin Fischer, *Campaign bill goes to Bush*, Charleston Daily Mail, Mar. 21, 2002, at A1.

591.    Karin Fischer, *Race may have been different, campaign reform could have altered race for Congress*, Charleston Daily Mail, Mar. 21, 2001, at A1.

592.    147 CONG. REC. S2857 (daily ed. Mar. 26, 2001) (statement of Sen. Byrd).

593.    147 CONG. REC. S2856 (daily ed. Mar. 26, 2001) (statement of Sen. Byrd).

594.    For instance, Darrell's wife Jorea, a former Kanawha County superintendent of schools, and Warren's wife Peggy, a former school teacher, are both classy, energetic, and intelligent women and two of the friendliest people you would ever want to meet. Warren's son Randolph, a former State House of Delegates member, and his sister Suzanne, a current Family Court Judge, are both more than capable lawyers and good people. I became acquainted with Randolph when he was in the Legislature and with Suzanne years earlier when I was working for Governor Caperton and she was working as a lawyer to the State Legislature. Randolph is exceptionally friendly just as Suzanne is highly intelligent with a first-class personality.

595.    Toby Coleman, *Attorney general's letter called political*, Charleston Gazette, October 19, 2004, at A1.

596.    *Id.*

597.    Staff Reports, *McGraw letter criticized as campaign maneuver*, Charleston Daily Mail, Oct. 20, 2004, at A7.

598.    Editorial, *McGraw's Name Game*, Parkersburg News, Aug. 22, 2003, at A4.

599.    Josh Hafenbrack, *McGraw's ad cost skyrocket, Attorney general's office says money from settlements*, Charleston Daily Mail, Mar. 5, 2004, at A1.

600.    Kris Wise, *Lawmakers want hand in fund allocation*, Charleston Daily Mail, Feb. 20, 2006, at A1; Editorial, *This is misuse of state power*, Charleston Daily Mail, Feb. 21, 2006, at A4; Editorial, *The Legislature must do its job*, Charleston Daily Mail, Feb. 10, 2006, at A4.

601.    Deanna Wrenn, *buying air time, Chamber president questions timing of advertisements*, Charleston Daily Mail, Mar. 5, 2003, at A1; *see also* Associated Press, *McGraw ad campaign plan criticized, Public awareness shots give unfair advantage, official says*, Charleston Gazette, Aug. 19, 2003, at A1.

602.    Josh Hafenbrack, *McGraw spending grows, GOP critics allege political motive for advertising*, Charleston Daily Mail, Mar. 9, 2004, at A1.

603.    Editorial, *Promotion, The McGraw brothers should pay for their own political ads*, Charleston Daily Mail, Mar. 8, 2004, at A4.

604.    Editorial, *McGraw's ads, Unseemly amid campaign*, Charleston Gazette, Mar. 11, 2004, at A4.

605.    Phil Kabler, *Statehouse Beat, Public service ads not cheap*, Charleston Gazette, Nov. 3, 2003, at A4.

606.    Associated Press, *Fired worker alleges McGraw uses office for re-election effort, group says it has filed ethics complaint over attorney general's actions*, Charleston Daily Mail, Oct. 7, 2004, at A1; Staff, *McGraw Staffer Says AG Will Be Cleared*, MetroNews Talkline, (Oct. 14, 2004, <www.wvmetronews.com.>).

607.    Toby Coleman, *Whanger stunned by firing, Attorney general's office fires former school board member over purchases*, Charleston Daily Mail, Aug. 24, 2004, at A1; Staff, *McGraw Staffer Says AG Will Be Cleared*, MetroNews Talkline, (Oct. 14, 2004, <www.wvmetronews.com.>).

608.    Scott Finn, *McGraw aide dismissed*, Charleston Gazette, Aug. 24, 2004, at A1.

609.    Associated Press, *Fired worker alleges McGraw uses office for re-election effort, group says it has filed ethics complaint over attorney general's actions*, Charleston Daily Mail, Oct. 7, 2004, at A1.

610.    Staff Reports, *Statehouse Notebook: Shelley looked up to John Kerry*, Charleston Daily Mail, Aug. 30, 2004, at A4.

611.    Toby Coleman, *Whanger stunned by firing, Attorney general's office fires former school board member over purchases*, Charleston Daily Mail, Aug. 24, 2004, at A1; Associated Press, *Fired worker alleges McGraw uses office for re-election effort, group says it has filed ethics complaint over attorney general's actions*, Charleston Daily Mail, Oct. 7, 2004, at A1.

612.    Staff, *McGraw Watchdog Group Files Ethics Complaint*, MetroNews Talkline, (Oct. 6,

2004, <www.wvmetronews.com.>); Staff, *McGraw Staffer Says AG Will Be Cleared*, MetroNews Talkline, (Oct. 14, 2004, <www.wvmetronews.com.>); Toby Coleman, *Massey president Blankenship contributed to watchdog group, Groups ads helped defeat Warren McGraw at polls*, Charleston Gazette, Jan. 11, 2005, at A1.

613.  Associated Press, *Fired worker alleges McGraw uses office for re-election effort, group says it has filed ethics complaint over attorney general's actions*, Charleston Daily Mail, Oct. 7, 2004, at A1; Staff, *McGraw Watchdog Group Files Ethics Complaint*, MetroNews Talkline, (Oct. 6, 2004, <www.wvmetronews.com.>).

614.  *Id*; Staff Reports, *McGraw Staffer Says AG Will Be Cleared*, MetroNews Talkline, (Oct. 14, 2004, <www.wvmetronews.com.>).

615.  Staff Reports, *McGraw Watchdog Group Files Ethics Complaint*, MetroNews Talkline, (Oct. 6, 2004, <www.wvmetronews.com.>); Associated Press, *Fired worker alleges McGraw uses office for re-election effort, group says it has filed ethics complaint over attorney general's actions*, Charleston Daily Mail, Oct. 7, 2004, at A1; Scott Finn, *McGraw aide dismissed*, Charleston Gazette, Aug. 24, 2004, at A1; Editorial, *Another misuse of public funds, Spending $141,815 in public funds for personal promotion is wrong*, Charleston Daily Mail, Aug. 25, 2004, at A4; Toby Coleman, *Whanger stunned by firing, Attorney general's office fires former school board member over purchases*, Charleston Daily Mail, Aug. 24, 2004, at A1; *see also* (<www.wvwantstoknow.com>) (visited November 16, 2004)). According to the West Virginia Wants To Know website, it is "an organization dedicated to insuring public moneys are spent according to their intended purpose."

616.  Toby Coleman, *Attorney General's Office to use promotional items after election*, Charleston Daily Mail, Aug. 25, 2004, at A1; *see also* Scott Finn, *McGraw aide dismissed*, Charleston Gazette, Aug. 24, 2004, at A1; Editorial, *Another misuse of public funds, Spending $141,815 in public funds for personal promotion is wrong*, Charleston Daily Mail, Aug. 25, 2004, at A4; Toby Coleman, *Whanger stunned by firing, Attorney general's office fires former school board member over purchases*, Charleston Daily Mail, Aug. 24, 2004, at A1.

617.  Phil Kabler, *McGraw's office just makes payroll*, Charleston Gazette, Jan. 19, 2006, at A1.

618.  Terry Burns, *Attorney General Under Fire For Shopping Bags*, The Times (Northwest Indiana), July 25, 2000, at A1; Staff Reports, *GOP keeps heat on Attorney General, Republicans ask Freeman-Wilson to reimburse State for shopping bags*, The Times (Northwest Indiana), Aug. 12, 2000, at A1; Staff Reports, *Giveaway prompts political tempest*, Indianapolis Star, July 20, 2000, at A4.

619.  Editorial, *Another misuse of public funds, Spending $141,815 in public funds for personal promotion is wrong*, Charleston Daily Mail, Aug. 25, 2004, at A4.

620.  Robert Mauk, *McGraw's ads are an abuse, Remember $15,280 for all the magnets at campaign time?*, Charleston Daily Mail, Sept. 4, 2003, at A4; *see also* Associated Press, *McGraw's television spot raises questions*, Oct. 19, 1998, at A3; Rebecca Catalanello, *McGraw ad stirs debate–Announcement seems like political ad to some stations*, Charleston Daily Mail, Oct. 17, 1998, at A1; Editorial, *Tactics*, Charleston Daily Mail, Oct. 19, 1998, at A4; Stacey Ruckle, *Many officials hand out trinkets, Tax money often pays for personalized items*, Charleston Daily Mail, Apr. 16, 1998, at A1; Associated Press, *McGraw magnets attract detractors: High court candidates say attorney general trying to help brother's campaign*, Charleston Gazette, Apr. 14, 1998, at A1; Editorial, *Trinkets: For the money they pay in taxes, people deserve more than key chains*, Charleston Daily Mail, Apr. 18, 1998, at A4; Stacey Ruckle, *McGraw giving out 160,000 magnets*, Charleston Daily Mail, Apr. 9, 1998, at A1; Ken Thomas, *Magnets attract criticism: Court candidates say McGraw using mailings, TV ads to help brother*, Charleston Daily Mail, Apr. 13, 1998, at A1.

621.  Associated Press, *McGraw magnets attract detractors: High court candidates say attorney general trying to help brother's campaign*, Charleston Gazette, Apr. 14, 1998, at A1.

622.  Staff Reports, *McGraw Refuses Debate Invitation*, Charleston Daily Mail, Mar. 19, 1988, at A1.

623.  Editorial, *McGraw's Treatment of Secretary Raises Questions*, Charleston Daily Mail, April 08, 1992, at A4; Editorial, *Equal Justice Is a Myth*, Charleston Daily Mail, January 24, 1997, at A4; *McGraw's Ex-secretary Won Settlement*, Charleston Gazette, Apr. 4, 1992, at A1; Norman Oder, *McGraw Faces Referendum on Himself in Supreme Court Race*, May 6, 1988, at A10.

624.  *See* Jack Deutsch, *Court officials recall McGraw's behavior*, Charleston Daily Mail, Apr. 3, 1992, at A10; Jack Deutsch, *'He's a Bully,' Ex-secretary Says*, Charleston Daily Mail, Apr. 29, 1988, at C1.

625.  Jack Deutsch, *McGraw Falls 1 Year Short of Pension*, Charleston Daily Mail, May 13, 1988, at A1; Editorial, *McGraw the official State pest*, Charleston Daily Mail, Mar. 29, 1990, at A4.

626.    Richard Ballad, *State Supreme Court Justice Darrell McGraw*, Penthouse Magazine, September 1978.

627.    Jack Deutsch, *McGraw Paid by State for Books He Got Free*, Charleston Daily Mail, Mar. 12, 1992, at A1.

628.    Editorial, *McGraw*, Charleston Daily Mail, Mar. 20, 1992, at A4; Jack Deutsch, *McGraw Retained Books at Fraction of the Price*, Charleston Daily Mail, Mar. 19, 1992, at A1.

629.    Kay Michael, *McGraw orders article Reprints for $3,614*, Charleston Daily Mail, Mar. 6, 1987, at A1; Editorial, *McGraw Spent $3,614 of the little people's money*, Charleston Daily Mail, Mar. 11, 1987, at A4; Jack Deutsch, *McGraw Buys Most Stationery*, Charleston Daily Mail, Feb. 24, 1988, at D3.

630.    Jack Deutsch, *'He's a Bully,' Ex-secretary Says*, Charleston Daily Mail, Apr. 29, 1988, at C1.

631.    Editorial, *McGraw Doesn't Lack Name Recognition*, Charleston Daily Mail, Apr. 29, 1988, at A4; Jack Deutsch, *McGraw says Reporter made Harassing calls*, Charleston Daily Mail, July 10, 1987, at A1; Jack Deutsch, *Police say McGraw uncooperative in probe*, Charleston Daily Mail, July 16, 1987, at A1.

632.    Associated Press, *Attorney General Alleges Incidents of Harassment*, Charleston Daily Mail, Apr. 13, 1995, at A1; Associated Press, *McGraw Says 'Efficiency' Led to '88 Loss*, Charleston Daily Mail, Apr. 14, 1995, at A1.

633.    Fanny Seiler, *McGraw Critical of Sweepstakes Operator's Tactics*, Charleston Gazette, Sept. 5, 1996, at A7; McGraw v. Imperial Marketing, 203 W.Va. 203, 506 S.E.2d 799 (1998); McGraw v. Imperial Marketing, 196 W.Va. 346, 472 S.E.2d 792 (1996).

634.    Associated Press, *Suarez Protests order to seize mail*, Charleston Daily Mail, Dec. 12, 1994, at A9.

635.    Suarez Corporation Industries v. McGraw, 71 F.Supp.2d 769 (N.D. Ohio 1999).

636.    David Adams, *Direct-Mail Company Gives West Virginia Officials A Tough Time*, Akron Beacon Journal (Ohio), Apr. 20, 1996, at A1; *see also* Paul J. Nyden, *Palmetto Poker: Machines pumping cash into South Carolina governor's race*, Sunday Charleston Gazette-Mail, Oct. 18, 1998, at A1.

637.    Fanny Seiler, *McGraw Critical of Sweepstakes Operator's Tactics*, Charleston Gazette, Sept. 5, 1996, at A7; Editorial, *Conspiracies?  More Tangled Accusations*, Charleston Gazette, Sept. 12, 1996, at A4.

638.    Leslie Wayne, *Where playing the stock market is really risky*, New York Times, May 1, 1995, at D5.

639.    Kay Michael, *McGraw Pleads No Contest after Incident on Turnpike*, Charleston Daily Mail, Jan. 7, 1992, at A1.

640.    Lawyer Disciplinary Board v. McGraw, 194 W.Va. 788, 461 S.E.2d 850 (1995).

641.    Brent Cunningham, *Impeachment possible, but unlikely for McGraw*, Charleston Daily Mail, Jan. 26, 1994, at A1; *see also* Jack Deutsch, *Ethics Panel Outlines Charges Against McGraw*, Charleston Gazette, Feb. 3, 1994, at A1; Philip Nussel, *McGraw Ethics Charges Fuel Debate*, Charleston Daily Mail, Jan. 25, 1994, at A1; Brent Cunningham, *Impeachment Possible, but Unlikely for McGraw*, Charleston Daily Mail, Jan. 26, 1994, at A1.

642.    Jack Deutsch, *McGraw Wants Ethics Hearing Blocked*, Charleston Daily Mail, Mar. 5, 1994, at A7.

643.    Steve Roberts, *Another McGraw sits on court to hear case: Attorney general's power play could be a family affair*, Charleston Gazette, Nov. 16, 2001, at A5; *see also* Sam Tranum, *McGraw says he's just protecting office*, Charleston Daily Mail, Sept. 28, 2001, at A1; Chris Stirewalt, *Case before justice affects his brother*, Charleston Daily Mail, Sept. 28, 2001, at A1; Chris Stirewalt, *Professor's ideas may be tested: Essay helped lay groundwork for suit by attorney general*, Charleston Daily Mail, Oct. 12, 2001, at A1.

644.    Editorial, *McGraw: His quest to expand his powers as attorney general is dangerous*, Charleston Daily Mail, Oct. 1, 2001, at A4.

645.    Chris Stirewalt, *Lawmakers critical of decision*, Charleston Daily Mail, Nov. 9, 2001, at A1.

646.    Editorial, *Potpourri*, Charleston Gazette, Dec. 10, 2001, at A4.

647.    Editorial, *McGraw: His quest to expand his powers as attorney general is dangerous*, Charleston Daily Mail, Oct. 1, 2001, at A4; Fanny Seiler, *BIC to oppose McGraw's legal suit*, Charleston Gazette, Nov. 30, 2001, at A1.

648.    Chris Stirewalt, *McGraw suit may alter government*, Charleston Daily Mail, Feb. 5, 2002, at A1.

649. Fanny Seiler, *BIC to oppose McGraw's legal suit*, Charleston Gazette, Nov. 30, 2001, at A1.

650. Steve Roberts, *Another McGraw sits on court to hear case: Attorney general's power play could be a family affair*, Charleston Gazette, Nov. 16, 2001, at A5.

651. H. John Rogers, *McGraw's petition aimed at restoring the status quo*, Charleston Gazette, Jan. 28, 2002, at A5.

652. Steve Roberts, *Another McGraw sits on court to hear case: Attorney general's power play could be a family affair*, Charleston Gazette, Nov. 16, 2001, at A5.

653. Jack McCarthy, *McGraw Defends Use Of "Outside Lawyers"*, Charleston Gazette, Aug. 27, 1994, at A1; Editorial, *$33.5 million: What kind of legal work justifies that kind of money*, Charleston Daily Mail, Oct. 19, 2001, at A4.

654. Sam Tranum, *Lawmaker questions legal fees*, Charleston Daily Mail, Oct. 18, 2001, at A1.

655. Juliet A. Terry, *Lawmaker Asks Members for 'Will to Act,'* The State Journal, Mar. 10, 2006, at 19; Delegate Bob Ashley's March 7, 2006, speech on the floor of the House of Delegates Chamber.

656. Rist v. Underwood, 206 W.Va. 258, 260, 273, 524 S.E.2d 179, 181, 194 (1999). The Emoluments Clause provides:

> No senator or delegate, during the term for which he shall have been elected, shall be elected or appointed to any civil office of profit under this State, which has been created, or the emoluments of which have been increased during such term, except offices to be filled by election by the people.

657. Carenbauer v. Hechler, 208 W.Va. 584, 542 S.E.2d 405 (2000).

658. Associated Press, *Taking McGraw's name off ballots a costly ordeal, clerks say*, Charleston Gazette, Apr. 6, 2000, at A1.

659. Toby Coleman, *Court attack ads part of a trend, Crime cases are common target in national efforts to unseat justices*, Charleston Sunday Gazette-Mail, Oct. 3, 2004, at A1; Toby Coleman, *Decision to make convicted man a janitor disputed*, Charleston Sunday Gazette-Mail, Oct. 3, 2004, at A1; Toby Coleman, *Ads may affect race, Warren McGraw could be hurt by campaign spots*, Charleston Gazette, Sept. 25, 2004, at A1.

660. Brad McElhinny, *Ad blasts McGraw brothers*, Charleston Daily Mail, Sept. 21, 2004, at A1; Toby Coleman, *Court race focus stays on case, McGraw defends decision; Benjamin says he is qualified*, Charleston Gazette, Oct. 7, 2004, at A1; *see* State v. Arbaugh, 215 W.Va. 132, 595 S.E.2d 289 (2004); *see also* Arbaugh v. Board of Education, 214 W.Va. 677, 591 S.E.2d 235 (2003).

661. Toby Coleman, *Court race focus stays on case, McGraw defends decision; Benjamin says he is qualified*, Charleston Gazette, Oct. 7, 2004, at A1.

662. Brad McElhinny, *Benjamin to continue ads on sex felon*, Charleston Daily Mail, Sept. 24, 2004, at A1.

663. Chris Stirewalt, *McGraw finds out what ugly really is, Conspiracy theories can be appealing, but are distracting*, Charleston Daily Mail, Sept. 28, 2004, at A4.

664. Toby Coleman, *Court race focus stays on case, McGraw defends decision; Benjamin says he is qualified*, Charleston Gazette, Oct. 7, 2004, at A1.

665. Paul J. Nyden, *Justice says ads factually wrong, Group continues to target McGraw, Starcher defends*, Charleston Sunday Gazette-Mail, Sept. 26, 2004, at A1.

666. Brad McElhinny, *Justice defends position on ruling, Davis says politics not involved in writing decision on sex offender*, Charleston Daily Mail, Sept. 30, 2004, at A1; *see also* Lawrence Messina, *Arbaugh opinion's author takes offense*, Charleston Gazette, Oct. 1, 2004, at A1.

667. Charles McElwee, *What is this about a 'bogus opinion'?*, Charleston Daily Mail, Oct.13, 2004, at A1.

668. Editorial, *Tragic, Politics mire sad case*, Charleston Gazette, Sept. 27, 2004, at A4 ("Since the ads appeared, Arbaugh has lost his job at a fruit and vegetable business. He told reported Paul J. Nyden that neighbors hurry their children inside when he comes out. A police officer watched him play basketball for an unnerving 30 minutes."); *see also* Brad McElhinny, *Benjamin to continue ads on sex felon*, Charleston Daily Mail, Sept. 24, 2004, at A1.

669. Associated Press, *Critics 'smear' McGraw: Incumbent justice tough on criminals, state records show*, Charleston Gazette, Oct. 11, 2004, at A1.

670. Toby Coleman, *Whanger stunned by firing, Attorney general's office fires former school*

*board member over purchases*, Charleston Daily Mail, Aug. 24, 2004, at A1; Associated Press, *Critics 'smear' McGraw: Incumbent justice tough on criminals, state records show*, Charleston Gazette, Oct. 11, 2004, at A1.

671. Associated Press, *Critics 'smear' McGraw: Incumbent justice tough on criminals, state records show*, Charleston Gazette, Oct. 11, 2004, at A1.

672. Staff Reports, *Statehouse Notebook: Hot words are making the national news, Supreme Court race draws TV, magazine coverage*, Charleston Daily Mail, Oct. 25, 2004, at A4.

673. Paul J. Nyden, *Other coal interests spread campaign contributions*, Charleston Sunday Gazette-Mail, Oct. 17, 2004, at A1.

674. Toby Coleman, *Massey CEO gives $1.7 million to anti-Warren McGraw group*, Charleston Gazette, October 15, 2004, at A1; *see also* Brad McElhinny, *Massey chief pours $1.7 million into race*, Charleston Daily Mail, Oct. 15, 2004, at A1 ("According to the financial Internet site Forbes.com, Blankenship in 2003 received $5.7 million for his work at Massey and holds stock options of $3.7 million.").

675. *Id*; Brad McElhinny, *Massey chief pours $1.7 million into race*, Charleston Daily Mail, Oct. 15, 2004, at A1 ("The group also received donations from other coal executives, as well as $745,000 from Doctors for Justice, a Wheeling-based organization of physicians who are concerned about the increasing cost of medical malpractice insurance."); Ken Ward Jr., *West Virginia 'open for business' Coal Leaders say, Industry welcomes Bush victory, McGraw defeat*, Charleston Gazette, Nov. 11, 2004, at A1; Ken Ward Jr., *Flood lawyer wants Maynard off case*, Charleston Gazette, Nov. 12, 2004, at A1; Ken Ward Jr., *Massey agrees to suspension of permit*, Charleston Gazette, Nov. 9, 2004, at A1.

676. Staff Reports, *Local briefs, Groups donated money to help defeat McGraw*, Charleston Daily Mail, Jan. 7, 2005, at A2.

677. Toby Coleman, *Will Benjamin be a reliable pro-business vote on court? Some fear he will defer to his election backers*, Charleston Gazette, Jan. 11, 2005, at A1.

678. Toby Coleman, *Massey CEO gives $1.7 million to anti-Warren McGraw group*, Charleston Gazette, October 15, 2004, at A1.

679. Toby Coleman, *Will Benjamin be a reliable pro-business vote on court? Some fear he will defer to his election backers*, Charleston Gazette, Jan. 11, 2005, at A1; Brad McElhinny, *Massey lawyers seek to have justice removed from case*, Charleston Daily Mail, Nov. 30, 2004, at A1; Toby Coleman, *Coal case creates recusal issue, Massey CEO at center of another controversy*, Charleston Gazette, Dec. 1, 2004, at A1.

680. *Id*.

681. Paul J. Nyden, *Brent Benjamin raking in heaviest contributions*, Charleston Gazette, Oct. 15, 2004, at A1; *see also* Ken Ward Jr., *Massey to go before Supreme Court, Energy plant fighting permit suspension ordered by DEP because of violations*, Charleston Gazette, Oct. 26, 2004, at A1; Toby Coleman, *Benjamin may face bias questions, Court winner says he is 'not bought by anybody,'* Charleston Gazette, Nov. 04, 2004, at A1.

682. Toby Coleman, *Massey CEO gives $1.7 million to anti-Warren McGraw group*, Charleston Gazette, October 15, 2004, at A1; Brad McElhinny, *Massey chief pours $1.7 million into race*, Charleston Daily Mail, Oct. 15, 2004, at A1.

683. Brad McElhinny, *Massey chief pours $1.7 million into race*, Charleston Daily Mail, Oct. 15, 2004, at A1.

684. *Id*.

685. Staff Reports, *Statehouse Notebook: Hot words are making the national news, Supreme Court race draws TV, magazine coverage*, Charleston Daily Mail, Oct. 25, 2004, at A4.

686. George Carenbauer, *Why focus on Justice Warren McGraw? West Virginians deserve justice that is impartial*, Charleston Daily Mail, Oct. 25, 2004, at A5.

687. Brad McElhinny, *High court ad war intensifies, McGraw, Benjamin deny the claims made in opponents' spots*, Charleston Daily Mail, Oct. 22, 2004, at A4.

688. *Id*.

689. Toby Coleman, *Court race focus stays on case, McGraw defends decision; Benjamin says he is qualified*, Charleston Gazette, Oct. 7, 2004, at A1.

690. Toby Coleman, *Benjamin statement questioned, Records show candidate hasn't had oral arguments before Supreme Court*, Charleston Gazette, Oct. 20, 2004, at A1.

691. *Id*; Staff, *Benjamin Camp Sticking With Previous Comments*, MetroNews Talkline Hoppy Kercheval, Oct. 20, 2004 (www.wvmetronews.com).

692. Toby Coleman, *Benjamin statement questioned, Records show candidate hasn't had oral arguments before Supreme Court*, Charleston Gazette, Oct. 20, 2004, at A1; Staff,

*Benjamin Camp Sticking With Previous Comments*, MetroNews Talkline Hoppy Kercheval, Oct. 20, 2004 (www.wvmetronews.com).

693. Staff Reports, *Lawyers disagree on Benjamin appearance*, Charleston Daily Mail, Oct. 28, 2004, at A1.

694. Editorial, *More arrogance from a McGraw, West Virginians don't have justice; they have an entitlement mentality*, Charleston Daily Mail, Aug. 19, 2004, at A4.

695. Brad McElhinny, *Ad blasts McGraw brothers*, Charleston Daily Mail, Sept. 21, 2004, at A1.

696. Brad McElhinny, *McGraw Campaign cries fowl*, Charleston Daily Mail, Sept. 22, 2004, at A1.

697. Brad McElhinny and Chris Stirewalt, *Statehouse Notebook: Potshots continue in high court race*, Oct. 18, 2004, at A4; *see also* Editorial, *Mass mail, Legislation needed*, Charleston Sunday Gazette-Mail, Oct. 24, 2004, at C1.

698. Associated Press, *Bar 'unhappy' with conduct in race*, Charleston Daily Mail, October 19, 2004, at A1.

699. Associated Press, *High court, high cost, Race to be state justice as pricey as it is messy*, Charleston Gazette, Oct. 4, 2004, at A1; *see also* Brad McElhinny, *McGraw Backers call 'emergency meeting,'* Charleston Daily Mail, Sept. 24, 2004, at A1.

700. Tom Searls, *Rowe outspent McGraw to lose state court race*, Charleston Gazette, June 15, 2004, at A1.

701. *Id.*

702. Brad McElhinny, *Benjamin knocks Warren McGraw off Supreme Court*, Charleston Daily Mail, Nov. 3, 2004, at A1.

703. Phil Kabler, *Statehouse Beat, Some predictions for 2005 at the Statehouse*, Charleston Gazette, January 3, 2005, at A4.

704. Brad McElhinny, *McGraw sues over TV ads, Case targets spots that led to justice's defeat*, Charleston Daily Mail, Dec. 2, 2004, at A1; *see also* Toby Coleman, *McGraw files attack-ad libel suit*, Charleston Gazette, Dec. 3, 2004, at A1.

705. Paul Nyden, *Lawsuit aims to 'set limits on sound bites' Neely hopes McGraw case reaches U.S. justices well before '08 election*, Charleston Gazette, Jan. 16, 2005, at A1.

706. Associated Press, *Massey, its Head, Sue for Damages Blankenship Sues Charleston Gazette*, Charleston Gazette, June 16, 2005, at C2; Associated Press, *Massey suit alleges defamation*, Charleston Daily Mail, June 16, 2005, at A1. Blankenship spoke about the lawsuit with numerous media outlets such as MetroNews Talkline with Hoppy Kercheval.

707. *See* In the Matter of Joseph G. Troisi, 202 W.Va. 390, 392, 504 S.E.2d 625, 627 (1998); Hugh Davies, *US judge gives the law some extra bite*, London Telegraph, Oct. 11, 1997, at A1; Lawrence Messina, *Troisi Quits over Nose-biting Snit Judge Pleads No Contest in Incident*, Charleston Gazette, Oct. 24, 1997, at A1; Jennifer Bundy, Associated Press, *Troisi Hit with Ethics Charges*, Charleston Gazette, July 17, 1997, at C1; Lawrence Messina, *Troisi Wasn't Himself, Psychiatrist Says*, Charleston Gazette, May 4, 1998, at A1; Lawrence Messina, *Troisi's Trial Date on Schedule Judge in Nose-biting Case in Court May 4*, Charleston Gazette, April 23, 1998, at A5; Maryclaire Dale, *Judge Troisi Investigated in Attack*, Charleston Gazette, July 2, 1997, at A1; Lawrence Messina, *Grand Jury Indicts Troisi Biting Incident Violated Rights, Prosecutor Charges*, Charleston Gazette, October 10, 1997, at A1; Dan Radmacher, *Biting Judge Resignation Shouldn't End Case*, Charleston Gazette, October 28, 1997, at A6; Kay Michael, *Anybody but a Judge 'Would Have Been Arrested' in Pleasants Courtroom*, Charleston Gazette, September 17, 1997, at A1; Editorial, *A biting matter. Judge should have stepped down sooner after losing temper in court*, Martinsburg Journal, Oct. 27, 1997, at A4; Editorial, n *Troisi. Judges have enormous power; they must meet high standards*, Charleston Daily Mail, Nov. 24, 1997, at A4 ; Editorial, *It's time Troisi resigns his post*, Register-Herald, Oct. 13, 1997, at A4; Editorial, *A judge is benched*, Clarksburg Exponent, Sept. 22, 1997, at A4; Editorial, *Troisi. Justices correctly suspended the pay of this troubled judge*, Charleston Daily Mail, Sept. 22, 1997, at A4; Editorial, *Biting judge. Suspend Troisi without pay*, Charleston Gazette, Aug. 13, 1997, at A4; Editorial, *Troisi. Nose-biting aside, this judge needs to develop his self-control*, Charleston Daily Mail, July 19, 1997, at A4; Staff Reports, *Statehouse Notebook: 'Vote Naked' is fun, up to a point*, Charleston Daily Mail, Apr. 19, 2004, at A4.

708. Kent R. Spellman, *Bizarre Biting Incident, Draws National Attention*, Ritchie Gazette, July 3, 1997, at 1.

709. *Id.*

710. Staff Reports, *Judge Appointed to Oversee Extortion Case*, Charleston Gazette, July 8,

1994, at C2; Lawrence Messina, *Nose-biting Judge Gets 5 Days in Jail Troisi Gets Same Length Sentence as He Gave John Hey*, Charleston Gazette, November 27, 1997, at A1; Kent R. Spellman, *Bizarre Biting Incident, Draws National Attention*, Ritchie Gazette, July 3, 1997, at 1; Staff Reports, *Statehouse Notebook: 'Vote Naked' is fun, up to a point*, Charleston Daily Mail, Apr. 19, 2004, at A4. Former-Kanawha County Circuit Judge John Hey eventually lost his license after being accused of being drunk on the bench and sexually harassing women in the courthouse.

711.  Kent R. Spellman, *Troisi Resigns in Plea Bargain, Judge still faces ethics, civil rights charges*, Ritchie Gazette, Oct. 30, 1997, at 1; *see also* Staff Reports, *Troisi Civil-rights Trial Set for May 4*, Charleston Gazette, April 21, 1998, at A7; Kent R. Spellman, *Bizarre Biting Incident, Draws National Attention*, Ritchie Gazette, July 3, 1997, at 1.

712.  *Id.*

713.  Kent R. Spellman, *Troisi Resigns in Plea Bargain, Judge still faces ethics, civil rights charges*, Ritchie Gazette, Oct. 30, 1997, at 1; *see also* Kay Michael, *Troisi's Bite Was Unintentional, His Lawyer Says*, Charleston Gazette, August 27, 1997, at C1; Kay Michael, *Judge Troisi Promises to Clean up His Act Didn't Intend to Bite Defendant's Nose, Pleasants Judge Says*, Charleston Gazette, August 30, 1997, at C7.

714.  Lawrence Messina, *Troisi May Get to Keep Law License Proposed Deal Now Goes to State Court*, Charleston Gazette, November 04, 1997, at A1.

715.  Kent R. Spellman, *Troisi Resigns in Plea Bargain, Judge still faces ethics, civil rights charges*, Ritchie Gazette, Oct. 30, 1997, at 1.

716.  202 W.Va. at 400, 504 S.E.2d at 634; Lawrence Messina, *Nose-biting Judge Gets 5 Days in Jail Troisi Gets Same Length Sentence as He Gave John Hey*, Charleston Gazette, November 27, 1997, at A1; Kay Michael, *Troisi Will Stay in Pleasants County Jail*, Charleston Gazette, Sept. 2, 1998, at D4; Kent R. Spellman, *Troisi Sentenced to Jail Time, "We can not and will not have two standards of justice." Former Judge Apologizes to Defendant and Court for Nose-Biting Incident*, Ritchie Gazette, Dec. 4, 1997, at 1.

717.  Kent R. Spellman, *Troisi Sentenced to Jail Time, "We can not and will not have two standards of justice." Former Judge Apologizes to Defendant and Court for Nose-Biting Incident*, Ritchie Gazette, Dec. 4, 1997, at 1.

718.  Staff Reports, *Nose-biter Turned 'Model Prisoner' Released Early*, Charleston Gazette, Dec. 29, 1998, at A1; *see also* 202 W.Va. at 400, 504 S.E.2d at 634; Staff Reports, *Pleasants Judge Troisi Freed from Jail*, Charleston Gazette, Dec. 6, 1997, at A6; Associated Press, *Troisi's Lawyer Denies Contact Between Client and Deputy Clerk*, Charleston Gazette, July 17, 1998, at A7; Kay Michael, *Troisi Chest-bumped Him, Clerk Alleges*, Charleston Gazette, July 11, 1998, at A1; Kay Michael, *Troisi's Law License up for Review by State Bar Former Pleasants Judge Fails Probation Test with Recent Outburst*, Charleston Gazette, Aug. 6, 1998, at A3; Staff Reports, *Former Judge Sent to Jail Confrontation with Court Clerk Violates Parole*, Charleston Gazette, July 30, 1998, at A1. Judge Troisi's wife, Thomasine Troisi, also received her own negative headlines during a time when she worked as a substitute teacher in the Pleasants County schools. She resigned as a substitute in 2004 following an accusation from a student who said "Mrs. Troisi choked her, knocked her to the floor, and dragged her to the principal's office." Mrs. Troisi denied the charges and told the *St. Marys Oracle* she resigned to pursue graduate education. Staff Reports, *Statehouse Notebook: 'Vote Naked' is fun, up to a point*, Charleston Daily Mail, Apr. 19, 2004, at A4.

719.  A.V. Gallagher, Associated Press, *Neely to End 22-year W.Va. Court Term*, News-Register (Beckley, WV), Apr. 3, 1995, at A13.

720.  Matter of Neely, 178 W.Va. 722, 723, 364 S.E.2d 250, 251 (1987).

721.  *Id.* Neely was charged with violating Canons 1 and 2 of the Code of Judicial Conduct. The Supreme Court found that Neely did not violate Canon 1, but did violate Canon 2 of the Code. Canon 1 provides, "An independent and honorable judiciary is indispensable to justice in our society. A judge should participate in establishing, maintaining, and enforcing high standards of conduct, and shall personally observe those standards so that the integrity and independence of the judiciary will be preserved. The provisions of this Code are to be construed and applied to further that objective." Canon 2 provides, "A judge shall respect and comply with the law, shall avoid impropriety and the appearance of impropriety in all of the judge's activities, and shall act at all times in a manner that promotes public confidence in the integrity and impartiality of the judiciary."

722.  *Id.* at 726, 364 S.E.2d at 254.

723.  A.V. Gallagher, Associated Press, *Neely to End 22-year W.Va. Court Term*, News-Register (Beckley, WV), Apr. 3, 1995, at A13; *see also* Richard Neely, *Take Back Your Neighborhood* (Donald Fine Inc., New York: 1990).

724.  *Id*; David Margolick, *Neely's imaginative campaign keeps reeling in clerks*, Charleston

Gazette, July 11, 1991, at D6; Lawrence Messina, *Outspoken, outgoing justice still unafraid to rock the bench*, Charleston Gazette, Apr. 17, 1995, at C1.

725.    1994 WL267860; 96 W.Va.L.Rev. 873 (1994) ("An article by Justice Richard Neely, West Virginia Supreme Court of Appeals, entitled, *Insider Trading Prosecutions Under the Misappropriation Theory: New York's Joke on Heartland America*, was originally scheduled for publication in this issue. Justice Neely decided not to publish this article due to a dispute over its editing, a dispute that did not involve the Executive Board of Volume 96."). According to students who attended law school at West Virginia University in 1994, the administration of the law school refused to allow law review student members to publish Justice Neely's article.

726.    Lisa A. Stamm, *Chief Justice Richard Neely "Uniquely Unconventional,"* W.Va. Lawyer, January 8, 1995, at 16.

727.    *Id.*

728.    Matter of Grubb, 187 W.Va. 228, 417 S.E.2d 919 (1992); *see also* Associated Press, *Ex-judge Grubb Dies*, Charleston Gazette, Apr. 17, 1997, at C1; (At the time of his arrest, James Ned Grubb was an elected circuit judge of the Seventh Judicial Circuit of West Virginia, located in Logan County.); Ron Hutchinson, *Ex-Judge Ordered To Court: Doctor says Grubb's Health would be hurt if sent back to prison*, Charleston Daily Mail, Jan. 10, 1997, at A2; United States v. Grubb, 11 F.3d 426 (4th Cir. 1993); United States v. Grubb, 11 F.3d 426, 430 (4th Cir. 1993); Associated Press, *W. Virginia Judge Found Guilty in Corruption Case*, Los Angeles Times, May 7, 1992, at A33.

729.    United States v. Grubb, 11 F.3d at 432.

730.    *Id.* at 432, n.2 ("Under West Virginia law, any candidate or person supporting a candidate must keep detailed accounts of monies received and spent and must file a report of the receipts and expenditures with the West Virginia Secretary of State. W.Va. Code §§ 3-8-5, 5(a), 5(b), and 7. Furthermore, W.Va. Code §§ 3-8-5d and 3-8-12(f) limit individual contributions to $50 cash and $1,000 per candidate. W.Va. Code § 3-8-11 makes it illegal for any person to solicit money from a candidate in exchange for support unless that person is a duly appointed and designated member of a political party committee."); (As part of a plea agreement to a charge of conspiracy to transport stolen coal across state lines, Adams agreed to meet with Grubb and tape their conversations.).

731.    Associated Press, *Ex-Judge Grubb Dies*, Charleston Gazette, Apr. 17, 1997, at C1.

732.    Grubb, 11 F.3d at 430, 431.

733.    *Id.* at 430, n.1. The West Virginia Code of Judicial Conduct was revised effective January 1, 1993, after the West Virginia Supreme Court authored its Opinion in Judge Grubb's case. As such, while the substance of Canon 2 may be the same, it is located within another Canon. Likewise, much of then Canon 7 is included within Canon 5 of the current West Virginia Code of Judicial Conduct. Canon 2 of the West Virginia Code of Judicial Ethics (1991) provides a standard that.

> A judge should respect and comply with the law and should conduct himself at all times in a manner that promotes public confidences and integrity in the impartiality of the judiciary. A judge should not allow his family, social, or other relationships to influence his judicial conduct or judgment. He should not lend the prestige of his office to advance the private interests of others nor should he convey or permit others to convey the impression that they are in a special position to influence him.

Canon 7 provides that a judge who is not a candidate for election or re-election should not:

> (a) act as a leader or hold any office in a political organization;
>
> (b) make speeches for a political organization or candidate or publicly endorse a candidate for public office except as permitted in [another section].

734.    *Id.* at 431. When Burgess filed the campaign finance report required by West Virginia law, he omitted reporting this illegal cash payment to Grubb, as well as Grubb's expenditure of those funds in behalf of Burgess and the slate. Burgess mailed this report to the West Virginia Secretary of State. Burgess testified at trial that the reason he did not report the $10,000 cash given to Grubb was because he was "dealing with a judge."

735.    Committee on Legal Ethics v. Hobbs, 190 W.Va. 606, 608, 439 S.E.2d 629, 631 (1993).

736.    *Id.* at 609, 439 S.E.2d at 632; *see* In the Matter of Codispoti, 186 W.Va. 710, 414 S.E.2d 628 (1992), In the Matter of Codispoti, 190 W.Va. 369, 438 S.E.2d 549 (1993).

737.    Fleming, *supra* note 12, at 117.

738.    *Id.*

739.    Associated Press, *Jury Convicts Logan Judge, Acquits Wife*, Charleston Gazette, May 7, 1992, at A1; *see also* United States v. Grubb, 11 F.3d 426 (4th Cir. 1993) (the court affirmed the conviction of Circuit Judge Grubb under § 666(a)(2).); Associated Press, *Judge Gets Fine, Prison for Corruption Conviction*, Orlando Sentinel, July 21, 1992, at A7; Staff Reports, *West Virginia*, USA Today, Apr. 29, 1992, at A7; Associated Press, *W. Virginia Judge Found Guilty in Corruption Case*, Los Angeles Times, May 7, 1992, at A33.

740.    The 1974 Judicial Reorganization Amendment produced changes in the judicial system. The State's judicial functions are now integrated into a single system which is fully controlled by the State Supreme Court of Appeals. There are three levels of courts in West Virginia, the Supreme Court of Appeals of West Virginia, Circuit Courts, and Magistrates. The Magistrate system replaced Justice of the Peace Courts.

741.    *See* State v. Good, 151 W.Va. 813, 156 S.E.2d 8 (1967) (Delmar Good, a Justice of the Peace in Ripley, West Virginia received a speeding ticket and paid money to another Justice of the peace Dovenor E. Jarrell to influence the decision against him. During the time of the payment from Good to Jarrell, the case was initially assigned to Justice of the Peace Gay H. Duke. The West Virginia Supreme Court held that Good's payment did not amount to a bribe as provided by West Virginia Code § 61-5-7, as when the payment was made, Jarrell had not yet been assigned he case and thus was not "acting or is to act" before the offense can be committed. That same statute did not apply in *State v. General Daniel Morgan Post No 548*, 144 W.Va. 137, 107 S.E.2d 353 (1959), where a county sheriff who received money for influence because the language of the statute "referred only to a state officer of the nature therein described or a member of the legislature.").

742.    Christopher Tritto, *Testimony begins in racketeering trial of Logan magistrate*, Charleston Gazette, Feb. 26, 2003, at A1.

743.    Chris Stratton, *Jury hears testimony in Wells trial*, The Logan Banner, March 4, 2003, at 1.

744.    Toby Coleman, *Ex-Logan mayor charged in link to Wells' extortion*, Charleston Gazette, Jan. 11, 2005, at A1; Associated Press, *Magistrate's lawyers promise to appeal, ex-Logan county official found guilty of racketeering*, Charleston Daily Mail, Mar. 4, 2003, at A1; Associated Press, *Convicted Logan Magistrate Resigns*, Charleston Daily Mail, Mar. 28, 2003, at A2; Staff Reports, *Ex-Logan Bailiff Charged with Lying to FBI*, Charleston Gazette, Jan. 27, 2005, at A1.

745.    Tom Searls, *Sting affected election*, Charleston Sunday Gazette-Mail, Nov. 20, 2005, at A1; Michael E. Ruane, *FBI's Sham Candidate Crawled Under W.Va.'s Political Rock*, The Washington Post, Dec. 2, 2005, at A1.

746.    Associated Press, *State election fraud informant gets probation*, Charleston Gazette, Jan. 11, 2006, at A1.

747.    J.D. Charles, *Wells arrested again*, The Logan Banner, Jan. 24, 2003, at 1.

748.    Staff Reports, *Ex-Magistrate Sues Police Officers*, Chapmanville, Charleston Gazette, June 26, 2004, at A2.

749.    Staff Reports, *Ex-Logan Magistrate Wells Sues Justices in Suspension*, Charleston Gazette, June 3, 2004, at A2.

750.    Staff Reports, *Former Logan County bailiff sentenced to six months*, Charleston Daily Mail, June 3, 2005, at A2; Staff Reports, *Former Logan marshal sentenced for lying*, Charleston Gazette, June 3, 2005, at A2.

751.    Associated Press, *Magistrate accused of harassment*, Charleston Daily Mail, Sept. 24, 2003, at A1; *see also* Associated Press, *Magistrate in Wayne Faces Sex Harassment Complaints*, Charleston Gazette, Sept. 24, 2003, at A1; Associated Press, *Acquitted Wayne Magistrate Seeks Reinstatement*, Apr. 27, 2005, at A1; Associated Press, *Wayne Magistrate Faces Sex-bribery Indictment*, Charleston Gazette, July 13, 2004, at A1; Staff Reports, *Police Briefs*, Charleston Gazette, July 16, 2004, at A1.

752.    Matter of Toler, __W.Va.__, 625 S.E.2d 731 (slip. op., December 5, 2005, No. 31797).

753.    In the Matter of Riffle, 210 W.Va. 591 n.8, 558 S.E.2d 590 n.8 (2001).

754.    Matter of Atkinson, 193 W.Va. 358, 456 S.E.2d 202 (1995).

755.    Staff Reports, *Looking Back: A decade of crimes*, Charleston Daily Mail, Aug. 5, 1999, at A1.

756.    Matter of Mendez, 176 W.Va. 401, 402, 344 S.E.2d 396, 397 (1985).

757.    Associated Press, *Logan County sheriff charged again, John Mendez implicated in two cases of vote buying*, Charleston Sunday Gazette-Mail, May 9, 2004, at A1; State Briefs, *State doesn't want ex-sheriff to get pension*, Charleston Daily Mail, Oct. 14, 2004, at A7;

Chris Wetterich, *Logan Sheriff pleads guilty, Mendez resigns, will cooperate in vote-buying investigation*, Charleston Gazette, July 20, 2004, at A1.

758. Associated Press, *Supreme Court Changes Law Licensing Standards*, Charleston Gazette, Dec. 12, 2000, at A1.

759. Lawrence Messina, *Court rethinks barring felons from law*, Charleston Gazette, Aug. 1, 2001, at A5.

760. Chris Stirewalt, *State branded 'hellhole,' Business group says W.Va's legal climate is unfair*, Charleston Daily Mail, Nov. 6, 2003, at A1; *see also* Toby Coleman, *National tort reform group criticizes state courts again*, Charleston Gazette, Dec. 16. 2004, at A1; Steve Roberts, *Commentary: To change W.Va., change the court*, Charleston Daily Mail, Sept. 30, 2004, at A5; Editorial, *Attitude, West Virginians still have a reputation for suit-happiness*, Charleston Saturday Gazette-Mail, Dec. 18, 2004, at A4. In 2004, West Virginia is the only entire state to be so listed; Ken Ward Jr., *Tort reform group criticized W.Va. for Fla. lawsuit*, Charleston Gazette, Dec. 15, 2005, at A1.

761. Editorial, *Court contest is about jobs, McGraw's home cooking costs West Virginians dearly*, Charleston Daily Mail, Oct. 1, 2004, at A4.

762. Chris Stirewalt, *State branded 'hellhole,' Business group says W.Va's legal climate is unfair*, Charleston Daily Mail, Nov. 6, 2003, at A1.

763. Chris Wetterich, *Chief Justice criticized money in judge races*, Charleston Daily Mail, Apr. 21, 2004, at A1; *see also* Toby Coleman, *Justice says judiciary's reputation is at stake, Experts discuss problems with partisan elections*, Charleston Daily Mail, Apr. 21, 2004, at A1.

764. Toby Coleman, *Justice says judiciary's reputation is at stake, Experts discuss problems with partisan elections*, Charleston Daily Mail, Apr. 21, 2004, at A1; Chris Wetterich, *Chief Justice criticized money in judge races*, Charleston Daily Mail, Apr. 21, 2004, at A1.

765. Editorial, *Judges, West Virginia is an aberration in the partisan election of judges*, Charleston Daily Mail, Apr. 19, 2004, at A4.

766. Editorial, *Brent Benjamin is the only choice, Change the state Supreme Court to change West Virginia's economy*, Charleston Daily Mail, Oct. 18, 2004, at A4.

767. *Id.*

768. Brennan Center for Justice at New York University School of Law, *The New Politics of Judicial Elections 2004*, June 27, 2005 (www.brennancenter.org).

769. Rice, *supra* note 110, at 307; *see also Snapshots of the Twentieth century*, Charleston Gazette, Feb. 13, 1999, at A12; (<http://www.wvgazette.com/static/century/GZ0213.html>) (visited Mar. 15, 2003.).

770. *Jack's W. Va. Jack Returned Hundred Fold*, The West Virginia Hillbilly, Jan 16, 1961, at 11

771. Staff Reports, *Governor William Wallace Barron's Inaugural Address*, The West Virginia Hillbilly, Jan. 16, 1961, at 7; *see also* West Virginia Archives and History (Visited Mar. 16, 2003 <http://www.wvculture.org/history/barron.html>.).

772. Bob Mellace, *Barron's Aides Advised He Isn't Running Again: Governor Ready to Put Himself Out Of Politics*, Charleston Daily Mail, July 2, 1962, at A1.

773. UPI, *'Serenity' Back Home Barron Aim: Return to Elkins 'Would Be Ideal'*, Charleston Gazette-Mail, Oct. 8, 1978, at A1; James A. Haught, *Barron Years Real Estate Web: City House: Pathetic Monument*, Charleston Gazette, December 17, 1971, at A1.

774. Associated Press, *Moore not first ex-governor to face prison*, Fairmont Times-West Virginian, July 11, 1990, at A12; Michael L. White, *Barron Pleads Guilty; Perry, Brown Also Cited in Charges*, Charleston Gazette, Mar. 30, 1971, at A1.

775. Staff Reports, *'I remember how gracious he was...,'* Charleston Gazette, Nov. 15, 2002, at A1.

776. L.T. Anderson, *Two Baffling loose Ends Remain*, Charleston Gazette, Apr. 7, 1971, at A4.

777. Michael L. White, *Barron Pleads Guilty; Perry, Brown Also Cited in Charges*, Charleston Gazette, Mar. 30, 1971, at A1; State v. Dandy, 151 W.Va. 547, 153 S.E.2d 507, (1967); State ex rel. Brown v. Thompson, 149 W.Va. 649, 142 S.E.2d 711 (1965).

778. UPI, *'Serenity' Back Home Barron Aim: Return to Elkins 'Would Be Ideal'*, Charleston Gazette-Mail, Oct. 8, 1978, at A1; *see also* Michael L. White, *Barron Pleads Guilty; Perry, Brown Also Cited in Charges*, Charleston Gazette, Mar. 30, 1971, at A1.

779. In re Barron, 155 W.Va. 98, 181 S.E.2d 273, 275 (1971).

780. In re Brown, 166 W.Va. 226, 233 273 S.E.2d 567, 574, (1980).

781.    Paul J. Nyden, *Ex-Underwood researcher later served as political spy for Nixon*, Charleston Gazette-Mail, Sept. 29, 1996, at C4.

782.    Staff Reports, *Barron, 16 others have faced courts*, Charleston Gazette, Feb. 15, 1968, at A1.

783.    L.T. Anderson, *Two Baffling loose Ends Remain*, Charleston Gazette, Apr. 7, 1971, at A4.

784.    Staff Reports, *'I remember how gracious he was...*,' Charleston Gazette, Nov. 15, 2002, at A1.

785.    Editorial, *Potpourri*, Charleston Gazette, Apr. 15, 2001, at A4.

786.    Staff Reports, *Barron figure Sawyers dies*, Charleston Gazette, Aug. 15, 2002, at C2.

787.    Editorial, *The Scale Is Unbalanced*, Charleston Sunday Gazette-Mail, Jan. 23, 1972, at A4.

788.    Staff Reports, *'I remember how gracious he was . . .*,' Charleston Gazette, Nov. 15, 2002, at A1.

789.    Bob Kittle, *Pomp and Circumstance*, Charleston Daily Mail, Dec. 9, 1976, at Al.

790.    UPI, *'Serenity' Back Home Barron Aim: Return to Elkins 'Would Be Ideal'*, Charleston Gazette-Mail, Oct. 8, 1978, at A1.  Barron received headlines in 1986 when his daughter and son-in-law were facing murder charges that were later dropped.  *See* Staff Reports, *Murder Charges Dropped Against Daughter, Son-in-law of Ex-Gov. Wally Barron*, Elkins Inter-Mountain, Mar. 29, 1986, at A1; Staff Reports, *Ex-Gov. Barron's Daughter Charged Murder of Dunbar Woman*, Elkins Inter-Mountain, Mar. 18, 1986, at A1; Staff Reports, *Ex-Gov. Barron's Daughter, Husband Jailed Without Bond in Woman's Murder*, Elkins Inter-Mountain, Mar. 19, 1986, at A1.

791.    Associated Press, *Ex-attorney General Robertson Dies at 69*, Charleston Daily Mail, Apr. 29, 1996, at B6; In re Robertson, 156 W.Va. 463, 194 S.E.2d 650 (1973).

792.    Committee on Legal Ethics of West Virginia State Bar v. Graziani, 157 W.Va. 167, 168-169, 200 S.E.2d 353, 354-355 (1973); Graziani v. Committee on Legal Ethics of West Virginia State Bar, 416 U.S. 995 (1974).

793.    Staff Reports, *Ex-lawyer, State Official Graziani Dies*, Charleston Gazette, Feb. 04, 1992, at A2; Staff Reports, *Former Attorney General Dead at 69*, Charleston Gazette, April 29, 1996, at A2; Staff Reports, *Controversial Ex-state Official Graziani Dies*, Charleston Daily Mail, Feb. 3, 1992, at A2.

794.    U.S. v. Truslow, 530 F.2d 257 (4th Cir. 1975).

795.    State ex rel. Truslow v. Boles, 148 W.Va. 707, 708, 137 S.E.2d 235, 236 (1964).

796.    Matter of Adoption of Truslow, 167 W.Va. 696, 697, 280 S.E.2d 312, 313 (1981); Staff Reports, *Rockefeller Grants Conditional Pardon*, Charleston Daily Mail, Jan. 16, 1985, at A2.

797.    Staff Reports, *Fugitive Robber Captured at Mother's House*, Charleston Gazette, Jan. 8, 1999, at A2.

798.    U.S. v. Truslow, 530 F.2d 257 (4th Cir. 1975).

799.    *Id.*

800.    *Id.*

801.    *Id*

802.    156 W.Va. at 464, 194 S.E.2d at 651.

803.    Associated Press, *Ex-attorney General Robertson Dies at 69*, Charleston Daily Mail, Apr. 29, 1996, at B6.

804.    Staff Reports, *ReBrook Says Depositions Invalid*, Charleston Gazette, Oct. 27, 1993, at A1; Staff Reports, *ReBrook: Caperton Avoiding Subpoena*, Charleston Gazette, Nov. 3, 1993, at A1; Staff Reports, *ReBrook Trial to Stay in State; Judge Refuses to Drop Charges*, Charleston Gazette, Oct. 29, 1993, at A1; Staff Reports, *Embattled ReBrook Subpoenas Reporters in Video Lottery Case*, Charleston Gazette, Oct. 30, 1993, at A1; Staff Reports, *ReBrook Guilty; Probe to Continue*, Charleston Gazette, Nov. 6, 1993, at A1; Staff Reports, *Week in Review*, Charleston Gazette, Sept. 12, 1993, at A2.

805.    Staff Reports, *Brown Indicted for Soliciting Contributions*, Charleston Gazette, Feb. 11, 1986, at A1; Staff Reports, *Brown Pleads Innocent to Election Law Charge*, Charleston Daily Mail, Feb. 22, 1986, at A1; Editorial, *Brown Endorsed*, Charleston Gazette, Apr. 28, 1988, at A4.

806.    *Meet the Kellys*, The West Virginia Hillbilly, Jan. 16, 1961, at 10; Topper Sherwood, *Kennedy in West Virginia*, Goldenseal, Fall 2000 at 17.

807.    United States v. Caldwell, 544 F.2d 691, 693 n.1 (4th Cir.1976).

808. *Id.*

809. McCormick v. United States, 500 U.S. 257, 260, 271-74 (1991); *see also* Ron Hutchison, *Jury indicts legislator for extortion*, Charleston Daily Mail, Sept. 10, 1988, at A1; Ron Hutchison, *Investigation targets other legislators*, Charleston Daily Mail, Dec. 9, 1988, at B1; Jack McCarthy, *Delegate found guilty of extortion, tax evasion*, Charleston Gazette, Dec. 8, 1988, at A1; Richard Grimes, *McCormick unsure about quitting*, Charleston Daily Mail, Jan. 5, 1989; Andy Wessels, *Former Delegate McCormick on Probation, fined $50,000*, Charleston Gazette, Feb. 9, 1989, at A1.

810. *Id.*

811. *Id.*

812. Fanny Seiler, *McCormick quits seat in Legislature*, Charleston Gazette, Jan. 21, 1989, at A1.

813. 500 U.S. at 260.

814. Staff Reports, *Former Delegate McCormick dies*, Charleston Gazette, June 21, 2004, at A2 (McCormick died on June 19, 2004.).

815. Jonathan Gill, Associated Press, *W. Va. Attorney General Resigns to Halt Criminal Investigation*, Charleston Daily Mail, Aug. 21, 1989, at A1.

816. Ron Hutchison, *Boettner cops plea with feds*, Charleston Daily Mail, Aug. 30, 1989, at A1; Jonathan Gill, Associated Press, *W. Va. Attorney General Resigns to halt Criminal Investigation*, Charleston Daily Mail, Aug. 21, 1989, at A1.

817. Editorial, *Brown Endorsed*, Charleston Gazette, Apr. 28, 1988, at A4.

818. Jonathan Gill, Associated Press, *W. Va. Attorney General Resigns to halt Criminal Investigation*, Charleston Daily Mail, Aug. 21, 1989, at A1; Barry Bearak, *Corruption in West Virginia: Scandals as Thick as Coal Dust*, Los Angeles Times, July 8, 1990, at A1.

819. UPI, *Charlie Brown Argues With Judge*, Inter-Mountain (Elkins, West Virginia), Nov. 14, 1986, at A1.

820. UPI, *'I do not Believe I have violated law,' Brown Testifies*, Inter-Mountain, Nov. 18, 1986, at A1; UPI, *Brown Indicted*, Inter-Mountain, Feb. 10, 1986, at A1.

821. Barry Bearak, *Corruption in West Virginia: Scandals as Thick as Coal Dust*, Los Angeles Times, July 8, 1990, at A1; Jonathan Gill, Associated Press, *W. Va. Attorney General Resigns to halt Criminal Investigation*, Charleston Daily Mail, Aug. 21, 1989, at A1 (The secretary in question, Brenda K. Simon, denied the allegations as reported by the *Charleston Gazette* and filed a $3 million libel suit against the newspaper.).

822. From News Services, *West Virginia Attorney General Resigns*, The Washington Post, Aug. 23, 1989, at A5.

823. Barry Bearak, *Corruption in West Virginia: Scandals as Thick as Coal Dust*, Los Angeles Times, July 8, 1990, at A1.

824. Stephen Hudak, *Brown views campaign as a crossroads in his career*, The Plain Dealer (Cleveland OH), Sept. 27, 1992, at A1.

825. Mark Kindt, Opinion Editorial, *View from the inside–Looking Back, Charlie Brown a committed public servant*, Oct. 15, 1998, at A5.

826. *Id.*

827. Editorial, *Bribery – World cleanup effort*, Charleston Gazette, Dec. 10, 1998, at A4.

828. L.T. Anderson, *Someone must be discounting the price on state senators these days*, Charleston Gazette, Feb. 1, 2000, at C1; Jennifer Bundy, Associated Press, *Federal Prosecutors seek information from Greenbrier*, Charleston Gazette, Sept. 14, 1999, at A1; Lawrence Messina, *Schoonover sentenced to 18 months – Ex-senator bribed by LeRose family member to get towing business*, Charleston Gazette, Jan. 25, 2000, at A1.

829. Jennifer Bundy, Associated Press, *Federal prosecutors seek information from Greenbrier*, Charleston Gazette, Sept. 14, 1999, at A1 (The article also noted that Senator Schoonover sponsored a controversial Greenbrier Gambling Bill that would allow a casino at the states only five-star establishment.).

830. Jennifer Bundy, Associated Press, *Former senator leaves prison*, Charleston Gazette, Feb. 21, 2001, at A2.

831. Lawrence Messina, *Schoonover sentenced to 18 months – Ex-senator bribed by LeRose family member to get towing business*, Charleston Gazette, Jan. 25, 2000, at A1.

832. Randy Coleman, Associated Press, *Out of prison, ex-senator builds new life*, Charleston Gazette, June 18, 2001, at A1; Associated Press, *Former state senator released from prison*, Feb. 22, 2001, at A1; Lawrence Messina, *Schoonover sentenced to 18 months – Ex-*

*senator bribed by LeRose family member to get towing business*, Charleston Gazette, Jan. 25, 2000, at A1; Randy Coleman, Associated Press, *Out of prison, ex-senator builds new life*, Charleston Gazette, June 18, 2001, at A1.

833.    L.T. Anderson, *Someone must be discounting the price on state senators these days*, Charleston Daily Mail, Feb. 1, 2000, at C1.

834.    Randy Coleman, Associated Press, *Out of prison, ex-senator builds new life*, Charleston Gazette, June 18, 2001, at A1.

835.    Tom Searls, *Mingo County clerk resigns under cloud*, Charleston Gazette, Jan. 31, 2002, at A11.

836.    *Id.*

837.    Fanny Seiler, *Chafin foe made threats, Mingo man says*, Charleston Gazette, Oct. 2, 2001, at A1.

838.    Jennifer Bennett, *Lloyd may have embezzled $200,000 from Randolph*, Inter-Mountain, Sept. 28, 2005, at A1; Julieanne Cooper, *Randolph Commissioner Wants Questions Answered Before Making Further Plans*, Inter-Mountain, Dec. 30, 2004, at A1; Ben Simmons, *Attorney General's Office: Elkins Residents Upset over Lloyd Case Can File Civil Suit*, Inter-Mountain, Dec. 30, 2004, at A1; Jennifer Bennett, *Unclear if Lloyd will receive full retirement*, Inter-Mountain, Dec. 23, 2004, at A1; Linda Howell *Skidmore, Auditors Eyed Previous Problems in Lloyd's Office*, Inter-Mountain, Dec. 18, 2004, at A1; Linda Howell Skidmore, *Randolph Prosecutor: Lloyd Embezzlement Case Began This Summer*, Inter-Mountain, Dec. 15, 2004, at A1; Julieanne Cooper; *New Randolph Clerk Says She Is Ready to Serve the Public*, Inter-Mountain, Dec. 16, 2004, at A1; Jennifer Bennett, *Lloyd Makes $48,000 Restitution to Randolph*, Inter-Mountain, Feb. 2, 2006, at A1.

839.    Staff Reports, *Marshall official faces fraud, other charges*, Charleston Daily Mail, Apr. 16, 1992, at B5; Associated Press, *Write-in Marshall Assessor Candidate Placed Distant Third*, Charleston Gazette, Nov. 5, 1992, at A2; Associated Press, *Ousted in Primary, Indicted Assessor mulls write-in bid*, Charleston Gazette, Sept. 16, 1992, at A1; Associated Press, *Indicted Assessor confirms write-in run*, Charleston Gazette, Oct. 20, 1992, at A1; Associated Press, *Official says indictment is personal retribution*, Charleston Daily Mail, Apr. 28, 1992, at A1; Associated Press, *Assessor says charges result from a vendetta*, Charleston Daily Mail, Apr. 28, 1992, at A1. On another occasion, Marshall County's commission and insurance carrier were forced to pay $8,000 to settle a lawsuit against Assessor Clark and his deputies for running up bills at a conference at Wheeling's Oglebay Park during a State Tax Department conference and not paying them. They were accused of accumulating a bill of more than $2,000 during the conference which was held just a few miles from Marshall County. Clark said the charges against him amounted to "nitpicking."

840.    James Haught, *Assessor Errors*, Charleston Gazette, Jan. 25, 1987, at A4.

841.    Associated Press, *Ex-assessor pleads guilty to tampering*, Charleston Gazette, Aug. 1, 1995, at A1; Associated Press, *Marshall-assessor Clark faces new charges*, Charleston Gazette, Aug. 1, 1995, at A1.

842.    Committee on Legal Ethics of the West Virginia State Bar v. White, 189 W.Va. 135, 136, 428 S.E.2d 556, 557 (1993); Staff Reports, *Marshall Prosecutor Quits in Drug Plea*, Charleston Daily Mail, Jan. 7, 1992, at A1.

843.    *See* New Vrindaban Community, Inc. v. Rose, 187 W.Va. 410, 419 S.E.2d 478 (1992); State ex rel. Drescher v. Hedrick, 180 W.Va. 35, 375 S.E.2d 213 (1988); Committee on Legal Ethics v. Karl, 192 W.Va. 23, 449 S.E.2d 277 (1994).

844.    Staff Reports, *Krishna leader cleared of arson charges*, Boston Globe, Dec. 16,1987, at A1; Paul Nyden, *Political Machine*, Charleston Gazette, July 13, 1986, at A2; Paul Nyden, *Commissioner Loath to Pay for Park Trip*, Charleston Gazette, August 3, 1986, at A2; Paul Nyden, *Suit against Marshall Assessor costs $8,000*, Charleston Gazette, Sept. 8, 1987, at A2; United Press International, *Krishna Community Gives Assessor Cool Reception*, Charleston Gazette, July 2, 1987, at A2; United Press International, *Legal Fight Against Krishna's Continues*, Charleston Gazette, Feb. 3, 1988, at A2; Associated Press, *Grand Jury Indicts Marshall Assessor*, Charleston Gazette, Apr. 16, 1992, at A1; Editorial, *Demagogue-2*, Charleston Gazette, Apr. 21, 1992, at A4; Associated Press, *Marshall Assessor faces new charges*, Charleston Gazette, Apr. 23, 1992, at A1; Associated Press, *Violence Prompts Fears of 'Holy War' in Sect*, Charleston Gazette, July 6, 1986, at A1; Associated Press, *Has Krishna Gold Tarnished or will community shine?*, Charleston Gazette, Jan. 25, 1987, at A2; James Haught, *Explanations*, Charleston Gazette, Jan. 25, 1987, at A4; James Haught, *Assessor Errors*, Charleston Gazette, Jan. 25, 1987, at A4; Associated Press, *Assessor Faces New Charges*, Charleston Daily Mail, May 23, 1992, at A7; Staff Reports, *Official Says Indictments 'Personal Retribution,'* Charleston Daily Mail, Apr. 28, 1992, at A5; Staff Reports, *State Backs Hare Krishna Assessment*, Charleston Daily Mail, Mar. 12, 1985, at A2.

845. Associated Press, *House of Delegates–Republicans*, Charleston Gazette, May 12, 2004, at A2.

846. Staff Reports, *Prosecutor pays for cell calls*, Charleston Daily Mail, June 7, 2005, at A1.

847. Scott Finn, *Ban on personal calls urged for state-paid cell phones*, Charleston Gazette, June 13, 2005, at A1; Scott Finn, *Lawyer wants Charnock timesheets*, Charleston Saturday Gazette-Mail, Nov. 26, 2005, at A1.

848. Scott Finn, *Charnock was warned*, Charleston Gazette, Nov. 15, 2005, at A1.

849. Tom Searls, *Prosecutor's campaign under investigation*, Charleston Gazette, Nov. 9, 2005, at A1.

850. Scott Finn, *Two state agencies investigating prosecutor*, Charleston Gazette, Nov. 16, 2005, at A1; Editorial, *Prosecutor, Public needs answers*, Charleston Gazette, Nov. 15, 2005, at A1; Kris Wise, *Prosecutor says enemies behind investigation*, Charleston Daily Mail, Nov. 14, 2005, at A1; Scott Finn, *Charnock used state resources for campaigns, audit alleges*, Charleston Gazette, Nov. 14, 2005, at A1.

851. Tom Searls, *Prosecutor's campaign under investigation*, Charleston Gazette, Nov. 9, 2005, at A1.

852. Scott Finn, *Prosecutor apologizes*, Charleston Gazette, Nov. 18, 2005, at A1.

853. Editorial, *Potpourri*, Charleston Gazette, Nov. 21, 2005, at A4.

854. Bill Charnock, *Charnock's Statement*, Charleston Daily Mail, Nov. 17, 2005, at A1; Jake Stump, *Charnock reports targeted*, Charleston Daily Mail, Nov. 18, 2005, at A1; Scott Finn, *Prosecutor apologizes*, Charleston Gazette, Nov. 18, 2005, at A1; Jake Stump, *Charnock apologizes for use of state resources*, Charleston Daily Mail, Nov. 17, 2005, at A1; Justin D. Anderson, *Judges ready for Charnock inquiry*, Charleston Daily Mail, Nov. 22, 2005, at A1; Justin D. Anderson, *Judge doesn't plan Charnock inquiry*, Charleston Daily Mail, Nov. 22, 2005, at A1; Associated Press, *Agency confirms Charnock inquiry*, Charleston Daily Mail, Nov. 16, 2005, at A1; Scott Finn, *GOP rubuts Charnock flap*, Charleston Sunday Gazette-Mail, Nov. 20, 2005, at A1; Scott Finn, *Charnock computer files turned over to State Police*, Charleston Gazette, Nov. 29, 2005, at A1; Tom Searls, *Charnock under investigation*, Charleston Gazette, Nov. 29, 2005, at A1; Lawrence Messina, Associated Press, *Charnock takes steps to keep report in headlines*, Charleston Daily Mail, Nov. 21, 2005, at A1; Scott Finn, *Group requests special prosecutor*, Charleston Gazette, Nov. 17, 2005, at A1; Associated Press, *Charnock case gets special prosecutor*, Charleston Gazette, Dec. 23, 2005, at A1.

855. Scott Finn, *Prosecutor drove man from scene of WVU tailgate fight*, Charleston Gazette, Dec. 16, 2005, at A1.

856. Associated Press, *Makeshift studio, piracy software found at Capitol*, Charleston Gazette, Jan. 18, 2006, at A1; see also Scott Finn, *Capitol worker let go, Shop for copying DVDs found in Capitol basement*, Charleston Gazette, Jan. 19, 2006, at A1; Associated Press, *Ex-official fired after shop found*, Charleston Daily Mail, Jan. 19, 2006, at A1.

857. Scott Finn, *Workers paid OT without working*, Charleston Gazette, Jan. 10, 2006, at A1; see also Scott Finn, *Asbestos contracts rigged?*, Charleston Gazette, Dec. 12, 2005, at A1; Scott Finn, *Asbestos overseer received good pay, OT*, Charleston Gazette, Dec. 13, 2005, at A1; Associated Press, *Audit casts doubt on bids for asbestos removal*, Charleston Gazette, Dec. 12, 2005, at A1.

858. Anna Mallory, *Money missing from agency $1 million in education funds unaccounted for*, Charleston Gazette, Feb. 9, 2006, at A1; see also Associated Press, *$1 million missing from education agency*, Charleston Daily Mail, Feb. 9, 2006, at A1; Jessica Karmasek, *Irregular finances targeted*, Charleston Daily Mail, Feb. 10, 2006, at A1; Editorial, *RESAs, no longer needed*, Charleston Gazette, Feb. 10, 2006, at A4; Associated Press, *State to take over RESA 1's finances*, Charleston Gazette, Feb. 10, 2006, at A1.

859. Tom Searls, *Misspent security funds probe started*, Charleston Gazette, Mar. 9, 2006, at A1.

860. *Express Line*, Charleston Gazette, May 1, 1996, at A5.

861. Associated Press, *Former Lottery Director Convicted of Fraud Charges*, Los Angeles Times, Sept. 26, 1993, at A24; Associated Press, *Ex-Lottery Officials Sentenced*, The Washington Post, Feb. 8, 1994, at A7.

862. United States v. Bryan, 58 F.3d 933, 937 (4th Cir. 1995) (In agreement with other circuits, the Fourth Circuit held in, that various kinds of dishonesty by public officials are denials of the "honest services" of 18 U.S.C. § 1346 and therefore prosecutable as mail fraud.); Ron Lewis, *Bryan architect or scapegoat?*, Intelligencer, Sept. 24, 1993, at A1; see also Pat Doyle, *State lottery may end ties with Atlanta Software Firm*, Star Tribune (Minneapolis, MN), Aug. 11, 1996, at A1 (AWI, a subsidiary of Video Lottery

Technologies, was barred from doing business in Australia for more than a year because of improper activities by its former president as Bryan was convicted of corruption charges for manipulating the contract-procurement process.).

863. United States v. ReBrook, III, 58 F.3d 961, 963 (4th Cir. 1995); United States v. Bryan, 837 F. Supp.162 (S.D. W.Va. 1993.); Associated Press, *Court Rules in Rebrook Case*, Charleston Daily Mail, July 1, 1995, at B5; United States v. Bryan, 837 F. Supp.162 (S.D. W.Va. 1993.); Staff Reports, *Rebrook Says Depositions Invalid*, Charleston Gazette, Oct. 27, 1993, at A1; Staff Reports, *Rebrook: Caperton Avoiding Subpoena*, Charleston Gazette, Nov. 3, 1993, at A1; Staff Reports, *Rebrook Trial to Stay in State; Judge Refuses to Drop Charges*, Charleston Gazette, Oct. 29, 1993, at A1; Staff Reports, *Embattled ReBrook Subpoenas Reporters in Video Lottery Case*, Charleston Gazette, Oct. 30, 1993, at A1; Staff Reports, *Rebrook Guilty; Probe to Continue*, Charleston Gazette, Nov. 6, 1993, at A1; Staff Reports, *Week in Review*, Charleston Gazette, Sept. 12, 1993, at A2.

864. Lawrence Messina, *Court lets ReBrook practice law*, Charleston Gazette, May 10, 2001, at A1; Jeanne Kennedy, *The Anatomy of an Election Eve Story*, Charleston Daily Mail, May 21, 1992, at A1; Howard Kurtz, *Late sex allegations increasingly familiar*, Charleston Daily Mail, May 14, 1992, at B6; Paul Nyden, *ReBrook is accused of sexual harassment*, Charleston Gazette, May 9, 1992, at A12; United States v. ReBrook, III, 58 F.3d 961, 963 (4th Cir. 1995); United States v. Bryan, 837 F. Supp.162 (S.D. W.Va. 1993.). During his trial, ReBrook said he believed in the Code of Omerta, an Italian term for his belief in not ratting on friends with whom one may have committed a crime. *See* Staff Reports, *Rebrook Gets Immunity For Testimony*, Charleston Gazette, Dec. 17, 1993, at A1; Staff Reports, *No 'Secret Plan,' Caperton Says Heywood Contradicts Governor's Testimony*, Charleston Gazette, Nov. 5, 1993, at A1; Associated Press, *Rebrook Guilty; Probe to Continue*, Charleston Gazette, Nov. 6, 1993, at A1.

865. Lee, *supra* note 176, at 122.

866. *Id.*

867. *Id.* at 122, 123.

868. Fleming, *supra* note 12, at 68, 69 (Harry Hamm interview by Dan Fleming, Jr., Wheeling, West Virginia, August 24, 1985.).

869. *Id.* at 77.

870. United States v. Altomare, 625 F.2d 5, 7 (4th Cir.1980).

871. West Virginia Public Employees Retirement System v. Dodd, 396 S.E.2d 725 (W.Va. 1990).

872. U.S. v. Ellis, 91 F.3d 135 (4th Cir. 1996) (unpublished); Ron Hutchison, *Ellis' Bid For Freedom Denied By Judges: Ex-City Businessman To Remain In Prison*, Charleston Daily Mail, July 25, 1996, at A6.

873. Ron Hutchison, *Ellis' Bid For Freedom Denied By Judges: Ex-City Businessman To Remain In Prison*, Charleston Daily Mail, July 25, 1996, at A6; Lawrence Messina, *2nd District ads heat up airwaves: Humphreys answers Capito attack within day*, Charleston Gazette, Oct. 4, 2000, at A8.

874. *Id*; Lawrence Messina, *2nd District ads heat up airwaves: Humphreys answers Capito attack within day*, Charleston Gazette, Oct. 4, 2000, at A8.

875. *West Virginian In Corruption Inquiry Is Punished by Court*, New York Times, Feb. 16, 1989, at A14 (following federal probe of corruption in West Virginia legislature, former President of State Senate, Dan Tonkovich, sentenced for extortion; during same week, former State Senate President Larry Tucker sentenced for taking illegal payment from gambling interests, and former State Senate Majority Leader Si Boettner sentenced for income tax evasion); *see also West Virginia Senate Head Is Fourth Leader to Resign*, New York Times, Sept. 9, 1989, at A8 (West Virginia's Attorney General and Treasurer were also investigated.); A.V. Gallagher, Associated Press, *"Former W. Va. Senate President Sentenced to 5 Years, Fined $10,000,"* Dec. 14, 1989, at A1.

876. Jack McCarthy, *Political Family Scion Making A Go For The Big Time*, Charleston Gazette, Dec. 27, 1995, at A1.

877. Cheryl Caswell, *Ex Politicos Rebound After Fall From Grace*, Charleston Daily Mail, Sept. 6, 1994, at A1; Jack Deutsch, *Tucker quits as he admits taking cash*, Charleston Daily Mail, Sept. 8, 1989, at A1; Grant Parsons, *Tucker pleads guilty, apologizes*, Charleston Gazette, Sept. 12, 1989, at B1; Fanny Seiler, *Senate president resigns after guilty plea*, Charleston Gazette, Sept. 8, 1989, at A1; Chicago Tribune wires, *Ex-W. Virginia Senate leader sent to prison*, Chicago Tribune, Mar. 19, 1991, at C6.

878. Ron Hutchison, *Official says Tucker lied about money*, Charleston Daily Mail, Dec. 14, 1989, at A1.

879.  *Id*; *see also* U.S. v. Ellis, 91 F.3d 135 (4th Cir. 1996) (unpublished).

880.  Staff Reports, *West Virginia Senate's Ex-Leader Enters Guilty Plea*, The Washington Post, Apr. 13, 1990, at A18; Ron Hutchison, *Tonkovich pleads guilty to extortion*, Charleston Daily Mail, Sept. 14, 1989, at A1; Jeffrey Bair, *Grand jury indicts Tonkovich*, Charleston Daily Mail, June 2, 1989, at A1; Ron Hutchison, *Former Tonkovich aide key witness in trial*, Charleston Daily Mail, Sept. 6, 1989, at A1; Jack McCarthy, *Prosecutors link Tonkovich, career gambler*, Charleston Gazette, Aug. 4, 1989, at A1; Ron Hutchison, *Tonkovich's term stiffest in fed probe*, Charleston Daily Mail, Dec. 15, 1989, at A1.

881.  Jack McCarthy, *Tonkovich gets five years for extortion*, Charleston Gazette, Dec. 14, 1989, at A1.

882.  Paul Nyden, *Boettner still fights to reverse tax conviction*, Charleston Sunday Gazette-Mail, Mar. 17, 1991, at C1; Boettner, v. Comm. Of Internal Revenue, 1998 WL 712526 (U.S. Tax Ct.) 76 T.C.M. (CCH) 622 (1998); U.S. v. Ellis 91 F.3d 135 (4th Cir. 1996) (unpublished); Committee on Legal Ethics of the West Virginia State Bar v. Boettner, 188 W.Va. 1, 3, 422 S.E.2d 478, 480 (1992); Committee on Legal Ethics v. Boettner, 183 W.Va. 136, 394 S.E.2d 735, 738 (1990); U.S. v. Boettner 52 F.3d 322 (Table) (4th Cir. 1995).

883.  Jack McCarthy, *Boettner unindicted abettor*, Charleston Gazette, Aug. 3, 1989, at A1; Ron Hutchison, *Boettner cops plea with feds*, Charleston Daily Mail, Aug. 30, 1989, at A1. 26 U.S.C. § 7201 provides:

> Any person who willfully attempts in any manner to evade or defeat any tax imposed by this title or the payment thereof shall, in addition to other penalties provided by law, be guilty of a felony and, upon conviction thereof, shall be fined not more than $100,000 ($500,000 in the case of a corporation), or imprisoned not more than 5 years, or both, together with the costs of prosecution.

884.  Chris Knap, *Boettner to move out of lobbyist's house*, Charleston Gazette, May 6, 1987, at A1; Richard Grimes, *Ethics Panel To Include Boettner*, Charleston Daily Mail, July 15, 1987, at A1.

885.  Fanny Seiler, *Affairs of State*, Charleston Gazette-Mail, Nov. 13, 1994, at B1; State ex rel. Owens v. Brown, 177 W.Va. 225, 351 S.E.2d 412 (1986).

886.  *Id*; Fanny Seiler, *Greyhound breeders' '01 payouts set a record*, Charleston Gazette, Mar. 4, 2002, at C1.

887.  James A. Haught, *Video Poker $300 Million A Year*, Charleston Gazette, Mar. 29, 1995, at A4.

888.  Fanny Seiler, *Affairs of State*, Charleston Gazette-Mail, Nov. 13, 1994, at B1; Fanny Seiler, *Power ready to shift in Senate to the southern counties*, Charleston Gazette, Nov. 12, 1994, at B1.

889.  James A. Haught, *Video Poker $300 Million A Year*, Charleston Gazette, Mar. 29, 1995, at A4; Paul J. Nyden, *Video Gambling: W. Va.'s dirty, untaxed little secret*, Sunday Charleston Gazette-Mail, Mar. 26, 1995, at A1.

890.  Fanny Seiler, *Affairs of State*, Charleston Gazette-Mail, Nov. 13, 1994, at B1; Paul J. Nyden, *Video poker debate likely to be lively: 'Gray machine' owners want to keep control if state makes payouts legal*, Sunday Charleston Gazette-Mail, Jan. 3, 1999, at A1; Editorial, *Gray machines: State should take over*, Charleston Gazette, Jan. 27, 1999, at A4; James A. Haught, *Video Poker $300 Million A Year*, Charleston Gazette, Mar. 29, 1995, at A4.

891.  James A. Haught, *Video Poker $300 Million A Year*, Charleston Gazette, Mar. 29, 1995, at A4.

892.  *Id*; Paul J. Nyden, *Video poker in gray area west Virginia*, Charleston Gazette, Aug. 27, 1998, at A1; Fanny Seiler, *Logan Delegate Aims for Senate*, Charleston Gazette, Aug. 29, 2001, at C1; Editorial, *Liar: Ferrell breaks promise*, Charleston Gazette, Aug. 30, 2001, at A4; *Coal Operators Told to Pay*, Charleston Daily Mail, Jan. 16, 1997, at A5 (Ferrell and former Logan County Commissioner Jack Robertson were ordered by the federal district court to pay $543,731 to Catepillar Financial Services for money that Ferrell and Robertson borrowed to purchase heavy mining equipment in March of 1991.); Paul J. Nyden, *Video poker in gray area West Virginia*, Charleston Gazette, Aug. 27, 1998, at A1.

893.  Fanny Seiler, *State Police raid Logan stores for gray machines*, Charleston Sunday Gazette-Mail, June 17, 2001, at C3; *see also* Randy Coleman, Associated Press, *Lottery Commission issues license to Logan delegate for video poker*, Charleston Gazette, Sept. 29, 2001, at A7.

894.  Fanny Seiler, *Logan Delegate Aims for Senate*, Charleston Gazette, Aug. 29, 2001, at C1; Editorial, *Liar: Ferrell breaks promise*, Charleston Gazette, Aug. 30, 2001, at A4; Fanny Seiler, *Judicial system complaints will be aired at rally*, Charleston Gazette, Feb. 17, 1998,

at C1; Paul J. Nyden, *Ferrell may have an out for office run*, Sunday Charleston Gazette-Mail, Sept. 6, 1998, at C1; United States v. Grubb, 11 F.3d 426 (4th Cir. 1993).

895.    *Id*; Fanny Seiler, *Needs for library surprise lawmaker*, Charleston Gazette, Apr. 27, 1998, at C1.

896.    Paul J. Nyden, *Ferrell may have an out for office run*, Sunday Charleston Gazette-Mail, Sept. 6, 1998, at C1.

897.    Editorial, *Liar: Ferrell breaks promise*, Charleston Gazette, Aug. 30, 2001, at A4.

898.    Fanny Seiler, *Logan Delegate Aims for Senate*, Charleston Gazette, Aug. 29, 2001, at A4; Fanny Seiler, *Weirton office site considered*, Charleston Gazette, Aug. 20, 2001, at C1.

899.    Editorial, *Liar: Ferrell breaks promise*, Charleston Gazette, Aug. 30, 2001, at A4.

900.    Tom Searls, *Delegate's business searched; no one says why*, Charleston Gazette, June 30, 2005, at A1.

901.    Phil Kabler, *House gives video poker its support Delegates vote 66-34 to OK bill consistent with Wise's concerns*, Apr. 7, 2001, at A1.

902.    Fanny Seiler, *Racing Commission chairman forced to resign*, Charleston Gazette, Jan. 23, 2002, at A1.

903.    Jennifer Bundy, Associated Press, *Casino bill under investigation, report says*, Charleston Gazette, Sept. 14, 1999, at A1.

904.    Tom Miller, *Under the Dome: A look back*, Charleston Gazette, Dec. 26, 2000, at A5.

905.    141 Cong. Rec. E86-02, at 6 (daily ed. Jan. 11, 1995) (statement of Representative Wolf); *see also* Staff Reports, *A Look at State Gambling Corruption*, Gannett News Serv., Sept. 23, 1995, 1995 WL 2906999 (listing gambling-related public corruption scandals in South Carolina, Kentucky, West Virginia, Louisiana, Illinois, Minnesota and Missouri).

906.    *Wise Supports Proposed Gambling Commission*, Charleston Daily Mail, Oct. 4, 1995, at A2.

907.    Editorial, *Results?, What's happening?*, Charleston Gazette, Mar. 30, 2001, at A4.

908.    Dan Radamacher, *Video Poker Profiteers Criminals*, Charleston Gazette, Mar. 30, 2001, at A4.

909.    Associated Press, *The task: harnessing video poker: Former S.C. governor raises caution flag*, Charleston Gazette, Mar. 10, 2001, at A1; *see also* Paul J. Nyden, *Palmetto Poker: Machines pumping cash into South Carolina governor's race*, Sunday Charleston Gazette-Mail, Oct. 18, 1998, at A1 (Governor Beasley's press secretary estimated that at least fifty percent of the contributions received by his election opponent came from "people who make money from video poker machines." He also argued that seventy-five percent of the $1,000 or more contributions came from gambling interests.); Paul Owens, *Gray Machines unmanageable, ex-governor says*, Charleston Daily Mail, Mar. 9, 2001, at A1.

910.    Paul Owens, *Gray Machines unmanageable, ex-governor says*, Charleston Daily Mail, Mar. 9, 2001, at A1.

911.    Associated Press, *The task: harnessing video poker: Former S.C. governor raises caution flag*, Charleston Gazette, Mar. 10, 2001, at A1.

912.    Editorial, *Potpourri*, Charleston Gazette, Dec. 17, 2001, at A4.

913.    Patricia Nealon, *Prosecutor ends a job of conviction*, The Boston Globe, Nov. 23, 1996, at B1.

914.    Terry Horne, *Why Riverboat Gambling Is Wrong*, Charleston Daily Mail, Feb. 6, 1995, at A4.

915.    Editorial, *Riverboats this is an economic development that West Virginia can ill afford*, Charleston Daily Mail, Jan. 24, 1995, at A4.

916.    Chris Stirewalt and Jim Wallace, *Wise: "I Was Not Faithful,"* Charleston Daily Mail, May 12, 2003, at A1.

917.    *Id*; Phil Kabler, *Governor admits to affair: He 'absolutely' won't resign, aide says; alleged accuser denies naming Wise*, Charleston Gazette, May 13, 2003, at A1; Scott Finn, *An unlikely couple behind Wise affair*, Charleston Gazette, May 13, 2003, at A1; Deanna Wrenn, *Reactions fly, details stall, What are their stories?*, Charleston Daily Mail, May 13, 2003, at A1; Toby Coleman, *Details often murky: Like many cases, Frye divorce may be out of public eye*, Charleston Daily Mail, May 14, 2003, at A1; Deanna Wrenn, *Analysts say Wise should face fallout: Governor advised to remain in public, answer questions*, Charleston Daily Mail, May 14, 2003, at A1.

918.    *Id*; Phil Kabler, *Not much unusual in Wise trips: Governor's travel plans often matched alleged paramour's*, Charleston Gazette, May 14, 2003, at A1; *see also* Rebeccah

Cantley-Falk, *Admission's effects on Wise's 2004 re-election bid uncertain*, The Herald-Dispatch (Huntington, WV), May 13, 2003, at A1; Jim Wallace, *Political implications of situation still unclear to many lawmakers*, Charleston Daily Mail, May 13, 2003, at A1; Deanna Wrenn, *Talk, opinions swirl over Wise*, Charleston Daily Mail, May 13, 2003, at A1; Jim Wallace, *Gainer says "everything looks appropriate: on Wise trip: Official says records show Wise, woman together in Spain*, Charleston Daily Mail, May 13, 2003, at A1; Deanna Wrenn, *Mascia-Frye accompanied Wise on plane, Both attended development meeting in Detroit*, Charleston Daily Mail, May 21, 2003, at A1.

919.   Deanna Wrenn, *Admitting affairs seems to be key move: Kentucky's Patton, President Clinton first denied affairs*, Charleston Daily Mail, May 13, 2003, at A1; *see also* Associated Press, *Sandy Wise's actions vital to governor's political future, consultants say*, Charleston Daily Mail, May 15, 2003, at A1; Jim Wallace, *Wise troubles affect campaigns: Candidate says it's too early to tell if issue alters race*, Charleston Daily Mail, May 15, 2003, at A1.

920.   WVAH Fox 10:00 p.m. News Broadcast, May 12, 2003 (airing Wise's September 14, 1998 comments).

921.   *See* West Virginia Archives and History, (visited May 15, 2003, <http://www.wvculture.org/history/wiseia.html>).

922.   Karin Fischer, *Wise situation shocks senators Byrd, Rockefeller react: to reports of unfaithfulness*, Charleston Daily Mail, May 14, 2003, at A1.

923.   Editorial, *Wise: The governor should go further to restore people's trust in him*, Charleston Daily Mail, May 14, 2003, at A4.

924.   Jim Wallace, *Former leader sorry for Wise: Caperton feels empathy for Wise's personal problems*, Charleston Daily Mail, May 15, 2003, at A1.

925.   Charles Shumaker, *Parody takes jab at Wise*, Charleston Gazette, May 31, 2003, at A1.

926.   Hoppy Kercheval, *Hoppy's Daily Commentary For Thursday*, Metronews Talkline, May 15, 2003, (<www.wvmetronews.com> (visited May 15, 2003)).

927.   *Id.*

928.   Interview of Governor Wise by Allen H. Loughry II, December 15, 2004, in the Governor's Office.

929.   Charleston Daily Mail, *Wise Staffer faces prostitution charge*, Charleston Daily Mail, Jan. 12, 2002, at C6.

930.   Hoppy Kercheval, *Hoppy's Daily Commentary For Thursday*, Metronews Talkline, Jan. 13, 2005, (<www.wvmetronews.com> (visited Jan. 13, 2005)).

931.   *See* Phil Kabler, *Wise gives farewell address*, Charleston Gazette, Jan. 13, 2005, at A1.

932.   State v. Richey, 171 W.Va. 342, 345, 298 S.E.2d 879, 882 (1982)

933.   State ex rel. Richey v. Hill, 216 W.Va. 155, 603 S.E.2d.177 (2004).

934.   171 W.Va. at 345, 298 S.E.2d at 882; State ex rel. Richey v. Hill, 216 W.Va. 155, 603 S.E.2d.177 (2004).

935.   171 W.Va. at 347, 353, 298 S.E.2d at 884, 890 (Since Richey did not put his character in issue, the book could not be used because the trial court ruled it could prejudice the jury against him.).

936.   *See* Hursty Richey, *Near Fatal Attraction* (Ashley Books, Inc.: Hollywood, FL 1977) (ISBN: 0879490764) ("The 'hunter and prey' game played in secret by youthful members of Boy Scout Troop 44 has resulted in a series of gruesome tragedies, and as the now-adult Troop members try to cope with their past, tragedy strikes again.").

937.   State ex rel. Richey v. Hill, 216 W.Va. 155, 603 S.E.2d.177 (2004).

938.   Lawrence Messina, *Court rethinks barring felons from law*, Charleston Gazette, Aug. 1, 2001, at A5; Charles Shumaker, *Ex-judge current on fines*, Charleston Gazette, Sept. 24, 2003, at A1; Editorial, *John Hey, Good moral character should be required of every lawyer in the state*, Charleston Daily Mail, Oct. 15, 2003, at A4.

939.   Chris Stirewalt, *Pick for Hey prosecutor questioned, former judge may face witness intimidation charge*, Charleston Daily Mail, Mar. 28, 2001, at A1; Lawrence Messina, *Berger gets 'A' for job on bench*, Charleston Gazette, July 5, 1995, at A1.

940.   Don Marsh, *Caperton didn't change the system–it changed him*, Charleston Gazette, July 17, 1995, at A5.

941.   Lawrence Messina, *Court rethinks barring felons from law*, Charleston Gazette, Aug. 1, 2001, at A5; Staff Reports, *Panel says Hey should regain his law license*, Charleston Daily Mail, Sept. 19, 2003, at A1; Associated Press, *Hey gets his license back, Supreme Court votes 3-2 in ex-judge's favor*, Charleston Gazette, Oct. 11, 2003, at A1. The *Hey* decision

was disposed of by a memorandum order in the recent case of *Lawyer Disciplinary Board v. Hey* (No. 28239, October 10, 2003).

942.    Associated Press, *Hey gets his license back, Supreme Court votes 3-2 in ex-judge's favor*, Charleston Gazette, Oct. 11, 2003, at A1.

943.    Editorial, *John Hey, Good moral character should be required of every lawyer in the state*, Charleston Daily Mail, Oct. 15, 2003, at A4.

944.    George Gannon, *Forbes says Hey should apologize*, Charleston Daily Mail, Sept. 20, 2003, at A1; *see also* Carol Sue Burdette, *Letters to the Editor, Can lawbreaking ever be honorable?*, Charleston Daily Mail, Oct. 21, 2003, at A5.

945.    Chris Stirewalt, *Pick for Hey prosecutor questioned: Former judge may face witness intimidation charge*, Charleston Daily Mail, Mar. 28, 2001, at A1.

946.    George Gannon, *Forbes says Hey should apologize*, Charleston Daily Mail, Sept. 20, 2003, at A1.

947.    In the matter of Hey, 188 W.Va. 545, 546, 425 S.E.2d 221, 222.

948.    *Id.* at 547, 425 S.E.2d at 223.

949.    Toby Coleman, *Embattled ex-Judge Hey settles lawsuit*, Charleston Saturday Gazette-Mail, Nov. 6, 2004, at A1.

950.    188 W.Va. at 549, 425 S.E.2d at 225. Canon 3A(6) of the Judicial Code of Ethics, in part, provides: "A judge should abstain from public comment about a pending or impending proceeding in any court. . . ."

951.    Toby Coleman, *Comments on CNN show hypothetical, Hey says in slander case*, Charleston Gazette, Nov. 4, 2004, at A1.

952.    Fanny Seiler, *Chafin foe made threats, Mingo man says*, Charleston Gazette, Oct. 2, 2001, at A1.

953.    State ex rel. Chafin v. Mingo County Com'n, 189 W.Va. 680, 682, 434 S.E.2d 40, 42 (1993).

954.    Staff Reports, *W.Va.'s all-star lineup*, Charleston Daily Mail, Aug. 5, 1997, at C1.

955.    *Majority Leader's Job In Hand Of Legislature: Senate To Vote On Employment If Chafin Convicted Of Charges*, Charleston Daily Mail, Mar. 21, 1995, at A1.

956.    Maryclaire Dale, *Chafin investigator gets 2 months in wiretapping*, Charleston Gazette, Jan. 30, 1996, at A1; Associated Press, *Chafin pleads not guilty to charges*, Herald Dispatch (Huntington, WV), Mar. 31, 1995, at A1; Associated Press, *Chafin re-charged in wiretapping case*, Parkersburg Sentinel, Sept. 20, 1995, at A6.

957.    *Id.*

958.    McMillian v. Ashley, 193 W.Va. 269, 273, 455 S.E.2d 921, 925 (1995).

959.    Associated Press, *Ex-private detective becomes eligible to practice law*, Charleston Daily Mail, June 22, 2005, at A1; In Re McMillian's Eligibility, 217 W.Va. 277, 617 S.E.2d 824 (2005).

960.    Toby Coleman, *Chafin's divorce back in court*, Charleston Daily Mail, Nov. 6, 2003, at A1.

961.    Staff Reports, *Ethics Commission Praised For Levying Fines Without Trial*, Charleston Gazette, June 8, 1990, at A1; Staff Reports, *$65,000 Collected by Fraudulent Billings*, Charleston Gazette, Apr. 30, 1988; Staff Reports, *Report Awaited in Speedway Case*, Charleston Gazette, Jan. 11, 1988, at A1; Staff Reports, *Public Defenders Testify in Involved Hearing*, Charleston Gazette, January 30, 1988, at A1; Staff Reports, *State Bar to judge Ranson*, Charleston Gazette, August 19, 1997, at A1; Staff Reports, *Resignation casts shadow over Ranson's career accomplishments*, Charleston Gazette, June 26, 1997, at A1; Staff Reports, *Probe forces judge to resign*, Charleston Gazette, June 26, 1997, at A1.

962.    Therese Smith, *Sprouse's colleague back him*, Charleston Daily Mail, Mar. 8, 2005, at A1; *see also* Therese Smith, *Father-in-law wants Sprouse to step down*, Charleston Daily Mail, Mar. 7, 2005, at A1; Associated Press, *Sprouse Expects Republicans to Judge him on Performance*, Charleston Gazette, Mar. 8, 2005, at A1; Phil Kabler, *Statehouse Beat*, Charleston Gazette, Mar. 7, 2005, at A5; Editorial, *Potpourri*, Charleston Gazette, Mar. 14, 2005, at A4; Editorial, *Potpourri*, Charleston Gazette, Mar. 7, 2005, at A4; Tom Searls, *'Bad Faith' Lawsuit Hearin is Thursday*, Charleston Gazette, Mar. 16, 2005, at A1; Phil Kabler, *Statehouse beat: Super credits waning*, Charleston Gazette, Mar. 14, 2005, at A5.

963.    Phil Kabler, *Statehouse beat: Senators antsy about Sprouse*, Charleston Gazette, Mar. 7, 2005, at A5; Associated Press, *Sprouse Expects Republicans to Judge him on Performance*; Charleston Gazette, Mar. 8, 2005, at A1.

964.    Staff Reports, *Senate Panel OKS Judicial Pay Raises*; Charleston Gazette, Apr. 6, 2005, at

A1, Staff Reports, *Pay Raise Bill has Backing From Unions*, Charleston Daily Mail, Apr. 6, 2005, at A1; Staff Reports, *Father-in-law wants Sprouse to step down*, Charleston Daily Mail, Mar. 7, 2005, at A1; Sebastian Tutte, *Commentary: Vic Mouse: Cheesy as Ever*, Bluefield News, April 16, 2005, at A5.

965. Staff Reports, *Bill on divorce passes*, Charleston Gazette, Mar. 4, 1999, at A1.

966. Staff Reports, *Father-in-law wants Sprouse to step down*, Charleston Daily Mail, Mar. 7, 2005, at A1; Staff Reports, *Local Briefs*, Charleston Daily Mail, Mar. 3, 2003, at A7.

967. Fanny Seiler, *Delegate's Passion is Politics*, Charleston Gazette, Mar. 26, 1996, at C1; Editorial, *Potpourri*, Charleston Gazette, Apr. 1, 1996, at A4; Staff Reports, *With Friends Like These, The GOP Doesn't Need Enemies*, Charleston Gazette, Oct. 21, 1996, at A1; Editorial, *Sex Hunt Open Season On Politicos*, Charleston Gazette, Sept. 11, 1998, at A4.

968. Tom Searls, *State trooper who "polices the police" target of inquiry*, Charleston Gazette, April 25, 2003, at A1.

969. Associated Press, *Suits against State Police cost $5 million*, Charleston Gazette, Apr. 29, 2002, at A1.

970. Editorial, *State Police: Discipline sorely needed*, Charleston Gazette, Feb. 1, 2002, at A4.

971. Christopher Tritto, *Hardy wants Clifford to submit resignation, while Clifford asks for investigation of Hardy*, Charleston Gazette, Jan. 17, 2003, at A1; *see also* Editorial, *Clifford Bar ethics inquiry*, Charleston Gazette, Oct. 11, 2002, at A4 (The *Charleston Gazette* called the allegations against Clifford "crude, obscene, disgusting, scatological behavior" and said that if true he should resign or be removed from office.).

972. Editorial, *Enough Clifford must go*, Charleston Gazette, Jan. 15, 2003, at A4; *see also* Charles Shumaker, *Clifford settles gas tab*, Charleston Gazette, Jan. 15, 2003, at A1.

973. Charles Shumaker, *Clifford ruling goes to high court*, Charleston Gazette, Nov. 1, 2003, at A1; Staff Reports, *Judges debate status of prosecuting attorney*, Charleston Gazette, Sept. 13, 2003, at A1; Jim Wallace, *Clifford denies allegations of retaliation*, Charleston Daily Mail, Sept. 15, 2004, at A1; Charles Shumaker, *Bid to oust Clifford will go to high court*, Charleston Gazette, Oct. 9, 2003, at A1.

974. Toby Coleman, *High court asked to hear Clifford case*, Charleston Daily Mail, Nov. 1, 2003, at A1; Toby Coleman, *Lawyers still after Clifford*, Charleston Daily Mail, Oct. 8, 2003, at A1; Toby Coleman, *Clifford survives effort at ouster*, Charleston Daily Mail, Oct. 4, 2003, at A1; Charles Shumaker, *Prosecutor keeps his job*, Charleston Gazette, Oct. 4, 2003, at A1.

975. Toby Coleman, *Clifford survives effort at ouster*, Charleston Daily Mail, Oct. 4, 2003, at A1.

976. Editorial, *Disgusting record*, Charleston Gazette, Oct. 8, 2003, at A4.

977. Toby Coleman, *Prosecutor's office barred from case*, Charleston Daily Mail, Dec. 14, 2001, at A2; *see also* Christopher Tritto, *Hardy wants Clifford to submit resignation, while Clifford asks for investigation of Hardy*, Charleston Gazette, Jan. 17, 2003, at A1; Editorial, *Potpourri*, Charleston Gazette, Oct. 29, 2001, at A4.

978. Brad Johnson, *Mayor, Clerk Accuse Each Other of Sexual Misconduct*, Inter-Mountain, Dec. 20, 2002, at A1.

979. *Id*; Staff Reports, *State Briefs*, Charleston Gazette, Jan. 3, 2003, at A2; Staff Reports, *State Briefs*, Charleston Gazette, Jan. 29, 2003, at A2; Staff Reports, *State Briefs*, Charleston Gazette, Nov. 12, 2004, at A2; Staff Reports, *Former Mayor Sues Elkins Current Mayor also named in Case,* Charleston Gazette, Mar. 22, 2004, at A2.

980. Brad Johnson, *City Controversy Expected to be Made Public Tonight*, Inter-Mountain, Dec. 19, 2002, at A1.

981. Staff Reports, *State Briefs, Former mayor of Elkins, city reach settlement*, Charleston Daily Mail, Mar. 21, 2005, at A7.

982. Heath Quint, *Judge Blasts Elkins Clerk in Retaliation Ruling*, Inter-Mountain, Feb. 2, 2006, at A1.

983. Dave Gustafson, *Jefferson officer has recent misdemeanor*, Charleston Gazette, Mar. 22, 2004, at A2.

984. Associated Press, *Ex-Mayor enters no contest plea over illegal account*, Charleston Daily Mail, Aug. 17, 2002, at A1; Staff Reports, *Jefferson Mayor put on probation for 5 years*, Charleston Daily Mail, Oct. 22, 2002, at A1; Rachelle Bott, *Jefferson mayor indicted*, Charleston Gazette, Oct. 26, 2001, at C1; Chris Stirewalt, *Ex-Jefferson Mayor faces new charges*, Charleston Daily Mail, Apr. 25, 2002, at A1.

985. Dave Gustafson, *Judges remove Jefferson's town recorder from office*, Charleston Gazette,

Jan. 12, 2005, at A1; Jim Wallace, *Town of Jefferson under review*, Charleston Daily Mail, Jan. 12, 2005, at A1; Jim Wallace, *Clerk says she can't afford to defend herself*, Charleston Daily Mail, Jan. 14, 2005, at A1; Editorial, *'Lawless town,' End Jefferson's misery*, Charleston Gazette, Jan. 14, 2005, at A4.

986.    Jim Wallace, *Town of Jefferson under review*, Charleston Daily Mail, Jan. 12, 2005, at A1.

987.    Rachelle Bott, *Jefferson mayor indicted*, Charleston Gazette, Oct. 26, 2001, at C1.

988.    Jim Wallace, *Town of Jefferson under review*, Charleston Daily Mail, Jan. 12, 2005, at A1.

989.    Dave Gustafson, *Receivership OK'd for Jefferson; vote expected Friday*, Charleston Gazette, June 29, 2005, at A1; Dave Gustafson, *Jefferson debts near $100,000, county told*, Charleston Gazette, July 22, 2005, at A1.

990.    Staff Reports, *Jefferson councilman arrested*, Charleston Gazette, May 7, 2005, at A2.

991.    Staff Reports, *Ex-Jefferson councilman pleads guilty to battery*, Charleston Gazette, Nov. 17, 2005, at A2.

992.    Chris Stirewalt, *Embattled delegate Mezzatesta announces cancer diagnosis*, Charleston Daily Mail, Sept. 23, 2004, at A1; Associated Press, *Speaker delaying action on Mezzatesta inquiry*, Charleston Daily Mail, Sept. 28, 2004, at A1; Eric Eyre, *Mezzatesta's letter to Ethics might have discrepancy, Letterhead was not in use at letter's stated date of origin*, Charleston Gazette, Aug. 3, 2004, at A1.

993.    The author of this book attended the press conference held by Speaker of the House Bob Kiss (State Capitol, Sept. 23, 2004).

994.    Eric Eyre, *Probe: Letter fabricated, Hampshire delegate Mezzatesta took part in cover-up, House report says*, Charleston Gazette, Sept. 24, 2004, at A1.

995.    Kris Wise, *Lawmakers say report will cast shadow*, Charleston Daily Mail, Sept. 24, 2004, at A1.

996.    Associated Press, *Speaker delaying action on Mezzatesta inquiry*, Charleston Daily Mail, Sept. 28, 2004, at A1.

997.    Chris Stirewalt, *Embattled delegate Mezzatesta announces cancer diagnosis*, Charleston Daily Mail, Sept. 23, 2004, at A1; Staff Reports, *Mezzatesta says he has cancer*, Charleston Gazette, Sept. 23, 2004, at A1.

998.    Eric Eyre, *Mezzatesta knew about faked letter, witnesses say*, Charleston Gazette, Sept. 29, 2004, at A1; Eric Eyre, *More letters may be falsified*, Charleston Gazette, Oct. 7, 2004, at A1; Associated Press, *Speaker delaying action on Mezzatesta inquiry*, Charleston Daily Mail, Sept. 28, 2004, at A1; Eric Eyre, *Letters contradict Mezzatesta, Delegate told Ethics panel he did not solicit grants for Hampshire County*, Charleston Gazette, July 1, 2004, at A1; Associated Press, *Mezzatesta affidavits challenged, Ex[candidate says legislator sought funds for county*, Charleston Daily Mail, July 2, 2004, at A1.

999.    Associated Press, *Speaker delaying action on Mezzatesta inquiry*, Charleston Daily Mail, Sept. 28, 2004, at A1.

1000.    Kris Wise, *Leaders hope Mezzatesta's empty position filled soon*, Charleston Daily Mail, Aug. 18, 2004, at A1; Eric Eyre, *State board reviewing school grants, Mezzatesta controversy prompts oversight of legislators' funding requests*, Charleston Gazette, Sept. 22, 2004, at A1; Eric Eyre, *Fifth of teacher grants went to Hampshire*, Charleston Gazette, July 8, 2004, at Al.

1001.    Associated Press, *Witness altered statements in Mezzatesta probe*, Charleston Daily Mail, Sept. 27, 2004, at A1; Eric Eyre, *Stewart backed Mezzatesta*, Charleston Gazette, June 20, 2004, at A1; Eric Eyre, *Part of Mezzatesta case given to Hampshire*, Charleston Gazette, Oct. 8, 2004, at A1; Associated Press, *Stewart sees nothing wrong with Mezzatesta's paychecks*, Charleston Daily Mail, Sept. 21, 2004, at A1; Eric Eyre, *Mezzatesta's pay gets mixed opinion from schools chief, Law doesn't ban double dipping, superintendent says*, Charleston Gazette, Sept. 21, 2004, at A1.

1002.    Associated Press, *Witness altered statements in Mezzatesta probe*, Charleston Daily Mail, Sept. 27, 2004, at A1; Eric Eyre, *Letters contradict Mezzatesta, Delegate told Ethics panel he did not solicit grants for Hampshire County*, Charleston Gazette, July 1, 2004, at A1; Editorial, *Mess-atesta, Still more problems*, Charleston Gazette, July 12, 2004, at A4.

1003.    Editorial, *Falsity, Major probe needed*, Charleston Gazette, June 20, 2004, at A4.

1004.    Eric Eyre, *Stewart backed Mezzatesta*, Charleston Gazette, Oct. 8, 2004, at A1.

1005.    Eric Eyre, *Ethics agency renews Mezzatesta Inquiry*, Charleston Gazette, Aug. 6, 2004, at A1; Eric Eyre, *Part of Mezzatesta case given to Hampshire*, Charleston Gazette, Oct. 8, 2004, at A1; Josh Hafenbrack, *Mezzatesta's wife works for House*, Charleston Daily Mail, Apr. 6, 2004, at A1; Associated Press, *Witness altered statements in Mezzatesta probe*, Charleston Daily Mail, Sept. 27, 2004, at A1; Associated Press, *Speaker delaying action on Mezzatesta inquiry*, Charleston Daily Mail, Sept. 28, 2004, at A1.

1006. Associated Press, *Witness altered statements in Mezzatesta probe*, Charleston Daily Mail, Sept. 27, 2004, at A1; Eric Eyre, *Fake letter plagued Mezzatesta workers, Statements reveal details of scheme*, Charleston Gazette, Dec. 12, 2004, at A1.

1007. Eric Eyre, *Probe: Letter fabricated, Hampshire delegate Mezzatesta took part in cover-up, House report says*, Charleston Gazette, Sept. 24, 2004, at A1.

1008. Eric Eyre, *Porn on House computer criticized, Legislators don't have restrictions on Internet use*, Charleston Gazette, Nov. 21, 2004, at A1.

1009. Eric Eyre, *'Just bring it on,' Mezzatesta says, Lawmaker denies he solicited grants, calls reports 'wrong,'*, Charleston Gazette, Sept. 21, 2004, at A1; Associated Press, *Mezzatesta affidavits challenged, Ex-candidate says legislator sought funds for county*, Charleston Daily Mail, July 2, 2004, at A1.

1010. Eric Eyre, *Mezzatesta knew about faked letter, witnesses say*, Charleston Gazette, Sept. 29, 2004, at A1; Eric Eyre, *More letters may be falsified*, Charleston Gazette, Oct. 7, 2004, at A1; Eric Eyre, *Part of Mezzatesta case given to Hampshire*, Charleston Gazette, Oct. 8, 2004, at A1.

1011. Eric Eyre, *Mezzatesta knew about faked letter, witnesses say*, Charleston Gazette, Sept. 29, 2004, at A1; *see also* Kris Wise, *Lawmakers say report will cast shadow*, Charleston Daily Mail, Sept. 24, 2004, at A1.

1012. Dave Gustafson, *Carney, Jarvis to be arraigned today in Mingo*, Charleston Gazette, Aug. 4, 2005, at A1; Lawrence Messina, Associated Press, *Jarvis, Carney face burglary charges*, Charleston Daily Mail, Aug. 4, 2005, at A1; Tom Searls, *Pair told to back off*, Charleston Gazette, Aug. 5, 2005, at A1.

1013. Dave Gustafson, *Carney countersues Nitro councilman*, Charleston Saturday Gazette-Mail, Apr. 30, 2005, at A1; Dave Gustafson, *Watchdog alleges Nitro phone misuse*, Charleston Saturday Gazette-Mail, May 4, 2005, at A1; Jake Stump, *Abuse of cell phones probed*, Charleston Daily Mail, May 23, 2005, at A1; Editorial, *Cell phones cost money*, Charleston Daily Mail, May 24, 2005, at A4.

1014. Eric Eyre, *Part of Mezzatesta case given to Hampshire*, Charleston Gazette, Oct. 8, 2004, at A1; Associated Press, *Speaker delaying action on Mezzatesta inquiry*, Charleston Daily Mail, Sept. 28, 2004, at A1; Eric Eyre, *Mezzatesta might face additional charges, Clifford appointed special prosecutor*, Charleston Gazette, Dec. 9, 2004, at A1; Associated Press, *Clifford handing over Mezzatesta investigation to Charnock*, Charleston Daily Mail, Dec. 9, 2004, at A1; Eric Eyre, *Mezzatesta seeks tapes of meetings*, Charleston Gazette, January 7, 2005, at A1; Staff Reports, *Mezzatestas sentenced, Former House Education chairman,wife fined, receive probation*, Charleston Daily Mail, Nov. 29, 2004, at A1; Eric Eyre, *Mezzatesta, wife get probation in alleged cover-up*, Charleston Gazette, Nov. 30, 2004, at A1; Editorial, *Sleaze, Mezzatesta lesson*, Charleston Gazette, Nov. 30, 2004 at A4; Therese Smith, *Plea's fallout unclear*, Charleston Daily Mail, Dec. 1, 2004, at A1; Eric Eyre, *Mezzatesta knew about faked letter, witnesses say*, Charleston Gazette, Sept. 29, 2004, at A1; Kris Wise, *Lawmakers say report will cast shadow*, Charleston Daily Mail, Sept. 24, 2004, at A1; Eric Eyre, *Inquiry focuses on Mezzatesta, 4 others*, Charleston Gazette, Sept. 28, 2004, at A1.

1015. Staff Reports, *Mezzatesta And Wife Agree To Plea Bargain*, MetroNews, Nov. 17, 2004 (<www.wvmetronews.com>); Eric Eyre, *Mezzatesta, wife to plead no contest, Ex-House Education chairman works out deal in response to misdemeanor*, Charleston Gazette, Nov. 18, 2004, at A1.

1016. Eric Eyre, *Mezzatesta seeks 'duty' pay for day he was sentenced*, Charleston Gazette, Dec. 1, 2004, at A1.

1017. Editorial, *Gall, Mezzatesta mess*, Charleston Gazette, Dec. 2, 2004, at A4; Therese Smith, *Mezzatesta pay request will get scrutiny*, Charleston Daily Mail, Dec. 2, 2004, at A1; Editorial, *Final insult*, Charleston Saturday Gazette-Mail, Dec. 11, 2004, at A4.

1018. Eric Eyre, *Ethics panel investigating delegate's wife, Complaint alleges Mary Lou Mezzatesta used Capitol office for private business*, Charleston Gazette, Dec. 15, 2004, at A1.

1019. Eric Eyre, *Could Mezzatesta be off the hook in home county?*, Charleston Gazette, Feb. 8, 2005, at A1.

1020. Eric Eyre, *Former delegate still faces charges*, Charleston Gazette, Mar. 2, 2005, at A1.

1021. Eric Eyre, *Could Mezzatesta be off the hook in home county?*, Charleston Gazette, Feb. 8, 2005, at A1.

1022. Eric Eyre, *Mezzatesta indicted*, Charleston Gazette, Apr. 21, 2005, at A1; Allison Barker, Associated Press, *Grand jury indicts Mezzatesta*, Charleston Daily Mail, Apr. 21, 2005, at

A1; Associated Press, *Judge asks to be excused from Jerry Mezzatesta cases*, Charleston Daily Mail, July 5, 2005, at Al; Eric Eyre, *Mezzatesta false swearing charge tossed*, Charleston Saturday Gazette-Mail, July 30, 2005, at A1.

1023.    Eric Eyre, *Mezzatesta refuses to pay fine*, Charleston Gazette, Mar. 6, 2005, at Al; Associated Press, *Mezzatesta, state ethics panel may go to court over fine*, Charleston Daily Mail, Apr. 13, 2005, at Al; Eric Eyre, *Mezzatesta given deadline to pay fine*, Charleston Gazette, Mar. 23, 2005, at Al; Eric Eyre, *Former delegate fined, reprimanded by board*, Charleston Gazette, Mar. 4, 2005, at Al; Associated Press, *Mezzatesta slapped with fine, reprimand*, Charleston Daily Mail, Mar. 4, 2005, at Al; Phil Kabler, *Ethics panel to sue for fines*, Charleston Gazette, May 6, 2005, at Al.

1024.    Scott Finn, *Lawmakers want Charnock investigated*, Charleston Gazette, May 16, 2005, at A1; Associated Press, Lawrence Messina, *Audit alleges prosecutor misused cell phone*, Charleston Daily Mail, May 16, 2005, at A1.

1025.    State Delegates have a base salary of $15,000, however, they receive additional money for attending various meetings including Interim Meetings. Information regarding salaries of many State office can be found on the West Virginia Secretary of State's website at www.wvsos.com. *See* Eric Eyre, *Mezzatesta's pay gets mixed opinion from schools chief, Law doesn't ban double dipping, superintendent says*, Charleston Gazette, Sept. 21, 2004, at A1; Associated Press, *Stewart sees nothing wrong with Mezzatesta's paychecks*, Charleston Daily Mail, Sept. 21, 2004, at A1; Editorial, *Mezzatesta is not the victim; it is W.Va. taxpayers who are*, Charleston Daily Mail, June 10, 2004, at A4.

1026.    Eric Eyre, *Little proof of Mezzatesta's board work, six form letters sent in four years*, Charleston Gazette, Aug. 1, 2004, at A1; Editorial, *Oh, for pity sake, it's an abuse, Voters need to weigh in on Delegate Jerry Mezzatesta*, Charleston Daily Mail, Sept. 22, 2004, at A4; Associated Press, *Stewart sees nothing wrong with Mezzatesta's paychecks*, Charleston Daily Mail, Sept. 21, 2004, at A1.

1027.    Editorial, *Integrity, W.Va. gets an F*, Charleston Gazette, Oct. 4, 2004, at A4; Editorial, *Double dip, Ethics ruling welcome, W.Va. gets an F*, Charleston Gazette, Mar. 31, 2004, at A4; Eric Eyre, *Complaint filed against delegate over his salaries*, Charleston Gazette, Mar. 31, 2004, at A1; Eric Eyre, *Mezzatesta's pay gets mixed opinion from schools chief, Law doesn't ban double dipping, superintendent says*, Charleston Gazette, Sept. 21, 2004, at A1.

1028.    Editorial, *Mezzatesta is not the victim; it is W.Va. taxpayers who are*, Charleston Daily Mail, June 10, 2004, at A4; Editorial, *Mezzatesta, If a person isn't needed 14 weeks a year, why is he paid $60,000*, Charleston Daily Mail, June 25, 2004, at A4.

1029.    Editorial, *Oh, for pity sake, it's an abuse, Voters need to weigh in on Delegate Jerry Mezzatesta*, Charleston Daily Mail, Sept. 22, 2004, at A4.

1030.    Eric Eyre, *School employee/legislators vow: No double dipping*, Charleston Gazette, June 10, 2004, at A1; Staff Reports, *One Lawmaker-Educator says Double Dipping Wrong*, MetroNews, Nov. 5, 2004 (www.wvmetronews.com).

1031.    Eric Eyre, *Probe of Hampshire schools urged*, Charleston Gazette, Sept. 10, 2004, at A1; *see also* Eric Eyre, *State board reviewing school grants, Mezzatesta controversy prompts oversight of legislators' funding requests*, Charleston Gazette, Sept. 22, 2004, at A1; Eric Eyre, *Mezzatesta diverted school money to fire departments*, Charleston Gazette, Apr. 21, 2004, at A1; Eric Eyre, *More ethics doubts arise, Mezzatesta solicited state grant despite county's vow he would not*, Charleston Gazette, Apr. 1, 2004, at A1.

1032.    Eric Eyre, *U.S. Agents intensify Mezzatesta grant probe*, Charleston Saturday Gazette-Mail, Oct. 8, 2005, at A1.

1033.    *See* Chapter Sixteen, Follow the Money.

1034.    Eric Eyre, *Mezzatesta keeps support at home*, Charleston Gazette, Oct. 31, 2003, at A1.

1035.    Eric Eyre, *Teachers' union chief urges Mezzatesta to quit*, Charleston Gazette, Oct. 1, 2004, at A1.

1036.    Editorial, *Mezzatesta, Don't stop the probes*, Charleston Gazette, Aug. 18, 2004, at A4; *see also* Chris Stirewalt, *Embattled delegate Mezzatesta announces cancer diagnosis*, Charleston Daily Mail, Sept. 23, 2004, at A1; Eric Eyre, *Mezzatests's pay gets mixed opinion from schools chief, Law doesn't ban double dipping, superintendent says*, Charleston Gazette, Sept. 21, 2004, at A1; Phil Kabler, *Mezzatesta loses education post, Ethics probe prompts Kiss to strip chairmanship from delegate*, Charleston Gazette, Aug. 18, 2004, at A1.

1037.    Chris Stirewalt, *Union official wants Mezzatesta out, Teachers group worried about embattled delegate's role in setting budget*, Charleston Daily Mail, Oct. 6, 2004, at A1.

1038.    Eric Eyre, *Kanawha board wants Mezzatesta out as education chairman*, Aug. 3, 2004, at A1; Staff Reports, *Lincoln school board asks for removal of Mezzatesta*, Charleston

Gazette, Aug. 17, 2004, at A2; Morgan Kelly, *School board may call for Mezzatesta's removal*, July 16, 2004, at A1; Eric Eyre, *County wants Mezzatesta out as education chairman, Braxton school board asks Speaker Kiss for replacement*, Charleston Gazette, July 13, 2004, at A1; Eric Eyre, *Monroe board seconds call for ouster of Mezzatesta*, Charleston Gazette, July 21, 2004, at A1.

1039.   Eric Eyre, *Mezzatesta seeks tapes of meetings*, Charleston Gazette, January 7, 2005, at A1.

1040.   Vicki Smith, *School board silences Mezzatesta critics*, Charleston Gazette, Mar. 10, 2005, at A1; Editorial, *Mess-atesta, Nightmare gets worse*, Charleston Gazette, Mar. 11, 2005, at A4; Associated Press, *Public silenced at board meeting*, Charleston Gazette, Mar. 10, 2005, at A1; Editorial, *Off the rails in Hampshire*, Charleston Daily Mail, Mar. 11, 2005, at A4.

1041.   Eric Eyre, *Hampshire schools in crisis, State of emergency declared, Mezzatesta, superintendent named in audit report*, Charleston Gazette, Feb. 10, 2005, at A1; *see also* Associated Press, *Two county school systems cited*, Charleston Daily Mail, Feb. 10, 2005, at A1; Editorial, *Hampshire is highly irregular*, Charleston Daily Mail, Mar. 18, 2005, at A4; Eric Eyre, *Hampshire told to pay back grant*, Charleston Gazette, Apr. 15, 2005, at A1; Editorial, *Shabby, Hampshire school mess*, Charleston Gazette, Mar. 18, 2005, at A4; Associated Press, *Review shows Hampshire spending violated rules*, Charleston Daily Mail, Mar. 11, 2005, at A1 ("A $100,000 "staff development" grant from the Department of Education went to pay substitute teachers. Most of a $75,000 grant intended for special education students went to seven volunteer fire departments in Hampshire County. Mezzatesta diverted the education funds to the fire departments, letters show.").

1042.   *Id.*

1043.   *Id*; Eric Eyre, *Hampshire finds Mezzatesta a job*, Charleston Gazette, Mar. 17, 2005, at A1; Editorial, *Hampshire bus drivers upset over Mezzatesta's new job*, Charleston Daily Mail, Mar. 17, 2005, at A4.

1044.   Eric Eyre, *Hampshire fires Mezzatesta*, Charleston Gazette, Apr. 23, 2005, at A1.

1045.   Allison Barker, Associated Press, *Board OK's partial seizure*, Charleston Daily Mail, Jan. 12, 2006, at A1.

1046.   Eric Eyre, *Schools chief resigns*, Charleston Gazette, Jan. 4, 2006, at A1.

1047.   Eric Eyre, *More information sought on Marockie's spending, Federal jury is looking into his use of expense accounts*, Charleston Gazette, Jan. 24, 2001, at C1.

1048.   Eric Eyre, *Former school official indicted*, Charleston Gazette, Jan. 28, 2005, at A1.

1049.   *Id*; Associated Press, *Businessman Booth dies at 55 of heart attack*, Charleston Daily Mail, June 20, 2005, at A1; Eric Eyre, *Convicted businessman 'Pork Chop' Booth dies*, Charleston Gazette, June 20, 2005, at A1; Eric Eyre, *McClung pleads guilty to extortion*, Charleston Gazette, May 24, 2005, at A1; Associated Press, *Former state schools official pleads guilty*, Charleston Daily Mail, May 24, 2005, at A1.

1050.   Eric Eyre, *McClung receives 7 years in prison*, Charleston Gazette, Aug. 30, 2005, at A1; Associated Press, *McClung gets seven-year jail sentence*, Charleston Daily Mail, Aug. 30, 2005, at A1.

1051.   Associated Press, *Former official getting 'stern letter' for action*, Charleston Daily Mail, Oct. 20, 2005, at A1.

1052.   Editorial, *Expenses, Abuse of the taxpayer just kills the case for higher taxes*, Charleston Gazette, May 27, 2003, at A4.

1053.   *Id.*

1054.   Eric Eyre, *Funeral attendance billed to state*, Charleston Sunday Gazette-Mail, May 25, 2003, at A1.

1055.   Christopher Tritto, *Official quits under a cloud*, Charleston Gazette, Oct. 11, 2002, at A1.

1056.   West Virginia Constitution, Art. XII, § 1 (1872).

1057.   Editorial, *Public funds need oversight, Here's to the state for imposing some rules on senior agencies*, Charleston Daily Mail, Oct. 8, 2004, at A4; Chris Wetterich, *Travels of seniors chief scrutinized*, Charleston Gazette, Mar. 26, 2004, at A1; *see also* Chris Wetterich, *A tale of two Boards, Lincoln not Wyoming, panel says*, Charleston Gazette, Mar. 12, 2004, at A1; Kris Wise, *Agency team to investigate program*, Charleston Daily Mail, Mar. 4, 2004, at A1; Kris Wise, *Graham's departure sought*, Charleston Daily Mail, Mar. 4, 2004, at A1; Kris Wise, *Federal probe sought*, Charleston Daily Mail, Mar. 5, 2004, at A1; Editorial, *Seniors, This scandal is a five-alarm fire for confidence in government*, Charleston Daily Mail, Mar. 5, 2004, at A4; Editorial, *$301,728, Calls for an investigation by Capito, Wise are a good start*, Charleston Daily Mail, Mar. 2, 2004, at A4; Eric Eyre, *Graham could reap $241,000 in sick pay*, Charleston Gazette, Mar. 2, 2004, at A1; Editorial, *What? The*

*Legislature needs to take corrective action this session*, Charleston Daily Mail, Mar. 3, 2004, at A4; Editorial, *Age-old problem, Nonprofit directors lax*, Charleston Gazette, Mar. 4, 2004, at A4; Chris Wetterich, *Aging agency director defends salary, controversy on pay, perks is overblown, Wyoming official says*, Charleston Gazette, Mar. 2, 2004, at A1.

1058.    Editorial, *Public funds need oversight, Here's to the state for imposing some rules on senior agencies*, Charleston Daily Mail, Oct. 8, 2004, at A4; Editorial, *No action? Federal and state officials stop the lunacy in Wyoming County*, Charleston Daily Mail, Mar. 6, at A4; Toby Coleman, *Graham fighting legal battle to keep job*, Charleston Saturday Gazette-Mail, Mar. 12, 2005, at A1.

1059.    Editorial, *No action? Federal and state officials stop the lunacy in Wyoming County*, Charleston Daily Mail, Mar. 6, 2004, at A4; Chris Wetterich, *Travels of seniors chief scrutinized*, Charleston Gazette, Mar. 26, 2004, at A1; Chris Wetterich and Eric Eyre, *Seniors chief's '03 pay $457 K*, Charleston Gazette, Mar. 25, 2004, at A1; Kris Wise, *Special session sought on salary*, Charleston Daily Mail, Mar. 25, 2004, at A1; Chris Wetterich, *Wyoming seniors chief silent on $301,728 salary, But he does admonish Wise on Medicaid savings*, Charleston Gazette, Feb. 27, 2004, at A1.

1060.    Editorial, *No action? Federal and state officials stop the lunacy in Wyoming County*, Charleston Daily Mail, Mar. 6, 2004, at A4.

1061.    Information on the salaries of West Virginia's elected officials is available on the West Virginia Secretary of State's website (<www.wvsos.org.>).

1062.    Editorial, *No Action? Federal and state officials stop the lunacy in Wyoming County*, Charleston Daily Mail, Mar. 6, 2004, at A4; Chris Wetterich, *Travels of seniors chief scrutinized*, Charleston Gazette, Mar. 26, 2004, at A1.

1063.    Eric Eyre, *Princeton High now in seniors mess*, Charleston Gazette, Mar. 12, 2004, at A1; Chris Wetterich, *Travels of seniors chief scrutinized*, Charleston Gazette, Mar. 26, 2004, at A1.

1064.    Chris Wetterich and Eric Eyre, *Seniors chief's '03 pay $457 K*, Charleston Gazette, Mar. 25, 2004, at A1.

1065.    Kris Wise, *Wyoming nonprofit leaders fear reactions to salary issue*, Charleston Daily Mail, Mar. 3, 2004, at A1.

1066.    Chris Wetterich and Eric Eyre, *Seniors chief vows to stay, Wyoming County agency board member quits; Graham says he might cut his compensation*, Charleston Gazette, Mar. 5, 2004, at A1; *see also* Kris Wise, *Resignation encouraged, Senator calls for Graham to step down from job*, Charleston Daily Mail, Mar. 3, 2004, at A1.

1067.    Editorial, *Profiteering, Riches from tax money*, Charleston Gazette, June 9, 2005, at A4.

1068.    Brad McElhinny, *Graham's wife's pay, perks detailed*, Charleston Daily Mail, June 6, 2005, at A1.

1069.    Kris Wise, *Graham faces embezzlement, tax charges*, Charleston Daily Mail, Jan. 27, 2006, at A1; Tom Searls, *Aging's Graham indicted*, Charleston Gazette, Jan. 27, 2006, at A1; Editorials, *Bob Graham did not act alone*, Charleston Daily Mail, Jan. 30, 2006, at A4.

1070.    Eric Eyre, *Graham blames others for legal woes*, Charleston Gazette, Jan. 31, 2006, at A1; Associated Press, *Graham sues Wise, other ex-officials*, Charleston Daily Mail, Jan. 31, 2006, at A1.

1071.    Kris Wise, *Graham on leave from job*, Charleston Daily Mail, Feb. 9, 2006, at A1; *see also* Kris Wise, *State seeking to oust Graham*, Charleston Daily Mail, Feb. 10, 2006, at A1.

1072.    Kris Warner, *Aren't we missing the real story?*, Charleston Daily Mail, Mar. 5, 2004, at A5; Editorial, *Porkbarrel, Budget Digest, Graham*, Charleston Gazette, Jan. 30, 2006, at A4.

1073.    Kris Wise, *Senator says he didn't know about salary*, Charleston Daily Mail, Mar. 2, 2004, at A1; *see also* Phil Kabler, *Senator got $415,000 in funding for agency*, Charleston Gazette, Mar. 2, 2004, at A1; Kris Warner, *Aren't we missing the real story?*, Charleston Daily Mail, Mar. 5, 2004, at A5.

1074.    *See* Tom Searls, *Wyoming County senator discounts ethics charge*, Charleston Saturday Gazette-Mail, Aug. 27, 2005, at A1; Editorial, *Ethics complaint proceeding against state senator*, Charleston Gazette, September 28, 2005, at A4; Kris Wise, *Bailey's dual role under scrutiny*, Charleston Daily Mail, Aug. 26, 2005, at A1; Kris Wise, *Senator cooks, serves for $25 an hour*, Charleston Daily Mail, Aug. 25, 2005, at A1; Kris Wise, *Graham's agency gets cash in Digest*, Charleston Daily Mail, Aug. 24, 2005, at A1.

1075.    Editorial, *Government ethics, West Virginia style*, Charleston Daily Mail, Dec. 27, 2005, at A4; *see also* Associated Press, *Panel clears senator of ethics complaint*, Charleston Daily Mail, Dec. 23, 2005, at A1; Eric Eyre, *State ethics panel rules for senator*, Charleston Gazette, Dec. 23, 2005, at A1.

1076. Editorial, *Potpourri*, Charleston Gazette, Dec. 26, 2005, at A4.

1077. Kris Warner, *Aren't we missing the real story?*, Charleston Daily Mail, Mar. 5, 2004, at A5.

1078. Jim Wallace, *Senator leaving board job*, Charleston Daily Mail, Mar. 3, 2005, at A1.

1079. Editorial, *Seniors, This scandal is a five-alarm fire for confidence in government*, Charleston Daily Mail, Mar. 5, 2004, at A4.

1080. Scott Finn, *WBOY-TV funded Mexico trip for Marion Delegate, both sides' actions' inappropriate,' parent company president says*, April 11, 2004, at A1; Scott Finn, *Marion delegate pays back cost of Mexico trip*, Charleston Gazette, April 14, 2004, at A1; Scott Finn, *Nonprofits lucrative for some insiders*, Charleston Gazette, April 14, 2004, at A1.

1081. A.V. Gallagher, Associated Press, *Harman respected during impeachment drive*, Sunday Gazette-Mail, Feb. 26, 1989, at A2; Daniel Bice, *Accounting style altered, witness says*, Charleston Daily Mail, Mar. 8, 1989, at A1; Richard Grimes, *Manchin book portrays office in severe turmoil*, Charleston Daily Mail, June 20, 1990, at A1.

1082. Fanny Seiler, *Treasurer records falsified*, Charleston Gazette, Feb. 9, 1989, at A1.

1083. James B. Lees, *Special prosecutor summarizes Manchin case*, Charleston Gazette, July 15, 1989, at A2; *see also* A.V. Gallagher, Associated Press, *Report accuses Manchin of cover-up*, Charleston Daily Mail, July 11, 1989, at A1; Patty Vandergrift, *Manchin tried to hush losses, panel told*, Charleston Gazette, Mar. 16, 1989, at A1.

1084. Jack McCarthy, *Political Family Scion Making A Go For The Big Time*, Charleston Gazette, Dec. 27, 1995, at A1; Cheryl Caswell, *Ex Politicos Rebound After Fall From Grace*, Charleston Daily Mail, Sept. 6, 1994, at A1 ("Margolin spent time at a half way house in St. Albans upon his release from the federal facility at Ashland two months early for good behavior."); Associated Press, *W. Va. Attorney General Resigns to halt Criminal Investigation*, Charleston Daily Mail, Aug. 21, 1989, at A1; Barry Bearak, *Corruption in West Virginia: Scandals as Thick as Coal Dust*, Los Angeles Times, July 8, 1990, at A1.

1085. Barry Bearak, *Corruption in West Virginia: Scandals as Thick as Coal Dust*, Los Angeles Times, July 8, 1990, at A1.

1086. Cheryl Caswell, *Ex Politicos Rebound After Fall From Grace*, Charleston Daily Mail, Sept. 6, 1994, at A1; *see also* Leslie Wayne, *Wall Street Broker Vs. Mountain State May Set Fiscal Precedent*, Charleston Gazette, Apr. 25, 1995, at D6; Phil Kabler, *A. James Manchin, 1927-2003, Unique politician was always campaigning, always onstage*, Charleston Gazette, Nov. 4, 2003, at A1.

1087. James B. Lees, *Investment funds found used for self-promotion*, Charleston Gazette, July 21, 1989, at A6.

1088. Fanny Seiler, *Investing fees went for car washes, trips around country*, Charleston Gazette, Jan. 13, 1989, at A9.

1089. James B. Lees, *Investment funds found used for self-promotion*, Charleston Gazette, July 21, 1989, at A6.

1090. *Id.*

1091. John Kimelman, *Manchin Continues Handing Out Paraphernalia*, July 11, 1985, at B1.

1092. Paul Nyden, *Debate over Manchin's award, trinket expenditures continues*, Sunday Gazette-Mail, Aug. 7, 1988, at A7.

1093. Phil Kabler, *Manchin's expenses for travel, memorabilia totaled $209,682*, Charleston Gazette, July 21, 1989, at A1; Richard Grimes, *Manchin says he will retire July 9*, Charleston Daily Mail, July 8, 1989, at A1; Leslie Wayne, *Wall Street Broker Vs. Mountain State May Set Fiscal Precedent*, Charleston Gazette, Apr. 25, 1995, at D6; *see also* Darrell E. Holmes, West Virginia Blue Book 414 n. 47 (Chapman Printing, Charleston, WV, 1997) (Special Session held by Senate for the trial of A. James Manchin, upon Articles of Impeachment July 10, 1989-July 10, 1989.); Jack McCarthy, *Political Family Scion Making A Go For The Big Time*, Charleston Gazette, Dec. 27, 1995, at A1; Associated Press, *W. Va. Attorney General Resigns to halt Criminal Investigation*, Charleston Daily Mail, Aug. 21, 1989, at A1.

1094. Sam Tranum, *House approves measure to move funds to treasurer*, Charleston Daily Mail, Mar. 2, 2002, at C5; Manchin was West Virginia Secretary of State from 1977 to 1985 as well as serving a previous term in the West Virginia House of Representatives. Manchin's nephew Joe Manchin, III, former State Senator from Marion County ran unsuccessfully for Governor in 1996 and was successfully elected during the 2000 election to serve as West Virginia Secretary of State and elected in 2004 as Governor; *see also* Greg Icenhower, *A. James Manchin: A Biography of Controversy* (Terra, Alta, West Virginia: Headline Books, 1990.).

1095. Staff Reports, *Loehr Orders Settlement Be Paid*, Charleston Gazette, July 28, 1989, at A4;

Editorial, *Pay, Manchin*, Charleston Gazette, May 25, 1988, at A4; Staff Reports, *Finance Too High for Man of Mementos*, Charleston Gazette, Mar. 26, 1989, at A1; Staff Reports, *Fired Workers' Settlement May Be Challenged*, Charleston Gazette, May 27, 1988, at A1; Patty Vandergrift, *Five Fired Workers Sue Manchin*, Charleston Gazette, Sept. 21, 1985, at A1; Staff Reports, *Cna Won't Say If Check Written in Manchin Case*, Charleston Gazette, June 1, 1988, at A1; Editorial, *Manchin Outrage*, Charleston Gazette, June 2, 1988, at A4; Fanny Seiler, *35 Workers Fired in Treasurer's Office*, Charleston Gazette, January 4, 1985, at A4; Editorial, *Spoils System*, Charleston Gazette, June 29, 1990, at A4; Editorial, *Boone Outrage*, Charleston Gazette, Jan. 5, 1989, at A4; Staff Reports, *Suit Settled Without Attorney General's ok*, Charleston Gazette, May 24, 1988, at A1; Staff Reports, *Shafting the People Time after Time, Politicians Commit*, Charleston Gazette, Dec. 16, 1988, at A1.

1096.    Phil Kabler, *A. James Manchin, 1927-2003, Unique politician was always campaigning, always onstage*, Charleston Gazette, Nov. 4, 2003, at A1.

1097.    UPI, *Manchin defends flag, ribbon money*, Charleston Gazette, July 15, 1982, at A1.

1098.    Fanny Seiler, *Manchin's expenses questioned*, Charleston Gazette, July 14, 1982, at A1.

1099.    UPI, *Manchin defends flag, ribbon money*, Charleston Gazette, July 15, 1982, at A1.

1100.    Cheryl Caswell, *REAPing the benefits*, Charleston Daily Mail, Feb. 11, 2005, at A1; *see also* Phil Kabler, *A. James Manchin, 1927-2003, Unique politician was always campaigning, always onstage*, Charleston Gazette, Nov. 4, 2003, at A1.

1101.    Editorial, *Manchin, This funny, canny politician never stopped serving W.Va.*, Nov. 4, 2003, at A4.

1102.    Bob Kelly, *Antonio James Manchin, R.I.P.*, Charleston Daily Mail, Nov. 4, 2003, at A4.

1103.    Deanna Wrenn, *Legendary figure dies at 76*, Charleston Daily Mail, Nov. 3, 2003, at A1.

1104.    Interview of United States Senator Edward M. Kennedy by Allen H. Loughry II, October 30, 2004, Holiday Inn Charleston House, Charleston, West Virginia (Following a Democratic Rally that included Senator John D. Rockefeller, IV, Senator Robert C. Byrd, and various other candidates. Kennedy recalled being in the home of Governor Joe Manchin, III in 1960 eating spaghetti, with his brothers John and Robert Kennedy.); *see also* United States Senator Edward M. Kennedy, Letter to the Editor, *A. James Manchin devoted to W.Va.*, Charleston Gazette, Nov. 7, 2003, at A5.

1105.    UPI, *Manchin defends flag, ribbon money*, Charleston Gazette, July 15, 1982, at A1.

1106.    It is widely known in political circles that Manchin employed full-time State employees to scour daily and weekly newspapers to gather names of individuals celebrating birthdays, anniversaries, milestones, or some other event or award received, in order to subsequently mail them one of the multitudes of taxpayer paid-for trinkets and certificates that most West Virginians have received at one time during their lives.

1107.    *See* Greg Icenhower, *A. James Manchin: A Biography of Controversy* (Terra, Alta, W.Va.: Headline Books, 1990.).

1108.    *Ex-Governor Cecil Underwood Makes His Farewell Address*, The West Virginia Hillbilly, Jan. 16, 1961, at 13.

1109.    Fanny Seiler, *Logan neighbors wrangle over paving of road*, Charleston Sunday Gazette-Mail, June 24, 2001, at 3C.

1110.    Fanny Seiler, *Weirton office site considered*, Charleston Gazette, Aug. 20, 2001, at C1.

1111.    Lawrence Messina, *Second murder's sentence was commuted: Man who killed Nicholas county woman in 1980 robbery is now eligible for parole*, Charleston Gazette, Feb. 7, 2001, at C1.

1112.    Ferrell v. Duncil, 230 F.3d 1352 (4th Cir. W.Va. 2000); Ferrell v. Duncil, No. CA-97-79-2 (N.D. W.Va. Aug. 16, 1999).

1113.    Lawrence Messina, *Underwood decision draws criticism: Ex-governor acted rashly in changing murderer's sentence, officials say*, Feb. 6, 2001, at A1; Associated Press, *Former governor defends changing sentence: Man convicted of murder to be eligible for parole*, Charleston Daily Mail, Feb. 6, 2001, at A1.

1114.    Telephone interview by Allen H. Loughry II with Grant County Prosecuting Attorney Dennis DiBenedetto (February 5, 2001). DiBinedetto, who tried the original criminal appeal, had spoken with the family members of the Victim as well as to members of the West Virginia Parole Board and concluded that not a single person had been contacted by the Governor's Office with regard to the commutation of Paul Ferrell's sentence; *see also* Lawrence Messina, *Underwood decision draws criticism: Ex-governor acted rashly in changing murderer's sentence, officials say*, Feb. 6, 2001, at A1; Associated Press, *Former governor defends changing sentence: Man convicted of murder to be eligible for parole*, Charleston Daily Mail, Feb. 6, 2001, at A1; Lawrence Messina, *Second murder's sentence was commuted: Man who killed Nicholas county woman in 1980 robbery is now eligible for parole*, Charleston Gazette, Feb. 7, 2001, at C1 (Governor Underwood also commuted the sentence of Clarence Bertchell Hall, who was in prison for killing a Nicholas County woman during a 1980 robbery.).

1115.   Anonymous interview by author held at the State Capitol in Charleston, West Virginia, on January 31, 2001; Second anonymous interview by author, held the same day at the State Capitol in Charleston, West Virginia.

1116.   Lawrence Messina, *Underwood decision draws criticism: Ex-governor acted rashly in changing murderer's sentence, officials say*, Feb. 6, 2001, at A1.

1117.   Editorial, *Pardons*, Charleston Gazette, Dec. 23, 1997, at A4.

1118.   Lawrence Messina, *Underwood decision draws criticism: Ex-governor acted rashly in changing murderer's sentence, officials say*, Charleston Gazette, Feb. 6, 2001, at A1; Telephone interview by author of Grant County Prosecuting Attorney Dennis DiBenedetto, Feb. 2, 2001; *see also* Associated Press, *Ex-Deputy granted parole in 1980s murder case*, Charleston Daily Mail, May 26, 2004, at A1.

1119.   Editorials, *Pardons: Maybe governors don't use the power to pardon because they don't need to*, Charleston Daily Mail, Dec. 23, 1997, at A4; Paul Owens, *Ads Called Untrue: Pritt Campaign Implies Underwood Soft on Crime*, Charleston Daily Mail, Nov. 1, 1996, at C1; Paul Owens, *Underwood Fires Back With Anti-Crime Ad: Miffed over Pritt Claim, GOP Hopeful Launches Counter Ad*, Charleston Daily Mail, Nov. 4, 1996, at A12 (Underwood's predecessor, Gaston Caperton, who served from 1989 to 1997, had granted a total of fourteen pardons.); Lawrence Messina, *Second murder's sentence was commuted: Man who killed Nicholas County woman in 1980 robbery is now eligible for parole*, Charleston Gazette, Feb. 7, 2001, at C1 (Underwood addressed five other criminal convictions on his last day in office including commuting the sentence of convicted murder Clarence Bertchell Hall, who was imprisoned for slaying a Nicholas County woman during a 1980 robbery. Moreover, according to records in the Secretary of State's Office, Underwood intervened in forty-eight criminal cases since 1998, which included pardons, commutation of two murderers sentences, and granted twelve medical respites or reprieves to seriously ill or older inmates to either receive treatment or to die outside of the prison walls.).

1120.   Phil Kabler, *Governor's contingency fund running on fumes*, Charleston Gazette, Jan. 17, 2001, at A2 (quote from Paul Mollohan); *see also* Phil Kabler, *Underwood's top-ranking aides cash in: Late payments put Wise administration in bind*, Charleston Gazette, Jan 18. 2001, at A1.

1121.   Editorial, *Handouts, Campaigning with tax money*, Charleston Gazette, Oct. 25, 2000, at A4; *see also* Phil Kabler, *'Stop the insanity,' Underwood told, Wise, Gainer blast governor's election-season use of contingency fund*, Charleston Gazette, Oct. 25, 2000, at C1.

1122.   Sam Tranum, *Former governor lashes out*, Charleston Daily Mail, Oct. 19, 2001, at A1.

1123.   Phil Kabler, *Governor's contingency fund running on fumes*, Charleston Gazette, Jan. 17, 2001, at A2; Phil Kabler, *Underwood's top-ranking aides cash in: Late payments put Wise administration in bind*, Charleston Gazette, Jan 18. 2001, at A1.

1124.   Phil Kabler, *Underwood documents 'sequestered', Former chief of staff won't discuss comp time; auditors secure records*, Charleston Gazette, Jan. 24, 2001, at A1.

1125.   Fanny Seiler, *Underwood staff overpaid more than $186,000*, Charleston Sunday Gazette-Mail, Apr. 1, 2001, at C3; Phil Kabler, *Underwood documents 'sequestered', Former chief of staff won't discuss comp time; auditors secure records*, Charleston Gazette, Jan. 24, 2001, at A1; Fanny Seiller, *Former Underwood aides owe $136,476*, Charleston Gazette, June 14, 2001, at A1; Fanny Seiler, *Wise's office to decide on Underwood staff overpayments*, Charleston Gazette, July 10, 2001, at A3 (The article reports that Wise's office determined that $136,476 was the total after deductions for taxes, Social Security and Medicaid, while Legislative Auditors arrived at a total of $186,749 that was overpaid.); Fanny Seiler, *Underwood staffers owe thousands*, Charleston Gazette, Apr. 9, 2001, at C1; Editorial, *What a mess: Underwood fallout*, Charleston Gazette, July 27, 2001, at A4; Phil Kabler, *Underwood's top-ranking aides cash in: Late payments put Wise administration in bind*, Charleston Gazette, Jan 18. 2001, at A1; Associated Press, *Most comp money still not returned*, Charleston Gazette, June 7, 2001, at A5; Randy Coleman, Associated Press, *Out of prison, ex-senator builds new life*, Charleston Gazette, June 18, 2001, at A1.

1126.   Phil Kabler, *Underwood's top-ranking aides cash in: Late payments put Wise administration in bind*, Charleston Gazette, Jan 18. 2001, at A1.

1127.   Sam Tranum, *Former governor lashes out*, Charleston Daily Mail, Oct. 19, 2001, at A1.

1128.   Paul J. Nyden, *Secret Coal Deals Made, Official Says, Approval of Workers' comp agreement was not sought by Vieweg, successor says*, Charleston Gazette, Mar. 28, 2001, at A1.

1129.    Editorial, *Probe? Ugly allegations*, Charleston Gazette, June 14, 2001, at A4; Paul J. Nyden, *Vieweg 'deceptive' in dismissing suits, official says*, June 7, 2001, at C1; Editorial, *Handouts, Campaigning with tax money*, Charleston Gazette, Oct. 25, 2000, at A4.

1130.    Editorial, *What a mess: Underwood fallout*, Charleston Gazette, July 27, 2001, at A4 (Vieweg was also charged with buying a $13 million State computer that "doesn't work properly" and that has triggered lawsuits and forced a grand jury probe. In addition, $3.6 million was paid to Connecticut consultants at nearly $200 an hour "to coach Workers' Compensation employees on how to do their jobs." Current Commissioner Robert Smith fired the consultants saying that "the experts did little of value."); *see also* Paul J. Nyden, *Secret Coal Deals Made, Official Says, Approval of Workers' comp agreement was not sought by Vieweg, successor says*, Charleston Gazette, Mar. 28, 2001, at A1 (Buyouts by self-insured employers should cover all long-term disability and medical benefits that will be paid to injured workers in the future.); Paul J. Nyden, *Arch Coal says Vieweg deals saved firm $21 million*, Charleston Sunday Gazette-Mail, May 6, 2001, at B1; Paul J. Nyden, *Vieweg wants his coal suit testimony kept secret*, Charleston Gazette, June 22, 2001, at A5; Editorial, *What a mess: Underwood fallout*, Charleston Gazette, July 27, 2001, at A4.

1131.    Ken Ward Jr., *$41 million in mine fines tossed: Underwood administration wrote off in 2000*, Charleston Sunday Gazette-Mail, May 26, 2002, at A1.

1132.    Fanny Seiler, *Unpaid phone bills probed: Audit finds problems that led to over $5 million being owed by state*, Charleston Gazette, May 8, 2001, at C1; Fanny Seiler, *Verizon: state owes millions*, Charleston Gazette, Mar. 20, 2001, at C1; Editorial, *What a mess: Underwood fallout*, Charleston Gazette, July 27, 2001, at A4; Phil Kabler, *Unpaid phone bills under Underwood total nearly $4 million*, Charleston Gazette, Jan. 18, 2002, at A1; Phil Kabler, *State untangles $10.28 million in claims for back phone bills*, Charleston Gazette, Nov. 18, 2003, at A1; Editorial, *The State should pay its phone bills*, Charleston Daily Mail, Mar. 21, 2005, at A4.

1133.    Scott Finn, *Grant to cabinet maker sets Sunny Day Fund record*, Charleston Gazette, Jan. 5, 2005, at A1.

1134.    Editorial, *Budget Digest*, Charleston Daily Mail, May 8, 2002, at A4.

1135.    Dan Radmacher, *Budget Digest simply a tool of coercion*, Charleston Gazette, Oct. 6, 2000, at A4.

1136.    Phil Kabler, *Budget Digest OK'd*, Charleston Gazette, July 26, 2005, at A1; Lawrence Messina, Associated Press, *Manchin says digest not aimed at bypassing him*, Charleston Daily Mail; Aug. 1, 2005, at A1; Lawrence Messina, Associated Press, *Legislators allot $26.5 million for budget digest*, Charleston Daily Mail, July 26, 2005, at A1.

1137.    Editorial, *Budget Digest*, Charleston Daily Mail, May 8, 2002, at A4.

1138.    Editorial, *Public cash, Used for political gain*, Charleston Sunday Gazette-Mail, May 9, 2004, at C1.

1139.    Phil Kabler, *Budget Digest no record: Allocations slightly larger than last year's*, Charleston Gazette, June 29, 2001, at A1; Phil Kabler, *Lean finances again limit Budget Digest*, Charleston Gazette, June 29, 2004, at A1; Phil Kabler, *Warner Vows to end state Budget Digest*, Charleston Gazette, Sept. 29, 2004, at A1; Associated Press, *Budget Digest gets nod from lawmakers*, Charleston Daily Mail, June 29, 2004, at A1.

1140.    Associated Press, *Budget Digest pared down to $21 million, Several programs, communities hope to see part of funds*, Charleston Gazette, May 24, 2003, at A1.

1141.    Fanny Seiler, *Democrats looking for Minear opponent; Staggers a possibility*, Charleston Sunday Gazette-Mail, July 13, 1997, at B8; Fanny Seiler, *Staggers weighs his options, including a shot at Wise seat*, Charleston Sunday Gazette-Mail, Oct. 5, 1997, at B8; Fanny Seiler, *Humphreys and Workman conduct early polls*, Charleston Gazette, Dec. 23, 2001, at A5.

1142.    Phil Kabler, *Lean finances again limit Budget Digest*, Charleston Gazette, June 29, 2004, at A1; Phil Kabler, *Warner Vows to end state Budget Digest*, Charleston Gazette, Sept. 29, 2004, at A1; Associated Press, *Budget Digest gets nod from lawmakers*, Charleston Daily Mail, June 29, 2004, at A1.

1143.    Editorial, *Budget Digest: Court should order reform*, Charleston Gazette, July 18, 2000, at A4.

1144.    Phil Kabler, *Statehouse Beat, Digest mentality plays part in uproar*, Charleston Gazette, Aug. 9, 2004, at A4.

1145.    Editorial, *Eastern College never approved*, Charleston Gazette-Mail, July 2, 2000, at A4.

1146.    Editorial, *Rewards*, Charleston Gazette, Mar. 31, 2005, at A4.

1147.    Editorial, *King Harold must be reined in*, Charleston Daily Mail, Mar. 29, 2005, at A4.

1148.   Eric Eyre, *Delegate controls $8 million in education accounts*, Charleston Gazette, Mar. 28, 2005, at A1.

1149.   Eric Eyre, *Michael dips into fund most*, Charleston Gazette, Mar. 27, 2005, at A1.

1150.   Fanny Seiler, *Manchin wants new doorway*, Charleston Gazette, Apr. 10, 2001, at A4.

1151.   Interview of Delegate Johnson by author, August 5, 2000, Barboursville Veterans Home, Barboursville, West Virginia, following a town hall meeting held by United States Senator John McCain.

1152.   Brad McElhinny, *Court upholds Budget Digest in 3-1 ruling*, Charleston Daily Mail, Mar. 26, 2001, at A1; Phil Kabler, *Johnson doesn't plan to quit budget lawsuit*, Charleston Gazette, Feb. 13, 2001, at A1.

1153.   State ex rel. League of Women Voters of West Virginia v. Tomblin, 209 W.Va. 565, 578, 550 S.E.2d 355, 369 (2001).

1154.   Rist v. Underwood, 206 W.Va. 258, 260, 524 S.E.2d 179, 181 (1999).

1155.   Common Cause of West Virginia v. Tomblin, 186 W.Va. 537, 540, 413 S. E.2d 358, 401 (1991) (Miller, J., Dissenting).

1156.   Phil Kabler, *Chemical plants among winners in Budget Digest: Despite high court ruling, allocation of state funds differs little from past*, Charleston Gazette, June 28, 2001, at A1; Phil Kabler, *Budget Digest no record: Allocations slightly larger than last year's*, Charleston Gazette, June 29, 2001, at A1; Phil Kabler, *Legislators pick up Budget Digest draft*, Charleston Gazette, June 27, 2001, at A1.

1157.   Phil Kabler, *Budget Digest rules ignored*, Charleston Gazette, June 16, 2005, at A1; Scott Finn, *Court frees Budget Digest Funds*, Charleston Gazette, June 30, 2005, at A1; Toby Coleman, *State high court to hear case on legality of Budget Digest*, Charleston Daily Mail, July 1, 2004, at A1; Associated Press, *Lawmakers challenge Budget Digest freeze*, Charleston Gazette, May 26, 2005, at A1; *see also* State ex. rel. Podelco v. Tomblin, et al., ___W.Va.___, ___S.E.2d.___ (2005) (The case was sent from the State Supreme Court to a lower court to hold hearings and make factual findings to then be sent back to the State Supreme Court.).

1158.   Editorial, *Slush fund, Buying voter gratitude*, Charleston Gazette, Aug. 3, 2004, at A4.

1159.   *Id.*

1160.   Jim Wallace, *Insignia, a hot-button issue*, Charleston Daily Mail, Nov. 30, 2004, at A1; *see also* Jim Wallace, *Outgoing sheriff spending more than $2,000 from pistol fund for patches, hat shields*, Charleston Daily Mail, Nov. 20, 2004, at A1; Editorial, *Gun fund law at issue*, Charleston Daily Mail, Dec. 20, 2004, at A4.

1161.   Editorial, *Pistol fund, Here's to greater accountability under Sheriff Mike Rutherford*, Charleston Saturday Gazette-Mail, Dec. 18, 2004, at A4; Chris Shumaker, *Gun fund expenditures detailed*, Charleston Gazette, May 9, 2002, at A1, Editorial, *Smiles and Scowls*, Charleston Gazette, May 11, 2002, at A4; Jim Wallace, *Pistol permit funds used for tepees*, Charleston Daily Mail, Dec. 16, 2004, at A1.

1162.   Jim Wallace, *Tucker defends tepees*, Charleston Daily Mail, Dec. 17, 2004, at A1.

1163.   Jim Wallace, *Pistol permit funds used for tepees*, Charleston Daily Mail, Dec. 16, 2004, at A1.

1164.   Randy Coleman, Associated Press, *Workman wants to depose House leaders about Budget Digest*, Charleston Gazette, Dec. 12, 2000, at A1; Randy Coleman, Associated Press, *Court refuses Workman petition*, Charleston Gazette, Dec. 14, 2000, at A1; Phil Kabler, *'098' account's days numbered, Bill to eliminate infamous fund passes Senate, goes to governor*, Charleston Gazette, Feb. 24, 2001, at A1 (The Senate did not have an equivalent account.).

1165.   Fanny Seiler, *Workman asks for contingency fund papers*, Charleston Gazette, Dec. 22, 2000, at A1.

1166.   Randy Coleman, Associated Press, *Workman wants to depose House leaders about Budget Digest*, Charleston Gazette, Dec. 12, 2000, at A1.

1167.   Fanny Seiler, *Workman asks for contingency fund papers*, Charleston Gazette, Dec. 22, 2000, at A1.

1168.   Fanny Seiler, *'098' empty, brief moot, Underwood lawyer says*, Charleston Gazette, Jan. 18, 2001, at A2.

1169.   Fanny Seiler, *Workman asks for contingency fund papers*, Charleston Gazette, Dec. 22, 2000, at A1.

1170.   Todd C. Frankel, *Once again, the inaugural cash flows: Celebration costs expected to be half of 1997 event*, Charleston Daily Mail, Jan. 17, 2001, at A1; Associated Press,

*Inauguration costs now top $600,000*, Charleston Daily Mail, Jan. 7, 2005, at A1.

1171.     Staff Reports, *If a governor gives $440,000...*, Charleston Gazette, June 14, 2001, at A3; Todd C. Frankel, *Once again, the inaugural cash flows: Celebration costs expected to be half of 1997 event*, Charleston Daily Mail, Jan. 17, 2001, at A1.

1172.     Associated Press, *Inauguration costs now top $600,000, Private donors have given about $900,000, committee officials say*, Charleston Daily Mail, Jan. 7, 2005, at A1; Associated Press, Michelle Saxton, *Work on Governor's Mansion planned*, Charleston Daily Mail, June 24, 2005, at A1; Phil Kabler, *Commission approves $1 million to upgrade Governor's Mansion*, Charleston Gazette, June 24, 2005, at A1; Associated Press, *Mansion Under Repair*, Charleston Daily Mail, Feb. 22, 2005, at A1.

1173.     Eric Eyre, *Mansion for rent*, Charleston Gazette, June 30, 2005, at A1.

1174.     Associated Press, *Gov.-elect to host party for inaugural event's financial contributors*, Charleston Daily Mail, Jan. 14, 2005, at A1.

1175.     Staff Reports, *Mansion may benefit from inaugural gifts*, Charleston Daily Mail, Jan. 20, 2005, at A1.

1176.     Paul Owens, *Bring that idea up again*, Charleston Daily Mail, Mar. 27, 1998, at C1.

1177.     Editorial, *Handouts, Campaigning with tax money*, Charleston Gazette, Oct. 25, 2000, at A4.

1178.     Stacey Ruckle, *Many officials hand out trinkets, Tax money often pays for personalized items*, Charleston Daily Mail, Apr. 16, 1998, at A1 (Kiss admits that he does keep some West Virginia flags on hand in his Capitol office because that's a common request among civic groups.).

1179.     Editorial, *Trinkets: For the money they pay in taxes, people deserve more than key chains*, Charleston Daily Mail, Apr. 18, 1998, at A4.

1180.     Editorial, *No Fair: Gainer, Perdue and McGraw spent your money to promote themselves*, Charleston Daily Mail, Sept. 10, 2001, at A4.

1181.     Associated Press, *Power family, W.Va. voters tend to keep electing names they know*, Sunday Charleston Gazette-Mail, July 11, 2004, at A1. Capito's father, Arch Moore is the daughter of former three-term Governor who also served in Congress from 1957 to 1968. Alan Mollohan's father, Robert, retired in 1982 after eighteen years in Congress.

1182.     Fanny Seiler, *Clay Ridge Residents Wrangle Over Water*, Charleston Gazette, Apr. 22, 2002, at C1.

1183.     Editorial, *Smears: Campaign 'attack ads'*, Charleston Gazette, Oct. 9, 2002, at A4.

1184.     Editorial, *Dumbed down, $4 million worth of TV ads won't fix what's wrong with this state*, Charleston Daily Mail, May 4, 2004, at A4.

1185.     Lawrence Messina, *Campaign finance bill means changes here*, Charleston Gazette, Mar. 24, 2002, at A1 (Only three states–Montana, Virginia, and Louisiana–saw such contributions equal a larger share of their Gross State Product as West Virginia, whose GSP ranks 40th overall.).

1186.     Karin Fischer, *TV war has two fronts: Capito, GOP outspending Humphreys in recent weeks*, Charleston Daily Mail, Sep. 22, 2000, at A1; Lawrence Messina, *House race in dead heat: Expensive fight for 2nd Congressional District goes down to wire*, Charleston Gazette, Nov. 8, 2000, at A1 (Campaign finance filings indicate that Humphreys was worth at least $43 million, most of which he gained by handling thousands of asbestos claims by his law firm.); Phil Kabler, *2nd District race will be among most costly*, Charleston Gazette, Sept. 28, 2002, at A1.

1187.     Lawrence Messina, *House race in dead heat: Expensive fight for 2nd Congressional District goes down to wire*, Charleston Gazette, Nov. 8, 2000, at A1; Lawrence Messina, *GOP money, mud beat him, Humphreys says*, Charleston Gazette, Nov. 10, 2000, at C1; Lawrence Messina, *Capito is already running for 2002*, Charleston Gazette, May 23, 2001, at D6.

1188.     Editorial, *Politics: $20 million enterprise?*, Charleston Gazette, Aug. 19, 2001, at A4.

1189.     Lawrence Messina, *GOP money, mud beat him, Humphreys says*, Charleston Gazette, Nov. 10, 2000, at C1; Lawrence Messina, *Out-of-state funds drop into political coffers*, Sunday Gazette-Mail, June 25, 2001, at A1; Karin Fischer, *Race may have been different, campaign reform could have altered race for Congress*, Charleston Daily Mail, Mar. 21, 2001, at A1; Lawrence Messina, *House race in dead heat: Expensive fight for 2nd Congressional District goes down to wire*, Charleston Gazette, Nov. 8, 2000, at A1; Lawrence Messina, *2nd District ads heat up airwaves: Humphreys answers Capito attack within day*, Charleston Gazette, Oct. 4, 2000, at A8; Lawrence Messina, *Capito and Humphreys continue to attack: Back taxes? Patients' rights? Corruption? Here's the background on the candidates ads*, Charleston Gazette, Oct. 13, 2000, at A16.

1190.     Lawrence Messina, *2nd District ads heat up airwaves: Humphreys answers Capito attack within day*, Charleston Gazette, Oct. 4, 2000, at A8; Lawrence Messina, *Capito and Humphreys continue to attack: Back taxes? Patients' rights? Corruption? Here's the background on the candidates ads*, Charleston Gazette, Oct. 13, 2000, at A16; Lawrence Messina, *House race in dead heat: Expensive fight for 2nd Congressional District goes down to wire*, Charleston Gazette, Nov. 8, 2000, at A1.

1191.     Lawrence Messina, *Common Cause urges Capito to join reform push*, Charleston Gazette, June 1, 2001, at C1.

1192.     Editorial, *Campaign finance: What will Capito do?*, Charleston Gazette, June 5, 2001, at A4. On October 6, 2004, Majority Leader Delay received his third rebuke from the House of Delegates Ethics Committee. His third rebuke resulted from Delay's "asking federal aviation officials to track an airplane involved in a Texas political spat, and for conduct that suggested political donations might influence legislative action." Charles Babington, *Delay Draws Third Rebuke*, The Washington Post, October 7, 2004, at A1; *see also* Charles Babington and Juliet Eilperin *Democrat Leaders Call for Delay's Ouster*, The Washington Post, October 8, 2004, at A4; Editorial, *Laundering*, Charleston Gazette, July 16, 2004, at A4.

1193.     Editorial, *Campaign finance: What will Capito do?*, Charleston Gazette, June 5, 2001, at A4; (The article was referring to John McCain providing moral and political support by appearing on Capito's behalf in several West Virginia locations.).

1194.     *See* Lawrence Messina, *GOP money, mud beat him, Humphreys says*, Charleston Gazette, Nov. 10, 2000, at C1; Randy Coleman, Associated Press, *Will Arch hurt Shelley's chances? Some state Republicans think convicted ex-governor should stay in background*, Charleston Gazette, June 13, 2000, at C1(Her sister Lucy Moore Durbin pleaded guilty to drug dealing charges in a 1993 federal cocaine case.); Tom Miller, *Under the Dome: A look back*, Charleston Gazette, Dec. 26, 2000, at A5 (Moore was also the first Republican to hold a West Virginia Congressional seat in nearly twenty years.); Associated Press, *Capito Piling Up Cash for Next Race*, The Inter-Mountain (Elkins, WV), Aug. 2, 2001, at A6; Lawrence Messina, *Facing re-election, Capito challenged on soft-money issue*, Charleston Sunday Gazette-Mail, Feb. 10, 2002, at A1 (As of June 30, 2001, West Virginia's Third District Congressman Nick Joe Rahall had 1.5 million in his campaign fund while First District Congressman Mollohan listed $46,615 in his campaign fund, and United States Senator had $936,000 in his campaign fund.).

1195.     Lawrence Messina, *Facing re-election, Capito challenged on soft-money issue*, Charleston Sunday Gazette-Mail, Feb. 10, 2002, at A1.

1196.     Karin Fischer, *Capito leads race for cash*, Charleston Daily Mail, Feb. 1, 2002, at A1; Phil Kabler, *2nd District race will be among most costly*, Charleston Gazette, Sept. 28, 2002, at A1.

1197.     Tara Tuckwiller, *Cheney stumps in city*, Charleston Gazette, Apr. 13, 2002, at A1, Josh Hafenbrack, *Cheney gives Capito a boost*, Charleston Daily Mail, Apr. 13, 2002, at A1.

1198.     Phil Kabler, *Bush urges voters to re-elect Capito*, Charleston Gazette, Nov. 1, 2002, at A1; *see also* Fanny Seiler, *Bush to visit July 4, Ripley mayor says*, Charleston Gazette, June 28, 2002, at A1; Phil Kabler, *Bush visits city today*, Charleston Gazette, Oct. 31, 2002, at A1.

1199.     Lawrence Messina, *Questions arise about Workman loan*, Charleston Gazette, Apr. 20, 2000, at A1; Karin Fischer, *Workman says loan came from joint account: Candidate says $500,000 is eligible for campaign loan*, Charleston Daily Mail, Apr. 25, 2002, at A1.

1200.     Karin Fischer, *TV war has two fronts: Capito, GOP outspending Humphreys in recent weeks*, Charleston Daily Mail, Sep. 22, 2000, at A1.

1201.     Lawrence Messina, *Capito is already running for 2002*, Charleston Gazette, May 23, 2001, at D6.

1202.     Chris Stirewalt, *Capito race still her own: Democratic foe has till not entered 2nd District race*, Charleston Daily Mail, Sept. 16, 2003, at A1.

1203.     Brad McElhinny, *For once, Capito's bankroll fatter, At $1 million, war chest for congresswoman's re-election bid dwarfs that of D*, Charleston Daily Mail, Aug. 16, 2004, at A1 ("Her largest donors include Leadership political action committee with $10,000; KPMG Partners political action committee with $10,000; National Air Traffic Controllers political action committee with $10,000; United Parcel Service's political action committee with $10,000; Goldman Sach's political action committee with $9,000; Massachusetts Mutual Life's political action committee with $9,000; Bank One's political action committee with $7,000; and Dominion's political action committee with $7,000.").

1204.     Chris Stirewalt, *Capito race still her own: Democratic foe has till not entered 2nd District race*, Charleston Daily Mail, Sept. 16, 2003, at A1.

1205.   *Id.*

1206.   Tom Searls, *Perdue cancels run for governor*, Charleston Gazette, Sept. 5, 2003, at A1.

1207.   Deanna Wrenn, *Manchin supports campaign funding*, Charleston Daily Mail, Sept. 5, 2003, at A1.

1208.   Tom Searls, *Some defeated candidates end primary race in the red*, Charleston Gazette, June 14, 2004, at A1.

1209.   Tom Searls, *Manchin won although he was outspent*, Charleston Gazette, June 16, 2004, at A1.

1210.   Tom Searls, *Some defeated candidates end primary race in the red*, Charleston Gazette, June 14, 2004, at A1.

1211.   Chris Stirewalt, *Warner remains in limbo, Gubernatorial debate neither finishes off nor resurrects campaign*, Charleston Daily Mail, Oct. 7, 2004, at A1; Associated Press, *Monty Warner levels charges of vote buying in Lincoln County, Republican candidate for governor releases list of people he alleges have already bought votes*, Charleston Daily Mail, Oct. 13, 2004, at A1; Associated Press, *Monty Warner considers clean campaign plan*, Charleston Daily Mail, June 7, 2004, at A1.

1212.   Associated Press, *Monty Warner levels charges of vote buying in Lincoln County, Republican candidate for governor releases list of people he alleges have already bought votes*, Charleston Daily Mail, Oct. 13, 2004, at A1.

1213.   Phil Kabler, *Campaigns trade barbs over Warner allegations*, Oct. 8, 2004, at A1.

1214.   Phil Kabler, *Manchin, Warner spar over issues, Republican attacks longtime political career; Democrat outlines economic proposal*, Charleston Gazette, Oct. 7, 2004, at A1; Chris Stirewalt, *Warner remains in limbo, Gubernatorial debate neither finishes off nor resurrects campaign*, Charleston Daily Mail, Oct. 7, 2004, at A1. The author of this book attended this October 7, 2004, debate which was held at the State Cultural Center located beside the State Capitol in Charleston, West Virginia.

1215.   Chris Stratton, *Manchin lashes out at Sloan*, The Logan Banner, Jan. 14, 2003, at 1.

1216.   Chris Stratton, *Secretary of State sued*, The Logan Banner, Jan. 10, 2003, at 1.

1217.   *Id; see also* Associated Press, *Judge Tosses Ex-manchin Worker's Lawsuit*, Charleston Daily Mail, Jan. 16, 2004, at A1; Staff Reports, *Firing Suit Decided in Manchin's Favor*, Charleston Gazette, January 16, 2004, at A4; Staff Reports, *Ex-Election Fraud Official Says Firing Was Political*, Charleston Gazette, Jan. 8, 2003, at A1; Staff Reports, *Candidates Support Election Fraud Power Hechler, Ireland Both Want Secretary of State to Have Prosecutorial Powers*, Charleston Gazette, Aug. 4, 2004, at A1; Associated Press, *Governor's Race Warner Criticizes Manchin Republican Blasts Secretary of State's Record on Investigations of Possible Election Fraud*, Charleston Gazette, July 26, 2004, at A1.

1218.   Scott Finn, *GOP chief's family properties show tax irregularities, Warners pay under $6 on valuable site in Philippi, owe thousands on others*, Charleston Gazette, May 4, 2004, at A1.

1219.   Tom Searls, *Some defeated candidates end primary race in the red*, Charleston Gazette, June 14, 2004, at A1; Associated Press, *Warner launches TV campaign as Manchin sticks to jobs issue*, Charleston Daily Mail, Oct. 20, 2004, at A1.

1220.   Scott Finn, *GOP chief's family properties show tax irregularities, Warners pay under $6 on valuable site in Philippi, owe thousands on others*, Charleston Gazette, May 4, 2004, at A1.

1221.   Associated Press, *Manchin Disputes some Warner signs*, Charleston Gazette, Oct. 23, 2004, at A1; Scott Finn, *Kris Warner got e-mail about campaign yard signs*, Charleston Gazette, Dec. 21, 2004, at A1; Staff Reports, *Campaign Briefs*, Charleston Gazette, Oct. 22, 2004, at A2; Associated Press, *Warner ads to air today, candidate to pay for most of $100,000 spots*, Charleston Gazette, Oct. 20, 2004, at A1; Associated Press, *Republicans registered more new voters*, Charleston Gazette, Oct. 26, 2004, at A1.

1222.   Scott Finn, *GOP chief denies Manchin probe*, Charleston Gazette, Dec. 29, 2004, at A1; Scott Finn, *Warner campaign director to sue party chief*, Charleston Gazette, Dec. 28, 2004, at A1.

1223.   Scott Finn, *Warner investigation sought, GOP chairman sent check from brother's campaign to PAC*, Charleston Gazette, Jan. 7, 2005, at A1.

1224.   Scott Finn, *GOP chief tested in party republicans call confidence vote on Kris Warner*, Charleston Gazette, Dec. 20, 2004, at A1; Associated Press, *Warner Brothers are under siege six months ago, their futures seemed bright*, Charleston Daily Mail, Dec. 20, 2004, at A1.

1225.   Scott Finn, *Kris Warner got e-mail about campaign yard signs*, Charleston Gazette, Dec.

21, 2004, at A1; Scott Finn, *Former staffer files complaint against Monty Warner*, Charleston Gazette, Dec. 24, 2004, at A1.

1226.    Scott Finn, *Warner campaign director to sue party chief*, Charleston Gazette, Dec. 28, 2004, at A1; *see also* Scott Finn, *Kris Warner got e-mail about campaign yard signs*, Charleston Gazette, Dec. 21, 2004, at A1; Scott Finn, *Former staffer files complaint against Monty Warner*, Charleston Gazette, Dec. 24, 2004, at A1.

1227.    *Id*; Scott Finn, *Former staffer files complaint against Monty Warner*, Charleston Gazette, Dec. 24, 2004, at A1; Scott Finn, *Warner campaign director to sue party chief*, Charleston Gazette, Dec. 28, 2004, at A1; *see also* Don Surber, *How two guys tuned W.Va. upside down*, Charleston Daily Mail, June 23, 2005, at A5; Gary Abernathy, *Leadership took state GOP in the wrong direction*, Charleston Gazette, Feb. 17, 2005, at A5.

1228.    Associated Press, *Warner adds to debt report*, Charleston Gazette, Dec. 23, 2004, at A1 (Warner's initial campaign report did not include nearly $300,000 in unpaid bills. Warner updated the report following complaints from former Warner campaign staffers.); Scott Finn, *Former staffer files complaint against Monty Warner*, Charleston Gazette, Dec. 24, 2004, at A1 ("Pimm said he is owed $55,000 from the Warner campaign. He has struggled to pay for Christmas presents for his two children and make his child-support payments since the end of the campaign.").

1229.    Staff Reports, *former campaign aide sued Money Warner*, Charleston Gazette, Mar. 1, 2005, at A7.

1230.    Scott Finn, *GOP chief denies Manchin probe*, Charleston Gazette, Dec. 29, 2004, at A1.

1231.    Tom Searls, *Warner Remains Silent on Future*, Charleston Gazette, July 20, 2005, at A1; George Gannon, *Kasey Warner is no longer U.S. attorney*, Charleston Daily Mail, Aug. 1, 2005, at A1; Matthew Thompson, *Charnock calling jabs partisan*, Charleston Daily Mail, Aug. 3, 2005, at A1.

1232.    Associated Press, *Political Briefs from the 2000 campaign trail*, Charleston Gazette, May 3, 2000, at A1.

1233.    Associated Press, *Wise sets high bar in fundraising, Governor's coffers 5 times more than potential opponents*, Charleston Daily Mail, Apr. 21, 2003, at A1.

1234.    Tom Searls, *Perdue cancels run for governor*, Charleston Gazette, Sept. 5, 2003, at A1;Josh Hafenbrack, *Wise issues refund checks, Checks sent out to contributors to defunct campaign*, Charleston Daily Mail, Sept. 25, 2003, at A1.

1235.    Interview number 1 of Governor Bob Wise, December 7, 2004, in the Governor's Office; Interview number two of Bob Wise, December 15, 2004, in the Governor's Office.

1236.    John Heys, *Underwood talks of post-governor life; no plans to run*, Charleston Gazette, Oct. 8, 2003, at A1; Josh Hafenbrack, *Underwood compares terms, Ex-governor gives credit to wife at UC speaker series*, Charleston Daily Mail, Oct. 8, 2003, at A1.

1237.    Josh Hafenbrack, *Wise issues refund checks, Checks sent out to contributors to defunct campaign*, Charleston Daily Mail, Sept. 25, 2003, at A1.

1238.    Paul Owens, *Pritt Camp Says Manchin's Consultant A Felon*, Charleston Daily Mail, Feb. 21, 1996, at A1.

1239.    Editorial, *Potpourri*, Charleston Gazette, Feb. 26, 1996, at A4.

1240.    Paul Owens, *Pritt Camp Says Manchin's Consultant A Felon*, Charleston Daily Mail, Feb. 21, 1996, at A1.

1241.    Susan Williams, *Workman is co-counsel for Pritt in GOP ad suit*, Charleston Gazette, May 2, 2001, at A5; Associated Press, *Court reinstates Pritt's ad lawsuit: GOP accused of running false ads with actual malice*, Charleston Daily Mail, Dec. 13, 2001, at A2; Pritt v. The Republican National Committee, 1 F. Supp. 2d 590 (S.D. W.Va. 1998).

1242.    Pritt v. The Republican National Committee, 1 F. Supp. 2d 590 (S.D. W.Va. 1998); Susan Williams, *Workman is co-counsel for Pritt in GOP ad suit*, Charleston Gazette, May 2, 2001, at A5.

1243.    Martha Bryson Hodel, Associated Press, *Pritt wants time for ad suit*, Charleston Gazette, Sept. 10, 2003, at A1; Associated Press, *Pritt can seek testimony in lawsuit, justices say*, Charleston Daily Mail, Oct. 11, 2003, at A1.

1244.    Editorial, *Smears: Campaign 'attack ads'*, Charleston Gazette, Oct. 9, 2002, at A4.

1245.    Editorial, *Smear: Campaign hatchet job*, Charleston Gazette, Oct. 9, 2002, at A4; *see also* Susan Williams, *Workman is co-counsel for Pritt in GOP ad suit*, Charleston Gazette, May 2, 2001, at A5; Associated Press, *Court reinstates Pritt's ad lawsuit: GOP accused of running false ads with actual malice*, Charleston Daily Mail, Dec. 13, 2001, at A2; Associated Press, *Pritt can seek testimony in lawsuit, justices say*, Charleston Daily Mail, Oct. 11, 2003, at A1.

1246.      Paul Owens, *Underwood Fires Back With Anti-Crime Ad: Miffed Over Pritt Claim, GOP Hopeful Launches Counter Ad*, Charleston Daily Mail, Nov. 4, 1996, at A12. Pritt explained she was not calling for the legalization of marijuana. She insists she merely said West Virginia could grow marijuana for sale if the federal government were to legalize it for medicinal uses. Pritt also said she voted against a bill that would have banned the sale or advertisement of drug paraphernalia, because it was overly broad and probably unconstitutional. Pritt's campaign consultant called the bill "fatally flawed." Pritt states she voted against a bill that reduced workers' compensation benefits for hearing loss saying supporters of the bill said the benefits were too liberal. The bill also happened to include a provision that denied workers' compensation benefits to State prisoners. Pritt campaign consultant, Mike Plante, said the provision was added by supporters of the bill to discourage opponents from voting against it.

1247.      State ex rel. Pritt v. Vickers, 214 W.Va. 221, 588 S.E.2d 210 (2003); Pritt v. Republican Nat. Committee, 210 W.Va. 446, 557 S.E.2d 853 (2001); Associated Press, *Pritt can seek testimony in lawsuit, justices say*, Charleston Daily Mail, Oct. 11, 2003, at A1.

1248.      Susan Williams, *GOP ads hurtful, untrue, Pritt says, Former candidate testifies at trial*, Charleston Gazette, Mar. 08, 2006, at A1; *see also* Susan Williams, *Pritt libel case begins 8 years later*, Charleston Saturday Gazette-Mail, Mar. 4, 2006, at A1; Susan Williams, *Pritt jury goes back to work Monday*, Charleston Saturday Gazette-Mail, Mar. 11, 2006, at A1; Susan Williams, *Pritt libel case set for jury today*, Charleston Gazette, Mar. 10, 2006, at A1.

1249.      Matthew Hill, *Former governor testifies in Pritt suit*, The Register-Herald, Mar. 7, 2006, at A1.

1250.      Susan Leffler, *Cash flow in politics targeted, Reformers try to persuade candidates to reduce spending*, Charleston Sunday Gazette-Mail, Aug. 30, 1992, at B1.

1251.      Associated Press, *Primary race for governor tops spending record*, Charleston Gazette, May 10, 2004, at A1.

1252.      Lloyd Grove, *Election case study in TV politics*, Charleston Gazette, May 13, 1988, at A1.

1253.      Grimes, *supra* note 560, at 111 (Moore received 423,817 votes while Rockefeller received 350,462.).

1254.      Paul J. Nyden, *Legislative candidates given $6 million, research shows*, Charleston Sunday Gazette-Mail, Oct. 5, 2003, at A1; Associated Press, *Nearly $6 million raised for races*, Charleston Daily Mail, Jan. 2, 2003, at A1.

1255.      Editorial, *Cash, Political bonanza*, Charleston Gazette, Dec. 19, 2002, at A4.

1256.      Tom Searls, *Former Putnam senator indicted*, Charleston Gazette, Jan. 11, 2006, at A1; Associated Press, *Ex-State senator, husband face federal trials on April 4*, Charleston Daily Mail, Jan. 27, 2006, at A1.

1257.      Associated Press, *Nearly $6 million raised for races*, Charleston Daily Mail, Jan. 2, 2003, at A1.

1258.      Phil Kabler, *Bitter fight in Mingo*, Charleston Gazette, May 13, 2002, at A1.

1259.      Toby Coleman, *Ex-coroner pleads guilty in tax scheme*, Charleston Daily Mail, Nov. 4, 2003, at A1.

1260.      Fanny Seiler, *Airport contract criticized*, Charleston Gazette, June 19, 2000, at C1.

1261.      Associated Press, *Nearly $6 million raised for races*, Charleston Daily Mail, Jan. 2, 2003, at A1.

1262.      Fanny Seiler, *Campaign cost high, Foster says*, Charleston Gazette, May 21, 2002, at C1.

1263.      Kris Wise, *Races more costly, Campaign finance reports indicate increased spending*, Charleston Daily Mail, June 23, 2004, at A1.

1264.      Josh Hafenbrack, *Jones spent $188,776 on campaign*, Charleston Daily Mail, June 19, 2003, at A1.

1265.      Moffat, *supra* note 18, at 267; Hechler had previously served in the United States House of Representatives in West Virginia from 1959 to 1977. While Hechler served in many different occupations including being an instructor at Columbia University and an assistant professor at Princeton University, he also served as research director and special assistant to President Harry S. Truman from 1947 to 1953. *See also* Fanny Seiler, *Hechler plans to teach two classes at W.Va. State*, Charleston Gazette, Oct. 12, 2000, at A9.

1266.      *Id.* at 268.

1267.      Tom Searls, *Manchin won although he was outspent*, Charleston Gazette, June 16, 2004, at A1.

1268.      Phil Kabler, *Final candidate disclosures in McGraw, Hechler each surpass $1 million in* *spending*, Charleston Gazette, Oct. 26, 2004, at A1; Associated Press, *Secretary of State candidates spar over spending*, Charleston Daily Mail, Sept. 23, 2004, at A1.

1269.    Editorial, *Secretary of State Elections Officer, For Republican Betty Ireland, the focus will be on doing the job,* Charleston Daily Mail, Oct. 21, 2004, at A4.

1270.    Phil Kabler, *Ireland priorities: Updating voting machines, anti-fraud*, Charleston Gazette, Oct. 12, 2004, at A1.

1271.    Associated Press, *Secretary of State candidates spar over spending*, Charleston Daily Mail, Sept. 23, 2004, at A1. West Virginia Code § 3-1B-5, in part, provides:

> I PERSONALLY SUPPORT a limit on campaign expenditures that when reasonable, sufficient and fairly applied, does not limit or restrict the expression of ideas of the candidate or others on behalf of the candidate, but instead challenges individuals to engage in open dialogue on the issues rather than merely to purchase the excessive repetition of images and slogans.

> ACCORDINGLY, IF I AM A CANDIDATE for one of the offices listed below, I will, in conjunction with the committee or committees organized on my behalf, adhere to the following limitations on campaign spending specified for the office I seek:

The prescribed limitations for the Primary and General elections include $1 million for Governor; $150,000 for Attorney General, Secretary of State, State Auditor, State Treasurer, Commissioner of Agriculture, and Supreme Court of Appeals; a $50,000 limit for Circuit Judges and State Senate candidates; and a $25,000 limit for House of Delegates candidates.

1272.    Associated Press, *Ken Hechler, Betty Ireland debate the role of secretary of state*, Charleston Daily Mail, Oct. 15, 2004, at A1.

1273.    *See* Editorial, *Spending: Why Break the Limit*, Charleston Gazette, Nov. 2, 1996, at A4.

1274.    Associated Press, *Candidates ignore campaign code*, Charleston Daily Mail, May 3, 2004, at A1. The author of this book also obtained a copy of Hechler's signed Code of Fair Campaign Practices form from the West Virginia Secretary of State's Office on October 26, 2004.

1275.    Associated Press, *Secretary of State candidates spar over spending*, Charleston Daily Mail, Sept. 23, 2004, at A1.

1276.    Ken Hechler, *Letter to the Editor, Hechler ads serve purpose*, Charleston Gazette, Apr. 14, 2004, at A5.

1277.    Associated Press, *Secretary of state candidates spar over spending*, Charleston Daily Mail, Sept. 23, 2004, at A1; Associated Press, *Ken Hechler, Betty Ireland debate the role of secretary of state*, Charleston Daily Mail, Oct. 15, 2004, at A1.

1278.    Moffat, *supra* note 18, at 312-313.

1279.    West Virginia Code § 3-1-37 (2004); *see also, generally*, Chafin, *supra* note 43.

1280.    Jennifer Bundy, Associated Press, *Logan Politics Hits the Light in Boss' Book*, Sunday Gazette-Mail, July 17, 1994, at A1.

1281.    Interview of United States Senator Robert C. Byrd by author, Oct. 30, 2004 (Charleston House Holiday Inn, Charleston, WV).

1282.    Fanny Seiler, *Underwood slow to pay debts, businesses say*, Charleston Gazette, July 8, 2001, at C3; Fanny Seiler, *Bush's picks for U.S. attorney ruffle feathers*, Charleston Gazette, July 1, 2001, at C3.

1283.    Associated Press, *Nearly $6 million raised for races*, Charleston Daily Mail, Jan. 2, 2003, at A1. As of January 2009, the Governor's salary will be $150,000.

1284.    Paul Nyden, *Debate over Manchin's award, trinket expenditures continues*, Sunday Gazette-Mail, Aug. 7, 1988, at A7.

1285.    Editorial, *Ethics Law needs more teeth*, Charleston Gazette, July 27, 2000, at A4; *see also* West Virginia Ethics Commission's Internet website (<http://www.wvethicscommission.org>). "The WV Ethics Commission was created in 1989 to implement and enforce a code of ethical conduct enacted by the Legislature for public servants. (WV Code 6B-1-1, *et seq.*)."

1286.    Bill McAllister, *Ex-Gov. Moore Agrees to Plead Guilty; W. Virginian Charged With Fraud, Extortion*, The Washington Post, Apr. 13, 1990, at A1.

1287.    Dan Radmacher, *Ethics Commission Return Investigatory Powers*, Charleston Gazette, Dec. 6, 1994, at A4.

1288.    Scott Finn, *Cycle of Influence: Ethics law falling short of promise to clean up government, critics say*, Charleston Gazette, July 23, 2000, at A1.

1289.    Editorial, *Mezzatesta perfects the legislator-lobbyist, Not having ethics pays very well today and carries a pension*, Charleston Daily Mail, July 16, 2004, at A4.

1290.    Josh Hafenbrack, *Ethics panel assailed, Some say ethics commission is ineffective, should dissolve*, Charleston Daily Mail, June 18, 2004, at A4; Chris Stirewalt, *Ethics panel formed in tough times, Committee lost some power over the years*, Charleston Daily Mail, July 20, 2004, at A1; Associated Press, *State Ethics Commission target of criticism*, Charleston Daily Mail, Dec. 13, 2001, at C6; Scott Finn, *Manchin won't bring progress, Warner says in debate*, Charleston Gazette, Oct. 25, 2004, at A1.

1291.    Dan Radmacher, *Ethics Commission Return Investigatory Powers*, Charleston Gazette, Dec. 6, 1994, at A4.

1292.    Staff Reports, *Legislative Survey*, Charleston Sunday Gazette-Mail, Jan. 8, 1995, at C1 (The telephone survey was conducted by the *Sunday-Gazette Mail* over the course of eight days in December and January. Eighty-five legislators participated.).

1293.    Therese Smith Cox, *Ethics changes may face hurdles*, Charleston Gazette, Jan. 18, 2005, at A1.

1294.    Associated Press, *Manchin signs his first ethics bill*, Charleston Daily Mail, Feb. 11, 2005, at A1; *see also* Phil Kabler, *Legislator clarifies 'gag order' in bill*, Charleston Gazette, Feb. 2, 2005, at A1; Phil Kabler, *House, Senate approve tougher ethics bill*, Jan. 30, 2005, at A1; Associated Press, *Senate passes its own version of ethics legislation*, Charleston Daily Mail, Jan. 27, 2005, at A1; Phil Kabler, *Ethics bill to be signed now, fixed later*, Charleston Gazette, Feb. 4, 2005, at A1; Associated Press, *Manchin pledges to target ethics bill's 'gag order,'* Charleston Daily Mail, Feb. 4, 2005, at A1.

1295.    U.S. Const. First Amendment; *see also* West Virginia Const. Art. III, § 7.

1296.    Hoppy Kercheval, *Hoppy's Commentary for Tuesday*, MetroNews, Feb. 1, 2005 (www.metronews.com); Scott Finn, *Ethics bills gag order illegal, law professor says*, Charleston Gazette, Feb. 1, 2005, at A1.

1297.    Phil Kabler, *Statehouse Beat*, Charleston Gazette, Oct. 11, 2004, at A4.

1298.    Phil Kabler, *Ethics Budget Request Chopped*, Charleston Gazette, Apr. 19, 2005, at A1; Tom Searls, *Ethics Amendment die in committee*, Charleston Gazette, Mar. 12, 2005, at A1; Phil Kabler, *Employers, lobbyists focus in ethics bill*, Charleston Gazette, May 24, 2005, at A1.

1299.    Chris Stirewalt, *Ethics panel formed in tough times, Committee lost some power over the years*, Charleston Daily Mail, July 20, 2004, at A1; Associated Press, *State Ethics Commission target of criticism*, Charleston Daily Mail, Dec. 13, 2001, at C6; Editorial, *Smiles and Scowls*, Charleston Gazette, Dec. 15, 2001, at A4; Scott Finn, *Ethics panel not catching violators*, Charleston Gazette, Dec. 13, 2001, at C1.

1300.    Phil Kabler, *10 legislative receptions cost more than $100,000*, Charleston Gazette, Mar. 2, 2004, at A1; Associated Press, *Lobbyists spending thousands on legislative parties*, Charleston Daily Mail, Mar. 2, 2004, at A1.

1301.    Therese Smith Cox, *Wining, dining at issue*, Charleston Daily Mail, Jan. 25, 2005, at A1; *see also* Phil Kabler, *Amendment to ethics bill targets free food, drink, Lawmakers would be barred from such lobbyist receptions*, Charleston Gazette, Jan. 26, 2005, at A1; Therese Smith Cox, *Ethics changes may face hurdles*, Charleston Gazette, Jan. 18, 2005, at A1.

1302.    Associated Press, *Interim session finds lawmakers working under scrutiny*, Charleston Daily Mail, Aug. 23, 2004, at A1.

1303.    Phil Kabler, *Statehouse Beat, Interims sponsor system defended*, Charleston Gazette, Aug. 30, 2004, at A4.

1304.    *Id.*

1305.    Editorial, *Ethics panel, By giving Mezzatesta a pass, the panel shows its worthlessness*, Charleston Daily Mail, June 21, 2004, at A4.

1306.    Josh Hafenbrack, *Ethics panel assailed, Some say ethics commission is ineffective, should dissolve*, Charleston Daily Mail, June 18, 2004, at A4.

1307.    Editorial, *Ethics panel, By giving Mezzatesta a pass, the panel shows its worthlessness*, Charleston Daily Mail, June 21, 2004, at A4.

1308.    Josh Hafenbrack, *Ethics panel assailed, Some say ethics commission is ineffective, should dissolve*, Charleston Daily Mail, June 18, 2004, at A4.

1309.    *Id.*

1310.    *Id*; "The Commission consists of twelve members appointed to five year terms by the Governor with the advice and consent of the Senate. The commission meets monthly, generally on the first Thursday, and is supported by a small full time staff (an executive director, part-time legal counsel, and administrative secretary). Investigators are hired on a contractual basis as needed." *See* Ethics Commission's Internet website (<http://www.wvethicscommission.org/geninfo.htm>).

1311.  Phil Kabler, *Review sought on ethics of MU job*, Charleston Gazette, Sept. 23, 2004, at A1.

1312.  *Id*; *see also* Phil Kabler, *Statehouse beat, Is being legislator a plus on job front?*, Charleston Gazette, Sept. 6, 2004, at A4.

1313.  Editorial, *Mess-atesta, More absurdity*, Charleston Gazette, June 5, 2004, at A4; *see also* Josh Hafenbrack, *Ethics panel assailed, Some say ethics commission is ineffective, should dissolve*, Charleston Daily Mail, June 18, 2004, at A4; Chris Stirewalt, *Ethics panel formed in tough times, Committee lost some power over the years*, Charleston Daily Mail, July 20, 2004, at A1.

1314.  Phil Kabler, *Ethics revision to include penalties for lying*, Charleston Gazette, Sept. 3, 2004, at A1.

1315.  Editorial, *Private gain? Home cooking in Hardy*, Charleston Gazette, Sept. 16, 2003, at A4.

1316.  Scott Finn, *Lawmaker resigns from Summit Financial Group Board*, Charleston Gazette, Mar. 8, 2006, at A1.

1317.  Editorial, *Private gain? Home cooking in Hardy*, Charleston Gazette, Sept. 16, 2003, at A4.

1318.  Editorial, *Outrage, Harold Michael U.*, Charleston Gazette, Sept. 16, 2003, at A4. My father, Allen H. Loughry Sr., was appointed in 2001 by Governor Bob Wise to serve a four-year term on the Board of Governors of the Eastern West Virginia Community and Technical College. After serving part of his term on the Board, Loughry asked not to be reappointed to a subsequent term.

1319.  Associated Press, *Interim session finds lawmakers working under scrutiny*, Charleston Daily Mail, Aug. 23, 2004, at A1; Associated Press, *Legislators urged to look at ethics, Steenstra calls for changes to commission that investigates charges*, Charleston Daily Mail, Aug. 20, 2004, at A1.

1320.  Associated Press, *Ethics panel says Sen. Mike Ross must answer for golf course vote*, Charleston Daily Mail, Aug. 19, 2004, at A1; *see also* Phil Kabler, *Ethics panel to investigate senator over Pete Dye vote*, Charleston Gazette, Aug. 19, 2004, at A4; Phil Kabler, *Statehouse beat, Mezzatesta could have put positive spin on case*, Charleston Gazette, Aug. 23, 2004, at A4; Scott Finn, *Senator's golf vote questioned, State to fund tournament where Ross owns land*, Charleston Gazette, Apr. 2, 2004, at A1.

1321.  *Id.*

1322.  Phil Kabler, *Ethics panel to investigate senator over Pete Dye vote*, Charleston Gazette, Aug. 19, 2004, at A4; *see also* Scott Finn, *Senator's golf vote questioned, State to fund tournament where Ross owns land*, Charleston Gazette, Apr. 2, 2004, at A1.

1323.  Scott Finn, *Senator denies benefiting from pro golf tournament, Ross voted funds for golf club owned by business associates*, Charleston Gazette, Dec. 15, 2004, at A1.

1324.  Scott Finn, *Senator's golf vote questioned, State to fund tournament where Ross owns land*, Charleston Gazette, Apr. 2, 2004, at A1.

1325.  Associated Press, *Ethics panel says Sen. Mike Ross must answer for golf course vote*, Charleston Daily Mail, Aug. 19, 2004, at A1.

1326.  Phil Kabler, *Ethics panel to investigate senator over Pete Dye vote*, Charleston Gazette, Aug. 19, 2004, at A4; Associated Press, *Ethics panel says Sen. Mike Ross must answer for golf course vote*, Charleston Daily Mail, Aug. 19, 2004, at A1.

1327.  Associated Press, *Legislators urged to look at ethics, Steenstra calls for changes to commission that investigates charges*, Charleston Daily Mail, Aug. 20, 2004, at A1.

1328.  Scott Finn, *Senator's golf vote questioned, State to fund tournament where Ross owns land*, Charleston Gazette, Apr. 2, 2004, at A1; Editorial, *good ol' boys, Golf perks look shabby*, Charleston Gazette, May 4, 2004, at A4.

1329.  Associated Press, *Legislators urged to look at ethics, Steenstra calls for changes to commission that investigates charges*, Charleston Daily Mail, Aug. 20, 2004, at A1.

1330.  Scott Finn, *Senator denies benefiting from pro golf tournament, Ross voted funds for golf club owned by business associates*, Charleston Gazette, Dec. 15, 2004, at A1.

1331.  Phil Kabler: *Statehouse beat, Golf tourney grants detailed*, Charleston Gazette, Dec. 13, 2004, at A1.

1332.  Associated Press, *Ethics Complaint over Senator's Golf vote dismissed*, Charleston Gazette, Apr. 8, 2005, at A1; Scott Finn, *Ross didn't benefit from vote, hearing examiner says,* Charleston Gazette, Mar. 16, 2005, at A1; Editorial, *Potpourri,* Charleston Gazette, Mar. 21, 2005, at A4; Associated Press, *Ethics case dropped against ex-official over golf course ties,* Charleston Daily Mail, Apr. 8, 2005, at A1.

1333.    Eric Eyre, *Senator wrongly reports mileage, Facemyer overstated distance from home,* Charleston Gazette, Apr. 14, 2005, at A1; Lawrence Messina, Associated Press, *Lawmakers back peer on expense reporting,* Charleston Daily Mail, Apr. 15, 2005, at A1.

1334.    Lawrence Messina, Associated Press, *Lawmakers back peer on expense reporting,* Charleston Daily Mail, Apr. 15, 2005, at A1; *see also* Eric Eyre, *Senator not billing for expenses during probe,* Charleston Gazette, June 26, 2005, at A1.

1335.    Eric Eyre, *Ethics Commission Dismisses Complaint Against Facemyer,* Charleston Gazette, July 18, 2005, at A1.

1336.    Associated Press, *Many state lawmakers face potential conflicts, report says,* Charleston Daily Mail, Sept. 24, 2004, at A1; Editorial, *Ethics Law needs more teeth,* Charleston Gazette, July 27, 2000, at A4.

1337.    *Id*; Editorial, *Ethics Law needs more teeth,* Charleston Gazette, July 27, 2000, at A4; Scott Finn, *Legislators' conflicts can cut both ways,* Charleston Gazette, Mar. 28, 2000, at A1.

1338.    Editorial, *Ethics: Law needs more teeth,* Charleston Gazette, July 27, 2000, at A4.

1339.    Scott Finn, *Cycle of Influence: Ethics law falling short of promise to clean up government, critics say,* Charleston Gazette, July 23, 2000, at A1.

1340.    Former House Speaker Lewis McManus died December 18, 2002. Following his death, former fellow-Delegate and current State Senate Clerk, Darrell Holmes, said, "Lew was one of the most credible and honest people I have ever met." United States Senator Jay Rockefeller, who served one term in the House with McManus, said he was "a giant in the political realm [and] a true statesman and a gentleman." United States Senator Robert C. Byrd said, "Lew and I both grew up in coal towns. We both represented Raleigh County in the West Virginia House of Delegates. And we both shared an unabated love for the Mountain State." Associated Press, *Former House Speaker Lewis McManus Dies,* Inter-Mountain (Elkins, WV), Dec. 19, 2002, at A5.

1341.    Scott Finn, *Cycle of Influence: Ethics law falling short of promise to clean up government, critics say,* Charleston Gazette, July 23, 2000, at A1.

1342.    Jim Wallace, *State ethics commission reverses itself on interpretation,* Charleston Daily Mail, May 3, 2002, at A1.

1343.    Scott Finn, *Peach case fuzzy; ethics panel to sort it out,* Charleston Gazette, Mar. 21, 2001, at A1; *see also* Shelby Young, *It was a Republican night in Putnam County, Peachie' Arthur the lone Democratic winner at county level,* Charleston Daily Mail, Nov. 3, 2004, at A1; Evadna Bartlett, *Putnam assessor fined for using peach logo,* Charleston Daily Mail, Apr. 7, 2001, at A2.

1344.    Michael W. Carey, Larry R. Ellis, Joseph F. Savage, Jr., *Federal Prosecution of State and Local Public Officials: The Obstacles To Punishing Breaches of the Public Turst And A Proposal For Reform, Part One,* 94 W.Va. L. Rev. 301, 304-309 (1992). Each State has a separate Constitution along with statutory laws whereby it is determined what responsibilities and powers are to be bestowed upon each of their constitutional offices. Many state's attorneys general are given criminal prosecutorial powers. West Virginia, however, is not one of those states.

1345.    Associated Press, *State seeks rehearing in Moore's sentencing,* Times-West Virginian (Fairmont, WV), July 14, 1990, at A1.

1346.    Moffat, *supra* note 18, at 310.

1347.    Dan Radmacher, *Ballistic Feat McGraw Shot Self In Foot,* Charleston Gazette, May 27, 1994, at A4.

1348.    Lawrence Messina, *Ex-prosecutor settles seduction suit,* Charleston Gazette, May 31, 2001, at A11.

1349.    David M. Herszenhorn, *Ex-U.S. Attorney Admits Investor Fraud,* New York Times, Dec. 17, 1998, at C4.

1350.    In re an Investigation of the W Va State Police Crime Lab, Serology Div., 190 W.Va. 392, 397, 438 S.E.2d 501, 506 (1993); *see also* In the Matter of Investigation of WV State Police Crime Lab, 191 W.Va. 224, 445 S.E.2d 165 (1994).

1351.    190 W.Va. 392, 399, 411, 438 S.E.2d 501, 508, 520; *see also* Lawrence I. Shulruff, *Lab Evidence Questioned,* 80 A.B.A. J. 16 (July 1994); *Corrupt Forensic Scientist Contaminates Hundreds of Convictions in West Virginia and Texas,* 18 The Champion 56 (June 1994); Associated Press, *Zain trial nears end as jury begins deliberations,* Charleston Gazette, Sept. 18, 2001, at C1.

1352.    Editorial, *Crime lab: More problems*, Charleston Gazette, Mar. 18, 2002, at A4.

1353.    Associated Press, *Zain trial nears end as jury begins deliberations*, Charleston Gazette, Sept. 18, 2001, at C1; Richard Grimes, *Crime labs should be independent: Scientific evidence should be examined by a neutral party*, Charleston Daily Mail, June 10, 1997, at A4.

1354.    Associated Press, *Conviction based on Zain testimony is overturned*, Charleston Daily Mail, Sept. 20 2003, at A1.

1355.    Lawrence Messina, *Lawyer sought to 'bury this thing' trooper testified*, Charleston Gazette, Feb. 20, 2002, at A1; Fanny Seiler, *Delegate Asks Ashcroft to investigate Steptoe*, Charleston Gazette, Mar. 3, 2002, at C1; Martha Bryson Hodel, Associated Press, *Trooper: Police Knew Zain Falsified Evidence*, Inter-Mountain (Elkins, WV), Sept. 7, 2001, at A1.

1356.    Lawrence Messina, *McGraw sues Steptoe & Johnson over Zain case*, Charleston Gazette, Feb. 20, 2002, at A1.

1357.    Rachelle Bott, *Zain enhanced lab test results, co-worker says*, Charleston Gazette, Sept. 7, 2001, at A1. Editorial, *Fallout: Zain mess worsens*, Charleston Gazette, Feb. 22, 2002, at A4.

1358.    Editorial, *Fallout: Zain mess worsens*, Charleston Gazette, Feb. 22, 2002, at A4.

1359.    *Id*; Bob Schwarz, *Palumbo gala to benefit muscular dystrophy research*, Sunday Charleston Gazette-Mail, Oct. 7, 2001, at B2; Lawrence Messina, *Firm accused in Zain case points to Palumbo*, Charleston Gazette, Feb. 8, 2002, at A1; *see also* Bob Schwartz, *Mario, Louis Palumbo die just a day apart*, Charleston Gazette, July 5, 2004, at A1.

1360.    Editorial, *Fallout: Zain mess worsens*, Charleston Gazette, Feb. 22, 2002, at A4.

1361.    Editorial, *Buckalew Zain Role Not Forgotten*, Charleston Gazette, May 23, 2000, at A4; Associated Press, *Buckalew Claimed Immunity, Senator Refused to Testify Again in Fred Zain Case*, Charleston Gazette, Oct. 6, 1998, at A1; Editorial, *Immunity, Buckalew Hid*, Charleston Gazette, Oct. 7, 1998, at A4; Editorial, *Zain Zoo, Will there be no Justice*, Charleston Gazette, Dec. 16, 1998, at A4.

1362.    Lawrence Messina, *Zain has cancer: Retrial suspended*, Charleston Gazette, Mar. 23, 2002, at A1; Leslie Baldacci, *Justice's scales a delicate balance*, Chicago Sun-Times, May 21, 1999, at A47; Staff Reports, *Discredited chemist Fred Zain, 52, dies*, Charleston Gazette, Dec. 4, 2002, at A1 (Attorneys for the Prosecution, Jim Lees and Steve Jury, pursued a strategy "that Zain defrauded the State by accepting pay, raises and promotions in exchange for his shoddy services."); Rachelle Bott, *Jurors divided on Zain*, Charleston Gazette, Sept. 19, 2001, at A1.

1363.    Editorial, *Crime lab: More problems*, Charleston Gazette, Mar. 18, 2002, at A4; Lawrence Messina, *Another shake-up at State Police lab*, Charleston Gazette, May 25, 2002, at A1; Sam Tranum, *State lab in trouble again: Two workers put on leave after discrepancy found*, Charleston Daily Mail, Mar. 12, 2002, at A1; Paul J. Nyden, *Crime lab back in court*, Sunday Charleston Gazette-Mail, Apr. 2, 2006, at A1.

1364.    Richard Grimes, *Crime labs should be independent: Scientific evidence should be examined by a neutral party*, Charleston Daily Mail, June 10, 1997, at A4.

1365.    Committee on Legal Ethics of West Virginia State Bar v. Roark, 181 W.Va. 260, 261, 262, 382 S.E.2d 313, 314, 315 (1989).

1366.    *Id*. at 265, 382 S.E.2d at 318.

1367.    Staff Reports, *Sheriff says police chief leaked report*, Charleston Daily Mail, Nov. 18, 1987, at A1; Staff Reports, *Mike Roark lived life of contradiction*, Charleston Gazette, Nov. 22, 1987, at A1; *see also* Greg Stone, *Jones not running from past*, Charleston Gazette, Nov. 14, 2002, at A1; Trina Kleist, *Sheriff Jones won't run for re-election*, Charleston Gazette, Jan. 22, 1988, at A1; Staff Reports, *Kanawha Sheriff Details Drug Use*, Charleston Gazette, Sept. 27, 1987, at A1; Fanny Seiler, *Person who leaked Jones file deserves medal*, Charleston Gazette, Oct. 4, 1987, at A1; Staff Reports, *Carey withdrew from friend's drug case*, Charleston Gazette, Sept. 29, 1987, at A1; Staff Reports, *Carey calls for help in probe of leak*, Charleston Daily Mail, Oct. 1, 1987, at A1.

1368.    Staff Reports, *What an education on the danger of drugs*, Charleston Daily Mail, Dec. 4, 1987, at A1.

1369.    Editorial, *Mingo: Trust the police?*, Charleston Gazette, Feb. 21, 2001, at A4.

1370.    Staff Reports, *Looking Back: A decade of crimes*, Charleston Daily Mail, Aug. 5, 1999 (Jerry Bradberry, former director of the State tax division was convicted of perjury and sentenced to one year probation, six months work release.).

1371.    Patty Vandergrift, *7 in Kermit plead guilty in drug ring*, Charleston Gazette, Oct. 15, 1986, at A1; Associated Press, *Police, Fire Chief charged in Kermit*, Charleston Gazette, May 31, 1986, at A1; Associated Press, *Kermit's ex-Fire Chief pleads innocent*, Charleston Gazette, July 4, 1986, at A1; Associated Press, *Kermit pair convicted on drug, tax charges*,

Charleston Gazette, June 18, 1987, at A1; Associated Press, *Trial*, Charleston Gazette, June 14, 1987, at A1.

1372.　Patricia Nealon, *Prosecutor ends a job of conviction*, Boston Globe, Nov. 23, 1996, at B1.

1373.　Sylvan Barnet, *The Complete Signet Classic Shakespeare: The Tragedy of Julius Caesar* 825 (Harcourt Brace Jovanovich, Inc.: San Diego, CA).

1374.　Lawrence Messina, Associated Press, *Delegate named a co-conspirator*, Charleston Daily Mail, Oct. 20, 2005, at A1.

1375.　Buckley v. Valeo, 424 U.S. 1 (1976).

1376.　Landell v. Sorrell, 382 F.3d 91 (2004); Landell v. Sorrell, 406 F.3d 159 (2nd Cir. Vt.).

1377.　West Virginia Code § 3-8-11 (c) currently provides that: "Any person who shall, knowingly, make or publish, or cause to be made or published, any false statement in regard to any candidate . . . is guilty of a misdemeanor." This change would significantly strengthen the penalties for such a violation.

1378.　L.T. Anderson, *Without Embarrassment: A Lobbyist's Handouts*, Charleston Daily Mail, May 4, 1990, at A4; Barry Bearak, *West Virginia Caught in Tide of Political Scandals*, Charleston Daily Mail, July 9, 1990, at A1.

1379.　Cartoon, *Special Interests 2000*, Charleston Daily Mail, Aug. 29, 2000, at A4.

1380.　Lisa A. Stamm, *Chief Justice Richard Neely "Uniquely Unconventional,"* W.Va. Lawyer, January 8, 1995, at 16.

1381.　*See* Buckley v. Valeo, 424 U.S. 1, 66-68 (1976); Louis D. Brandeis, "What Publicity Can Do," *Other People's Money*, chapter 5, p. 92 (Washington, D.C., National Home Library Foundation 1933) (First published in Harper's Weekly, December 20, 1913.).

1382.　Editorial, *Bad idea, West Virginians should not be forced to subsidize politicians*, Charleston Daily Mail, Dec. 9, 2003, at A1.

1383.　Debate, *Maine aims to clean up system*, USA Today, May 2, 2000, at A15; *see also* ME ST T. 21-A §1121 (1995).

1384.　Interview of Boyd Marley by author, University of Charleston, Geary Student Union, 2nd Floor, Charleston, West Virginia, Feb. 2, 2003.

1385.　Phil Kabler, *Voter apathy: Senators try to boost turnout*, Charleston Gazette, Feb. 24, 2001, at A9.

1386.　Chafin, *supra* note 43, at xiii.

1387.　Adkins v. Miller, 187 W.Va. 774, 781, 421 S.E.2d 682, 689 (1992) (J. Neely Dissent).

1388　The State motto of West Virginia *Montani Semper Liberi* is included on the official State seal. *See* W.Va. Const. Art. II § 7 (1872).

1389　Chicago Tribune wires, *Sentencing, guilty plea latest in a county's corruption saga*, Chicago Tribune, Apr. 19, 1988, at A14.

1390　Leslie Baldacci, *Justice's scales a delicate balance*, Chicago Sun-Times, May 21, 1999, at A47.

1391　Barry Bearak, *Corruption in West Virginia: Scandals as Thick as Coal Dust*, Los Angeles Times, July 8, 1990, at A1.

1392　Michael Shannon Friedman, *Elusive Appalachia: Writer wrestles with what it means to be from here*, Charleston Gazette-Mail, Aug. 19, 2001, at F4.

1393　Editorial, *Bribery: World cleanup effort*, Charleston Gazette, Dec. 10, 1998, at A4.

1394　White, *surpra* note 3, at 97.

1395　Fleming, *supra* note 12, at 101.

1396　Harold L. Ickes, *The Secret Diary of Harold L. Ickes: The Inside Struggle* 71 (New York: Simon and Schuster, 1954).

1397　M. Charles Bakst, *Glib Dick Morris takes cheap shot at Rhode Island*, The Providence Journal-Bulletin (R.I.), Nov. 25, 1997, at B1.

1398　Paul Owens, *Caperton Tells 'Real Story' to N.Y. Paper*, Charleston Daily Mail, June 22, 1994, at A1.

1399　Xan Smiley, *Who killed the newsman who shamed Klan?*, The Sunday Telegraph (London, England), May 17, 1992, at A18.

1400　Peter Carlson, *The Magic and the Misery*, The Washington Post Sunday-Magazine, Nov. 22, 1992, at W9.

1401　Bill McAllister, *Ex-Gov. Moore Agrees to Plead Guilty; W. Virginian Charged With Fraud,*

*Extortion*, The Washington Post, Apr. 13, 1990, at A1; *see also* Jill Wilson, Associated Press, *W. Virginia indicts former governor*, The Phoenix Gazette, Apr. 13, 1990, at C2; Moreover, the *Phoenix Gazette* reported:

> Many West Virginia politicians have either become involved in corruption scandals or resigned recently. Since December 1988, a state attorney general, a state treasurer, two state Senate presidents, a Senate majority leader, a top aide to a Senate president, a House member and two lobbyists have lost their jobs.

*See also Ex-West Virginia Governor Admits Corruption Schemes*, New York Times, Apr. 13, 1990, Abstracts at 8; Bill McAllister, *Ex-Gov. Moore Agrees to Plead Guilty; W. Virginian Charged With Fraud, Extortion*, The Washington Post, Apr. 13, 1990, at A1.

1402 Joe Urschel, *Shock jock for high office? He'll fit right in*, USA Today, Mar. 24, 1994, at A12.

1403 Rick Steelhammer, *It's time to get to the root of the hall of fame issue*, Sunday Gazette-Mail, Feb. 4, 1996, at C1.

1404 Dorris Haddock, *Granny D: Walking Across America in my Ninetieth Year* (Villard 2001); Dorris Haddock, *Granny D: You're Never Too Old To Raise a Little Hell* (Villard 2003).

1405 Interview of Doris Haddock (Granny D) by author, at the Kanawha County Senior Center, 2428 Kanawha Boulevard, Charleston, West Virginia, December 14, 2001, at 2:00 p.m.

1406 *See* (<www.teachingamericanhistory.org>) (From the December 10, 1856, speech at a Republican Banquet in Chicago, Illinois.).

1407 Archer H. Shaw, *The Lincoln Encyclopedia* 64 (The Macmillian Company: New York 1950); (Abraham Lincoln Speech, given in Springfield, Dec. 20, 1839.)

1408 Winkler v. State School Bldg. Authority, 189 W.Va. 748, 767, 434 S.E.2d 420, 439 (1993) (J. Neely Concurrence).

# INDEX

# ABOUT THE AUTHOR

Dr. Allen H. Loughry II, holds four separate law degrees including an S.J.D (Doctor of Juridical Science) from The American University, Washington College of Law; an LL.M. (Master of Laws in Criminology and Criminal Justice) from the University of London; an LL.M. (Master of Laws in Law and Government) from The American University, Washington College of Law; and a JD from Capital University School of Law. In addition, he has studied law at the University of Oxford and holds a B.S. in Journalism from West Virginia University. He is currently a law clerk to Justice Elliott "Spike" Maynard of the West Virginia Supreme Court. He has served as a Senior Assistant Attorney General in the West Virginia Attorney General's Office, and has argued more than twenty cases before the West Virginia Supreme Court as well as argued or filed legal pleadings in the Supreme Court of the United States, the United States Court of Appeals for the Fourth Circuit, the United States District Courts for the Southern and Northern Districts of West Virginia, the Southern District of Florida, and various other legal forums. Dr. Loughry also worked as a Special Assistant/Deputy Press Secretary to United States Congressman Harley O. Staggers, Jr. and as a Direct Aide to West Virginia Governor Gaston Caperton. Moreover, he has worked for the Ohio Supreme Court; served as a personal assistant to a county prosecutor; was appointed as a special prosecuting attorney; wrote for two newspapers and the *Associated Press*; and assisted with or ran various political campaigns at local, state, and national levels.